MAJORITY-MINORITY RELATIONS

John E. Farley

Southern Illinois University
at Edwardsville

Prentice-Hall, Inc.   Englewood Cliffs, N. J. 07632

Library of Congress Cataloging in Publication Data

FARLEY, JOHN E.
  Majority-minority relations.

  Bibliography: p.
  Includes index.
    1. United States—Race relations. 2. United States—
Ethnic relations. 3. Minorities—United States.
I. Title.
E184.A1F34   305.8′00973   81-13893
ISBN 0-13-545574-X   AACR2

Production Editor: Alison Gnerre/Dee Josephson
Photo Researcher: Anita Duncan
Manufacturing Buyer: John Hall

Printed in the United States of America
10 9 8 7 6 5 4 3 2 1

Prentice-Hall International, Inc., *London*
Prentice-Hall of Australia Pty. Limited, *Sydney*
Prentice-Hall of Canada, Ltd., *Toronto*
Prentice-Hall of India Private Limited, *New Delhi*
Prentice-Hall of Japan, Inc., *Tokyo*
Prentice-Hall of Southeast Asia Pte. Ltd., *Singapore*
Whitehall Books Limited, Wellington, *New Zealand*

CONTENTS

PREFACE

This book is designed to enable the reader to understand the principles and processes which shape the patterns of relations between racial, ethnic, and other groups in society. It is not a study of any one racial or ethnic group, though a wide variety of information is indeed provided about a number of groups. Rather, it is intended to enhance the reader's understanding of why such groups interact as they do. The primary emphasis is on the relationships between dominant (majority) and subordinate (minority) racial and ethnic groups in the United States. However, thorough understanding of the dynamics of intergroup relations cannot be obtained by looking at only one society. Accordingly, a full chapter has been devoted to the examination of intergroup relations in societies other than the United States. There is also attention, particularly in the closing chapter, to minority groups other than racial and ethnic ones.

The book is divided into four major parts. In Part I (Chapters 2 and 3) the attitudes and beliefs of the individual concerning intergroup relations are explored using a variety of social psychological approaches. The concept of prejudice is examined and various theories about the causes of prejudice are presented and evaluated. There is also attention to ways in which prejudice may be combated, and to the relationship between intergroup attitudes and intergroup behavior. In Part II (Chapters 4–7) the emphasis shifts to the larger societal arena. Two major sociological perspectives, order and conflict, are introduced here. These perspectives, and more specific kinds of theory arising from them, are used throughout the book as a means of understanding intergroup relations in society. In the balance of Part II, the history of U. S. majority-minority relations is explored and analyzed using the two perspectives, and the theories arising from the perspectives are tested and refined using this historical material. The theories are further refined through examination of cross-cultural variations in intergroup relations in the closing chapter of Part II.

The major concern in Part III of the book (Chapters 8–11) is with present day intergroup relations in the United States. This part begins with a compilation of data concerning the numbers, characteristics, and social statuses of a wide range of American racial and ethnic groups, including some material from the 1980 census. The remainder of Part III consists of an extensive discussion of institutional discrimination in America. Analysts of intergroup relations are in relatively broad agreement that institutional discrimination has become more important than individual discrimination in the maintenance of racial and ethnic inequality in America. That fact is not, however, reflected in the content of most of the general works on intergroup relations now available. This book attempts to remedy that deficiency through extensive discussion of processes thaat create or maintain such inequality of the political, legal, economic, health care, and educational institutions. All of these areas, as well as housing discrimination and its causes and effects, are discussed and analyzed in Chapters 8–11.

In Part IV of the book, issues of controversy in the present and future of U.S. intergroup relations are explored. In Chapter 12, three models of intergroup relations—assimilation, pluralism, and separatism—are explored with attention to their influence in the history of the United States. Chapter 13 explores several controversies concerning intergroup relations, including arguments for and against each of the models discussed in Chapter 12, the affirmative action controversy (with extensive discussion of the *Bakke* and *Weber* cases), the extension of legal protection to nonracial minorities such as women, the disabled, and homosexuals, the future of U. S. immigration policy, and the relative importance of race and class in American society.

To enhance the reader's awareness of essential concepts used throughout the book, definitions of important new terms are introduced at the end of each chapter. Major ideas throughout the book have been illustrated photographically, and the extensive list of references has been grouped together at the end of this book so any reference can be easily located. For the instructor, a test manual co-authored by the author of this book is available.

An undertaking such as the writing of this book would be impossible without the assistance of many people. In the early stages of developing ideas for this book I received encouragement and helpful advice from Hugh Barlow, Joel Charon, and Charles Tilly. Donald Noel, Howard Schuman, Lyle Shannon, Richard Cramer, David Willman, Katherine O'Sullivan See, and Betsey Useem each read and commented upon part of all of earlier versions of the manuscript. The book has benefited greatly from their insightful observations; the shortcomings that remain are entirely the responsibility of the author. Portions of the manuscript were typed by Sherrie Williams, Kathy Howlatt, Lynn Krieger, Krista Wright, and Marilyn Morrison. Brenda Eich assisted in the compilation of the reference list. The capable editorial staff at Prentice-Hall, including Sociology Editor Ed Stanford, his assistant Irene Fraga, and Production Editor Alison Gnerre, has been a pleasure to work with. Last but far from least, I am grateful to my wife Margi for putting up with far more lost evenings and weekends than any wife should have to put up with in the first year of marriage. It is to her that this book is lovingly dedicated.

To her and all the other people mentioned here, many thanks.

Orientation: Basic Terms and Concepts

1

WHY STUDY RACE AND ETHNIC RELATIONS?

When the project of writing this book was undertaken, ethnic relations had largely faded from the forefront of public consciousness. During the late 1970s, newspaper headlines dealt not with minority protest and ghetto rebellions, but rather with tax revolt, runaway inflation, and energy shortages. Public opinion polls showed that racial and ethnic problems had virtually disappeared as public concerns—replaced by inflation, taxes, and energy as the issues most people perceived to be our most serious problems. Does this mean that racial and ethnic relations in fact no longer present a serious problem in the United States? The answer, in the judgment of the author, is clearly no. In many ways, racial and ethnic problems continue to be critical to the future of the United States and should therefore be studied by anyone concerned with the quality of life in this country.

In 1981, as this book is about to go to press, the truth of the observations above has been all too tragically demonstrated by the events of the first year and a half of the new decade. In Miami, the start of the new decade brought the bloodiest racial violence seen in this country in more than a dozen years. At least fifteen people were killed, hundreds were injured, and large areas of the city were destroyed. Smaller outbreaks of violence followed in other cities. At the same time, the membership and influence of racist organizations such as the Ku Klux Klan and Nazis appeared to be on the increase. Persons openly proclaiming to be KKK members received major party nominations for the U.S. Congress in California and Michigan, and an avowed Nazi narrowly missed getting the Republican nomination for attorney general of North Carolina, carrying nearly half of that state's counties. The Klan and the Nazis have been involved in several violent incidents, including an armed attack on a group of leftist demonstrators in Greensboro, North Carolina, which resulted in the death of several people in the group that was attacked. Also in 1980, civil rights leader Vernon Jordan was shot in Fort Wayne, Indiana, and, as of May, 1981, a string of murders that have taken the lives of more than two dozen young blacks in Atlanta remained unsolved. All of these tragic incidents point to the same conclusion: America's racial problem is with us today as much as ever, and it simply will not go away.

The most basic fact, which will be amply demonstrated in later chapters of this book, is that fundamental and critical inequalities based on race and ethnicity continue to exist in American society. This remains true in spite of the substantial elimination of overt discrimination; in spite of hundreds of civil rights laws, ordinances, and court decisions at the federal, state and local levels; and in spite of the fact that conditions have substantially improved for some minority group members. In spite of all this, the aggregate pattern remains one of racial and ethnic inequality. This is true whether we talk about income, education, political representation, or any other measure of status in American society. Furthermore, for many minority group members, conditions have not improved, and for some, they have actually gotten worse.

These basic facts carry serious implications for all Americans. For some minority group members, they mean that life is a day-to-day struggle for survival. For all minority group members, they mean facing socially imposed disadvantages that they would not face if they were white. For majority group members, it means the continued dilemma of living in a society that preaches equality but in large part fails to practice it. Furthermore, it means facing the near certainty of turmoil and social upheaval at some time in the future. As long as the fundamental inequalities that led to past upheavals remain, the potential—indeed the strong likelihood—of future turmoil remains. All that is needed is the correct set of precipitating social conditions to set off the spark. The conclusion is inescapable: The issue of racial and ethnic relations will somehow affect the life of nearly every American in the coming years.

Another reason that racial and ethnic relations continue to be of concern can be found in the changing racial and ethnic composition of the United States. For a number of reasons, a growing percentage of the American population will be composed of racial and ethnic minorities in coming years. Most notable is the growing percentage of the population made up of Spanish-speaking ethnic groups. Increasingly, the United States—particularly in certain regions—may become a bilingual society. This is something largely new to this country, a situation that will require sizeable adjustments. It will also require a greater understanding by all Americans of the ethnic and cultural issues that are raised when two linguistically different groups interact in one society.

Finally, it must be understood that many of the contemporary "hot issues" which are not essentially racial or ethnic in character nonetheless carry significant racial or ethnic overtones. The "tax revolt" of 1978 can be used as an example. The tax-cutting Proposition 13 passed by California voters was not, on its face, a racial or ethnic issue. In the view of its prime mover, Howard Jarvis, it was aimed at high taxes and wasteful government spending. Nonetheless, if one examines the cuts in programs and services that resulted, one discovers that a disproportionate number of those programs and services that were cut affected members of the state's minority groups: blacks, Chicanos (Mexican-Americans), and Asian-Americans. Thus, an issue that apparently was not racial or ethnic turns out—in one way—to have been racial and ethnic.

For all these reasons, there remains a critical need for understanding of racial and ethnic dynamics in America. The goal of this book is to contribute to such understanding. In the remainder of this introductory chapter, we will describe the emphases of the book and the approaches to the study of racial and ethnic relations that it will stress. Finally, we will define and discuss some basic concepts which will be used throughout the book and which one must thoroughly understand to study racial and ethnic relations effectively.

EMPHASIS AND APPROACH OF THE BOOK

As is evident by now, this book is mainly concerned with race and ethnic relations in the United States. Nonetheless, while the U.S. situation is emphasized, this is not exclusively a book about American race relations. The fundamental objective of the book is to understand the dynamics of race and ethnic relations. This could never be accomplished by looking at only one society. How ethnic groups interact with one another varies from one society to another according to the social, economic, cultural, and political conditions found in those societies. Racial and ethnic relations—including the American case—can therefore be best understood through comparison of what has happened in different times and places. Accordingly, the emphasis of this book upon the American situation cannot and does not exclude comparative analysis of racial and ethnic relations in different kinds of societies.

A second major characteristic of this book is that it is concerned with analysis and explanation rather than merely description. In other words, the major concern is with understanding *why* race relations work the way they do, not merely with describing the pattern of American race relations or with presenting a detailed descriptive history of various American ethnic groups. (The size of the book would not permit us to do justice to the varied and rich histories of the multiplicity of

American ethnic groups, in any case.)[1] If we are to understand and deal with racial and ethnic problems, we must know not only what those problems are, but how they developed, and what are the social forces that cause them to persist. Thus, ours is a search for principles and regularities in patterns of ethnic relations: For example, what are the social conditions under which segregation develops? What changes are associated with declines in segregation? Only through this approach, which stresses the "whys" of race relations, can we begin to understand and deal with the problems we face today.

A third important characteristic of the book is that it will enable us to examine race and ethnic relations on both the individual and societal levels. Some people who study race relations look mainly at the behaviors and prejudices of individuals, asking why a person is prejudiced and what we can do about it. Others look mainly at groups and societies, stressing economic and political systems, or such trends as urbanization and industrialization, asking how these large-scale factors influence the interaction of the ethnic groups in a society. The plan of this book is to begin at the individual level, then move to analyses on a larger scale. We shall examine theory and research about individual thinking and behavior regarding race and ethnicity, then theories and research about the larger societal factors and race and ethnicity. Having laid this groundwork, we will examine the status of various racial and ethnic groups in American society today and examine ways in which major American social institutions influence the status of these groups.

BASIC TERMS AND CONCEPTS

In any field of study, one must understand certain terms and concepts to make sense of the subject. The field of racial and ethnic relations is certainly no exception. Unfortunately, in this field more than most, any particular term may be given a wide variety of meanings by different scholars. Therefore, it is probably impossible to come up with definitions on which all would agree. Still, we must know what is meant by the terms we are using. Accordingly, we present the following definitions with the understandings that:

1. It is unlikely that every social scientist studying race and ethnic relations would agree on all of these definitions, or on any set of definitions.
2. The definitions, insofar as possible, reflect current trends in common usage among those who study race and ethnic relations.
3. The reasons for using a particular definition will be explained.
4. The definitions are stated in such a way that, once they are understood, it should be quite possible for any reader to say who or what fits the definition and who or what does not.

[1]For those interested in historical information on a wide variety of racial and ethnic groups in America, an excellent source is the Harvard Encyclopedia of American Ethnic Groups (Thernstrom et al., 1980).

Race and Ethnicity

A *race* can be defined as a grouping of people who (1) are generally considered to be physically distinct in some way, such as skin color, hair texture, or facial features, from other groupings, *and* (2) are generally considered by themselves and/or others to be a distinct group. Thus, the concept of race has two components: physical and social. The physical component involves the fact that every race is generally regarded as being somehow different in appearance from other races. The social component involves the fact that, in order to be considered a race, the group must be recognized by its own members or by others as in some way being a group, or at least sharing some characteristics (physical and perhaps other characteristics) in common. Without such social recognition, a grouping of people will not be identified as a race.

This definition conflicts with the way many members of the general public (and, at one time, many scientists as well) have thought of race. Race was seen as being entirely a matter of physical or biological characteristics, as being something that is genetically determined. Although it is true, as we have seen, that race is *partly* a matter of physical characteristics, it can be readily shown that it is not entirely physical or genetic. The best illustration of this is the inability of geneticists, anthropologists, or sociologists to agree on how many races there are in the world's population. The estimates range anywhere from the common notion of three races (black, white, and yellow) to thirty-four races (Dobzhansky, 1962) or more. Furthermore, the particular physical characteristics that are used to define a race are arbitrary and vary from one classification scheme to the next. Finally, long-term interbreeding between races has in many cases made the notion of races as discrete biological categories meaningless. All in all, it is hard to avoid concluding that social factors are just as important as physical or biological ones in determining the meaning of race. Physical characteristics partially define race, *but only in the context of a decision by society to consider those physical characteristics relevant.*

Another distinction is sometimes raised by social scientists between a *race* and a *racial group.* This distinction is well illustrated by Spencer (1979, p. 274). She presents the example of an Eskimo girl raised in a white American family in the South, never exposed to Eskimo culture or society. This girl's race might be considered Eskimo (she has physical features and parentage that would define her as Eskimo), but she is not part of Eskimo society or culture and would not, on first contact with Eskimo society, understand it any more than anyone else in the South. She would, therefore, not be considered a member of the Eskimo racial group. Thus, a racial group might be defined as a group of people of the same race who interact with one another and who develop some common cultural characteristics. In actual practice, many sociologists see the distinction between race and racial group as being more a matter of degree than anything else. In other words, races differ in the degree of group identity they develop, and individuals also differ in the degree to which they are exposed to or identify with a racial group. Whether or not one emphasizes the distinction between a race and a racial group, the important principle is that groups and individuals do vary in their degree of identification with a race and on the degree to which they develop cultural characteristics shared by other members of the same race.

A concept closely related to race is that of an ethnic group. An *ethnic group* may be defined as a grouping of people who are generally recognized by themselves and/or by others as a distinct group, with such recognition occurring on the basis of social or cultural characteristics. The most common of these characteristics are nationality, language, and religion. Ethnic groups tend to be, at least to some degree, biologically self-perpetuating, so that ethnicity is a social characteristic that passes from generation to generation. In the United States, Irish-Americans, Jewish-Americans, and Italian-Americans would be examples of ethnic groups. Unlike races or racial groups, physical traits are not necessarily a part of the definition of an ethnic group. In the case of ethnic groups such as Jews or Irish Catholics, it is impossible to reliably tell, on the basis of appearance alone, who belongs and who does not. It is perhaps ironic that Hitler, who always insisted that Jews were a race, ultimately turned to a classification based on parentage to determine who was Jewish (you were Jewish if one or more of your grandparents identified with the Jewish faith), because it was impossible to tell by appearance.

Sociologists disagree on whether ethnicity is a broad concept that includes race or whether races and ethnic groups are two different things. Some (Gordon, 1964; Glazer, 1971) argue that races are a particular type of ethnic group. Under this definition, some ethnic groups are not races (for example, Mennonites, Polish-Americans), but all races are ethnic groups. Other social scientists make a distinction, arguing that if physical characteristics are involved, the group is a race (blacks, whites), but if the group is based solely on social/cultural characteristics, the group is an ethnic group (French-Canadians, German-Americans). Examples of this can be seen in the writings of Warner and Srole (1945) and Van den Berghe (1967). Because it makes a good deal of difference in terms of intergroup relations whether or not a group is identifiable on the basis of appearance, we shall use this approach in this book unless expressly indicated otherwise. For purposes of this book, races are defined on the basis of both physical and social characteristics; ethnic groups purely on the basis of social or cultural characteristics.

Majority and Minority Groups

Two terms used throughout this book are *majority group* and *minority group*. When sociologists use these terms, they are not speaking strictly in the numerical sense in which the terms *majority* and *minority* are ordinarily used. The sociological meaning of *majority group,* as used in this book, is any group which is dominant in society—that is, any group that enjoys more than a proportionate share of the wealth, power, and/or social status in that society. Typically, a majority group is in a position to dominate or exercise power over other groups in society. A *minority group* may be defined as any group that is assigned an inferior status in

Ethnicity is based on cultural, rather than physical, characteristics. Could you identify the ethnicity of this group of people without the ethnic dress? Mac Anderson; 1980.

society—that is, any group that has less than its proportionate share of wealth, power, and/or social status. Frequently, minority group members are discriminated against by those in the majority.

A number of important points can be made about majority and minority groups. First, majorities and minorities are very frequently determined by race or ethnicity, but they may be determined on the basis of many other factors, such as sex, physical disability, lifestyle, or sexual preference (homosexuality or heterosexuality). Much of what is true, for example, about relations between blacks and whites is also true about relations between males and females, disabled and non-disabled, "gays" and "straights." We have chosen to title this book in terms of majority-minority relations precisely for this reason: the dynamics of relations between majority groups and minority groups are in many ways similar, regardless of how those groups are formed. Accordingly, it should be kept in mind that, although this book is mainly about race and ethnic relations, many of the principles apply to other kinds of majority-minority relations, or intergroup relations, as well.

We noted earlier that the sociological usage of the terms *majority* and *minority* differs from the common numerical usage. It is quite possible for a group to be a numerical majority but still a minority group in the sociological sense. Several familiar examples come to mind. Perhaps the best known example is the

7

position of blacks in South Africa. Although over 80 percent of the population is black, the political system is totally controlled by whites. Racial separation and discrimination against blacks have been written into South African law for years, and the country's wealth is almost totally controlled by whites. Thus, although blacks are an overwhelming majority numerically, they are a minority group in the sociological sense because they have been forced into a *subordinate* role in South Africa's social system. Another instance of a numerical majority that is a sociological minority group is women in the United States. Women actually make up slightly over half of the U.S. population, but few hold offices in the nation's higher political governing bodies (such as the U.S. Congress). They have long been subject to discrimination (as of early 1981, a U.S. constitutional amendment to ban sexual discrimination remained stalled), and men continue to own and control most of the nation's wealth (historically, women have been heavily dependent on wage-earning men for economic support and sustenance). Thus, even though they are a numerical majority, women have in many ways been relegated to a subordinate and dependent role in American society. Accordingly, they can be regarded as a minority group in the sociological sense.

The important thing to keep in mind, then, is that it is a group's role and status, not its numbers, that make it a majority group or a minority group. A helpful way to think of this, suggested by Yetman and Steele (1975), is to think of *majority* as a synonym for *dominant*, and *minority* as a synonym for *subordinate*. Occasionally, a society may have relatively peaceful and egalitarian relations among its racial or ethnic groups, so that no group is dominant or subordinate. However, the more common pattern in diverse societies is for some groups to dominate others, so that in such societies majority (dominant) and minority (subordinate) groups can be identified. Accordingly, interracial or interethnic relations will usually fall into the larger category of majority-minority relations. Unless we are talking specifically about cases where the three concepts—race and ethnic relations, majority-minority relations, and intergroup relations—do *not* overlap, we shall use these terms more or less interchangeably to avoid the fatigue that frequently results from repeated use of the same term. This is not meant in any way to negate the important facts that not *all* race and ethnic relations are marked by domination and subordination, and that many intergroup relations besides race and ethnic relations operate according to the majority-minority model.

Racism

Perhaps no term in recent years has been used in as many different ways as the term *racism*. Any definition of this term would be subject to controversy; for this reason we have chosen to give this term a very broad definition, then to present further definitions to identify different forms of racism. Accordingly, *racism* may be defined as any attitude, belief, behavior, or institutional arrangement that tends to favor one race or ethnic group (usually a majority group) over another (usually a minority group). By favoring one group over another, we are talking not only about intentions but also about consequences: If the result of something is that one race or ethnic group gets a disproportionate share of scarce resources (money, education, political power, social status), we would have an example of racism. It would also be a case of racism if the consequence of an arrangement were to give one group greater freedom than another. Thus, by this broad definition, something or someone can be racist either on the basis of intentions or on the basis of results. Accordingly, it follows that sometimes racism (and similar phenomena such as sexism) are conscious and deliberate; at other times they are not. The unfortunate fact is that if one is the victim of racism or sexism, it makes relatively little difference whether the resultant disadvantage was intentionally imposed or not: It is still a disadvantage. (For further discussion of this broad concept of racism, see Yetman and Steele, 1975; Jones, 1972; and U.S. Commission on Civil Rights, 1970.)

Within this broad definition of racism, we can identify several specific kinds of racism. Among these are (1) attitudinal racism, or racial prejudice, (2) ideological racism, or racist ideology, (3) individual racist behavior, or individual discrimination, and (4) institutional racism or discrimination.

Prejudice   *Attitudinal racism,* or *prejudice,* refers to people's thinking: their attitudes and beliefs which tend to favor one group over another, or which tend to cause unequal treatment on the basis of race. Prejudice can be direct or overt, such as disliking a group or believing that it is inherently inferior. However, it also can be subtle. Examples of subtle prejudice would be the belief that a group that has been discriminated against is to blame for its own troubles, the feelings that a group protesting its subordinate status is "causing trouble," and the practice of stereotyping, of assuming that "all of them are alike." Thus, two critical things should be kept in mind about the meaning of *prejudice*. First, the term refers to people's thinking—their attitudes and beliefs—and not their behavior. Second, prejudice can be overt and very obvious, or it can be subtle and indirect.

Ideological Racism   Closely related to the concept of prejudice is the more specific concept of *ideological racism,* or *racist ideology.* These terms refer specifically to the belief that one race is biologically, intellectually, or culturally inferior to another. The term *racism* was originally used to mean this type of ideology that views various races as superior or inferior to one another, and some social scientists continue to prefer this narrower definition. In any case, it is unfortunately true that racist ideology has been widely advocated and widely believed, particularly in Europe and North America. Frequently, such racist ideology has been elevated to the status of "scientific theory," giving rise to what has been called *scientific racism.* The idea here is that science supposedly proves that some groups are innately superior to others. It is significant that such ideologies always define the race of the "scientist" as superior. An example of this can be seen in social Darwinism, which argues on the basis of "survival of the fittest" that the wealthiest and most powerful groups are biologically the "most fit." This ideology was widely used to justify domination and colonization of the natives of Asia, Africa, the Americas, and Oceania by white Europeans. In fact, it is an important characteristic of ideological racism that its main function is to justify domination and exploitation of one group by another by showing that group superiority/ inferiority is in the natural way of things (Wilson, 1973, pp. 32−35). When it has served dominant group interests to do so, claims of innate inferiority have been made at various times in the United States against a wide variety of groups, including Irish, Italian, Polish, Portuguese, and Jewish Americans, as well as blacks, Chicanos, and American Indians. The rise of the anti-immigration and anti-Catholic Know Nothing Party around 1850 and the Ku Klux Klan in the early twentieth century marked high points of ideological racism in the United States. Elsewhere, ideological racism was at the heart of German Nazism, arguing that Germans were part of a superior "Aryan" race, and that Jews, blacks, and others were innately inferior. Notions of race superiority were also used to justify Japanese expansionism during World War II.

Despite the advocacy of scientific racism in Europe, America, and elsewhere for over a hundred years (Grant, 1916; Gobineau, 1915; Stoddard, 1920; Hitler, 1940), careful scientific analysis does not support the notion of innate biological, intellectual, cultural, temperamental, or moral superiority of any racial or ethnic group over another (cf. Montague, 1963, 1964; UNESCO, 1950, 1952).[2] Ideological racism is best understood as a means by which members of dominant groups attempt to make acceptable their domination of other groups. Unfortunately, the label of science has often been used to legitimize such ideological racism.

Obviously, ideological racism is in many regards similar to some types of racial prejudice. The differences are that ideological racism has become institutionalized (in other words, it has become a widely-accepted element within a culture), and/or it is used to justify behavior whereby one group dominates or exploits another. Prejudice, on the other hand, can exist in the absence of both of these conditions.

Individual Discrimination   Another form of racism is referred to as *individual discrimination*. When we talk about discrimination, we are talking about behavior, not beliefs or attitudes. *Individual discrimination* can be defined as any behavior on the part of an individual which leads to unequal treatment on the basis of race or ethnicity. Examples would be a homeowner's refusal to sell his or her home to a Jew, a taxi-driver's refusing to pick up blacks, or an employer's paying lower wages to Chicanos than to Anglos for comparable work. The important distinction here is that we are talking about what people actually do—their behavior—rather than what they think. The two are not always the same.

---

[2]It is true that average scores on particular tests designed to measure intelligence and achievement vary from group to group. However, as we shall see in a later chapter, these differences are best explained by the testing process and by cultural variations between groups which render any one test useless as a measure for all groups.

Institutional Racism   The fourth form of racism, and perhaps the least understood, is *institutional racism,* or *institutional discrimination.* It has been pointed out by Carmichael and Hamilton (1967) that not all—and perhaps not even most—discrimination is perpetrated by individuals. Our basic *social institutions*— well-established structures such as the family, the state, the educational system, the economic system, and religion, which perform basic functions in our society—play a critical role in the creation and perpetration of racial inequality. Accordingly, we can define *institutional racism* as arrangements or practices in social institutions and their related organizations that tend to favor one racial or ethnic group (usually the majority group) over another. Institutional racism is sometimes conscious and deliberate, as in the legally required school segregation that existed in some Southern states before the 1954 Supreme Court decision banning such segregation. Frequently, however, institutional practices develop without any conscious racist intent which nonetheless tend to place or keep minority groups in a subordinate position. An example can be seen in the high cost of a college education. This may not come about from any intention to discriminate, but the result is to do exactly that. Since blacks, Chicanos, and American Indians are less able to afford the cost than whites, they are placed at a disadvantage. It is the view of many social scientists, including the author of this book, that institutional racism—including that which is not necessarily conscious or deliberate—plays a critical role in the continuing pattern of racial and ethnic inequality in the United States. Every available measure shows major reductions in prejudice in general and in the belief in racist ideologies in particular over the past twenty to thirty years in the United States. Deliberate racial discrimination in virtually every form has been illegal for years. Yet, as we indicated at the beginning of the chapter, racial inequality continues in America today, and, for many minority group members, the situation is probably getting worse. In the judgment of the author, the explanation probably is to be found in our social institutions and related organizations. Thus, our concern in this book cannot focus exclusively on the prejudice, the racist ideology, or the deliberate instances of individual discrimination that have been the main focus of the study of majority-minority relations in the past. We must also examine our political, economic, educational, and other institutions to identify ways in which they unconsciously serve to perpetuate racial inequality. Without such analysis, the problem of racial inequality in the America of the 1980s can be neither understood nor effectively attacked.

SUMMARY AND CONCLUSION

In this chapter, we have examined some of the reasons for studying race relations in contemporary America and discussed some of the ways this book will approach the study of majority-minority relations. We have also defined some basic terms that will be encountered throughout the book. Your understanding of the terms presented in this chapter is critical, both because the terms are used throughout the book and because you must understand what is meant by the terms if you are to understand the principles of intergroup relations in later parts of the book. As you proceed through the book, you will encounter additional definitions related to each topic. The concepts presented in this chapter, however, are crucial to your understanding of virtually all topics in the book. To facilitate your understanding of both the concepts presented here and in later chapters, a list of definitions is presented at the end of each chapter where new terminology is introduced. It is hoped that this will be a handy reference to help you keep track of concepts that are critical to your understanding of majority-minority relations.

In the next two chapters, we will be concerned primarily with the first of the four kinds of racism: racial or ethnic prejudice. We shall try to identify what causes prejudice, what can be done about it, and how it is related to the problem of racial and ethnic discrimination.

GLOSSARY

Attitudinal racism   Racial or ethnic prejudice. See prejudice.

Dominant group   Similar in meaning to *majority group*.

Ethnic group   A group of people who are generally regarded by themselves or others as a distinct group, with such recognition based on social or cultural characteristics such as nationality, language, and religion. Ethnicity, like race, tends to be passed from generation to generation and is ordinarily not an affiliation that one can freely drop.

Ideological racism, or **racist ideology**   The belief that one race is superior to another biologically, intellectually, culturally, temperamentally, or morally. Such ideologies usually exist in order to rationalize or justify domination of one race or ethnic group by another, and tend to become institutionalized, or widely accepted within a culture.

Individual racial discrimination, or **individual behavioral racism**   Any behavior by individuals that leads to unequal treatment on the basis of race or ethnicity. A restaurant owner's refusal to serve Chinese-Americans would be an example.

Institutional racism, or **institutional discrimination**   Any arrangement or practice within a social institution or its related organizations that tends to favor one race or ethnic group (usually the majority group) over another. Institutional racism may be conscious and deliberate, as in discriminatory voting laws, or subtle and perhaps unintended, as in industrial location decisions that favor suburban whites over inner-city blacks.

Majority group   Any social group that is dominant in a society; i.e., it enjoys more than a proportionate share of the wealth, power, and/or social status in that society. Although majority groups in this sense are frequently a numerical majority, this is not always the case.

Minority group   Any group that is assigned to a subordinate role in society; i.e. it has less than its proportionate share of wealth, power, and/or social status. Minority groups are frequently, but not necessarily, a numerical minority in society. Blacks in South Africa would be an example of a minority group that is a numerical majority.

Prejudice   Any attitude or belief that tends to favor one group over another, or to lead to unequal treatment. Prejudice usually involves a tendency to overgeneralize, i.e., to assume that all members of any given group are much the same.

Race   A grouping of people generally considered to be physically distinct in some way from others and regarded by themselves or others to be a distinct group.

Racial group   A group of people who develop a group identity and/or common culture based on race. The main difference between a racial group and a race is that one need not have a strong group identity or be part of a cultural group in order to be a member of a race.

Racism   Any attitude, belief, behavior, or institutional arrangement that tends to favor one racial or ethnic group (usually a majority group) over another (usually a minority group). See also the four types of racism: prejudice (attitudinal racism); ideological racism; individual discrimination (individual behavioral racism); and institutional racism.

Social institution   A well-established structure, or form of organization, with supporting norms and values, which performs a central function in society. Examples would include religion, the family, and the economic, political, legal, educational, and health care systems.

Subordinate group   Similar in meaning to *minority group*.

SOCIAL-PSYCHOLOGICAL
PERSPECTIVES ON
MAJORITY-MINORITY RELATIONS
THE STUDY OF PREJUDICE

Causes and Dynamics of Prejudice

2

One of the first things most people think of when they think about race and ethnic relations is *prejudice*. We are all familiar with the concept of prejudice, and we have all seen numerous examples of it, both in individuals we know and in examples from the popular media. At the most basic level, nearly everyone knows that the term *prejudice* means just what it suggests: a tendency to prejudge people, usually negatively and usually on the basis of a single personal characteristic (such as race, sex, religion, hair length, etc.), without any objective basis for making such a judgment. When prejudice is further investigated, however, many different types of prejudice turn up, and not all types are found in the same people. The objectives of this chapter will be to investigate those different types of prejudice, illustrate some of the ways they differ, and try to find at least some tentative answers to the ever-present question, "Why are people prejudiced?"

FORMS OF PREJUDICE

As indicated in the previous chapter, prejudice is basically in the mind: The term refers not to behavior but rather to beliefs and attitudes, to what people think. What people think can be divided into at least three dimensions: What they believe is true (*cognitive*), what they like or dislike (*affective*), and how they are inclined to behave (*conative*). This suggests three types of prejudice, each slightly different from the others: Prejudice toward a group may take the form of having negative beliefs concerning what is true about a group (cognitive prejudice), disliking a group (affective prejudice), or wanting to discriminate against or show aggression toward a group (conative prejudice) (Kramer, 1949; Triandis, 1971). Although the three are correlated, it is quite possible for an individual to be prejudiced in one of the above three ways without being prejudiced in another. An individual might, for example, believe that most members of a particular race lack intelligence without feeling any dislike toward them and without any desire to discriminate. In a somewhat different example, someone might feel strong dislike for a particular ethnic group because he or she is in intense competition with members of the group (for scarce jobs, for example) without believing that members of the group are stupid, clannish, greedy, immoral, or anything else bad. The distinction among these types of prejudice can be important, because it may sometimes be possible to reduce one type without having much effect on another. We might, for example, correct a white person's incorrect beliefs about black people without reducing his or her dislike for them. The common factor in each type of prejudice—cognitive, affective, and conative—is that the beliefs, attitudes, or tendencies toward discrimination are applied toward the group as a whole, without recognition of wide variations that exist in individuals in any group (Allport, 1954, Chapter 1). This tendency to overcategorize is common to all types of prejudice.

STEREOTYPES

One form of cognitive prejudice of special interest to those who study race relations is called *stereotyping*. Various definitions of *stereotype* are possible, but Allport's (1954) will do quite well: A stereotype is an exaggerated belief associated with a category (a group of people, such as a racial, ethnic, or religious group). This short definition implies several important characteristics. First, it refers to *exaggerated* beliefs. It is true sometimes that groups are stereotyped in ways that bear absolutely no resemblance to reality. At other times there are real cultural differences between racial and ethnic groups, and some stereotypes do contain, as Allport puts it, a "kernel of truth." It is true, for example, that black Americans are more likely to support liberal political candidates than are white Americans. That does not, however, justify the stereotype that all blacks are liberals or radicals: many are not. The difference between a stereotype and a legitimate observation about group differences is that the latter allows for the considerable variation in cultural traits that occurs from one individual to another in any group; the former does not.

As suggested in the discussion above, a second characteristic of a stereotype is that it is associated with a *category* of people: blacks, whites, Jews, Americans, Germans, homosexuals, or whatever. The stereotyped thinker tends to categorize people, assuming that they have whatever characteristic he or she associates with the category. For example, if John believes that Jewish people are money-hungry (a common stereotype among people prejudiced against Jews), he will tend, more or less without thinking about it, to assume that any Jewish person he encounters will be money-hungry. In other words, he has come to more or less automatically associate the characteristic ''money-hungry'' with the category ''Jew.''

Not all stereotypes are negative or derogatory. Frequently, we tend to form positive or complimentary stereotypes of our own group (what social psychologists call the *in-group*) and negative or derogatory stereotypes of groups of which we are not a member and that are different from our own. (These are called *out-groups*.) An example of this can be seen in surveys of college students in the United States (Katz and Braley, 1933; Gilbert, 1951) in which students chose highly positive adjectives to describe ''Americans,'' but much less positive and frequently negative terms to describe ''Chinese,'' ''Jews,'' ''Negroes,'' and ''Turks.'' (Interestingly, more recent studies have shown drastic changes in these stereotyping patterns, which will be discussed in a later chapter.) It is also true that the identical trait may be given positive connotations for an in-group, but negative connotations for an out-group. A widely used example suggested by Robert Merton (1949: pp. 426−430) points to the characteristics admired in Abraham Lincoln: thrift, ambition, hard work. Stereotyped thinkers often see these same characteristics in Jews, for example, or Asian-Americans. In these out-groups, however, the characteristics are seen not as admirable traits but as greed, tightfistedness, pushiness, being unfairly competitive. In other words, the *same* stereotypes that make Abraham Lincoln admirable are labeled so as to make Jewish or Asian Americans undesirable. To summarize, then, a stereotype may be either favorable or unfavorable. Frequently, we stereotype so as to create a positive image of our own group and a negative image of others—sometimes even when the stereotypes of in-groups and out-groups refer to essentially the same traits.

In some cases, even stereotypes of out-groups are positive. Blacks, for example, are often stereotyped by whites as being ''musical'' or ''good dancers.'' Such stereotypes, however, are at best mixed blessings for the group to which they are applied. First, they serve to rationalize the more common negative stereotypes and make the prejudiced person appear a bit more ''reasonable.'' Second, they deny individuals in the group the freedom to be what they are, demanding instead that they live up to the stereotypical expectation. This was graphically illustrated in the television epic *Roots, Part II*, where a black college president was made to tap dance to please a group of white benefactors.

CAUSES OF PREJUDICE

It has often been suggested that people form prejudices because they observe characteristics they do not like in members of the group against whom they are prejudiced. Put slightly differently, it is argued that prejudice should be explained not in terms of the characteristics of those who are prejudiced, but rather in terms of the characteristics of the group they are prejudiced against. In other words, if a researcher wants to find out why people are prejudiced against, for example, Turks, he or she should study the Turks rather than the prejudiced people. There are several problems with this line of reasoning. Although it is undoubtedly true that individual encounters shape many people's thinking about out-groups, prejudice involves unfounded generalizations about groups and does not allow for individual variations within those groups. Many people may have unpleasant experiences with individual members of out-groups, but only *some* of those individuals respond with the irrational generalizations that we call prejudice. Another fact that calls into question the view that the cause of prejudice is to be found in the out-group is illustrated in a fascinating study by Hartley (1946); see also Jahoda (1960). In this study, respondents were asked about their attitudes concerning a variety of ethnic groups, including "Danireans," "Piraneans," and "Wallonians." The study found that people who were antagonistic toward blacks and Jews were also antagonistic toward these other three groups, sometimes even advocating that restrictive measures be taken against them. The catch is that none of the three groups exist! In other words, people who are prejudiced against real groups are also quite capable of being prejudiced against nonexistent groups. This suggests very strongly that the causes of prejudice must be sought in the characteristics and experiences of those who are prejudiced—*not* the characteristics of those they are prejudiced against.

In our discussion of causes of prejudice, we shall focus on three general kinds of theories. One of these approaches, which applies some basic ideas from Freudian psychology to the problem of prejudice, sees prejudice primarily as something that meets the personality needs of individuals with certain kinds of experiences. A second approach views prejudice as being something that is learned from others and that develops largely out of the need to conform to group pressures. A third approach sees the source of prejudice primarily in a person's position in the larger social structure (one's economic position, for example). In the remainder of this chapter, we shall discuss and evaluate each of these three major kinds of theories about why people are prejudiced.

THEORIES ABOUT PERSONALTY AND PREJUDICE

One of the most influential studies ever done on the subject of prejudice was published in 1950 in a book by Theodor Adorno, Else Frenkel-Brunswick, and associates entitled *The Authoritarian Personality*. This book, which today remains a basic study in the understanding of prejudice, made the fundamental argument that people are prejudiced because their prejudices meet certain needs associated with their personality. The questions these researchers sought to answer were (1) Is there a personality type associated with prejudice? and (2) If so, how is such a personality acquired?

Is Prejudice Generalized?

Adorno and his associates began with the assumption that, if there is a prejudiced personality type, it ought to be possible to show that a person prejudiced against one out-group is likely to be prejudiced against out-groups in general. In other words, if being prejudiced is a personality characteristic, as the researchers thought, we would expect that a person with this personality characteristic would be prejudiced not just against one particular out-group, but against people or groups in general who are culturally or ethnically different. To test this assumption, they developed questionnaires designed to measure two forms of prejudice. One questionnaire measured *anti-Semitism*, which refers to prejudice against Jews.[1] The other measured a somewhat more complex and generalized form of prejudice called *ethnocentrism*. Ethnocentrism refers to a tendency to view one's own group as the norm and other groups as not only different, but also strange and, usually, inferior. One's own ways of doing things are seen not only as the best, but as the normal, natural way of doing things, as a standard against which the ways of other groups are to be judged. (The concept of ethnocentrism is extremely important in the study of majority-minority relations and will be widely utilized throughout this book.)

Both questionnaires consisted of sets of statements to which respondents could choose one of six responses ranging from strong agreement to strong disagreement. There was no "neutral" choice. The anti-Semitism, or AS, Scale included such items as the following:

1. One trouble with Jewish businessmen is that they stick together and connive so that a Gentile doesn't have a fair chance in competition.
2. I can hardly imagine myself marrying a Jew.
3. No matter how Americanized a Jew may seem to be, there is always something different and strange, something basically Jewish underneath.
4. The trouble with letting Jews into a nice neighborhood is that they gradually give it a typical Jewish atmosphere.

The last item above is suggestive of the sometimes subtle nature of prejudice. Certainly it does not indicate a fierce hatred of Jewish people or a malicious intent to do harm. Nonetheless, it does reflect some deep-seated prejudices. The phrase "letting into," for example, suggests that Gentiles are or should be in a position of greater power and also suggests a belief in a certain "pushiness" or intrusiveness in Jews. The term "nice neighborhood" suggests that the neighborhood might become otherwise if Jewish people move in, and the word "typical" is indicative of stereotyped thinking.

The ethnocentrism, or E-scale items are of a similar nature, but they are

---

[1] Actually, the term *Semitic* properly refers to a variety of people of East-Mediterranean stock, including both Jews and Arabs, but in common usage, anti-Semitism has come to refer to prejudice against Jews.

designed to measure both the in-group's feelings of superiority and its distrust of out-groups, traits that characterize ethnocentrism. Examples of items include:

1. Negroes have their rights, but it is best to keep them in their own districts and schools and to avoid too much contact with whites.
2. Certain religious sects who refuse to salute the flag should be forced to conform to such a patriotic action or else be abolished.
3. America may not be perfect, but the American Way has brought us about as close as human beings can get to a perfect society.

If prejudice is a generalized attitude, as Adorno believed, then a person prejudiced against Jews would also be prejudiced against blacks, Mexican-Americans, foreigners, and so on. If this were the case, we would expect two things to be true with regard to the AS and E scales. First, the E-scale (ethnocentrism) items should be highly correlated to one another—that is, a person agreeing with one of them should tend toward agreement with most of the rest of them. Second, we would expect that people scoring high on the AS-scale would tend to score high on the E-scale, and that people scoring low on one would tend to score low on the other. It turns out indeed that *both* of these things were true. In fact, a high correlation (0.80) between E-scale and AS-scale scores was obtained.[2] This finding, (along with other similar findings) supports the view that prejudice is largely a personal characteristic of the prejudiced person directed at a variety of out-groups rather than an attitude resulting from a person's particular experiences with one specific group. If a person is prejudiced against one group, she or he is very likely to be prejudiced to some degree against a wide variety of groups. (It should, however, be kept in mind that there is not a perfect relationship between different types of prejudice and that there are people who are highly prejudiced against one group but not others—cf. Ehrlich, 1973.)

Adorno and his colleagues also developed a measure of political and economic conservatism to see if prejudice might simply be an indication of conservatism. They found that it was not. More conservative people did tend to be somewhat more prejudiced, but it was far from a perfect relationship: some ''conservatives'' turned out to be not at all prejudiced and some ''liberals'' turned out to be quite prejudiced.

The Authoritarian Personality

At this point, Adorno and his colleagues were ready to test their theory that prejudice was produced by some particular personality pattern or type. They were able to identify certain themes that appeared with some regularity in the speeches

---

[2]A correlation, or correlation coefficient, is a statistical measure of the strength and direction of a relationship between any two variables that can be expressed as numbers. It can range from $+1.0$ (perfect positive relationship) through 0 (no relationship) to -1.0 (perfect negative relationship). Since many studies in the social sciences base their findings on correlations as weak as .20 to .40, a correlation of .80 would be considered a very strong positive relationship.

and writings of fascists and anti-Semitic agitators, and they hypothesized that these themes might be indicative of the characteristics of a prejudiced or authoritarian personality type. A questionnaire similar to the E scale and AS scale was developed to test for and measure this personality type. This questionnaire was called the F scale (for potential for fascism); it is now commonly referred to as the authoritarianism scale (Brown, 1965). The basic characteristics Adorno believed associated with the authoritarian personality and some of the F-scale items used to measure them are shown below:

1. Conventionalism: Rigid adherence to conventional values
   a. Obedience and respect for authority are the most important virtues children should learn.
   b. A person who has bad manners, habits, and breeding can hardly expect to get along with decent people.
   c. The businessman and the manufacturer are much more important to society than the artist and the professor.
2. Authoritarian submission: Uncritical acceptance of authority
   a. Every person should have complete faith in some supernatural power whose decisions he obeys without question.
   b. Young people sometimes get rebellious ideas, but as they grow up, they ought to get over them and settle down.
3. Authoritatian aggression: Aggressiveness toward people who do not conform to authority or conventional norms
   a. An insult to our honor should always be punished.
   b. There is hardly anything lower than a person who does not feel a great love, gratitude, and respect for his parents.
4. Anti-intraception: Opposition to the subjective or imaginative; rejection of self-analysis
   a. When a person has a problem or worry, it is best for him not to think about it, but to keep busy with more cheerful things.
   b. Nowadays more and more people are prying into matters that should remain personal and private.
5. Superstition and stereotypical thinking
   a. Some people are born with an urge to jump from high places.
   b. Someday it will probably be shown that astrology can explain a lot of things.
6. Concern with power and toughness
   a. An insult to our honor should always be punished.
   b. People can be divided into two distinct classes: the weak and the strong.
7. Destructiveness and cynicism
   a. Human nature being what it is, there will always be war and conflict.
   b. Familiarity breeds contempt.
8. Projectivity: Projection outward of unconscious emotions; belief that the world is wild and dangerous place
   a. Nowadays when so many different kinds of people move around and mix together so much, a person has to protect himself especially carefully against catching an infection or disease from them.

    b. Most people don't realize how much our lives are controlled by plots hatched in secret places.

9. Exaggerated concern with sexual "goings-on."
    a. Sex crimes, such as rape and attacks on children, deserve more than imprisonment; such criminals ought to be publicly whipped or worse.
    b. The wild sex life of the old Greeks and Romans was tame compared to some of the goings-on in this country, even in places where people might least expect it.

    Unlike the AS scale, which measured attitudes toward Jews, or the E scale, which measured attitudes toward out-groups in general, the F scale does not attempt to measure any one type of attitude. Rather, it measures a *set* of attitudes and beliefs that do not necessarily follow *logically* from one another (one does not logically have to be superstitious to be submissive to authority), but nonetheless are believed to occur together in the same people. It is this fact that makes the F scale a *personality* measure, which the others are not; only the F scale measures a set of logically diverse or unrelated attitudes and beliefs that are nonetheless found together in the same persons. Adorno and his colleagues were able to show that the F scale was indeed a valid measure of personality: The various attitudes and beliefs measured by the F scale did tend to "hang together" as they expected. Specifically, they were able to show that if a person agreed with one of the items, he or she was likely to agree with most of the rest. Furthermore, Adorno was able to show that people who scored high on the F scale were substantially more likely than others to be prejudiced: High F scale scores tended to be strongly associated with high AS-scale (anti-Semitism) and E-scale (ethnocentrism) scores. Accordingly, Adorno had established significant evidence supporting the following generalizations:

1. Prejudice is an attitude or set of attitudes that tends to be generalized to a wide variety of out-groups rather than a specific attitudinal response based on experiences with members of a particular out-group.
2. There is a personality type (he called it the authoritarian personality) that tends to be associated with prejudice.

Explaining Prejudice: Scapegoating and Projection

    It should be noted here that Adorno is not without his critics, and some of the major criticisms will be discussed as we look at other thories about the causes of prejudice. Nonetheless, it appears that Adorno was able to mount substantial, if not conclusive, evidence in support of the generalizations above. If we were to stop here, however, there would be something fundamentally dissatisfying or incomplete about the knowledge. While it may be interesting (and perhaps self-satisfying to the unprejudiced person, if such exists) to know that prejudice is associated with a personality type, it leaves unanswered the basic question of how that personality type comes into being. Fortunately, Adorno did not stop with the conclusion that there is a personality type associated with prejudice. Indeed, probably the most useful—and most controversial—part of Adorno's work addresses the question of how people acquire the personality pattern associated with prejudice. Adorno's theories in this regard illustrate two of the most widely analyzed processes that lead to prejudice: *scapegoating,* or *displaced aggression*, and *projection. Scapegoating,* or *displaced aggression* (the terms are used almost interchangeably), refers to a tendency to take out one's feelings of frustration and aggression on someone other than the true scource of the frustration. Often, this someone is an out-group or a relatively powerless minority group. The process of *projection* is related but somewhat different. Projection is a process in which we forget about, minimize, or deny characteristics we find undesirable in ourselves by exaggerating these same characteristics in others. Again, the others in whom these "undesirable" characteristics are exaggerated are often members of cultural or ethnic groups other than one's own. Adorno argues—based largely on the theories of Sigmund Freud—that people with authoritarian personalities are people who have unusually strong personality needs for scapegoating and projection. Like Freud, Adorno felt that adult personalities largely reflect childhood experiences. A major aspect of Freudian theory is the notion that people are born with strong innate needs or drives, such as aggressiveness and sexuality. Freud felt that if these drives are too severely repressed in childhood, frustrations result that remain throughout life and are reflected in adult personality problems (see Freud, 1930).

The Development of Prejudiced Personalities

Using this as a theoretical starting point, Adorno explored the childhood experiences and the personalities of highly prejudiced and relatively unprejudiced subjects through open-ended questions and projective methods. The latter included the Thematic Apperception Test (TAT), in which subjects are shown pictures and asked to tell stories about them, and questions such as "We all have times when we feel below par. What moods or feelings are most unpleasant or disturbing to you?" This part of Adorno's study revealed a number of additional findings that are useful in explaining how people may develop a personality type that predisposes them toward prejudice. Among these findings:

1. Prejudiced subjects were generally unwilling to acknowledge faults in themselves, whereas unprejudiced subjects tended to be more objective in self-evaluation, seeing both good and bad in themselves.
2. Perhaps to an even greater degree, prejudiced subjects tended to idealize their parents. These subjects appeared unable to view their parents critically; unprejudiced subjects, on the other hand, tended to be able to talk about both desirable and undesirable characteristics in their parents.

3. On those occasions when prejudiced subjects did say something that might appear critical of themselves or their parents, they tended to quickly qualify it or explain it away. In themselves, they tended to view negative qualities as coming from some external force, making statements such as "I let my carnal self get away from me," or "It's the Latin in me," or "I got that from the other side of the family." When they criticized their parents, they tended to withdraw or qualify the criticism quickly: "He forced some decisions on me," followed quickly by "but he allowed me to do as I pleased."

4. While prejudiced subjects were unlikely to see faults in themselves or their parents or quickly down-played or explained away such faults, they were *very* likely to find faults in out-groups. Their references, for example, to "oversexed Negroes" and "pushy Jews" showed up in this open-ended part of the research as well as on the fixed-response questionnaires discussed earlier.

These four findings are strongly supportive of the notion that projection is an important process in the thinking of prejudiced people. They down-play faults in themselves and those close to them by exaggerating the same characteristics in others, particularly in others who are culturally, racially, ethnically, or religiously different. Indeed, a wide variety of research (for a thorough review, see Ehrlich, 1973) shows that people who are insecure about their own qualities or are inwardly lacking in self-esteem are the people who are most often prejudiced. It is among such people that the need for projection is likely to be greatest—particularly if they are unable to accept the negative aspects of their personalities. Two other findings from the subjective part of Adorno's research cast additional light on the dynamics of prejudice.

First, the responses to open-ended and projective questions indicated that the prejudiced subjects were highly concerned about status. They appeared to have a strong need to rank people and showed evidence of having learned to be very concerned about their own status at an early age. Frequently, they talked about the importance of never doing anything that would reflect negatively on their family.

The second pattern Adorno noticed was that nearly all the prejudiced subjects come from very strict homes. As children, they had been severely punished and taught to obey without arguing or asking why.

In these findings, Adorno and his colleagues felt that they had identified the process by which prejudiced persons had developed personality needs for projection and scapegoating. The process may be sketched as follows:

1. Very strict childrearing practices generate feelings of frustration and aggression. This occurs due to the severity of punishment and the highly restrictive rules characteristic of very strict families.

2. At the same time, children are taught strong norms (rules) about respecting authority. They are also taught to believe in the justness and legitimacy of society's ranking systems. Eventually, they come to internalize (accept in their own minds) these norms and beliefs.

3. These conditions create a situation where feelings of frustration and aggression

build up but cannot be released against the authority figures who are the source of the strict rules and severe punishment.

4. As a consequence, a process of displacement, or scapegoating, occurs: the aggression is taken out against those who are low in the individual's ranking system (racial, ethnic, or religious minorities, or other out-groups).

5. Because of the concern with ranking and the learned need to avoid bringing shame on themselves or their families, faults in the self are minimized (or the admission of them is avoided entirely) by exaggerating those faults in out-groups. (This is the process of projection discussed earlier.) This projection is especially noticeable in the areas of sexual behavior and agression.

Evaluation of Personality Theory of Prejudice

Certainly, the authoritarian personality studies have been subjected to considerable criticism, both of the methods employed and the underlying theories on which they are based. Methodologically, for example, the study has been criticized because, on three of the four scales, the prejudiced or authoritarian

Overly strict childrearing may be an important cause of the development of prejudiced personalities, because it frequently leads to a tendency toward displacement of aggression. Frequently, minority groups become scapegoats toward whom such displaced aggression is expressed. Mimi Forsyth from Monkmeyer Press Photo Service.

response was always to "agree" with the statements presented. Some people, commonly known as "yeasayers," will agree with almost any statement that they are presented with (Cronbach, 1946). Thus, the scales may to some degree have been measuring "yeasaying" rather than prejudice or authoritarianism (Cohn, 1953). A common substantive criticism has been that the theory deals only with right-wing or fascist authoritarianism, when it may be true that those on the left—liberals and radicals—can be rigid and authoritarian, too. This has sparked considerable sociological and psychological debate as to whether there are authoritarians of the left as well as the right (for a detailed discussion of these and other criticisms, see Brown, 1965, pp. 509−544). Despite the criticisms, few social scientists would totally negate the notion that prejudice meets basic personality needs in some individuals. It is also widely agreed that displacement, or scapegoating, and projection are important processes leading to prejudice (see, for example, Simpson and Yinger, 1972, pp. 67−77; Allport, 1954, Chapters 21 and 24). The major debate centers around the relative importance of personality needs compared to other factors in causing prejudice. One example of this can be found in the observation that people who feel insecure about their status are more likely to be prejudiced. Although this can be readily interpreted as evidence that personality problems lead to prejudice, there are other ways of looking at it. It could be argued that people who feel insecure about their status frequently *are* in more insecure social and economic positions, and that they will feel (perhaps with some justification) that any gains by minority groups are likely to come at *their* expense rather than at the expense of those who are better off. Indeed, people who are in marginal economic positions *do* tend to be more prejudiced. Thus, it is reasonable to conclude that some of the patterns observed by Adorno may be the results of the larger social structure rather than being entirely the products of individual personalities. Clearly, no single factor can entirely explain prejudice, and there is much debate about the relative importance of different processes and factors that are associated with prejudice. We shall turn now to some of the other causes of prejudice that have been identified by social scientists.

SOCIAL LEARNING AND CONFORMITY AS CAUSES OF PREJUDICE

Rather than focusing on the personality needs of the individual, social scientists who study social learning and conformity as causes of prejudice usually look at the social environment. Their belief is that an environment where prejudice is the norm will tend to produce prejudiced individuals—even if those individuals have no particular personality need to be prejudiced.

One way this happens is through the childhood socialization process. In a variety of ways, agents of socialization—parents, peers, schools, the media—transmit *their* values and behavior patterns to the child. One of the most important processes by which this happens is that of selective exposure and modeling. By this, we mean that children are exposed to certain kinds of values and behaviors but not others. Sometimes this reflects a deliberate effort on the part of parents seeking to "protect" or shelter children. However, such exposure is often quite unintentional, reflecting homogeneity among peer groups, parents, and other agents of socialization. In any case, if a child is exposed over a long period of time to one set of values or one way of doing things, he or she is likely to eventually come to view that as the natural way or the only way. This is particularly true when the models (those from whom the values or behaviors are learned) are people with whom the child feels a close identification, such as parents or close friends (Bandura and Walters, 1963; Allport, 1954). The parents, for example, can do a great many things that a young child cannot, and of course are the main source of assistance and support. Frequently, young children see their parents as all-knowing and all-powerful. Thus, the parents' prejudices are taken for truth by the children, often with very little thought or awareness of what has happened (Allport, 1954, Chapter 17).

In addition to these effects of selective exposure and modeling, we may add patterns of reward and punishment. All agents of socialization reward behavior and expression of attitudes that conform to their norms and punish those that do not. As with selective exposure, these patterns of reward and punishment are sometimes very deliberate and planned but at other times very informal and impromptu. Among peer groups it may be as simple as mild derision or "kidding" when nonconforming views are expressed or a friendly handshake or backslap in response to a conforming view. Either way, the message gets across: Conform and you will be rewarded; dissent and you will be punished. Research on moral and cognitive development of children, moreover, shows that while children may initially conform merely to get reward or avoid punishment, they will eventually internalize (come to accept on their own) the conforming beliefs, values, and norms about behavior (Piaget, 1932; Kohlberg, 1969).

Prejudice may be seen as just one of many kinds of beliefs and attitudes that are learned through such socialization processes as selective exposure, modeling, reward and punishment, and internalization. This suggests that one source of prejudice is the experience of growing up in prejudiced environments: families, peer groups, schools, and other places where prejudice is the norm. Children growing up in such environments are in fact likely to express considerable prejudice (see for example, Richert, 1974; Allport, 1954; Blake and Dennis, 1943); to the degree that they internalize prejudiced beliefs and attitudes, they may retain these biases into their adult lives. Indeed, it has been shown by numerous studies that people's ethnic attitudes—even in adulthood—are substantially influenced by the attitudes of their parents. (For a review of this literature, see Ehrlich, 1973.) Of course, there are many other factors in adult life that will determine the actual level of prejudice, but it does appear that social learning from parents and other agents of childhood socialization lays a groundwork that significantly predisposes people toward being prejudiced or unprejudiced later on.

Not all social learning and pressures for conformity occur in childhood, however. Indeed, social scientists today recognize that socialization is a lifelong process. Moreover, it seems fair to say that the attitudes prevailing in an adult's *present* social environment can be at least as important in shaping her or his attitudes as anything learned in childhood. Put simply, most people are concerned about what others think of them and will tend to conform to gain or keep the acceptance of others. The strength of these pressures for conformity have been demonstrated in a famous experiment by Asch (1956) showing that people will actually give a description contrary to what they can plainly see if the pressures for conformity are strong enough. In Asch's experiment, seven confederates (accomplices of the researcher posing as subjects) gave an obviously wrong answer concerning the relative length of lines shown to research subjects. When the real subjects were asked the answer, about a third of them conformed to the unanimous opinion of the others and agreed with the clearly wrong answer given by the others. (In a control group, less than 1 percent of subjects gave wrong answers.) This tendency toward conformity has been widely confirmed by other research.

These general principles about the tendency of attitudes to conform to those of *reference others* (other people with whom we have contact, who are meaningful to us, and whose judgments are important to us) have been shown to be true for prejudice as well as for other types of attitudes and beliefs. This can be illustrated in several ways. First, it appears that in settings where strong prejudice is the norm, personality factors are less valid predictors of one's level of prejudice. In the southern United States in the 1950s, for example, the pressures to conform were so strong that the overwhelming majority expressed prejudiced views (see, for example, Prothro, 1952). In that setting, one definitely did not have to have an authoritarian personality in order to score high on a scale measuring antiblack or anti-Semitic attitudes and beliefs (Pettigrew, 1971, Chapter 5).

The tendency to conform to the norms of reference of others on racial and ethnic issues can also be seen in a set of studies in which college students were asked to commit themselves to public actions supporting harmonious race relations. Examples included appearing in a newspaper ad supporting tolerance with a person of the opposite race and sex, participating in a civil rights demonstration, and giving a speech on television advocating tolerance. (For examples of this type of research, see DeFleur and Westie, 1958; Fendrich, 1967; Ewens and Ehrlich, 1969). These studies found that individual attitudes and beliefs could not completely predict willingness to take such actions. Furthermore, the perceived attitudes of reference others—friends, parents, acquaintances—were a significant factor influencing such willingness. Taken together, the various items of research on conformity and prejudice suggest that ethnic attitudes, beliefs, and predispositions to behave are all shaped by the dominant norms of one's reference others. In other words, they are significantly influenced by pressures for conformity.

This suggests two generalizations about prejudice. First, as we have already observed, people who grow up in social settings where prejudice is the norm will tend to be prejudiced both in childhood and in their adult lives. Second, anyone in an environment where prejudice is the norm will experience pressures to be prejudiced. Thus, people in such settings will tend to be more prejudiced than people in settings without norms favoring prejudice. There are of course rebels: Some people in prejudiced environments are unprejudiced, and some people in tolerant settings are prejudiced. Social learning and conformity clearly do not totally explain human behavior. Nonetheless, people will, in the absence of some social or psychological force to the contrary, usually tend to conform.

Comparison of Personality Theory and Social Learning Theory

It is difficult to evaluate the relative importance of personality needs as opposed to social learning and conformity pressures as causes of prejudice. Some have suggested that social learning offers a simpler explanation for some of the relationships observed in the authoritarian personality studies than the rather complex Freudian theories suggested by Adorno. If, as Adorno found, authoritarian people are prejudiced, and prejudiced people tend to have been raised in authoritarian homes, is it not possible that they simply learned prejudice from their parents? This is an appealing suggestion and probably is of merit in some cases. The problem with it is that some people who grow up in prejudiced homes retain their prejudices throughout life and others do not. One explanation of this is that people who have a strong personality need to be prejudiced tend to remain prejudiced even when the social environment is *not* supportive, whereas people who are prejudiced mainly for reasons of conformity tend more often to change as the environment changes. There is in fact good evidence that many people of both types exist (Pettigrew, 1976, pp. 486–489). Personality needs, then, suggest one reason why, in spite of the general tendency toward conformity, many people do not conform, even when the social environment offers clear norms.

Of course, it is more often than not true that in homes where children are strictly raised and severely punished (which leads to prejudice-prone personality types), the parents also tend to be more prejudiced (see, for example, Allport, 1954, Chapter 18). Thus, both personality dynamics *and* social learning patterns tend to create prejudice in the same individuals, and it is often difficult to sort out the influences of the two factors. In spite of this difficulty, it does seem clear that prejudice which meets some basic personality needs (such as scapegoating or projection) is more difficult to change than prejudice that is mainly the result of social learning and conformity. The latter can frequently be unlearned in an unprejudiced environment; the former cannot.

Before moving on, we should point to one further pattern that suggests that neither personality theory nor social learning–conformity theory can give us the whole picture of prejudice. This pattern is easy to understand and quite well known: Various social groups differ drastically in their degree of prejudice toward groups and individuals who differ from them. Such group differences cannot be explained

on the basis of individual personality differences, and social learning and conformity do not offer a very good explanation either. They can, of course, explain why
people *within* a group tend to hold similar attitudes, but they *cannot* explain how
different groups developed different attitudes and beliefs in the first place. In other
words, why is it that some social, economic, cultural, and religious groups tend
generally to be open and tolerant toward others, while other groups tend to be
narrow and intolerant? It would appear that the answer to this must be sought in
variations in the collective experiences of the groups, or in the larger social structure
within which the groups exist. This approach will be given greater emphasis in later
chapters, but we shall explore one aspect of it in the remainder of this chapter.

SOCIOECONOMIC STATUS
AND PREJUDICE

One of the fundamental criteria on which people in any society tend to group
themselves together is socioeconomic status (often abbreviated SES). By
socioeconomic status, we mean one's position in society's ranking system as
represented particularly by such criteria as income, educational level, and occupation. It has been shown, quite consistently, that the various forms of prejudice are
quite strongly related to socioeconomic status. Persons in lower SES groups tend to
report more negative views toward out-groups, to be more ethnocentric, and to
express more stereotyped thinking (see, for example, Brown, 1965, pp. 518–523;
Simpson and Yinger, 1972, pp. 131–138). Some critics of this view have
suggested that the relationships researchers have found reflect sophistication more
than actual prejudice: Middle and upper class participants in present-day social
research ''know better'' than to make strongly or clearly prejudiced statements.
There are, however, several reasons to believe that the SES-prejudice relationship
cannot be dismissed so readily. First, many characteristics known to be related to
prejudice are also related to social class: Authoritarianism and the related
dimensions, rigidity of thinking, and status concern coupled with insecurity are
examples (MacKinnon and Centers, 1956; Lipset, 1959). Furthermore, there are a
number of logical explanations for the relationship. For one, people of higher SES
have more education, and education is widely seen as a way of breaking down
oversimplified, stereotyped thinking. Studies do show that persons of higher
education tend to be less prejudiced, though the relationship is not always strong
(Allport, 1954).

Another explanation can be found in the relationship between feelings of
status insecurity and prejudice. If persons who feel insecure about their status are
indeed more prejudiced, it is hardly surprising that persons of lower SES are more
prejudiced: their position in life is in fact more marginal and insecure than that of
people who are economically ''better off.'' As a result, they may attempt to make
themselves feel better about their status by invidious comparisons with minority

group members: "I may not be much, but at least I'm better than a lousy (fill in the blank)." Still another explanation for the tendency toward an inverse relationship between SES and prejudice is also to be found in the structural position of the lower- or working-class person. As we shall show in considerable detail in subsequent chapters, society is organized so that most of the time it is the *least advantaged* members of the majority group who are forced to compete with minority group members for such resources as jobs, education, and housing. This view suggests that the source of working-class prejudice is not to be found mainly in personality or psycholgical factors, but rather in the fact that working class whites are structured into competing with minorities in a way that others are not (Ransford, 1972). If we understand this, we can perhaps see why it is that lower status members of majority groups tend to see minorities as threats, even enemies—and develop the prejudiced attitudes consistent with that view.

SUMMARY AND CONCLUSION

In this chapter we have examined the meaning of the concept of prejudice and seen the various forms that prejudice can take. We have seen that one reason people are prejudiced is that prejudice meets some people's personality needs, which have developed as a result of certain kinds of experiences in life. Nonetheless, not all people who are prejudiced have a psychlogcial need for prejudice: Some are prejudiced either because they learned prejudice from their parents, peers, or other agents of socialization, or because they live in a social environment where prejudice is the norm. Finally, we have introduced the idea—to be explored in greater detail in later chapters—that prejudice can be a result of one's position in the socioeconomic hierarchy. This can occur either because of effects of education, which is believed to make people more open-minded, or because of structured competition between minority groups and lower status majority group members. In addition, downgrading of minorities may serve the psychological function of easing dissatisfaction with one's own low status.

This chapter has concerned itself mainly with the nature of prejudice and with its causes; the next chapter will turn to two important questions about prejudice that we have not yet discussed: First, how can existing prejudice be effectively combated or reduced? Second, what is the relationship between prejudiced attitudes and discriminatory behavior?

GLOSSARY

Anti-Semitism   Prejudice and discrimination against Jewish people.
Displacement, or Displaced aggression   Similar in meaning to scapegoating.
Ethnocentrism   A tendency to view one's own group as the norm or standard

and to view out-groups as not just different but also strange and usually inferior. The ways of the in-group are viewed as the natural way or the only way of doing things and become a standard against which out-groups are judged.

In-group   A group of which a person is a member, or with which he or she identifies.

Out-group   A group to which one does not belong and with which one does not identify. Frequently, this group is culturally or racially different from and/or in competition with the in-group.

Prejudice   A tendency to think in a particular way, usually negative, toward an entire group. Prejudice can be cognative (involving beliefs about a group), affective (involving dislike of a group), or conative (involving the desire to behave negatively toward a group).

Projection   A process whereby people minimize or deny characteristics they see as undesirable in themselves by exaggerating these same characteristics in others. Since such characteristics are often projected onto members of out-groups, projection appears to be a significant factor in the dynamics of prejudice.

Stereotype   An exaggerated belief associated with a category such as a group of people. It is a tendency to believe that anyone or almost anyone who belongs to a particular group will have a certain characteristic; e.g., "Jews are money-hungry."

Scapegoating   A tendency to take out one's feelings of frustration and aggression against someone or something other than the true source of the feelings. Often, racial, ethnic, or religious minorities are made the scapegoat for feelings of anger and frustration that have built up for reasons unrelated to the minority groups.

Combating Prejudice; How Important Is Prejudice?

3

Having examined some of the causes of prejudice and the ways in which people become prejudiced, we shall now examine two other important issues. First, we shall examine and evaluate various approaches to combating or reducing prejudice. Second, we shall examine the relationship between prejudice and behavior and attempt to answer the question, how important is prejudice as a cause of racial and ethnic discrimination?

REDUCING PREJUDICE—SOME PRINCIPLES AND APPROACHES

Two important principles were presented in the previous chapter: (1) There are several different kinds of prejudice: cognitive (involving beliefs), affective (involving dislike), and conative (wanting to discriminate). (2) Prejudice of any kind has multiple causes, such as personality needs, social learning and conformity, and the nature of a society and its institutions. Taken together, these facts suggest some important principles about combating or reducing prejudice. First, there is no one approach which is *the* solution to the problem of prejudice. There are simply too many kinds of prejudice, and too many reasons why people are prejudiced, for any one approach to always work. Thus, such statements as "The answer is education" or "If only people would get to know each other, they'd get along" are oversimplifications. They are true in some situations but clearly not in others.

A second general principle about combating prejudice is that the approaches that work best vary from case to case, depending on the type of prejudice and its main causes in any given case. An example may help to illustrate this principle. If some personality need underlies a person's prejudice, neither education nor contact with minorities is likely to reduce that prejudice. The most effective approach in such a case may be some type of individual or group therapy to resolve the personality problem causing the prejudice. However, if a person is prejudiced mainly as a result of social learning or pressures for conformity, personal therapy aimed at personality change may be quite ineffective. A better solution in this case could be either an educational effort aimed at correcting false stereotypes or an effort to change the environment to make it more favorable to open-mindedness, either by reducing pressures to discriminate or to express prejudiced views or by creating counterpressures in the opposite direction. (Conformity pressures can tend to make people unprejudiced as well as prejudiced.) Another important situation is one in which prejudice serves mainly as a mechanism to justify or support discriminatory behavior. In this case, direct attempts to change the prejudice may not be effective at all: The behavior is the source of the problem, and it is the behavior which needs to be changed. The important point is that what may work to eliminate one type of prejudice may be ineffective against another type; therefore, the approach used must always be geared to the particular situation.

We can identify at least four major kinds of approaches that are frequently suggested as possible ways of reducing racial and ethnic prejudice. These are persuasive communications, education, intergroup contact, and therapy. All share the common assumption that, while prejudice may serve some important individual or social functions, prejudice fundamentally involves invalid or irrational thinking and is therefore vulnerable to attack. Some examples of this were illustrated in Chapter 2. We showed, for example, that prejudiced people frequently express prejudices against nonexistent groups, and that the same quality is often labeled positively for the in-group but negatively for the out-group. It can also be shown that stereotyping frequently is contradictory, so that, for example, anti-Semitic persons view Jews as "pushing in where they don't belong" but also "sticking to themselves and refusing to assimilate," or as being "ruthless capitalists and unfair businessmen" but also "communistic" (Adorno et al., 1950; Allport, 1954). In theory, then, pointing out the fallacies of prejudiced thinking ought to have some potential for reducing the level of prejudice. All the methods mentioned— persuasive communication, education, intergroup contact, and therapy—seek to do this in some way. Therapy, in addition, may seek to resolve personality problems that may be causing prejudice. In practice, the effectiveness of each of these techniques varies widely. This is partly a function of how the techniques are used. It is also partly determined by the type of prejudice and the causes of the prejudice encountered in any given case—and as we have noted, these vary widely. In the following pages, we shall discuss and evaluate each of these four approaches to the reduction of prejudice.

Persuasive Communications

A *persuasive communication* can be broadly defined as any communication—written, oral, audio-visual, or whatever—which is specifically intended to influence attitudes, beliefs, or behavior. The key defining characteristic here is intent. A speech, movie, or book clearly aimed at reducing prejudice would be a persuasive communication; a college course on race relations, designed only to impart information, would not, even if it did bring about a change in students' attitudes. (Of course, this example is not an accurate description of all college courses; some are designed with the intent of changing people's minds.) Some social scientists, such as Yinger and Simpson (1974) further subdivide persuasive communications into such categories as exhortation (direct pleading or argument of a viewpoint to a person or audience) and propaganda (large-scale and organized efforts, frequently involving the mass media). Although such a distinction is useful for some purposes, the general principles regarding the effectiveness of the communication are quite similar for either type. Accordingly, we shall treat these two subtypes together in this chapter under the general heading of persuasive communications.

Perhaps the best way to begin our evaluation of persuasive communications as a means of reducing prejudice is to examine what is known about the effectiveness of persuasive communications in general. We can start with some principles that establish minimum conditions necessary for a persuasive communication to be successful (Flowerman, 1947; Hovland, Janis, and Kelley, 1953; McGuire, 1968). First, a communication must be heard and paid attention to. This is no small requirement, because in a society where advertising and propaganda are pervasive, most people have developed considerable skill at avoiding or ignoring persuasive communications. Second, the message must be correctly understood. If a pleasant story with the moral that prejudice is bad is understood only as a pleasant story—that is, if the message about prejudice is totally missed—it cannot be effective in changing people's minds. Third, receiving the communication must in some way be a positive experience: The message must be enjoyed or seen as presenting "a good idea." Finally, the message must be retained and internalized so that the desired effect lasts more than a few minutes after the end of the communication. A failure at any one of these points means that the communication is not going to be successful in changing attitudes or beliefs. The likelihood that these conditions will be met depends on a number of factors, including (1) the source of the communication, (2) the content of the message, (3) the process in which the message is presented, and (4) the characteristics of the audience—that is, the person or persons receiving the message (Triandis, 1971).

Having outlined these general principles about persuasive communications and attitude change, we can move to several more specific observations. One is that people tend to expose themselves to messages that are consistent with what they already believe. They also tend to pay better attention to, and to retain longer, messages that support their preexisting viewpoints. These tendencies vary according to personality and situation (Triandis, 1971, Chapter 6), but overall, we see, pay attention to, and remember things that reinforce what we already believe. Thus, those who receive the most antiprejudice communications tend to be people who are already least prejudiced. Furthermore, the tendency will be for those who are *most* strongly prejudiced to be the least exposed and the most resistant to antiprejudice communications. The reasons for this are that people tend not to like to have their beliefs seriously challenged (so they avoid communications that do so), and they tend to resolve inconsistencies by ignoring or rationalizing away communications that are inconsistent with their attitudes and beliefs rather than by changing their thinking. In other words, attitudes tend to be resistant to change, even if they are, *logically* speaking, vulnerable to attack. Thus, the prospect for changing a strongly prejudiced person through persuasion is usually not good. The potential of persuasive communication appears to be greatest as a means of reinforcing open-mindedness in relatively unprejudiced persons. It can sometimes reduce prejudice in mildly prejudiced persons, but not usually in ones with strong prejudices (Yinger and Simpson, 1974).

A further point relating to the question of exposure is that the main sources of information for most people—books, newspapers, television, and movies—are generally privately controlled and enjoy constitutional guarantees of freedom of expression. Thus, there is no easy way to force these media to expose people to antiprejudice communications. In fact, the messages people receive will tend to reflect the interests and values of those who produce the media as well as the values already present in the larger culture (since the media producers want to sell their product). The likelihood that people will be exposed to antiprejudice messages depends very much on the wishes of media owners and producers and on the general social and cultural atmosphere at any given time. It follows, unhappily, that in times when prejudice is most widespread, the media will be least likely to send antiprejudice messages.

The personality characteristics of the person receiving the message also influence the effectiveness of persuasive communication aimed at reducing prejudice. In general, people who have a strong personality need for prejudice will tend to be resistant to persuasion. Such people are prejudiced mainly because prejudice serves a psychological function for them—not because they are persuaded by the logic of prejudiced arguments. There may, however, be some effective ways to use persuasion in such cases. One such way is to persuade the person to adopt some other viewpoint that meets his or her personality needs more effectively than prejudice, though this can in practice be difficult if the personality need is related to self-image (Triandis, 1971, p. 144), as it often is in prejudiced persons. With authoritarian personalities, another approach is to alter the source of the communication. In this case, a message from a respected authority figure might be better received than would otherwise be the case.

As the last illustration suggests, the source can be highly important in determining the effectiveness of antiprejudice persuasion. The prestige, credibility, attractiveness, and power of the person or source presenting the message can all influence how the message is received. A group of conservative whites, for example, would ordinarily respond more favorably to an antiprejudice communication from the American Legion than to the identical message from the Black Panthers. Of the various factors mentioned, research suggests that the most important one for bringing about long-term attitude change is the credibility of the source (Kelman, 1958). Sources that are persuasive because they are powerful retain their effectiveness only as long as they maintain some control over their audiences; thus, power does not appear to be effective in getting people to internalize the message of a persuasive communication.

To summarize, antiprejudice persuasion appears most effective when the audience is initially not highly prejudiced, when the message is enjoyable and does not conflict with personality needs of the recipient, and when the source of the communication is seen as highly credible by the recipient. Repetition of the message over an extended period is also helpful. All of this suggests that the effectiveness of persuasion as a way of reducing prejudice, while variable, is quite limited, particularly among the most prejudiced people. They are least likely to be exposed to the message, and if they are exposed, they are least likely to understand it (Cooper and Jahoda, 1947; Kendall and Wolf, 1949), enjoy it, or be persuaded by it. They are particularly resistant to persuasion if their prejudices are meeting basic personality needs.

We should not conclude, however, that persuasion can never lead people to become less prejudiced. Studies have shown, for example, that people can become somewhat less prejudiced as a result of viewing a film with a theme of tolerance. In one instance, students shown a popular Hollywood movie that took a strong strand against anti-Semitism became somewhat less prejudiced against not only Jews but also blacks, even though antiblack prejudice was not dealt with in the film (Middleton, 1960). As expected, persons highly concerned about status—a characteristic associated with authoritarian personalities—were least affected by the film. There was, however, no follow-up to see whether the reduction of prejudice remained over an extended time. A similar study (Mittnick and McGinnes, 1958) indicated that some of the reduction in prejudice resulting from a film remained a month later, if the film was followed by a discussion of prejudice.

All in all, we can conclude that persuasive communication can—under certain circumstances—lead to some reduction in prejudice and can reinforce open-mindedness in those who are already relatively unprejudiced. However, the effectiveness of this approach seems very limited when prejudice is strong and in cases where prejudice is meeting some personality need.

Education

Education about majority-minority relations works in ways somewhat similar to persuasion, in that it imparts information that may help to break down incorrect stereotypes and irrational prejudices. Certainly, it is subject to some of the same limitations as persuasion. It cannot, for example, by itself resolve personality needs that cause people to be prejudiced. The main definitional difference between persuasion and education is that education does not, per se, attempt to change people's attitudes. Its objective is to bring about learning, to impart information. As it is actually practiced, it often does have a latent objective of changing people's minds. For the purposes of definition, however, the objective of education is to teach rather than persuade. Nevertheless, in real life, much of what is called education is in fact a mixture of education and persuasion.

Many of the principles pertaining to persuasion also apply to education, but we can make some generalizations that apply specifically to education. Our focus here will be mainly on education about intergroup relations; we shall discuss the effects of educational level later when we examine the influence of social structure, including socioeconomic status, on intergroup relations, and in the chapter on education and intergroup relations.

One principle is that education in intergroup relations is most effective in reducing prejudice (and this also applies to persuasion) when it minimizes the stress associated with admitting previous error. In other words, such education should not make people feel defensive or threaten their egos. The best results are obtained if the person feels he or she is participating in the process of learning new ideas that may be contrary to old ones (Lewin, 1948; Fineburg, 1949).

Teachers, like other people, are sometimes themselves prejudiced—a fact that potentially limits the effect of intergroup relations education. Also, minority group members are underrepresented in the teaching profession. Although substantial improvement has been made in recent years, underrepresentation of minorities remains a problem, particularly in the higher levels of education such as colleges and universities. The evident presence of prejudice or discrimination in the teacher or a teaching staff that is all or mostly white can offset any positive effects of the educational program. Thus, it is important that minorities be appropriately represented on intergroup relations teaching staffs, and that the teachers in such courses be as free from racial and ethnic prejudices as is humanly possible. School materials must also be free from stereotypical portrayals of minorities or from the equally common pattern of ignoring minorities altogether (see, for example, Lessing and Clark, 1976). These principles apply not only to intergroup relations courses and materials but to the entire curriculum. If the learning that occurs in the race relations course is offset by prejudiced teachers, discriminatory practices, and stereotypical books and materials elsewhere in the curriculum, it is unlikely that students will become less prejudiced.

Another problem with the use of education to reduce prejudice—particularly at the college level, where courses are frequently taken on an elective basis—is the familiar one of self-selection. People who take courses in majority-minority relations or related topics probably tend to be less prejudiced than others to begin with. Thus, as with persuasion, education frequently does not reach the most prejudiced people. A similar pattern may develop at the elementary and secondary levels, although for different reasons. At those levels, the school districts that do the most to teach intergroup relations tend to be the more liberal ones where prejudice may be somewhat less widespread to begin with. School districts where prejudice is more widespread (among parents as well as children) may do less to teach intergroup relations simply because the decision makers reflect the general opinion of people in the school district. They frequently tend to view intergroup relations education as unnecessary and perhaps even undesirable, since it detracts from time spent on "reading, writing, and arithmetic" and might lead children to develop "unconventional" ideas, contrary to those of their parents. *The Autobiography of Malcom X* (Haley, 1964), for example, has been a frequent target of protesting parents who object to their children's being exposed to that important work concerning white racism, the black experience, and the black power movement.

Of the research studies that have been done on the effects of education about intergroup relations on prejudice, studies that show a reduction in prejudice outnumber those that do not by about two to one (Ashmore, 1970; Harding et al., 1969). Such educational programs appear most effective in communities that are not highly polarized racially (Litcher and Johnson, 1969) and least effective in communities experiencing racial tensions and polarization (Lessing and Clarke, 1976). As we have suggested earlier, the educational approach also appears more effective when prejudice is relatively mild and does not arise out of personality needs. Dent (1975), for example, found that an education program in intergroup relations was somewhat effective in lowering prejudice levels in people with relatively low F-scale (authoritarianism) scores, but among those with high F-scale scores, the education made no significant difference. These results suggest that —like persuasion—the educational approach to reducing prejudice can be effective, but only up to a point and only in certain situations. Where prejudice is strongest and most deeply entrenched, the educational approach is least effective.

Intergroup Contact

One of the remedies most frequently suggested for reducing racial and ethnic prejudices is intergroup contact. It is felt that intergroup contact, perhaps even more than persuasion and education, can break down people's prejudices by showing them that their stereotypes and their fears about out-groups are unfounded. Indeed, some impressive findings from social science lend support to this notion (often referred to as the "contact hypothesis"). Studies have shown, for example, that people living in integrated public housing projects are less prejudiced and interact more closely with persons of the opposite race than people who live in segregated (all-white or all-black) projects (Deutsch and Collins, 1951; Wilner et al., 1955).

Similar results have been obtained in studies of military personnel where a change from segregated to integrated troop units and living quarters led to substantial declines in prejudice among white soldiers (Stouffer et al., 1949; Mandelbaum, 1952). In studies of other areas of life, the results have been less consistent, but there is considerable evidence that reductions in prejudice—or increased acceptance of racial and ethnic groups other than one's own—result from contact in educational, employment, recreational, and other settings. One problem, however, is that increased contact in a particular setting may lead to increased acceptance only in that situation (Ashmore, 1970). In other words, a white person who works with black people might come to favor integrated workplaces but continue to object to integrated neighborhoods.

Contact between two racial or ethnic groups does not *always* lead to reduced prejudice or improved relations between the groups. There are clearly instances where this is not so. An example can be seen in the intense and sometimes violent conflicts accompanying school desegregation in Boston, Louisville, Pontiac,

Intergroup contact often leads to intergroup friendships, as with these children in a Bronx, New York school. Under the right circumstances, such contact can lead to improved inter-group relations and to reduced prejudice. United Nations/ Macia Weinstein.

Michigan, and elsewhere. Accordingly, research exploring the contact hypothesis has sought to identify the conditions under which contact is likely to reduce prejudice. One essential condition is *equal status*. In other words, people from the racial or ethnic groups involved must be similar in status and power and must not be in a position where one can dominate or exercise authority over the other. Persons working on the same jobs for the same pay or renting similar apartments in the same building would present an example of equal-status contact. A supervisor-employee relationship would be a clear case of unequal status contact. If the people are not of equal status, contact is likely to foster resentment among those in the subordinate role and to reinforce stereotypes about group superiority, or dominance, and inferiority and submission. Since, in a society marked by racial inequality, much intergroup contact is on an unequal basis, the requirement that contact be on an equal level significantly limits the effectiveness of intergroup contact as a way of reducing prejudice. In some cases, contact situations *designed* to create equal status fail to do so because cultural or institutionalized status differences carry over into the situation. Thus, groups designed to create equal status majority-minority contact frequently end up being dominated by majority group members (Cohen, 1972). Accordingly, special efforts may be necessary to insure that truly equal status contact occurs. Research by Cohen et al. (1976) suggests that one way to do this may be to present role models or experiences that contradict the generalized cultural pattern, such as having black students act as ''teachers'' and white students as ''learners'' in training exercises involving unfamiliar tasks or knowledge.

　　Another essential condition is that contact be noncompetitive and nonthreatening for both groups involved. Any contact that evokes fear and defensiveness runs the risk of making intergroup relations worse, not better. Racial prejudice is sometimes strong in working-class whites because they fear they will lose their jobs or lose control of their schools or neighborhoods to blacks, Chicanos, Puerto Ricans, or other minorities. Contact that intensifies such fears can often make prejudiced people even more prejudiced. Some school desegregation conflicts illustrate this. The city of Boston experienced intense conflict and a number of violent incidents during the implementation of a school desegregation plan in the mid-1970s. Although the plan involved numerous neighborhoods and schools, the violence centered around a very few schools and neighborhoods. The conflict was most intense in the white districts of South Boston, and to a lesser degree, Charlestown, East Boston, and Hyde Park, and in the black neighborhood of Roxbury. Most of these neighborhoods shared certain characteristics that explain why they experienced great turbulence while the rest of the city remained quiet. Most were poor or near-poor neighborhoods, where people had little security or control in their jobs and their economic situations. The neighborhoods were for the most part ethnically homogeneous (South Boston, for example, was heavily Irish), and ethnicity formed a basis for solidarity. In addition, the neighborhoods were grossly underrepresented in the city's political and educational power structure. They did, however, have a strong sense of community within the neighborhood— perhaps even a sense of ''turf.'' Indeed, the residents (the whites particularly) perceived their immediate neighborhood—symbolized by the neighborhood school—as one of the very few places where they did have control. Finally, there was a widespread belief, both among the poor blacks in Roxbury and the poor whites in South Boston and similar neighborhoods, that they were in intense job competition with the other race. As is frequently the case with the urban working and lower classes, each race tended to see the other as a threat to already-limited employment opportunities. To whites in South Boston, school desegregation took away one of the few remaining areas where they felt they had control. When combined with their generally insecure position and their fears and prejudices toward blacks, this created an explosive mix. Antiblack feelings soared and exploded into violence. Blacks, who certainly felt equally threatened and power-less, responded with violence of their own. The result was several mass attacks on black people in South Boston, followed by attacks on whites in Roxbury. As we shall see when we study the busing issue in a later chapter, it is questionable whether much could have been gained by including such poverty-stricken white neighborhoods in the busing plan. The particular characteristics of the neighbor-hoods made them ones where desegregation was viewed as an intense threat, and where intergroup contact led to worse, not better race relations, at least in the first year or two of the plan. The difference between these neighborhoods and most Boston neighborhoods (where little or no real conflict accompanied desegregation) illustrates well the point that intergroup contact must be noncompetitive and nonthreatening to both groups. If this condition is not met, the contact is unlikely to lead to improved attitudes and can, in fact, make racial attitudes much less favorable.

Before moving on, it should be pointed out that even a situation where intergroup contact is highly threatening to both groups does not have to remain that way forever. If the initial storm can be weathered, people can sometimes overcome their fears so that they see less threat or no threat in a particular kind of contact. An example can be seen in another northern school desegregation case, this one in Pontiac, Michigan. Several years before the Boston controversy, a desegregation plan that, like Boston's, involving busing, was implemented under court order in Pontiac. The plan brought intense conflict, climaxed by a bombing of several school buses by Ku Klux Klan members. Within a few years, however, people had accommodated themselves to the plan and many felt that, although they would rather have done without it, it did not really pose a great threat to the quality of their lives. Many observers in the community also felt that racial conflict in Pontiac was greatly reduced in the several years following implementation of the desegregation plan.

To summarize, then, contact must be noncompetitive and nonthreatening if it is to lead to improved intergroup attitudes and beliefs. However, it should be added that what is initially a threatening contact does not always have to remain so.

Intergroup contact must also be more than superficial if it is to lead to reduced prejudice. Studies of interracial camping situations have shown, for example, that sharing a room or tent led to a greater reduction in prejudice and stereotyping than merely playing games together. This is probably because—given their preexisting prejudices—people will tend to avoid getting to know members of the other race very well if the situation permits such avoidance. This is probably why interracial housing arrangements generally lead to a greater reduction in prejudice than other forms of contact (Harding et al., 1969).

It has become increasingly clear that the most effective contact in reducing prejudice is contact that not only meets all of the above conditions but also makes members of the two groups dependent on one another and demands cooperation. This principle was illustrated in a fascinating study by Sherif et al. (1961) known as the Robbers Cave experiment. Sherif and his colleagues arranged for a group of boys attending scout camp to be divided into two groups (the Rattlers and the Eagles), then placed the groups in numerous competitive and sometimes frustrating situations. In addition to competitive games between the two groups, situations were arranged such as one where one group arrived first at a party and ate most of the food before the other arrived. This caused strong group identities to form within each group and considerable hostility to develop between the groups. Eventually, the experimenters ended the competition and brought the groups together in common, noncompetitive situations. This had no effect. The groups continued to maintain their identities, and members of each remained hostile and cold toward members of the others. It was not until a third stage of the experiment that a significant change occurred. In this stage, the experimenters cleverly created situations in which members of the two groups *had* to cooperate in order to achieve some shared goal. For example, on a trip a truck stalled and members of both groups had to cooperate in pulling it up a hill until it would start. In another instance, the experimenters secretly disrupted the camp's water supply, and members of the two groups had to cooperate in restoring the supply. After a series of similar incidents, the hostility had almost entirely melted away. No longer were members of the opposite group shunned and ridiculed. Instead, friendships developed between members of opposite groups. In this experiment, equal-status contact alone was not sufficient to break down the intense intergroup hostility which had developed. Only when the two groups were *interdependent* and had to cooperate did the hostilities break down.

Although the Sherif experiment involved groups "artificially" created by an experimenter rather than real racial and ethnic groups, there is ample evidence that interdependency is important in reducing real-life racial and ethnic prejudices. This is illustrated, for example, by the reductions in racial prejudice among black and white soldiers who have depended on one another in combat situations (Stouffer et al., 1949)—perhaps the prototypical case of a situation demanding cooperation for a common goal.

To summarize, then, contact can be an important force for reducing prejudice under the right conditions. In order to reduce prejudice, intergroup contact must be on an equal-status basis, it must be more than superficial, and it must be nonthreatening and noncompetitive. It is most effective when, in addition, the contact is such that members of the groups must cooperate to reach some common

Army recruiters. Although racial conflict is not uncommon in the military, interracial units in *combat* situations often lead to a reduction in prejudice, since the soldiers are "all in the same boat together" and depend upon one another for survival. Marc Anderson.

goal. Unfortunately, much of the contact between racial and ethnic groups in America today does not meet these conditions. Moreover, because of the largely segregated nature of our social institutions, many whites have very little contact with minority group members other than the most superficial types.

Many of the research studies we have discussed have focused mainly on the prejudices of majority group members. Indeed, the intergroup attitudes of whites have been studied much more extensively than those of minority group members. This is partly because the problem of racial discrimination is by its nature mainly a majority group problem. Subordinated minorities simply do not have comparable power to discriminate, even if they are so inclined. Nonetheless, the research that has recently been undertaken in the understudied area of minority-group attitudes has yielded some interesting findings. One is that the attitudes of blacks toward whites appear less subject to change by education (Robinson and Preston, 1976) and by intergroup contact (Robinson and Preston, 1976; Ford, 1973) than do the attitudes of whites about blacks. This could be interpreted as meaning blacks are less flexible in their thinking than whites, but the studies suggest that other explanations are more plausible. Both studies showed that blacks were less prejudiced to begin with, so they had less room for improvement. It also turns out that what whites see as equal-status contact does not seem equal to blacks, who perceive—often with some basis in fact—subtle acts of condenscension or superiority and dominance on the part of whites (cf. Cohen and Roper, 1972; Riordan and Ruggiero, 1980). Finally, the ''prejudices'' among blacks turn out to be mainly the perception that whites will behave in a discriminatory, paternalistic, or egotistical manner toward blacks. Since whites have a disproportionate share of power, and since many (though certainly not all) whites do behave in these ways, the negative interracial attitudes of blacks would appear to be largely a cautious approach of tending to withhold trust until they are confident that trust is warranted. If this is prejudice, it is certainly qualitatively different from the kinds of prejudice whites frequently display toward blacks. In any case, research on minority group attitudes toward the majority group is increasingly showing that processes by which ethnic attitudes are formed and altered can be quite different for minority group members than for majority group members.

THERAPY

To a large degree, various forms of therapy are aimed at a different kind of prejudice than are the methods previously discussed. Persuasion, education, and intergroup contact, as we have seen, all appear to be most useful when prejudice arises from causes other than personality needs. When prejudice is serving mainly as a way of adapting to personal feelings of insecurity or low self-esteem, undermining the logic of prejudice is unlikely to have much effect. It simply does not deal with the needs and functions that prejudice is serving for the person. Rather, when prejudice is arising from personality needs, many social psychologists feel that some form of individual or group therapy may be the best approach. Such therapy may be aimed at resolving the personality problems that are causing people to be prejudiced or, more conservatively, at convincing the prejudiced person that prejudice is not a rational way of dealing with one's problems and insecurities. Although there is some evidence that individual therapy can sometimes reduce prejudice (Allport, 1954, Chapter 30), group therapy is most commonly used to reduce prejudice, partly because persons rarely if ever seek individual therapy primarily to change their ethnic attitudes. When individual therapy does deal with ethnic attitudes, it is usually in relation to some other problem that caused the person to seek therapy. Another reason for the emphasis on group therapy is that the intense, one-to-one, and frequently long-term interaction between patient and therapist necessary in individual therapy simply would not permit it to reach any sizable proportion of the large number of prejudiced persons in the population. Accordingly, group therapy is more widely used to reduce prejudice, and its use for that purpose has been more widely evaluated. There is evidence that both group therapy aimed at personality change (Haimowitz and Haimowitz, 1950; Pearl, 1954; Rubin, 1967) and group therapy aimed at showing that prejudice is a poor way of adjusting by revealing the personality dynamics of prejudice (Katz et al., 1956; Stotland et al., 1959) can be effective in reducing prejudice. Ashmore (1970), however, has pointed out two potential limitations of such studies. First, several of the studies involved interracial groups, so it is difficult to sort out the effects of group therapy from those of intergroup contact. It is true, however, that in some of the studies subjects showed indications of better personality adjustment along with reductions in prejudice. Second, most of the groups were composed of either highly educated persons or college students. Although such biases are common in social psychological studies, they may be especially important here, since such persons may be motivated more than the average person both to understand their own personalities and to reduce their prejudices.

Another way that has been suggested to reduce personality-related prejudice is to induce people to change their child-rearing practices. As we saw in Chapter 2, those with prejudiced personalities have frequently grown up in an overtly strict, authoritarian home. Unfortunately, however, those parents who are most authoritarian are least likely to be influenced by the child-rearing advice of psychologists and sociologists.

Overview

We have seen that—depending on the situation, the kind of prejudice, the reasons a person is prejudiced, and other factors—persuasion, education, contact, and therapy can be effective in reducing prejudice. None of these approaches however, offers great promise for making inroads on the strongest or most deeply entrenched kinds of prejudice. Many sociologists believe that the causes of prejudice are largely to be found in features of the larger society, such as competition between blacks and whites for scarce jobs. These sociologists believe that the most promising approach to reducing prejudice is to alter the features of society that cause people to be prejudiced. This view will be extensively explored in later portions of this book.

Another view, closely related to this one, is that prejudiced attitudes are largely produced by discriminatory behavior (Raab and Lipset, 1959). According to this view, prejudiced attitudes develop largely to support or rationalize discriminatory behavior that has become institutionalized in some social settings. According to this view, such strategies as therapy, education, and persuasion are unlikely to succeed unless accompanied by efforts to prevent discriminatory behavior, because it is largely the discrimination that causes the prejudice.

A question which follows from this one is whether or not prejudice is really an important cause of discriminatory behavior. Although it is popularly believed that attitudes cause behavior, there is some reason to question whether or not they really do. In the remainder of the chapter, we shall focus on questions relating to the importance of prejudice as a cause of discrimination, and to the reverse possibility, that discrimination may in some cases be a cause of prejudice.

HOW IMPORTANT IS PREJUDICE?

Just how important is prejudice as a cause of discriminatory behavior? A cassic study by La Piere (1936) illustrates dramatically that discrimination does not always follow from prejudice. La Piere, a white man, traveled around the United States with a Chinese couple. They visited sixty-six hotels and motels and one hundred eighty-four restaurants. Of all the establishments, only one refused them service. Six months later, he sent a letter to each establishment asking whether it would give service to Chinese guests. Only about half of them answered the letter, but of those that did answer 92 percent indicated that they would *not* serve Chinese guests. (Obviously, such a response would be illegal today, but at that time it was not.) Kutner and his colleagues (1952) obtained substantially the same results in visits to restaurants by a group of blacks and whites. It is evident that the operators of the establishments had some racial prejudices and *preferred* not to serve Chinese-Americans or blacks. When presented with an actual face-to-face encounter, however, they did. Why is this so? There are several possibilities. Perhaps in the actual face-to-face situation, the proprietors did not have the nerve to say no. Other values—the desire to avoid a hassle or not to seem unkind—may have outweighed the prejudice. Perhaps, too, the presence of a white person with the Chinese or black persons made a difference. It could be that when the operators of the establishments answered the letters, they did not envision the possibility of a racially mixed group of customers. To a prejudiced white, a Chinese person with a white person along to "keep an eye on him or her" may not have seemed as bad as a Chinese person alone.

Whatever the reasons, these studies show that prejudiced attitudes supportive of discrimination do not always lead to actual discrimination.

Merton's Typology on Prejudice and Discrimination

Robert Merton (1949) developed a useful typology based on the principle that prejudice and discrimination do not always occur together. Merton developed four classifications concerning prejudice and discrimination (see Figure 3.1). Type 1, the unprejudiced nondiscriminator, or all-weather liberal, behaves consistently

	DOES NOT DISCRIMINATE	DISCRIMINATES
UNPREJUDICED	1. Unprejudiced nondiscriminator. (all-weather liberal)	2. Unprejudiced discriminator. (fair-weather liberal)
PREJUDICED	3. Prejudiced nondiscriminator. (timid bigot)	4. Prejudiced discriminator. (all-weather bigot)

Figure 3.1   Robert Merton's Typology on Prejudice and Discrimination

with his or her beliefs, as does Type 4, the prejudiced discriminator. Many people—perhaps most—do not fit into either of these categories, however. Some people (Type 2) are fair-weather liberals: They are not prejudiced, but they discriminate anyway. Others (Type 3) are timid bigots: They are prejudiced but do not discriminate. How can the behavior of fair-weather liberals and timid bigots be explained? In both cases, the answer is likely to be found in social pressures that influence behavior so that people's behavior does not always reflect their beliefs. The fair-weather liberal (unprejudiced discriminator) may discriminate because his or her friends or work associates discriminate and expect others to. It is simply easier to discriminate than to risk the ridicule or criticism that could result from doing otherwise. For fair-weather liberals, social policies that create counterpressures *not* to discriminate, or that reduce the pressures to discriminate, may be very effective in reducing or eliminating discriminatory behavior. Greater contact with all-weather liberals may also reduce discrimination among such people, since such contact would strengthen and reinforce their unprejudiced attitudes and perhaps make them aware of the inconsistency of their behavior. The timid bigots (prejudiced nondiscriminators) are also inconsistent in their behavior. Although they would like to discriminate, they don't because they fear running afoul of civil rights laws or, like La Piere's subjects, they are simply too uncomfortable to discriminate in the face-to-face situation. If they are businesspeople, they might avoid discrimination for fear of losing minority business. Because timid bigots will not discriminate as long as they fear the consequences of doing so, antidiscrimination laws are probably an important means of preventing such people from discriminating.

Very few people, of course, fit unambiguously into any one category all of the time. The lines between categories can be fuzzy, behavior often varies from one time to the next, and both prejudice and discrimination are partly a matter of degree. The important point is that prejudice and discrimination do not always go together. In any particular case, the presence or absence of discrimination will be influenced by a number of factors other than prejudice. The pressures of any given situation can influence behavior as much as or more than personal attitudes. Furthermore, other personal attitudes—for example the desire to please others—may conflict with one's ethnic attitudes. How one behaves in such situations may be largely determined by which of the conflicting attitudes is stronger or more salient in the situation at hand.

Can Behavior Determine Attitudes?

We have established that ethnic attitudes do not always determine ethnic behavior. We can now go a step further and ask whether ethnic behavior can sometimes determine ethnic attitudes. A social psychological theory known as *cognitive dissonance theory* (Festinger, 1957) is relevant to this question. Dissonance theory says that we want to believe that our behavior is consistent with our attitudes. Accordingly, if—due to social pressure or whatever reason—we repeatedly behave in a manner inconsistent with our attitudes, we tend to unconsciously change our *attitudes* so that our attitudes and behavior are again consistent. Festinger and Carlsmith (1959) found, for instance, that laboratory subjects who were asked to do a boring task and did so, decided afterwards that the task had really been quite interesting—even when given very little reward for doing it. Moreover, other subjects who had been well paid for doing the same task later said that it had been dull and boring. The difference was that these subjects could say "It was stupid, but I did it for the money," but the poorly paid subjects could make no such rationalization. They could either say "I did this dumb task and got almost nothing for doing it," or "That was really fun." Most chose the latter. The application of this finding to race relations can perhaps be best seen in the American South. The most dramatic declines in prejudice and discrimination in the United States since World War II have been in the South. The decline did not occur as a result of voluntary attitude change. Rather, the South was more or less forced to change by federal legislation, court orders, and at times intervention of federal marshals and federal troops under the order of the President. *After* overt discrimination had been outlawed and had largely disappeared, attitudes changed to become consistent with behavior. In effect, it was easier to say "We don't discriminate because we know now that discrimination is wrong" than to say "We really want to discriminate, but we don't because the Washington bureaucrats told us we can't." Indeed, the new viewpoint even puts Southerners in a position to tell whites protesting school desegregation in Boston or Michigan to "practice what you preach; we are." Indeed, the experiences of the United States South since World War II seriously question the old truism that "legislation can't change people's minds." Although we are not arguing that prejudice has been eliminated in the South (or any other part of the country, for that matter), it is evident that prejudice has been substantially reduced. It also appears that an important cause of this reduction was legislation that forced behavior to change by banning open and deliberate forms of discrimination. In short, a change in behavior led to a change in attitudes (for further discussion of these issues, see Bem, 1970, pp. 68–69; Sheatsley, 1966).

Prejudice and Discrimination in America Today

Because prejudice is not always accompanied by discrimination and because a reduction in discrimination can cause a reduction in prejudice, many social scientists believe that prejudice is not really an important cause of discrimination.

More important, they argue, are characteristics of the larger society, such as the relative power and numbers of different races and ethnic groups, and the degree of competition between groups for scarce resources such as jobs or housing. Furthermore, a strong argument can be made that both prejudice and open, deliberate discrimination are much less important today as causes of racial and ethnic inequality than they were in the past.

For one thing, we know that absolute levels of prejudice are much lower today than they were in the past. This is evident in several ways. Studies of cognitive forms of prejudice show, for example, that negative stereotyping of minority groups, once commonplace, is much less so today. A series of studies of Princeton University students in 1933, 1951, and 1967 graphically illustrates the change. Students were given lists of traits and asked to mark those that were true of each of a variety of ethnic groups. Table 3.1 presents data from these studies showing a steady decline in negative stereotyping of blacks. The same studies showed similar tendencies regarding stereotypes of Chinese (sharp reductions in checking of "superstitious" and "sly"), Jews (greatly reduced tendency to mark "shrewd" and "mercenary"), and Turks (large reduction in marking of "cruel"). On the other hand, there appears to have been an increased tendency to attribute more positive stereotypes to minority groups such as "musical" for blacks, "ambitious" for Jews, and "loyal to family ties" for Chinese. This suggests that people still think in stereotypes, but they are considerably less willing today than in the past to stereotype minority groups negatively. The opposite may be true of stereotypes of the majority group. There was a large reduction in the marking of "industrious" and "intelligent" for "Americans," and an even larger increase in marking of "materialistic" for them: By 1967 it was marked more than twice as often as any other trait. A reduction in cognitive prejudices toward minorities—at least the negative type—can also be seen in the first part of Table 3.2, which shows a huge increase in the percentage of whites agreeing that blacks are as intelligent as whites. In 1942 fewer than half of white Americans agreed with such a statement; since the mid-1950s studies have consistently shown about four out of five whites agreeing with it.

Table 3.1   Characteristics Assigned to Blacks by White Princeton University Students (by marking a checklist)

	1933	1951	1967
Superstitious	84%	41%	13%
Lazy	75	31	26
Happy-go-lucky	38	17	27
Ignorant	38	24	11
Musical	26	33	47

Source: Adapted from Marvin Karlins, Thomas Coffman, and Gary Walters, "On the Fading of Social Stereotypes: Studies of Three Generations of College Students," *Journal of Personality and Social Psychology* 13:1-6. Copyright 1969 by the American Psychological Association. Reprinted by permission.

Table 3.2   Percentage of Whites Agreeing with Statements about Blacks
in U.S. National Samples

Blacks are as intelligent as whites.*
1942: 42%
1956: 78

I would not object if a black of the same income and education as mine moved onto my block.†
1942: 35%
1956: 51
1968: 65
1972: 84

White children and black children should attend the same schools.††
1942: 30%
1956: 48
1968: 60
1970: 73
1972: 84

Sources: *Hyman and Sheatsley, 1964.
†1942–1968: Skolnick, 1969, pp. 179–182; 1972: Farley, 1977.
††1942–1968: Skolnick, 1969; 1970; Greeley and Sheatsley, 1971; 1972; Farley, 1970.

As indicated in Chapter 2, another slightly different form of prejudice is conative prejudice, a tendency to behave in a particular way toward a group. The findings in Table 3.2 show that there has been a major change here too. Compared to the early 1940s, in 1972 far fewer whites indicated a preference to discriminate in the areas of schools and housing, with more than four out of five favoring a nondiscriminatory position. A similar tendency can be seen in measures of *social distance*. The concept of social distance refers to a preference to avoid certain kinds of contact with minority groups. In general, the closer the contact (for example, living next door as opposed to shopping in the same store), the greater the tendency to maintain social distance or avoid contact. One commonly used measure of social distance developed by Bogardus was administered to U.S. college students in 1926, 1946, 1956, and 1966. The items on this scale range from "would marry into group" to "would debar from my nation." The results of these studies for selected groups are presented in Table 3.3. They show a reduction in social distance scores (the higher the score, the greater the social distance) for blacks, Mexican-Americans, American Indians, and Japanese-Americans. The average social distance for the thirty groups studied also declined. Certainly, this study does not indicate anything like a total elimination of prejudice, but it does indicate a consistent pattern of reduced prejudice toward a wide variety of minority groups. A more recent study reported by Bahr and his colleagues (1979) suggests that the desire to maintain social distance has probably decreased further since 1966. This study, using a different measure of social distance and focusing on American Indians, showed that two-thirds of the Seattle whites responding were willing to have their children date Indians, with substantially greater acceptance of other forms of contact (see Table 3.4).

Table 3.3   Bogardus Social Distance Scores for Selected Groups, U.S. National Samples of College Students

	1926	1946	1956	1966
White Americans	1.10	1.04	1.08	1.07
Negroes	3.28	3.60	2.74	2.56
Mexican Americans	—	2.52	2.51	2.37
American Indians	2.38	2.45	2.35	2.12
Japanese Americans	—	2.90	2.34	2.14
Mean, 30 groups	2.14*	2.12	2.08	1.92

*28 groups
Source: Bogardus, 1968.

Table 3.4   Social Distance toward American Indians: Percentage of Whites Agreeing with Selected Statements, Seattle, 1971 (N=304).

I would not mind sitting next to an Indian at lunch in a restaurant or lunch counter.	97%
I would enjoy having an Indian couple come to my home for a visit.	93
I would enjoy being invited to dinner at the home of an Indian family.	91
I would not mind my children dating Indian young people.	65
I would *dislike* going out for an evening of entertainment with a group which included some Indian couples.	12
I would *not* like living next door to a family of Indians.	13
I would *not* want my children going to a school where over half the students were Indians.	18

Source: Reprinted by permission of the publisher, from *American Ethnicity* by Howard M. Bahr, Bruce A. Chadwick, and Joseph H. Strauss (Lexington, Mass.: D. C. Heath and Company, 1979).

Do Attitudes Cause Intergroup Inequality?

Attitude surveys over the past thirty years—those mentioned here and others—consistently indicate a reduction among Americans in the expression of stereotyped thinking and in the desire to discriminate. In spite of this change, racial and ethnic inequalities persist. In Chapter 8 we shall explore in detail the status of a variety of American minority groups. A fair summary of that material is that, despite improvement in some areas, very substantial inequalities persist, and in some areas there has been no real improvement. This brings us back to the question raised at the beginning of this chapter: If prejudice has declined but inequality persists, just how important can majority group attitudes be as a cause of racial inequality? Social scientists answer this question in two ways, and there is no unanimous belief about which answer is better

The Affirmative Answer: Attitudes Do Cause Inequality   Several kinds of arguments are made by those who support the view that white attitudes are an important cause of minority disadvantage, even today when surveys indicate that majority group prejudices have decreased. First, people of this viewpoint are quick to point out that prejudice is by no means eliminated, despite the changes. The social distance scores for blacks, Chicanos, American Indians, and Japanese-Americans remain much higher than those for "white Americans" and for European groups, despite the decreases. Furthermore, there is a notable unwillingness on the part of whites to support efforts aimed at *undoing* the effects of discrimination. Busing and hiring and admissions programs giving preference to minorities who have been victimized by discrimination are opposed by the great majority (many surveys indicate about 80 percent) of whites. Furthermore, research by Schuman (1975) indicates that most whites in 1968 saw blacks as mainly responsible for their own disadvantage (see Table 3.5). A similar study by Feagin (1972) indicated that whites, in particular, also tend more generally to say that poor people are at fault for their own poverty. All in all, many observers would argue that, while blatant prejudices have decreased, white attitudes are still not favorable to the kinds of changes that would be necessary to bring about equality and that whites continue on the whole to blame minorities for their own disadvantage. Furthermore, the "closer to home," or more personal, the issue becomes, the greater the white defensiveness.

In a society where majority rules (at least in part), attitudes can be important. Those in positions of political power must pay attention to what their constituents think, and elections have been won and lost on such issues as busing and affirmative action. The race of the candidate is also frequently an important factor determining how people vote.

Research also indicates that racial attitudes are an important factor influencing the behavior of whites in the workplace toward minority coworkers and subordinates (Harding et al., 1969). Since blocked mobility in the work place—being trapped in low-status, low-paying jobs—is an important source of minority disadvantage, it would appear that majority group attitudes may be contributing to racial inequality in this area. Finally, research also indicates that one of the areas where attitudes are most related to behavior toward minorities is that of friendly association (Harding et al., 1969). Prejudiced people simply avoid friendly contact with members of groups other than their own. To the degree that this promotes separate institutions and the exclusion of minorities, it may contribute to racial inequality.

All and all, it is probably an overstatement to say that racial attitudes have no

Table 3.5 White Opinions about Who is Mainly to Blame for Black Disadvantage "in this City."

Discrimination (by whites)	19
Negroes themselves	54
Mixture of both	19
Denied disadvantage/refused to answer	4
Don't know	4

Source: Schuman, 1975.

effect on racial inequality: We have seen several areas in which they do likely have an effect. On the other hand, how large and how important this effect is, is open to serious question. Attitudes should not be ignored as a cause of racial and ethnic inequality, but neither should they be overplayed. Other factors may be of equal or greater importance than attitudes, as we shall see in the following section.

The Negative Answer: Attitudes Are Not an Important Cause of Inequality Social scientists who do not see individual attitudes as an important cause of inequality generally tend to see larger-scale characteristics of ethnic groups and entire societies as the main causes of inequality. This idea will be explored in detail in the next few chapters; the main objective here is to outline why individual attitudes are not in this view an important cause of racial and ethnic stratification and conflict. Basically, two kinds of arguments are made, and both have already at least been hinted at. One argument centers around a fact we examined earlier in the chapter: Attitudes and beliefs often change to conform to behavior (as they have in the South since discrimination was made illegal) rather than the other way around. Social scientists who hold this view will tend to ask, "What came first, the attitude or the behavior?" If racist attitudes develop merely as a way of rationalizing racist behavior that is already present for some other reason, such as personal gain, then the attitudes cannot be the cause of the racist behavior. They are merely a supporting mechanism.

The other argument acknowledges that racist attitudes may sometimes lead to racist behavior but questions where the attitudes came from in the first place. If intergroup competition or social and economic insecurity, for example, are the ultimate causes of people's prejudices, then it is not productive to point fingers at prejudice as the cause of racial inequality and conflict. The cause runs deeper. Social scientists who hold this view generally tend to downplay the study of prejudice and in particular do not emphasize personality needs or social learning as the root causes of prejudice. Instead, they see prejudice, discrimination, and intergroup conflict as all being caused by larger social forces that can only be .

understood by being aware of how entire societies operate. These social scientists point out—with some good reason—that in the popular mind problems of race relations are frequently equated with problems of prejudice. Whatever importance prejudice may have, we cannot have a full understanding of majority-minority relations without also understanding how the characteristics of whole societies shape the relations between the racial and ethnic groups within them.

SUMMARY AND CONCLUSIONS

In the latter part of this chapter we have seen that, while there is some relationship between prejudiced attitudes and discriminatory behavior, it is far from a one-to-one relationship. In any given case, a person's prejudice is only one of several factors that determine whether or not that person actually discriminates. Moreover, at the larger societal level, there is far from a one-to-one relationship between the degree or prevalence of prejudice and the degree of actual racial inequality in society. Prejudices, at least of some kinds, have greatly declined in the United States compared to thirty or forty years ago, but inequality persists. Thus, factors other than prejudice may account at least for the persistence, if not the original development, of racial inequality. Finally, we have seen that attitudes sometimes change to conform to behavior rather than the other way around. For all these reasons, prejudice *alone* cannot totally explain racial and ethnic inequality and conflict. We must also look at larger societal forces, which we shall do in the next part of the book.

GLOSSARY

Cognitive dissonance theory   A theory that says we strive to make our attitudes consistent with our behavior, frequently by developing attitudes to support or justify preexisting behavior. This theory suggests that nondiscriminatory behavior (e.g., to comply with the law) may lead to unprejudiced attitudes. Similarly, racist behavior (e.g., for personal gain) may lead to racist attitudes as a justifying mechanism

Intergroup education   Any effort, by whatever means, to bring about factual learning about intergroup relations. Education is not primarily intended to change attitudes or opinions, although this may be a common result and is sometimes a latent objective.

Persuasive communication   Any communication—written, oral, audio-visual, or otherwise—that is specifically intended to influence attitudes, beliefs, or behavior.

SOCIAL-STRUCTURAL PERSPECTIVES ON MAJORITY-MINORITY RELATIONS

Sociological
Perspectives: The Order
and Conflict Models

4

SOCIOLOGICAL VERSUS SOCIAL-PSYCHOLOGICAL APPROACHES TO MAJORITY-MINORITY RELATIONS

In Chapters 2 and 3 we have primarily employed a *social-psychological* approach to race and ethnic relations. By this we mean that our concern has been with socially learned attitudes and beliefs in *individuals*. We have looked at how individuals develop negative attitudes and beliefs concerning out-groups, how those attitudes and beliefs may be changed once they have become established, and how they relate to an individual's behavior toward out-groups. Throughout the discussion, we have been talking mainly about *individuals*: their attitudes and beliefs, their experiences, their behavior.

In this chapter, we wish to introduce an alternative approach. This approach is *sociological* because, rather than studying individuals, it focuses on *collectivities* of people: groups and societies. It suggests that the nature of interaction between racial and ethnic groups is determined *not* by the characteristics of individuals in such groups, but rather by the nature of the groups themselves and the society in which they are found. Those who study majority-minority relations from a *sociological* perspective are concerned with such variables as the social, political, and economic organization of a society, the roles played by various ethnic groups within that society, the social organization within the ethnic groups, and the cultures of both the society as a whole and the various groups that compose that society.

The sociological approach assumes that the attitudes of individuals are for the most part shaped by these larger social forces, and that the patterns of ethnic relations also are largely determined by such social forces. In other words, the general characteristics of a society at a given point in time, and the position of a social group (let's say Wallonians) within that society will determine (1) the relationship of the Wallonian group toward other groups in society, (2) the pattern of attitudes held by individual Wallonians toward other groups, and (3) the attitudes of individuals elsewhere in society toward Wallonians. The sociological view, then, sees individual attitudes as being relatively unimportant in *causing* patterns of intergroup relations to develop. These patterns of intergroup relations, instead of being caused by individual attitudes, are caused by the nature of the society as a whole and the nature of the groups within it. These characteristics of the society and its constituent groups are also seen as the major factor determining individual attitudes.

To present a simple example of this, let us consider black-white relations in the United States. If relations between blacks and whites are marked by conflict and exploitation, it is not—according to this sociological or social-structural view—because individual blacks or whites are prejudiced against the other race. Rather, the reasons for the conflict and exploitation are to be found in the characteristics (relative power, culture, or history, for example) of the two groups and in the characteristics of the larger society (the United States) within which both groups exist.

Accordingly, those who take this sociological, or social structural, approach toward studying race relations analyze groups and societies rather than individuals. They seek, first, to describe accurately the patterns of relations between the racial and ethnic groups in a society and, second, to explain the reasons for the particular pattern of relationships found in a society. In making such explanations, they emphasize characteristics of the society and characteristics of the groups in that society—*not* the characteristics of individuals, which are seen for the most part as resulting from, not causing, the group and societywide patterns.

Perhaps an example will help to illustrate the principle. Let us imagine a hypothetical society in which there are two ethnic groups—let us say Wallonians and Piraneans. The first task of the social scientist would probably be to describe the nature of the relationship between the two ethnic groups. It might be the case, for example, that the Wallonians generally dominate the Piraneans. Most of the better jobs and positions of authority are held by Wallonians, and Wallonians have higher incomes and better education. Furthermore, although not all Wallonians are wealthy, nearly all the means of production (such as factories, land, and natural resources) are owned by Wallonians. Furthermore, Wallonians frequently discriminate against Piraneans, though there is no formal code requiring discrimination. Sometimes the Piraneans respond to their subordinate position with organized protest, but they usually try to adapt and make the best of their situation.

The above would be an example (abbreviated and simplified) of a description of a relationship between two ethnic groups in a society. Indeed, if one were to substitute "whites" for Wallonians and "blacks" for Piraneans, the description would be similar in several regards to the relationship between blacks and whites in the United States during recent decades. As you can see, the emphasis is not on individual behavior but on group characteristics and on interaction between two groups, including their roles and statuses in the larger society. In this case, we might summarize the relationship as being one of subtle but nonetheless real domination of one group by another, with the subordinate group responding to the domination with a mixture of protest and adaptation.

Factors Shaping Patterns of Majority-Minority Relations: The Sociological View

The *reasons* for the existence of this pattern would similarly be sought in the characteristics of the society and of the two ethnic groups. Among the things a sociologist would look for would be the following:

1. The basis of economic production in the society: Is the society an industrial society? An agricultural society? A colony? Closely related, what is the level of technology and productivity in the society? Is the society highly complex and specialized, or small and simple without great specialization? Such factors will influence the roles that may be filled by the social groups within that society, and thereby influence the way the groups relate to one another.
2. The nature of the political system: Is it, for example, a democracy, dictatorship, or monarchy? What are the power relationships between groups? What degree of political freedom is permitted in the society?
3. The nature of the economic system: Is it capitalist, feudal, socialist, or some other system? Of particular importance would be the overall distribution of income and wealth, particularly ownership of the basic means of production.
4. Characteristics of other basic institutions in society, such as religion, the family, and education.
5. The predominant culture in the society, including particularly the shared beliefs about reality and the value systems in the society.
6. Characteristics related to culture and social organization that are internal to each of the various ethnic groups that make up the society. Examples might be the existence of aggressive or warlike values in a group, a history within a group of doing a certain kind of work, a shared belief in a particular religion, and so on.

If we wanted, then, to explain why, in our imaginary society, Wallonians and Piraneans relate to one another as they do, and if our approach was a sociological or social structural one, we would ask questions such as those outlined above. All of the questions pertain to characteristics either of the society as a whole or to whole groups within that society—*not* to the characteristics of individual members of the society.

PERSPECTIVES IN SOCIOLOGY

Those who study racial and ethnic relations from a social structural approach may be further divided into at least two differing and often clashing groups. These groups are said to represent competing *perspectives* within sociology. In this section we shall briefly explain what is meant by a perspective; in the remainder of this chapter we shall describe, illustrate, and compare the two dominant perspectives used by those who take a sociological approach to the study of majority-minority relations.

A *perspective*, in the most literal sense, is a way of looking at a question or problem. In large part, that is what the term means when it is applied to sociology. A "way of looking at a problem" may, however, be broken down into at least three parts. The first part involves what questions we ask about a problem or issue. (In a sense, the "answer" we get always depends in part on the question we ask.) The second involves what we *believe* to be true about the issue. When we put together a complex set of propositions that we believe to be true about some topic, we say we have developed a *theory* about that topic. Ideally, a theory is testable: We can evaluate to what degree it accurately describes reality. The third part of a "way of looking at a problem" often implies that we may like or dislike what we see—that is, we may believe that it is "good" or "bad." This opinion is *not* something that can be proven or disproven; it is a matter of personal preference, perhaps a personal moral code. When we talk about personal preferences and opinions that carry notions of good or bad, right and wrong, we are talking about *values* (sometimes referred to as *ideologies*). A perspective, then, is usually composed of three elements:

1. An approach to a topic that helps to determine the kinds of questions that are asked about the topic
2. A theory or set of theories describing what are believed to be the realities of the topic
3. Stated or unstated values concerning potentially controversial issues related to the topic

It is, of course, sometimes asserted that the social sciences are or should be free of values. In real life, however, this is rarely possible. Even the topic a researcher chooses and the questions he or she asks about it are always determined at least partly by personal values. Furthermore, it will be evident as we discuss and illustrate the major perspectives in sociology and how they apply to race relations that these perspectives are far from value free. This does not imply, of course, that they are *only* value judgments or "just a matter of opinion": They do reflect actual theories about the reality of how societies in general and majority-minority relations in particular work. However, they—like most human creations—also reflect the values of the people who developed them.

ORDER AND CONFLICT:
TWO SOCIOLOGICAL PERSPECTIVES

In macrosociology (the study of large-scale, social-structural issues), two perspectives—order and conflict—have been particularly influential. Furthermore, in the particular area of racial and ethnic relations, most social theorizing has utilized one or the other of the two perspectives or has attempted to achieve a synthesis of the two. We shall describe in general terms each of the two perspectives, then attempt to show the major ways in which each has been applied to the study of race and ethnic relations.

The Order Perspective

The first perspective we wish to discuss is known by a variety of names. It has at various times been called the order perspective, structural-functionalism (or simply functionalism), consensus theory, equilibrium theory, or system theory. It arises largely from the theories of Emile Durkheim; however, it has been further developed and greatly elaborated upon by Talcott Parsons and numerous other contemporary sociologists. As we shall also see, it has been widely applied to race and ethnic relations, particularly but not exclusively in the United States. This perspective, like others, should be seen not necessarily as one clear, unified, all-encompassing theory, but rather as a set of related theories (and sometimes value judgments) arising from certain common premises. We shall attempt to state those premises as concisely as possible, keeping in mind that different theorists stress different aspects of the general perspective. In the most basic sense, the common notion underlying this perspective is that society is the way it is *not* by chance but for very specific reasons. Social arrangements exist because they perform some *function* for society: They meet some need of the society or somehow enable the society to operate more smoothly and efficiently than would otherwise be possible. The order, or functionalist, perspective involves a number of assumptions related to this basic premise; most important are the following:

1. Society is made up of a number of interdependent parts. The functioning of society depends on the operation and coordination of all these interdependent segments. Because different parts of society depend upon one another, a change at one point in society will have impacts elsewhere. This is especially true in large, modern, complex, specialized societies.

2. Every aspect of the social structure performs some function for the social system: Somehow, it meets a need or contributes to making the system work or holding it together. A frequently unstated but implicit notion is that society usually tends to work for the greatest good of the largest number of its members.

3. Societies tend toward stability and equilibrium. Because each part is performing a function (making a contribution to society) and is somehow related to other parts, it will tend toward stability and balance: A drastic change would usually be dysfunctional (prevent the system from meeting its basic needs).

4. Society tends toward consensus, at least on certain basic values. This consensus is necessary for cooperation, which in turn is necessary because the people and groups in the social system depend on one another to meet their basic needs.

5. Consensus and stability are desirable in society (a value judgment) because they facilitate the cooperation necessary to meet individual, group, and system needs.

In large part because of the final assumption listed above, the order, or functionalist, perspective is frequently associated with political conservatism, or at most with a cautious type of liberalism advocating minor adjustment but not wholesale change in the social, political, and economic system. Because of its emphasis on stability and its belief that social structure as it is meets basic social needs, the order perspective frequently values stability over social equality, which often requires conflict, change, and struggle. For this reason, critics point out that the perspective reflects certain values as well as sociological theory (see, for example, Horton, 1966), even though some of its proponents purport it to be value free. The functionalist perspective has been dominant throughout most of the history of American sociology. However, for a variety of reasons, including the fact that order theory did not predict (and had a hard time explaining) the social upheavals of the 1960s and early 1970s, its alternative, the conflict perspective, was "rediscovered" in the 1960s and has taken on a growing importance in American sociology over the past fifteen years.

The Conflict Perspective

The major competing approach to the order perspective is known as the conflict, or power and conflict, perspective. This approach arises largely, though not entirely, out of the theories of Karl Marx and has been elaborated upon by such modern sociologists as C. Wright Mills and Ralf Dahrendorf. As with the order approach, the conflict perspective is best seen not as one unified, totally coherent theory but as a set of related theories that share certain common premises and assumptions. The most basic premise underlying this approach is that society is as it is because the arrangements in society favor certain powerful and advantaged groups who exercise control over most aspects of society. Associated with this premise are the following assumptions:

1. Because of the control exercised by the powerful groups, most or all aspects of the social structure operate in such a way that they serve the interests of the dominant group. As a result, this dominant group (usually small relative to the entire population) controls a vastly disproportionate share of such scarce resources as wealth and social status.
2. Conflict is built into society; that is, societies naturally tend toward conflict. This is because wealth and power are distributed unequally; therefore, different social groups have different and conflicting self-interests.
3. When consensus does appear in society, it is artificial and unlikely to persist over the long run. The usual causes of apparent consensus in society are either coercion and repression by the dominant group or an acceptance by disadvantaged groups of ideologies not in their self-interest. The latter occurs because dominant groups exert disproportionate control over the sources of influence over public opinion. In either case, the consensus lacks a fundamental stability and is unlikely to persist over the longer run.
4. Conflict in society is desirable (a value judgment) because it makes possible social change, which may lead to a more equitable distribution of wealth and power.

As can be seen from the last assumption, the conflict perspective also makes some value judgments. Because social change and equality are valued over stability, the conflict perspective tends toward a radical (or at the very least, strongly reformist) political orientation: It argues that if the social structure promotes the interests of a dominant few at the expense of others, it must be changed—often in very basic and fundamental ways.

As noted, one social theorist, Karl Marx, has had an especially strong influence over the conflict perspective. Although by no means are all conflict-oriented theories based on Marx, his theories are relevant to race and ethnic relations, and they have influenced many modern conflict theories. Hence, some elaboration of these theories appears useful. A central assumption of Marxian theory is that the distribution of wealth by and large determines other aspects of society, such as the political system and the culture, including social norms, values, and beliefs (Marx, 1964, 1967, 1971), which Marx referred to as *ideology*. In particular, Marx focused on ownership of the *means of production,* by which he meant whatever one had to own or control to produce things of economic value. This varies with technology and the system of production. For example, in an agricultural society the means of production is mainly land; in an industrial society it is *capital*: ownership of factories, stores, natural resources, and such, or the money with which to purchase them. According to Marx, then, the political system, social institutions, and culture all tend to support the economic system: Specifically, they serve the interests of those who control the means of production. In effect, the system by which wealth (means of production) is distributed determines the political system, social institutions, and culture. These in turn support and reinforce the economic system and protect the interests of those who control the means of production.

Some sociologists would look at this picture and see cooperation, exchange, and interdependency. Others would look at it and see unequal power, possibly even domination. What do you see? Marc Anderson.

Perhaps an example will illustrate this principle. A common religious belief in the Middle Ages concerned the "divine right" of kings. According to this principle, kings were appointed to their royal positions through the will of God. Accordingly, anyone who challenged the right of a king to rule, or objected to the system of royalty and nobility, was going against the will of God. In effect, the royalty and nobility, who amassed wealth by controlling the means of production (land), were able to create an ideology—the divine right of kings—that served their own economic interests. Furthermore, this belief was generally accepted in the societies of the time—even by the peasant class, who provided the labor that enriched the landowners but received very little reward themselves.

According to Marx and his followers, this pattern of a subordinate group's accepting an ideology that goes against its own self-interest is not unusual. It is, in fact, common enough that they have a name for it—*false consciousness*. The existence of false consciousness among subordinate groups is not limited to societies in the past. In fact, an example can be seen in recent American history. In the 1972 presidential election, the Democratic candidate, Senator George McGovern, proposed a 100 percent taxation on all inheritance over $500,000; the practical effect would have been to make that the maximum amount an individual could inherit. Although this would have sharply limited the perpetuation of concentrated wealth through inheritance and would probably have benefited the working class through lower taxes or improved services, the *strongest* opposition to it came not from the elite, who had the most to lose, but from the working class, who stood to gain (Dushkin Publishing Group, 1977). Apparently, blue-collar workers wanted to *believe* they had the chance of amassing such a fortune and passing it along to their children—even though the real chance of any particular blue collar worker ever attaining such wealth was very close to zero. The consequence, of course, is that the attitudes of the masses helped to preserve the right of a very wealthy few to pass their wealth down from generation to generation.

A Comparison

Before moving on to apply the order and conflict perspectives more specifically to majority-minority relations, several general observations can be made. First, the two are in many ways competing perspectives. The order, or functionalist, approach sees society as basically stable and orderly, arranged in ways that meet its basic needs and marked by value consensus. The conflict approach, on the other hand, sees society as being arranged in ways that meet the needs of a powerful few, often marked by sharply conflicting values and power conflicts that arise from the unequal distribution of resources. Conflict theorists believe that because of these struggles, society tends toward change, sometimes drastic change. Furthermore, the two approaches often involve conflicting values and political orientations. Nonetheless, the fact that the two perspectives frequently compete and disagree does not necessarily make them completely incompatible—a fact that leading social theorists increasingly emphasize (Schermerhorn, 1978; Williams, 1977). This is true in several ways. First, it is quite possible that any given aspect of social structure or of culture may operate the way *both* perspectives say it should. In other words, it may *both* meet some need—say, contributing to overall efficiency—of the society as a whole *and* tend to keep wealth and power in the hands of a few. The task of the serious researcher is to try to answer the question, "how much of each?" and to identify the process by which it works both ways. Second, it is evident even to a casual student of history that in any given society—take the United States as an example—there are periods of relative stability and periods marked by conflict and upheaval. Obviously, then, there are *both* forces for stability and forces for change at work in the same society, albeit in different amounts at different times. Again, then, the task of the serious student of society is to identify these forces and determine why some predominate at one time and others predominate at another time. Similarly, some societies have relatively equalitarian intergroup relations; others are marked by brutal exploitation and intense conflict. Again, it becomes a matter of identifying basic differences between the societies that cause one to have peace and the other to have conflict. Throughout much of the rest of the book, we will engage in analyses such as those described previously, using the order and conflict approaches together to identify the basic dynamics of interaction between different racial and ethnic groups in different societies. Because it is anticipated that most readers of this book will be Americans, the greatest emphasis will be on intergroup relations in the United States.

THE SOCIAL-STRUCTURAL PERSPECTIVES AND SOCIAL PROBLEMS

The sociology of racial and ethnic relations is viewed by many sociologists as one part of a somewhat larger area: the study of social problems. We, too, shall begin our study of how order and conflict perspectives are applied to intergroup relations by determining how they apply more generally to the study of social problems. In the study of social problems the two perspectives tend strongly toward disagreement in two particular areas. One is in the *definition* of social problems, which is mostly a matter of values; the other is in the *location* of social problems, which is—or should be—an issue of scientific theory and empirical research.

The Definition of Social Problems

When we talk about defining social problems, we simply mean asking, "What is considered to be a problem?" At this point, we are primarily talking about a value judgment: Something is a problem if it has (or can be expected to have) some consequence that we don't like. However, what people "don't like" is not always the same. Accordingly, it is primarily the human reaction to some fact or event (i.e., people "do not like" its consequences) that makes it a problem, and this reaction is not the same for everyone. What the order perspective sees as a social problem is not necessarily a problem from the conflict perspective. Furthermore, even when both agree that something is a problem, they may not agree on *how serious* that problem is, or even *why* it is a problem. In general, to the order, or functionalist, sociologist, the most serious social problems are those that threaten the smooth or efficient functioning of society or that threaten to cause such drastic social change that a new, less well-adapted form of society may result. For this reason, social protest—especially if it is violent or demands radical change—is seen as potentially a very serious problem. Conflict in society is usually seen as a problem for the same reason (for an example of this viewpoint, see Lipset and Raab's, 1973, analysis of social conflicts underlying the Watergate case). To the conflict sociologist, on the other hand, the most serious social problems involve such concerns as poverty, racism, and, more generally, exploitation of subordinate groups and inequitable distributions of scarce resources. Conflict and social movements are generally *not* seen as significant social problems. In part, this is because conflict and change are seen as built into society, as an ordinary part of society that does not threaten the existence of a smoothly operating society. More fundamentally, however, the conflict theorist believes *only* conflict and change can bring about a fairer and more equitable distribution of resources. For this reason, then, many conflict theorists actually view protest and conflict as *desirable,* because they offer the possibility of reducing the social inequality that the conflict theorist usually sees as the most serious social problem.

The Location of Social Problems

While the definition of social problems is mainly a matter of values, the *location* of social problems involves a theoretical or empirical question: Where should we look to find the source of a social problem, or, put differently, what is the cause of some phenomenon that we have decided is a problem? Since this is a *factual* question, it is—in the ideal sense—a theoretical-empirical question, not a matter of values. However, values still have some influence. First, there are different places one might look or different questions one might ask in seeking the cause of some social problem. An order sociologist and a conflict sociologist probably would begin their analysis of a problem by asking different questions. Second, almost any problem in real life has multiple causes, and functionalists and conflict theorists would be apt to emphasize different causes.

Concretely, the major differences between the order and conflict perspectives concerning the location of social problems can be summarized as follows: The order, or functionalist, sociologist will tend to seek the causes for a social problem in the characteristics of a disadvantaged group. Such a group might be disadvantaged because it collectively *lacks* the necessary skills to perform a function for which it would be rewarded, or perhaps it has been excluded because its culture is incompatible with the general culture that exists in a society. In each case, the burden of change is placed mainly on the disadvantaged group, not on the dominant group and certainly not on the society as a whole. In fact, the functionalist would counsel *against* major changes in the society itself: The society is the way it is because it works well that way (its various elements perform functions necessary to the system as a whole), and if it is substantially changed, this functioning is likely to be disrupted or impaired.

The conflict theorist, on the other hand, does not seek the source of social problems in the characteristics of disadvantaged groups. These groups are seen as the victims of exploitation by the powerful: To seek the causes of social problems in these subordinate groups is somewhat akin to blaming the victim of a crime for the crime (for a forceful statement of this view, see Ryan, 1971). In the view of the conflict theorists, the source of social problems is to be found in the exploitative behavior of the dominant or ruling class: It is assumed that if someone is suffering or placed in a disadvantaged position, there is more than likely someone else more powerful who is benefiting from it (see, for example, Gans's, 1971, analysis of who benefits from poverty). Furthermore, since, as we have seen, conflict theorists frequently assume that a society's institutions are arranged so that they serve the needs of the dominant elite, these institutions are seen as an important source of the problem. If such social problems as poverty and racism are to be effectively combatted, argues the conflict sociologist, the only workable solution is to make fundamental changes in the social, political, and economic institutions that are believed to be an important source of the problems.

With regard to the location of social problems, the positions argued by the order and conflict perspective are, at least in theory, empirically testable. A supporter of the functionalist view should be able to identify what characteristics of a subordinate group cause it to be disadvantaged, to show that these really are true characteristics of the group, and to demonstrate how these characteristics place the group at a disadvantage. A conflict theorist should be able to show that someone else is indeed benefiting from the disadvantaged position of a subordinate group and to show the means by which social institutions actually work both to benefit the dominant group and to keep down the subordinate group. Of course, supporters of each view will frequently advance their position by trying to disprove arguments made in support of the opposite view. Once again it should be emphasized that in most instances neither one perspective nor the other is "totally right." Social problems may well be caused in part by the behavior of subordinate groups and in part by the behavior of dominant groups and by the structure of society's institutions. The job of the researcher is to answer the question: How much of each, and in what ways? The present state of sociological knowledge about the answer leaves room for a spirited debate between functionalist and conflict sociologists. In the remainder of this chapter we shall examine this debate as it applies to race and ethnic relations.

THE SOCIAL-STRUCTURAL PERSPECTIVES AND MAJORITY-MINORITY RELATIONS

As was the case when we spoke of social problems in the more general sense, we can best start a discussion of the order and conflict approaches to majority-minority relations by looking at their definitions of the problem. In other words, *why* do majority-minority relations constitute a social problem? (Keep in mind that when we talk about *definitions* of social problems, we are primarily talking about value judgments.) Before we try to answer the question, we should stress that the different answers given by the order, or functionalist, and conflict perspectives are more a matter of *emphasis* than of total disagreement. In general, however, functionalist sociologists will tend to be *most* concerned about majority-minority problems because of their potential for serious disruption—and in severe cases, even the destruction—of society. In other words, it is simply not rational or functional for society to become severely divided along lines of race, ethnicity, or religion. When such division becomes sufficiently deep, a society can simply no longer function normally. One might point to Northern Ireland, Lebanon, or Iran in recent years as examples to support this viewpoint.

Conflict theorists tend to see majority-minority relations as a source of social problems for somewhat different reasons. The conflict sociologist looks at majority-minority relations as a case of domination and exploitation. The problem is that the majority group—or some elite within the majority group—enhances its own position by placing or keeping the minority group in a disadvantaged position. The conflict sociologist is likely to view intergroup relations as a problem because the minority group is treated unfairly or because its members are harmed by the exploitative behavior of the dominant group. From this perspective, racial or ethnic conflict is often seen as desirable because the position of the minority group may be improved through such conflict.

We turn now to the actual theories about intergroup relations offered by the two sociological perspectives. Of all the substantive areas in sociology, race and ethnic relations is one of the areas where the two theoretical perspectives have been most widely applied. As with other areas in sociology, the order, or functionalist, approach to race and ethnic relations was the much more widely used of the two, especially in American sociology, until the changes of the 1960s challenged many assumptions of this approach. This is not to say the conflict approach had no adherents; some important analyses of intergroup relations did use this approach (see, for example, Cox, 1948). On the whole, however, approaches to the study of intergroup relations using the conflict perspective have been much more common since the mid-1960s. Today, it is fair to say that in the area of ethnic relations each approach has many adherents and that there is also a large and growing number of sociologists attempting to achieve a synthesis of the two approaches.

Functionalist Theories about Majority-Minority Relations

Such phenomena as racial and ethnic inequality, prejudice, and ethnocentrism can be explained along quite different lines, depending on one's theoretical perspective. Let us first examine the approach taken to these phenomena by the order, or functionalist, perspective. We shall begin with the example of *ethnic stratification*. By ethnic stratification, we mean any system that distributes scarce resources (such as wealth, income, and power) on an unequal basis according to race or ethnicity. The more commonly used term—racial inequality—would simply be a special case of ethnic stratification in which the inequality is based on race. While the conflict theorist would tend to see such inequality as mainly a case of domination and exploitation, the functionalist is more likely to suggest that if a society has racial inequality (or, more generally, ethnic stratification), that inequality must be meeting some kind of social need in that society. If we start by examining inequality in the general sense (that is, stratification or inequality *not* necessarily based on race or ethnicity), several possibilities come to mind. In one of the best known (and most controversial) sociological articles ever written, Davis and Moore (1945) presented a functionalist theory of stratification. They argued that the existence of social inequality is necessary to create incentives. Some jobs are more critical to the functioning of society and require longer, more difficult periods of training than others. To ensure that these more critical and more demanding jobs are filled by competent individuals, they must carry greater rewards. Accordingly, socioeconomic inequality is necessary and inevitable in a modern society. This, of course, does not explain why stratification should occur on the basis of race or ethnicity (in fact, we will see later that it suggests this should *not* be the case), but it does clearly suggest that any modern society needs to and will tend to have socioeconomic inequality. Other considerations, however, do suggest some reasons for racial and ethnic inequality. One argument suggests that ethnic minorities fill an important need in society by being willing to work at jobs and/or wages that are unattractive to others. This may be particularly true of immigrant minorities who view such positions as better than those that were available in their place of origin; the same argument is applied to rural migrants to the city. Were it not for such minorities, these jobs—ones that need to be done but are unattractive—would go unfilled.

Another explanation of ethnic stratification arising from the order perspective stresses *ethnocentrism*. (For a detailed discussion of this concept, see Chapter 2.) Although ethnocentrism obviously can be dysfunctional if it causes ethnic conflict that threatens to tear a society apart, a manageable amount of it is often seen as functional, or useful, for society (Sumner, 1906, p. 13; Catton, 1961; Simpson and Yinger, 1972, Chapter 4). The reason is seen in a society's need for consensus and a shared identity, or a "we" feeling. Durkheim (1964, 1965) and numerous order theorists since his time have argued that cooperation within a society is only possible when the members of the society share certain basic values and feel a sense of common or shared identity. Ethnocentrism can contribute to this in several ways. First, it highlights the nature of that common culture and group identity. It helps to illustrate, for example, what is "true American" by illustrating what is un-American. Furthermore, it can create unity and cooperation within the in-group by defining the out-group as a threat or by promoting hostility toward the out-group. Perhaps the best example of this can be seen in the characterization of "the enemy" in times of war. For all these reasons there is some tendency for ethnocentrism to develop in any society (see, for example, Williams, 1977, pp. 18–19). But, however functional or necessary this may or may not be, it also can create problems. The two most obvious are that it can get a society into conflict with another society when such conflict might otherwise not happen, and—our present concern—it can lead to ethnic stratification (and therefore ethnic conflict) within a society. This is because ethnocentrism in reality is directed not only at other societies perceived as enemies, but also at minority groups within the society who are different from the dominant group in culture or appearance. As a result of such generalized ethnocentrism, the minority groups against whom it is directed are placed in a disadvantaged position. In other words, ethnic stratification results.

Ethnocentrism and War

One of the best illustrations of the functions of ethnocentrism can be seen in characterizations of the enemy during periods of war. Baldridge (1976, pp. 110–111) uses war posters to illustrate this. Some posters from World War I, for example, characterized the enemy as "Huns." One read "Hun or Home?"; another showed a newspaper headline reading "Huns Kill Women and Children" and an angry American reader, with the caption, "Tell that to the Marines." A British poster read "Wounded and a Prisoner, Our Soldier Cries for Water. The German 'Sister' Pours it on the Ground Before His Eyes. There is No Woman in Britain Who Would Do It. There Is No Woman In Britain Who Will Forget." Of course, in wartime situations such ethnocentrism is usually mutual. One German poster, for example, depicted U.S. President Woodrow Wilson as a dragon.

Most functionalist sociologists would agree that ethnic stratification is a problem and that it ought to be minimized. However, many of them see it as inevitable as long as there is diversity within society. Because of the need for consensus and group identity, ethnocentrism will always tend to occur. As long as there are cultural minorities[1] within the society, they will tend to become the objects of ethnocentrism. The best ways to minimize this, then, are (1) to reduce the cultural differences between the dominant group and the minorities, (2) to eliminate legal and other barriers set up by the dominant group to exclude the minority, and (3) to develop in the minority groups any skills they may be lacking to enable them to participate in the society. This approach will result in *assimilation:* The minority group will gradually become integrated into the system, and the need for drastic changes that threaten the system will be avoided. Furthermore, by becoming culturally similar to the majority group, the minority group eliminates itself as a potential target of ethnocentrism. However, since both stratification and ethnocentrism are seen by functionalists as necessary for society, this view sees ethnic stratification as more or less unavoidable in any culturally diverse society—the only possible way out is through assimilation.

Because they emphasize the need for assimilation, functionalist theories about majority-minority relations have frequently been criticized for placing most of the burden of change on minority groups. If stratification and ethnocentrism are indeed more or less inevitable in any society, it seems to follow that minorities will experience hostility (and probably subordination) as long as they remain different from the majority group. Therefore, it appears to follow from this viewpoint that for equality to occur, minorities must become more similar to the majority. It is not particularly surprising that some people find this view offensive; furthermore, not all sociologists accept this view. For an alternative interpretation, we shall now turn to the conflict perspective.

---

[1]Keep in mind that here and throughout the chapter we are using the "minority" in the sociological sense as explained in Chapter 1.

Conflict Theories
about Majority-Minority Relations

Compared to order theorists, conflict theorists are much less supportive of the notions that stratification and ethnocentrism are functional and necessary in any society. Ethnic stratification is seen not as an unfortunate byproduct of social diversity, but rather as a pattern that exists mainly because it serves the interests of some dominant elite. According to this view, the basic cause of the problem is to be found in the exploitative behavior of either the majority group as a whole or some very wealthy and powerful (though possibly very small) segment of the majority group. Minority groups are subordinated because that subordination provides some benefit to the elite and because the minority either lacks the power or the awareness to prevent such exploitation.

As suggested above, conflict theorists are generally unpersuaded by functionalist arguments about the necessity of stratification for a productive, efficient society. Tumin (1953) and others have raised a number of criticisms, arguing that Davis and Moore's functionalist theory cannot explain anywhere near the degree of stratification that is found in most societies, including that of the United States. First of all, they argue, stratification cannot possibly act as an incentive in the way Davis and Moore argue, because most inequality is inherited rather than earned. For the system to work as the functionalists claim, there would have to be free mobility between generations so that, for example, a well-qualified son or daughter of a sharecropper would have the same chance of becoming a medical doctor as anyone else. In reality, this rarely happens. A further barrier to the mobility that would be necessary for inequality to work as an incentive is the existence of ethnic stratification. If high income is to reward hard work, it must be equally available to anyone who is capable and works hard.

It is also argued by Tumin and other critics that shortages of personnel in highly demanding jobs often exist because professional organizations restrict entry into the profession—*not* because there is a shortage of motivated and capable people seeking entry. Two other observations can be made. First, some occupations, which carry relatively little economic reward in relation to the training required, are nonetheless crowded because they are rewarding in themselves, or because they carry prestige. Social workers and college professors are frequently cited as examples. Secondly, it can be demonstrated that there is considerable variation in the degree of stratification in societies with similar levels of productivity. Sweden, for example, has lesser extremes of wealth and, particularly, poverty than the United States, yet its per capita gross national product in 1977 was actually somewhat higher than that of the United States (Population Reference Bureau, 1979). Considering all these arguments, conflict theorists conclude that stratification is much less necessary than the functionalist view suggests, and that it exists mainly because it benefits the wealthy and powerful elite at the upper end of the scale. It is doubtful whether the society as a whole—and particularly those, including racial and cultural minorities, who are in the lower part of the wealth and income distributions—really benefit from the degree of social inequality that exists.

According to conflict theorists, then, stratification exists not because it meets the needs of society as a whole, but because it serves the interest of some group that is dominant in terms of wealth, income, and/or power. Similarly, if inequality occurs along the lines of race or ethnicity, it is because such ethnic stratification serves the interests of some advantaged group—usually either the majority group as a whole or some elite among the majority group. This viewpoint does not see ethnocentrism primarily as a way of promoting social solidarity and thereby contributing to society's ability to function. Rather, it claims that ethnocentrism and other forms of prejudice develop as a way of rationalizing exploitation of the minority group or groups.

In fact, ethnocentrism and prejudice can be seen as just one example of a general principle discussed earlier in this chapter: According to Marx and other conflict theorists, a society's ideology (system of beliefs and values) tends to support its distribution of resources. In general, the elite or advantaged group will—consciously or otherwise—promote the beliefs and values that serve its own self-interests, which usually conflict with those of subordinate groups.

For this reason, among others, many conflict theorists—and many members of minority groups themselves—are skeptical of the argument that racial or ethnic equality can best be brought about by assimilation. If the Marxian theory that a society's ideology generally supports the interests of an elite over all others is correct, then it would be foolhardy for any disadvantaged or exploited group to buy into that ideology. Indeed, it would be a classic case of false consciousness: supporting a system of beliefs and values that goes against one's own self-interests. Fundamentally, if a social system is built upon inequality, domination, and exploitation, the best way for a minority group to achieve equality is not to try to become part of that system, not to adopt the ideologies created by that system. Rather, according to the conflict theorist, the answer is to take action seeking to make fundamental changes in the way that system works and in the way resources are distributed in the system. In effect, this means a challenge to the power of the dominant group.

Because the self-interests of subordinate groups (ethnic or otherwise) lie in challenging the power structure, conflict theorists believe that any society with stratification (ethnic or otherwise) will sooner or later experience social conflict. If there is racial or ethnic stratification in a society, that society will very likely experience conflict along racial or ethnic lines. Conflict theorists do not see anything wrong with this; indeed, they tend to view it as desirable. The most effective strategy for a minority group, they argue, is to challenge the power structure that keeps the minority group disadvantaged. It is *not* to accept the ideologies of the dominant society, which may actually be used against the minority group.

There is a further reason why many conflict theorists are skeptical of assimilation. Fundamentally, this comes down to the notion of "blaming the victim" discussed earlier. If, as those who support the conflict perspective believe, racial inequality results from exploitation of the minority group by the majority group, then the cause of the inequality is primarily to be found in the behavior of the majority group. Assimilation, however, typically demands that the minority group make most or all of the changes in behavior; it must change its ways in order to "fit in." Many see this as both being illogical and making an unfair demand on minority groups whose subordinate position is, after all, not their fault.

Competing Perspectives: Is Synthesis Possible?

To briefly summarize the chapter thus far, we have outlined two competing perspectives in sociology and examined how they apply to majority-minority relations. One, the order, or functionalist, perspective, sees society as basically stable and orderly. Society does tend to have inequality and ethnocentrism, but they exist because they perform certain functions for society. This often leads to ethnic stratification, which is seen as a social problem for several reasons, but most particularly because the resultant internal divisions can inhibit the effectiveness and productivity of the society and, in severe cases, can even destroy the society. The functionalist perspective sees the best solution to the problem to be a gradual process of assimilation, whereby minorities come to accept and be accepted into the dominant society and culture.

Conflict theory, on the other hand, sees society as tending—over the long run—toward instability and change. This is because most societies have marked inequality between those who own and control resources and those who do not. This comes about mainly because such an arrangement favors the interests of the elite, who are powerful enough to hold on to what they have. A society's institutions and culture (ideology) tend to serve the interests of that elite. Accordingly, acceptance of dominant ideologies and institutions is not in the interests of those who lack resources, including racial and ethnic minority groups. Rather, their interests are best served by challenging the power structure and seeking to alter the distribution of resources. Such conflict is both natural and desirable. Rather than viewing it as a threat to society, conflict theorists see it as a way to create a better, more egalitarian society, free of inequality and racism.

Obviously, the two perspectives are fundamentally opposed in many ways. By now you may be wondering if any synthesis is possible. Many strong adherents of each perspective would say no: They are saying opposite things, and one is right and the other wrong. Yet, as we have mentioned, many sociologists, including race and ethnic relations specialists such as Williams (1977) and Schermerhorn (1978), have been seeking to attain such a synthesis. There are probably two ways such common ground might be found. First, it is possible that the two perspectives could, on any given point, each be partially correct. For example, a given institution or ideology might both promote the efficiency of the society as a whole (as functionalists argue) *and* serve the interests of the dominant elite in particular (as conflict theorists argue). The task here is to identify, as precisely as possible, the ways in which it does each.

The second source of common ground can be found in the fact that under different circumstances, people and societies behave differently. Thus, as Schermerhorn points out, a society may at one point in its history and under one set of circumstances be stable and orderly, with ethnic minorities seeking—and to some extent gaining—equality through assimilation. At another point in time, the same society might be marked by disorder and conflict, with minority groups seeking— and again to some extent gaining—equality through conflict and use of power. Here, the key task for sociologists is to identify the circumstances that produce one outcome or the other.

In much of the rest of this book, we will be seeking to answer the following questions:

1. In what ways do racial and ethnic relations occur in ways consistent with the predictions of order theories? Of conflict theories?
2. Under what circumstances do racial and ethnic relations tend to follow patterns predicted by order theorists? By conflict theorists?

In the remainder of the chapter, we shall present an example that concretely illustrates the differences and disagreements between the two perspectives and that shows some ways in which sociological research can be used to test competing theories arising from the two perspectives.

AN ILLUSTRATION OF THE DEBATE: "CULTURE OF POVERTY" THEORY AND THE MOYNIHAN REPORT

A debate among sociologists concerned with race and ethnic relations that illustrates the arguments of the two sociological perspectives as well as any centers around a concept known as the "culture of poverty" and, in particular, the Moynihan Report, a government report on the black family (U.S. Department of Labor, 1965). We shall begin our discussion of this debate with a general overview of culture of poverty theory, then proceed to a more specific presentation of the debate over the Moynihan Report.

Culture of Poverty Theory

The term "culture of poverty" arises from the work of Oscar Lewis (1959, 1965). Lewis and other social researchers have observed certain cultural characteristics among poor people in industrial, capitalist societies. These characteristics have been observed in a number of such societies, and across a wide variety of racial and ethnic groups. Furthermore, according to Lewis and other culture of poverty theorists, poor people in such societies display cultural characteristics and values that are not held by the nonpoor in those same societies. Among these characteristics are:

> the absence of childhood as a specially prolonged and protected stage in the lifecycle, early initiation into sex, free unions or consensual marriages, a relatively high incidence of abandonment of wives and children, a trend toward female—or mother-centered families . . . , a strong predisposition toward authoritarianism, lack of privacy, verbal emphasis upon family solidarity which is only rarely achieved because of sibling rivalry, and competition for limited goods and maternal affection (Lewis, 1965, p. xvii).

Such cultural characteristics are predominant among the poor, according to culture of poverty theory, because they enable poor people to adapt to difficulties arising from poverty. At the same time as they permit people to adapt, however, it is argued that they make it more difficult for poor people to do what they have to do to escape from poverty. Therefore, the net effect of the culture of poverty is to keep poor people poor and to cause poverty to be passed from generation to generation. Accordingly, many culture of poverty theorists conclude that as long as poor people retain the culture of poverty, they will remain poor. The way to enable poor people to escape poverty, therefore, is to change the culture of poverty.

As you can see, this theory is closely associated with the functionalist perspective. Poor people are kept poor because their culture deviates from the norm; therefore, the solution to the problem of poverty is to change the culture of poor people so it more closely fits the dominant culture. In other words, poor people need to be assimilated. Not surprisingly, this view has come under both ideological and theoretical attack from social scientists associated with the conflict perspective. They argue that this approach (1) blames the poor for their poverty, when the true cause is to be found in the exploitative behavior of those who benefit from poverty, and (2) suggests an ineffective approach to solving the problems of poverty, since acceptance of an ideology and system that serves mainly the interests of the "haves" cannot possibly serve the interests of the "have-nots." Examples of such criticism can be seen in the writings of Valentine (1968), Ryan (1971), and Gans (1973, Chapter 4).

The Moynihan Report and the Black Family

The Moynihan Report (U.S. Department of Labor, 1965) used the general approach of the culture of poverty theory but applied it more specifically to the issue of race and poverty. The author, Daniel Patrick Moynihan, has served as a policy advisor to four presidents (Kennedy, Johnson, Nixon, and Ford) and has held university professorships in the social sciences. In 1976 he was elected to the U.S. Senate from New York State. Thus, his interests lie both in academic social science and in the formulation of public policy. Working for the federal government,

Moynihan sought to identify some of the reasons—and some possible solutions—for the disproportionately high incidence of poverty among black Americans. Although Moynihan examined many factors in black poverty, his main focus, along the lines of the culture of poverty approach, was on the structure of the black family in America. Moynihan presented various statistics showing higher than average incidences of divorce and separation, births out of wedlock, female family headship, and single parenthood among blacks. According to Moynihan, these patterns were particularly prevalent in urban areas and among lower-income blacks. Moynihan suggested several reasons for these racial differences in family structure. One was the history of black slavery, which regularly and consciously broke up black families. Other reasons were discrimination and violence against black males and high rates of unemployment among blacks, all of which made it extremely difficult for many black males to fill the traditional role of family provider.

Moynihan, however, did not merely present statistics. One of the most controversial aspects of the Moynihan report was the conclusion that the fundamental cause of continuing black poverty in the 1960s was the structure of the black family. Moynihan wrote:

> At the heart of the deterioration of the fabric of Negro society is the deterioration of the Negro family.
>
> It is the fundamental source of the weakness of the Negro community at the present time (U.S. Department of Labor, 1965, p. 5).

In the introduction to the report, Moynihan stated:

> The gap between the Negro and most other groups in American society is widening.
>
> The fundamental problem, in which this is most clearly the case, is that of family structure. The evidence—not final, but powerfully persuasive—is that the Negro family in the urban ghettos is crumbling. . . . So long as this situation persists, the cycle of poverty and disadvantage will continue to repeat itself.

From these words and other parts of the Moynihan report, the conclusion is clear: Blacks cannot escape poverty unless their family structure is altered. The relationship of Moynihan's view to the culture of poverty theory specifically and the order perspective more generally is evident. Blacks developed a family structure different from that of whites as a consequence of or adaptation to poverty and discrimination. That family structure has now become, however, a barrier to blacks' escaping poverty. The solution: Alter black family structure so it fits more closely to the two-parent family, which is the norm in American society.

Critique of the Moynihan Report

In part because of this conclusion, and in part because of other aspects of the Moynihan report, it became highly controversial even before it was issued publicly. Minority group spokespersons, many social scientists, and others have criticized the report on a number of grounds (Rainwater and Yancy, 1967). Many of these critics argued, implicitly or explicitly, from a conflict perspective, and the resultant confrontation is a classic example of an order versus conflict perspective debate.

One of the most important criticisms of the report was that it at least implicitly placed the burden for solving black poverty on blacks themselves. Although it is clear from other sources that Moynihan did favor welfare reform and government programs aimed at reducing unemployment among blacks (Rainwater and Yancey, 1967), he did not make any such recommendations in the report. His reason for this decision was that he did not want to detract from his key point, which was that the most crucial aspect of the problem was what he saw as deterioration of the black family. The tone of the report, consequently, was such that it gave subtle support to the notion that the burden of change was now on blacks: No amount of governmental programs, institutional reforms, or changes in white society could effectively combat black poverty if the cause was to be found in black family structure. By providing ammunition for such an argument, Moynihan had surely given aid to those who opposed efforts for racial equality, whether he intended to or not (Gans, 1967; Ryan, 1967). As such, the report was seen by many as serving the interest of a dominant group over a subordinate group.

Aside from this argument that the Moynihan Report in effect "blamed the victim," serious questions have been raised as to whether the consequences of being raised in one-parent and/or a female-headed family are anywhere near as severe as Moynihan claimed. Moynihan presented precious little evidence to show that this was the case; for the most part he assumed it. However, there is good reason to question such an assumption. Gans, in his critique of the Moynihan report, cites studies showing that single-parent families are not strongly linked to such problems as poor school performance (mentioned by Moynihan) and mental illness, particularly when compared with such factors as poverty and low social status. Although divorces and separations are frequently stressful to children (Neuhaus and Neuhaus, 1974), there is also evidence that a separation or divorce frequently leads to equal or better adjustment in children than that found in homes where the parents remain married unhappily (Landis, 1962; Burgess, 1970). Accordingly, it cannot be assumed that parents' divorce or separation, or the experience of growing up in single-parent families, is "pathological" in the sense that Moynihan argued.

Furthermore, as Gans points out, the higher incidence among blacks of single-parent, female-headed families does not necessarily mean that such families are unstable. The role of the extended family as a source of strength and stability in the black family has been noted by many sociologists, with grandmothers and aunts playing a particularly important role (Gans, 1967; Hill, 1972; Frazier, 1966; Staples, 1973). The absence of a father in the female-headed family also does not imply the absence of male role models. Male relatives or friends of the mother are frequently in contact with children in those black families where the father is absent (Hannerz, 1969). If a female parent can provide adequate images of the male role through such friends and relatives, the children may be greatly assisted in their own relationships with the opposite sex (Burgess, 1970). Considering all these factors, Moynihan's argument about the negative consequences of growing up in single parent families cannot be supported on the basis of present sociological evidence. Indeed, two leading family sociologists concluded that "Research does not support the idea that a child of a one-parent family will inevitably develop in a significantly different manner than other children, nor does it support the notion that the one-parent child will necessarily be less well adjusted than the two-parent child" (Stinnett and Walters, 1977, p. 432).

We have, then, identified two major sociological problems that have been raised by critics of the Moynihan report. First, its emphasis on black family structure as the "fundamental source of weakness" in the black community ignored the importance of continuing, socially imposed disadvantages as causes of black poverty, and (probably unintentionally) gave support to those who wanted to place all the burden for change on blacks themselves. In effect, it supported the notion that the black family, not the social structure and not the behavior of whites, was

An impoverished black family. The Moynihan Report argued that black poverty is perpetuated by certain features of the black family. Critics of this view suggest that if the black family is different from the white family, the difference is a *result* of poverty rather than a *cause* of poverty. United Nations/S. Rotner.

mainly responsible for continuing black poverty. Second, it failed to prove that single-parent and/or female-headed families were harmful in the ways it argued.

Beyond these sociological criticisms, minority spokespersons and conflict theorists such as Ryan raised a number of other points about the Moynihan Report. The most fundamental one is that its dramatic tone created the image in the public mind that most black families are broken or headed by a female. Moynihan's own statistics showed that this was not true, but the tone of the report contributed to an incorrect stereotype of the black family. The fact is that—then and now—most black families are husband-wife families, as are most white families (Scanzoni, 1977). This remains true even though the incidence of divorce and single-parent families has risen since then both among blacks and whites (U.S. Bureau of the Census, 1978).[2] Furthermore, Moynihan's use of such value-laden terms as "tangle of pathology" led many readers to ignore the many strengths of the black family and the black community. It also led many to associate with all blacks characteristics true of only a minority of blacks, usually those with the lowest income. Accordingly, the report was roundly criticized for its tone as well as its content, a tone many felt contributed strongly to stereotyping and antiblack racial prejudice.

What would conflict theorists argue is the best approach to the issue of race and poverty? Rather than focusing on characteristics of blacks (or more generally, of any disadvantaged or exploited group), sociologists should direct attention to aspects of the social structure that place the group at a disadvantage. Conflict theorists would argue that blacks are disproportionately poor because whites (at least some) are benefiting from that fact and have been for years. By Moynihan's own admission, the differences in structure that do exist between black and white families are largely a product of racial discrimination and the historic exploitation of black people in the United States. Among these factors are the deliberate disruption of black families under slavery, discrimination and violence against black males (which certainly has weakened their ability to act as "leaders" of traditional families), and high black unemployment. To these factors one might add welfare laws that encourage the break-up of husband-wife families. For all these reasons, it is highly unrealistic to treat the black family as if it were independent of the social forces acting upon it.

The solution, in the view of the conflict theorist, is to make fundamental changes in the aspects of the economic and political system that place blacks at a disadvantage. Ordinarily, this will involve a challenge to the existing power structure. Whatever difficulties this may entail, conflict theorists see it as preferable to urging blacks (or other minorities) to conform to the majority group's cultural and institutional patterns, since they beleive there is no reason to conclude that such conformity will lead to an improvement in the group's situation.

[2]Some observers have pointed out that in recent years, increasing numbers of whites have begun to adopt family patterns similar to those Moynihan attributed to the black family.

SUMMARY AND CONCLUSION

In this chapter, we began by contrasting a sociological approach to majority-minority relations, which stresses social organization, institutions, and culture, with a social-psychological approach, which stresses individual attitudes and beliefs, including racial and ethnic prejudice. We then outlined two major perspectives within the sociological, or social-structural, approach. The order, or functionalist, approach stresses order, stability, interdependency, and the need for shared values and beliefs in society. The conflict perspective stresses inequality, conflict, and biases supporting the dominant group in a society's social structure and culture. We examined how these approaches disagree about definitions and the causes of social problems, first in general, then specifically in the area of race relations. The culture of poverty issue and, specifically, the controversy over the Moynihan Report illustrates this disagreement. The culture of poverty approach, represented by Moynihan, focuses on ways minority groups (or the poor in general) do not conform to a society's culture or institutions. This view is closely aligned with the functionalist perspective. The critics of Moynihan and the culture of poverty approach—mostly aligned more closely with the conflict perspective—argue that an emphasis on assimilation or "fitting in" is misplaced, and that minority groups (and disadvantaged groups in general) can improve their position only by challenging the power structure and attempting to change the social institutions and/or dominant group behavior.

Having outlined and illustrated these two major sociological perspectives in this chapter, we shall use them (and, where appropriate, the social-psychological approach as well) in following chapters to enhance our understanding of how minorities and majorities relate to one another in a variety of situations.

GLOSSARY

Assimilation   A process whereby a minority group is gradually integrated into the culture and social system of the dominant group. Although the dominant group may adapt itself to the minority or absorb certain cultural characteristics of the minority group, it is more often the minority group that must adapt to fit into the culture and social system of the majority.

Conflict perspective   A sociological perspective that sees society as dominated by a powerful elite, which controls most of the wealth and power in the society, to the disadvantage of other, less powerful members of the society. Because of this inequality, society tends toward conflict and change, though the power and/or prestige of the dominant group may for a time lead to a consensus in society, or the appearance thereof. This consensus, however, is temporary; the long-term tendency is toward conflict and change.

False consciousness   The acceptance—usually by a subordinate group—of values, beliefs, or ideologies that do not serve the self-interest of that group. In Marxian analysis, false consciousness frequently occurs when subordinate groups accept ideologies promoted by the wealthy elite to serve the interests of the elite at the expense of the subordinate groups.

Functionalist perspective   A sociological perspective stressing the notions that society is made up of interrelated parts that contribute to the effectiveness of the society, and that society tends toward consensus, order, and stability. These tendencies are seen as necessary if society is to be effective and efficient. According to this perspective, the absence of these conditions can pose a serious threat to the quality of life in the society and even to the society's ability to continue to function.

Order perspective   See *Functionalist perspective*.

Perspective   A general approach to or way of looking at an issue. A perspective consists of a set of questions to be asked about a topic, a theory or set of theories about realities concerning that topic, and a set of values concerning potentially controversial issues related to the topic.

Sociological, or social structural, approach   An approach to the study of majority-minority relations that emphasizes the characteristics of collectivities of people (e.g., groups, societies) rather than the characteristics of individuals. Issues of interest concern how a group or society is organized, its base of economic productivity, its power structure, its social institutions, and its culture.

Theory   A set of interrelated propositions about some topic or issue that are believed to be true. Ideally, a theory should be testable, i.e., possible to evaluate in terms of its accuracy in describing reality.

Value   A personal preference or an opinion or moral belief concerning goodness or badness, right or wrong, etc. A value, being a matter of personal preference, cannot be tested, proven, or disproven.

Origins and Causes
of Ethnic Stratification

5

INTRODUCTION

We all know that in societies with more than one ethnic or racial group—such as the United States—there is frequently inequality and/or conflict along the lines of race and ethnicity. We know, too, that the basic patterns of intergroup relations vary over time in any given society and also vary from one society to another. Black-white relations in the United States, for example, are quite different from black-white relations in Brazil. Today's race relations in the United States are also quite different from what they were before the Civil War, and both today's race relations and antebellum (before the Civil War) race relations differ markedly from those of the period between World War I and World War II.

In the next three chapters, we will examine some of the major ways race relations differ in various time periods and various societies. We will also try to find some of the reasons for these variations. In this chapter, we will introduce some major patterns of race and ethnic relations that have been identified by social scientists and seem to appear repeatedly in a number of places. We will also examine the circumstances associated with the development of racial inequality in early American history. Using the theoretical perspectives outlined in previous chapters, we will try to answer the question, "How and why did racial and ethnic inequality first develop in the United States?" In Chapters 6 and 7, we shall examine how and why race relations have changed in the United States, and how and why intergroup relations vary from one country to another in today's world.

PATTERNS OF RACE/ETHNIC RELATIONS

Caste Versus Class Systems of Stratification

Sociologists who study stratification, or social inequality, frequently try to place societies along a continuum or range that runs from *caste* systems at one end to *class* systems at the other. A *caste system* is one that has two or more rigidly defined and unequal groups in which membership is passed from generation to generation. The group into which one is born determines one's status for life. In this type of system, one's legal rights, job, marriage partner, and even where and when one may be present are all determined by caste membership. Caste membership is rigid and cannot be changed at any time throughout life. *Ascribed status*—the group into which one is born—totally determines one's opportunities throughout life. In caste systems, caste membership may be determined according to religious criteria, as it was in the caste system once legally in effect (and today far from totally eradicated) in India. However, many of the more rigid systems of racial inequality, such as that of South Africa, operate in much the same way as caste systems. In fact, many social scientists consider them to be a slightly different form of caste system.

At the opposite end of the scale is the *class system*. In a class system, there is also inequality, but—ideally at least—one's status is not determined by birth. In a class system, *achieved status* is emphasized. This refers to status one gains through one's own actions, not the status one is born into. Theoretically, in class societies people are not born into rigid groups that influence their statuses for life. Rather, ideally everyone has the same chance, depending on what they do in life.

Of course, reality does not always match the ideal. Both caste system and class system are "ideal types," or abstract conceptualizations that do not exist as pure types in real life. Most societies lie somewhere between the caste system and the class system. Even though this is true, caste and class are still useful concepts in describing real societies. In comparing any two societies it is frequently quite possible to describe one as being more castelike, the other as more classlike.

Three Common Patterns of Race Relations

Borrowing from the work of sociologists Pierre L. van den Berghe (1958, 1978) and William J. Wilson (1973, 1978), we can identify three major patterns of race/ethnic relations that are found in various societies. Initially, van den Berghe outlined two patterns, which he called paternalistic and competitive systems of race relations. Wilson expanded on the competitive system dividing it into relatively rigid competitive and fluid competitive systems. We shall discuss in turn each of the three patterns: paternalistic race relations, rigid competitive race relations, and fluid competitive race relations. As with caste and class, keep in mind that these terms represent ideal types, and that, in real life, societies exist along a range, or continuum. Roughly speaking, paternalistic systems are at one end of the continuum, fluid competitive systems are at the other end, and rigid competitive systems are somewhere in the middle.

Paternalistic Race Relations   A paternalistic system of race relations can be seen as a kind of caste system. In this system, one's race pretty well determines one's status for life, and that of one's children as well. In a paternalistic system, the roles and statuses that belong to each race or ethnic group are known and understood by all in both the majority group and the minority group. These roles and statuses are supported by a complex system of "racial etiquette," which specifies the manner in which minority group members may speak to and behave toward majority group members. As the terminology suggests, there is a great deal of paternalism toward minority group members. It is frequently claimed that members of the subordinate group are childlike and helpless, so that dominant group members are doing them a great favor by providing them with shelter and work and teaching them the ways of civilization. In societies of this type, there is usually little or no visible racial conflict or competition. The roles of majority and minority groups are structured in such a way that minorities are not permitted to compete with the dominant group for jobs, housing, and such. There are two important reasons for the lack of conflict. Most important is the fact that the penalty for anyone who steps out of line is severe—often death. Another reason is that the ideology of dominant-group superiority, along with the idea that they are doing the minority group a favor by sheltering and civilizing its members, is sometimes accepted even by some minority group members. In some instances, it is the only mode of thinking to which they have been exposed. Of course, it is frequently true that minority group members may play along with the system to gain favors or avoid punishment without ever really accepting it.

Competitive Race Relations   In competitive systems of race relations, on the other hand, there is open conflict and competition between the races. This is true of both the rigid and fluid forms of competitive race relations. On a number of other criteria, however, these two patterns are quite different.

Rigid Competitive Race Relations   The rigid competitive form of race relations, like the paternalistic form, closely resembles a caste system. For the most part, one's social status is determined by one's race. However, this system differs from the paternalistic system in at least two very important ways. First, majority and minority group members compete in some important areas. They may, for example, work at similar jobs in the same factory. Typically, the jobs held by minority group members have different job titles and pay less than those held by majority group members. There is still at least implicit competition, however, because there is always the possibility that the factory owner might fire members of the majority group and replace them with lower-paid minority group members. They may also compete for housing if the population of either the majority or minority group (or both) increases rapidly in an area with limited housing. When such competition threatens the dominant group, it often responds by demanding increased discrimination against the subordinate group. In fact, one of the main ways this pattern differs from the paternalistic one is that the dominant group usually feels more immediately threatened by minority group competition. Partly for this reason, conflict between majority and minority groups is much more open under this system. This tendency toward conflict is the second major way the rigid competitive system is different from the paternalistic. In rigid competitive race relations, both groups are aware that, despite the discrimination and racial inequality in this system, there is always the possibility of majority-minority competition, which was not the case in the paternalistic system. This makes the dominant group feel more threatened, and it makes the minority group feel more powerful and therefore assertive. Hence, there is more conflict. This conflict carries the possibility of mass violence between majority and minority groups and also the possibility of severe repression of the minority by the majority. Perhaps this pattern can be best described as an unstable form of caste system. There is still gross racial inequality and formalized discrimination, but the system is beginning to come under attack by the minority and the majority knows it. As a result, this pattern, unlike the paternalistic one, is marked by extensive open conflict.

Fluid Competitive Race Relations   Considerable conflict and intergroup competition are also found under the fluid competitive pattern of majority-minority relations. This pattern, however, has more of the elements of a class system, though some castelike qualities remain. The main difference between fluid and rigid competitive race relations is that, under the fluid pattern, formalized discrimination has been largely eliminated—perhaps even outlawed. In *theory*, members of both the minority and majority group are free to pursue any endeavor and to be judged on their own merits. In practice, however, it doesn't quite work that way. Typically, minority groups start out with fewer resources because of past discrimination. Furthermore, the majority group usually controls the major social institutions and runs them in ways that serve its own interests first. Finally, for a variety of reasons, some majority group members do discriminate, even though discrimination is not socially approved. People also certainly continue to think of themselves in terms of their racial identity, so that when jobs, housing, or educational opportunities are in short supply, there is competition between racial groups for those resources. Frequently this leads to racial or ethnic conflict. Another source of conflict comes from protests by minority group members against their generally disadvantaged position in the system, even in the absence of formalized discrimination. To summarize, under the fluid competitive system, minorities are much less restricted than under either the paternalistic or rigid competitive systems, but the fluid competitive system is still a system of racial inequality. Like the rigid competitive system, there is considerable racial competition and conflict. In fact, the fluid competitive pattern usually has even more competition and conflict, because minorities are freer both to compete with the majority and to protest their generally disadvantaged position.

Some Further Comparisons of Paternalistic, Rigid Competitive, and Fluid Competitive Race Relations   In the preceding sections we have seen some of the basic elements of each of the three "ideal type" patterns of majority-minority relations. We shall now compare the three patterns on the basis of a number of characteristics on which they differ.

Economic Systems   Patterns of majority-minority relations tend to differ according to a society's economic system, or system of production. The paternalistic system is most commonly found in rural, agricultural societies with large-scale land ownership. As you may have surmised, the system of slavery in the United States before the Civil War is frequently given as an example of a paternalistic system of race relations. For reasons we will explore in considerable detail in the next two chapters, a society tends to move to competitive race relations when it urbanizes and industrializes. The rigid competitive pattern is associated with early stages of urbanization and industrialization. As society becomes more complex, diverse, and technologically sophisticated, it tends to move toward fluid competitive relations.

Relative Size of Majority Group and Minority Group   Sociohistorical studies have shown that the paternalistic pattern occurs most often when the majority group in the sociological sense (the dominant group) is small in size relative to the subordinate, or minority, group. Frequently in paternalistic systems, the dominant group is actually a numerical minority. It is also not unusual for the dominant group to be a numerical minority in rigid competitive systems. In general, when a numerical minority is dominant, race relations tend to be castelike. When a dominant group is outnumbered, it requires more stringent social control to maintain its advantaged position. Any strengthening of the position of the subordinate group could lead to a breakdown of the dominant group's advantaged position. In the fluid competitive pattern of race relations, on the other hand, the dominant group is usually also the numerical majority. Here, superior numbers are often enough to assure a somewhat advantaged position.

Stratification   In paternalistic systems of race relations, stratification is very much linked to race. There is a very large gap between the social and economic status of the majority and minority groups, with very little difference within the minority group, where status is quite uniformly low. In the rigid competitive system, there is also considerable racial stratification. Typically, a few members of the minority group attain relatively high status, but the great majority remain near the "bottom of the ladder." Under the fluid competitive pattern there is also racial stratification, but there is a wider variation of statuses within both the majority group and the minority group. A sizable proportion of the subordinate group may attain relatively high status, but the *average* status remains substantially lower in the subordinate group than in the dominant or majority group.

Division of Labor   In general, under the paternalistic pattern of majority-minority relations, division of labor is relatively simple because the society is not complex or highly specialized. Furthermore, division of labor is very much along racial lines, so that certain types of work are always or almost always done by members of the subordinate group, and other kinds of work are done by members of the dominant group. In rigid competitive race relations, there is more complex specialization of labor, and division of labor is less along the lines of race or ethnicity. Although the jobs may carry different titles and pay, members of the majority and minority groups may do quite similar kinds of work. As one moves toward the fluid pattern of race relations, division of labor becomes more complex and less tied to race, although even at the fluid competitive end of the continuum one's race has some influence on the kind of work one does.

Mobility   Both geographic and socioeconomic mobility tend to increase as one moves from paternalistic race relations through rigid competitive toward more fluid race relations. Under the paternalistic pattern, the majority group generally determines where members of the minority group will live. It is a rural agricultural society in which there is little residential moving; people know what their social status is from early childhood and pass that same status on to their children. Statuses tend to be less tied to birth as one moves through the competitive pattern, particularly toward the fluid competitive. There is also increasing geographic mobility as one moves through rigid competitive relations toward the fluid competitive pattern.

Racial Interaction   One of the major differences among the three systems is in how the races interact with one another. As noted, in the paternalistic system a complex racial etiquette specifies exactly how minority group members may speak and behave toward majority group members. This system also permits majority group members—within certain rules—to give orders to minority group members and to extract favors from them. This system can best be described as one in which there is a great deal of contact between majority and minority, but the contact always unequal, reminding the minority of its subordinate status. There is relatively little racial separation or segregation, other than living in separate homes: It is so clearly understood that the dominant and subordinate groups have unequal status that the dominant group feels no need to impose segregation to prove it. Even sexual contact is commonplace, but again, it is of an unequal nature: Minority women must submit to the sexual desires of dominant group men. Of course, subordinate group males are strictly forbidden sexual access to majority group females, and violation of this rule results in severe punishment.

In the rigid competitive system the races become much more separated. Frequently, jobs and other statuses are not as distinct as under the paternalistic pattern. Consequently, the majority group tries to protect and maintain its favored status by mandating a doctrine of "separate and unequal." It is under a system of rigid competitive race relations that segregation becomes most intense, as the majority group tries to protect its threatened status. What the majority group has lost in social deference and advantaged social standing automatically conferred by race, it tries to make up for by requiring the minority to live in separate (and physically inferior) neighborhoods and to use separate and inferior public facilities.

Under the fluid competitive system, strict segregation has broken down under the pressures of a modern, complex, mobile society, and there is more interracial contact than under the rigid competitive pattern. That contact tends much more to be equal-status contact than under either of the other patterns. Still, to a large degree the majority and minority groups form separate subsocieties, and close, personal contact between racial groups outside work and business settings is more the exception than the rule.

Value Consensus versus Conflict   As we have already noted, there is usually little or no open conflict under the paternalistic pattern. It is difficult to tell to what degree this reflects a value consensus and to what degree it results from forced conformity. Quite likely, it is some of both. In such societies, people are usually exposed only to one way of thinking, so they come to accept it as the natural way of things. All institutions—scientific, religious, legal, educational—support the dominant group ideology. Even if people are inclined to disagree with the accepted mode of thought and behavior, the penalties for expressing such disagreement are severe enough to discourage most people. As we have noted, it is not unusual for minority group members to play along in order to avoid punishment or get what favors they can from the dominant group, even when they do not really believe in the dominant ideology. Thus, what appears to be consensus may in fact be conformity for the sake of survival. This question will be explored further in a later part of this chapter when we discuss the experiences of specific minority groups in American society.

Under competitive patterns of majority-minority relations, there is usually a good deal of open conflict, and value systems tend to differ on some key points between majority and minority groups. Although conflict occasionally reaches great intensity in rigid competitive systems, with outbreaks of mass violence between majority and minority groups, it is probably more widespread and continuous under the fluid competitive pattern. Societies of this type frequently have institutionalized ways of handling conflict (courts, civil rights commissions, collective bargaining) that regularize conflict and also serve to keep it within acceptable bounds and prevent it from threatening the basic operation of the social system. Nonetheless, conflict sometimes becomes too intense for these mechanisms to handle and spills over into collective violence, as happened in United States cities in the middle and late 1960s.

These patterns are summarized in Table 5.1; in addition, countries and time periods that offer examples of each pattern are listed. In the next three chapters, we shall examine American history and compare different countries in today's world to find some reasons why each pattern has appeared in the times, places, and situations that it has.

Table 5.1   Summary of Characteristics Associated with Three Patterns of Race/Ethnic Relations

	PATERNALISTIC	RIGID COMPETITIVE	FLUID COMPETITIVE
1. System of production	Agricultural, usually plantation or feudal	Early urban Industrial	Advanced industrial/corporate
2. Relative size of group	Dominant group usually numerical minority	Variable, but dominant group often numerically small	Dominant group usually numerical majority
3. Stratification	Caste; group determines status	Unstable caste; group usually determines status with some exceptions	Mixture of caste and class, considerable within-group status variation, but still racial stratification.
4. Division of labor	By race; simple division of labor	Mostly by race, but some jobs done by both dominant and subordinate groups. More complex division of labor.	Complex specialization; race only moderately related to type of work done; wide variation within all racial groups
5. Mobility	Very low	Low to moderate	Relatively high
6. Racial interaction	Much interaction, but highly unequal; Little separation of races	Little and mostly unequal interaction: almost total separation of races	More interaction than rigid, less than paternalistic; more equal interaction than either of the others.
7. Consensus vs. conflict	Little outward conflict; apparent consensus on most issues	Some racial conflict, occasional violent outbursts	Diverse values, institutionalized conflict in racial and other areas.
8. Examples	United States South during slavery	Unites States South after slavery; South Africa today	United States today

(Note: Material presented in this table is drawn primarily from van den Berghe, 1958, 1967, and Wilson, 1973, 1978.)

THE DEVELOPMENT OF ETHNIC
STRATIFICATION

As Table 5.1 indicates, each of the three patterns described above has been found in some times and places in American history. In fact, a strong argument can be made that in the history of the United States and some other societies, some very regular sequences of events can be found in which the three patterns appear in fairly regular order. This may be summarized as follows:

1. Diverse racial or ethnic groups come into contact with one another. Usually the initial contact is marked by curiosity and frequently by some degree of accommodation. Frequently, early contact has elements of both conflict and cooperation.
2. Under certain circumstances, one group becomes subordinated. When this happens, relations between the dominant and subordinate group quickly become castelike, and, depending on the social setting, either a paternalistic or rigid competitive system is established.
3. As the society modernizes, urbanizes, and industrializes, race relations become more classlike, with competitive systems replacing paternalistic ones and becoming increasingly fluid. Fewer and fewer formal restrictions are placed on the minority group and its social movements become larger and stronger.

In the United States three of the groups that best fit the definition of *minority group,* or *subordinate group,* presented in Chapter 1 are blacks, American Indians, or Native Americans, and Chicanos, or Mexican Americans. We shall examine the history of these groups to see to what degree the general historical pattern described above fits their particular histories. We shall also try to identify some of the reasons *why* these groups experienced the history of subordination that they did, and we shall use this knowledge to test competing theories about the causes of ethnic stratification.

Initial Contact between Racial/Ethnic Groups

Obviously, before any kind of intergroup relations can occur, two or more racial or ethnic groups must come in contact with one another. There are a number of ways this can happen, and how it happens can have a big effect on the subsequent relations between the two groups (Schermerhorn, 1978, Chapter 3; Feagin, 1978, pp. 20–25; Blauner, 1972). Essentially, for any two groups to come into contact, one or both of them must migrate. Either one group must move into an area where the other group is already present, or both groups must move into the same area. When these migration patterns occur, they can result in several types of contact, which may be classified as colonization, voluntary and involuntary annexation, and voluntary and involuntary immigration. *Colonization* occurs when one group migrates into an area where another group is present and conquers and subordinates that indigenous group. *Annexation* occurs when one group expands it territory to take over control of an area formerly under the control of another group. This can occur by military action (conquest), in which case the outcome may be very similar to colonization, or it can be voluntary, as when residents of an area petition to be annexed. Many cases of annexation, such as land purchases, fall somewhere between fully voluntary and fully involuntary actions. *Immigration* occurs when a group migrates into an area where another group is established and becomes a part of the indigenous group's society. Like annexation, migration may be voluntary, as when people move to a new country in search of better economic opportunity, or involuntary, as when they are imported as slaves. Again, there are intermediate cases, such as contract or indentured labor and political refugees. As we shall see, the degree to which an ethnic group is voluntarily a part of a society will have a major influence on that group's status in the society. There is a tendency for greater stratification to exist when contact originally occurred through colonization, involuntary annexation, or involuntary migration. However, this alone will not *always* determine the outcome of contact, and it is certainly true that contact does not *always* lead to ethnic stratification.

Origins of Ethnic Stratification

Perhaps there is no better way to identify the causes of racial or ethnic inequality than to examine how it begins. You will recall from previous chapters that the different theoretical perspectives we have examined offer different explanations of why there is racial inequality. The social-psychological approach stresses individual prejudices and suggests that inequality can occur if a sufficient number of individuals are racially or ethnically prejudiced. The order, or functionalist, approach also stresses attitudes and beliefs, but on a larger scale: It suggests that ethnocentrism toward out-groups becomes generalized in a society because it meets needs for cohesiveness and cooperation in a society. This ethnocentrism will tend to cause discrimination against those who are racially or culturally different from the majority and will cause stratification (which is seen as normal and necessary) to occur along the lines of race or ethnicity. The conflict perspective, unlike the other two, does not stress prejudice or ethnocentrism as important causes of ethnic stratification. Rather, it stresses the idea that the dominant group benefits from ethnic stratification and is in a position to impose a subordinate role on the minority group. Thus, majorities subordinate minorities because they can gain from doing so.

Noel (1968) has drawn on both the order and conflict perspectives to develop an important theory of the origins of ethnic stratification. According to Noel, three conditions must be present for intergroup contact to lead to ethnic stratification. First, there must be *ethnocentrism,* as the order perspective suggests. This alone, however, will not cause ethnic stratification: Noel cites examples of initially ethnocentric groups that have lived side by side in peace over long periods. Second, there must be *competition* or opportunity for exploitation between ethnic groups. This occurs whenever two groups both desire the same scarce resource or have mutually exclusive needs or desires, or when one group has some resource (such as land or labor) that the other group wants. In short, the situation must be such that one group can benefit by subordinating the other. This, of course, is one of the main explanations given by the conflict perspective for social inequality. However, even the presence of ethnocentrism and competition does not guarantee that there will be ethnic stratification. If the groups involved have relatively equal power—if neither can impose its will on the other—ethnic stratification will not occur. Accordingly, the third condition that must be present for ethnic stratification to occur is *unequal power:* One group must be powerful enough to dominate or subordinate the other. To summarize, Noel's theory argues that we cannot explain racial/ethnic inequality on the basis of prejudice or ethnocentrism alone, as the social psychological or functionalist perspectives might suggest. There must also be competition or opportunity for exploitation *and* unequal power, as suggested by the conflict perspective. In short, notions arising from *both* the order and the conflict theoretical approaches must be used to understand how racial inequality begins.

ORIGINS OF ETHNIC STRATIFICATION IN THE UNITED STATES

We have argued that initial contact between diverse racial or ethnic groups frequently does not involve stratification. Ethnic stratification—the dominance of one group by another—occurs only when certain conditions are met—namely, ethnocentrism, competition, and unequal power. When ethnic stratification first occurs, the pattern is frequently castelike: paternalistic or rigid competitive. In the the remainder of this chapter, we shall examine the histories of interactions between whites and the three minorities mentioned earlier, blacks, American Indians, and Chicanos, to see to what degree the history of each group actually fits the theoretical pattern outlined above.

Afro-Americans

Historians generally agree that blacks first arrived in what is now the United States in 1619 in the colony of Virginia. Since they were brought here involuntarily, racial inequality existed from the start. However, considerable evidence suggests that the racial inequality in that early period was quite mild compared to that which developed later. During the first generation or two of black presence here, many and perhaps all blacks had a status comparable to that of English indentured servants (Franklin, 1969, p. 71). While this was certainly involuntary servitude, it was not comparable to the system of chattel slavery that existed later. First, many blacks were servants for a limited period of time, after which they became free and received land of their own (Franklin, 1969, p. 71). Furthermore, the status of blacks was not very different from that of a great many whites, who frequently were under some form of involuntary servitude and were sometimes brought involuntarily to the New World. Handlin and Handlin (1950) note for example, that "nearly everyone" in the Virginia colony in the mid-seventeenth century was under some form of indenture or involuntary servitude. Thus, although the blacks were generally not free, they were also not very different in status from many whites. The amount of racial inequality, or stratification, was quite small *compared to what was to come later*. (For further discussion of this point see Degler, 1959a and b; Elkins, 1959; and Jordan, 1962, 1968).

Within two or three generations of the first arrival of blacks, the situation had changed drastically. By the 1660s several colonies had passed laws sanctioning the enslavement of blacks, and the principle was rapidly evolving that slaves were property and therefore had few or no legal rights. By this time, slavery had become a status from which one could not escape, and which was automatically passed on to one's children.

Why the change? Most sociologists and historians focus on two major factors. First, the plantation system that was evolving in the South could be most profitable under a system that provided massive amounts of low-cost labor. Second, other groups were, for various reasons, not as easy to enslave and force to do plantation work as were blacks involuntarily imported from Africa. A third contributory factor was ethnocentrism, though it alone would not have been sufficient to bring about slavery. Let us examine each of these factors in greater detail.

The Plantation System   The economic predominance of the plantation system coupled with the fact that the economic elite who controlled the system were dependent upon slavery as a means of amassing their wealth, is probably the most important reason for the development of chattel slavery in the southern United States. In fact, it is probably safe to say that without the plantation system, slavery as it developed in this country would never have happened. This can be illustrated in several ways. As the plantation system became the dominant mode of economic production in the South, two important things happened. First, the plantation-owning class became the dominant economic and political elite in the South. Wilson (1978, p. 25) tells us that "by the end of the eighteenth century, the Southern slaveholders had clearly established themselves as a regional ruling class. The economic system, the political system, and the juridicial system were all controlled and shaped by the slaveholding elite." The plantation system owned by this elite required cheap and dependable labor in order to amass wealth for its owners. This explains why slavery was never institutionalized in the North to the degree that it was in the South: In the North, slaves were largely a luxury for a few wealthy individuals; they were not crucial to the power elite for amassing its wealth. Consequently, northern states never passed laws—as the South did—legislating all blacks into slavery. The plantation's need for labor also explains why most southern whites did not own any slaves at all, and why most slaves belonged to plantation owners. Only one fourth of all southern white families owned slaves, and over half the slaves were owned by "planter class" white families who owned more than twenty slaves. Only about 3 percent of the white southern population owned this many slaves, yet this small group, almost all plantation owners, owned over half the slaves (Stampp, 1956, pp. 29–31). It seems clear that the self-interests of a small, wealthy, powerful elite were a critical factor leading to the creation of black slavery. In short, slavery was created because an elite could benefit from it. This indicates that one of Noel's three conditions for the development of ethnic stratification was clearly present: The elite group among the whites could benefit from the subordination and enslavement of blacks in the South.

Why Blacks?   But the question remains: Why were blacks enslaved rather than some other groups? One of Noel's other two conditions, ethnocentrism, suggests part of the answer: The elite required cheap labor, and blacks became the source because people were prejudiced against them. The answer, however, is not that simple. As Noel (1968) demonstrates, the prejudice and ethnocentrism among the British colonists were not directed toward blacks particularly more than toward some other groups, though there were certainly antiblack prejudices (Jordan, 1968, Chapter 1). Certainly there was a comparable amount of ethnocentrism toward Indians, and the crucial prejudice of the period was against non-Christian "heathens," be they black, Indian, or otherwise (Boskin, 1965, p. 453; Jordan, 1968, pp. 85–92). Even non-English white Christians such as the Irish were subjected to some, though less, ethnocentrism. Thus, while ethnocentrism undoubtedly played an important role in the enslavement of blacks, it alone cannot account for the enslavement of blacks. Noel's third factor, unequal power, appears to complete the explanation. The most obvious alternative groups that might have been enslaved on the plantations were white indentured servants and American Indians. However, both of these groups were in a better position to resist enslavement than were blacks. If indentured servants were permanently enslaved, there was the very real possibility that the supply of servants would be cut off: English debtors would no longer be willing to come to the colonies to work off their debts. Indeed, the supply of servants was in fact threatened by rumors of harsh treatment and permanent enslavement. Enslavement of Indians proved difficult due to the ease with which Indians could run away and rejoin their tribal groups, and the constant threat that Indians would attack the plantations to free their people. Furthermore, whites were often dependent on Indians for trade. None of these problems existed with blacks: There was nothing voluntary about their immigration and once here they were in a strange land with no possibility of running off to rejoin their people. They lacked the group cohesion of the Indian tribes, since black family and tribal groupings were often deliberately broken up. In short, the power balance was so heavily weighted against blacks that they were the easiest group to enslave. Thus, we see that Noel's third condition, unequal power, was also a crucial factor in the development of

United States slave trade, 1830.

black slavery. An additional factor was that black Africans knew hot-weather farming techniques unknown to either the Indians or Europeans, which made them even more desirable as a source of plantation labor. Finally, they were available in much larger numbers than were Indians. Thus, it seems safe to conclude that black enslavement was only in part due to ethnocentrism: the labor needs of the economic elite and the blacks' relative lack of power to avoid enslavement were the crucial factors. Thus we see that neither the order perspective, stressing cultural differences and ethnocentrism, nor the conflict perspective, stressing the dominant group's self interests and the unequal power between races, is sufficient by itself to understand slavery: Both theories must be used to understand the origins of black-white inequality in the United States.

Institutionalization of Paternalistic Caste Relations   Over the two hundred or so years after slavery was legally established in the 1660s, slavery became increasingly more institutionalized in the southern United States, and the plantation became even more the dominant mode of economic production in the South. The invention of the cotton gin in 1793, for example, altered the economics of southern agriculture further in favor of the large-scale plantation, thereby increasing the demand for black slaves (Franklin, 1969, p. 149). During the era of slavery antiblack racism gradually intensified so that by the mid-nineteenth century there was a pervasive racist ideology in the South unlike anything that existed when slavery was first established (Wilson, 1973, pp. 76–81; Jordan, 1968, Chapter 2).

Among the ideologies that became widespread *after* the establishment of slavery were the beliefs that blacks were innately inferior to whites, lacking in intelligence, and incapable of developing a civilized society. As is usually true of racist ideologies, these beliefs came into being mainly to justify slavery, which was beginning to come under attack from northern abolitionists. As Davis (1966) notes, many whites would find unacceptable the enslaving of human beings with the same abilities and human rights as themselves. If, however, they could convince themselves that slaves were less than human, that they were heathens and savages incapable of being civilized, they might be able to convince themselves and others that slavery was not so bad. Indeed, they could even claim it was morally good, since it taught the slaves about as much as they could learn about the ways of "civilized" society. Thus, we see that ideological racism and intense antiblack prejudice were not so much the cause of slavery as the result of it: They developed in large part as a way for whites to rationalize or justify to themselves the brutal and total subjugation of other human beings that was slavery. This illustrates again that racial attitudes are as often the result of behavior as the cause, and that a common function of racist ideology is to justify racist behavior (see, for example, Noel, 1972a).

In most regards, slavery in the South between the mid-seventeenth and mid-nineteenth centuries closely resembled Van den Berghe's concept of a paternalistic system of race relations. The status of slave was totally determined by race, with laws in most southern states aimed at assigning slave status to all blacks. A complex racial etiquette developed specifying when and how blacks could approach and address whites. In general, there was little outward racial conflict, although serious slave uprisings did occasionally occur. Certainly the planter class lived in constant fear of such uprisings. Especially during the latter portion of the period of slavery, the fear sometimes approached paranoia. This concern was increased by the realization that, in some parts of the South, blacks substantially outnumbered whites, as is frequently true under the paternalistic pattern of majority-minority relations.

Some historians have made much of the fact that there were relatively few slave revolts in the United States compared to Latin America. The major reason why so few slaves revolted appears not to be that most blacks accepted the status of slave, though in the controlled ideological setting of the Southern plantation, some probably did.[1] Rather, the main reason is probably found in the power situation: There was virtually no opportunity for successful revolt. This was true for several reasons. First, blacks in the southern United States were, overall, a numerical minority, even though they outnumbered whites in some smaller areas. Being outnumbered, and with whites controlling the guns, blacks were in a poor position to revolt. Secondly, blacks were highly fragmented and scattered about in a white-dominated region. Slave codes forbade slaves to travel alone, so they lacked the mobility necessary to plan revolts on any regional scale. Even contact with slaves on a nearby plantation was very difficult. Furthermore, nearly half the slaves were on small plantations with fewer than twenty slaves, unlike South America, where the average plantation had about two hundred slaves. Finally, the agricultural development of the southern United States was such that runaway slaves could

---

[1]A related factor noted by Wilson (1973) is the relative lack in the United States of newly imported slaves who remembered their freedom, compared to the predominance of such slaves in Latin America.

never be far from whites who supported slavery (including nonslaveholders). Escaping and plotting a rebellion was very difficult. The rebellions that did occur all ultimately ended in failure, and they were frequently followed by witch hunts in which any slave even suspected of supporting the uprising was in danger of losing his or her life. For these reasons, there was—as is typically the case with paternalistic, castelike race relations—relatively little open conflict in the South during the slavery era. This does not mean that most slaves willingly accepted their status. Subtle resistance in the form of sabotage, playing on white prejudices to avoid work or gain favor, running away, and even self-mutilation were not uncommon.

LIFE UNDER SLAVERY

To understand majority-minority relations in the United States, one must be aware of the reasons for the emergence of black slavery; however, a sociological analysis cannot describe what slavery was like on a day-to-day basis, nor can it adequately depict what a dehumanizing institution slavery was. To truly understand the black experience in America, some awareness of the day-to-day operation of that institution is necessary. Such a description is presented vividly in the following excerpt from *The Peculiar Institution* by Kenneth Stampp.

The Peculiar Institution: Slavery in the Ante-Bellum South*

It would not be too much to say that masters usually demanded from their slaves a long day of hard work and managed by some means or others to get it. The evidence does not sustain the belief that free laborers generally worked longer hours and at a brisker pace than the unfree. During the months when crops were being cultivated or harvested the slaves commonly were in the fields fifteen or sixteen hours a day, including time allowed for meals and rest.[2] By ante-bellum standards this may not have been excessive, but it was not a light work routine by the standards of that or any other day.

In instructions to overseers, planters almost always cautioned against overwork, yet insisted that the hands be made to labor vigorously as many hours as there was daylight. Overseers who could not accomplish this were discharged. An Arkansas master described a work day that was in no sense unusual on the plantations of the Deep South: "We get up before day every morning and eat breakfast before day and have everybody at work before day dawns. I am never caught in bed after day light nor is any body else on the place, and we continue in the cotton fields when we can have fair weather till it is so dark we cant see to work, and this history of one day is the history of every day."[3]

Planters who contributed articles on the management of slaves to southern

---

*Copyright © 1956 by Kenneth Stampp. Reprinted by permission of Alfred A. Knopf, Inc.

[2]Gray, *History of Agriculture*, I, pp. 556–57.

[3]Gustavus A. Henry to his wife, November 27, 1860, Henry Papers.

periodicals took this routine for granted. "It is expected," one of them wrote, "that servants should rise early enough to be at work by the time it is light. . . . While at work, they should be brisk. . . . I have no objection to their whistling or singing some lively tune, but no *drawling* tunes are allowed in the field, for their motions are almost certain to keep time with the music."[4] These planters had the businessman's interest in maximum production without injury to their capital.

The work schedule was not strikingly different on the plantations of the Upper South. Here too it was a common practice to regulate the hours of labor in accordance with the amount of daylight. A former slave on a Missouri tobacco and hemp plantation recalled that the field-hands began their work at half past four in the morning. Such rules were far more common on Virginia plantations than were the customs of languid patricians. An ex-slave in Hanover County, Virginia, remembered seeing slave women hurrying to their work in the early morning "with their shoes and stockings in their hands, and a petticoat wrapped over their shoulders, to dress in the field the best way they could."[5] The bulk of the Virginia planters were businessmen too.

Planters who were concerned about the physical condition of their slaves permitted them to rest at noon after eating their dinners in the fields. "In the Winter," advised one expert on slave management, "a hand may be pressed all day, but not so in Summer. . . . In May, from one and a half to two hours; in June, two and a half; in July and August, three hours rest [should be given] at noon."[6] Except for certain essential chores, Sunday work was uncommon but not unheard of if the crops required it. On Saturdays slaves were often permitted to quit the fields at noon. They were also given holidays, most commonly at Christmas and after the crops were laid by.

But a holiday was not always a time for rest and relaxation. Many planters encouraged their bondsmen to cultivate small crops during their "leisure" to provide some of their own food. Thus a North Carolina planter instructed his overseer: "As soon as you have laid by the crop give the people 2 days but . . . they must work their own crops." Another planter gave his slaves a "holiday to plant their potatoes," and another "holiday to get in their potatoes." James H. Hammond once wrote in disgust: "Holiday for the negroes who fenced in their gardens. Lazy devils they did nothing after 12 o'clock." In addition, slave women had to devote part of their time when they were not in the fields to washing clothes, cooking, and cleaning their cabins. An Alabama planter wrote: "I always give them half of each Saturday, and often the whole day, at which time . . . the women do their household work; therefore they are never idle."[7]

Planters avoided night work as much as they felt they could, but slaves rarely escaped it entirely. Night work was almost universal on sugar plantations during the grinding season, and on cotton plantations when the crop was being picked, ginned, and packed. A Mississippi planter did not hesitate to keep his hands hauling fodder until ten o'clock at night when the hours of daylight were not sufficient for his work schedule.[8]

Occasionally a planter hired free laborers for such heavy work as ditching in

---

[4]*Southern Cultivator*, VIII (1850), p. 163.

[5]William W. Brown, *Narrative of William W. Brown, a Fugitive Slave* (Boston, 1847), p. 14; Olmsted, *Seaboard*, p. 109; *De Bow's Review*, XIV (1853), pp. 176–78; Benjamin Drew, *The Refugee: or the Narratives of Fugitive Slaves in Canada* (Boston, 1856), p. 162.

[6]*Southern Cultivator*, VIII (1850), p. 163.

[7]Henry K. Burgwyn to Arthur Souter, August 6, 1843, Henry King Burgwyn Papers; John C. Jenkins Diary, entries for November 15, 1845; April 22, 1854; Hammond Diary, entry for May 12, 1832; *De Bow's Review*, XIII (1852), pp. 193–94.

[8]Jenkins Diary, entry for August 7, 1843.

order to protect his slave property. But, contrary to the legend, this was not a common practice. Most planters used their own field-hands for ditching and for clearing new ground. Moreover, they often assigned slave women to this type of labor as well as to plowing. On one plantation Olmsted saw twenty women operating heavy plows with double teams: "They were superintended by a male negro driver, who carried a whip, which he frequently cracked at them, permitting no dawdling or delay at the turning."[9]

Among the smaller planters and slaveholding farmers there was generally no appreciable relaxation of this normal labor routine. Their production records, their diaries and farm journals, and the testimony of their slaves all suggest the same dawn-to-dusk regimen that prevailed on the large plantations.[10] This was also the experience of most slaves engaged in nonagricultural occupations. Everywhere, then, masters normally expected from their slaves, in accordance with the standards of their time, a full stint of labor from "day clean" to "first dark."

Some, however, demanded more than this. Continuously, or at least for long intervals, they drove their slaves at a pace that was bound, sooner, or later, to injure their health. Such hard driving seldom occurred on the smaller plantations and farms or in urban centers; it was decidedly a phenomenon of the large plantations. Though the majority of planters did not sanction it, more of them tolerated excessively heavy labor routines than is generally realized. The records of the plantation regime clearly indicate that slaves were more frequently overworked by calloused tyrants than overindulged by mellowed patriarchs.

That a large number of southern bondsmen were worked severely during the colonial period is beyond dispute. The South Carolina code of 1740 charged that "many owners . . . do confine them so closely to hard labor, that they have not sufficient time for natural rest."[11] In the nineteenth century conditions seemed to have improved, especially in the older regions of the South. Unquestionably the ante-bellum planter who coveted a high rank in society responded to subtle pressures that others did not feel. The closing of the African slave trade and the steady rise of slave prices were additional restraining influences. "The time has been," wrote a planter in 1849, "that the farmer could kill up and wear out one Negro to buy another; but it is not so now. Negroes are too high in proportion to the price of cotton, and it behooves those who own them to make them last as long as possible."[12]

But neither public opinion nor high prices prevented some of the bondsmen from suffering physical breakdowns and early deaths because of overwork. The abolitionists never proved their claim that many sugar and cotton growers deliberately worked their slaves to death every seven years with the intention of replacing them from profits. Yet some of the great planters came close to accomplishing that result without designing it. In the "race for wealth" in which, according to one Louisiana planter, all were enlisted, few proprietors managed their estates according to the code of the patricians.[13] They were sometimes remarkably shortsighted in the use of their investments.

Irresponsible overseers, who had no permanent interest in slave property, were frequently blamed for the overworking of slaves. Since this was a common complaint, it is important to remember that nearly half of the slaves lived on plantations of the size

[9]Olmsted, *Back Country*, p. 81; Sydnor, *Slavery in Mississippi*, p. 12.

[10]See, for example, Marston Papers; Torbert Plantation Diary; *De Bow's Review*, XI (1851), pp. 369–72; Drew, *Refugee*; Douglass, *My Bondage*, p. 215; Trexler, *Slavery in Missouri*, pp. 97–98.

[11]Hurd, *Law of Freedom and Bondage*, 1, p. 307; Flanders, *Plantation Slavery in Georgia*, p. 42.

[12]*Southern Cultivator*, VII (1849), p. 69.

[13]Kenneth M. Clark to Lewis Thompson, December 29, 1859, Thompson Papers.

that ordinarily employed overseers. But planters could not escape responsibility for these conditions simply because their written instructions usually prohibited excessive driving. For they often demanded crop yields that could be achieved by no other method.

Most overseers believed (with good reason) that their success was measured by how much they produced, and that merely having the slave force in good condition at the end of the year would not guarantee re-employment. A Mississippi overseer with sixteen years of experience confirmed this belief in defending his profession: "When I came to Mississippi, I found that the overseer who could have the most cotton bales ready for market by Christmas, was considered best qualified for the business—consequently, every overseer gave his whole attention to cotton bales, to the exclusion of everything else."[14]

More than a few planters agreed that this was true. A committee of an Alabama agricultural society reported: "It is too commonly the case that masters look only to the yearly products of their farms, and praise or condemn their overseers by this standard alone, without ever once troubling themselves to inquire into the manner in which things are managed on their plantations, and whether he may have lost more in the diminished value of his slaves by over-work than he has gained by his large crop." This being the case, it was understandably of no consequence to the overseer that the old hands were "worked down" and the young ones "overstrained," that the "breeding women" miscarried, and that the "sucklers" lost their children. "So that he has the requisite number of cotton bags, all is overlooked; he is re-employed at an advanced salary, and his reputation increased."[15]

2

A wise master did not take seriously the belief that Negroes were natural-born slaves. He knew better. He knew that Negroes freshly imported from Africa had to be broken in to bondage; that each succeeding generation had to be carefully trained. This was no easy task, for the bondsman rarely submitted willingly. Moreover, he rarely submitted completely. In most cases there was no end to the need for control—at least not until old age reduced the slave to a condition of helplessness.

Masters revealed the qualities they sought to develop in slaves when they singled out certain ones for special commendation. A small Mississippi planter mourned the death of his "faithful and dearly beloved servant" Jack: "Since I have owned him he has been true to me in all respects. He was an obedient trusty servant. . . . I never knew him to steal nor lie and he ever set a moral and industrious example to those around him. . . . I shall ever cherish his memory." A Louisiana sugar planter lost a "very valuable Boy" through an accident: "His life was a very great one. I have always found him willing and obedient and never knew him to fail to do anything he was put to do."[16] These were "ideal" slaves, the models slaveholders had in mind as they trained and governed their workers.

How might this ideal be approached? The first step, advised those who wrote discourses on the management of slaves, was to establish and maintain strict discipline. An Arkansas master suggested the adoption of the "Army Regulations as to the discipline in Forts." "They must obey at all times, and under all circumstances, cheerfully and with alacrity," affirmed a Virginia slaveholder. "It greatly impairs the happiness of a negro, to

[14]*American Cotton Planter and Soil of the South*, II (1858), pp. 112–13.

[15]*American Farmer*, II (1846), p. 78; *Southern Cultivator*, II (1844), pp. 97, 107.

[16]Baker Diary, entry for July 1, 1854; Alexander Franklin Pugh Ms. Plantation Diary, entry for June 21, 1860.

be allowed to cultivate an insubordinate temper. Unconditional submission is the only footing upon which slavery should be placed. It is precisely similar to the attitude of a minor to his parent, or a soldier to his general." A South Carolinian limned a perfect relationship between a slave and his master: "that the slave should know that his master is to govern absolutely, and he is to obey implicitly. That he is never for a moment to exercise either his will or judgment in opposition to a positive order."[17]

The second step was to implant in the bondsmen themselves a consciousness of personal inferiority. The had "to know and keep their places," to "feel the difference between master and slave," to understand that bondage was their natural status. They had to feel that African ancestry tainted them, that their color was a badge of degradation. In the country they were to show respect for even their master's nonslaveholding neighbors; in the towns they were to give way on the streets to the most wretched white man. The line between the races must never be crossed, for familiarity caused slaves to forget their lowly station and to become "impudent."[18]

Frederick Douglass explained that a slave might commit the offense of impudence in various ways: "in the tone of an answer; in answering at all; in not answering; in the expression of countenance; in the motion of the head; in the gait, manner and bearing of the slave." Any of these acts, in some subtle way, might indicate the absence of proper subordination. "In a well regulated community," wrote a Texan, "a negro takes off his hat in addressing a white man. . . . Where this is not enforced, we may always look for impudent and rebellious negroes."[19]

The third step in the training of slaves was to awe them with a sense of their master's enormous power. The only principle upon which slavery could be maintained, reported a group of Charlestonians, was the "principle of fear." In tis defense of slavery James H. Hammond admitted that this, unfortunately, was true but put the responsibility upon the abolitionists. Antislavery agitation had forced masters to strengthen their authority: "We have to rely more and more on the power of fear. . . . We are determined to continue masters, and to do so we have to draw the reign tighter and tighter day by day to be assured that we hold them in complete check." A North Carolina mistress, after subduing a troublesome domestic, realized that it was essential "to make them stand in fear"![20]

In this the slaveholders had considerable success. Frederick Douglass believed that most slaves stood "in awe" of white men; few could free themselves altogether from the notion that their masters were "invested with a sort of sacredness." Olmsted saw a small white girl stop a slave on the road and boldly order him to return to his plantation. The slave fearfully obeyed her command. A visitor in Mississippi claimed that a master, armed only with a whip or cane, could throw himself among a score of bondsmen and cause them to "flee with terror." He accomplished this by the "peculiar tone of authority" with which he spoke. "Fear, awe, and obedience . . . are interwoven into the very nature of the slave."[21]

The fourth step was to persuade the bondsmen to take an interest in the master's

[17]*Southern Cultivator*, IV (1846), pp. 43–44; XVIII (1860), pp. 304–305; *Farmers' Register*, V (1837), p. 32.

[18]*Southern Planter*, XII (1852), pp. 376–79; *Southern Cultivator*, VIII (1850), p. 163; *Farmers' Register*, I (1834), pp. 564–65.

[19]Douglass, *My Bondage*, p. 92; Austin *Texas State Gazette*, October 10, 1857.

[20]Phillips (ed.). *Plantation and Frontier*, II, pp. 108–11; *De Bow's Review*, VII (1849), p. 498; Mary W. Bryan to Ebenezer Pettigrew, October 20, 1835, Pettigrew Family Papers.

[21]Douglass, *My Bondage*, pp. 250–51; Olmsted, *Back Country*, pp. 444–45; [Ingraham], *South-West*, II, pp. 260–61.

enterprise and to accept his standards of good conduct. A South Carolina planter explained: "The master should make it his business to show his slaves, that the advancement of his individual interest, is at the same time an advancement of theirs. Once they feel this, it will require but little compulsion to make them act as it becomes them."[22] Though slaveholders induced only a few chattels to respond to this appeal, these few were useful examples for others.

The final step was to impress Negroes with their helplessness, to create in them "a habit of perfect dependence" upon their masters.[23] Many believed it dangerous to train slaves to be skilled artisans in the towns, because they tended to become self-reliant. Some thought it equally dangerous to hire them to factory owners. In the Richmond tobacco factories they were alarmingly independent and "insolent." A Virginian was dismayed to find that his bondsmen, while working at an iron furnace, "got a habit of roaming about and *taking care of themselves.*" Permitting them to hire their own time produced even worse results. "No higher evidence can be furnished of its baneful effects," wrote a Charlestonian, "than the unwillingness it produces in the slave, to return to the regular life and domestic control of the master."[24]

"Chains and irons," James H. Hammond correctly explained, were used chiefly to control and discipline runaways. "You will admit," he argued logically enough, "that if we pretend to own slaves, they must not be permitted to abscond whenever they see fit; and that if nothing else will prevent it these means must be resorted to."[25] Three entries in Hammond's diary, in 1844, indicated that he practiced what he preached. July 17: "Alonzo runaway with his irons on." July 30: "Alonzo came in with his irons off." July 31: ". . . re-ironed Alonzo."

Hammond was but one of many masters who gave critics of the peculiar institution a poignant symbol — the fettered slave. A Mississippian had his runaway Maria "Ironed with a shackle on each leg connected with a chain." When he caught Albert he "had an iron collar put on his neck"; on Woodson, a habitual runaway, he "put the ball and chain." A Kentuckian recalled seeing slaves in his state wearing iron collars, some of them with bells attached. The fetters, however, did not always accomplish their purpose, for numerous advertisements stated that fugitives wore these encumbrances when they escaped. For example, Peter, a Louisiana runaway, "Had on each foot when leaving, an iron ring, with a small chain attached to it."[26]

But the whip was the most common instrument of punishment—indeed, it was the emblem of the master's authority. Nearly every slaveholder used it, and few grown slaves escaped it entirely. Defenders of the institution conceded that corporal punishment was essential in certain situations; some were convinced that it was better than any other remedy. If slavery were right, argued an Arkansas planter, means had to be found to keep slaves in subjugation, "and my opinion is, the lash—not used murderously, as would-be philanthropists assert, is the most effectual." A Virginian agreed: "A great deal of whipping is not necessary; *some* is."[27]

The majority seemed to think that the certainty, and not the severity, of physical

[22]*Farmers' Register,* IV (1837), p. 574.

[23]*Southern Cultivator,* IV (1846), p. 44.

[24]*Southern Planter,* XII (1852), pp. 376–79; Olmsted, *Seaboard,* pp. 58–59; Charleston *Courier,* September 12, 1850.

[25]*De Bow's Review,* VII (1849), p. 500.

[26]Nevitt Plantation Journal, entries for November 9, 1827; March, 28, 1831; July 18, 1832; Coleman, *Slavery Times in Kentucky,* pp. 248–49; New Orleans *Picayune,* December 26, 1847.

[27]*Southern Cultivator,* XVIII (1860). p. 239–40; *Southern Planter,* XII (1852), p. 107.

"correction" was what made it effective. While no offense could go unpunished, the number of lashes should be in proportion to the nature of the offense and the character of the offender. The master should control his temper. "Never inflict punishment when in a passion," advised a Louisiana slaveholder, "but wait until perfectly cool, and until it can be done rather in sorrow than in anger." Many urged, therefore, that time be permitted to elapse between the misdeed and the flogging. A Georgian required his driver to do the whipping so that his bondsmen would not think that it was "for the pleasure of punishing, rather than for the purpose of enforcing obedience."[28]

Planters who employed overseers often fixed the number of stripes they could inflict for each specific offense, or a maximum number whatever the offense. On Pierce Butler's Georgia plantation each driver could administer twelve lashes, the head driver thirty-six, and the overseer fifty. A South Carolinian instructed his overseer to ask permission before going beyond fifteen. "The highest punishment must not exceed 100 lashes in one day and to that extent only in extreme cases," wrote James H. Hammond. "In general 15 to 20 lashes will be a sufficient flogging."[29]

The significance of these numbers depended in part upon the kind of whip that was used. The "rawhide," or "cowskin," was a savage instrument requiring only a few strokes to provide a chastisement that a slave would not soon forget. A former bondsman remembered that it was made of about three feet of untanned ox hide, an inch thick at the butt end, and tapering to a point which made it "quite elastic and springy."[30]

Many slaveholders would not use the rawhide because it lacerated the skin. One recommended, instead, a leather strap, eighteen inches long and two and a half inches wide, fastened to a wooden handle. In Mississippi, according to a visitor, the whip in general use consisted of a "stout flexible stalk" covered with a tapering leather plait, about three and a half feet in length, which formed the lash. "To the end of the lash is attached a soft, dry, buckskin cracker, about three eighths of an inch wide and ten or twelve inches long, which is the only part allowed to strike, in whipping on the bare skin. . . . When it is used by an experienced hand it makes a very loud report, and stings, or 'burns' the skin smartly, but does not bruise it."[31]

How frequently a master resorted to the whip depended upon his temperament and his methods of management. On some establishments long periods of time elapsed with relatively few whippings—until, as a rice planter explained, it seemed "as if the devil had got into" the hands, and for a time there was "a good deal of it." Or, occasionally, a normally amiable slave got out of hand and had to be flogged. "Had to whip my Man Willis for insolence to the overseer," wrote a Tennesseean. "This I done with much regret as he was never whipped before."[32]

On other establishments the whip was in constant use. The size of the estate may have had some relationship to the amount of whipping, but the disposition of the proprietor was decidedly more crucial. Small farmers, as well as large planters, often relied upon corporal punishment as their chief method of enforcing discipline. Southern women were sometimes equally prone to use the lash upon errant domestics.

Some overseers, upon assuming control, thought it wise to whip every hand on the plantation to let them know who was in command. Some masters used the lash as a

[28]*De Bow's Review,* XXII (1857). pp. 376–79; *Southern Agriculturist* IV (1831), p. 350.

[29]Kemble, *Journal,* pp. 42–43; Phillips (ed.), *Plantation and Frontier,* I, pp. 116–22; Plantation Manual in Hammond Papers.

[30]Douglass, *My Bondage,* p. 103.

[31]*Southern Cultivator,* VII (1849), p. 135; [Ingraham], *South-West,* II, pp. 287–88.

[32]Olmsted, *Seaboard,* pp. 438–39; Bills Diary, entry for March 30, 1860.

form of incentive by flogging the last slave out of his cabin in the morning.[33] Many used it to "break in" a young slave and to "break the spirit" of an insubordinate older one. "If the negro is humble and appears duly sensible of the impropriety of his conduct, a very moderate chastisement will answer better than a severe one," advised a planter. "If, however, he is stubborn . . . a slight punishment will only make bad worse." Slaves had to be flogged, explained an Alabamian, until they manifested "submission and penitence."[34]

In short, the infliction of stripes curbed many a bondsman who could not be influenced by any other technique. Whipping had a dispiriting effect upon most of them. "Had to administer a little rod to Bob this morning," reported a Virginian. "Have seen for more than 3 months I should have to humble him some, hope it may benefit him."[35]

We have seen, then, that ethnocentrism, competition, and unequal power combined to take blacks from a status not too different from that of white indentured servants to that of white people's property with no recognized human rights. When it was profitable for the white power elite (remember, most slaves were owned by a tiny percentage of the white population) to do so, and they had the power to do so, blacks were relegated to the unfortunate status of a minority group in a paternalistic system of race relations. Only after this system of racial inequality and exploitation was established did intense antiblack prejudices become widespread, apparently as a way of justifying the exploitation. (For further discussion of the origins of black-white inequality, including reprints of several articles cited in this section, see Noel, 1972b.) In the following section, we shall examine the subordination of Indian people in America, to look for similarities and differences in the ways racial inequality developed in the cases of these two very different groups.

Native Americans

Early Contact　　The first thing to keep in mind about the history of relations between Native Americans and European whites in North America is that it is an incredibly complex history, with considerable variations in events from one area to another. North America's native people, who numbered at least one million (Collier, 1947, p. 172) and possibly several times that many (Josephy, 1968, pp. 50−51; Garbarino, 1976, p. 72), were organized into about six hundred independent nations that varied tremendously in culture, social organization, and mode of economic production. Three major national groups of Europeans—Spanish, French, and British—were involved in the conquest and settlement of North America by whites, and here, too, there was great variation within the three groups. Because of this historical complexity, almost any generalization one might make has its exceptions. Nonetheless, certain patterns and regularities in Indian-white

---

[33]*Southern Cultivator*, II (1844), pp. 169−70; Davis, *Cotton Kingdom in Alabama*, pp. 54−55.

[34]*Southern Cultivator*, VIII (1850), p. 164; William P. Gould Ms. Plantation Rules.

[35]Adams Diary, entry for July 2, 1860.

relations in North America held more often than not, and these may enable us to understand some of the causes of the oppression and subordination of Indian people in the United States. Of the three major European colonial groups that settled in the United States, the one that had the dominant influence on Indian-white relations was the British. The Spanish played an important role in Florida and the Southwest, and the French for a time in the Northeast. However, in this country, most white contact with Native Americans involved British colonists or their descendents.

The Spanish, French, and British all had somewhat different objectives in coming to the New World. The Spanish came mainly to seek wealth, and secondarily to convert souls to Christianity (Garbarino, 1976). In Latin America, the Spanish also sought to conquer and control land (and the land's population), but basically to extract its wealth, rather than to establish a self-supporting system of production (Josephy, 1968, Chapter 25). This led the Spanish to immediately conquer whatever populations they encountered in Latin America, plunder the highly developed and often wealthy cities of the Aztecs, Incas, and Mayas, and force the natives into slavery or peonage. In North America, the Spanish for the most part did not become sufficiently well-established to do this (except in parts of the Southwest), and their contact with the native peoples tended to take one of two forms. When the Spanish periodically sent expeditions through North America seeking wealth, such as those of De Soto and various slave catchers in Florida, Indian people were sometimes brutally attacked, tortured, and killed. (Coronado's famous expedition in the western and plains states was a notable exception to this rule.) The other type of contact was more benevolent, and took the form of missionaries seeking to convert the native peoples to Christianity.

Among both the French and British, trading with the Indians was an important objective. Accordingly, both groups enjoyed relatively harmonious relations with Indian people at first, and in these early years, both groups largely depended on Indian people for their survival. It is unlikely, for example, that the Pilgrims at Plymouth could have survived the winter of 1621−22 without their assistance (Josephy, 1968, p. 301). The French depended largely on the fur trade as a source of economic support, and many British settlers also relied on trade with the Indians. Indian people, too, often found the early contact beneficial, particularly those tribes that were hunters and could benefit from the fur trade (Lurie, 1975). This relationship, marked by substantial but not total cooperation, did not last long, however. It soon changed to one of conflict and led to the conquest of the native people by the Europeans, particularly the British. However, the existence of this period of relative cooperation does illustrate one sociological point: Even where there are two greatly different cultural groups and considerable ethnocentrism, ethnic conflict and stratification does not automatically occur. It is clear that the British, especially, took a highly ethnocentric view of Native Americans, sometimes seeing them as ungodly heathens not subject to conversion or worthy of human association. Under the influence of Calvinism, the Protestant British regarded conversion largely as a matter of predestination: either one was part of God's chosen people or one was not, and attempting to convert those who were not chosen was a waste of time. For the most part, this led to the view that the British were chosen, and the Indians were not. Indeed, the same generalized prejudice against non-Christians that shaped British attitudes toward blacks also shaped their attitudes toward Indians.

The Catholic French, on the other hand, were like their fellow Catholic missionaries from Spain: They viewed the Indians as fellow human beings with souls, and hence, they were obligated to give them the message of Christianity. Accordingly, the French had a milder prejudice against the Indians than did the British. Another fact, however, was of even greater importance in shaping the history of these two European groups' relations with Native Americans. The French were not mainly interested in settling land: They were traders. Thus, their livelihood depended on reasonably good relations with the native hunting peoples, who provided them with their source of wealth. The British, on the other hand, mainly wanted to settle land. They were largely agriculturalists, and the opportunity to own land was one of the major attractive features of North America to British settlers (Garbarino, 1976, p. 44). When *added to* the ethnocentrism already mentioned, this factor made it inevitable that conflict would eventually break out between the British colonists and Indian people. As more and more British settlers arrived, Indian people began to be forced off their land (Josephy, 1968, Chapter 26). Since the Europeans controlled the firearms, the power balance was grossly unequal. The outcome could never have been in serious doubt once the British began to arrive in large numbers. Accordingly, the seeds of over two centuries of conquest and domination had now been sown. The basic approaches of making treaties with Indians to gain their land and of establishing Indian reservations were largely established under the British before the Revolutionary War (Garbarino, 1976, p. 440; Lurie, 1975, p. 173).

One disastrous effect of the displacement of Indian people by whites was an increase in rivalries between the various Indian nations. At first, conflicts arose over who would have control of trading with the whites. Later, as Indian people began to be displaced from their homelands, conflicts over land flared between various Indian tribes. A tragic consequence was a tremendous escalation of warfare among the various Native American groups. In the past, conflict had been controlled and somewhat ritualistic. Now, struggle had become a matter of life and death. In addition to the deaths directly resulting from the struggle, the tribal warfare made it nearly impossible for Indian people to mount a unified defense against the incursions of the whites. Largely because of animosities that had built up against Indian allies of the French, the Iroquois nations supported (in fact, if not openly) the British in the French and Indian War (Garbarino, 1976, p. 437; Josephy, 1968, pp. 311–312). This support was a critical factor, and as a result of this war, the French lost control of eastern North America.

In addition to intertribal conflicts, another disastrous result of white-Indian contacts was disease. Most historians agree that more Indians died of white people's diseases than were killed in warfare. Indian people had no immunity to these European diseases, and when Europeans brought their diseases to the Americas,

Indian people died by the thousands. In some areas, 90 percent of the indigenous population was lost (Garbarino, 1976, p. 438), and in at least one case, an entire tribe was wiped out (Debo, 1970).

A Trail of Broken Treaties   A recent American Indian protest campaign referred to itself as the "trail of broken treaties." This name is a fitting description of Indian-white relations from before the Revolutionary War until the end of the nineteenth century. Again and again, treaties were made with Indian nations, requiring the Indian people to give up their land with only the smallest compensation and move to new land, which was promised to be theirs forever. Again and again, the demands for land by a swelling white population led to displacement of the Indian people from these "promised lands." This system of treaties was fundamentally deceptive to Indian people, for two major reasons. First, Indian nations generally had a system of common ownership of land. Often, they believed they were letting whites *use* commonly owned land, not giving it up. Secondly, Indian people generally signed treaties in good faith, expecting them to be kept. In Indian societies, a person's word was enough. Whites, on the other hand, often saw the treaties as stopgap measures to get the Indians out of the way. They could always be renegotiated later when whites needed more land (Lurie, 1975, p. 176).

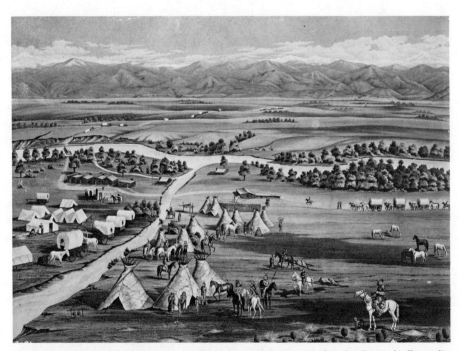

Denver in 1859. Note the process of white encroachment on Indian land. Gradually, Indians were displaced from most of the desirable locations and forced into small areas on the least desirable land. Library of Congress.

Gradually, as whites increased their population and their desire for land, Indian nations were forced to move farther and farther west, often displacing other Indian nations in the process. Some were forced to move, ultimately, as far as from Georgia to Oklahoma. One-fourth of the Cherokees died on one such forced trek (Josephy, 1968, p. 323). Certainly, it is one of history's worst examples of the forced migration of an indigenous population by an invading population.

Causes of the Subordination of Indian People   In analyzing the causes of this forced migration and subordination of America's native peoples, the same three factors stand out as with the establishment of slavery. First, there was ethnocentrism, as there usually is when two very different cultures come into contact. This, in and of itself, did not lead to widesparead subordination of the Native American peoples. This only happened when population pressures in the land-settling British (and later American) population brought this group into competition with the Indians over land. In other words, whites had something to gain—land—by subordinating the Indians, just as the Southern plantation owners had something to gain by enslaving blacks. Firearms gave the whites the power to take the land from Indians, and they used this power. Thus, the same three factors—ethnocentrism, competition, and unequal power—seem important in explaining the displacement and conquest of Indians as explained the enslavement of blacks. As Lurie (1975, p. 174, 176) points out, this can be illustrated by comparing white-Indian relations in the United States to those in Canada, where white pressure for land was never as great. There, too, Indian people were often deprived of their land, but they were given more desirable land than the American Indian, with reserves "located in the tribes' homelands or nearby ecologically similar areas" (Lurie, 1975, p. 174). Furthermore, once treaties were established, they were generally honored, and Indian people were not forced to move repeatedly from place to place as they were in the United States. A major factor in this milder treatment of the native population in Canada appears to be the fact that there has always been much less pressure for land in that country, which has both a much smaller population and less reliance on the land-based enterprise of agriculture than the United States.

The Reservation System   As Indians were forced off their land in the United States from the late eighteenth through the nineteenth century, more and more of them found themselves living on reservations. As white population increased, the reservations were increasingly relegated to land the whites considered worthless or uninhabitable. The reservations also became more and more prisonlike, with Indian people having fewer and fewer recognized legal rights. In 1871 Congress abolished the practice of making treaties with the Indians. This even further stripped Indians of their rights, since whites tended to view the "agreements" made after this change as legally and morally even less binding than the earlier treaties (Lurie, 1975). Another unfortunate development during this period was the government's designation of Indian people as "wards" of the government in 1862. While paternalism and a general effort to get Indians to surrender their own culture and adopt the white man's ways had always been a key part of European colonial and later, American, policy toward Indian people, this became even more prevalent from the 1860s on. By the latter 1800s, most Indians had been forced onto reservations, often after ferocious warfare and great bloodshed on both sides. In California, for example, it is estimated that 70,000 Indian people lost their lives in the ten years immediately after the 1849 Gold Rush, the period of greatest white population expansion (Garbarino, 1976). By the end of this period, most of those who survived had been forced onto Indian reservations. The Indian reservation of the latter nineteenth century, if it existed today, would probably be called a concentration camp. The reservations more often than not were heavily guarded by U.S. Army troops, and Indian people could not leave the reservation without a pass. Practice of native religions and other displays of Indian culture were forbidden. The Sun Dance, an annual religious ritual practiced by many plains tribes, was banned. The reason given was that the ceremony frequently involved some elements of self-torture, but the fact remains that it was a freely chosen and crucial aspect of the culture and belief of many tribes, and nobody was compelled to participate in the self-torture aspects. Indian children on reservations were frequently taken from their homes and forced to attend boarding schools run by whites. At these schools, they were required to speak only English; if they were caught speaking their native language, they were severely punished. Finally, Indian people were denied the right to vote. They could not vote in state and federal elections because they were not regarded as U.S. citizens, and they were allowed no input into the running of reservations, either, even though the reservations were supposedly their land. Even those who sought to help Indian people usually ended up exercising social control over them instead. This was because even philanthropists, some policy makers, and missionaries who meant well generally assumed that the best way to improve the conditions of Indian people was to get them to accept the "civilized" ways of the whites. Beginning in 1887, a policy known as "allotment" was initiated. The purpose of this program was to set Indians up as individual landowning farmers who would make a living by growing and selling agricultural products from their own land. Because it simply attempted to model itself after the social and economic organization of white culture without understanding the situation of the people it was supposed to help, the program was a miserable failure (Garbarino, 1976, p. 442). To begin with, it was applied indiscriminately to all tribes, whether they had any history of agriculture or not. Second, it imposed the white concept of land ownership, which was different from the usual Indian concept of commonly owned land. Also, in many Indian cultures women cultivated while men hunted or were warriors, so European-style farming was contrary to long-held notions about sex roles. Finally, many Indians were encouraged to become indebted to whites, who then took the land for payment (Lurie, 1975, p. 180). All these factors combined to make this well-intended but highly ethnocentric program a failure: Its main result was to transfer thousands of acres of Indian land to whites. Thus, we see that even when intentions were good (and, as we have seen, they usually were not), the white people's behavior and policy toward Indian people was so shaped by paternalism and ethnocentrism that it ended up serving white interests rather than Indian.

The Indian Reservation and the Slave
Plantation: A Comparison

We shall end our discussion of American Indian history up to 1900 with a comparison of the Indian reservation of the late nineteenth century to the slave plantation of the early nineteenth century. In many regards, the reservation fits model of the paternalistic pattern of race relations almost as well as the slave plantation, though it is less often given as an example and there are some differences. In both systems status was determined totally on the basis of racial or ethnic identity. Indians were expected to go to the reservations, just as antebellum Southern blacks were automatically slaves. In both cases group culture was severely repressed, and an ideology of paternalism—the belief that "we're doing them a favor by civilizing them"—was pervasive. This was to justify the exploitation of the minority group, which is the final common element in the two systems. Here, though was an important difference: Blacks were exploited totally for their labor; they had no land in this country that could be taken away. Indian people, on the other hand, were exploited mostly for their land, though a few were made slaves, both by British and white American settlers in the Southeast and Spanish settlers in the Southeast and Southwest. For the most part, however, Indians were not enslaved, for the reasons mentioned earlier in our discussion of slavery. This explains the other major difference between the two systems. Under slavery, there was continuous contact between whites and blacks, who, as indicated earlier, lived close by one another in a hierarchical system where everyone was expected to know her or his place. This was necessary if whites were to exploit blacks for their labor on the plantation. The effort in the case of Native Americans, however, was to separate them from the white population; to force them onto white-controlled reservations. The main concern was with getting them out of the way, so whites could safely farm the land that had been taken from the Indian people. Thus, the different economic objective of the dominant group—land versus labor—led to a difference in the pattern of racial inequality that resulted. The black-white pattern almost totally resembled the paternalistic form; the Indian-white pattern might best be described as basically paternalistic with the one difference being the racial separation that is more characteristic of the rigid competitive model. The important fact remains that when whites were in a position to benefit and when, with their firearms, they had the power to do so, they set up rigid systems of inequality, subordinating both black people and Indian people. Despite the many differences in the two histories, the crucial elements of ethnocentrism, unequal power, and competition or potential gain were present in both. In the case of black people the objective was labor; in the case of Indian people it was land. In both cases too, intense racist ideologies developed as a way of rationalizing or justifying the exploitation. The original ethnocentrism greatly increased after the pattern of exploitation developed.[36] As Nash (1970, Chapter 1) points out, the English settlers

[36]The different nature of the contact with and exploitation of the two groups resulted in somewhat different racist stereotypes. For further discussion of this point, see Nash, (1970), Chapter One.

were aware that they were taking land away from an established people. To justify this, they developed an image of the Native American as a helpless savage who could only benefit from being Christianized, civilized, and brought into a modern agricultural system. As pressures for land increased, so did racist stereotyping of Indian people, and the image of the Indian as a lawless barbarian replaced the earlier image of the ''noble savage.''

Mexican-Americans

Early Contacts   The first contact between Mexicans and Americans came about in what is now the southwestern United States. This contact increased to a sizable scale in the early 1800s, as the Mexican population expanded northward and the American population expanded westward. This Mexican population was mostly mestizo, a mixture of Spanish and Indian, which was by that time the overwhelming majority of the Mexican population. There were also, however, some recent white immigrants from Spain, who preferred to think of themselves as Spanish rather than Mexican and were generally so recognized. At this time, the present-day states of Texas, California, New Mexico, Arizona, and Utah were all part of Mexico, as were most of Colorado and small parts of three other states. The relationship between white Americans, or Anglos, and Mexicans during this period might best be described as having elements of both cooperation and competition. There was a certain amount of competition, but there was little ethnic stratification between Mexicans and Anglos. Both groups were landowners, farmers, and ranchers; Mexicans were operating ranches on a large scale in Texas by the late eighteenth century, and later in California, especially after Mexico became independent from Spain in 1822 (Meier and Rivera, 1972, Chapter 3). In addition to the general absence of ethnic inequality, the competition between Anglos and Mexicans was limited and—as we have indicated—was counterbalanced by significant elements of cooperation. Two examples illustrate this principle. One example can be seen in the occasional instances of ''filibustering'' by some American settlers in Texas. This referred to insurrections aimed at separating from the authority of the Mexican government. When these uprisings occurred, however, other Anglos generally helped the Mexican authorities put them down. One influential U.S. citizen who received a number of land grants, Stephen Austin, was instrumental in helping control a revolt of this type in 1826, the Fredonia Revolt, which had the support of a number of recent American immigrants. Austin also was helpful in his efforts to assure that immigrants respected the terms of their land grants and swore an oath of loyalty to Mexico (Meier and Rivera, 1972, p. 58). The overall tone is such that one expert in Chicano (Mexican-American) history has observed that ''the *general* tone of the times was one of intercultural cooperation'' (Alvarez, 1973, p. 922). In California in the 1820s and 1830s, there is similar evidence of cooperation. In fact, the Anglo immigrants of this period were often quite completely assimilated into Mexican life. Frequently they became Mexican citizens, married Mexicans, and received land grants; occasionally they even held public office (Meier and Rivera, 1972, p. 67).

To summarize, then, Mexican and Anglo residents in the early stages of southwestern settlement lived side by side in relatively equal status, with relatively cooperative relationships. In each of the three major areas (Texas, California, and Nuevo Mexico, which largely comprised present-day Arizona and New Mexico) the life style and mode of production was somewhat different, but in all three, the pattern was one of relative equality with substantial elements of cooperation. Of course both groups in different ways oppressed the southwestern Indian people, but they treated and regarded one another as relative equals.

Origins of Ethnic Stratification

Texas. During the 1830s, a chain of events began that was to prove disastrous for Mexicans living in Aztlan, as the region of Mexico that became part of the United States is sometimes called. By the early 1830s, conflict had arisen in Mexico over the role of that country's national government. Some Mexicans, the centralists, wanted a strong national government that would exercise close administrative control over all of Mexico. Others, the federalists, wanted a looser confederation with greater local autonomy, not unlike the system of the United States. Most Texans—both Mexican and Anglo—favored the latter approach and sided with the federalists. Ultimately, centralists came to control Mexico's national government. The army came to Texas to control the dissident federalists, but in the process spilled so much blood that a revolution was started and Texas ended up—for a short time—as an independent nation (Alvarez, 1973). This chain of events upset the power balance, creating new demands for land among whites in Texas in a way that resulted almost overnight in gross social inequality between Anglos and Mexicans. Why, did this happen? First, Texas's independence from Mexico accelerated the influx of white immigrants, mostly from the United States South. Before long, Anglos outnumbered Mexicans in Texas by a ratio of five to one. (Grebler et al., 1970, p. 40). These immigrants brought with them the prejudices of the South as well as a tremendous demand for land. Many sought to set up a plantation system for raising cotton, similar to the pattern in the South. Outnumbering the Mexicans as they did, they soon appealed for admission to the United States, and in 1845 Texas was annexed. The situation now was totally changed, and the past cooperation of the Mexicans with the Anglos was forgotten. Most Mexicans were quickly deprived of their land, either by force or by American law (backed by force), which consistently served Anglo, not Mexican, interests. By 1900 even the largest and wealthiest Mexican landowners had generally been deprived of their land (Alvarez, 1973).

During this period, there was also a great upsurge in anti-Mexican prejudice, which further contributed to the subordination of the now Mexican-American people in Texas. Alvarez (1973) cites three major reasons for this upsurge in prejudice. First, the warfare with Mexico had led most Anglos to view *all* Mexicans as former enemies, even though most of them had also opposed Mexico's centralist government and many had fought for Texas's independence from Mexico. Second, as noted, many had learned intense race prejudice in the United States South and readily applied notions of racial inferiority to Mexicans. Finally, racist ideology served an economic purpose in supporting and rationalizing the Anglos' actions of taking land from the Mexicans.

California and Nuevo Mexico   Most of the rest of the Southwest— California and Nuevo Mexico—became part of the United States in 1848 as a result of the Treaty of Guadalupe Hidalgo, which ended the Mexican War. This war was the result of a number of factors, particularly Mexican objections to the annexation of Texas by the United States, American desire to expand westward into Nuevo Mexico and California, and border disputes all along the U.S.-Mexican border (Meier and Rivera, 1972, Chapter 4). During this war, Nuevo Mexico surrendered itself to the United States without a fight, in part because of opposition to the centralist government of Mexico. In California, the situation was somewhat different. The cooperation between Anglos and *Californios* (Mexican settlers in California) during the 1820s and 1830s increasingly turned to conflict during the 1840s, as more and more Anglo settlers came to northern California via the Oregon trail. Here, too, opposition to the centrists among both Anglos and Mexicans was strong enough that California declared its independence from Mexico in 1836. In 1840, however, California returned to Mexican control. But increasingly, the influx of white settlers caused Anglo-*Californio* conflicts which ended any cooperation between the two, even though both had opposed the centrists in Mexico. In 1846 a new independence movement known as the Bear Flag Revolt took place. This movement came to be pretty much controlled by Anglos, who soon antagonized *Californios* in Los Angeles so strongly that they rebelled against the Anglos, who by now were openly proclaiming California to be United States territory. This led to the only serious fighting of the part of the Mexican War that occurred in what is now the United States, and led to effective American control of California by 1847. Meanwhile, the major fighting of the war was taking place in Mexico, which had been invaded by U.S. troops. In 1847 Mexico City was captured, and a year later the Treaty of Guadalupe Hidalgo was signed and ratified. This treaty ceded most of California and Nuevo Mexico to the United States, formally recognized American sovereignty over Texas, and resolved the border disputes along the Texas-Mexico boundary in favor of the United States. In protocol accompanying the treaty, the United States agreed in writing to recognize the land ownership of Mexicans in the ceded territories. The 80,000 Mexicans living in the ceded territories also were given U.S. citizenship rights, and most became citizens.[37] A few years later, the present United States—Mexican border was established when the Gadsden Purchase (1853) ceded the southern parts of present-day Arizona and New Mexico to the United States.

As was the case a few years earlier in Texas, the annexation of Nuevo Mexico and California caused a critical change in the power structure, which sooner or later proved disastrous for the Mexican people living in these two territories. The familiar pattern was repeated: Once there was a sizable influx of Anglos into an area, the

---

[37]Although Indians in the ceded territories who previously had the right of Mexican citizenship, did not receive the right of U.S. citizenship (Meier and Rivera, 1972, p. 70).

Anglos and Mexican-Americans came into competition over land. Once this happened, the Mexican-Americans were nearly always deprived of their land, despite the international agreement (and numerous verbal promises) that this would not happen. Sometimes the land was simply taken by force. At other times, the legal system accomplished the same result. This was possible because the Mexican and American concepts of land ownership were different, as were the methods for legally proving a land claim (Meier and Rivera, 1972). Thus, many Mexicans who could easily have proven their claims in Mexican courts could not do so in American courts. It is also true, of course, that judges and magistrates were usually Anglo and protected Anglo interests, and that Anglo landowners were often better able to afford quality lawyers. Furthermore, even when Mexican-Americans did eventually win their claims, they were so deeply in debt from the cost of the legal battle—some dragged on for as long as seventeen years—that they often lost part or all of their land because of the debt (Meier and Rivera, 1972, p. 80). Put simply, the balance of power was totally on the side of the Anglo-Americans.

As we said, this process of competition for land and displacement of Mexican-American landowners was closely associated with the influx of Anglo population into an area. This first occurred on a large scale in northern California during the Gold Rush, which began in 1849. In southern California, few Anglos were present; the process occurred more slowly. *Californios* and new immigrants from Mexico were in the majority until the 1870s, but the building of transcontinental railroads brought more whites to the region; by 1880 three fourths of the population was Anglo. (Meier and Rivera, 1973, chapter 5). With this influx of whites, *Californio* wealth, land ownership, and cultural influence over the region were largely lost. The process was sped up in the 1860s by floods, droughts, and declining farm prices, which put many *Californio* landowners in debt (Grebler et al., 1970, pp. 49–50). By the 1880s, Anglos were quite solidly in control of the region. The area slowest to come under Anglo domination was the present-day state of New Mexico, largely because there were fewer whites and a larger Mexican-American population here than elsewhere. About 60,000 of the 80,000 or so Mexican-Americans in 1848 lived in New Mexico (Moore, 1976, pp. 12, 15). Except on the ranchlands of eastern New Mexico near Texas, there was not the influx of whites seen in Texas and California. A wealthy class of Mexican-American urbanites—who usually preferred to think of themselves as Spanish rather than Mexican—was present here and highly influential in the region's politics past the turn of the century. Even today there is a larger and more powerful Mexican-American elite here than anywhere else in the country. Even here, Anglos eventually came to dominate. One example can be seen in the fact that by 1910, fewer than a third of the parcels of land owned by Mexicans before annexation to the U.S. remained in the hands of the Mexican owners (Gonzales, 1967, p. 29).

Causes of Anglo—Chicano Inequality   This brief discussion of the early history of Anglo-Chicano relations is sufficient to confirm that Noel's (1968) theory about the origins of ethnic stratification can be applied to Mexican-Americans as well as to other U.S. minorities.[38] Only in the presence of all three elements cited by Noel—ethnocentrism, competition, and unequal power—did patterns of near-total domination of Chicanos by Anglos emerge. Early competition for land and the whites' superior power and numbers brought this about first in Texas. The Treaty of Guadalupe Hidalgo gave political and legal power to whites throughout the Southwest, but this did not immediately cause great ethnic inequality except in northern California, where the Gold Rush began almost immediately after the treaty. In other areas, subordination of the Mexican-American population tended to come when there was a sizable influx of whites—the 1870s and 1880s in southern California, later in New Mexico. This influx added the element of competition as whites wanting land deprived Mexican-Americans of their land claims. It also increased both white ethnocentrism and the inequality of the power balance. As with blacks and Indians, racist stereotypes developed and were used to justify mistreatment of Chicanos. Another form of ethnocentrism was the concept of "manifest destiny," which was used to justify annexation of Mexican territory and to displace both Mexican-Americans and Indians from their lands. This view was that the white man's supernaturally willed destiny was to rule and "civilize" all of North America, from coast to coast. Thus, the conquest of indigenous Indian and Mexican-American populations and the taking of their lands could be justified—it was God's will. The other factor, unequal power, was also increased with a large influx of whites. Whites became a numerical majority, which augmented the legal and political power they already held. For all these reasons, there was a close association between the numerical balance of Anglos and Chicanos and the amount of inequality between the two groups in various times and places throughout the Southwest. In some regards, the history of Chicanos is very different from that of blacks and Native Americans. Only Chicano history involves the conquest by force of a sovereign, internationally recognized nation-state and the abrogation of rights accorded to its citizens by that nation. In spite of this and other differences, however, the origin of Anglo-Chicano inequality seems to involve the same three elements as the other two groups we have examined: Afro-Americans and Native Americans.

Exploitation of Chicanos for Labor   Another way in which Mexican-Americans are unique among the three groups discussed is that only they were exploited on a large scale for *both* their land and their labor in this country. Blacks had no land here because they were not indigenous: They were brought here under a system of forced migration to be exploited for their labor. Indians, for reasons discussed earlier in the chapter, were never enslaved on a large scale, and their resistance to forced assimilation, as well as their forced isolation on the reservation, generally kept white employers from seeing them as an easy source of cheap labor. Mexican-Americans, however, soon came to be exploited for their labor as well as

[38]For more complete discussions of Chicano history, see the previously cited publications as well as McWilliams, 1949, which is considered by some to be the best general work on Mexican-American history in the southwest.

their land. We have already discussed at length the exploitation of Chicanos for their land and the reasons behind it. In the remainder of this section, we shall examine the ways in which Anglos took advantage of Mexican-Americans as a source of cheap labor.

As Mexican-Americans were being displaced from their land by whites during the 1850−1900 period, whites in the Southwest were developing an economic system largely built around mining, large-scale agriculture, and railroad transportation. These types of economic activity, especially mining and large-scale agriculture, are highly labor-intensive and are most profitable when there is a large labor supply. The owners of the ranches and mines accordingly sought a supply of laborers willing to do hard, dirty work for low wages (Grebler et al., 1970, p. 51). Although bonded laborers from Asia were brought to the west to do some of this work, Mexican-Americans became the most important source of such labor. Those Mexican-Americans who were displaced from their land when the United States took over the Southwest were placed in a desperate economic position and became a major source of farm and mine labor during the latter half of the nineteenth century. After the turn of the century, the Mexican Revolution of 1909−1910 caused massive displacements and widespread economic distress in Mexico. For political and economic reasons, as well as simply for their personal safety, thousands of Mexicans fled to this country during and after that upheaval. This massive wave of immigration continued through the 1920s. This made even more Mexican-Americans available as a source of cheap labor. Furthermore, fears about competition with whites had led to tight restrictions on Asian immigration, so Asians were now less available as an alternative source of labor (see, for example, Camarillo, 1979).[39]

By the early twentieth century, the Chicano agricultural laborer was in a position only marginally better than slavery, in a system that in some ways resembled the paternalistic pattern of race relations. To a large degree, Mexican-Americans were restricted to certain low-paying, low-status jobs, so that ethnicity largely determined one's status and economic position. Frequently, the total control over minority group life associated with paternalistic systems was present for farm and mine workers, who were required to buy their goods at inflated prices at the company or ranch store and were closely supervised by labor contractors. Frequently, too, the system of labor was more unfree than free, since workers were often bound to their employers to work off the debts incurred at these company stores. Finally, there was the paternalism—the constant assertion by ranch, farm, and mine owners that their Mexican-American workers were happy, that the owners had their best interests at heart, and that the workers needed "close supervision" because they were incapable of functioning on their own. And, of course, there was the oft-repeated claim that Mexican-Americans were incapable of work other than

---

[39] Similar efforts were also directed at Mexicans, but had less effect. Immigration across the border was harder to control, and—especially in agriculture—Chicanos largely held jobs whites were unwilling to accept, so whites were less concerned about their competition.

Child migrant workers being driven to the fields. Chicanos are unique among minorities in the sense that they were systematically exploited first for their land and later for their labor. United Nations/S. Rotner.

unskilled farm or labor work and that they were especially suited to this type of work. It should be pointed out that in other regards, the pattern did not resemble Van den Berghe's paternalistic system. For one thing, there was typically a good deal of geographic mobility. Although one's movement might be quite restricted while working at any one ranch, Chicano farm labor in the early twentieth century (and since) was highly migratory. There was much movement from job to job as different crops came due to be planted or harvested. There was also much movement between the city and rural areas, with many of the farm workers spending much of the off seasons in the city, working at low-skill jobs and living in the Mexican-American neighborhoods known as *barrios* (Grebler, et al., 1970). Regardless of just how closely it resembled the paternalistic pattern, it is clear that for Chicano farm workers and many mine and railroad workers, the situation was highly exploitative. Hours were long, pay exceedingly low, food and housing were poor, and education was practically nonexistent. Especially in the rural areas, few Chicanos were permitted to rise above this status, so that the system of stratification closely fit the caste model: One's status was pretty well determined by one's ethnic group. In the mining and railroad industries and in the city, the pattern was often more like the rigid competitive pattern than the paternalistic, but here, too, Mexican-Americans were seen by employers as a source of cheap labor (Camarillo, 1979).[40] In either case, most Mexican-Americans in the latter nineteenth and early twentieth centuries found themselves in a caste system with little chance of advancement.

SUMMARY AND CONCLUSION

In this chapter, we have examined different patterns of race relations and the conditions under which these patterns tend to appear. We have discussed a theory of ethnic stratification that argues that three conditions must be present for ethnic stratification or racial inequality to develop: ethnocentrism; competition, or the opportunity for one group to gain at the other's expense; and unequal power. The order perspective stresses ethnocentrism in a situation where different cultures come into contact as the major reason for racial inequality. This approach suggests that to reduce racial inequality, assimilation must come about: Minority groups must be absorbed into the system and become culturally similar to the majority (though the majority may also borrow from the minority culture). The conflict perspective argues that racial inequality occurs because one group is in a position to gain by dominating or exploiting another, and because groups are not equal in power. In such a context, the more powerful group will gain and the less powerful group will become subordinate. This approach suggests that assimilation cannot solve the problem of racial inequality because cultural differences are not the cause of the problem. Only a change in the power balance or a redistribution of resources can solve the problem.

Our examination suggests that each view is partially correct. The histories of the three American groups we have examined, while varying greatly in many regards, all support Noel's thesis that ethnocentrism, competition, and unequal power must *all* be present before substantial racial or ethnic inequality will appear. Thus, the once-common view that eliminating prejudices and encouraging assimilation can by themselves eliminate racial inequality seems unlikely: Prejudices and cultural differences did not *by themselves* cause racial inequality. It is only in the context of competition and unequal power that ethnocentrism seems to result in race stratification. In other words, racial or ethnic inequality will occur only when, in addition to the presence of ethnocentrism, one group can benefit from dominating or oppressing another and is powerful enough to do so. This would seem to suggest

---

[40]The experience of this segment of the Mexican American population will be discussed in Chapter 6.

that part of the solution to the problem of racial inequality must be sought in the basic power structure of a society, and that changes deeper than simple attitudinal and cultural change may be necessary to solve the problem.

In the next chapter, we shall examine more recent American history to identify some of the factors associated with change in patterns of racial inequality once they have been established. It is clear that majority-minority relations today are different from majority-minority relations fifty or one hundred years ago. In the next chapter, we will try to find out some of the reasons why.

GLOSSARY

Achieved status   A position or status attained by something a person does or accomplishes rather than by birth. In class systems, social standing is determined largely by achieved statuses, though ascribed statuses also have a sizable influence.

Annexation   An expansion of territory by one group to take control over territory formerly under control of another group. This may be through military conquest, in which the outcome is much the same as in colonization. It may also be voluntary, as when residents of an area ask to be annexed. Some cases, such as purchases, fall somewhere between.

Ascribed status   Any characteristic or status determined by birth, such as race, sex, or who one's parents are. In caste systems, one's social standing is determined on the basis of ascribed statuses.

Caste system   A system of social inequality with two or more rigidly defined and unequal groups, membership in which is determined by birth and passed from generation to generation. There is ordinarily no opportunity for a person in one group to move to another group of higher status.

Class system   A system of loosely defined, unequal groups in which there is significant, but not unlimited opportunity to move to a higher or lower status.

Colonization   A form of intergroup contact that occurs when one group migrates into an area occupied by another group and subordinates that indigenous group.

Fluid competitive race relations   A pattern of race relations best described as a class system with racial inequalities remaining from a past racial caste system. There is little official segregation but often much de facto segregation. Minority groups have middle classes but are disproportionately poor. Racial conflict is present but usually kept to a controlled level.

Immigration   Migration of one group into an area controlled by another group. The entering group becomes a part of the indigenous group's society. Immigration may be either voluntary or, as in the case of slave importation, involuntary. Bonded or indentured laborers and political refugees are cases that fall somewhere between voluntary and involuntary.

Paternalistic race relations   A pattern of intergroup relations usually found in agricultural, preindustrial societies. It is a form of caste system characterized by clearly defined and well-understood racial roles and much contact between races, but also with much ritual or etiquette denoting inequality, paternalism, and little outward conflict.

Rigid competitve race relations   A pattern of race relations resembling an unstable caste system. Race largely but not totally defines roles and statuses; division of labor is more complex than in the paternalistic patttern, with majority and minority workers sometimes competing because they do similar work, though usually at different wages. Strict segregation usually accompanies this pattern, as a way the majority group protects its threatened social status. The potential for major conflict is nearly always present. This pattern is usually found in newly industrializing societies.

Changing Patterns
of Majority-Minority
Relations in the
United States

6

In the previous chapter, we examined the origins of racial and ethnic inequality in the United States. We traced the early development of relations between whites and three minority groups—blacks, American Indians, and Chicanos—through an era of castelike relationships with gross racial inequality. In this chapter, we shall examine changes over the past seventy-five to one hundred years, a period in which American race relations have gradually changed to a more fluid, classlike pattern. Race relations today, while still marked by great inequality, are in a number of ways fundamentally different from what they were in the late nineteenth century. In this chapter, we shall try to find out how and why we got from where we were then to where we are now.

Where we are now, of course, has been partly determined by our earlier patterns of racial inequality. Accordingly, we shall start this chapter by examining how the origins of ethnic stratification discussed at length in the previous chapter influence today's majority-minority relations. We shall then examine how we got from the castelike patterns discussed in the previous chapter to the more classlike race relations of today.

ORIGINS OF CONTACT
AND MODERN-DAY RACE RELATIONS:
A THEORY OF INTERNAL COLONIALISM

In the previous chapter, we discussed a number of different ways that two groups can come in contact, ranging from voluntary to involuntary. Robert Blauner (1972) has developed a theory about the development of American race relations that places crucial importance on the nature of this initial contact. Blauner's theory of *internal colonialism* distinguishes between those conquered peoples who became part of the United States (or any other country) involuntarily and those who entered voluntarily. A group that is conquered, or annexed by force, is referred to as a *colonized minority*; one which entered willingly is called an *immigrant minority*. As we have seen, Afro-Americans, Mexican-Americans, and Native Americans all fit the category of colonized minorities. The Chicano and Indian people were conquered and forced into subordinate status in much the same way as native peoples in Asia, Africa, Latin America, and Oceania when the Europeans colonized those areas. A major difference is that in the United States the white Europeans became a majority more quickly and declared independence from the mother country more quickly than in some of the other areas. They treated the indigenous populations they conquered—Indians and Mexicans—much as colonizers did in other parts of the world, however.

Some critics argue that blacks do not fit the model because they were not conquered and enslaved on their own land. Blauner replies that this does not change the basic fact that they were conquered and forced into a subordinate status in this country. This experience—forced entry into American society—distinguishes blacks, Chicanos, and Indians from *all* other American ethnic groups. However much discrimination the various European immigrant groups may have suffered, their entry here was voluntary. They did not have the status of a conquered people. Blauner argues that this difference between immigrant and colonized minorities created vast differences in their position in American society, some of which persist today. According to Blauner, certain things always happen to ethnic or racial groups when they are conquered and colonized. First, they are forced to participate in somebody else's society, whether they want to or not. Second, they are subjected to some form of unfree labor, which "greatly restricts the social mobility of the group and its participation in the political arena" (Blauner, 1972, p. 53). Often, the colonized group is isolated in the least advanced sector of the society, away from the areas of growth and opportunity. Finally, the culture and social institutions of the colonized group are subjected to attack by the colonizer. The colonizer's objective is to *force* the group to give up its ways and accept the "superior" ways of the colonizer. As a result the colonized minority is frequently subjected to the castelike patterns of intergroup relations discussed in the previous chapter. As we saw in the previous chapter, *all* of these things happened to each of the groups discussed: blacks, Chicanos, and American Indians.

It has been argued by some (see, for example, Murguria, 1975, Chapter 3) that Mexican-Americans fall somewhere between the colonial and immigrant classifications, largely because, despite their initial involuntarily presence, Mexicans have been voluntarily immigrating into the United States ever since the Southwest was annexed. It is, however, true that the *initial* mode of contact—which for Chicanos was involuntary—shapes all subsequent contact. For these reasons, and because of the distinct Chicano history of subordination and subjection to unfree labor, many argue that the internal colonialism model describes very well the Chicano experience (Barrera, 1979; Moore, 1970). Although we must admit that there is debate on the matter, Mexican-Americans would appear to fit the description of a colonized minority more closely than they fit the description of an immigrant minority.

The experience of blacks, American Indians, and Chicanos presents a sharp contrast when compared to that of the European ethnic immigrants. For whatever reason, they came voluntarily. In some cases, their culture was closer to America's dominant culture than that of the other groups, but the criticial difference is that they *chose* to enter and learn American culture. However much they may have been discriminated against, they never experienced the complete social control of the plantation or Indian reservation. They never experienced the unfree labor situation of the slave or the migrant farmworker. Their families and religious institutions were never systematically attacked as were those of black people and Indian people. Finally, they were never restricted to jobs outside the industrial mainstream, as were so many blacks, Indians, and Chicanos. To all these differences, we must add that a majority tends to have different and more intense prejudices toward a conquered and subordinated people than it has toward an immigrant people. Blauner's main point is actually quite simple: These tremendous historical differences place modern-day blacks, Chicanos, and Native Americans in a very different social position than their counterparts among the European ethnics. They have been, and are, subject to a number of socially imposed disadvantages that the immigrant groups are not, no matter how much they may have been discriminated against. Furthermore, their relationship to the dominant society is and always has been fundamentally different. Blauner and others feel this offers one answer to two oft-repeated questions: (1) Why have blacks, Chicanos, and Indians not assimilated to the degree that other groups have? (2) Why do these three groups remain socially and economically disadvantaged when other groups, such as Irish and Italian-Americans, have enjoyed rising status? These sociologists believe that these differences result from the differences in the historical experience of *immigrant minorities* and *colonized minorities*. (Blauner, 1972, discusses all of these differences between European immigrant groups and the three colonized minorities at greater length.)

We have considered blacks, Chicanos, Indians, and European immigrants in terms of the immigrant versus colonized minority dichotomy. By now, you may be wondering where Asian-Americans fit in. The answer seems to be somewhere between an immigrant minority and a colonized minority. It is hard to classify their original presence in the United States as either completely voluntary or completely involuntary. The majority of Chinese immigrants during the peak period of migration in the nineteenth century came as indentured laborers or contract laborers. These immigrants were bound to creditors in China, to whom they had to pay off debt incurred for travel to the United States. Some of the contract laborers, who were referred to as "coolies," were actually forced into their servitude (Barth, 1964, pp. 50–59). The same was true of some—though far fewer—Japanese immigrants—mostly those who came by way of Hawaii (Ichihashi, 1969, Chapter 5). The early immigration of Filipinos, whose homeland was in fact made into a colony of the United States, was also often less than voluntary.

These groups might be classified as falling somewhere between immigrant and colonized minorities, and their experience since their arrival in America supports that view. Their labor was often unfree, with many tied to job and employer until their debts, contracts, or indentures were paid off. They were largely isolated in low-pay, labor-intensive sectors of the economy, as were blacks and Chicanos. On the other hand, they were not forcibly deprived of their land or subjected to the total control of slavery or the Indian reservation as were the other groups,[1] so they were in a more favorable position to retain their social organization and ways of life. Since many of them did come voluntarily, they were also more inclined to make some voluntary adaptation to American culture and institutions. In short, both the nature of their arrival and their experiences after arriving in America suggest that the experience of Chinese-, Japanese-, and Filipino-Americans falls somewhere between the colonialized experience of blacks, Chicanos, and Indians and the immigrant experience of the European ethnics.

Another group that falls somewhere between an immigrant and colonized minority is Puerto Ricans in the United States. Their homeland was, like the Philippines, made into a colony of the United States. Their migration to the United States, however, seems to have been quite voluntary (Blauner, 1972). As with the Asian groups, their experience since migration seems to fall somewhere between that of the immigrant and colonized minorities.

Regardless of the exact position of any group on the immigrant versus colonized-minority continuum, Blauner's basic point seems to be correct. The experiences of those who entered America voluntarily have been quite different from the experiences of those who did not. Not only were they forced into American society against their will in the first place, but colonized minorities have also had imposed on them disadvantages, social control, and attacks on their culture that immigrant groups have not. These differences have led to less assimilation, greater exploitation, and lower status, even to the present day, among colonized minorities as compared to immigrant minorities. It further appears that the situation *today* of those groups whose initial presence falls between immigration and colonization remains somewhere between that of the colonized racial minorities and the immigrants from Europe. To summarize, the position of any racial or ethnic group in America today cannot be understood without some examination of that

---

[1] A notable exception is the imprisonment of Japanese-Americans in concentration camps during World War II, which is discussed later in this chapter.

group's history, going all the way back to how it first came into contact with American society.

EVOLVING PATTERNS OF BLACK-WHITE RACE RELATIONS

Caste Relations Become Unstable: The Development of Rigid Competitive Race Relations, 1860–1945

As America moved through the latter half of the nineteenth century and into the twentieth century, a number of important social changes were taking place. Throughout the Western world, including the United States, urbanization, industrialization, and an increase in the complexity of social organization were taking place. The dominant mode of production was shifting from agriculture—where ownership of land was crucial—to industry and commerce, where ownership of capital was crucial. In some ways it was a gradual, evolutionary process. In other ways, there were abrupt, cataclysmic changes. The Civil War, for example, is seen by most historians not simply as a struggle to free the slaves but as a more basic conflict between the rural, agrarian, landowning interests of the South and the rising industrial and commercial interests of the North. The North's victory is sometimes seen as a triumph of capitalism over feudalism, analogous in some ways with the outcome of the French Revolution. Both the abrupt changes that came with the Civil War and the more gradual changes that took place over a longer time caused important changes in the pattern of majority-minority relations in America, and those changes are the main subject of this chapter.

The main effect of these changes was a destabilization of, but not—for a very long time—a real move toward elimination of castelike race relations. During the latter part of the nineteenth and early part of the twentieth centuries, the dominant pattern of American race relations came to resemble the rigid competitive pattern. This was most clearly true with regard to Afro-Americans and later, Mexican Americans, but it was also partially true for Native Americans, Puerto Ricans, and Asian-Americans. Although the characteristics of rigid competitive patterns of race relations were described in some detail in the previous chapter, they can be briefly listed here:

1. Status is determined mostly, but not totally, by race. Small elites appear among generally disadvantaged minority groups.
2. Division of labor is largely but not totally by race. In some situations, both majority and minority group members are doing the same kind of work, although the minority group members are nearly always paid less for the same work. (This is called a *dual wage market*.) Also, the job titles are frequently different for majority and minority group members even when the work is the same.

3. Separation of the races, or *segregation,* is extensive. The majority group imposes this segregation as a way of protecting its threatened status against the upward mobility of the minority group.
4. The competition over jobs (since in some situations both majority and minority are seeking and doing similar work) and other scarce resources carries the potential for severe conflict. Major outbursts of violence—usually attacks by majority group members against minorities—occur periodically.

The Antebellum North   Perhaps the development of this pattern can be seen most clearly by examining the history of black-white relations of the nineteenth century and the first half of the twentieth century. The pattern was already well developed in the North before the Civil War. After slavery was abolished in the North—by 1804 in most of those areas where it had ever existed—blacks and whites, particularly lower-status whites who had recently immigrated from Europe, began to compete for jobs. Numerous discriminatory laws and practices were developed to protect white workers from black competition. In 1862, Irish longshoremen threatened to shut down the port of New York unless all black workers were fired (Bloch, 1969, p. 34). Earlier, laws had been passed in Illinois, Indiana, and Oregon banning black people from entering those states (Wilson, 1973, p. 95). By the time of the Civil War, the pattern of race riots was also becoming established in the North. In 1863 the worst riot in American history occurred in New York City as thousands of whites went on a rampage to protest being drafted to fight in the Civil War. It is estimated that two thousand people died in the violence (Bahr et al., 1979). Although this was not ostensibly a race riot, it had considerable racial overtones. First, it was largely a protest by whites against what they saw as being forced to fight a war to free black slaves. Second, like later race riots, it involved numerous attacks against blacks. Many blacks were beaten to death, and the homes of blacks were destroyed. Clearly, then, racial resentment was a major factor in the violence. (For further discussion of northern race relations before the Civil War, see Litwack, 1961).

The Postbellum South   When the Civil War brought an end to slavery in the South, many hoped that it would result in major changes for the better in the pattern of race relations in the South. For a brief period of time known as Reconstruction, there were indications that such a positive change was happening. This period did not last, however, and before long, prejudice and racist ideology in the South intensified, and black-white segregation increased to a level beyond anything that existed under slavery. There are several important reasons why the Civil War did not bring an end to pervasive racial inequality in the South.

First, the elite planter class did not disappear at the end of the Civil War, though its power was certainly somewhat reduced. This class still retained enough influence immediately after the Civil War to pass a series of laws in southern states sometimes called Black Codes, aimed at keeping the black population in a subordinate status and, more specifically, at keeping blacks as a cheap source of labor (Wilson, 1973, p. 99; 1978, pp. 52–53; Woodward, 1971, pp. 251–252).

These laws passed in 1865–66, were designed to force all blacks to work whether they wanted to or not, by providing for arrest and imprisonment of blacks who quit their jobs, and by permitting those who refused to work to be fined and/or bound out to labor contractors (Wilson, 1973, p. 99; Franklin, 1969, p. 303). There were also laws passed which deprived blacks of the rights of voting, officeholding, military service, jury duty, testifying against whites in court, and freedom of travel (Gossett, 1963, Meier and Rudwick, 1970a).

These laws were rather quickly nullified by federal (that is, northern) intervention, which initiated Reconstruction. Partly for ideological reasons, but also in large part for political purposes (to strengthen their position nationally by giving the vote to southern blacks), the Republicans who controlled the U.S. Congress passed a series of laws protecting the rights of southern blacks. A series of civil rights laws and Reconstruction bills were passed that not only guaranteed protection of the rights of southern blacks and nullified the Black Codes, but also established martial law in the South to enforce the federal policy. In addition, the Freedmen's Bureau was established to provide food, education, medical care, transportation, and, in some cases land, to freed slaves (and to many needy whites as well).

Reconstruction substantially improved the condition of southern blacks, both economically and politically. Blacks, for example, served in legislatures of southern states, occasionally in large numbers. At sometime or other between 1869 and 1901, two blacks (Hiram R. Revels and Blanche K. Bruce, both from Mississippi) served in the U.S. Senate, and twenty blacks served in the U.S. House of Representatives. In spite of these improvements, Reconstruction did not last very long, and was soon replaced by a new version of the old order of racial inequality.

After about 1870 it gradually became evident that Reconstruction was on its way out. In the North, political changes were causing the federal government to lose its will to enforce the policies of Reconstruction. In the South two important things began to happen. First, old Confederate officials and supporters—many of whom lost the right to vote at the start of Reconstruction—were given back the vote under amnesty or policies of universal male suffrage. This strengthened the political power of antiblack southern white Democrats. Second, southern whites opposed to Reconstruction took the law into their own hands by forming the Ku Klux Klan and a host of other violent secret societies that kept blacks from voting and exercising other rights.

Although historians debate which segment of the white population was responsible for and benefited from the establishment of racial segregation in the South, it is clear that both the upper and lower segment of the white population felt that they were benefiting from the reestablishment of strict racial inequality in the South. There is little doubt that the main strength of the Ku Klux Klan and the loudest demand for segregation laws came from poor and working-class whites in the South. It was these whites who were in direct competition with freed blacks for land, under the sharecropping system, and for jobs. Thus, they sought to shield themselves from such competition through discrimination. The reaction of poorer whites to such competition was all the stronger because they had never had to compete directly with blacks in these ways before.

At the same time, the ruling class of the South—now composed both of the old planter class and a growing industrial elite—was happy to sit back and benefit from racism. As long as working-class whites and blacks saw each other as the enemy, there was little chance of a united, class-based movement against those who controlled the real wealth of the South. Thus, although the elite was willing to side at times with blacks against working-class whites to keep the latter under control, it was most definitely *not* willing to act effectively to prevent the emergence of a system of racial inequality that divided the poor and the working class along racial lines. Thus, both competition between lower-status whites and the freed blacks *and* the desire of the upper economic class to protect its position by dividing its potential opposition helped to create and maintain the rigid system of segregation that developed in the South following the brief period of Reconstruction after the Civil War. (For further discussion of this period see Wilson, 1978, Chapter 3; and Woodward, 1971, 1966). Divisions and competition between poorer members of the majority group and minority group members are critical elements in a rigid competitive system of race relations, and divisions of this type are a crucial reason for the emergence of such a system after Reconstruction.

After Rutherford Hayes became president in 1876, federal troops were withdrawn from the South, and the reforms of Reconstruction were gradually undone. During the 1880s, blacks gradually lost the vote; segregation appeared and gradually became widespread in education and public facilities (Franklin, 1969, pp. 330–343). The Supreme Court began to strike down civil rights legislation that had been passed during Reconstruction, and finally gave its full stamp of approval to segregation in the *Plessy* v. *Ferguson* case in 1896. In this ruling the Court established the "separate but equal" doctrine, which upheld segregated facilities as long as the facilities available to each race were equal. As a practical matter, however, very little attention was paid to the "equal" part, and separate and *unequal* facilities became the rule throughout the South. By thirty-five years after the Civil War, a system of segregation existed that was unlike anything that had existed before, even under slavery. Prejudice and ideological racism (the belief that blacks were innately inferior) also rose to levels of intensity beyond even those of the slavery period. We have already seen part of the reason for this—the new competition between lower-status whites and freed blacks, along with the desire of the elite to maintain its dominance by encouraging racial divisions in the working class.

There was, however, also an attempt by whites more generally to maintain a system where whiteness conferred status; a system of *social distance*. Under slavery that had been easy—everyone knew that whites were masters and blacks were slaves. This in itself created the unequal relationship from which the whites gained psychological and material benefit. If whites were to maintain such a relationship *after* slavery, however, they would have to find a new way to proclaim and enforce the norm of racial inequality. They did this by establishing segregation—in effect by replacing social distance with physical distance. Now, white superiority was proclaimed by setting up places and situations where only whites could go—and where blacks were defined as unworthy and unacceptable. In effect, society would be remade into a private club that only whites were good enough to enter. Special privilege and physical separation rather than a master-slave relationship were now the indicators of a system of white dominance and white superiority. Along with the policy of segregation came an intensified ideology of racism, as whites tried, through promoting notions of biological superiority, to retain the image of dominance and superiority that being a slaveowner race had given them. In short, the intensified racism and the rise of segregation after the Civil War represented an attempt by whites to hang onto the favored social and economic status that was threatened by the end of slavery.

There were some attempts during the post–Civil War period to break through the racial division and unify poor whites and blacks on the basis of class. Probably the most notable of these was the Populist party, which gained some degree of success in getting the votes of both blacks and poor whites. The Populist appeal was clearly class-based, arguing that the rural poor of both races should unite to defeat the wealthy elite that ruled them. Consider, for example, the following statement by Populist leader Tom Watson: "You are made to hate each other because upon that hatred is rested the keystone of the arch of financial despotism which enslaves you both. You are deceived and blinded that you may not see how this race antagonism perpetuates a monetary system which beggars you both." (quoted in Woodward, 1966, p. 63). Watson gained substantial black support in Georgia, and a coalition of Populists and the remnants of Reconstruction-era liberal Republican organizations briefly gained control of the North Carolina legislature in 1894, resulting in the appointment of numerous black public officials (Franklin, 1969, p. 337). Ultimately, however, the Populists did not succeed. It became clear to them that wealthy, southern Democratic elite could use laws designed to deny blacks the vote against poor whites, too. The elite's implicit threat to do so if the Populists continued to appeal to the black vote caused the Populists to back off this strategy in most areas. In addition, the Populists in many areas were hurt by the fraudulent use of black votes by the conservative Democrats. Thus, the Populists were both weakened and frightened away from the black vote. In short, the strategy of the wealthy white elite to divide and conquer, though briefly threatened, was ultimately successful. As a consequence, black political power was thwarted, and the white working class was kept largely powerless and increasingly resentful of the threat of competition from blacks (for further discussion of the Populists, see Franklin, 1969, pp. 335–338; Wilson, 1973, pp. 102–103; 1978, pp. 58–59; Woodward, 1966, pp. 60–65).

In short, then, the power of the elite to divide and conquer the poor on the basis of race, combined with the real fear of the black population by working-class and poor whites who were forced into competition with it after the Civil War, led to a pattern of intensified prejudice, racism, and segregation by about thirty years after the Civil War. We can see again that the social-structural factors of unequal power, intergroup competition, and the opportunity for one group to gain by subordinating another played a crucial role in maintaining racial inequality in the South. Because the competition took a new form (the competition between poor whites and blacks for land and jobs) and because of federal intervention, which ended slavery, racial inequality took a new form. The old paternalistic system of slavery was replaced by a rigid competitive system of race relations, marked by strict segregation, heightened prejudice and ideological racism, and more intergroup conflict.

During the 1890s, most southern states went the final step and deprived blacks of the right to vote. Thus, on top of the new system of total segregation and the intensification of prejudice and racial ideologies we have already mentioned, blacks lost virtually all of their political power in the South. Before long, nearly all of the many blacks who had been elected to public office were gone. In effect, the racial caste system of the South was rather quickly restored in a new form. Because their status had been threatened by the end of slavery and by the competition we have already discussed, whites now resorted to more violence against blacks than ever. According to Franklin (1969, p. 439), there were over 2,500 lynchings in the last sixteen years of the nineteenth century. The great majority of the victims were black, and most of the lynchings took place in the South.

The following selection, drawn from black author Richard Wright's essay, "The Ethics of Living Jim Crow," provides a graphic description of what black people experienced during the era of Jim Crow segregation. It also illustrates a number of features we have identified as characteristic of rigid competitive race relations: the fear of minority competition in the white working class, the ideology of racial superiority, the separation of blacks and whites, and the exclusion of blacks from white society. (From pp. xiii—xxx in "The Ethics of Living Jim Crow," from *Uncle Tom's Children* by Richard Wright. Copyright 1937 by Richard Wright; renewed 1965 by Ellen Wright. Reprinted by permission of Harper and Row, Publishers, Inc.)

THE ETHICS OF LIVING JIM CROW

There is but one place where a black boy who knows no trade can get a job, and that's where the houses and faces are white, where the trees, lawns, and hedges are green. My first job was with an optical company in Jackson, Mississippi. The morning I applied I stood straight and neat before the boss, answering all his questions with sharp yessirs and nosirs. I was very careful to pronounce my *sirs* distinctly, in order that he might know that I was polite, that I knew where I was, and that I knew he was a *white* man. I wanted that job badly.

He looked me over as though he were examining a prize poodle. He questioned me closely about my schooling, being particularly insistent about how much mathematics I had had. He seemed very pleased when I told him I had had two years of algebra.

"Boy, how would you like to try to learn something around here?" he asked me.

"I'd like it fine, sir," I said, happy. I had visions of "working my way up." Even Negroes have those visions.

"All right," he said, "Come on."

I followed him to the small factory.

"Pease," he said to a white man of about thirty-five, "this is Richard. He's going to work for us."

Pease looked at me and nodded.

I was then taken to a white boy of about seventeen.

"Morrie, this is Richard, who's going to work for us."

"Whut yuh sayin' there, boy!" Morrie boomed at me.

"Fine!" I answered.

The boss instructed these two to help me, teach me, give me jobs to do, and let me learn what I could in my spare time.

My wages were five dollars a week.

I worked hard, trying to please. For the first month I got along O.K. Both Pease and Morrie seemed to like me. But one thing was missing. And I kept thinking about it. I was not learning anything and nobody was volunteering to help me. Thinking they had forgotten that I was to learn something about the mechanics of grinding lenses, I asked Morrie one day to tell me about the work. He grew red.

"Whut yuh tryin' t' do, nigger, get smart?" he asked.

"Naw; I ain' tryin' t' git smart," I said.

"Well, don't, if yuh know whut's good for yuh!"

I was puzzled. Maybe he just doesn't want to help me, I thought. I went to Pease.

"Say, are yuh crazy, you black bastard?" Pease asked me, his gray eyes growing hard.

I spoke out, reminding him that the boss had said I was to be given a chance to learn something.

"Nigger, you think you're *white,* don't you?"

"Naw, sir!"

"Well, you're acting mighty like it!"

"But, Mr. Pease, the boss said . . ."

Pease shook his fist in my face.

"This is a *white* man's work around here, and you better watch yourself!"

From then on they changed toward me. They said good-morning no more. When I was just a bit slow in performing some duty, I was called a lazy son-of-a-bitch.

Once I thought of reporting all this to the boss. But the mere idea of what would happen to me if Pease and Morrie should learn that I had "snitched" stopped me. And after all the boss was a white man, too. What was the use?

The climax came at noon one summer day. Pease called me to his workbench. To get to him I had to go between two narrow benches and stand with my back against a wall.

"Yes, sir," I said.

"Richard, I want to ask you something." Pease began pleasantly, not looking up from his work.

"Yes, sir," I said again.

Morrie came over, blocking the narrow passage between the benches. He folded his arms, staring at me solemnly.

I looked from one to the other, sensing that something was coming.

"Yes, sir," I said for the third time

Pease looked up and spoke very slowly.

"Richard, *Mr.* Morrie here tells me you called me *Pease.*"

I stiffened. A void seemed to open up in me. I knew this was the show-down.

He meant that I had failed to call him Mr. Pease. I looked at Morrie. He was gripping a steel bar in his hands. I opened my mouth to speak, to protest, to assure Pease that I had never called him simply *Pease,* and that I had never had any intentions of doing so, when Morrie grabbed me by the collar, ramming my head against the wall.

"Now, be careful, nigger!" snarled Morrie, baring his teeth. "*I heard yuh call 'im Pease!* 'N' if yuh say yuh didn't, yuh're callin' me a *lie,* see?" He waved the steel bar threateningly.

If I had said: No sir, Mr. Pease, I never called you *Pease,* I would have been automatically calling Morrie a liar. And if I had said: Yes sir, Mr. Pease, I called you *Pease,* I would have been pleading guilty to having uttered the worst insult that a Negro can utter to a southern white man. I stood hesitating, trying to frame a neutral reply.

"Richard, I asked you a question!" said Pease. Anger was creeping into his voice.

"I don't remember calling you *Pease,* Mr. Pease," I said cautiously. "And if I did, I sure didn't mean . . ."

"You black son-of-a-bitch! You called me *Pease,* then!" he spat, slapping me till I bent sideways over a bench. Morrie was on top of me, demanding:

"Didn't yuh call 'im *Pease*? If yuh say yuh didn't, I'll rip yo' gut string loose with this bar, you black granny dodger! Yuh can't call a white man a lie 'n' git erway with it, you black son-of-a-bitch!"

I wilted. I begged them not to bother me. I knew what they wanted. They wanted me to leave.

"I'll leave," I promised, "I'll leave right *now.*"

They gave me a minute to get out of the factory. I was warned not to show up again, or tell the boss.

I went.

When I told the folks at home what had happened, they called me a fool. They told me that I must never again attempt to exceed my boundaries. When you are working for white folks, they said, you got to "stay in your place" if you want to keep working.

II

My Jim Crow education continued on my next job, which was portering in a clothing store. One morning, while polishing brass out front, the boss and his twenty-year-old son got out of their car and half dragged and half kicked a Negro woman into the store. A policeman standing at the corner looked on, twirling his night-stick. I watched out of the corner of my eye, never slackening the strokes of my chamois upon the brass. After a few minutes, I heard shrill screams coming from the rear of the store. Later the woman stumbled out, bleeding, crying, and holding her stomach. When she reached the end of the block, the policeman grabbed her and accused her of being drunk. Silently, I watched him throw her into a patrol wagon.

When I went to the rear of the store, the boss and his son were washing their hands at the sink. They were chuckling. The floor was bloody and strewn with wisps of hair and clothing. No doubt I must have appeared pretty shocked, for the boss slapped me reassuringly on the back.

"Boy, that's what we do to niggers when they don't want to pay their bills," he said, laughing.

His son looked at me and grinned.

"Here, hava cigarette," he said.

Not knowing what to do, I took it. He lit his and held the match for me. This was a gesture of kindness, indicating that even if they had beaten the poor old woman, they would not beat me if I knew enough to keep my mouth shut.

"Yes, sir," I said, and asked no questions.

After they had gone, I sat on the edge of the packing box and stared at the bloody floor till the cigarette went out.

That day at noon, while eating in a hamburger joint, I told my fellow Negro porters what had happened. No one seemed surprised. One fellow, after swallowing a huge bite, turned to me and asked:

"Huh! is tha' all they did t' her?"

"Yeah. Wasn't tha' enough?" I asked.

"Shucks! Man, she's a lucky bitch!" he said, burying his lips deep into a juicy hamburger. "Hell, it's a wonder they din't lay her when they got through."

III

I was learning fast, but not quite fast enough. One day, while I was delivering packages in the suburbs, my bicycle tire was punctured. I walked along the hot, dusty road, sweating and leading my bicycle by the handle-bars.

A car slowed at my side.

"What's the matter, boy?" a white man called.

I told him my bicycle was broken and I was walking back to town.

"That's too bad," he said. "Hop on the running board."

He stopped the car. I clutched hard at my bicycle with one hand and clung to the side of the car with the other.

"All set?"

"Yes sir," I anwered. The car started.

It was full of young white men. They were drinking. I watched the flask pass from mouth to mouth.

"Wanna drink, boy?" one asked.

I laughed as the wind whipped my face. Instinctively obeying the freshly planted precepts of my mother, I said:

"Oh, no!"

The words were hardly out of my mouth before I felt something hard and cold smash me between the eyes. It was an empty whisky bottle. I saw stars, and fell backwards from the speeding car into the dust of the road, my feet becoming entangled in the steel spokes of my bicycle. The white men piled out and stood over me.

"Nigger, ain' yuh learned no better sense'n tha' yet?" asked the man who hit me. "Ain' yuh learned t' say *sir* t' a white man yet?"

Dazed, I pulled to my feet. My elbows and legs were bleeding. Fists doubled, the white man advanced kicking my bicycle out of the way.

"Aw, leave the bastard alone. He's got enough," said one.

They stood looking at me. I rubbed my shins, trying to stop the flow of blood. No doubt they felt a sort of contemptuous pity, for one asked:

"Yuh wanna ride t' town now, nigger? Yuh reckon yuh know enough t' ride now?"

"I wanna walk," I said, simply.

Maybe it sounded funny. They laughed.

"Well, walk, yuh black son-of-a-bitch!"

When they left they comforted me with:

"Nigger, yuh sho better be damn glad it wuz us yuh talked t' tha' way. Yuh're a lucky bastard, 'cause if yuh'd said tha' t' somebody else, yuh might've been a dead nigger now."

IV

Negroes who have lived South know the dread of being caught alone upon the streets in white neighborhoods after the sun has set. In such a simple situation as this the plight of the Negro in America is graphically symbolized. While white strangers may be in these neighborhoods trying to get home, they can pass unmolested. But the color of a Negro's skin makes him easily recognizable, makes him suspect, converts him into a defenseless target.

Late one Saturday night I made some deliveries in a white neighborhood. I was pedaling my bicycle back to the store as fast as I could, when a police car, swerving toward me, jammed me into the curbing.

"Get down and put up your hands" the policemen ordered.

I did. They climbed out of the car, guns drawn, faces set, and advanced slowly.

"Keep still!" they ordered.

I reached my hands higher. They searched my pockets and packages. They seemed dissatisfied when they could find nothing incriminating. Finally, one of them said:

"Boy, tell your boss not to send you out in white neighborhoods after sundown."

As usual, I said:

"Yes, sir."

V

My next job was a hall-boy in a hotel. Here my Jim Crow education broadened and deepened. When the bell-boys were busy, I was often called to assist them. As many of the rooms in the hotel were occupied by prostitutes, I was constantly called to carry them liquor and cigarettes. These women were nude most of the time. They did not bother about clothing, even for bell-boys. When you went into their rooms, you were supposed to take their nakedness for granted, as though it startled you no more than a blue vase or a red rug. Your presence awoke in them no sense of shame, for you were not regarded as human. If they were alone, you could steal sidelong glimpses at them. But if they were receiving men, not a flicker of your eyelids could show. I remember one incident vividly. A new woman, a huge, snowy-skinned blonde, took a room on my floor. I was sent to wait upon her. She was in bed with a thickset man; both were nude and uncovered. She said she wanted some liquor and slid out of bed and waddled across the floor to get her money from a dresser drawer. I watched her.

"Nigger, what in hell you looking at?" the white man asked me, raising himself upon his elbows.

"Nothing," I answered, looking miles deep into the blank wall of the room.

"Keep your eyes where they belong, if you want to be healthy!" he said.

"Yes, sir."

VI

One of the bell-boys I knew in this hotel was keeping steady company with one of the Negro maids. Out of a clear sky the police descended upon his home and arrested him, accusing him of bastardy. The poor boy swore he had had no intimate relations with the girl. Nevertheless, they forced him to marry her. When the child arrived, it was found to be much lighter in complexion than either of the two supposedly legal parents. The white men around the hotel made a great joke of it. They spread the rumor that some white cow must have scared the poor girl while she was carrying the baby. If you were in their presence when this explanation was offered, you were supposed to laugh.

VII

One of the bell-boys was caught in bed with a white prostitute. He was castrated and run out of town. Immediately after this all the bell-boys and hall-boys were called together and warned. We were given to understand that the boy who had been castrated was a "mightly, mighty lucky bastard." We were impressed with the fact that next time the management of the hotel would not be responsible for the lives of "trouble-makin' niggers." We were silent.

VIII

One night, just as I was about to go home, I met one of the Negro maids. She lived in my direction, and we fell in to walk part of the way home together. As we passed the white nightwatchman, he slapped the maid on her buttock. I turned around, amazed. The watchman looked at me with a long, hard, fixed-under stare. Suddenly he pulled his gun and asked:

"Nigger, don't yuh like it?"

I hesitated.

"I asked yuh don't yuh like it?" he asked again, stepping forward.

"Yes, sir," I mumbled.

"Talk like it, then!"

"Oh, yes, sir!" I said with as much heartiness as I could muster.

Outside, I walked ahead of the girl, ashamed to face her. She caught up with me and said:

"Don't be a fool! Yuh couldn't help it!"

This watchman boasted of having killed two Negroes in self-defense.

Yet, in spite of all this, the life of the hotel ran with an amazing smoothness. It would have been impossible for a stranger to detect anything. The maids, the hall-boys, and the bell-boys were all smiles. They had to be.

IX

I had learned my Jim Crow lessons so thoroughly that I kept the hotel job till I left Jackson for Memphis. It so happened that while in Memphis I applied for a job at a branch of the optical company. I was hired. And for some reason, as long as I worked there, they never brought my past against me.

Here Jim Crow education assumed quite a different form. It was no longer brutally cruel, but subtly cruel. Here I learned to lie, to steal, to dissemble. I learned to play that dual role which every Negro must play if he wants to eat and live.

For example, it was almost impossible to get a book to read. It was assumed that after a Negro had imbibed what scanty schooling the state furnished he had no further need for books. I was always borrowing books from men on the job. One day I mustered enough courage to ask one of the men to let me get books from the library in his name. Surprisingly, he consented because he was a Roman Catholic and felt a vague sympathy for Negroes, being himself an object of hatred. Armed with a library card, I obtained books in the following manner: I would write a note to the librarian, saying: "Please let this nigger boy have the following books." I would then sign it with the white man's name.

When I went to the library, I would stand at the desk, hat in hand, looking as unbookish as possible. When I received the books desired I would take them home. If the books listed in the note happened to be out, I would sneak into the lobby and forge a new one. I never took any chances guessing with the white librarian about what the fictitious white man would want to read. No doubt if any of the white patrons had suspected that some of the volumes they enjoyed had been in the home of a Negro, they would not have tolerated it for an instant.

The factory force of the optical company in Memphis was much larger than that in Jackson, and more urbanized. At least they liked to talk, and would engage the Negro help in conversation whenever possible. By this means I found that many subjects were taboo from the white man's point of view. Among the topics they did not like to discuss with Negroes were the following: American white women; the Ku Klux Klan; France, and how Negro soldiers fared while there; French women; Jack Johnson; the entire northern part of the United States; the Civil War; Abraham Lincoln; U.S. Grant; General

Sherman; Catholics; the Pope; Jews; the Republican Party; slavery; social equality; Communism; Socialism; the 13th and 14th Amendments to the Constitution; or any topic calling for positive knowledge or manly self-assertion on the part of the Negro. The most accepted topics were sex and religion.

There were many times when I had to exercise a great deal of ingenuity to keep out of trouble. It is southern custom that all men must take off their hats when they enter an elevator. And especially did this apply to us blacks with rigid force. One day I stepped into an elevator with my arms full of packages. I was forced to ride with my hat on. Two white men stared at me coldly. Then one of them very kindly lifted my hat and placed it upon my armful of packages. Now the most accepted response for a Negro to make under such circumstances is to look at the white man out of the corner of his eye and grin. To have said: "Thank you!" would have made the white man *think* that you *thought* you were receiving from him a personal service. For such an act I have seen Negroes take a blow in the mouth. Finding the first alternative distasteful, and the second dangerous, I hit upon an acceptable course of action which fell safely between these two poles. I immediately—no sooner than my hat was lifted—pretended that my packages were about to spill, and appeared deeply distressed with keeping them in my arms. In this fashion I evaded having to acknowledge his service, and, in spite of adverse circumstances, salvaged a slender shred of personal pride.

How do Negroes feel about the way they have to live? How do they discuss it when alone among themselves? I think this question can be answered in a single sentence. A friend of mine who ran an elevator once told me:

"Lawd, man! Ef it wuzn't fer them polices 'n' them ol' lynch-mobs, there wouldn't be nothin' but uproar down here!"

The Postbellum North   In the North as in the South, the period immediately after the Civil War brought a short-lived easing of racial restrictions. The Reconstruction policies of the federal government, aimed at transforming the South, had their effects in the North, too. For a time, about 1870−1890, race relations in the North became more fluid—that is, less restrictive. Accounts of racial violence during this period (see, for example, Grimshaw, 1959) focus mainly on the South, and Spear (1971, p. 154) reports that "there was probably more contact between the races [in the North] during this time than at any other time before or since." Following 1890, however, northern race relations took an abrupt turn for the worse, with a great upsurge in both prejudice and discrimination. Discriminatory devices of every type were used to keep blacks at a distance from whites and to protect whites from the perceived threat of black competition. It is significant to note that during this period, there was also intensified prejudice and discrimination against other racial and ethnic minorities, notably Chinese- and Japanese-Americans in the West and Jewish and Catholic Americans in the East. Sentiment against immigration was strong, and ideologies of race superiority/inferiority were given legitimacy by scientific racists, who argued that science "proved" racial superiority (of their own race, of course).

There seem to be a number of reasons for this change, and it is striking that most of them in some way arose from the economics of the era, from some kind of competition for scarce resources. To begin with, this was a period of unrestricted capitalism that led to some of the grossest exploitation of labor in American history. Accordingly, deep resentment developed among the working class (which in the North was still overwhelmingly white), and the beginnings of the American labor union movement were under way. At the same time, difficult conditions in the South were causing an increasing number of blacks to migrate to the North. They came to northern cities in sufficient numbers to be seen as a threat by whites, but not yet in sufficient numbers to be a major political force. At the same time, the large numbers of immigrants were arriving or had recently arrived on the East and West coasts.

The consequence was intense competition for jobs and housing, especially between white immigrants and blacks. This was made worse by labor and management practices. Most white workers saw blacks as a threat and tried to keep them out of the workplace. As a consequence, most of the labor unions discriminated against blacks and would not accept them as members. The blacks arriving from the South, desparately poor, were often willing to work for lower wages than whites. Accordingly, dual wage systems developed, in which blacks were paid less than whites for doing the same work. In other cases, blacks were kept out of certain "white jobs," at least until the white workers went on strike. For several reasons, blacks newly arriving in northern cities often ended up working as strikebreakers. First, their poverty often placed them in a position where they had little choice but to work any job that was offered. Second, because most unions excluded blacks, blacks were distrustful of and unsympathetic toward unions and therefore willing to break their strikes. Third, being a strikebreaker was often the only way to get into certain better jobs that were normally reserved for whites. Finally, many employers actively sought out blacks to break their employees' strikes, realizing that their bargaining position would be enhanced if the working classes could be divided along the lines of race. In some cases, blacks in the South were promised jobs if they moved north, without being told that they would be breaking a strike.

For all these reasons, the use of blacks as strikebreakers stirred up racial tensions in northern cities large and small in the early twentieth century. In 1910 blacks were brought to Waterloo, Iowa, by the Illinois Central Railroad to break a strike by white workers (Kloss et al., 1976). Railroads repeated that tactic in Chicago in 1916, and in the following ten years blacks were used to break six more strikes in that city (Bonacich, 1976). In East St. Louis, Illinois, use of blacks as strikebreakers in the meat-packing industry in 1916 and in the aluminum industry in 1917 was a significant factor contributing to that city's bloody race riot of 1917 (Rudwick, 1964). The most widespread instance of this practice occurred in 1919, when a nationwide steel strike was broken largely by the use of black strikebreakers. The steel companies brought an estimated 30,000 to 40,000 blacks into the mills, mostly from the South, to break the strike (Foster, 1920). Of course, not all strikebreakers were blacks, and most black workers were not strikebreakers. Still, the use of blacks as strikebreakers was common enough to worsen the already tense race relations of the era. Of course, the only real winners in these situations were the owners of the plants, mills, railroads, and so on. Black and white workers, because of their mutual fear and mistrust of one another—and their inherently weak bargaining position in an era of low wages and surplus labor—were easily played off against one another.

These conflicts and similar ones over housing and other resources led whites—especially working-class and immigrant whites—to take drastic measures to protect their status from the real or perceived threats that blacks represented. Blacks were forced out of white neighborhoods by every means from boycotts to bombs. Juries and public officials stopped enforcing civil rights laws (Wilson, 1973, p. 104), and most public and private facilities became segregated. Even churches pushed out their black members. In short, there was in the North from 1890 on the move toward segregation that characterized rigid competitive systems of race relations. Another characteristic of this pattern that was sadly evident was periodic severe outbursts of violence. Lynchings increased in the North, and the period from 1917—1919 included some of the bloodiest race riots in American history. Unlike the riots of the 1960s and 1970s, these riots involved mass fighting between blacks and whites, and the targets of the mobs were people, not property. Usually the riots broke out in cities where the black population was increasing and blacks and whites were competing for jobs. Fears of a sexual nature were also significant: Some of the riots started after rumors of attacks by blacks on white women were circulated in the white community. Nearly always the riots began with white mobs attacking blacks, and most of the victims were black. The two worst were in the Illinois cities of East St. Louis in 1917 and Chicago in 1919. The East St. Louis riot had the highest death toll of any U.S. riot clearly classifiable as a race riot, and among American riots of all types, it was exceeded in carnage only by the New York draft riot of 1863, discussed earlier in the chapter. The East St. Louis riot took forty-eight lives—thirty-nine black and nine white. The chilling accounts of the observers of this riot described the actions of whites as having a visible coolness and premeditation about it. "'. . . this was not the hectic and raving demonstration of men suddenly gone mad" (Rudwick, 1964, quoting reporters describing the violence). Two years later in Chicago, the violence was repeated. This riot was touched off when a group of black children swam into a white area on a Lake Michigan beach and were attacked by a white mob. Three days of violence ensued, with white mobs attacking blacks and black mobs striking back at whites. In this mayhem, thirty-eight people were killed: fifteen whites and twenty-three blacks. In both the Chicago and East St. Louis riots—and most of the other two dozen or so riots that occurred during this era—police did little or nothing to stop the white mobs from attacking blacks. They only moved in when the blacks began to strike back.

Although the tensions eased somewhat after 1920, the general pattern of discrimination, segregation, and periodic violent outbursts associated with the rigid competitive pattern of race relations continued until World War II. In 1943, in a situation of racial competition similar to the earlier situation in East St. Louis and Chicago, a bloody race riot erupted in Detroit. In this violence, twenty-five blacks and nine whites were killed.

RIGID COMPETITIVE RACE RELATIONS
AND OTHER RACIAL/ETHNIC GROUPS

We have discussed the pattern of rigid competitive race relations mainly in terms of black-white relations, but from about 1880 to 1945 the pattern applied to a number of other minorities as well. In both the East and West, immigration was seen as a threat to the status of white workers and was widely opposed. Eastern Europeans and—largely by association—Catholics and Jews, were the target in the East, Asian-Americans in the West. In the East, strong opposition to immigration and accompanying surges of anti-Catholicism and anti-Semitism arose during periods of economic instability or downturn. Such periods occurred in the 1830s and the 1850s, from 1880 to 1900, and in the 1920s and 1930s (Simpson and Yinger, 1972, p. 116).

It was in the West, however, that anti-immigrant sentiments were the strongest. The opposition to Asian immigrants became so strong that the U.S. Congress eventually passed racist laws forbidding Asians to immigrate to the United States. The first such law, passed in 1882, banned Chinese immigration. It was to last ten years, but was repeatedly renewed until 1904, when it was made permanent. Immigration by Japanese was also gradually restricted after 1900, until it was ended entirely in 1924 by a quota system that banned all Asians from migrating to the United States.

While ethnic prejudices per se played an important role in the development of exclusionist sentiment, economic competition between whites and Asian-Americans was probably the biggest cause of it. Of course, this competition was also a major cause of the prejudice. In any case, there was intense competition for jobs between whites and Asian-Americans from the 1870s on. Asians, often in debt for passage to the United States, were frequently willing to work for lower wages than whites. This greatly aggravated the tensions between the two groups, and among most whites highly negative stereotypes (deceitful, opium smugglers, clannish) replaced the earlier, more positive stereotypes. As had happened with blacks, considerable violence and mob action was directed against Asian-Americans. Anti-Chinese riots broke out in San Francisco, Los Angeles, and a number of other areas. In San Francisco, white laborers rioted against the presence of Chinese workers in certain industries (Barth, 1964, p. 143). The Los Angeles riot of 1871 resulted in the death of twenty Chinese-Americans (Kitano, 1974, p. 196). The Japanese were also sometimes the victims of violence: In 1890 fifteen Japanese cobblers were violently attacked by members of the shoemaker's union (Ichihashi, 1969). Boycotts of Japanese restaurants and other businesses were common in the early 1900s; in one case the boycotters handed out matchboxes bearing the slogan, "White men and women, patronize your own race" (Ichihashi, 1969, p. 235).

In 1906 the city of San Francisco banned all Japanese, Chinese, and Korean children from attending school with white students. The Asian-American students were required to attend a separate "Oriental school." In general, not only in education but in a number of areas, whites enforced a system that segregated Asian-Americans much as had been done to blacks in other areas. These events set the stage for one of the most disgraceful events in all American history. During World War II, all persons in the western United States of Japanese ancestry (defined as one-eighth or more Japanese) were required by presidential order to be relocated to prison camps. By November 1942, nine months after the order, some 110,000 West Coast Japanese—most of them American citizens—were in the camps. They remained there for over two years. Many lost their incomes and possessions during the ordeal. One did not have to show any evidence of questionable loyalty to be in the camps—one only had to be Japanese. It is also significant that no such imprisonment was used against German-Americans, even though we were also at war with Germany. Racism appears to have been a crucial factor in the imprisonment of Japanese-Americans.

The patterns of competition, segregation, and occasional violent attacks that marked white-Asian relations also were evident in Anglo-Chicano relations. As with other groups, competition for jobs was an important cause of friction. Since many employers used a dual wage system, paying Mexican-Americans less than Anglos, many whites believed that the Mexicans were responsible for low wages. Anglo labor unions also opposed immigration of Mexicans, on the grounds that such immigration created a labor surplus that held down wages and raised unemployment. As had happened with blacks and Asian-Americans, segregation in housing, schools, and public accommodations was imposed on Chicanos. Chicanos were sometimes the victims of mass violence, as other minorities had been. The worst was a week-long series of disturbances in Los Angeles in 1943, which have come to be called the "zoot-suit riots." The trouble began when gangs of white servicemen attacked Chicano youth wearing "zoot suits," a form of dress especially popular among young Mexican-Americans. To many whites the zoot suits were a symbol of disrespect and lawlessness. As the riots worsened, civilian whites joined the servicemen, and Mexican-Americans were indiscriminately set upon and beaten, whether or not they were wearing the zoot suits that supposedly were the target of the rioters. Chicanos—and some blacks and Filipinos as well—were dragged from streetcars and theaters and beaten. The police generally did not interfere with the rioters, but they did arrest a number of injured Mexican-Americans after they had been beaten.

The press played a major role in inciting the race riot—for more than a year it had been headlining crime by Mexican youths and appealing to white fears. During the riots the servicemen were presented in the papers as heroes, giving the "lawless youth gangs" a well-deserved lesson. The press also announced that Mexican "gangs" were planning a counterattack, and even announced the times and places! These places then became the assembling points for mobs of whites who rampaged through the downtown area and Chicano neighborhoods beating and stripping people. The newspapers did not present the events as a race riot, but rather as the action of servicemen attempting to restore law and order. The true character of these events—a race riot initiated and sustained by whites in which only about half the Chicano victims even were wearing zoot suits—came out later. A committee appointed by the governor of California to investigate the riot concluded that it was a race riot, that Anglos were the main aggressors, and that the newspapers were largely to blame for the whole thing. This riot in Los Angeles triggered a number of similar disturbances in other western and midwestern cities and is seen by some as a contributing factor to Detroit's bloody race riot in 1943. (For a full account and analysis of the zoot suit riots, see McWilliams, 1948, Chapters 12 and 13).

To summarize briefly, we can say that the general period from the end of the Civil War to World War II is a classic case of rigid competitive race relations. The urban populations of blacks, Asian-Americans, and Chicanos increased rapidly at various places and times during this period, but their numbers were not yet great enough to give them much political power. All these groups were seen by whites as competition for jobs, housing, education, and public facilities. All were limited to restricted, low-wage job markets as whites attempted to maintain the advantages they received in a racial caste system. The maintenance of that caste system, however, was threatened by the increasing industrialization of this period. Employers saw the advantage in playing white and minority workers off against one another. Dual wage systems were set up in which minorities were paid less for the same work than whites. In addition to blatantly exploiting minority workers, this pattern also angered whites, who saw their wages and jobs threatened. They tried to

Streetcar terminal in Oklahoma City, July, 1939. Separate and usually unequal facilities were a predominant characteristic of the period of rigid competitive race relations in the United States. Russell Lee, FSA, Library of Congress.

Table 6.1 Major Riots in Which Whites Attacked Minority Group Members, 1860–1945.

DATE	PLACE	NOTES
1863	New York	Draft riot, mass attacks by whites on blacks; total death toll, about 2,000 (see text).
1871	Los Angeles	White mobs attacked Chinese-Americans; 20 Chinese-Americans killed (see text).
1898	Wilmington, N.C.	White attacks on blacks.
1906	Springfield, Ohio, and Atlanta	White mobs attacked blacks (Boskin, 1969).
1908	Springfield, Illinois	Mass attacks by whites on blacks, black neighborhood burned; 2 blacks lynched, 4 whites killed by stray bullets (Crouthamel, 1969).
1917	East St. Louis, Illinois, and other cities	Whites attacked blacks; 48 deaths (see text). Disturbances also occurred in Philadelphia and Chester, Pennsylvania.
1919	Chicago, Washington, D.C., and other cities.	White attacks on blacks and interracial fighting; 39 deaths in Chicago (see text); 2 whites and 2 blacks killed in Washington. Other riots in Omaha, Knoxville, Elaine, Arkansas, Charleston, and Longview, Texas (Franklin, 1969; U.S. National Advisory Commission on Civil Disorders, 1968).
1921	Tulsa, Oklahoma	Mob attacks on blacks by whites, including bombing from airplanes; 21 blacks, 9 whites killed (Franklin, 1969).
1943	Los Angeles, Detroit, and other cities	"Zoot-suit" riots; interracial fighting; 25 blacks and 9 whites killed in Detroit (see text; Franklin, 1969).

protect their status by segregating and excluding minorities; blacks, Asian-Americans, and Mexican-Americans all experienced segregation during at least part of this period. White ethnocentrism, combined with fears of minority competition, and white economic and political power produced not only segregation but also violent outbursts against minorities, with the minorities receiving little or no protection or support from the law or the news media. (For a summary, see Table 6.1) Thus, all the minorities mentioned became the targets of race riots, suffered most of the casualties, and frequently ended up getting blamed for the riots, which were in fact initiated by whites. These riots tended to occur during periods when a city's minority population was growing rapidly and when white and minority workers were competing for jobs (Allport, 1954, p. 59−61). At other times race relations, while more peaceful, were still unequal and mostly segregated. Despite periods of relative fluidity and rigidity, the overall pattern changed little until after World War II: Segregation was still the rule. It has, however, changed dramatically since that time, and that change will be explored in the following sections.

A SHIFT TO FLUID COMPETITIVE RACE RELATIONS: AMERICA SINCE WORLD WAR II

Since World War II dramatic changes have taken place in American race and ethnic relations. Debate continues over whether and to what degree race relations today are *better* than in the past, but there can be no question that race relations are substantially *different*. Today's majority-minority relations in the United States are an example of what Wilson (1973, 1978) calls fluid competitive race relations. Briefly, this may be classified as a system that is a mixture of caste and class, with open and relatively unrestricted intergroup competition and decreasing amounts of overt or deliberate discrimination. In fact, such discrimination may even be illegal in such a system, as it is in the United States. In the next few pages, we shall outline some of the major characteristics of present-day American intergroup relations and see how they represent changes from the past.

Changes in the Law: The Banning of Discrimination

As we have said, racial segregation and discrimination were the rule over most of the United States up to the time of World War II. In some areas, discrimination and segregation resulted from formal or informal practices in the private sector. Examples included unwillingness of many employers to hire blacks and other minority group members (or hiring them for only certain jobs), refusals of homeowners or realtors to sell to blacks, and segregated businesses, such as lunch counters. In other instances, discrimination was written into law. The laws of many southern states *required* discrimination in public facilities and education, and numerous state universities refused to accept blacks. These conditions remained largely in effect until the late 1940s to mid 1950s, and—in some cases—well beyond. In addition to this legally required discrimination, a great deal of private-sector discrimination operated with the support of the legal system. An example was the restrictive housing covenant. When a person purchased a house, she or he was frequently required—as a condition of purchase—to agree to a legally binding commitment not to sell the house to blacks, Jews, and/or other racial/ethnic minority group members. This agreement, called a restrictive covenant, had the backing of the law, so that it was actually illegal and punishable for the homeowner to sell to a minority group member. Without the backing of the law, the agreement would have been meaningless; accordingly, this private-sector discrimination was in fact made possible by the action of the public sector.

Beginning in the late 1930s, the stance of the law that at worst required and at best tolerated racial discrimination began to change. Court rulings in 1936 and 1938, while not challenging segregation, did put some enforcement in the "but equal" part of the old "separate but equal" doctrine. In 1936 the appellate court required that a black applicant be admitted to the University of Maryland Law School, because there was no comparable state-supported facility for blacks. In 1938 the Supreme Court ruled the same way in a case involving the University of Missouri's Law School (Johnson, 1943). In 1946 federal courts ruled that segregation on interstate travel regulated by the federal government was illegal (Simpson and Yinger, 1972, p. 417). In 1948 the Court ruled that states could no longer enforce restrictive housing covenants, though the writing of such agreements was not banned. The truly crucial ruling, however, came in 1954, in the *Brown v. Topeka Board of Education* case. This ruling abolished the concept of "separate but equal," as the court ruled unanimously that separate schools could not be equal because segregating children on the basis of race "generates a feeling of inferiority as to their status in the community that may affect their hearts and minds in a way unlikely ever to be undone." In this and a related case, the Court ruled that the equal protection clause of the Fourteenth Amendment and the due process clause of the Fifth Amendment forbade school segregation. Various legal rulings in the remainder of the 1950s and into the 1960s extended the *Brown* principle to all publicly operated programs and facilities, though some cities and states in the South defied these rulings well into the 1960s. In some cases, direct protest action was a significant factor in getting local and state governments in the South to comply with the federal law. In general, the action of the courts was a critical factor in the elimination of segregation and overt discrimination by state, federal, and local bodies of government.

The banning of overt discrimination and segregation in privately owned businesses came later, and legislation and direct protest action were both important factors in bringing about this change. Following the 1954 *Brown* decision, important civil rights laws were passed by the Congress in 1957, 1960, 1964, 1965, and 1968. These laws protected the voting rights of blacks and other minorities, which in some parts of the country had been almost totally blocked by various tactics such as poll taxes and literacy tests. (At one time, tactics such as "grandfather clauses"—one could vote if his or her grandfather had been a voter—and the "white primary" had been used to restrict black voting, but these had been ended by earlier court decisions.) These laws also extended the protection against discrimination beyond the public sector to the private sector: Employers were not to discriminate in hiring, businesses were not to discriminate in the sales of goods or services, and real estate owners and brokers were not to discriminate in the sale or rental of housing. These laws generally forbade discrimination on the basis of race, religion, color, or national origin. They did not, in general, deal with discrimination on the basis of

Legal and formal protection of the rights of minorities is typical of the fluid competitive pattern of race relations. Although such protection does make open and deliberate discrimination illegal, it by no means guarantees that minorities will enjoy a social and economic status equal to that of the dominant group. Irene Springer.

other characteristics, such as sex, age, disability, or sexual preference, though the 1964 law did ban sex discrimination in employment. At the local level, numerous ordinances and laws were also passed against discrimination on the basis of race and ethnicity and, in some cases, other characteristics as well. Although these laws have not always been effective, it is indeed significant that by 1968 the clear position of American law was against racial and ethnic discrimination. This represents a near total reversal of the situation twenty-five to thirty years earlier, when the position of American law had been somewhere between tolerating and requiring such discrimination. The change came about first by action of the courts and later through legislation by elected lawmaking bodies, with the help of court rulings legitimating and enforcing the legislation. It is important to stress that the court rulings and especially the legislation came largely in response to a powerful, articulate, and well-timed protest movement on the part of American minorities—a development that will be discussed at greater length later in this chapter. (The stance of American government and law toward minorities past and present, is discussed in greater length and detail in Chapter 10.)

Changes in Economics: The Development of Substantial Middle Classes among Minority Groups

While the status of minority groups in America will be discussed in greater detail in a later chapter, it should be stated here that one of the major changes in minority group status since World War II is the presence of a sizable and growing middle class. There have always been some members of each American minority group who have attained middle-class or elite status. However, until recently the pervasive race discrimination in American society has kept the proportion attaining such status very small. In recent years this has changed. Substantial middle classes exist among blacks and Chicanos, though the majority would still be classified as either working class or poor. Among the Chicanos, the educational gap with whites closed between 1950 and 1970, and the proportion of Chicanos in white-collar (professional, managerial, clerical, and sales) jobs increased, though improvement here was less extensive than in the educational area (Moore, 1976, pp. 64–67). Somewhat greater improvements were noted in the black population, especially in the job structure. Among black males, the percentage in white-collar jobs more than doubled from 8.6 percent in 1950 to 20.2 percent in 1970 (Wilson, 1978, p. 128). The comparable figure for Chicano males in the Southwest is 21.6 percent (Moore, 1976, p. 64), a rise from around 16 percent in 1950. It should be pointed out that, despite this substantial middle class among both groups, the comparable figures for white Anglos are much higher—over half of white males hold middle-class, white-collar jobs. Among Chinese- and Japanese-Americans, who were also victims of segregation and discrimination, the change has been such that both groups would be considered predominantly middle-class today by most criteria.

With the growth in minority middle classes has come an increase in social mobility among minorities. No longer are certain jobs reserved for whites or for minorities, as they frequently were before World War II. There is free competition for jobs, unrestricted by rules of discrimination. Wilson (1978) has summarized these changes in the black population by noting that today there is more class stratification *within* the black population than ever before. In other words, we are moving—as is ordinarily true when competitive race relations become more fluid—from a *racial caste system* toward a *class system*. That is not to say, however, we have moved all the way. As Wilson's critics (see, for example, Willie, 1979) point out—and Wilson himself does not deny—there remains in the black population (and the Chicano and Indian populations as well) a large group that is not enjoying the benefits of this fluidity of race relations. This group, which outnumbers the middle class among all three minorities, is commonly called the underclass. It is trapped in poverty, apparently unable to move up. (We shall examine the reasons for this in later chapters.) Still, *class* stratification has increased within the black and Chicano populations (but perhaps not in the American Indian population), and a portion of the black and Chicano populations have experienced increased social mobility. (The debate over the relative importance of race and class as causes of minority group disadvantage will be explored in greater detail in Chapter 13.)

Changes in Attitudes: Changes in the Kind and Degree of Prejudice among Whites

Another clear trend in the past thirty to forty years has been an apparent substantial change in the kind and degree of racial and ethnic prejudice. These changes were discussed in greater detail in Chapter 3, but the major points can be restated here. First, racial prejudice of all three types discussed in that chapter has declined: Cognitive prejudice (stereotypical or racist beliefs about minorities) has decreased, as Americans today show less tendency to agree with stereotypical statements about racial and ethnic groups. Affective prejudice (dislike of minorities) has also declined, as people report more willingness to associate with minorities on a friendly basis. Finally, conative prejudice (desire to act in a discriminatory way) has declined, as fewer and fewer whites express support for segregation and discrimination. This does not, of course, mean that prejudice has been eliminated, and part of the change might be a result of greater "sophistication" or unwillingness to openly express feelings of prejudice. Still, the change in what people say, at least, has been quite dramatic. The second change is in the kind of prejudice, or, more precisely, the kinds of racist ideologies or beliefs that are accepted. Forty years ago, it was widely believed among whites that blacks and other minorities were *biologically* or *genetically* inferior. Today, those beliefs have greatly declined, despite the arguments in support of genetic racial intelligence differences by a few advocates such as Jensen (1969, 1973) and Shockley (1971a, 1971b). However, another form of racism, which Wilson (1978) calls *cultural racism,* has come to predominate. This view argues that minorities have developed cultural characteristics that in some way place them at a disadvantage. In more extreme forms, this view holds that groups are culturally inferior; in milder forms they argue that minorities are placed at a disadvantage because of certain of their cultural characteristics. In other words, if people are poor (or a minority group is disproportionately poor), it is their own fault. Feagin (1972) and Schuman (1975) have demonstrated that this view is very widespread among whites—even ones who consider themselves unprejudiced—and that it is specifically used by many whites to explain black poverty. This allows whites to escape the burden of responsibility arising from the facts that whites, by discrimination and exploitation, created minority poverty in the first place and that many whites continue to benefit from it (see, for example, Gans, 1971).

FACTORS CAUSING THE CHANGES: THE EFFECTS OF URBANIZATION AND INDUSTRIALIZATION

The twentieth century has been a period of dramatic urbanization and industrialization in the United States. This process was already under way at the turn of the century, but at that time the United States was still a predominantly rural society. Today, it is overwhelmingly urban. Industry and technology have expanded tremendously in this century, and increasingly our productive capacity has come to be owned by massive corporations. For minority groups the transformation has been even more rapid. Early in the century, blacks and Mexican-Americans were more rural than the white population; today they are more urban. Much of the urbanization of these groups occurred between World War II and about 1970, though the process had begun earlier.

Among blacks, American Indians, and all major Hispanic and Asian-American groups, only Indians are not more urban than the white population. These trends of urbanization, modernization, and industrialization have influenced majority-minority relations in numerous ways, and can directly or indirectly explain much of the change. We have already noted that Van den Berghe and Wilson have argued that as urbanization proceeds, societies tend to move from castelike race relations toward increasingly classlike or fluid competitive race relations. We have seen that this type of change has corresponded to urbanization and industrialization in the United States. That, of course, does not prove that they caused the change. Nonetheless, a number of consequences of urbanization and industrialization do seem to push in the direction of more fluid race relations. In this section, we shall enumerate and briefly discuss some of these factors.

Requirement of Greater Mobility
and the Economic Irrationality of Discrimination

In order to operate effectively, industrial societies require greater mobility than do agricultural societies. Especially in the modern era of giant corporations and complex technology, employees are frequently recruited on a nationwide basis. Considerable geographic and social mobility is required to achieve the best match of person and job.

In addition, getting the best match of person to job suggests that such considerations as race, religion, and parentage—ascribed statuses—should not influence the hiring decision. Only job qualifications should matter. Considering ascribed statuses can only interfere with the best match. The same can be said of other kinds of activities and transactions. It does not make sense for a seller of goods or services to cut off potential buyers because of race, religion, or some other irrelevant factor. In short, a complex, modern society works at maximum efficiency when all irrelevant factors such as race are disregarded. This was recognized by the classic sociological theorist Max Weber (1968), who argued in the early twentieth century that such *rationalization* is the critical element in the emergence of industrial society.

If rationalization had been the only social force at work, however, it might not have been sufficient to cause the changes that have taken place. The social psychologist Herbert Blumer, in a widely cited article entitled "Industrialization and Race Relations" (1965), argues that the forces of modernization and rationalization do *not* always lead to more fluid race relations. Even with industrialization (and sometimes because of it), some elements within society perceive that they are gaining from the subordination of minorities, and these elements press for continued discrimination. We have already seen examples of white workers trying to shield themselves from black, Chicano, or Chinese competition. Thus, were it not for other changes that reduced majority demands for discrimination and created a situation conducive to the development of strong and effective minority group movements, the changes in majority-minority relations might never have occurred, even with industrialization.

Generally Rising Educational Levels

Another trend that has occurred throughout the twentieth century and become especially pronounced after World War II is a rising educational level. Among minority group members this has tended to promote greater assertiveness, as we shall see later in this chapter. Among the whites it has undoubtedly led to some increase in tolerance, as the irrationality of prejudice is revealed. We have already seen in Chapters 2 and 3 that there is some tendency for prejudice to decrease at higher levels of education. Thus, the inreasing educational level of the population has probably played some role in the reduction of prejudice and overt discrimination.

Postwar Economic Growth and Easing of Intergroup Competition

We have already seen that intergroup competition is an extremely important cause of intergroup prejudice, discrimination, and conflict. It therefore follows that when intergroup competition is reduced, intergroup relations should improve. Wilson (1978) makes a strong case that this is what happened during the 1950s and 1960s. In general, this was a prosperous time. The economy was growing rapidly, unemployment was for the most part fairly low, and the number of jobs was increasing, especially in the white-collar sector. This meant a number of things, all of which tended to bring about more fluid race relations. First, new opportunities were opened to blacks and other minorities in the expanding economy. Second, the position of minority group members was more secure, so it was safer for them to make demands for more equality. Third, whites—especially middle-class ones— were less threatened by minority gains than in the past. This meant they could be less prejudiced, more receptive to the demands made by minorities, and more accepting of court rulings against discrimination and segregation. In short, the expanding economy and reduced intergroup competition of the postwar period made the climate favorable for easing of the strict racial barriers of the prewar period.

Increased Assertiveness on the Part of Minorities

Probably very little if any of the changes in race relations would have come about were it not for one additional factor—the increased assertiveness of minorities, most notably the black civil rights movement of the 1950s and 1960s and the legal efforts of the NAACP (National Association for the Advancement of Colored People). These changes, too, arose in a sizable part from the postwar urbanization, industrialization, and economic growth. Both in and of itself and as a means of understanding the changing pattern of race relations after World War II, the rise of minority group social movements is of special importance. The remainder of this chapter will examine the response of minority groups to domination and subordination and how and why that response has changed since about the time of World War II.

THE RESPONSE OF MINORITY GROUPS TO SUBORDINATE STATUS

In this concluding section of Chapter 6, we shall examine the various ways that minority groups may respond to their subordinate status, what determines how they respond, and how and why the responses of American minorities have changed over time.

There are two basic ways that people can respond when they find themselves in undesirable situations. They can try to *adapt* to the situation—to attempt to get along as best they can in a bad situation—or they can try to *change* the situation. A person can decide that she or he is not willing to put up with the situation and is therefore going to change it to something more favorable. Basically, the responses of minority group members to the undesirable situation of being dominated or subordinated can be fit into one of these two approaches. Either they are *adaptive* strategies, which try to make the situation as tolerable as possible, or they are *change-oriented* strategies, which seek to change the situation for the better. In the following section, we shall discuss some responses that fit into each category.

Adaptive Responses

There are four common ways of responding to subordinate or minority status that are mainly adaptive. They are feigned or real *acceptance* of the status, *displaced aggression, avoidance* of the status, and *seeking assimilation* into or imitating the majority group. Each of these responses takes the system of unequal statuses as a given and attempts to adapt to or live with that system. Let us discuss each in somewhat more detail.

Acceptance   Probably the most clearly adaptive (as opposed to change-oriented) kind of response to a socially imposed position of disadvantage is to just accept it. When minorities choose to simply accept their lower status, there are several things that may be happening. One possibility is that they really have become convinced of the ideology that whites are superior and minorities deserve an inferior role. Such a response is certainly not unheard of among relatively powerless people. Clark and Clark's (1958) doll studies suggest that racism did result in a lower self-image among some black children during the 1950s. Many also point to the opposition of some women to the Equal Rights Amendment as an example of internal acceptance of a subordinate role.

A second, perhaps more common, response might be called resignation. One does not accept that one should have a lower status or that one is inferior, yet one recognizes the reality that he or she *does* have a lower status and believes that little can be done about it. In this case, the likely response will be to put up with the situation and try to make the best of it.

A third response of this type is to pretend to accept the status and play upon majority group prejudices. In effect, it says "if they think we're all stupid, then we'll pretend to be stupid, fool them, and use it to our advantage." It calls to mind the story (of unknown truth) about a Southern sheriff who stopped a black man for running a red light. The man responded, "But sir, I didn't want to go on the white folks' light [green]. I thought us black folks was supposed to wait for the other one." The sheriff, completely fooled, responded, "Well, OK, I guess you meant well. But from now on, I'm going to let you go on the white folks' light," and got in his car and drove off.

Displaced Aggression You will recall from Chapter 2 that when people feel frustrated, and consequently aggressive, but cannot take it out against the person or thing causing the frustration, they will take it out against some easier or more available target. This is called *displaced aggression,* or *scapegoating*, and as we have seen, it is a common cause of prejudice among majority group members. Such displacement of aggression also frequently occurs among minority group members. If they are oppressed by members of the dominant group and the power structure does not permit them to strike back, they may well displace the aggression. This helps to explain the tragic fact that minority group members frequently commit violence against other minority group members and, more generally, the fact that crime rates are frequently high among members of subordinate racial or ethnic groups. It may also explain high suicide rates among some ethnic minority groups, as one's feelings of frustration and aggression may even be turned against oneself.

Avoidance Another way of dealing with a bad situation is to try to avoid reminders of it, or to try to escape reality entirely. One way minority group members may try to avoid being reminded of their subordinate status is to avoid contacts with majority group members, which may remind them of their subordinate status. Others may turn to a more generalized kind of avoidance, or withdrawal from one's role entirely. They somehow attempt to separate or isolate themselves from society through such things as alcohol or drugs. It is frequently true that alcoholism and drug abuse rates are high among subordinate ethnic groups; apparently, such substance abuse offers the hope of escape from an unhappy situation not of one's own making.

Seeking Assimilation This response might best be classified as accepting the *system* but attempting to deny one's role within that system. In effect, the minority group member seeks either to become a member of the majority group or to become accepted in its culture and/or social institutions. In this case, no real attempt is made to change the system of majority-minority relations. Rather, the minority individual attempts to change his or her individual position or role within that system.

The most extreme form of this response is the practice of "passing." Sometimes minority group members who are close in appearance to whites have presented themselves to the world as whites—or passed as whites. This has enabled them to enjoy the advantaged status that is reserved only for members of the majority group. It is not known how many people do this, but it does at least occasionally happen. (For discussion of the extent of the practice among American blacks, see Simpson and Yinger, 1972, pp. 208–209, 507; Stuckert, 1958.)

More common is the practice of seeking cultural assimilation with the majority—adopting the life styles, fashions, and values of the majority group. Often, this is aimed at gaining acceptance with the majority group. This practice has been more common among the minority group middle classes than among the poor or working class. In fact, minority middle-class people may attempt to put distance between themselves and poor people of the same group. It has been noted, for example, that some black middle-class neighborhoods have resisted the introduction of low-cost, subsidized housing as strongly as have any white middle-class neighborhoods. Other evidence may be seen in the popularity of straightened hair ("process" haircuts) among many blacks in the 1950s and early 1960s and the practice of "Americanizing" ethnic names among a number of groups. Although some people in minority groups still seek assimilation with the majority, there has been some movement away from this pattern in the past decade. We shall examine the reasons for this change in a later chapter.

Change-oriented Responses

The alternative to trying to live with an unpleasant position is trying to change that situation. Change-oriented responses to minority status are ones that attempt to change the nature of majority-minority relations in a society and/or to change the role or position of the minority group in that system. Such efforts vary in both their *goals* and *strategies*. The *goal* of such a movement may be to bring about a systemwide *assimilation*—to create a society and culture that is common, shared, and equal among the former dominant and subordinate groups. This results in a cultural and social coming together of the two groups, although in practice the new culture and society usually resembles that of the old majority group more than that of the old minority. Other change-oriented responses seek a different outcome— they seek to build alternative, minority-controlled institutions. This approach aims to preserve and strengthen minority group culture and to build an independent power base that will ultimately make the minority politically, socially, and economically stronger. To some degree, this encourages movement toward separate or distinct minority and majority group social structure, rather than the single shared structure sought by assimilation. Of course, these goals are ideal types; real-life social movements most frequently fall somewhere between, with some elements of each approach.

The *strategies* of movements seeking change also vary. They may be legal and within the system, or they may go outside the system and use illegal strategies. Examples of within-the-system strategies include legal campaigns, such as lawsuits and judicial appeals, legislative campaigns (attempting to pass favorable legislation), voter registration and election efforts, legal strikes and boycotts, and peaceful legal protests that appeal but do not disrupt. Outside-the-system strategies include peaceful but illegal protests aimed at disruption (nonviolent sit-ins are a good example) and violent forms of protest such as riots and bombings.

A Shift Toward Change-oriented Responses

Minorities have always responded to subordinate status with both adaptive and change-oriented responses, and they continue to do so today. Nonetheless, there has been a shift in this century, and particularly since World War II, *away* from adaptation and *toward* seeking change. Largely because the power structure made it difficult or impossible to do otherwise, the earlier response by minorities to their socially imposed disadvantage fell more in the adaptive categories than in the change-oriented. This is not to say that most of them were satisfied with their roles; they were not. Furthermore, important efforts aimed at changing the system had been made by all minorities. We have already discussed slave rebellions among blacks before the Civil War; here we shall briefly note some of the protest movements of the period between the Civil War and World War II. In the late 1860s, and again from 1900 to 1906, boycotts and protests were carried on against segregated streetcar systems in southern and border cities (Wilson, 1973; Meier and Rudwick, 1969). The first wave of protest ended such segregation in New Orleans, Louisville, Charleston, Richmond, and Savannah. The later campaign, though less successful, involved fully twenty-six cities. In the 1870s, the Negro Convention Movement became an important political force seeking civil rights enforcement of the Fifteenth Amendment, which forbade racial discrimination in voting, and protesting violence against blacks. In the early twentieth century the social movements led by Marcus Garvey and W. E. B. Du Bois were important. Garvey's separatist "Back to Africa" movement enjoyed widespread support among low-income blacks, and W. E. B. Du Bois's militant movement for racial integration and equality helped lead to the founding of the NAACP.

Among Mexican-Americans, the amount of pre-World War II protest activity was less (Simpson and Yinger, 1972, pp. 411–412) but still significant. In the 1880s, the *Caballeros de Labor* sought to unionize Chicano workers and protest the taking of Chicano land by Anglos. In the teens, twenties, and particularly the thirties, Chicano farmworkers struck in California; the movement to unionize farmworkers, then as now, was largely led and coordinated by Mexican-Americans. In 1929 a number of organizations combined to form the League of United Latin American Citizens (LULAC). This organization combated segregated schools, exclusion of Mexican-Americans from jury duty, and exploitation of farm labor (Meier and Rivera, 1972, pp. 241–243).

Despite these and other pre-World War II minority group social movements, movements since World War II have been considerably more significant. Movements by blacks, Chicanos, Indians, and a number of other ethnic groups have been larger, more powerful, more widely supported, and more successful than ever before. Furthermore, more minority group people than ever before have rejected various ways of adapting to subordinate status. To these masses of people, adaptation is unacceptable because subordinate status is unacceptable. Since World War II, they have demanded change to an extent that has never been seen before.

The Rising Tide of Protest

It is impossible here to provide a detailed history of the protest movements of minority groups during the postwar era; to do so would fill volumes. We shall, however, attempt to present a brief overview of some of the major events since World War II.

Among blacks, the early activity during and after the war centered largely in the courts. The NAACP began to pursue legal efforts against discrimination more vigorously and more effectively in the 1940s and 1950s, and this effort led up to most of the important court rulings discussed earlier in the chapter, including the 1954 *Brown* decision. There were other efforts, too—most notably A. Philip Randolph's threat to organize a massive march on Washington if President Roosevelt did not ban job discrimination in military supply industries during World War II. (Under the threat of such an internationally embarassing demonstration, Roosevelt did issue an order banning such discrimination.)

Gradually, as the 1950s turned into the 1960s, such actions became more widespread. Court rulings were important, but their effectiveness was limited for two reasons. First, local governments—especially in the South—seldom complied promptly with the court orders. Typically, they stalled and looked for ways around the orders; sometimes they even defied them more or less openly. An example of this was seen in the Little Rock, Arkansas, school desegregation case. Governor Orval Faubus defied a federal court order in 1957 to desegregate a high school in that city; President Eisenhower had to send federal troops to the city to carry out the order. In the face of occasional open defiance and a near-universal pattern of stalling and avoidance, something more than court orders was needed. A second limitation of the courts was that their orders—before the civil rights laws of the 1960s— generally applied only to public-sector discrimination. They did not cover private businesses or organizations. For these reasons, the civil rights movement had to change its tactics to include direct action.

A crucial event took place in 1955, which precipitated a move toward direct-action protest movements. A black woman named Roza Parks refused to give up her seat on a bus in Montgomery, Alabama, to a white man. This led to a campaign to desegregate that city's bus system, which was joined by a young minister named Dr. Martin Luther King. Months later and bolstered by a federal court order, the battle was won. This victory led to similar campaigns around the country and helped catapult Dr. King into a position of national leadership. Applying the principles and philosophy of nonviolent resistance developed in India by Mahatma Gandhi, King led similar campaigns around the country. Notable among these was the 1963 struggle in Birmingham, Alabama, in which hundreds of peaceful protesters were jailed, beaten, and fire-hosed by police, and in which the motel where Dr. King was staying was bombed, as was his brother's house. These protests and others, along with a massive demonstration by about 250,000 blacks and whites in Washington later that year, helped bring about the Civil Rights Act of 1964. It was at this demonstration that Dr. King gave his famous "I have a dream" speech. Other major events in the civil rights movement included the student sit-ins at lunch counters and various public facilities in the early 1960s and the freedom rides to protest segregated transportation facilities. In 1965 Dr. King's famous march from Selma to Montgomery, Alabama, helped pass the 1965 Voting Rights Act.

Not all the action was in the South. Campaigns against discrimination were also carried on in a number of northern cities. A protest march against housing segregation led by Dr. King on Chicago's southwest side was attacked by a mob of angry whites, leading him to say he had never seen such race hatred anywhere in the South. By the mid-1960s, white resistance to civil rights had grown sufficiently strong that many blacks felt new tactics were needed; furthermore, a repeated pattern of violent attacks against peaceful protesters was raising tensions to a critical point. The objectives of the protesters began to change; "black power" replaced desegregation as a goal. During this period, leaders with a new, more militant message began to emerge. Black leaders such as Malcolm X and Stokely Carmichael began to stress survival, economic equality, and political power as the immediate goals of the black movement. These were goals that required changes far more drastic than civil rights laws, but they spoke directly to the immediate concerns of impoverished blacks in big city ghettoes.

At the same time, many blacks were beginning to question the value of nonviolence in light of the strong and often violent resistance to change on the part of whites. The failure of civil rights laws to bring change in the day-to-day life of poverty-stricken urban blacks also led to heightened frustration. Given the increasing anger and frustration of American blacks, it is not surprising that a wave of violent rebellions spread across the country during the period of 1964–1968. Violence broke out in hundreds of cities, and the rebellions resulted in scores of deaths (mostly blacks killed by law enforcement officials) and millions of dollars in property damage. The worst of these outbreaks were in the Watts district of Los Angeles in 1965 (thirty-four deaths) and in Newark (twenty-five deaths) and Detroit (forty-three deaths) in 1967 (U.S. National Advisory Commission, 1968). In 1968 Dr. Martin Luther King was shot to death on the balcony of a motel where he was staying in Memphis, Tennessee, to support a garbage collectors' strike. This violent attack on a man who had won the Nobel Prize for his advocacy of peaceful protest was, to many, the straw that broke the camel's back. Violent outbursts occurred in numerous cities, with especially severe ones in Washington and Chicago. More than ever, the effectiveness of peaceful protest was called into question. (For further discussions of the black civil rights and black power movements of the 1950s, 1960s and early 1970s, see Killian (1968, 1975); Meier and Rudwick (1970b); Pinkney (1975).

Blacks were not the only groups turning to change-oriented movements during this era. After World War II, Mexican-American veterans returning home to find discrimination formed the G.I. Forum, which became one of the most influential Chicano organizations of the 1950s and 1960s (Meier and Rivera, 1972, pp. 245–247). This organization fought discrimination at the local level and conducted voter registration drives and lobbying efforts throughout the Southwest. In the 1960s Chicanos increasingly turned to direct-action protest. Student walkouts and protests over discrimination, biased materials, and prejudiced teachers occurred in a number of areas. In California, a campaign to unionize agricultural laborers begun by Cesar Chavez led to massive strikes in 1965 and subsequent years and to nationwide boycotts of table grapes, lettuce, and certain wines. Like King, Chavez has practiced Gandhian nonviolence and even went on an extended fast (with some damage to his personal health) to protest violence in his movement. Like King's, Chavez's efforts have been met with considerable violence by Anglos. However, they have also been successful as never before in unionizing a sizable segment of farm labor.

Chicanos were carrying on other, more militant actions. In New Mexico a movement seeking restoration of land to Mexican-Americans claimed 20,000 members in the mid 1960s. Its leader, Reies Lopez Tijerina, led an occupation of Forest Service land in which several Forest Service rangers were taken captive. Tijerina and several others were arrested, but on June 5, 1967, they were freed in an armed raid on a New Mexico courthouse by a group of their followers. A force of six hundred state troopers and National Guardsmen eventually rounded them up (Meier and Rivera, 1972). As with blacks, continuous resistance by Anglos was causing frustration and stimulating a move toward violence. The most serious outburst occurred in Los Angeles in 1970. A massive demonstration called the Chicano Moratorium was called to protest the Vietnam War and its effects on Chicanos. Violence broke out between protesters and police, spread across the *barrio*, and continued for hours. At least one person, a Chicano journalist, was killed by police fire, and property damage was heavy.

Among Indian people, too, social action and protest has increased in recent years. The incidence of such protest gradually rose during the 1960s, frequently focusing on treaty rights to unrestricted fishing. This issue has led to conflicts in Michigan, Minnesota, and the Pacific Northwest. In 1968 the American Indian Movement (AIM) was founded in Minneapolis. It started out as a local organization but soon became national in scope and played a role in several major protests, most notably the 1973 occupation at Wounded Knee, South Dakota, which led to violent confrontations with federal authorities and two deaths. Other major protests by Indian people included a takeover of Alcatraz Island, a former federal prison on San Francisco Bay, under an 1868 treaty providing that surplus federal property could be claimed by the Sioux. This takeover lasted nearly two years. Indian protesters also occupied Fort Lawton, a military base in Washington state, after it was declared surplus in 1970 and eventually were granted part of that property (Bahr et al., 1979). One of the most widely publicized protests took place in 1972, when various problems confronting a national protest in Washington, called the "Trail of Broken Treaties," led to a takeover of the Bureau of Indian Affairs building.

Clearly, then, these three minority groups and others gradually changed their response to subordinate status from trying to adapt to it toward trying, with increasing insistence, to change it. In the remainder of the chapter, we shall examine some of the reasons why.

NECESSARY CONDITIONS
FOR SOCIAL MOVEMENTS

If we are to explain why minority groups have turned to social movements seeking change as they have over the past thirty-five years or so, a logical starting point is to ask, "What are the conditions under which social movements get started?" Social scientists have identified four major conditions which must be present for social movements to develop.

Dissatisfaction

The first condition that must be present for a social movement to form is dissatisfaction. People must *feel* that they are somehow being taken advantage of, or that their situation is unsatisfactory. Such feelings of dissatisfaction are not always found where people are the worst off in absolute terms. Rather, they are found when people feel badly off *relative* to others or to what they feel they *should* have. This helps to explain why social movements develop most readily when poverty is found in the midst of wealth or when things improve somewhat. In such situations expectations and feelings of *relative* deprivation are the greatest (for further discussion of the notion of relative deprivation, see Geschwender, 1964).

Communication Network

The second condition needed for a social movement to develop is a network of communication within the dissatisfied group. It does not matter how dissatisfied people are if they cannot communicate their dissatisfactions to one another. Without communication, they cannot act collectively to change the source of their dissatisfaction. To form a movement, dissatisfied people must be able to share their dissatisfactions, develop a group consciousness, and decide what they are going to do to change the source of their dissatisfaction.

Sense of Efficacy

Assuming that a group is dissatisfied and has adequate means of internal communication, it must still have what social scientists call a *sense of efficacy*. Put simply, this means that people must feel that they have something to gain by protest and that the potential gains outweigh any possible negative effects that might come as a result of the protest. No matter how dissatisfied people are, they are unlikely to become involved in a movement if they think the consequence will be to make them even worse off than they already are. They have to see a net gain.

Leadership

The final condition that must be present for social movements to develop is leadership. Somebody has to plan strategies, inspire the rank-and-file participants, and do the day-to-day work behind most successful movements. There is some question as to whether this factor is as critical as the other three—some say that under those conditions effective leadership will emerge—but it is clear that leadership is important both in getting a movement started and in making it effective once it is under way.

DEVELOPMENT OF THESE CONDITIONS AND THE FORMATION OF MINORITY SOCIAL MOVEMENTS IN THE UNITED STATES AFTER WORLD WAR II

In the twentieth century, and particularly after World War II, a number of changes occurred that helped bring about these four movement-facilitating conditions of dissatisfaction, communication, sense of efficacy, and effective leadership among American minorities. The most important were the trend towards urbanization and industrialization, economic expansion, mass telecommunications, rising levels of education, and international changes. Each helped in important ways to bring into being conditions favorable to the development of social movements among oppressed minorities.

Urbanization and Industrialization

The related trends of urbanization and industrialization were of great importance. We have already discussed the general trend of urbanization in the United States and the fact that most minority groups have undergone an even greater and more rapid transition from urban to rural than the white Anglo population (see Table 6.2). The pattern of rapid urbanization is particularly notable for blacks and Mexican-Americans, who as recently as 1930 were more rural than the overall population but who today are more urban. Rapid urbanization is also notable among the Japanese-American population and, since 1950, among the Native American population as well.

One of the effects of this urbanization was to increase feelings of relative deprivation, or dissatisfaction. Minority group members arriving in large cities were exposed to affluence and life styles they often had not seen before, an experience that undoubtedly makes people more conscious of what they *could* have and, consequently, less satisfied when they have less than their share. The mobility that goes with urbanization and industrialization also helps to raise expectations

(Williams, 1977, p. 28). If people enjoy greater freedom and have raised expectations but find that they must still accept a subordinate status, the potential for dissatisfaction becomes very great. In a society with racial inequality, urbanization has exactly this effect. Urbanization in the United States also increased competition between whites and minorities for the same jobs. Often, whites were hired ahead of others or received higher pay than others for the same work. These experiences undoubtedly added to feelings of dissatisfaction and relative deprivation among minority group members.

Urbanization also made it easier for minority group members to communicate their dissatisfactions to one another and to discuss what could be done. In the urban ghettos and *barrios,* masses of people with similar ethnic background were brought together with many others who had similar dissatisfactions. In addition, the greater freedom and independence of the urban setting made it safer to promote antiestablishment ideas. This presents a sharp contrast with the rural setting (especially on large-scale plantations and fruit and vegetable farming operations) where the close social control made even talking about protest risky. Thus, both the concentration of minority group members and the greater freedom of the city made it easier for minority people to communicate with one another about their dissatisfactions and what might be done about them.

It is also probably true that a social movement has, all else being equal, a greater chance of success in an urban setting than in a rural setting, partly because of the weaker social control in large cities. There are simply too many people there for any authority to be aware of what everyone is doing. The large numbers of people mean that, almost by definition, there must be more variety of opinions and lifestyles. Thus, a social movement in an urban area is less likely to be repressed by authorities than a similar movement in a rural area. Furthermore, the ability to mobilize large numbers of people, which exists in the city, is a source of power itself. People can vote; they can boycott businesses; they can pack public meetings; they can tie up city traffic. These actions are potentially a source of power for a social movement, and all are more effective when masses of people are involved. Thus, not only is a movement easier to organize in the city, it is also more likely to have some positive results. Undoubtedly these factors go a long way toward explaining why social movements and protests are nearly always disproportionately urban events (Tilly, 1974).

All of the above considerations point to the same conclusion: A society that attempts to maintain a pattern of racial inequality when it is urbanizing is likely to experience considerable minority group protest. Urbanization helps create most of the conditions necessary for social movements: feelings of dissatisfaction, ability to communicate among the dissatisfied, and a reasonable chance of success. It probably also helps to develop a leadership; even movements occurring in rural areas, such as the United Farm Workers and the Wounded Knee protest, have had leaders with a largely urban background. Another look at Table 6.2 will indicate not only that minorities became much more urbanized in the twentieth century, but that

Table 6.2   Percent Urban, 1910, 1930, 1950, and 1970, for Various American Ethnic Groups.

YEAR	TOTAL POPULATION	BLACKS	CHICANOS	INDIANS	CHINESE-AMERICANS	JAPANESE-AMERICANS
1910	46	27	32	4	76	49
1930	56	44	51	10	88	54
1950	64	62	66	16	93	71
1970	74	81	85	45	96	89

Source: U.S. Census of Population, 1970, 1950, 1930, 1910.

Contact among a great many people of diverse status and background occurs in urban settings. Frequently, this contact stimulates minority group protest by making people more aware of the inequalities that exist in society. United Nations, M. Tzovaras.

the period from 1950 to 1970 was a time of particularly rapid urbanization among the black, Chicano, and American Indian populations. It is hardly surprising that this period was an era of social movements among groups seeking change in their subordinate status.

Economic Expansion   Although the trend toward urbanization and industrialization played an important role in facilitating ethnic protest movements, it has not been the only factor. Many experts feel that another reason for the postwar trend toward social movements can be found in the economic expansion of the time. It has been shown by Wilson (1973, 1978) that both the extent and militancy of racial protest and its degree of success tend to be greater in times of relative economic expansion. In times of economic decline, minorities have tended to protest less and often have difficulty protecting their status against attacks by members of the majority group.

The 1950s and early 1960s were generally a time of economic expansion in the United States. Given Wilson's historical observations, it is hardly surprising that this was a period of rising ethnic protest. In addition to the historical relationship, there are a number of other reasons to believe that this economic growth probably did facilitate minority group social movements. First, such expansion tends to raise minority group expectations by opening up new positions to minority group members. At the same time, it makes the minority groups less of a threat to the majority, so that the majority group is more inclined to respond favorably to minority protest, increasing such protest's chance of success. Thus, one of the important conditions necessary for social movements to develop is brought about: a belief that the movement can succeed. Wilson argues that one reason for both the size and effectiveness of the civil rights movement of the 1950s and 1960s is the fact that black leaders correctly perceived that the social and economic climate was favorable for a successful movement. Of course, once one campaign has been successful, others will frequently follow, because people realize that the things they do *can* make a difference.

Mass Communications   Williams (1977) and others have commented on the importance of mass communications in stimulating social protest. The media can easily raise feelings of dissatisfaction or relative deprivation by making people more aware of the contrasts between the haves and the have-nots. This can facilitate the exchange of ideas among dissatisfied people, if only by exposing more people to the ideas of protest leaders. Finally, it can stimulate protest by making people aware of movements elsewhere and the successes of those movements. In effect, it helps people realize that "we could do that, too." Through the spread of radio and television, as well as the nearly universal availability of the telephone, mass communications since World War II have created a revolution in the ways people receive and exchange information. This change has very likely been an important stimulant to racial and other kinds of protest since World War II.

Rising Educational Levels   We have already discussed ways in which rising educational levels among both whites and people of color in the United States have contributed to the increasing fluidity of race relations in the twentieth century. More specifically, however, they have also contributed directly to the rising incidence of protest. For one thing, the increase in education among minority groups has helped in the development of leadership. As in all movements, the leaders of the civil rights and other minority group social movements have tended to be people of greater than average education. The increased education also has tended to increase feelings of relative deprivation as people in minority groups were made more aware of both the inequalities between them and the white majority and the ways in which minorities were treated unfairly or differently.

As we have suggested earlier, the increasing levels of education in the population have also influenced the thinking of the white population. Education, as we have seen, tends to lower the level of prejudice. It also may make whites more aware of unjust treatment of black people, Indian people, Chicanos, and others. This has undoubtedly made whites more responsive to minority demands. Furthermore, it helps to explain the considerable involvement by whites in protest movements on behalf of minorities. Thousands of whites were involved in the civil rights movement, in protests to increase numbers of minority students in universities during the 1960s, in the United Farm Workers' boycotts of grapes and lettuce in the 1960s and 1970s, and in other efforts. In general, white college students and more highly educated whites have been most involved in these efforts.

International Changes   A final important factor helping the development of minority group social movements since World War II can be found in certain international changes. Most important is the emergence of independent nations in formerly colonized areas in Africa and other Third World areas. This trend has had two important effects. First, it has presented minority Americans with important examples, or role models, of the successful exercise of power and self-governance by people of color. The emergence of self-determination for black Africans, for example, has strengthened the hopes of black Americans for greater self-determination. A second major effect has been to force the American government to be more supportive of the demands for equality by people of color here. The United States is competing with the Soviet Union and other powers for the support and friendship of Third World nations. If we lose that friendship, our position in the world may be seriously weakened. Indeed, because of our involvement in Vietnam, our support of the doomed government of the Shah of Iran, and other shortsighted foreign policies, our position *has* been somewhat weakened. One important facet of our relationships with Third World countries is how people of color are treated in this country. If we discriminate against blacks, we can hardly expect to maintain good relations with African nations. If we mistreat Chicanos, we can hardly expect unlimited oil from Mexico. If we antagonize Third World countries, we *can* expect that our competitors, such as the Soviet Union, will take advantage. Thus, the position of people of color in the United States has been helped by these concerns. Our government's concerns about international relations have undoubtedly made it somewhat more responsive to minority concerns. Thus, the prospects for success by minority social movements have been enhanced and such efforts undoubtedly encouraged.

We have seen that a number of changes have helped bring about the conditions necessary for the development of minority-group social movements that seek change in the patterns of majority-minority relations. Among these changes, which have been particularly notable since World War II, are urbanization and industrialization, economic expansion, the spread of mass communications, rising educational levels, and international changes. Together, these changes have heightened feelings of relative deprivation among minority groups, enabled communication and planning among those groups, improved the hopes of success for minority movements, and facilitated the development of effective minority leadership. The result has been a turn toward change-oriented social movements among Afro-Americans, Mexican-Americans, American Indians, and other groups since World War II.

SUMMARY AND CONCLUSIONS

In this chapter, we have examined changing patterns of race relations in the United States during the hundred years between the Civil War and the 1960s. In so doing, we have identified some of the major structural factors that determine the patterns of order and conflict between majority and minority groups. We have seen the continuing importance of economic factors—one group's opportunity to gain at another's expense—on majority-minority relations. We have observed a tendency toward intergroup violence when one group threatens another, as happened in such periods as 1910–1920, when strikebreaking and race riots spread across the country. We have observed, too, that in periods of expansion, such as the 1950s, whites have tended to be less resistant to minority demands. Thus, as the conflict theory predicts, competition for scarce resources and one group's opportunity to gain at the expense of another are important in determining the pattern of majority-minority relations. Also important is the balance of power. As social movements, concentrated population, and international changes have strengthened the *power* of minorities vis a vis that of whites, some movement in the direction of equality has occurred. On the other hand, as predicted by functionalist theory, cultural differences and ethnocentrism continued to play an important role in causing minority subordination during the early twentieth century. However, the explanatory power of these factors seems limited: As the power balance and degree of competition have shifted in favor of minorities since World War II, and as overt discrimination has decreased, prejudice and ethnocentrism have declined substantially. This suggests that such attitudinal and cultural factors may be as much an *effect* of discrimination and racial inequality as a cause. The *most* important determinants of racial inequality seem to be found in the factors that influence the degree of competition and the power balance between majority and minority groups. Ethnocentrism facilitates discrimination and tends to lead inequality to fall along racial or ethnic lines. It does not, however, cause or sustain inequality without the presence of the other factors—unequal power and competition or the opportunity for one group to gain at the other's expense.

In the last two chapters, we have sought to learn some principles of majority-minority relations by looking at American history. In the next chapter, we shall seek to learn more by comparing majority-minority relations in a number of different international settings.

Colonized minority   A minority group that initially became a part of the society it lives in through conquest or annexation. In addition to such forcible entry, colonized minorities are usually subjected to some form of unfree labor and to attacks on their culture and social institutions.

Immigrant minority   A minority group that voluntarily migrated into the country or society in which it lives. Ordinarily, these minorities are more readily assimilated into the dominant society than colonized minorities.

Cross-Cultural Studies of Majority-Minority Relations

7

In the previous two chapters, we have examined the changing patterns of majority-minority relations over the history of the United States and the earlier British Colonies, and we have identified a number of basic principles about majority-minority relations. By studying different periods of American history, we have seen some of the conditions that lead to racial or ethnic inequality, and we have seen that the form of inequality varies with the social and economic conditions present at the time. Although we have hopefully learned much about majority-minority relations, there is a limit to how much we can learn by looking only at American history. As we have seen, American society, and consequently American race relations, have been very different at different points in time, but we are still talking about one society. In a world with thousands of different societies, large and small, all kinds of social conditions exist that have never been seen in the United States. To fully understand the dynamics of race and ethnic relations, we must look at them in a wide range of social and cultural settings. We shall do so in this chapter. More specifically, we will try to accomplish two things in the chapter: (1) use international evidence to further test and refine major principles already identified in earlier chapters; and (2) use cross-cultural comparisons to identify additional principles about the dynamics of majority-minority relations.

CROSS-CULTURAL EVIDENCE
ON THE EFFECTS OF COLONIZATION

One principle we have identified in American race relations is that the racial or ethnic groups experiencing the greatest disadvantage, and which have had the greatest conflict with the majority, are those whose initial entry into American society was through conquest or colonization. This would seem to suggest that one very important cause of both racial-ethnic stratification and conflict is the conquest or colonization of one group by another. That, at least, is what U.S. history suggests. But is it true throughout the world?

Consider for a moment the racial or ethnic conflicts around the world that you have read or heard about in the last few years: Among the best known are conflicts between blacks and whites in South Africa and Zimbabwe (formerly Rhodesia); between Catholics and Protestants in Northern Ireland; between English-speakers and French-speakers in Quebec, Canada; and between Arabs (particularly Palestinian Arabs) and Jews in the Middle East. These groups and societies vary tremendously, but if we examine the situation closely, we find one common denominator: In each place, the intergroup conflict can be traced back to the colonization or conquest of one racial or ethnic group by another. Let us briefly examine the origins of ethnic stratification and conflict in each of the places mentioned.

South Africa

No other nation in the world today is known for having a system of racial inequality more rigid than that in South Africa. Although there has been a slight loosening in recent years, institutionalized and legally required racial inequality and segregation remains the way of life in South Africa. The law specifies who is black, white, Asian, or "coloured" (that is, a mixture of black and white); where people of a given race may live; and when black and coloured people may or may not be present in the downtown areas of cities. "Conspiring" to have sex relations with a person of another race is forbidden and can result in a stiff prison sentence, even if there was no actual sexual contact. The black population is restricted to the poorest housing and jobs (though the need for labor is causing some bending of this rule); they are forbidden effective political participation and are limited in land ownership to a tiny fraction (13 percent) of the land, and the worst land at that. All this is true in spite of the fact that over two thirds of the population is black, about 10 percent coloured, 3 percent Asian, and less than 20 percent white (Van den Berghe, 1978; Hunt and Walker, 1974).

This severe racial inequality has led to violent uprisings, particularly in the last two decades, as well as an increase in underground actions, such as sabotage. Thus, South Africa is a nation whose history has been marked by gross racial inequality and serious racial conflict.

The roots of this inequality and conflict originated with conquest of the indigenous black African population by white European populations. Although *apartheid* (formal and legally codified segregation) has been the law only since 1948, racial inequality has been deeply institutionalized since the Dutch began to colonize the area in the mid-1600s. Although the first Dutch settlers were mainly interested in supplying their ships passing the area, agricultural settlers began moving inland, or "trekking," which brought conflict with the natives and ultimately their conquest. It also frequently brought genocide, or mass killing of the native population. Close to the coast, a paternalistic system of slavery was developed, though the slaves were usually imported from other parts of Africa. Gradually and after a series of conflicts, the British gained control of the area from the Dutch, and attempted to treat the native population more liberally. This was not the actual result, however, for several reasons. First, the Dutch were pushed inland in further "treks" to avoid the British, conquering and subordinating still more of the native population. Included in this group was the large and well-organized Bantu nation, which fought fiercely and effectively for many years before final conquest. Second, the British ultimately became as dependent as the Dutch on white supremacy, and their attempts at liberalization always stopped well short of a point

South African law requires separate facilities for blacks and whites. Note the exclusion of "natives" from this park. United Nations, D. Boernstein.

that could have threatened the white power structure. In addition, the decendents of the Dutch settlers, known as Afrikaners, viewed the British as outsiders who threatened their way of life with their attempts at racial liberalism, and the Afrikaners responded by becoming even more repressive of the native population. Thus, the establishment of *apartheid* in 1948 when the Afrikaners regained full control was by and large a codification of what had already developed: a strict caste system of racial inequality that had changed mainly from paternalism to segregation (rigid competitive pattern) as the society changed from agricultural to urban. Over time, the caste system actually became more rigid, as whites came to see the native population as an ever-greater threat to their supremacy. The more blacks become able to do work that allows them to compete with whites and the more they become aware of their repression, the more of a threat they are to the dominant white minority. Despite these changes, and despite the conflict and shifting power balance between the British and Dutch, the presence of a racial caste system can be traced back to the conquest of the native population by the Dutch. In many ways, that conquest was similar to that of Indian people by whites in the United States. (For further discussion of South Africa, see Van den Berghe, 1965 and 1978, Chapter 5, and Hunt and Walker, 1974, Chapter 6.) Thus, while the pattern of conflict and inequality was changed and in many ways became worse, its origins can be directly traced to the country's colonial origins.

Zimbabwe

In 1979, a settlement was reached to bring majority rule to Zimbabwe (formerly Rhodesia), and the popular revolutionary leader, Robert Mugabe, was elected president. Although safeguards were provided to guarantee some continuing white representation in the government, black majority rule has become reality in Zimbabwe today. However, this settlement was reached only after a seven-year civil war that took more than 20,000 lives—one of the bloodiest racial conflicts in recent history. The roots of this long conflict again can be found in the conquest and colonization of native peoples by Europeans. Here, the colonial influence was mainly British, without a major Dutch presence. As in South Africa, however, the white, European colonialists built a society based on white supremacy. Although the discrimination was not as rigid or formalized as in South Africa, the ownership of land and capital and the control of the political structure were almost entirely in white hands. Furthermore, when Great Britian began to try to change these patterns in the 1960s, the white colonists responded by declaring independence and establishing the white-controlled nation of Rhodesia in 1965 (Hunt and Walker, 1974). To have altered the system of white supremacy would quite simply have been too harmful to the interests of the small but dominant white elite for them to have accepted it. In a situation where the near-total dominance of one racial group over another had been established by conquest and institutionalized by decades of colonialism, only an extended guerilla war and intense international pressure could bring about change. Indeed, by the late 1970s most observers of the situation in Zimbawe agreed that the situation could end only in a negotiated move to majority rule or a victory by the revolutionary forces after an extended and bloody escalation of the civil war. Fortunately, a negotiated settlement was reached, though not without good deal of death and bloodshed.

Northern Ireland

Not all instances of severe intergroup conflict or stratification in the world involves different races. In Nothern Ireland, a violent intergroup conflict that flared in the late 1960s continued throughout the 1970s and has showed no sign of an early resolution. Since 1968, over two thousand lives have been lost in that conflict. All participants are white and European. By all outward appearance, it is a religious conflict between Catholics and Protestants. However, a closer analysis of the situation shows there is much more to it than that. Indeed, the roots of today's conflict go all the way back to the sixteenth century, when Britain gradually asserted control over Ireland. Initially, an English colony was established in Ireland mainly for military and political reasons, since control of Ireland was advantageous in military conflicts with mainland European countries. Later, economic motivations also became important, as the English colonists established themselves as feudal landlords over the Irish population. It is important to note that the English colonists were Protestant (Anglican) and the Irish whom they conquered were Catholic. Later, the English settlers were joined by Scottish ones, who were also Protestant but Presbyterian. Many of the Scots settled in the six northern counties, which are today Northern Ireland. The Irish people never accepted domination by the British, and revolts and upheavals occurred intermittently. The Scottish Presbyterians, who occupied an intermediate position between the Anglicans from England and the Irish Catholics, also rebelled against the English periodically, but by the late eighteenth century the two Protestant groups were drawn together by the threat of increased Irish Catholic political power (Moore, 1972). Eventually, this polarization between the English and Scottish Protestants on one side and the native Irish Catholics led to violent and bloody conflict, which resulted in the division of Ireland. The six northern counties, known as Ulster or Northern Ireland, remained under partial British control and Protestant domination. The remainder of the country, heavily Catholic, became the Republic of Ireland. Since that time, the arena of conflict has been in the north. There the Protestants, a two-to-one majority, retain general control of the government and a position of social and economic advantage. Not all Protestants are wealthy or even middle-class, but most of the wealth is in Protestant hands. The Catholics demand equality, but lacking effective political power, they are unable to escape the low status of a subordinate group. Being a third of the population, they *can* cause a great deal of disruption. Consequently, the situation has remained a violence-ridden stalemate. This necessarily brief and somewhat superficial discussion[1] is sufficient to illustrate one very important point: The roots of the conflict are to be found in colonialism. Today's Irish Catholics (North and

---

[1]For more extensive discusson, see Moore (1972); Barrit and Carter (1962); Rose (1971).

South) are descendents of the native Irish who were conquered and colonized by British (Scottish and English) Protestants. Today's Irish Protestants are the descendents of the British colonizers and look upon the Irish Catholics as an inferior but dangerous and treacherous people. The history of conquest, rebellion, and conflict is central in the mind of both groups in Northern Ireland. Finally, the two groups largely retain the statuses associated with colonizers and colonized minorities. As a result, majority-minority relations in Northern Ireland, even though between two white, European, and Christian ethnic groups, have in many ways closely resembled race relations between blacks and whites in such places as South Africa, Rhodesia (Zimbabwe), and the United States (Moore, 1972).

Quebec, Canada

Quebec Province in Canada is unique among the areas we have discussed; not only is the conflict between two white, European, and Christian groups (English and French-speaking Canadians), but between two groups whose original presence in Canada was that of a colonizer rather than an indigenous population. Neither British nor French were native to Canada, and both (in somewhat different ways) colonized the native Canadian Indian population. The dominance of the English-speaking (a 20 percent minority of Quebec's population) over the much larger French-speaking population originated with the conquest of the French colonists by the British colonists in 1759. Since that time, the English-speaking Canadians have had a dominant social, economic, and until recently, political position. The great majority of the province's wealth, for example, is owned by the English-speaking population. Although English-French conflict has been muted by class divisions that do exist within the French population (Ossenberg, 1975), the English-French conflict has increased in recent decades. This led to violence by militant Quebec separatists in 1970 and in the 1970s brought to power the *Parti Quebecois,* which advocates separation of Quebec from the Canadian confederation (although a referendum on separation failed in 1980). The example of Quebec shows that considerable ethnic stratification and ethnic conflict can result from conquest and colonization, even when one colonizing group conquers another colonizing group and the groups are of the same race and only moderately different in cultural values. As we shall see later, language differences such as those in Quebec can greatly aggravate ethnic conflicts, but in the absence of colonization or conquest, they often do not have that result. The inequality and conflict in Quebec arise largely out of a situation in which one group conquered and colonized another over two hundred years ago.

The Middle East

Perhaps the most potentially explosive area of intergroup relations in today's world is the conflict between Arab and Jew in the Middle East. It is not entirely a problem of ethnic or racial relations, or even of majority-minority relations, because the conflict is in large part an international one between Israel and several of its Arab neighbors. It is, however, worth talking about in a book on majority-minority relations, for several reasons. First, the conflict is both internal and international—one fundamental question in the whole conflict is the status of Palestinian Arabs within the boundary of Israel, some of whom are even Israeli citizens. Second, the conflict is partly ethnic, in the sense that being Jewish or Arab will almost certainly determine where one stands in the conflict. Thirdly, even the international aspect of the conflict centers around jurisdiction over one land area to which both Jews and Palestinian Arabs feel they have a historical and legitimate claim and which each group regards fervently as its true homeland.

The origins of this conflict are more complex than the others we have examined. First, both the dominant group (Jews) and the subordinate group (Arabs) in today's Israel had some historical claim to the land prior to the establishment of the Israeli state in 1948. Israel or Palestine was the historic home of the Jewish people and has been the focal point of their religion throughout history. Nonetheless, there was until modern times no significant Jewish presence there after the conquest of Jerusalem in A.D. 70 (Douglas-Home, 1968, p. 14). During this long period, the only Jewish population was a handful of students and scholars of the Holy Writings (Dodd and Sales, 1970).

The Arab dominance of the region can be traced at least to the establishment of the Turkish and Islamic Ottoman Empire's rule over the region in the sixteenth century, though some trace it further back to the spread of Islamic and Arabic culture to the region in the seventh and eighth centuries (Epp, 1970). In any case, the area had unquestionably been predominantly Arab for hundreds of years before the Zionist movement of the twentieth century, even though it was often governed from outside and did not exist as a distinct Arab or Palestinian state. It should also be noted that the area had major religious significance for both Christians and Muslims as well as Jews. In any case, it is certainly fair to say that, at the time Israeli control of the area was established, both the Jewish and Arab populations viewed the area as their homeland and felt they had a legitimate claim to it. The same cannot be said for majority and minority groups in America or in the African colonies.

The Israeli situation also differs from the others we have studied in that the group that established dominance—the Jewish population—was in large part a displaced population that had experienced centuries of worldwide persecution. It had just suffered perhaps the worst incidence of genocide in the history of the world—the murder of six million Jews in the Holocaust. Thus, the impetus for the Jewish settlement came not from the expansionist desires of a colonial power but in large part from the desire of a persecuted people for a safe homeland.

In these regards, then, the origin of the Israeli state and the present-day Arab-Jewish conflict differed from the patterns of colonialism and conquest we have seen in the other societies. However, there are important similarities. When Zionism first became a serious movement in the late nineteenth century, the population of what is now Israel was overwhelmingly Arab and had been for hundreds of years. Furthermore, the establishment of the Jewish state of Israel was imposed against the will of that indigenous Arab population. It was accomplished through the actions of the United Nations, European powers (notably Britian and France), and ultimately, the armed struggle of the Jewish immigrants against the indigenous Arab population. In the end, much of that population fled, and those who stayed behind have occupied a subordinate role in Israeli society (though not to nearly the same extent as blacks in South Africa or Rhodesia, for example). Thus, while there are important differences between the Israeli case and the pattern of colonialism we have examined in other places, there are some important similarities as well. Most important, the problem did arise as a result of an indigenous population (Palestinian Arabs) coming under the domination of a new population (Jewish) through the use of force.

Some Comparisons and Contrasts

Sociologist Stanley Lieberson (1961) has examined majority-minority relations both historically within certain societies and comparatively between a number of societies. Lieberson concluded that when an *indigenous group*—one that is established in or native to an area—is made subordinate to another group entering from the outside, the result is usually conflict and ethnic inequality. Assimilation and intergroup cooperation are very difficult in this situation. Of course, such situations usually originate with the conquest or colonization of the indigenous population. In the reverse situation, where the indigenous group is dominant over the immigrant group, the situation is usually different. Unless the immigrant group was forced to immigrate, as in the case of slaves, a trend toward assimilation will usually emerge, with only mild and occasional ethnic conflict.

The societies we have examined in this section all fit Lieberson's first type, where the indigenous group was made subordinate to an immigrant or outside group. With the possible exception of Israel, they all have a history of colonialism. And, as we know, they are all among the world's most volatile flashpoints of intergroup conflict. A history of colonialism, conquest, or domination of an indigenous population by an immigrant one appears to be one of the factors most closely associated with cases of ethnic conflict and inequality in today's world. Not every country with such a history has a serious majority-minority problem, and not every country with such a problem has that type of history. The U.S. state of Hawaii and the countries of Mexico and Brazil, for example, all have a history of conquest of the native population by colonial powers, but are all frequently cited as cases of better-than-average intergroup relations. On the other hand, one of the most brutal examples of ethnic oppression in history, Hitler's genocidal campaign against Jews, occurred in a situation with no colonial history. It is thus important to keep in mind that *no one factor* taken alone can explain the pattern of intergroup relations in any society. Nonetheless, if we examine the broad range of societies in the world, it does seem clear that, *all else being equal,* the presence of a colonial history does seem to be associated with greater than average amounts of intergroup inequality and intergroup conflict. (For further discussion of this issue, see Kinloch, 1974; 1979, pp. 175–188; Mason, 1971, pp. 81–86.)

SOCIETIES WITH PEACEFUL INTERGROUP RELATIONS

The same point about the importance of history can be illustrated by looking at examples at the opposite end of the scale from those we have examined. One such example, cited by Hunt and Walker (1974, pp. 41–45) is Switzerland. That country has a number of different nationalities and religions, many of whom do not even speak the same language. Despite this diversity, relations between the groups are for the most part harmonious. According to Hunt and Walker, an important reason is that each of the various and ethnically diverse parts of the country came into confederation voluntarily, largely to seek protection. One rare exception to this is the Jura region, which is the one part of Switzerland where intergroup relations are not harmonious. This area was taken from France and made a part of Switzerland in 1815, against the will of its residents. As recently as the 1960s and 1970s, a social movement to separate the area from Swiss rule sparked violence.

Another relevant example is Hawaii. Although, as we have already noted, Hawaii did experience external colonization, its colonization was quite different from that of South Africa, Ireland, or the mainland United States. Berry and Tischler (1978, pp. 158–163) discuss Hawaii as an example of a society with relatively harmonious intergroup relations. Hawaii has greater ethnic diversity than any other state, yet, despite its social and cultural heterogeneity, it sets an admirable example of racial and ethnic harmony for the rest of the country. We are not saying that there is *no* racial problem—native Hawaiians do occupy a position subordinate to that of several newcomer groups—but racial harmony and tolerance do seem much more the rule than the exception. Certainly the norms against prejudice and discrimination are much stronger there than on the mainland, and contact among various racial groups is more commonplace and more harmonious than on the mainland. According to Berry and Tischler, much of the reason for this can be found in the islands' history. The local population, although subject to colonial influences, was never conquered and subordinated in a manner similar to, for example, the native populations of the mainland United States or South Africa. While there was considerable outside interest in Hawaii from 1778 on, the native population was well organized and had effective leaders who represented their interests well to the outsiders. The whites who came to Hawaii, in turn, respected and cooperated with the leadership. Indeed, friendship and marriage between the two groups was common and socially supported. This was in part because the early contact was with whites interested in trade rather than conquest. A variety of groups such as Chinese, Japanese, and Filipinos arrived later to meet the islands' labor needs, but no outside group ever took control and dominated the indigenous population. Consistent with Lieberson's theory, Berry and Tischler argue that this history is an important factor in Hawaii's harmonious racial and ethnic relations.

The first general pattern, then, that we see from international examination of intergroup relations is that colonization or conquest of an indigenous population tends to leave a legacy of majority-minority inequality and conflict that can persist for years, even centuries. In countries where groups have come together peaceably, intergroup relations tend to be more harmonious. Of course, this is not the only factor influencing intergroup relations, and other factors can and often do create exceptions. Still, the general rule holds more often than not.

CROSS-CULTURAL EVIDENCE ON THE EFFECTS OF URBANIZATION AND MODERNIZATION

In our study of the history of majority-minority relations in the United States we also examined the closely related trends of urbanization, industrialization, and modernization. In American history, these trends have been associated with a decrease in the rigidity in race relations. As we saw in detail in Chapter 6, this has been especially evident since World War II, though the shift from an agricultural society to an industrial one began to have important effects much earlier than that. In this section, we wish to explore the degree to which parallel changes have been taking place throughout the world. We cannot, of course, explore the history of every country in even the limited detail we have given to the United States. Nonetheless, some important worldwide trends have taken place that seem related to one another and that may provide some answers to the question of whether and how modernization and urbanization are related to intergroup relations.

Industrialized Countries

The first of these general kinds of changes involves those more developed countries of the world that have subordinate ethnic or racial minorities. In such countries, two things have tended to happen. First, the minority groups have increasingly turned to protest and to social and political action to improve their position. We have already discussed this trend in some detail for the United States; it is equally evident in a number of other developed countries. In Canada, the French-speaking minority, about 30 percent of the population, has become increasingly vocal in recent decades. Among the results have been legislation making French the only official language in Quebec province, where most of the French-speaking population lives, and the 1976 election victory of the Quebec separatist *Parti Quebecois*. Although Quebec voters have since voted against separation from the Canadian confederation, the rise to dominance of the *Parti Quebecois* and the passage of the language legislation clearly indicate heightened assertiveness among Canada's French-speaking minority. We have also discussed the violence in Northern Ireland in the 1960s and 1970s. In Quebec, the causes underlying the present-day protest and political change have been there for years, but the protest has surfaced only within the last twenty years. Although Northern Ireland has a long history of conflict, it has substantially escalated since 1968. Other examples of minority groups that have become increasingly vocal in recent years include blacks and Asians in Great Britain, the Flemish in Belgium (who have become a numerical majority but have historically been a subordinate group), the South Moluccans who have turned to terrorism in Holland, and the Jurans in Switzerland. In Great Britain, minority group dissatisfaction was an important contributing factor to widespread urban violence during the summer of 1981.

The other, related trend in the more developed countries has been a reduction in overt discrimination and prejudice and a move toward legal protection of the rights of minorities. The United States, Great Britian, Canada, and other Western countries have passed legislation banning racial and ethnic discrimination. In both Canada and Great Britain, the open expression of racial prejudice is generally frowned on, though both countries have experienced opposition to immigration, which in recent years has been predominantly black and Asian. Nonetheless, in most of the Western industrial nations, discrimination today is illegal, and open discrimination and prejudice are relatively rare compared to the past. Furthermore, as Kinloch (1979) points out, social differentiation in the more developed nations has tended to become more complex, and based on a wide range of factors including class, sex, and life style, with some decline in the importance of race and ethnicity.

Increasing Fluidity? Or Rigidity with Conflict?

In spite of these general patterns, it would be an overstatment to say that modernization always leads to increasingly fluid intergroup relations. The examples of South Africa and Northern Ireland show that rigid intergroup inequality and intergroup conflict can continue and even worsen in societies that have experienced considerable modernization and urbanization. A widely cited essay by Blumer (1965) suggests some of the reasons why. Blumer argues that industrialization is no guarantee of improved race relations because certain social forces tend to maintain inequality, even if discrimination is per se economically irrational in a modernizing society. First, there remain important elements of the traditional structure, including a desire for discrimination on the part of many majority group members, some of whom are directly benefiting from discrimination. An example of this would be the white industrial laborers in the early twentieth-century United States, who saw discrimination as a way of protecting themselves from competition from minority workers (for further discussion, see Chapter 6). Thus, in societies with a history of rigid discrimination, Blumer argues that dominant group members exert strong pressures for discrimination as a way of shielding themselves from potential competition from minority groups. As a result, it is often more economically rational for industrialists to continue discriminating than to put up with the conflict and protest they would get from elements of the majority group if they stopped discriminating. Thus, Blumer makes the point that it is by no means clear that discrimination is always economically irrational in industrial societies.

This suggests that there are two directions a country's intergroup relations may take as it modernizes. One possibility is that they may become increasingly fluid, though sometimes after a period of rigid competitive relations, as in the United States. The following conditions make such a pattern more likely:

1. Minority groups are in a position to generate effective protest. Among other factors, such protest is more likely to be a result of urbanization in countries allowing relatively great freedom of expression.
2. There is external pressure for more equal race relations. Blumer cites the pressures of northern liberals and the federal government on the South as examples of this. The desire of the United States, Britain, and other Western countries for good relations with African countries would be another example, since this exerted pressure on them to "get their own house in order" and improve race relations on the home front. A third example would be pressure exerted by Britain and the United States to get Rhodesia's white government to agree to majority rule.
3. The economy and/or social system is such that gains by minority group members are not viewed as a threat by majority group members. Wilson (1978) argues that this was the case in the United States during the late 1950s and much of the 1960s, because it was a period of economic growth with room for everyone to benefit. Thus, it was largely during this period that the United States moved from rigid to fluid competitive race relations. Bastide (1965, pp. 14–18) argues that one reason for Brazil's relatively harmonious intergroup relations is that until very recently, blacks were not seen as competitors by most whites. They largely did different kinds of work. Whites, for example, had little desire to work in the crafts or manual labor (the attitude toward work was totally different from that in the United States), so there was little objection to the movement of blacks into such jobs (Mason, 1971, p. 314). Even when blacks *did* compete with whites, they were not seen as a real threat because whites could shield themselves from blacks in their family settings even if not in their work settings, and the family, not the economy, has historically been the central institution in Brazil's social system. Recently, as blacks and whites have begun to compete more in the work setting and as the family has declined somewhat in importance, there have been some more noticeable instances of racial conflict.
4. The country does not have a history of highly rigid racial inequality. Blumer (1965, p. 23) suggests that ethnic distinctions in the United States and Canada have blurred more than racial ones in part because they did not have the same degree of rigidity to begin with. He cites the mingling of racial groups in Southeast Asia as another example of this.

The other possibility that may result from modernization, ubanization, and industrialization is continued rigid intergroup inequality, but with rising levels of conflict, protest and, often, violence. South Africa is probably the best example of this, though Northern Ireland is another example, and for a time, this was the pattern in the Southern United States and in Rhodesia (now Zimbabwe). The following conditions make this pattern most likely:

1. The dominant group has great power relative to the subordinate group(s).
2. The dominant group sees the subordinate group as a strong threat.
3. There is no effective source of external pressure for more fluid intergroup relations.
4. The country has a history of very rigid racial distinctions.

Not surprisingly, *all* of these conditions are very clearly present in South Africa. Historically, the power has always been on the side of whites, first through the possession of firearms and later through total control of the government and the military. Unlike countries that have constitutional guarantees of free speech for all, the subordinate groups in South Africa—blacks, coloreds, and Asians—have essentially no political or civil rights. In such totalitarian regimes, it is simply much more difficult for minorities to organize effective protest movements than it is where freedom of expression is guaranteed. In spite of this, violent outbursts do periodically occur; and in large part because whites are outnumbered four to one, the whites (probably correctly) see any move toward liberalism as a threat to their advantage. The attempts at liberalization on the part of the British—who were seen as outside impostors by the Afrikaner majority among the white population— probably heightened the perception among whites that their status was threatened. As a consequence, whites were not about to "take any chances" of losing their racial advantage. Thus, unlike several other parts of the world, racial discrimination in South Africa actually became more formalized and more rigid during the "modern" post-World War II era.

A final factor in this example is the absence of effective outside pressure. In the southern United States pressure from the North was an important cause of liberalization during the 1960s. In Rhodesia, pressure from Britain and the United States (along with an escalating civil war on the homefront) helped force the white minority government to give up power. In South Africa no comparable pressure had been exerted on the white regime by the early 1980s. Two *potential* sources of such pressure exist. One exists in the independent African nations adjacent to South Africa. All African nations strongly oppose the South African regime, but to date they have not exerted effective pressure on it to change. One reason is that some of them are economically dependent on South Africa, and another is that most are weaker militarily. They simply do not have the power to force it to change (see Mason, 1971, pp. 218–219; Legum, 1975, pp. 103–104).

The other potential source of pressure on South Africa is the superpowers. Here, too, however, effective pressure has not been forthcoming. Part of the reason can probably be found in economics: British, and to a lesser degree, American companies have substantial investments in South Africa under the present regime. A bigger part of the reason, however, is any *effective* pressure could involve military as well as economic costs, and as Legum (1975, p. 104) puts it, "No major power—black, white or brown; communist, capitalist, or nonaligned—has committed its resources to a warlike enterprise purely out of moral conviction. Nations undertake the use of force, military or economic, only when their national interests are threatened or can be greatly enhanced.'' He goes on to argue that unless or until the interests of Western nations are threatened by the South African situation, they are unlikely to get involved. The history of Zimbabwe illustrates this quite well: Only when that country's civil war threatened to lead to an anti-Western, pro-Communist state did the Western powers get involved. It can be argued that a major reason for their intervention was to prevent such an event, which would have given allies of the Soviet Union an important foothold in Africa. Should such a situation develop in South Africa, Western intervention is quite possible; without such a situation, it is unlikely. Thus, to date none of the situations necessary to bring about change in South Africa has come into being, and the result has been a continuing rigid pattern of racial domination, discrimination, and segregation.

The continuing pattern of domination has, however, been accompanied by a rising level of racial conflict. As we stated, urbanization and modernization usually give rise either to more fluid intergroup relations or to continued rigid intergroup relations but with rising levels of conflict—something like the rigid competitive pattern discussed in earlier chapters. Urbanization and modernization do facilitate protest by making the subordinate group more aware of inequalities and by bringing subordinate group members together in one place where they can plan and carry out protest activities. If they are frustrated in such efforts and/or if they sufficiently frighten the dominant group, the potential for violence can be great. South Africa illustrates this principle all too well: an attack by police on peaceful demonstrators in 1960 in Sharpeville resulted in the loss of sixty-seven lives (Wilson, 1973, p. 176), and bloody riots in Soweto and other black townships (regions around the major cities where urban black workers and their families are required to live) in 1976 and 1977 took hundreds more lives. The exact figure is hard to know since it is widely alleged that the government suppressed the true death toll. In 1980 there was further loss of life in incidents involving both black and coloured protestors.

In addition to these incidents, protest organizations have proliferated despite official repression, and there have been a number of incidents of sabotage. It would appear, then, that the maintenance of a rigid system of racial or ethnic discrimination in a context of modernization and urbanization will lead to a heightened level of conflict. (Rhodesia before majority rule and, to a lesser extent, Northern Ireland suggest the same thing.) Nonetheless, such systems of inequality can be very capable of resisting change if the power is sufficiently concentrated in the hands of the dominant group, if the dominant group feels highly threatened, and if there is little effective pressure for change from the outside.

Third World Countries

In the Third World, the change has been more dramatic than in the West, though its direction has been perhaps less uniform. Here, two major trends can be observed. First, there has been a great change away from colonialism toward national independence. The great colonial empires of the British, French, Portuguese, and Dutch have disappeared, or practically so. As recently as World War II, the European countries had dozens of colonies throughout the world; today, they have practically none. In some cases the colonies were relinquished voluntarily, but in others independence came about only after long periods of warfare.

Closely related to this has been the change in those places still under colonial influence. Most such situations that remain today take one of two forms. Sometimes a small minority of people ethnically associated with the colonial power dominate an indigenous majority population, even though the country is legally no longer a colony. The dominance of the ethnically British whites until recently in Zimbabwe and of the descendents of Dutch and British colonialists in South Africa provide two examples of this pattern. In other countries a government may be established and heavily influenced by a colonial power, even though the countries involved may never have been colonies of the power involved. Examples of this are the Thieu government in Vietnam and the monarchy of the Shah in Iran, both of which were established by action of the United States CIA and heavily supported and influenced by the U.S. government. In both types of "pseudocolonial" situation, there has since World War II been a marked increase in indigenous group opposition to the regimes. That has occurred to the point that the Vietnamese and Iranian governments were overthrown, and the white minority government of Rhodesia (now Zimbabwe) has been replaced by majority rule. Of the examples given, only South Africa has not had a change in government. While there is no evidence that the South African government is in immediate danger of collapse, an upsurge of both violent and nonviolent protest against that government has been evident in the past fifteen to twenty years. Recent history in other parts of the world does not suggest that the protest will permanently subside until majority rule is brought about.

These changes have come about during a period of rapid urbanization and modernization in the world. Certainly many parts of the world remain rural and traditional, but even these parts are undergoing rapid change. By 1979, the world's population was 39 percent urban, and even the two most rural continents, Africa and Asia, were 25 percent and 27 percent urban respectively (Population Reference Bureau, 1980). Even the predominantly rural countries today frequently have large cities. Bangladesh, for example, is only 9 percent urban, yet it has a city, Dacca, with a population of a million. China, India, Indonesia, Burma, and Vietnam all have cities among the world's fifty largest; none of these countries are more than 25 percent urban (Cousins and Nagpaul, 1979, pp. 9–11; Population Reference Bureau, 1980). Most of these cities have grown dramatically since World War II, as even the societies that are still predominantly rural have undergone considerable urbanization. Between 1950 and 1975, for example, the proportion of the world's population living in places with a population of 20,000 or more increased by nearly 50 percent. In the less developed parts of the world the increase was faster than that (Frisbie, 1977). Also notable during the period was social and technological modernization. The complexity of social organization increased throughout the world, mass communications such as radio and television spread to even some of the least developed parts of the world, and modern economic systems such as capitalism and socialism continued to spread, supplanting agrarian feudal systems. In most parts of the world, there has been more and more contact with influences from outside the local area, both national and international (Schermerhorn, 1978, p. 165).

Of course, the fact that the changes in majority-minority relations around the world have been happening at the same time as the urbanization and modernization trends does not prove that the changes were *caused* by those trends. Nonetheless, a thoughtful analysis of the issue does suggest some reasons for assuming they probably were, at least in part. One of the most important changes we have noted in majority-minority relations has been the move toward more minority assertiveness in developed countries and toward nationalism and anticolonialism in the Third World. We can identify a number of ways in which urbanization and modernization have brought these changes. Urbanization has brought people together in the cities where they can share ideas and organize protest. Mass communications have helped make people aware of inequalities and have contributed to rising expectations by showing subordinate peoples what life *could* be like. They have provided role models by showing people protests and revolutions over similar issues in other places. Finally, mass communications have facilitated communication and the use of propaganda by protest movements.

Industrialization and technological modernization have had more general effects. They have created demands for labor which open new opportunities to members of the native or colonized population—at times even when the colonial leadership would rather not create such opportunities. The white leadership in South Africa, for example, has been faced with the question of whether to leave jobs unfilled and suffer lowered productivity or to train and hire blacks for what were formerly "white jobs" (Hunt and Walker, 1974, pp. 187–191). They have also created a need for rising educational levels. This increase in education has had a number of important effects, both on minorities in developed countries and on indigenous populations in less developed, colonial societies. One general effect has been to raise expectations by heightening awareness of inequalities. Another important effect, particularly in the Third World, has been to provide leadership for protest movements. It is not at all unusual for leaders in revolutionary Third World movements to have been educated in developed Western nations. Some of the leaders of the 1979 revolution in Iran, for example, had attended institutions of higher education in the United States.

Another important trend associated with modernization has been greater contact among the nations of the world. This has tended to expose people to a wider range of social, religious, and political ideologies than ever before. This alone is likely to have some unsettling effects. When combined with the presence of big power competition in the world, the effect is even greater. As the United States, the Soviet Union, and to a lesser degree, China and some European nations seek political, economic, and military advantage around the world, they offer additional sources of aid to combatants in internal conflicts. The Soviet Union has frequently aided revolutionary movements aimed at overthrowing governments friendly to the

United States, though the ability of the Soviets to cause such events has been greatly exaggerated by political conservatives in the United States.

Although the United States has frequently supported colonialist or psuedocolonialist regimes in order to retain power overseas and control Soviet influence, there is some evidence that the policy changed after the Vietnam War, particularly under the Carter administration. When it became evident that the Somoza regime in Nicaraugua was in imminent danger of being overthrown, the U.S. government helped to persuade Somoza to surrender power, realizing that a failure to do so would probably have resulted in a government hostile to the United States. At the time of this writing, it remained to be seen whether a permanent shift in U.S. policy was under way. The election of conservative Ronald Reagan as president has brought a return toward a more procolonialist foreign policy. Regardless of the *degree* to which U.S. policy has changed, there is no doubt that the United States, because of big-power competition, has had to become more concerned about the thinking of anticolonialist elements around the world. This has undoubtedly had some effect of giving greater hope to such movements. Finally, in this era of international contact and mass communication, the spread of minority and anticolonial protest since World War II has developed a momentum largely of its own. This is not unlike the "contagion effect" on domestic protest in the United States, which we discussed in the last chapter. A successful protest or revolution in one place raises hopes for a similar action in another place where similar conditions exist. Thus, the rise of protest against one colonial or racist regime can, particularly if successful, lead to similar protest against others, given the amount of international contact and the extent of mass communications in today's world.

COMBINED EFFECTS OF COLONIALISM AND DEGREE OF MODERNIZATION

Graham Kinloch (1979, Chapter 12) has developed a useful model combining the effects of (1) whether a nation has a colonial history and (2) the degree of development or modernization in the country. As we have seen, Kinloch, along with most sociologists of race relations, argues that societies with a history of colonialism or conquest have more majority-minority inequality and more conflict than do countries without such a history. Within this group of societies, race and ethnicity are more important in the less developed, less modernized countries. As such countries modernize, they tend to become differentiated less on the basis of race and ethnicity and more on the basis of a wide range of factors including economics, behavior, sex, and age. Among countries without a colonial history— for example, Switzerland—there tends to be less division, and race and ethnicity are less important. Again, the degree of inequality and the lines along which society is divided vary with degree of development. Among underdeveloped societies with no history of colonialization, there may be very little stratification: There is barely enough to go around, and everyone shares pretty much equally. As Kinloch notes, such societies are an extreme rarity in today's world: Only some scattered tribal groups really fit this pattern. More common is the noncolonial developed society, which has relatively little racial or ethnic inequality but does tend to have inequalities based on class, behavior, sex, age, and so on.

NUMBER OF RACIAL AND ETHNIC GROUPS

Although many social scientists feel that the two most important factors in comparative studies of majority-minority relations are the nature of the original contact—whether or not it involved colonialism or conquest—and the degree of modernization and development of a society, other factors also seem to make important differences. One that many experts have emphasized is the number of racial or ethnic groups. In general, when a society has many groups that are generally recognized as distinct, it tends to have less racial and ethnic conflict and less inequality than when it has only two groups (Hunt and Walker, 1974, p. 235). When there are several groups, there is often no *one* group large or powerful enough to dominate the others. Furthermore, any group that discriminates against or shows hostility toward outgroups runs the risk of being treated the same way itself. When there are only two groups, it is much easier for one to discriminate against the other. It is also common for each group to see the other as the enemy and the cause of its troubles—this can happen much more readily in the "us versus them" mentality that can easily develop in the two-group situation.

Some of the places already mentioned as examples of harmonious race relations help to illustrate this principle. According to Smith (1942), one reason for Hawaii's harmonious race relations is that it has a large number of racial and ethnic groups, rather than just two. As of the 1970 census, no racial group accounted for than about 40 percent of the population, and the population included large numbers of whites, Japanese-Americans, native Hawaiians, Filipino-Americans, and Chinese-Americans. Also present, in relatively small numbers, were blacks and American Indians. The fact that no group is a majority in Hawaii makes the situation there particularly conducive to harmonious racial and ethnic relations. To a lesser degree, the presence of multiple ethnic and linguistic groups in Switzerland probably helps to explain that country's relative racial harmony.

In other examples, complex racial classification systems recognizing a number of distinct classifications have been suggested as causes of relative racial and ethnic harmony in the French Antilles and in Mexico (Hunt and Walker, 1974, pp. 155–156, 235). In Mexico, a multiple classification system that contained from ten to forty-six categories (Hunt and Walker, 1974, p. 139; Roncal, 1944, p. 533) became so confusing that it was generally disregarded, and the great bulk of the population came to be regarded as mestizo (mixed Indian and white). Ultimately, the result was considerable *amalgamation*—biological mixing that eliminated distinct racial categories. In the French Antilles (Guadalupe and Martinique), racial animosities were reduced as a result of a multiple classification system treating persons of mixed black and white ancestry as a separate group. This practice, which is also common in Latin America, helps "to blur racial distinctions rather than to sharpen them" (Hunt and Walker, 1974, p. 214). In general, if a society has multiple racial and ethnic groups or multiple racial and ethnic classifications, it will tend to have more harmonious intergroup relations. Often, it is not so much the number of groups present as it is the number of classifications that is important. In the United States, persons of European, African, and North American ancestry are socially classified in three major groupings: whites, blacks, and American Indians. In Mexico, however, the same population would be divided into *at least* six groups: whites (*Hispanos*), blacks (*Negros*), Indians (*Indios*), *mestizos* (Indian and white), *lobos* (Indian and black), and *mulattos* (white and black). In fact, the Mexican classification system has tended to be more complex than that, with mixtures such as Indian-mulatto recognized as separate groups and with region—and birthplace—also related to classification. The importance of classification is further illustrated in the South African system. Each of the four official groups—whites, blacks, coloureds, and Asians—has within it important ethnic divisions. Nonetheless, the classification system has come to blur these ethnic distinctions and heighten the racial ones: The European population has come to think of itself as white rather than as British or Afrikans, and the native population has moved away from ethnic or tribal identity toward black nationalism. These changes have been an important factor in the heightened level of conflict in South Africa in recent years.

The propensity for conflict may be especially great where the majority of the population falls into one of two classifications. Although both South Africa and the United States have multiple classifications, over 85 percent of South Africa's population is either black or white, and over 90 percent of the U.S. population is either white Anglo or black. Canada has many racial and ethnic groups, but in Quebec province, the great majority is either English or French. Finally, in Northern Ireland, nearly everyone self-identifies as either Catholic or Protestant. Undoubtedly, this factor is less important than others, such as the power balance and a history of colonialism, but the division of most of the population into two major divisions does appear to heighten the potential for polarization, whereas a multitude of classifications—with no one or two forming a large majority—frequently seems to lead to a blurring and softening of intergroup divisions.

CULTURAL AND DEMOGRAPHIC CHARACTERISTICS OF MAJORITY AND MINORITY GROUPS: THE EXAMPLES OF BRAZIL AND MEXICO

The cultural and demographic characteristics of the groups involved in any situation of intergroup relations will also help determine the kinds of relations that develop between groups. We shall illustrate this general principle with two examples from Latin America: Brazil and Mexico.

Brazil has often been cited as an example of successful assimilation between diverse groups. Extensive assimilation, including widespread intermarriage, took place between the white population and the native Indian population and between blacks and whites, even though blacks were originally brought to Brazil as slaves. This is not to deny that there is racial stratification in Brazil: In general, darker skin color is associated with lower status. Brazil did have a long period of slavery, and both blacks and Indians were forced to live under a paternalistic system of race relations (Van den Berghe, 1978, pp. 63−65). The blacks were slaves on the *fazendas*, or feudal plantations, as were some Indians. Most of the Indians, however, experienced paternalism in the *aldeas*, or Jesuit mission villages. Although this system had more benevolent objectives than the slave plantations, it too was a despotic system that forcibly took children from their parents and resocialized Indians to what the Jesuits viewed as the ideal culture. Nonetheless, there is no United States-style segregation and little overt discrimination. Indeed, to Brazilians, the major "problem" in intergroup relations is concern about groups unwilling to assimilate (Berry and Tischler, 1978, pp. 156−158).

Several characteristics of the ethnic groups involved (the majority group in particular) help to account for Brazil's pattern of assimilation. One is the very uneven sex ratio among the Portuguese who settled Brazil: They were overwhelmingly male. This encouraged considerable intermarriage between the male settlers and Indian women. Later, when more women did arrive, the pattern of intermarriage had become well established. In addition, this mixing of groups led to a considerable blurring of racial distinctions. In contrast to the Brazilian pattern is that of the United States, where English settlers much more frequently came over as families. As a result, intermarriage has been much less common in the United States.

Another factor noted by Pierson (1942) that supports a tendency toward assimilation in Brazil is the history of Moorish influence in Portugal. According to Pierson, this led to a tolerance of darker-skinned people, perhaps even a tendency to view dark skin as a source of prestige. In Brazil, for example, brown skin and straight hair are regarded as the standard of beauty, again reflecting the mixed composition of the population. To the degree that this was true, it certainly would have led the Portuguese colonists in Brazil to be more supportive of intermarriage and assimilation. Another factor that encouraged intermixing was the common Portuguese custom of concubinage, which often brought regular and somewhat institutionalized relationships between white males and racially mixed females.

A final important factor, noted by Kinloch (1974) was the Catholic religion of the Portuguese colonists. As in other parts of Latin America, the Catholic religion of the Portuguese led them to seek to assimilate the Indians and black slaves rather than to isolate and subordinate them. The Catholic religion emphasized human equality and the winning of souls. Consequently, an effort was made to convert the Indians and blacks and to integrate them into the Catholic culture and society of the Portuguese colonists. Protestant religions, some of which include notions of a select people, often tended to view people as either having received the word of God or not having received it, with the prescription to avoid those who are seen as not having received it. This has often been suggested as a reason for the *lack* of acceptance of racial minorities and the much greater segregation in the United States as compared to countries such as Brazil.

These cultural differences have helped lead to a milder form of intergroup inequality, and more harmonious intergroup relations, than are found in many other countries with a history of colonialism. As we have suggested, they made possible a greater degree of cultural assimilation and more amalgamation than is typically found elsewhere. Such cultural assimilation and interbreeding with whites (called *blanchiment*, meaning "bleaching" or "whitening") became a potential route of upward mobility for blacks and mulattos (Bastide, 1965, pp. 15−17).

Assimilation has been a limited source of mobility, to be sure, and one that requires a loss of one's racial identity. Nonetheless, it has been sufficient to prevent widespread protest on the part of blacks and to preserve the widespread image of Brazil as a racial paradise. In reality, it is not a racial paradise, but racial inequality there *is* less rigid than in other countries with a colonial history, and there is notably less racial conflict (though both are probably on the increase as the country moves

Sunbathing in Sao Paolo, Brazil. Assimilation and amalgamation of racial groups has proceeded farther in Brazil than in most societies. Nonetheless, there remains substantial class inequality and lighter-skinned people are overrepresented in the upper classes, darker-skinned people in the lower classes. United Nations, J. Frank.

toward a competitive, industrial system.) This pattern of less rigid inequality and less conflict is probably in large part the result of the cultural factors we have discussed.

Another country that is frequently cited as an example of successful assimilation is Mexico. Some of the reasons are the same as in Brazil: The colonizing population (Spanish) was mostly Catholic, so they believed that Indians had souls and that accordingly, there was an obligation to convert them. They were also mostly male, which encouraged racial mixing. There were, however, also, important characteristics of the indigenous or subordinate group, Indians, that contributed to the pattern of assimilation. In Mexico, the Aztec Indians had a highly developed and in many regards modern culture before the Spanish *conquistadores* arrived. Their chief city, Tenochitlan, (now Mexico City), had a population of over 300,000 and must be regarded as one of the great cities of the world at that time. Although the Indian society was quickly crushed by Spanish military force, the influence of the highly developed Indian culture lived on. Mexico's unique mixture of Spanish and Indian culture became a national symbol, the more so with time as intermixing between those of Indian and Spanish ancestry continued. The evolution of a Mexican or mestizo culture that was neither Spanish nor Indian but a mixture of both and the development of the culture into a symbol of national unity helped to contribute further to the disappearance of distinct racial categories in Mexico. Thus, we see from the example of Mexico that cultural and social organizational characteristics of both the majority group and the minority group had important effects on the relationship between the two groups. In this case, it led in large degree to an *amalgamation* of the two groups into one new group that became a symbol of national unity.

As a result, it became the rule in Mexico that one's group identity was determined by one's social roles and cultural attributes rather than one's genetic composition or physical appearance. Thus, a mestizo who married into a prominent Spanish family could come to be regarded as a Spaniard. An Indian who moved to the city and adopted the Spanish language, way of dressing, and customs would be regarded as a mestizo or Mexican, whereas one who remained in the rural village and kept the Indian culture would be regarded as a member of the *Indio* group. Today, the great majority of the Mexican population identifies with the mestizo, or simply Mexican, grouping, and it is this group that is regarded as representative of the Mexican culture. Nonetheless, despite a view that in Mexican history the Spanish are seen largely as villains and the Indians as heros, higher status attaches to Spanish appearance and culture than to Indian (Mason, 1971, p. 249). Furthermore, the 15 percent or so of Mexico's population that retains the *Indio* identity is the least well-off and is looked down upon somewhat by the rest of the population. Thus in Mexico, as in Brazil, movement toward the European group's culture is an important requisite for upward mobility. On the other hand, the group boundaries in both countries have greatly blurred, and Mexico is one of the closest approximations of the *amalgamation* model (loss of group distinctions through interbreeding) found anywhere in the world.

CROSS-CUTTING
VERSUS OVERLAPPING CLEAVAGES

Divisions, or *cleavages*, in society are sometimes described as being either *cross-cutting* or *overlapping*. Overlapping cleavages occur when, for example, racial, religious, class, and language divisions all cut the same way. Imagine a fictitious society made up of blacks and whites. Assume that all the blacks are wealthy, Muslim, and speak Swahili and that all whites are poor, Protestant, and speak German. In a society like this, the potential for conflict would be very high: No matter whether conflict occurred on the basis of race, religion, language, or economics, the division would always be the same. Nobody would be in a position of having mixed loyalties. Such a society would quickly divide into two mutually hostile and distrustful groups. The opposite kind of society is said to have cross-cutting cleavages: There is little or no relationship among race, income, religion, language, and so on. In a society like this, knowing that a person was black would tell you nothing about his or her income, language, or religion. Divisions along the lines of religion would be different from divisions along the lines of income, and both would be unrelated to racial divisions. In this kind of society, there would be relatively little conflict, because everyone would have mixed loyalties.

Of course few societies are as clearly delineated as those described here. Nonetheless, real-life societies do differ in the *degree* to which they have overlapping or cross-cutting cleavages, and there is considerable evidence that cross-cutting cleavages do tend to reduce intergroup conflict. This can be illustrated by two examples. We have already discussed the general pattern of ethnic harmony in Switzerland. That country has two religious groups, three nationalities, and four language groups. However, two of the three nationality groups, Germans and French, are religiously divided. Hunt and Walker (1974, p. 42) believe that these cross-cutting cleavages are an important reason for Switzerland's relatively harmonious ethnic relations, since those united by religion are often divided by language.

Another society where cross-cutting cleavages have muted ethnic conflict is Canada. The conflict between English- and French-speaking Canadians has heated up considerably over the last ten to fifteen years, but before that time it was very difficult for French-speaking Canadians to develop a unified movement. According to Ossenberg (1975), an important reason for this was the existence of class divisions within the French-speaking population. Although the French-speaking population as a whole was of lower socioeconomic status than the English-speaking, and the latter controlled the wealth, there was also a fairly wide range of socioeconomic status within the French-speaking population. This tended to prevent a unified French position against the dominant English-speaking group and thereby reduced the amount of English-French conflict.

TERRITORIAL ETHNIC BASE

Another factor that can influence the intensity of racial or ethnic conflict is whether ethnic minority groups are territorially based. When a subordinate group is concentrated in one part of a country and is a numerical majority in that area, its ability to mount an effective social movement is often strengthened. Its members are concentrated together and are frequently in a position to become dominant in their particular part of the country, even though they are subordinate in the nation as a whole. Accordingly, if ethnic conflicts exist, they may become more intense when the subordinate group is territorially based. Once English-French conflict in Canada came out into the open, the strength of the French-speaking group was enhanced by its concentration in Quebec province. This enabled the French speakers to elect leaders supportive of their cause and to change the province's language laws. As frequently happens when minorities are territorially based, a secessionist or separatist movement developed. Other minorities that have used a territorial base to develop powerful social movements include the Basques in northern Spain, the Flemish and Walloons in Belgium, and the Kurdish population in northwestern Iran.

LANGUAGE

When two ethnic groups speak different languages, the potential for conflict between them increases. Language has been the major bone of contention between French and English Canadians; it has also been a major source of conflict between the Flemish and Walloons in Belgium. In the United States, a growing Hispanic population has increasingly demanded bilingual education, has tended to continue to use Spanish, and has increasingly demanded ballots, social services materials, public documents, and product labels in Spanish. The intensity of debate on the issue observed by the author in his own race relations classes suggests that, as the Spanish population grows to become our largest minority group over the next twenty to thirty years, the potential for language-based conflict in the United States may greatly increase. Further evidence of this can be seen in the reaction of Dade Country, Florida, voters in the 1980 election to the growing Hispanic influence in the area. They voted to make English the county's only official language in an effort to end the county's practice of doing business on a bilingual basis.

INTERNATIONAL RELATIONSHIPS

Within any country, race and ethnic relations can be greatly influenced by international relations. In a nation that is in conflict with the country associated with one of its minority groups, members of that group are often in a very unenviable position. One of the clearest examples of this is the mass internment of Japanese-Americans—many of whom were U.S. citizens—in detention camps in the United States during World War II. In addition to being imprisoned for up to two years without trial or hearing, many American citizens of Japanese descent lost most of their possessions. Other groups placed at a disadvantage because of international conflicts include Chinese in Vietnam, Arabs in Israel, and Jews in Arab countries. In 1979 a number of Iranians (as well as some Latin Americans mistaken for Iranians) in the United States suffered physical attack or destruction of their property as a result of the taking of American hostages in Iran, even though some of the Iranians attacked did not even support the Iranian government with which the United States was at odds.

RACIAL VERSUS ETHNIC DIVISIONS

All else being equal, racial divisions tend to be more intense than ethnic divisions, if for no other reason than because race makes discrimination easier: It is possible to distinguish a racial group by appearance—something that is not possible with ethnic groups. Thus, the majority of the long, seemingly intractable intergroup conflicts in the world involve racial rather than ethnic divisions. An example of this was seen in the United States during World War II: Japanese-Americans, identifiable by appearance, were imprisoned in detention camps; German-Americans were not, even though the United States was at war with both Germany and Japan. This does not, of course, mean that ethnic conflicts can *never* become intense; Northern Ireland and Quebec clearly do have intense ethnic conflict. The point is that race, because of its visibility, can become a basis of discrimination and conflict more easily than ethnicity.

INTERNATIONAL PRESSURES

Finally, it is important to note another effect of international relations on majority-minority relations. In a highly complex world where no nation can afford to be isolated, international pressures can have important effects on race and ethnic relations within countries that are subjected to such pressures. Although just how effective such pressures can be is debatable, their importance cannot be totally discounted. Our discussion of Africa has already pointed to the potential importance of international pressures. International pressure from its African neighbors, the United States, Great Britain, and even to some extent South Africa, played a significant role in bringing about majority rule in Zimbabwe, though the threat of internal revolt was probably of greater importance. One reason for South Africa's ability to maintain white minority rule is that it has *not* been subjected to comparable pressure. Legum (1975) argues that a main factor in maintaining white supremacy in

South Africa is the absence of effective pressure from Western nations such as Britain and the United States. The United States, for example, continues to trade with South Africa, and American-owned corporations play an important role in the South African economy. Legum argues that only a real threat to Western interests (an example would be an immediate threat of a communist takeover in South Africa) will bring about Western intervention of a type that could bring about majority rule in South Africa. The recent history in Zimbabwe, where the threat of a guerrilla takeover moved Britain and the United States to pressure the Ian Smith government to surrender power, would appear to support Legum's view.

SUMMARY AND CONCLUSIONS

In this chapter, we have examined intergroup relations in a wide range of societies throughout the world. This examination has given rise to a number of generalizations. The most important one is that *no one factor* can explain the pattern of intergroup relations in any society: The factors involved in shaping a society's intergroup relations are always multiple and complex. Thus, *none of the generalizations we have made will hold for all societies*. In any society, there are counterforces that will modify the influence of any factor we might identify. Thus, while intense racial conflicts (that is, conflicts between groups different in appearance) develop more easily than intense ethnic conflicts, the particular history and social conditions present in Quebec and Northern Ireland have given rise to severe intergroup conflicts, even though both groups in both societies are white. With this caveat, we can summarize the generalizations arising from the societies we have examined in this chapter:

1. Societies in which the dominant group gained power through conquest or colonialism tend to have more racial or ethnic stratification and more intergroup conflict than societies without a history of colonialism or conquest. This is especially true if the subordinate group is indigenous to the area.
2. Modernization, urbanization, and development tend to facilitate the development of minority or indigenous group movements. This may, depending on a number of factors, lead either to increased fluidity of intergroup relations or to continued rigidity with rising levels of conflict. Typically, a move toward greater fluidity in racial or ethnic relations leads to social differentiation on the basis of a wider range of characteristics.
3. Societies with a large number of racial and ethnic classifications tend to have more harmonious intergroup relations than societies where the bulk of the populations is classified into two major groups. This is especially true where no group is a numerical majority.
4. The cultural and demographic characteristics of the two or more groups involved in intergroup relations will have important effects on the pattern of relations between the groups.

5. Societies with cross-cutting cleavages will experience less intergroup conflict than societies with overlapping cleavages.
6. Ethnic groups with a territorial base will tend to be in a stronger power position and will resort more readily to conflict strategies than will groups without a territorial base.
7. Ethnic conflicts tend to be more intense when the groups involved speak different languages.
8. International conflicts with a nation associated with a minority group tend to result in hostility toward and subordination of the minority group.
9. Racial divisions tend to be more intense than ethnic divisions.
10. International pressure can cause dominant groups to change their treatment of subordinate groups, though the degree to which this is true is uncertain.

These generalizations help us to further evaluate usefulness of the social-psychological, functionalist, and conflict perspectives for understanding the dynamics of intergroup relations. Item 4, and to a lesser extent, items 7 to 9, do suggest some importance of the patterns of attitude in a society, as the social psychological perspective suggests. However, attitudes relevant to these generalizations are determined to a considerable degree by large-scale characteristics of the society. Clearly, much that is attitudinal is a product of society; only through an understanding of culture and social structure can the pattern of intergroup relations in any society be understood. Within the broad area of social-structural effects, some support is found in these generalizations for both the functionalist and conflict perspectives. In support of the functionalist view, generalization 2, insofar as it concerns a move toward more fluid intergroup relations in some modern societies, recognizes that patterns of intergroup relations that may be functional in modern societies differ from those that are functional in traditional societies. Items 4, 7, 8, and 9 implicitly recognize the importance of ethnocentrism, which is stressed by the functionalist perspective as a cause of ethnic inequality and conflict. On the other hand, there is also considerable support for the importance of competition and conflict in majority-minority relations, as stressed by the conflict theory. Generalization 1, which is crucial, recognizes the importance of one group's (the colonizer) opportunity to benefit at the expense of another (the indigenous group) in a context of unequal power. Items 2, 3, 6, and 10 all stress the importance of power as a variable shaping intergroup relations throughout the world. Thus, three general conclusions regarding the major perspectives seem warranted. First, variations in large-scale social structure and culture seem to be the most important factors determining what kind of intergroup relations a society will have. Second, both the order (functionalist) and conflict perspectives make important contributions to the understanding of intergroup relations in a worldwide context. Third, the power relationship between two groups and whether or not one has ever been in a position to gain at the expense of the other are probably the most important factors determining the kind of relations any two groups will have.

Amalgamation The combination of two racial or ethnic groups into one through marriage or other sexual contact between the groups. Gradually, the distinction between the two groups becomes blurred, and they come to be regarded as a single group.

Cross-cutting cleavages The situation in which societal divisions such as race, language, religion, and class all cut along different lines; there are, for example, religious divisions within racial groups. Cross-cutting cleavages tend to hold down the amount of intergroup conflict, because people have divided loyalties.

Indigenous Group A racial or ethnic group that is well established in an area prior to the arrival of some new group. An indigenous group may be, but does not have to be, native to the area in which it is established.

Overlapping cleavages The situation in which societal divisions such as race, religion, class, and language all cut along the same lines. In this situation there tends to be a great deal of conflict because no matter what the issue, people are always on the same side.

MAJORITY-MINORITY
RELATIONS IN AMERICA TODAY:
THE ROLE OF INSTITUTIONAL
DISCRIMINATION

The Status of Majority and Minority Groups in the United States Today

8

MAJOR RACIAL AND ETHNIC GROUPS: OVERVIEW AND GENERAL STATISTICS

In Chapter 8 we shall examine the major racial and ethnic groups in American society today—who they are, their numbers and geographic distribution, and their social status. We shall also explore the current debate over whether the status of minority groups in American society is improving and, if so, by how much and in what areas. In this first section, we shall present general information about a number of racial and ethnic groups in American society. Some closely fit the definition of *minority group* presented in Chapter 1, some fit the definition of *majority, or dominant*, group, and some fall somewhere between.

Minority Groups

As we indicated in Chapter 1, the three groups that most closely fit the definition of minority group are blacks, or Afro-Americans; Latinos, or Hispanic Americans (actually composed of several distinct subgroups); and Indian people, or Native Americans (again, a larger grouping composed of many distinct sub-groups). We shall now present general information about each of these major groups.

Blacks   Blacks are the largest minority group in the United States. According to the 1980 Census, there are 26.5 million black people in the United States, which constitutes 11.7 percent of the total population (U.S. Bureau of the Census, 1981, p.1). For a variety of reasons, this estimate is probably somewhat low. The 1970 census, for example, apparently missed 7 to 8 percent of the black population; the 1960 census, 8 to 9 percent (U.S. Bureau of the Census, 1979a, p. 10). All indications are that this undercount has been reduced in the 1980 census, though it certainly has not been completely eliminated. It is believed that the 1980 census missed about 5% of the black population. Thus, it is possible that the true black population at the beginning of the 1980s may exceed 27 million, or 12 percent of the total population.

Today, as in the past, the majority of black people in the United States live in the South. According to the 1970 Census, 53 percent of the black population lived in the South (U.S. Bureau of the Census, 1979a). (See figure 8.1, p. 209.) That was the lowest percentage recorded by any census up to that time, reflecting the long period of black migration out of the South from the late nineteenth century to the mid-twentieth century (U.S. Bureau of Census, 1979a). All indications are that this black outmigration from the South ended in the early 1970s, and that since then, more black people have moved into than out of the South. Many who had previously moved out of the South have returned in recent years (Biggar, 1979, p. 29). Consequently, the 1980 Census also showed that 53 percent of the black population lived in the South (U.S. Bureau of the Census, 1981, p. 1). This reversal has occurred for several reasons. First, as it became apparent that the North was not the racial paradise that many southern blacks once believed it was, many black migrants found it very sensible to return to the South, where many of their families still resided and where the mores, life style, and, undoubtedly, the weather and climate were more familiar to them. Another important factor is the general nationwide pattern of jobs and population moving toward the Sun Belt. During the past decade economic growth has been greater in the South than in the North, and blacks, as well as others, have moved South to take advantage of the newly created opportunities. Indeed, the white population has also experienced substantial net migration into the South during the 1970s. In addition, there was also net black migration into the West during the middle and late 1970s (Biggar, 1979, p. 29).

The remainder—somewhat less than half—of the black population that lives outside the South is fairly evenly spread across the Northeast and Midwest, with a smaller but growing number in the West. In 1980, 18.3 percent of black people in the United States lived in the Northeast, 20.1 percent in the North Central states (Midwest), and 8.5 percent in the West (U.S. Bureau of the Census, 1981, p.6).

The black population is highly urbanized. Although it was more rural than the population as a whole during the early twentieth century, today it is more urban. As of 1978, 75 percent of all blacks in the United States lived in metropolitan areas, compared to 66 percent of all whites (U.S. Bureau of the Census, 1979b, p. 34). The black population is particularly concentrated in the large industrial cities of the

Great Lakes and Northeast regions, as well as the cities in the South (though there are more rural blacks in the South than anywhere else). Compared to the population as a whole, the black population is much more highly concentrated in large central cities and much less suburbanized. Over half (55 percent) of all blacks live in central cities. In the total population, only 28 percent live in central cities, and 39 percent in suburbs (U.S. Bureau of the Census, 1979b, p. 34). Although relatively few blacks live in suburbs (only about 5 percent of all suburbanites are black), black migration from the city to the suburbs has increased somewhat during the 1970s.

A final important observation can be made about the black population of the United States: It is younger than the population as a whole. In 1978, 37.9 percent of the black population was under eighteen years of age. This compares to 29.6 percent for the total population and 28.4 percent for the white population. The median age of the black population in 1980 was 24.9—five years younger than the median age for the total population, 30.0 (U.S. Bureau of the Census, 1981, p. 3).

Hispanic Americans   The second largest minority group in the United States is Hispanic Americans, also known as Latinos or as Americans of Spanish origin (the Census's Bureau's term). This umbrella label covers at least four distinct groups: Mexican-Americans, or Chicanos; Puerto Ricans; Cuban Americans; and Central and South Americans. There are also a number of Hispanic Americans who do not fit neatly into any of these categories. Table 8.1 presents Census Bureau estimates of the number of Hispanic Americans in 1979. As can be seen in the table, these estimates indicate a total of about twelve million Americans of Spanish origin, a majority of whom are Mexican-Americans. The total Hispanic population, according to this estimate, is about 5.5 percent of the U.S. population. More recent data from the 1980 census indicate that the Hispanic population as of 1980 is 14.6 million, or 6.4 percent of the United States population, though a breakdown by group was not available as of this writing. As is the case with Census Bureau statistics on blacks, it is known that these estimates are lower than the actual Spanish-origin population. For a number of reasons, including language barriers and the existence of some illegal immigration from Latin American countries in

Table 8.1   Americans of Spanish Origin

GROUP	1978 POPULATION IN MILLIONS	PERCENT OF TOTAL SPANISH ORIGIN
Chicanos	7.326	60.6%
Puerto Ricans	1.748	14.5
Cuban Americans	.794	6.6
Central and South American	.840	7.0
Other Spanish Origin	1.371	11.4
Total	12.079	100.0

Source: U.S. Bureau of the Census, 1980a, p.1.

recent years, the underestimate of the Spanish population is probably greater than the underestimate of the black population, though there is some disagreement on its exact size. There is little doubt, however, that the census figure is significantly below the true figure for persons of Spanish origin. It has been estimated, for example, that as many as 5 to 8 million persons of Spanish origin may be illegally present in the United States (St. Louis Post Dispatch, 1978; Des Moines Register, 1978), though some demographers regard these estimates as too high because they do not consider return migration out of the United States by illegal immigrants. In any case, there is little doubt that some of these illegal immigrants have tried to avoid being counted in the census for fear of detection, which in turn has caused the census figures to be lower than the actual Hispanic population. In spite of the illegal immigration, it should be stressed that the great majority of persons of Spanish origin in the United States are present legally; most are U.S. citizens, and some have lived in the United States for generations. If we correct for the census undercount of the Hispanic population, it appears likely that the true Hispanic population of the United States is in excess of 15 million, and possibly as high as 18 or 19 million.

The Hispanic population is one of the fastest-growing population groups in the United States, partly because Latinos have a relatively high birth rate, and partly because their immigration rate, both legal and illegal, has been among the highest of any group in recent years. Officially, the Hispanic population increased by about 50 percent between 1970 and 1980, and the actual rate of growth may have been even higher. Most experts believe that by sometime in the 1990s the Hispanic population will exceed the black population, making Latinos the nation's largest minority group.

The Hispanic population is even more urban than the black population. In 1978, fully 85 percent of the Spanish-origin population lived in metropolitan areas (U.S. Bureau of the Census, 1979c). Though there is some variation among the various groups, all Hispanic groups are over 80 percent urban. Although many people associate them with agricultural labor, 81 percent of all Mexican-Americans live in metropolitan areas. This percentage is higher than that of either the white or black population. Like blacks, Latinos are heavily concentrated in central cities; 51 percent of all Americans of Spanish origin lived in central cities in 1978, a figure that is almost as high as that for blacks and well above the figure for whites. Hispanic Americans are more suburbanized than blacks but less suburbanized than whites; 34 percent of the Hispanic population lived in suburbs in 1978 (U.S. Bureau of the Census, 1979b).

The Chicano population is heavily concentrated in five Southwestern states: California, Texas, Arizona, New Mexico, and Colorado; 60 percent of all Hispanic Americans and 87 percent of all Chicanos live in these five states (U.S. Bureau of the Census, 1979c). There are, however, also sizable concentrations of Mexican-Americans in several midwestern and northeastern states; Illinois and Michigan are notable examples.

Although Chicanos are often associated in the public mind with agricultural labor (and it is true that many farmworkers are Chicanos), the fact is that all three major Hispanic groups in the United States—Chicanos, Puerto Ricans, and Cuban-Americans—are more urbanized than the American population as a whole. Marc Anderson.

The Puerto Rican population is heavily concentrated in the urban Northeast, particularly the New York City area. As a result of this concentration, 11.4 percent of the total Latino population lives in New York State, giving it the third largest Latino population of any state, behind only California and Texas (U.S. Bureau of the Census, 1981, p.6). There are also sizable Puerto Rican populations in several other northeastern cities; Boston is a notable example.

The Cuban-American population, largely refugees from the Castro government and their descendants, is heavily concentrated in Florida, particularly the Miami area. According to the 1980 Census, over 850,000 Hispanic persons lived in Florida, the fourth largest total of any state. There are, however, also sizable numbers of Cuban-Americans in some parts of the Northeast.

As a whole, Latinos are one of the youngest ethnic groups in the United States. As of 1978, 42 percent of all Hispanic Americans were less than eighteen years old, which is a higher proportion than for blacks and about a time and a half as high as for whites. The median age of Hispanic Americans in 1980 was 23.2, about seven years younger than for the American population as a whole (U.S. Bureau of the Census, 1981, p. 3).

Indian People   Up-to-date and detailed statistics are more difficult to obtain for Indian people, because their relatively small numbers make it impossible to obtain reliable data on them from the Census Bureau's ongoing Current Population Surveys, the major source of current data on black and Hispanic Americans. The main source of data on Indian people is the U.S. Census, which has been taken every ten years but is now tentatively planned for every five years, with the first mid-decade census planned for 1985, depending on funding. According to the 1970 census, the Indian and Alaskan native population was about 793,000 (U.S. Bureau of the Census, 1972). By 1980, this population had risen to 1.4 million, or 0.6 percent of the U.S. population. In part this represents real growth, but much of the increase is probably the result of people of mixed parentage classifying themselves as Indian rather than white—the census determines race on the basis of self reports. In recent years, people of mixed parentage have increasingly come to think of themselves as Indian. The 1.4 million total today reflects substantial and real growth in the Indian population from a low point of around 250,000 just before the turn of the century (Driver, 1969). It is, however, no more than and probably substantially *less* than the Native American population prior to the decimation of the native population by warfare and, especially, European diseases that followed the arrival of whites on the continent. (Driver, 1969; Dobyns, 1966; Kroeber, 1939).

In 1980, 50.7 percent of the Indian population lived in the West, 26.2 percent in the South, 17.5 percent in the North Central states, and 5.5 percent in the Northeast. However, just three states, Oklahoma, California, and Arizona, account for fully 37 percent of the Indian population (U. S. Bureau of the Census, 1981, p.6). (The regional distribution of all three minority groups we have discussed is illustrated in Figure 8.1.)

American Indians are the only minority group that is *less* urbanized than the population as a whole. In 1970 fewer than half, 45 percent, of Indian people in the United States lived in urban areas; 55 percent lived in rural areas. Today, a majority of Indian people may live in urban areas; there was considerable urbanization between the 1960 and 1970 censuses and probably some further urbanization during the 1970s.

Not only are Indian people more rural than any other group, they also frequently become less permanently linked to the city even when they do move there. Urban Indians frequently live in cities near the reservation where they grew up. They tend to maintain close ties with the reservation, often remaining active in its cultural, social, and religious affairs. They also return to the reservation frequently for weekend visits and are visited by friends who still live on the reservation (Steele, 1972, 1975). Urban Indians also oftentimes view their residence in the city as a temporary sojourn and return to the reservation after a period of living in the city.

The Indian population is probably the youngest of any major American racial or ethnic group. As of the 1980 Census, 43.8 percent of all Indian people in the United States were under twenty. The median age of Native Americans was 23.0 (U.S. Bureau of the Census, 1981, p.3).

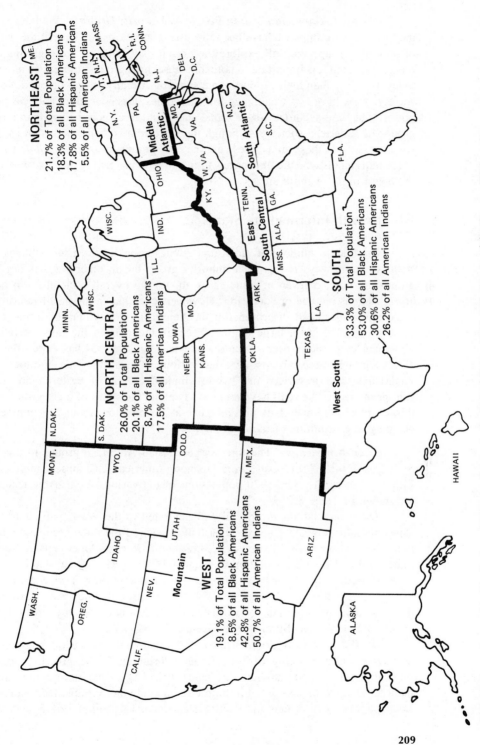

NORTHEAST

21.7% of Total Population
18.3% of all Black Americans
17.8% of all Hispanic Americans
5.5% of all American Indians

NORTH CENTRAL

26.0% of Total Population
20.1% of all Black Americans
8.7% of all Hispanic Americans
17.5% of all American Indians

SOUTH

33.3% of Total Population
53.0% of all Black Americans
30.6% of all Hispanic Americans
26.2% of all American Indians

WEST

19.1% of Total Population
8.5% of all Black Americans
42.8% of all Hispanic Americans
50.7% of all American Indians

ME.
N.H.
VT.
MASS.
R.I.
CONN.
N.Y.
PA.
N.J.
DEL.
MD.
D.C.
Middle Atlantic
N.C.
VA.
W. VA.
S.C.
FLA.
South Atlantic
KY.
TENN.
GA.
East South Central
ALA.
MISS.
ARK.
LA.
OKLA.
TEXAS
West South
OHIO
IND.
ILL.
WISC.
MINN.
WISC.
S. DAK.
IOWA
MO.
NEBR.
KANS.
N. DAK.
MONT.
WYO.
COLO.
N. MEX.
UTAH
IDAHO
NEV.
WASH.
OREG.
CALIF.
ARIZ.
Mountain
HAWAII
ALASKA

Figure 8.1 Geographic Distribution of Minority Groups in the United States, 1980. U.S. Bureau of the Census, 1981, p. 6.

209

Blacks, Latinos, and Indian People as Minority Groups   We have said that the three major groups we have been discussing are those that best fit the definition of minority group. We will explore the present-day status of these groups later in this chapter, but it is important to note that these three groups, more than any others, today have less than their proportionate share of virtually all resources in American society. They have less wealth and lower incomes, less education, and less political power. They are accorded lower social status and live shorter lives than any other groups in American society. Although there are some other groups that suffer low status in *some* of these areas, these are the only groups that, *on the whole* (there are many individuals who are exceptions to the general pattern) suffer low status across the board in *all* of these areas.

Groups with Intermediate Status

There are a number of racial and ethnic groups in the United States whose status in some ways is that of a minority group but in other ways is not. These groups are near, or even in some cases above, the overall societal norm in some areas, such as income or education. However, each has in the past been or is now subject to widespread discrimination in American society. Furthermore, each of these groups has, to a large degree, been excluded from the upper echelons of American corporate power structure, or what Mills (1956) has called the power elite. Among these groups are the various Asian-American groups, Jewish Americans, and a variety of "white ethnic" groups of eastern and southern European origin. We shall have more to say about the status of these groups later in this chapter; here we shall present general infromation about the numbers and geographic distribution of these groups.

Asian-Americans   The three largest Asian-American groups in the United States, as of the 1970 Census, were Japanese-Americans, Chinese-Americans, and Filipino-Americans. The 1970 populations of the various Asian-American groups are shown in Table 8.2.

These populations are heavily concentrated in the West, particularly in the states of California and Hawaii. Over half of each of the three groups live in these two states. There is also a large concentration of Chinese-Americans in New York State, with a Chinese population of over 80,000. Lesser but substantial numbers (over 10,000) of the other two groups are also found in New York State and of all three groups in Illinois. Overall, in 1980, 59.5 percent of Asian-Americans lived in the West, 16.0 percent in the Northeast, 13.4 percent in the South, and 11.1 percent in the Midwest (U.S. Bureau of the Census, 1981, p.6).

By 1980, a fourth group, Vietnamese Americans, had become numerous due to the large influx of refugees from Vietnam during the 1970s, growing rapidly to a population of several hundred thousand. This large-scale immigration of Vietnamese, along with substantial immigration among other groups, led to an increase in the population of Asians and Pacific Islanders to 3.4 million, or 1.5 percent of the

Table 8.2   1970 Population of Asian-American Groups (to nearest 1000)

Japanese-Americans	591,000
Chinese-Americans	435,000
Filipino-Americans	343,000

Source: U.S. Bureau of the Census, 1972.

U.S. population—about double the 1970 total (U.S. Bureau of the Census, 1981, p. 6).

All Asian-American groups are highly urban. Fully 97 percent of all Chinese-Americans live in urban areas. Among Japanese-Americans, the corresponding figure is 89 percent, and among Filipinos, 86 percent (Office of Special Concerns, 1974). Chinese-Americans predominantly live in central cities rather than suburbs; just over two thirds of all Chinese-Americans live in central cities. Four urban areas account for the majority of the Chinese-American population: San Francisco—Oakland, New York City, Honolulu, and Los Angeles—Long Beach. Most of these urban Chinese Americans live in the central-city neighborhoods known as the Chinatowns. In addition to the cities mentioned, Chicago and Boston also have sizable Chinatowns.

Compared to the Chinese, Japanese-Americans and Filipino-Americans are more suburbanized, but more of them live in central cities than anywhere else. About 48 percent of each of these groups live in central cities, compared to 28 percent of the total population (Office of Special Concerns, 1974).

Japanese Americans are, on the average, older than the population as a whole, with a median age of 32.4. Chinese- and Filipino-Americans, on the other hand, are somewhat younger than the population as a whole, with median ages of 26.7 and 26.1 respectively (U.S. Bureau of the Census, 1973b pp. 593—594).

Although the majority of Asian-Americans fit into one of the groups discussed above, there are some who do not. There were, for example, about 71,000 Korean-Americans living in the United States as of the 1970 Census (U.S. Bureau of the Census, 1973b, p. 594).

Jewish Americans   Accurate data on Jewish Americans and other white ethnic groups are more difficult to obtain and less reliable than data on the other groups we have been discussing. The Census does not ask people their religion, and only incomplete data (first- and second-generation immigrants) were obtained on nationality before the 1980 census.

The best guess is that the Jewish population of the United States is slightly above 6 million, or 3 percent of the U.S. population (Goren, 1980, p. 571). This is about half the world's Jewish population. The U.S. Jewish population is growing less rapidly than the population as a whole because of its relatively low birth rate.

The Jewish population is highly urbanized. In 1957, the last year for which good data are available, 96 percent of all Jewish Americans lived in urban areas (U.S. Bureau of the Census, 1958). In particular, a sizable proportion lives in the Greater New York City metropolitan area. This is reflected in the regional distribution of Jewish Americans: About 64 percent of them live in the Northeast. The remainder are somewhat evenly distributed through the Midwest, South, and West.

Eastern and Southern European "White Ethnics"   The term "white ethnics" is applied to a wide variety of groups from eastern and southern Europe. As a general rule, these groups have immigrated to the United States somewhat more recently than the groups from northern and western Europe. The bulk of the eastern and southern European migration arrived after 1900, during the early part of the twentieth century. Much of the Italian population, for example, came in one decade, 1901–1910. In contrast, immigration from Ireland peaked in the 1850s and immigration from Germany peaked in the 1880s (Thomlinson, 1976).

The eastern and southern European "white ethnics" include, among others, Italian, Polish, Greek, Russian, Hungarian, Czechoslovakian, and Ukrainian Americans. A 1972 survey by the Census Bureau indicated that the largest of these groups was Italian-Americans, with a population of about 8.8 million. Next came Polish-Americans at 5.1 million, and Russian-Americans at 2.2 million (U.S. Bureau of the Census, 1973b). Many of the latter group are also Jewish. Although this survey did not cover Greek-Americans, membership in the Greek Orthodox Church—nearly 2 million in 1977 (Jacquet, 1979)—is suggestive of the size of that group.

The majority of these ethnic groups are concentrated in the Northeast and in the Great Lakes states. This is reflected in 1970 statistics, which show that in Massachusetts, New York, Rhode Island, Connecticut, and New Jersey, 30 percent or more of the population was of foreign stock (U.S. Bureau of the Census, 1972b, p. 472). Eastern and southern Europeans also make up a substantial portion of the population in Illinois, Michigan, Wisconsin, and the northern parts of Ohio and Indiana. For the most part, these ethnic groups are highly urban; they are heavily concentrated in the large industrial cities of the above-mentioned regions.

A final important characteristic of these groups is that they generally belong to religions outside the Protestant majority in the United States. The majority of eastern and southern Europeans are Catholic. This is particularly true for Italians and Poles, though a sizable portion of the latter are Jewish. A large part of the Russian-American population also is Jewish; much of the remainder is Russian Orthodox. The various Slavic groups tend to belong to one of the Eastern Orthodox churches, as do Greek Americans, who typically belong to the Greek Orthodox Church.

Whites from Western and Northern Europe: A Dominant Group within a Dominant Group

In contemporary America the groups that most clearly fit the definition of majority or dominant group are whites from western and northern Europe. Certainly whites as a whole are in a dominant position relative to blacks, Chicanos, American

Indians and, to a lesser degree, Asian-Americans. Within that white population, however, the most advantaged groups are those from western and northern Europe. The largest and most established among these groups are the English, Scots, and Welsh, who totaled 29.5 million, or 14.4 percent of the population in 1972. Nearly as large a group are the Germans, who totaled 25.5 million, or 12.5 percent of the population. The Irish, who numbered 16.4 million, make up 8 percent of the population. Combined, these three groups are over one third of the U.S. population (U.S. Bureau of the Census, 1973b).

There are other, smaller, groups that also are of northern and western European origin; among these are Americans of French, Dutch, and Scandinavian (Swedish, Norwegian, and Danish) origin.

As a general rule, these groups immigrated earlier than most of the eastern and southern Europeans, though Scandinavians are something of an exception in this regard. Partly because of this, these groups tend to be more assimilated into American society and less conscious of ethnicity than other groups we have discussed, though some ethnic awareness persists in all American ethnic groups and may be on the rise in many.

The British groups (English, Scots, Welsh), a sizable proportion of the Germans, and the Scandinavians and Dutch are predominantly Protestant. These are the groups that form the core of the so-called WASP (white Anglo-Saxon Protestant) population. Most of the rest of the Germans and the majority of the Irish are Catholic, although there are many Irish, particularly in the South, who belong to fundamentalist Protestant churches.

For the most part, these groups are quite widely distributed geographically. The most notable exceptions are the Scandinavian groups, which are largely concentrated in the upper Midwest.

As we have indicated, these groups are generally in a dominant socioeconomic position. They tend to have relatively high economic, educational, and occupational levels, and relatively low rates of poverty, though there is some variation by both nationality and religion. Data from large scale surveys by the National Opinion Research Center indicate, for example, that among eleven white Catholic and Protestant ethnic groups, the four highest occupational prestige ratings were among British Protestants, Irish Catholics, German Catholics, and German Protestants in that order (Greeley, 1977, p. 60). In urban areas outside the South, Scandinavian Protestants also ranked close to these four groups (Greeley, 1977, p. 61; see also Greeley, 1974).

STATUS OF MINORITY GROUPS
IN AMERICA TODAY

In the following sections, we shall focus in greater detail on the racial and ethnic groups in American society that we have identified as minority groups. We shall examine in detail the social and economic status of these groups, with special attention to the growing debate over whether the status of minority groups in the United States has improved significantly. We shall first present evidence of improvement in the status of minorities, then examine some evidence of continuing racial and ethnic inequality in America. We shall then attempt to see how the two balance.

Evidence of Improvement in Minority Status

There are some social indicators that suggest substantial improvement in the status of minorities between about 1940 and 1980. Some of the trends are fairly recent; others have been under way since around World War II.

One indication of improved status among minorities can be seen in their occupational structure. One indicator of a group's occupational status is the number or proportion of group members who hold professional or managerial positions. Among blacks the number of persons in professional occupations more than tripled between 1960 and 1975. The number of blacks in management positions increased by about 2¼ times. Among whites; people in professional occupations increased by only about 1⅔ times; people in managerial positions, by about 1¼ times (U.S. Department of Commerce, 1977, p. 377). In other words, the number of blacks in high-status jobs grew at a relatively faster rate than did the number of whites in such jobs. Latinos, too, experienced a more rapid growth in high status jobs than did whites during this period (Moore, 1976, p. 64; U.S. Bureau of the Census, 1979c, p. 26). Thus, by the late 1970s, a substantially higher proportion of the black and Latino populations held high-status occupations in the United States than ever before, though that proportion was still lower for both blacks and Latinos than it was for whites.

Among those who are employed, the gap in individual incomes between minorities and whites has declined substantially over the past thirty years. In 1950, for example, the median income of employed black males was around 60 percent of the median income of employed white males. By 1975 it was nearly 75 percent—a substantial closing of the gap (U.S. Department of Commerce, 1977, p. 459; U.S. Bureau of the Census, 1979a; Freeman, 1978). In 1975 the income of employed black women was nearly as high as that of employed white women—97 percent, according to Freeman. In the early 1950s it was only about half as high. If we focus on the subgroup of *young* workers who have just recently *finished college,* the gap has been practically eliminated. As an example of this, black male college graduates between the ages of twenty-five and twenty-nine earn 93 percent as much as comparable white males (Freeman, 1978, p. 59).

In the area of political representation, there is also evidence of substantial minority gain. Between 1970 and 1977, the number of black elected officials in the United States more than tripled, rising from around 1,300 in 1970 to over 4,500 in 1979 (U.S. Bureau of the Census, 1979f). This figure includes 162 black mayors

(Hamilton, 1978). Among the major cities that have elected black mayors are Los Angeles, Detroit, Washington, Atlanta, New Orleans, and Birmingham, Alabama—the city that had been a national symbol of resistance to black rights during the early 1960s. During the 1970s two states, Arizona and New Mexico, elected Chicano governors. Between 1965 and 1973 the number of Spanish-surnamed legislators in five southwestern states nearly doubled, increasing from thirty-five to sixty-six (Moore, 1976, p. 156). In 1981, San Antonio became the first major city to elect a Chicano mayor. Thus, it is clear that both blacks and Chicanos have made very substantial gains in political representation during the past ten to fifteen years.

Finally, it is important to reiterate that deliberate racial discrimination is today illegal and less common than in the past. This in itself is a dramatic change, considering that as recently as thirty years ago, such discrimination was not only legal and widespread but, in some parts of the country, required by law. This decline in deliberate discrimination has, as we have indicated, been accompanied by some rather dramatic reductions in prejudice in the population.

It seems clear from these data, then, that in at least some areas there *has* been substantial improvement in the status of minority group members in America. An important factor in this improvement has been the rise of minority group social movements, which was discussed at length in Chapter 6.

Despite these apparent gains, some hard questions must still be asked. First, we must ask, despite whatever progress has occurred, how much inequality and racism still persists? More specifically, what is the standing of minorities relative to that of whites in America today? The fact that minorities have gained in certain areas does not necessarily mean either that they have caught up or that *all* minority group members have gained at all. Finally, we must ask what is the absolute level of living among minorities today? We shall turn to these questions in the next section.

Evidence of Continuing Majority-Minority Inequality

Economics   Despite the progress we have seen among some segments of the minority population, the overall picture today continues to be one of serious majority-minority inequality in the economic arena. One important indicator of economic well-being is median family income. The median family income for all white, black, and Spanish-origin families in 1978 is shown in Table 8.3. These data clearly show that, whatever gains have been made, the income of Latinos and, even more so, blacks, remains substantially below that of whites. Indeed, the figure for blacks represents only a small gain relative to whites over the past forty years: In the 1940s median family income for blacks was about 50 percent of what it was for whites. Today, it is about 59 percent.

Another indicator of the economic position of a group is the proportion of its members who are below the federally defined poverty level (approximately $6,200

Table 8.3   Median Family Income, 1978: Whites, Blacks, and Persons of Spanish Origin

	MEDIAN FAMILY INCOME	PERCENT OF WHITE MEDIAN FAMILY INCOME
White	$18,368	—
Black	10,879	58.6
Spanish Origin	12,566	68.4

Source: U.S. Bureau of the Census, 1980b.

for a family of four, $3100 for a single individual in 1977, but adjusted for inflation annually). In 1977, 8.9 percent of the white population, but 31.3 percent of the black population and 22.4 percent of the Spanish-origin population had incomes below the poverty level (U.S. Bureau of the Census, 1979e). In other words, black people are more than three times as likely as white people to be poor, and Latinos are about two and a half times as likely as Anglos to be poor. Recent statistics are not available for Indian people, but the 1970 Census indicated that in 1969, 39 percent of the Indian population had incomes below the poverty level—a higher percentage than any of the other groups.

A final indicator of economic status is the unemployment rate. Here, too, substantial inequalities are evident. For 1980 the unemployment rate for whites was 6.3 percent. For blacks and other races, it was 14.1 percent. For Hispanic Americans, it was 10.1 percent (Wescott and Bednarzik, 1981, p. 7). Among Indians on reservations in 1973 the unemployment rate was 38 percent. Thus, we see that the unemployment rate for blacks is more than twice as high as for whites; for Latinos, nearly twice as high, and, for reservation Indians, considerably higher, though recent data are not available.

In general, black unemployment has been about twice as high as white unemployment since the end of World War II. Prior to that time, during the 1920s and 1930s, blacks and whites had very similar unemployment rates (Wilson, 1978). However, since the war there has been a drastic reduction in the number of low-skill, low-pay, dead-end jobs that many blacks had occupied. In general, a sizable segment of the black population has continued to be excluded from the opportunity to learn skills necessary for better jobs, and the disappearance of the unskilled jobs has left many of those individuals unemployed (Wilson, 1978).

The problem of minority unemployment becomes even greater if we focus on particular segments of the minority population. Among young black urban males, for example, the unemployment rate is believed to be in the range of 40 percent to 50 percent.

Taken as a whole, these economic data indicate that very substantial inequalities between whites and minorities persist. While a segment of the black and Hispanic population today enjoys relatively high incomes and good jobs, another large segment of the minority population can only be described as trapped at the bottom of the socioeconomic structure. For this group things are not getting better;

In the United States today, there is a large and growing minority middle class. At the same time, however, other minority group members remain poor, and the proportion of minorities in the impoverished "underclass" is far greater than the proportion of whites in the underclass. Top, Marc Anderson; bottom, Irene Springer.

indeed, relative to everyone else they are probably getting worse. If we examine the minority population as a whole, two conclusions appear evident. First, among the black and Hispanic populations there is increasing stratification and a growing gap between a segment that is relatively well-off and another segment that is impoverished and struggling for survival. Second, if we take the overall minority population, the *average* economic positions of blacks, Latinos, and Indians remain substantially lower than the average position of whites, and the average positions have improved only marginally relative to the position of whites.

Political Representation   As we have seen earlier in this chapter, the political representation of black and Hispanic Americans has risen dramatically during the past decade. Nonetheless, the political representation of these groups remains well below their share of the population. In 1977, for example, there were sixteen blacks in the U.S. House of Representatives, and one in the U.S. Senate (Hamilton, 1978). These figures work out to about 4 percent and 1 percent, respectively, for a group that makes up nearly twelve percent of the population. In the Congress elected in 1978, there were still sixteen blacks in the House but none in the Senate—the only black senator was defeated in his reelection campaign. Overall, the total number of black elected officials is less than 1 percent of all elected officials (Joint Center for Political Studies, 1977). In 1980 there were still no black governors, and no black person had ever been elected President or Vice President or even received the Democratic or Republican nomination for either of these offices.

Among Hispanic Americans, the underrepresentation is even greater. In California, for example, 16 percent of the population is Chicano, but only 5 percent of the state legislature seats and 2 percent of all elected officials in the mid-1970s were Chicano. It is thus evident that for Chicanos, as for blacks, recent gains in political representation have not yet approached a share of representation proportionate to the group's population.

Education   Data on the educational attainment in 1979 for whites, blacks, and Americans of Spanish Origin are shown in Tables 8.4, 8.5, and 8.6. Table 8.4 shows median years of school completed—a good overall measure of a group's educational status. These data indicate that in the population over twenty-five, there is a gap of a little more than half a year between the median black position and the

Table 8.4   Median Years of School Completed by Age, for Whites, Blacks, and Americans of Spanish Origin, 1979

| | *AGE* | | |
	25+	**18+**	**20-24**
White	12.5	12.5	12.8
Black	11.9	12.1	12.5
Spanish Origin	10.3	11.3	12.3

Source: U.S. Bureau of the Census, 1980c, pp. 23-27.

Table 8.5   Percent High School Graduates by Age, for Whites,
              Blacks, and Americans of Spanish Origin, 1979

| | AGE | | |
	25+	18+	20-24
White	69.7	71.5	85.7
Black	49.4	53.6	75.0
Spanish Origin	42.0	45.7	61.7

Source: U.S. Bureau of the Census, 1980c, pp. 23-27.

Table 8.6   Percent of Population with Four or More Years
              of College by Age, for Whites, Blacks, and Americans
              of Spanish Origin, 1977

	25+	AGE	25-29
White	17.2		24.3
Black	7.9		12.4
Spanish Origin	6.7		7.3

Source: U.S. Bureau of the Census, 1980c, pp. 23-27

median white position, and more than a two year gap between Latinos and whites. However, if we add younger adults to the total and look at everyone over eighteen, the gap decreases to less than half a year for blacks and a year and a half for Latinos. This would appear to suggest that despite substantial educational inequality among the total population, the gap is decreasing among younger adults who have recently come through the educational system. This is confirmed by looking at the third column of Table 8.4, which shows that among young adults only (ages twenty to twenty-four), the gap is only three tenths of a year for blacks and half a year for Latinos. Thus, inequality in the *amount* of education has been greatly reduced (though not eliminated) among young black and Hispanic Americans who have recently come through the educational system. This pattern is confirmed in Table 8.5, which shows the percentage of the three groups who have graduated from high school. The intergroup gap is great when we look at the whole adult population, particularly those twenty-five and over who would have graduated by 1970 or 1971. Among *young* adults, however, the gap is again reduced but not eliminated. Note that Hispanic young adults, in particular, remain well below white young adults on this measure. Black young adults are also behind but not by as much.

The figures on college graduation indicate less improvement in the standing of blacks and Latinos relative to whites. While the proportion of college graduates among the younger population *relative to* the population over twenty-five shows somewhat more gain among blacks than among whites, the proportion of college graduates among young blacks (twenty-five to twenty-nine) remains only about half as high as among whites the same age. Among Latinos the picture is even more dismal. The percentage of Latinos between the ages of twenty-five and twenty-nine who have completed four years of college is barely higher than the percentage for all Latinos over twenty-five, and relative to the figures for the white population in the same age group, it is lower.

Data on current college enrollment are also instructive. In 1978, about 10.4 percent of U.S. college students were black. This is a substantial improvement over the statistics for years past: in 1974, 9.2 percent were black; in 1972, 8.9 percent; and, in 1966, only 4.7 percent (U.S. Bureau of the Census, 1980d; U.S. Bureau of the Census, 1979f). Nonetheless, blacks are still underrepresented among college students, since the college age population is 12.9 percent black (U.S. Bureau of the Census, 1980e). In addition, blacks are overrepresented in the less prestigious colleges and universities, and black enrollment actually fell during the late 1970s at a number of major state universities. Among Hispanic Americans, the un-derrepresentation is even greater; only 3.8 percent of U.S. college students were Hispanic in 1978 (U.S. Bureau of the Census, 1980d), despite that group's substantially larger representation in the college age population.

These data indicate that, while there has been some improvement in educational attainment in the black and Hispanic populations, serious inequalities remain. Among younger blacks and Latinos, particularly, the educational gap with whites has closed but not disappeared. However, these data suggest that, even in the younger population, there are far fewer college graduates among blacks than among whites. The gap is even greater among Hispanic Americans. Furthermore, there have been only modest gains among the black population and apparently none at all among the Latino population.

Unfortunately, data of this nature are not available for American Indians. All indications are, however, that the problem of unequal education is at least as great for Indian people as for blacks and Latinos. In the late 1960s fewer than half of all Indian youths entering high school were finishing. This would probably indicate high school graduation rates significantly lower than for either black or Hispanic Americans.

Of course, statistics about educational attainment cannot begin to tell the whole story about how well or poorly any group is being served by the educational system. Quality of education is as important as quantity, and even statistics showing that young blacks' educational levels are becoming closer to those of whites say nothing about the issue of educational quality. We know, for example, that black students are underrepresented in prestigious private colleges and major state universities and overrepresented in community colleges and smaller regional or commuter state colleges and universities. We shall explore in Chapter 11 the entire issue of how the operation of our educational system and the role of minorities within that system shape the status of minority groups in America today.

Health and Mortality   So far, we have seen evidence of continuing serious racial and ethnic inequality in the areas of economics, political representation, and education. In such situations, there is always the risk that such information will be seen by some as just so many more statistics in a world where we are daily bombarded by more and more statistics. However, one area, probably more than any other, shows the human dimension—and indeed the human tragedy—of racial and ethnic inequality. In the United States today, the racial or ethnic group to which one belongs even partially determines how long that person will live. It also influences the amount that person can expect to be ill in his or her lifetime and the likelihood that one or more of his or her children will die in infancy. As we shall see in considerably more detail in Chapter 9, these differences exist not because of biological racial differences, but rather because of social inequalities associated with race or ethnicity. We turn now to the grim statistics.

On the average, black Americans live about five years less than white Americans. In 1976 the male life expectancy for whites was 69.7 years; for blacks and other races, 64.1 years, a gap of 5.6 years. Among females the figures are 77.3 for whites and 72.6 for blacks and other races, a difference of 4.7 years (U.S. Department of Health, Education, and Welfare, 1978). Recent data are not available for American Indians, but the 1970 life expectancy for Indians (male and female) was 64.9. If the Indian life expectancy has followed the general trend in the population, it would be a year or two higher today, around 66 or 67. This would be six or seven years less than among the population as a whole.

Infant mortality is also higher among minority groups than it is among whites. The infant mortality rate (number of deaths per year to infants under one year old per thousand live births) was 13.3 for whites in 1976, but 25.5—nearly twice as high—for blacks (U.S. Department of Health, Education and Welfare, 1978). Among American Indians the rate is slightly lower than among black Americans— 23.8 in 1971; probably a little lower today (National Center for Health Statistics, 1976).

In addition to living shorter lives and experiencing a greater risk of infant death, members of minority groups experience more illness on the average than do whites. In 1976, black Americans on the average, experienced 23.3 days of restricted activity due to illness, and Hispanic Americans, 20.3 days. White Americans averaged 17.6 days (National Center for Health Statistics, 1976). If we consider only bed disability, we find a similar pattern. The average number of bed disability days was 9.9 for blacks and 9.3 for Latinos, but only 6.6 for whites (National Center for Health Statistics, 1976).

SUMMARY AND CONCLUSION

We have seen in the preceding pages that very serious racial and ethnic inequalities remain in the United States. It is true that racial and ethnic prejudice and deliberate discrimination have decreased considerably over the past two or three decades, though they have certainly not disappeared. It is true that increasing numbers of black and Hispanic Americans have attained middle-class status, and that some are wealthy and/or highly educated. However, there are still large segments of the black, Hispanic, and American Indian populations who have not shared in the progress and who are trapped at the bottom of the socioeconomic ladder. For them, things are not getting better; indeed, in some ways they are getting worse. Consequently, the overall position of the minority population remains one of substantial disadvantage. In some cases, the gap between the minority populations as a whole and the white population has narrowed only slightly.

The facts in this chapter carry some important implications about the social forces influencing majority-minority relations in America today. Considering the considerable decrease in deliberate discrimination, it would appear that *open and deliberate* acts of discrimination are probably not the main cause of continuing racial and ethnic inequality in America *today*. Rather, today's continuing inequality would appear to be largely the result of two factors. The first is the continuing effects of past discrimination. This discrimination has left a large portion of the minority population—particularly the "underclass," which is near or below the poverty level—without the resources necessary to enjoy a reasonable level of living or to offer one's children much chance for upward mobility. The second factor involves a host of institutional, social, and economic processes that have the *effect* (though often not the intention) of maintaining and sometimes worsening the racial and ethnic inequalities in our society. These processes, which are the legacy of past discrimination and exploitation, impact particularly heavily on the "underclass." Because these processes are so institutionalized and because some advantaged segments of the population benefit from them, there is frequently fierce resistance to any attempts to alter them in a way that would bring about greater equality. These institutional, social, and economic processes are a major concern of the remainder of this book.

The American Economic System and the Status of Minority Groups Today

9

As we have seen, a sizable gap remains between the average economic position of white people in America today and that of minority groups—most notably black, Indian, and Hispanic Americans. For some—particularly the younger college-educated segments of the minority population—the racial disparity has decreased. Nonetheless, if we look at the minority populations *as a whole,* the economic disparity is evident and not even greatly reduced from the past. A major part of this—discussed in greater detail in the previous chapter—is the existence within the minority population of a large, impoverished, and underemployed or unemployed "underclass." This group, falling below the federally defined poverty level, includes one-fourth of the Latino population, one-third of the black population, and an even larger segment of the Indian population. By comparison, it is only one-tenth of the white population.

It is also highly significant that minority groups have been virtually excluded from ownership or control of the major means of production in today's complex corporate economy. America's productive capacity today is overwhelmingly in the hands of a relatively small number of very large national or multinational corporations, exemplified by those included in the *Fortune 500.* Both the ownership and control of these organizations is in the hands of a relatively small elite, from which minority group members have been almost totally excluded. If, for example, we examine ownership of the corporations, we may think at first that ownership is fairly dispersed among the population. A great many Americans own corporate stock, including most certainly thousands of black and Latino Americans. Most of them, however, own only a small amount of stock. The great bulk of stock is owned by a small number of stockholders, and they are both very wealthy and overwhelmingly white. Estimates based on the compilation of various economic data indicate that the 1 percent of the adult population with the highest income owned about 42 percent of all corporate stock in 1970 (Lebergott, 1976, p. 242). Other estimates (Lampman, 1962) suggest that 2 to 5 percent of the population owns over 80 percent of all corporate stock. Precise data on stock ownership by race or ethnicity are not available, but Lebergott's data are instructive: Very few blacks, Latinos or Indians fall in the very high income levels where most of the corporate stock is owned. Thus, it appears safe to conclude that only a *very small* proportion of America's total corporate wealth is in the hands of minority group members.

Similarly, very few minority group members are to be found in positions of true power in the major corporations. A study by Egerton (1970), for example, found *no* black senior executives or members of boards of directors among the more than 1,300 persons holding such positions in the nation's twenty-five largest industrial corporations. Also without any black senior executives or board members were the five largest retailing companies, the six largest transportation companies, and the four largest utilities. The nation's six largest banks had one black among their roughly 950 board members and officers, and the nation's six largest life insurance companies had two blacks among their 475 directors and senior officers. Although there has probably been a slight increase since Egerton's survey, the actual number of minority board members and officers is still very small, particularly considering that a very few prominent blacks serve on several different corporate boards. On the whole, it is not an overstatement to say that minority group members have been almost totally excluded from the boards of directors and senior executive positions that form the center of power in the corporate structure.

THE ECONOMICS OF DISCRIMINATION: THREE THEORIES

Because major racial inequalities persist in the area of economics, it is important to try to answer the question, "What causes economic inequality or discrimination?" In this section, we shall discuss and evaluate three major theories about the economics of discrimination.

Gary Becker's Theory

The first major effort to construct an economic theory of discrimination was made by Gary Becker (1957). Becker drew on some important insights from both the social-psychological and functionalist perspectives on race and ethnic relations. Becker's starting point is that some people have a "taste for discrimination"—what we have called conative prejudice. This taste for discrimination on the part of employers, employees, or potential customers results in minority group members not being hired, or not being hired for certain (usually better) jobs. In effect, a *choice* is made to discriminate either because of the employer's prejudice or because of his or her concerns about the reactions of white employees or customers.

Such discrimination in hiring, however, is *dysfunctional* for both the employer and the society as a whole, because it stands in the way of getting the best-qualified employee. The employer hires on the basis of race rather than qualifications. This harms the productivity or efficiency of both the employer's enterprise and of the society at large, and it wastes valuable human resources. It also, of course, directly harms the minority workers, who end up underemployed, underpaid, or unemployed. The only potential beneficiaries are the white workers who get better jobs and more pay than they would in a rational, nondiscriminatory hiring system. Even they, however, are negatively affected by the lower overall productivity of the system.

Becker's theory implies that over the long run discrimination in a complex industrial society should gradually disappear because it is dysfunctional both for the employer and for the overall society. Accordingly, firms that do not discriminate should gain a competitive advantage over those that do (Welch, 1967; Arrow, 1972; Masters, 1975). We would therefore expect the discriminatory firms to either stop discriminating or go out of business, with the overall result being a gradual reduction in the amount of discrimination.

In actual fact, this has happened, but only to a rather limited degree. Open, deliberate policies and acts of discrimination have become illegal over the past forty years and have become less common. However, subtler forms of discrimination have persisted, and the overall extent of economic inequality remains substantial.

In a critical evaluation of Becker's theory, we must also question the central role Becker attributes to *attitudes*: the "taste for discrimination." As we have seen in earlier chapters, the degree to which attitudes produce behavior is questionable. Indeed, an equally strong case can be made that behavior produces attitudes. Thus, we cannot *assume,* as Becker seems to do, that attitudes or "tastes" are the main cause of discrimination.

Split Labor Market Theory

The latter criticism of Becker's theory may be largely answered in another theory of the economics of discrimination known as split labor market theory (Bonacich, 1972; 1975; 1976; Wilson, 1978; see also Blumer, 1965). This theory notes some of the same patterns as Becker's theory but attributes them to social structure rather than to individual preferences. It is a form of conflict theory in that it sees discrimination as a result of the clash of competing interest groups.

This model, unlike Becker's, argues that the business owner or capitalist *recognizes* that racial discrimination is dysfunctional for the business enterprise and prefers *not* to discriminate. The objective of the capitalist is to get the best worker for the cheapest wage, and it is therefore in the capitalist's interest *not* to discriminate because discrimination limits the pool of workers available for the position. Accordingly, those doing the hiring discriminate *not* because they have a "taste for discrimination," but rather because they are *forced* to do so by another interest group that does benefit from discrimination. This interest group is white laborers. Discrimination, in the view of this theory, is in the interest of white laborers because it insulates them from potential competition from minority group workers. Accordingly, white workers, if they are powerful enough to do so, demand the exclusion of minority group workers from certain more desirable jobs (or from industrial jobs altogether), in effect creating a system of "white jobs" with high pay and "black jobs" or "Latino jobs" with low pay.

In such a split labor market, the cost of white labor is higher than the cost of minority labor, still another reason why nondiscrimination would be in the interest of the employer or capitalist. But this is also largely why higher-paid white labor demands discrimination: Discrimination keeps their wages high by protecting them from the competition of lower-paid minority labor. Higher-paid white labor may be able to impose a system of discrimination in a number of ways. It might prevent minority group labor from obtaining skills by demanding educational discrimination. It might seek to exclude minority group members from a territory entirely: If they cannot move into an area, they cannot compete (Wilson, 1978, p. 7). It may also attempt to keep minority laborers out of its segment of the labor market by, for example, keeping them out of the labor unions. Exclusion of blacks from labor unions was commonplace in the United States prior to World War II (Bonacich, 1975, p. 38; Wesley, 1927, pp. 254–281). Brody (1960, p. 186) has also documented that in 1917 several steel firms refused to hire blacks because *they were afraid of the reaction of white workers*. In another part of the world, today's system of *apartheid* in South Africa has its roots partially in the demands of white labor unions for the exclusion of black workers during the 1920s (Wilson, 1973, p. 168; Van der Horst, 1967, pp. 117–118).

Apparently such strategies were effective for white laborers, at least in the short run (Marshall, 1965, pp. 22–23); over the long run, however, one must question their effectiveness: a frequent consequence of such discrimination was to so antagonize black laborers that they acted as strikebreakers, greatly weakening the position of the white workers' labor unions. This was especially common during the 1920s (Bonacich, 1976, p. 40; Wilson, 1978, p. 74), and it contributed significantly to the weakening of labor unions during that period (Wilson, 1978, p. 76). Thus, split labor market theory, too, appears to have some limitations, or at the very least, to describe some periods of history better than others.

Marxist Theory on Discrimination

A third theory, arising from a general Marxist perspective, differs from both theories we have examined thus far. It shares one element in common with split labor market theory: It is a conflict theory arguing that racial discrimination in employment is the result of the clash of competing interest groups. However, it disagrees with *both* of the other theories on who gains and who loses as a result of discrimination. Recall that both Becker's theory and the split labor market theory argue that white laborers gain and employers or capitalists lose as a result of discrimination. The Marxist theory argues precisely the opposite: Employers or capitalists gain and white workers lose as a result of discrimination (Baran and Sweezy, 1966; Reich, 1972). This is mainly because racial antagonisms divide workers and thereby weaken their power relative to that of their employers. A prime example can be seen in the strikebreaking of the early twentieth century. White unions excluded blacks, and blacks responded by acting as strikebreakers when the whites went on strike.[1] The consequence was the weakening of unions and lower wages for both blacks and whites. Eventually, many unions realized this (particularly the industrial unions of the CIO) and, with some encouragement from the Roosevelt administration, altered their policies to oppose discrimination. Reich (1972) argues that the theory continues to be relevant today, as conflicts over school busing and neighborhood racial change have mainly involved working-class blacks and whites. The consequence, according to Reich, is that working-class whites and blacks see each other as the enemy. Consequently, they fail to recognize their common self-interests and are unable to cooperate with each other to influence the political system or to protect their common self-interests against the opposing self-interests of their employers or, more generally, the wealthy elite.

Evaluating the Three Theories

Each of these three theories offers a different reason for the existence of economic racial and ethnic discrimination. According to Becker, discrimination occurs because some people have a "taste for discrimination"—in other words the cause lies in people's attitudes. According to split labor market theory, discrimination occurs because white workers benefit from it by eliminating minority competition. According to the Marxist theory, discrimination occurs because capitalists benefit from the divisions it creates in the working class, which weaken the bargaining position of workers and lead black and white workers to blame each other for their difficulties rather than blaming the capitalist class. With three such different explanations, who is right?

It would seem that, under different social conditions, each of the three theories can be correct. Discrimination *can* result from prejudiced attitudes, particularly when the culture is supportive. Certainly a culture that favored prejudice and discrimination led some employers to discriminate, regardless of the economic consequences, in the "Old South." Another example can be found in a personal experience of the author while conducting interviews in a survey of

---

[1] It is important, however, to note that this was not the *only* reason for black strikebreaking. Many did so out of desperation, and some took jobs in distant areas without being told they were breaking a strike until they arrived at the job site. Of course, many whites were also strikebreakers, and many blacks never worked as strikebreakers.

This girl has suffered brain damage from eating lead-based paint. Lead poisoning is a common problem among children of impoverished families in urban areas. Sociologists of the conflict perspective believe that such poverty and suffering exists because, somewhere in the social system, some more advantaged group of people is benefitting from it. United Nations, W.A. Graham.

employers in the Detroit area in 1972. One plant owner claimed that if the government told him he had to hire a certain number of blacks (at the time he had no black employees), he would simply close the plant and go out of business. It is hard to conclude that this employer was acting mainly on the basis of calculating his possible gains: He simply had a very strong opinion that made him willing (or so he said) to go out of business rather than change.

In other cases, however, individual attitudes are probably not the major cause of discriminatory behavior. We have noted documented cases where pressures from white labor did cause employers to discriminate, and where white labor was able to effectively control the hiring process, the strategy appears to have worked. Marshall

(1965, pp. 22–23) notes certain strong craft unions that were able to keep blacks out were able to maintain high wages and high membership during a period in the 1920s when most unions were losing ground. However, most unions do not have enough control over hiring to make such a strategy work. Both Reich (1972, p. 319) and Wilson (1978, p. 78) have noted that in recent years, the one element of white labor that has been able to use discrimination to its advantage is the craft unions such as the building trades, which control hiring through the union hiring hall.

The majority of workers, however, do not have such control over hiring, and in these cases, the Marxist theory may offer the best explanation of the causes and consequences of race discrimination. Racial divisions were disastrous for many unions during the 1920s, and since that time most unions (particularly industrywide unions such as the United Auto Workers) have taken an official stance against racial prejudice and discrimination. (Of course, white members do not always go along with the official position.)

There is also evidence that racial divisions continue to harm the economic position of the working and lower classes today. As we have seen, prejudice is strongest among these groups, at least by the usual measures of attitudes about intergroup relations. Social organizers, moreover, frequently lament the degree to which racial divisions keep poor blacks, whites, Latinos, and others from recognizing a common interest. Some empirical light is shed on the issue in a study by Reich (1972). Reich examined 1960 census data on the forty-eight largest metropolitan areas in the United States. For each area, he determined the ratio of black median family income to white median family income as a measure of *racial* economic inequality or discrimination. He also obtained two measures of income inequality *within the white population*. His interesting finding was that where black-white inequality or discrimination was great, income within the white population was indeed more concentrated: The wealthier segment had higher income and the poorer segment a lower income than in areas with less racial inequality. In Reich's judgment this finding supported the theory that wealthy whites and employers benefit from racism and the less wealthy and working-class whites are hurt by it. Reich concludes that discrimination is largely a product of capitalism because it serves the interests of the dominant economic class in that system. There are, however, other possible interpretations of Reich's findings. All his variables could be measuring the same thing: The overall amount of inequality in an area, an inequality that falls along both class and racial lines. Accordingly, Reich's study should be seen as one piece of evidence supporting the Marxist theory of discrimination, not conclusive proof of it. Regardless of this, it does appear true that one of the major effects of discrimination is to create divisions that potentially weaken the bargaining position of the working class.

Studies by Glenn (1963, 1966) and by Dowdall (1974) shed further light on the question and seem to support the view that both the Marxist and split labor market interpretations may be correct, depending on the situation. These studies showed that, given the level of discrimination in American society, whites in areas with *more* blacks enjoyed higher occupational status, income, and employment rates. To the degree that this was true because blacks took the burden of unemployment and underpaid work, freeing the whites for better jobs (and not being in much of a position to compete for those better jobs), the results would appear to support the split labor market theory. On the other hand, Dowdall (1974, p. 182) argues that the findings support the Marxist theory, in that it seems to be those at the top who benefit most from discrimination. Finally, it must be pointed out that the findings do not directly bear on the question of who would be better off with or without discrimination, because these studies do not measure or compare the amount of discrimination. They merely show that, *taking discrimination as a given,* the dominant group appears to come out better off when there are large numbers of subordinate group members present.

A more direct test of the effects of discrimination on the overall white population is provided by Szymanski (1976). Szymanski showed that in states with relatively high racial inequality in income, whites (1) had *lower* average incomes and (2) had a more *unequal* income distribution. This was *especially* true for those states with larger than average minority populations. This relationship was explained only partially by region; Szymanski's data indicated that the main reason for the pattern was that unions were weaker in states with great racial inequality. This set of findings, then, provides significant support for the Marxist theory of the economics of discrimination.

Taken as a whole, our discussion seems to point to the view that under different conditions, economic discrimination may operate according to any of the three models we have discussed. Nonetheless, Szymanski's study, the historical trends we have discussed, and the inability of labor (except some of the craft unions) to control the hiring process all suggest the possibility that in *today's* economy, the Marxist theory may be correct in more situations than either of the others. None of the three, however, can totally explain the economics of discrimination. A recent study by Beck (1980), for example, provides support for the notion that to some degree the economy still operates according to the split labor market model. Beck's study showed that comparing different points in time from 1947 to 1974, periods of relatively high unionization were accompanied by high black-white inequality, and vice versa. However, part of Beck's findings may result from the fact that changes in the job structure toward white-collar jobs have both reduced unionization and, as Wilson (1978) argues, opened new opportunities for the expansion of a black middle class. In any case, the evidence available does not indicate that the economics of discrimination operate entirely according to any one of the three models we have discussed.

RECENT TRENDS AND THEIR EFFECTS
ON RACIAL ECONOMIC INEQUALITY

Whatever the underlying causes of racial economic discrimination may be, there *are* some things we know about (1) the mechanisms that maintain racial economic inequality today and (2) the effects of recent social trends on patterns of economic inequality and discrimination along the lines of race. In the remainder of this chapter, these two closely related issues will be the focus of our concern.

Rising Educational Demands and the Employment of Minorities

As we have seen, the expansion of white-collar jobs has created the opportunity for a sizable minority middle class to develop. However, this expansion—because of the increase in educational requirements for employment that have accompanied it—has also created problems for a large segment of the minority population. These problems have been aggravated by the tendency of employers to demand higher levels of education for their jobs, whether or not the education is actually needed for the job. The tendency of employers to make such demands increases as the average educational level of the population increases, as it has over the past few decades. It also increases during periods of high unemployment—and unemployment has been relatively high since the late 1960s. An employer may want to hire a person with more education than is necessary to do the job for a variety of reasons. One very important factor—which will be discussed at greater length in a later chapter—is that employers frequently seek to hire workers with cultural values and work habits similar to their own. Thus, they prefer more educated employees not because they know more about the job, but because they will "fit in" better.

This practice, though usually not deliberately racist, does end up being racist in its *consequences*. As we have seen, average educational levels among blacks, Latinos, and American Indians are well below the average educational level of whites. When more education is demanded than the job requires, many people quite capable of doing the job are excluded (Berg, 1971), and a disproportionate number of them are members of minority groups. Thus, inflated educational requirements can be identified as one cause of the relatively high levels of unemployment and poverty among the black, Hispanic, and American Indian populations. Considered along with the increase in jobs that *do* actually require higher educational levels and the reduction in the number of unskilled jobs resulting from automation, this tendency helps to explain why the black unemployment rate rose to twice as high as the white unemployment rate after World War II and has been at least that high ever since.

Job Decentralization and Housing Segregation

As we have seen, the majority of all black Americans and about half of all Hispanic Americans live in the central cities of our metropolitan areas—compared to only a little more than a quarter of the white population. Between World War II and the 1970s, the black and Latino populations became increasingly concentrated in these central cities. During the same period and continuing into the 1980s, however, employment opportunities have been moving *out* of those central cities. This is true for business and retail sales jobs and also for the industrial jobs that have been especially important as a source of relatively high paying jobs for blacks and Latinos. This is especially true for the larger metropolitan areas, which are the home of a disproportionate share of blacks and Latinos (Sternleib and Hughes, 1976, p. 30). While the number of jobs has simply stopped growing in some of the smaller cities, it has actually fallen in many of the larger cities and in some smaller ones with large minority populations. New York City, for example, lost 380,000 jobs between 1970 and 1975 (Greenberg and Valente, 1976, p. 92). East St. Louis, Illinois, a relatively small industrial city that is overwhelmingly black, lost over half of its manufacturing jobs between 1950 and 1970 (Illinois Capital Development Board, 1977). Nationally, between 1947 and 1967, manufacturing employment in central cities declined by 4 percent; it rose by 94 percent in the suburbs during the

The problem of unemployment is especially widespread among the black and Hispanic populations in the United States. Marc Anderson.

same period. A similar trend to the suburbs can also be seen in wholesale and retail trade (Barabba, 1976, p. 56).

This shift to the suburbs harms minority group members because, just as they are *over*represented in the central cities, they are *under*represented in the suburbs. The net effect is to take jobs out of areas where blacks and Latinos live and to move them into areas where white Anglos live. In addition to suburbanizing, manufacturing is also moving to rural areas; it is moving away from the Midwest and Northeast and into the South and West. The move to rural areas probably hurts minorities: Relatively few blacks or Latinos live in rural areas anymore. Nor do Indians benefit much, because most rural Indian people live on reservations, which is not where the jobs are going. The southward and westward movement might at first glance appear to increase opportunities for blacks and Latinos, but this is in fact dubious. Firestine (1977) presents evidence that blacks have *not* gained substantially from industrial growth in the South. An important reason for this appears to be that industries moving to the South are locating in predominantly white areas: either suburbs or mainly white rural areas (Firestine, 1977; Thompson, 1976, p. 190).

There is little doubt that job shifts in recent decades have resulted in reduced opportunities for minority group members. This pattern raises two important questions: Why have these changes detrimental to minority group members happened? What, if anything, can minority group members do to minimize the effects on them of these job shifts?

Reasons for Job Shifts There are numerous reasons why employment opportunities have moved out of central cities and into suburbs and rural areas. Some have absolutely nothing to do with race or ethnicity; others, however, suggest at least some race-consciousness on the part of corporate decision makers.

One reason for the decentralization of manufacturing is that modern manufacturing is more efficient in sprawling, one-level factory complexes than in the once typical multistory factory. The one-story complexes require much more land than the old factories, and this land is available and affordable only in urban fringe areas and in rural areas. Nonetheless, the movement to rural and suburban areas would probably never have happened without the development of truck transportation and the interstate highway system. Because transportation is crucial to manufacturing, it was at one time necessary for industry to locate on a major waterway, at or near a rail junction, or both. Generally, this meant locating in a major city. Today, however, most industries can locate wherever there is an interstate highway, since much more shipping is done by truck. It is significant that the greatest growth in manufacturing activity and in population in rural areas has been in counties through which an interstate highway passes.

There are, however, other factors that may be more directly linked to race and ethnicity. Some movement is probably the result of prejudices and fears on the part of whites which make them reluctant to keep their businesses in predominantly black or Hispanic areas. Some employers have also complained about the work habits and life style of inner-city employees, which may be significantly different from their own. Finally, some of the movement seems aimed at avoiding unionization, and in some cases, this probably means deliberately avoiding black areas. In the South, particularly, white workers are less prounion than black workers, and this may be one reason that companies moving to the South largely locate in white areas (Thompson, 1976, p. 190).

The movement of retail and wholesale trade to the suburbs appears largely to be the result of the movement of population—especially the wealthier (and mostly white) population with money to spend—to the suburbs. Fear of crime and the reluctance of white shoppers to shop in minority neighborhoods may also be a factor in the decentralization of these businesses.

Whatever the *intent* of those who decide to relocate business and industry out of central cities, the *result* is clearly to contribute to racial inequality by taking jobs out of the areas where minorities live and into the areas where whites live. In the following section, we shall examine the alternatives available to minorities to adjust to this changing distribution of job opportunities.

Adjustment to Job Shifts   Two responses appear possible which might enable minority group members to adjust to the shifting distribution of employment opportunities. One response would be increased commuting from city to suburb. Undoubtedly, some minority workers have responded in this way, but a great many others cannot. Only a few American cities have rapid transit systems that would permit such commuting by public transit, and for many minority group members, private transportation is simply not an alternative. A surprising number of minority group members cannot afford to own an automobile. Statistics from the Detroit and St. Louis metropolitan areas—neither of which has public rapid transit—are a good example of this. In Detroit—the "Motor City"—37.5 percent of all black households do *not* own even one automobile. In some predominantly black neighborhoods, the majority of households do not have cars (U.S. Bureau of the Census, 1972c, Tables H2, H4). In St. Louis the picture is even worse: fully 48.6 percent of all black households are without automobiles. In nearby East St. Louis, over half are without cars (U.S. Bureau of the Census, 1972d, Tables H2, H4). Among those who do have cars, the rapidly rising cost of gasoline in recent years has sharply limited the feasibility of long-distance commuting.

The other alternative is to move to the areas where the jobs are located; however, the cost of the move is often prohibitive. Furthermore, restrictive zoning and public opposition to low-income housing have largely kept the minority poor out of the suburbs. There has been some increased migration of blacks to the suburbs in recent years, but much of it has been into "suburban ghettoes," large concentrations of black population, mostly in the older parts of the suburbs, which are also losing employment opportunities. Much of it, too, has involved those blacks who have already attained middle-class status and are least in need of employment opportunities.

Probably the most important factor keeping minorities from moving to follow jobs, however, is the pervasive pattern of discrimination and segregation in housing. This issue is of such importance, both in and of itself and as a factor potentially reducing minority employment opportunities, that we shall discuss it separately in the next section.

HOUSING DISCRIMINATION AND SEGREGATION

When sociologists talk about housing segregation, they are referring to the tendency for people in any two groups or races to live in separate areas. When, for example, all the blacks in a city live in one neighborhood or set of neighborhoods and all the whites live in other neighborhoods, we would have a highly segregated situation. Sociologists have a number of measures of residential segregation, but probably the most widely used is the *index of dissimilarity,* sometimes called the segregation index. This index can range from zero to one hundred, with zero being no segregation and one hundred being total segregation. This measure is based on city blocks or urban neighborhood areas called *census tracts*. For any two groups, such as blacks and whites, the segregation index tells us what percentage of a city's black *or* white population would have to move to another block or census tract in order to have no segregation at all.

This measure has been computed for every U.S. metropolitan area and for every city with a population over 50,000, using census data from 1950, 1960, and 1970. For all metropolitan areas in the United States, the 1970 segregation index, based on census tract data, averaged a little under 70, whether computed for the entire metropolitan areas or only for the central cities. This figure, based on 237 metropolitan areas, is slightly lower than the average segregation index of 75 (both central city and metropolitan-wide) for the 144 metropolitan areas that existed in 1960 (Van Valey, et. al., 1977, p. 837). This would seem to suggest a decrease in segregation during the 1960's, but that is not the case. Most of the difference results from the addition of the hundred or so areas that were defined as metropolitan areas between 1960 and 1970 (because their central cities reached a population of 50,000). These areas are smaller in population and generally have small black populations—and areas of this type do generally have less segregation. If we look only at those 137 areas that were defined as metropolitan areas both in 1960 and 1970, we find that there was no change: The average for both years was about 75 (Van Valey, et. al., 1977, p. 839). In other words, most areas in both years were about three quarters of the way toward the segregated end of the scale. Segregation indices for some representative cities are presented in Table 9.1. It should be noted again that these indices are based on census tract data. When segregation indices are computed using block data, they tend to be even higher, because block data permits the detection of patterns of segregation *within* the larger neighborhoods that form census tracts.

Table 9.1 Segregation Indices for Selected Metropolitan Areas and Central Cities, 1960 and 1970

CITY	METROPOLITAN AREA		CENTRAL CITY	
	1970	1960	1970	1960
Atlanta	81.7	77.1	83.4	83.1
Birmingham	67.6	64.1	70.9	69.0
Boston	79.3	80.8	81.2	83.9
Buffalo	85.7	86.8	83.4	84.5
Chicago	91.2	91.2	91.0	91.8
Cincinnati	81.8	83.2	74.3	81.2
Cleveland	90.2	89.6	86.7	85.6
Dallas	86.9	81.2	91.7	88.8
Denver	84.7	84.6	84.6	83.4
Des Moines	74.5	77.0	71.7	77.4
Detroit	88.9	87.1	78.2	80.4
Indianapolis	83.8	78.7	80.3	76.0
Little Rock	70.8	65.0	76.7	65.2
Los Angeles	88.5	89.2	88.6	85.4
Louisville	82.8	80.4	84.4	79.5
Milwaukee	89.5	90.4	87.0	88.4
Minneapolis	79.9	83.3	74.6	75.8
Newark	78.8	72.8	72.1	63.2
New Haven	67.0	65.4	73.0	53.5
New Orleans	74.2	65.0	70.9	67.7
New York	73.8	74.4	71.6	75.2
Philadelphia	78.0	77.1	76.8	79.0
Phoenix	75.4	81.1	77.7	85.4
Pittsburgh	74.5	74.4	79.2	81.1
Portland, Oregon	80.2	81.3	77.4	79.6
Richmond	76.6	74.9	83.2	79.5
Sacramento	66.1	72.1	61.0	60.1
St. Louis	86.5	85.9	83.8	85.4
San Diego	76.2	79.5	76.1	80.2
San Francisco	77.3	79.4	67.8	71.1
Seattle	78.1	83.3	76.7	82.2
Tucson	63.6	73.0	64.0	78.3

Source: Reprinted from Thomas L. Van Valey, Wade Clark Roof, and Jerome E. Wilcox, "Trends in Residential Segregation: 1960–1970," *American Journal of Sociology* 82: 830–835, by permission of The University of Chicago Press. Copyright 1977 by The University of Chicago.

It is obvious from these data that the level of housing segregation of blacks and whites in most American cities is quite high, and that in most cities there has been little reduction in the extent of segregation over the past decade or two. How can this persistence be explained? A number of possible explanations have been offered, and the topic has been researched widely enough to offer some fairly clear answers to some of the questions.

Economic Explanations of Housing Segregation

One explanation frequently offered for racial housing segregation is economic. As we have seen, the black population has a significantly lower average income than the white population. Accordingly, some people have argued that a major reason for housing segregation is that most blacks cannot afford to live in many of the neighborhoods where whites live.

It turns out that it is quite possible to measure the extent to which this is the case. Through use of a measure called *indirect standardization,* sociologists can estimate quite precisely the number of blacks and whites that one would *expect* to live in each neighborhood of a city based on the neighborhood's income distribution. From these estimates, it is in turn possible to compute *what the segregation index for the city would be* if income differences between blacks and whites were the only reason for housing segregation.

Using house value or rent as a substitute for income, Taeuber and Taeuber (1965) calculated expected segregation indices for fifteen major cities using 1960 census data and compared those to the actual segregation indices. They found that if economic inequality between blacks and whites had been the *only* reason for segregation in these cities, the 1960 segregation indices would have ranged from 8.5 to 30.4 and averaged 20.8. The *actual* segregation indices for the fifteen cities ranged from 67.8 to 87.1, and averaged 78.4 (Taeuber and Taeuber, 1965, p. 85). In other words, if economic inequality had been the only reason for black-white segregation, there would have been only a little more than one fourth as much segregation as there actually was.

The principle is further illustrated by a study conducted by the author concerning racial segregation in the Cleveland metropolitan area. Using the technique of indirect standardization and working with 1970 census data, I computed the number of blacks who would have lived in Cleveland and each of thirty-six suburbs if income differences had been the only cause of segregation. These numbers were converted to percentages and compared to the actual percentage of blacks living in the suburbs. The results of this analysis are presented in Table 9.2. As you can see, both Cleveland and East Cleveland—an industrial satellite—have far *more* blacks than would be expected on the basis of income. Of the remaining suburbs, thirty-two out of thirty-five have far *fewer* blacks than would be expected. Indeed, nineteen have essentially *no* black population (one tenth of one percent or less), even though based on their *income* distribution, we would expect these suburbs to be 10 to 14 percent black.

This study, that of Taeuber and Taeuber, and others (see Hermalin and Farley, 1973) show clearly that (1) only a small portion, perhaps one fourth, of racial housing segregation can be accounted for by income differences, and (2) housing segregation has largely restricted blacks to living in central cities, even

Table 9.2 Expected (Based on Income Distribution) and Actual Percent Black in Cleveland and its Suburbs, 1970.

CITY	EXPECTED PERCENT BLACK	ACTUAL PERCENT BLACK
Cleveland	18.6	35.9
Bay Village	9.6	<0.1
Bedford	13.5	<0.1
Bedford Heights	13.3	0.9
Berea	12.2	2.6
Broadview Heights	11.7	0.0
Brooklyn	13.1	0.2
Brook Park	12.1	<0.1
Cleveland Heights	12.7	2.3
East Cleveland	19.1	57.1
Eastlake	13.5	<0.1
Euclid	13.7	<0.1
Fairview Park	11.6	0.0
Garfield Heights	13.9	3.6
Lakewood	13.9	<0.1
Lyndhurst	10.8	<0.1
Maple Heights	13.6	1.8
Mayfield Heights	13.4	0.4
Mentor	12.3	0.1
Middleburg Heights	10.7	<0.1
North Olmstead	11.7	<0.1
North Royalton	12.1	0.0
Painesville	16.2	9.4
Parma	13.5	<0.1
Parma Heights	12.7	<0.1
Rocky River	11.1	<0.1
Seven Hills	10.5	0.1
Shaker Heights	10.6	13.2
Solon	11.0	<0.1
South Euclid	12.5	0.1
Strongsville	12.8	0.1
University Heights	10.8	0.4
Warrensville Heights	12.9	18.9
Westlake	12.1	1.1
Wickliffe	12.4	2.3
Willoughby	13.4	0.1
Willowick	12.4	0.2
All suburbs	12.8	3.7

Source: Analysis of 1970 census tract data by author.

though a great many of them can afford housing in the suburbs. The author's data, for example, indicate that if income differences were the only reason for housing segregation, half of the Cleveland area's blacks would have lived in the suburbs; in fact only 13 percent did. Hermalin and Farley's (1973) data showed that in Detroit, the expected proportion in the suburbs was 67 percent, while the actual figure was only 12 percent.

Black Preferences

Another explanation offered for housing segregation is that black people prefer to live in all black neighborhoods. Undoubtedly many do, but recent research suggests that this factor, too, probably cannot account for anywhere near the level of segregation that really exists. A team of researchers headed by Reynolds Farley (Farley et. al., 1978, 1979) recently conducted a large-scale survey of the housing and neighborhood preferences of blacks and whites in the Detroit metropolitan area. Blacks and whites responding to the survey were shown cards depicting various combinations of blacks and whites in hypothetical neighborhoods (see Figure 9.1). They were then asked about their willingness to live in the neighborhoods, and their neighborhood preferences. Blacks expressed a clear preference for integrated neighborhoods: 63 percent picked the 50 percent black and 50 percent white neighborhood as their first choice and fully 85 percent of the blacks chose integrated neighborhoods. Only 12 percent chose the all-black neighborhood and 2 percent chose an all-white neighborhood. The most common reason given for preferring integrated neighborhoods was the need to get along with whites. Clearly, then, this study would indicate that housing segregation cannot be explained by black preferences, and its findings are quite consistent with those of a number of previous studies (for a review, see Pettigrew, 1973, pp. 43−58).

White Preferences

Another commonly suggested explanation for housing segregation is that white residents prefer all-white neighborhoods, and behave in such a manner as to exclude blacks from their neighborhoods. The two studies by Farley and his associates (1978, 1979) provide significant evidence in support of this explanation. When whites who answered the survey in Detroit were shown cards depicting various neighborhood racial mixes, they expressed preferences very different from those of the blacks. Over one-fourth (27 percent) of the whites indicated that they would be unwilling to move a neighborhood with *one* black family and fully half would not be willing to move into a neighborhood that was 20 percent black. Almost three-fourths (73 percent) of the whites indicated that they would not be willing to move to a neighborhood that was one-third black, and 41 percent said they would try to move out of such a neighborhood if they already lived there (Farley et. al., 1979). Furthermore, for each neighborhood racial mix, the number of whites who said they would feel uncomfortable if their neighborhood developed such a mix was almost as great as the number who said they would not move into

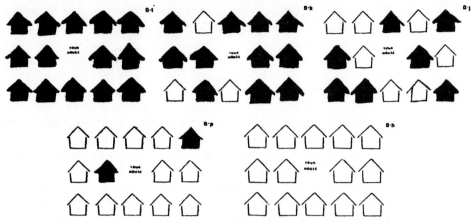

Neighborhood Diagrams for Black Respondents

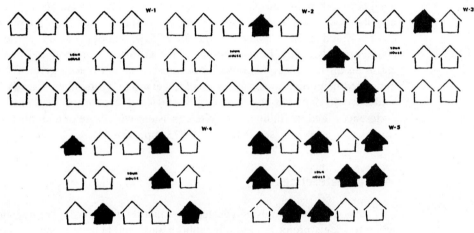

Neighborhood Diagrams for White Respondents

Figure 9.1 Pictures of neighborhood diagrams presented to black and white respondents. Source: Reprinted from "Barriers to the Racial Integration of Neighborhoods: The Detroit Case," by Reynoldo Farley, Suzanne Bianchi, and Diane Colasanto in volume 441 of *The Annals of the American Academy of Political and Social Science*. Copyright © 1979 by the American Academy of Political and Social Science.

such a neighborhood. Clearly, anything more than minimal integration in housing is unacceptable to the majority of whites, and a sizable minority rejects even minimal integration.

These findings are instructive in several respects. While they do show that some whites are willing to live in minimally integrated neighborhoods, they also show that most whites prefer exactly the kind of neighborhood they live in: all white. Furthermore, they show that the integrated neighborhoods that blacks prefer to move *into* are exactly the kind of neighborhoods that whites want to move *out of*, and even more so, refuse to move into. It appears that once a neighborhood becomes minimally integrated, the following things happen: (1) The neighborhood becomes more attractive to blacks, so blacks move in at an accelerated rate. (2) Whites stop moving into the neighborhood. (3) In some neighborhoods whites may move out at a faster than normal rate. Taken together, these processes tend to turn the neighborhood rather quickly from all-white to all-black, or nearly all black. Because the majority of whites are unwilling to move into integrated neighborhoods, it becomes difficult for neighborhoods to remain integrated once they have become integrated: For the neighborhood to stay integrated, both blacks and whites must continue moving in. The data show that most blacks will continue moving into an integrated neighborhood; most whites will not. Even in the absence of sizable white flight, the failure of whites to move into the neighborhood guarantees that it will become resegregated, only now predominately black (see Molotch, 1972).

The inability of neighborhoods to remain integrated is illustrated by research by Taeuber and Taeuber (1963, pp. 105–114). Of ten major cities, only six had *any* stable interracial areas where the number of blacks and whites stayed about the same between 1950 and 1960. In these six cities, only from 1 to 10 percent of the census tracts with a black population of 250 or more (out of an average population of around 4,000) were stably integrated. If we add those neighborhoods where both the black and white populations were stable or growing, but one at a faster pace than the other, we can account for another 20 percent of the census tracts, on the average. This leaves an average of about three-fourths of the tracts which have sizable black population in either established black neighborhoods, neighborhoods where blacks were moving in and whites moving out (over 40 percent of the neighborhoods, on the average), neighborhoods where whites were moving in and blacks moving out (a "displacement" pattern to be discussed later), or neighborhoods where both blacks and whites were moving out. Interestingly, this study found more stable integrated neighborhoods in the southern cities than in the North. Clearly, then, the unwillingness of most whites to move into integrated neighborhoods emerges as one important cause of racial housing segregation.

Another factor that undoubtedly serves to preserve the pattern of housing segregation is harassment by whites of blacks who move into all-white neighborhoods. Incidents of this nature have been reported in most large metropolitan areas and have continued to occur in various areas throughout the 1970s. Frequently such incidents are violent, with vandalism to homes, automobiles, and other property; in some cases shots have been fired through windows and houses burned down. Such incidents undoubtedly have had some effect of blocking the integration of all-white neighborhoods. The Detroit study (R. Farley, et. al., 1979) found that 90 percent of the blacks reluctant to move to all-white areas expressed the view that whites would not welcome them, and one-sixth expressed fears of serious violence against themselves or their house.

Practices in the Real Estate Business

Not all racial segregation can be explained by the behaviors and preferences of white residents, however. Although most whites do not want to live in integrated neighborhoods, there is clearly a significant minority of the white population that is willing and in some cases even desires to live in racially integrated neighborhoods (Taylor, 1979; Farley, et. al., 1979). Furthermore, a significant portion of the white objection to living in integrated neighborhoods arises from fears that the neighborhood will "tip" and become all black (Taylor, 1979).

This suggests that there may be other important reasons for the pattern of housing segregation, and one that has been most often suggested is the behavior of some real estate agents and speculators. Discrimination in the sale and rental of housing has been illegal in the United States since 1968, but there is ample evidence that such discrimination continues. One common practice is the selective showing of houses to blacks and whites, commonly referred to as *"racial steering."*

Pearce (1976) showed that this practice was widespread in the Detroit area. She had couples with similar social characteristics except race approach a number of realtors in the Detroit area. Each realtor was approached a few weeks apart by a black couple and a white couple. The results of the study were striking: The white couples were shown more houses, on the average, and blacks and whites were shown houses in different areas. The whites were shown houses in white neighborhoods; usually in the same community as the realtor's office. The black couples, on the other hand, were shown houses in either racially mixed or all-black neighborhoods, usually outside the community where the realtor's office was located. A CBS news team conducting an investigation for the program "60 Minutes" found essentially the same pattern in the Chicago area, also by sending black and white couples to realtors. Widespread discrimination and racial steering were found in both sale and rental housing in forty metropolitan areas in a recent study by the Department of Housing and Urban Development (1979). Even using a conservative approach, the researchers found that a black visiting six rental offices would have an 85 percent chance of encountering discrimination, and that a black visiting four real estate sales offices would have about a 50−50 chance of experiencing discrimination. Indeed, it is frequently difficult or impossible for whites wishing to buy in integrated or mostly black neighborhoods or blacks wishing to buy in all-white neighborhoods to do so: Realtors actively discourage such home buying. Although illegal, racial steering is difficult to prove to a court or civil rights commission: To do so would require a careful and time-consuming study such as those of Pearce and the CBS news team, and of course most potential complainants do not have the resources to do such a study. As an alternative, some Chicago suburbs (mostly in racially changing areas) have proposed ordinances to require that whites be made aware of available houses in racially integrated areas and that blacks be told about houses in all-white areas. These have led to charges of reverse steering or discrimination by some whites and blacks, particularly those who are associated with the real estate industry. However, unless effective measures are

242

taken to curb the practice of racial steering, substantial reduction in the amount of housing segregation is unlikely.

There were also efforts in 1980 to strengthen the 1968 Civil Rights Act, which prohibits discrimination in the sale and rental of housing. This act covers about 80 percent of the housing supply. The problem, as we have seen, is that enforcement of the 1968 law has been extremely difficult. A major objective of the proposed 1980 amendments was to make the law more enforceable by (1) giving the Department of Housing and Urban Development (HUD) direct enforcement powers—that is, the ability to issue orders and impose fines, (2) expanding the concept of legal standing to make it easier to sue for discrimination, (3) increasing the relief that can be obtained in court by those discriminated against, and (4) clarifying the prohibition against discrimination and redlining in the mortgage and real estate insurance businesses. These changes appeared to have an excellent chance of approval early in 1980, but they ultimately failed, apparently because of political fears arising from the defeat in the 1980 election of a number of "liberal" pro-civil rights senators and the election of Ronald Reagan to the presidency.

Racial discrimination can be highly profitable to some people in the real estate industry, as is shown by another common practice known as *blockbusting*. Blockbusting is a practice whereby unscrupulous realtors play on the fears of whites and the housing predicament of blacks to make a fast buck by encouraging the rapid turnover of a neighborhood from all-white to all-black. Typically, the process begins in an all-white neighborhood near a black neighborhood or a neighborhood undergoing change. Realtors or real estate speculators approach people living in the neighborhood and tell them that blacks are about to move into the neighborhood and that property values are going to go down. They tell the whites that they had better sell now, while they can still get their money out of the house. The object, of course, is to create panic so that the whites will sell their houses at a low price, often to a real estate speculator. Commissions can be collected, and often a shrewd speculator can sell the house to a black family for more than it is worth: Blacks typically must pay more for the same quality housing than whites because of the restricted housing market available to them due to discrimination. Of course, such practices are illegal under the 1968 law against housing discrimination, but again there are ways of getting around the law. In some cities, anonymous letters have been distributed in the middle of the night; anonymous phone calls saying "sell now" are not unheard of. Of course, not all realtors engage in blockbusting, but the practice has been wide-spread enough to be a significant factor in the patterns of housing segregation in many large cities.

The Marxist theory of the economics of discrimination (Reich, 1972) appears applicable to this issue. Both black and white homeowners are harmed by the practice: Whites sell their houses for less than they are worth, and blacks have to pay an inflated price. Furthermore, the practice would not work were it not for the fears and prejudices of the white population. If whites did not *believe* that blacks in the neighborhood lead to lowered property values, they could not be frightened into the panic selling that creates falling property values. In short, racial prejudice appears to serve the interests of the real estate speculators and unscrupulous realtors at the expense of both black and white homeowners.

To summarize briefly, in our investigation of housing segregation we have seen that income differences between blacks and whites and the preferences of blacks are relatively unimportant as causes of housing segregation. The main causes appear to be the preference of most whites not to live in substantially integrated neighborhoods, and real estate practices such as racial steering and blockbusting, which act to preserve the pattern of racial housing segregation.

Housing Segregation
Other than Black-White

Thus far, we have examined only black-white housing segregation. Other groups, however, have also encountered housing segregation similar to that encountered by black Americans.

Hispanic Americans have encountered considerable housing segregation. Using 1970 census data, Kantrowitz (1978, pp. 49−52) found that Chicanos and Puerto Ricans in the Boston area were nearly as segregated as were blacks. In Philadelphia Hershberg and his associates (1978) found Puerto Ricans even more segregated than blacks in 1970. Guest and Weed (1976) found much the same situation as in Boston, with segregation of Chicanos and Puerto Ricans in Cleveland slightly lower than blacks but much higher than for any white ethnic group. In Seattle the segregation of Puerto Ricans was comparable to that of blacks, but Chicanos were less segregated than either. They were, however, more segregated than any white ethnic group (see Table 9.3). As the figures from these three cities suggest, Moore (1976) reports that the Chicano population, while tending to be segregated, varies widely from city to city in the degree to which it is segregated. In the Southwest, the average segregation index between Chicanos and Anglos in 35 cities for 1960 was 54.5, compared to 80.1 between blacks and whites. Segregation tends to be especially high in Texas, where eight out of the ten most segregated cities in the southwest had Chicano-Anglo segregation indices of between 63 and 76 (Murguia, 1975; Grebler, et. al., 1970, p. 275).

In most cities white ethnic groups also show some degree of segregation. They are typically somewhat less segregated than Chicanos and considerably less segregated than either blacks or Puerto Ricans. When compared to the distribution of other ethnic groups or to the population as a whole, most of these groups have segregation indices about halfway between the integrated and segregated ends of the scale—typically in the range of 40−60 (Kantrowitz, 1978; Guest and Weed, 1976). (See again Table 9.3.) It can be assumed that these levels of segregation arise largely from group preferences to live in neighborhoods with others of the same group, since these groups have not been subject to significant levels of discrimination in recent years. The higher level of segregation among Chicanos and the considerably higher levels among Puerto Ricans and blacks, on the other hand, would appear to reflect discrimination of the types discussed in this chapter.

Table 9.3 Average Segregation Indices for Ethnic Groups in Selected Cities, 1970

ETHNIC GROUP	CLEVELAND	City BOSTON	SEATTLE
A. "Old" Immigrants			
1. Canada	50.5	48.7	37.4
2. Germany	46.5	49.2	37.2
3. Ireland	56.1	52.4	42.1
4. Sweden	60.1	53.5	39.9
5. United Kingdom	48.8	47.4	37.9
B. "New" Immigrants			
6. Austria	48.5	53.5	41.9
7. Czechoslovakia	52.3	66.5	47.7
8. Hungary	53.2	63.8	51.3
9. Italy	55.4	58.2	44.1
10. Poland	58.7	53.4	43.3
11. USSR	60.6	58.0	40.7
C. Minority groups			
12. Mexico	74.6	78.6	52.6
13. Black	85.5	81.3	74.9
14. Other non-white	56.1	58.4	49.6
15. Puerto Rico	77.9	77.6	82.0

Source: Adapted from Avery M. Guest and James A. Weed, "Ethnic Residential Segregation: Patterns of Change," *American Journal of Sociology* 18:1096, by permission of The University of Chicago Press. Copyright 1976 by The University of Chicago.

The Impact of Segregation on Employment

When the topic of housing segregation was introduced earlier in this chapter, it was done so in the context of factors limiting the economic opportunities of blacks and other minorities. Obviously, housing segregation is in certain ways harmful in and of itself: It deprives people—especially black people—of a free choice of places to live. Furthermore, it restricts the market of housing available to blacks and other minorities, thereby requiring them to pay more for housing of comparable quality. Above and beyond these factors, however, housing segregation can have an impact in two other important ways. First, it can lead to segregated schools, which are at the center of the busing controversy; this will be explored in a later chapter. Second, it can aggravate the minority unemployment problem by restricting minorities to living in exactly the areas where employment opportunities are disappearing.

As we have seen, jobs are moving away from the central city neighborhoods where most black and Hispanic Americans live. A sizable segment of the urban minority population cannot afford to own an automobile. Many cities lack adequate mass transportation. As a result, many minority workers cannot get employment unless they can move to the areas to which the employment opportunities are moving. Patterns of housing segregation, however, frequently make this impossible, restricting minorities to areas with increasingly fewer jobs. The studies of Cleveland and Detroit mentioned earlier, for example, indicate that housing segregation has kept the numbers of blacks in the suburbs far below what would be expected on the basis of the black and white income distributions. Over and above the restrictions resulting from housing discrimination, the high costs of moving and the exclusionary zoning practices make it even more difficult for lower-income minority people—the ones most in need of decent employment—to move to where the jobs are going.

Although the evidence is mixed, several studies suggest that these factors are an important cause of high black unemployment. Research by Kain (1968) in Chicago and Detroit indicates that housing segregation in those cities may have cost black workers 25,000 jobs in Chicago and 9,000 in Detroit. Limited access to jobs also was identified as an important cause of black unemployment in studies by Mooney (1969), Hutchinson (1974), and Shanahan (1976). A recent study by the author (Farley, 1981) using data from all U.S. metropolitan areas showed that black unemployment in 1970 was higher relative to white unemployment in areas where the black population was more concentrated in the central city, and where jobs were more suburbanized. It is uncertain at present just how important housing segregation and job access are relative to other factors such as limited opportunity to learn job-related skills. Nonetheless, the movement of jobs from minority neighborhoods and the inability of these workers either to commute to distant jobs or to move close to those jobs constitute one more major handicap that has been imposed on many urban blacks and Latinos. There may be little or no deliberate racial discrimination on the part of employers, but the result may still be fewer opportunities for blacks and Latinos to obtain meaningful employment.

In addition to whatever harmful effects housing segregation has on minority employment opportunities, it must be mentioned that it probably has affected the racial attitudes of both whites and minorities. It tends to greatly restrict the amount of day-to-day neighborly contact between the races, and contact can be an important source of improved race relations. In its absence, prejudices and stereotypes frequently go unchallenged. Furthermore, when housing is segregated, the racial contacts that *do* occur can be of a highly destructive type. Frequently, the racial composition of a neighborhood changes rapidly, as with blockbusting, creating a situation that is highly threatening to both blacks and whites and probably ends up making intergroup relations worse, not better. Finally, as we have mentioned, the school desegregation and busing controversy is largely rooted in the pervasive pattern of housing segregation in American cities.

THE FISCAL CRISIS OF CITIES AND ITS IMPACT ON MINORITIES

Thus far in this chapter, we have seen how a number of trends, practices, and patterns in contemporary society have contributed to the maintenance of racial and ethnic economic inequality. Among the important areas we have discussed are rising educational demands for prospective employees, the departure of jobs from the areas where minority group members live, and the widespread pattern of housing segregation in our major metropolitan areas. We shall next examine another significant economic pattern with especially dire implications for American minority groups: the fiscal crisis of American cities.

In recent years many large cities with substantial minority populations have experienced serious fiscal difficulties as revenue sources have been unable to match expenditures. The most highly publicized cases have been New York City and Cleveland, both of which reached the brink of bankruptcy, but numerous cities have had similar problems, particularly in the Northeast and Midwest. In recent years, for example, Detroit was forced to lay off a large portion of its police force, Chicago was unable to meet payrolls in its school system, and Toledo was forced to close its school system entirely from Thanksgiving until after New Year's Day.

The reasons for this fiscal crisis are complex, but to a large degree they arise from a tax system that requires local financing of city services combined with the dual trends of business, industry, and middle-class population leaving the city and of the lower-income population becoming increasingly concentrated in the city.

Although cities receive significant state and federal financial aid through such programs as revenue sharing and Community Development Block Grants, cities must still raise the majority of their revenue through local sources. As Table 9.4 shows, in the 1976–77 fiscal year, municipalities raised about 60 percent of their revenue locally. School districts raised about half of their revenue locally. For both, the property tax was the most important source of local revenue.

Because cities must raise most of their revenue locally, a situation is created whereby the areas with the *greatest* need for services are the *least* able to raise the revenue to pay for those services. The ability, for example, of the property tax to raise revenue is directly dependent on the value of the property in the city. As we have seen, business, industry, and the middle-class population have all left central cities (especially in the Midwest and Northeast) in large numbers since World War II. Their departure has left steadily less high-value property to tax in the city relative

Table 9.4   Sources of Local Government Revenue,* 1976–77 Fiscal Year.

Source	*Percent of Total Revenue*	
	MUNICIPALITIES	**SCHOOL DISTRICTS**
Inter-government	39.6%	50.4%
Federal	14.6	1.5
State	23.4	46.8
Local General Revenue	60.4	49.6
Taxes	42.8	43.0
Property Tax	25.7	42.0
Other Taxes	17.1	1.1
Miscellaneous charges	17.5	6.6

Source: U.S. Bureau of the Census, 1978b, p. 46.
*Excluding utilities

to the rate of growth in the cost of urban government resulting from inflation. Consequently, many central cities have had to raise their tax rates per dollar of assessed valuation substantially, yet are still less able to raise revenue than the wealthier suburbs, which have much more property to tax. One example of this can be seen in East St. Louis, Illinois, a city whose population is predominantly black and in large part poor. The city's tax effort (that is, the tax rate per total per capita assessed valuation) is *six and a half times* as great as the average for the county in which it is located (Illinois Capital Development Board, 1977, p. 56). In spite of this, the city's revenues fell well below that of neighboring communities, and in recent years the city has been chronically unable to raise enough revenue to meet its expenses.

Much the same problem exists with other local taxes, such as the local sales tax or local income tax. If retail business moves out of the city, there is less sales tax revenue. If the wealthier population moves out, there is less income tax revenue. Thus, the need to raise revenue locally has become a crucial fiscal handicap to large cities with large minority populations, particularly in the Midwest and Northeast.

As local sources of revenue have been shrinking in large cities, the expenses of those cities have been rising, in large part because they have increasingly become the home of the poor. This in turn has created a rising demand for welfare and for various programs and services aimed at reducing the harmful effects of poverty. In large part, too, this demand has increased because various functions that once were performed by someone else have been left to the local government in recent years. As Piven (1977, p. 134) notes, "In the era of the big city machine, municipal authorities managed to maintain a degree of consensus and allegiance among diverse groups by distributing public goods in the form of private favors. Today public goods are distributed through the service bureaucracies." In other words, they are distributed at the expense of local governments, rather than at private expense, as they once were.

As a result of all this, it costs big city governments more today than ever before to provide even a low level of services to the needy. At the same time, their sources of revenue have been drained to a greater degree than ever before. The consequence has been sizable cuts in services in the cities where much of the black and Latino population of the United States live. Police and fire protection have been reduced, education has been cut back, library hours have been reduced, and day-care centers and public hospitals have been closed. Black and Latino Americans have been disproportionately harmed for a number of reasons. Most obviously, a disproportionate number of them live in the cities where the cutbacks have taken place. Beyond this, however, they tend—because they are disproportionately poor—to be more reliant on public services than are others who can buy services such as health care and education in the private sector. The recent tax-cutting mood of the American public has made the problem even worse, as the most fiscally fragile communities are most harmed by the revenue losses resulting from tax-slashing efforts such as California's Proposition 13 and Proposition 2½ in Massachusetts.

Again, all this may well have happened with no conscious and deliberate intent to discriminate. Nonetheless, it appears certain that as long as the current trend in the distribution of population, industry, and business continues, the present system of taxation will work against the interest of black and Hispanic Americans who are concentrated in America's central cities. They will continue to pay at relatively higher tax rates and to receive lower levels of service. It appears that only some major change in the system of raising local revenue could meaningfully alter this pattern.

HEALTH CARE AND MINORITIES

Another major element of the American economic system that has critical implications for the welfare of minority citizens is our health care system. In the United States, health care is largely purchased according to one's ability to pay. This and other institutionalized patterns in our health care system have significant effects on the health and mortality of minority Americans. We shall begin our discussion with a brief reexamination of the health status of minorities in the United States.

As we saw in Chapter 8, minority group members suffer significant disadvantages relative to whites in health status. They live shorter lives, are more likely to die in infancy, and suffer more frequent and more serious illness. A brief look back at the figures in that chapter will remind us that blacks on the average live about five years less than whites in the United States, and Indians six to seven years less than whites. Black babies are about twice as likely as white babies to die during the first year of life, and the situation is almost as bad for Indian babies. The statistics on illness show a similar pattern. Blacks experience about 32 percent more days and Hispanics about 15 percent more days of restricted activity due to illness than do white Anglos. Both blacks and Hispanics on the average experience about one and a half times more bed disability than whites over the course of a year. Other health indicators show a similar picture. The 1970 census, for example, indicated that 14.6 percent of the adult nonelderly black population was handicapped or disabled, compared to only 10.4 percent of the white population (U.S. Bureau of the Census, 1973c).

Kitagawa's (1972) Index of Excess Mortality is a shocking indicator of the extent of racial and class inequality in the area of health. This measure compares the mortality rates among various groups in the population to the relatively low mortality among white adults with at least one year of college. It shows that if other groups had the same health advantages as this group, their mortality would be much lower, and about 19 percent of all deaths in 1960 would have been prevented. However, the variations among different racial and class groups are tremendous. Among whites, about 17 percent of 1960 deaths were preventable; among nonwhites, about 36 percent of all 1960 deaths could presumably have been prevented. Among nonwhite females with eight years of school or less, fully half of all deaths were preventable (Kitigawa, 1972; Kitigawa and Hauser, 1973).

There are, of course, many possible causes of health and mortality differentials between majority and minority groups, and some have nothing to do with the health care system. Some jobs, for example, are more dangerous than others, and minority group members are overrepresented among many of the manual occupations that carry danger of injury or exposure to toxic substances. Other factors are the poor nutrition and inadequate shelter that are frequently associated with poverty. (As we have seen, blacks, Latinos, and Indians are much more likely than whites to be poor.) Life is frequently stressful for minority group members, and they frequently suffer from stress-related diseases such as ulcers and hypertension (high blood pressure). Among the black population, the problem of hypertension is especially widespread. Between the ages of twenty-five and forty-four, blacks are fifteen to seventeen times as likely as whites to die of hypertension (Cockerham, 1978, p. 34). Among males, blacks are somewhat more likely than whites to smoke—behavior which may be a response to stress and which is known to be harmful to health. Finally, we have seen that minority group members are more likely than whites to be the victims of violent crimes. In 1974, for example, black Americans were more than six times as likely as white Americans to die as a result of homicide (U.S. Bureau of the Census, 1979a, p. 124).

All of the above notwithstanding, there is considerable reason to believe that a good deal of the differences between minorities and whites in health and mortality do result form the ways these groups are treated by our health care system. In the following sections we shall examine some of the ways the health care system treats majority and minority groups unequally.

Cost of Health Care

In the United States, health care is expensive. Furthermore, it is in large part based on ability to pay. It is provided by the public sector only for the elderly through Medicare and for the poorest of the poor (about 6 percent of the population) through Medicaid. For the great majority of the population, including millions with low and moderate incomes, getting health care is a matter of buying or arranging for private sector insurance, paying out of the pocket, or, most likely, some combination of the two. In this respect, the U.S. health care system is virtually unique: Among the major industrialized nations of the world, only the United States and South Africa retain systems of health care based on ability to pay. The remainder of the industrialized countries have either a system of socialized medicine, as does Great Britain, or of national health insurance, as does Canada. Under socialized medicine, doctors are essentially salaried employees who are paid out of tax revenues. This system is similar to a large-scale Health Maintenance Organization (HMO), in which a group of people join together to pay the salaries of medical personnel who provide them with health care services. The national health insurance system retains the fee-for-service (that is, so much paid for each service, such as an office visit, lab test, or operation), but the fee is paid by a governmental insurance agency. Generally, the entire population is required to participate in this public insurance program.

There is good reason to believe that the system in the United States is more expensive and less efficient than either of the other two systems. Research in the mid-1970s indicated that the United States spends a larger share of its resources on health care than any other nation in the world (Organization for Economic Cooperation and Development, 1977; U.S. Department of Health, Education, and Welfare, 1978). By 1977, we were spending 8.8 percent of our gross national product on health care (U.S. Department of Health, Education, and Welfare, 1978, p. 380). Unfortunately, we apparently do not get more for our money—a number of the nations that spend less have longer life expectancies and/or lower infant mortality rates (see Population Reference Bureau, 1980).

This kind of system can be expensive for everyone—in recent years, medical expenses have been the number one cause of personal bankruptcies in the United States (Blumenthal and Fallows, 1974). Furthermore, it is rapidly becoming even more expensive: During the late 1970s, health costs rose much more rapidly than the cost of living as a whole—around 15 percent per year. The burden is especially heavy, however, on those with relatively low incomes—a group among which minority group members are greatly overrepresented. According to Light and Keller (1979, p. 482), one family out of eight in the total population, but one out of three in the poor population, spends 15 percent or more of its income on health care expenses. Part of the reason that health care poses a special burden on the poor is that they are less likely to have insurance: In 1976, among families with incomes below $7,000, over 21 percent had no insurance—neither private, Medicare, nor Medicaid. Disproportionate poverty among minorities is reflected in the fact that 16.3 percent of all nonwhite Americans have no insurance, compared to only 10.2 percent of whites (U.S. Department of Health, Education, and Welfare, 1978, p. 404). Among those in minority groups who do have insurance, many encounter considerable expenses not covered by the insurance (nationally, about 30 percent of health care expenses are out-of-pocket), and many more are reliant on Medicaid. Although Medicaid represents a distinct improvement over the past, when no assistance was available to the poor, it carries considerable problems, which will be discussed in a later section. Furthermore, even this very limited program has been further reduced as a result of the Reagan budget cuts. To summarize the evidence presented here, it is clear that minorities are less likely to be covered by medical insurance, less able to afford to pay for health care out of pocket, but more likely to have to do exactly that. This represents a serious barrier to the ability of minority Americans, and poor Americans more generally, to obtain needed health care services.

Frequency of Seeking Medical Care

An obvious factor influencing health is the frequency with which people seek medical care, including preventive care, which can keep people from getting sick when they otherwise might. Because of their poverty, minority group members on the average receive medical care, and particularly preventive care, less frequently than whites. In the population as a whole, white people see doctors about 9 percent more often than do minority group members. Strikingly, most of the racial difference in visits to doctors is among children: minority children see doctors about 25 percent less often than do white children (U.S. Department of Health, Education, and Welfare, 1978, pp. 261, 269, 270). Hurley (1970) found that only 10 percent of poor children had *ever* been to a pediatrician. Although this has undoubtedly changed somewhat because of Medicaid, the more recent figures from the Department of Health, Education and Welfare (HEW) cited previously show that the problem has not been eliminated. For the poor person it often comes down to a choice of what will be the greater burden: being sick or paying money that one cannot afford in order to see the doctor. This is especially true if the patient suspects that the doctor will merely tell him or her to "wait and see what happens" (Blumenthal and Fallows, 1974). The extent to which medical costs prevent people from seeking care is well illustrated by an experiment in Saskatchewan Province, Canada. As a way of deterring unnecessary visits to the doctor, the province instituted a $1.50 fee to visit the doctor (it had been free). Much to their surprise, provincial officials found that it did not reduce visits to the doctor; it merely changed the characteristics of those who came. Poorer patients, especially with large families, in large part stopped coming to the doctor. Wealthier patients, however, took up the slack and came more often, figuring that they would not have to wait as long. In short, all the fee did was keep poor people away. It was subsequently abolished (Blumenthal and Fallows, 1974). A similar experiment in California under Medicaid also indicated that very small charges to the poor can have major effects on use of health care (Helms et al., 1978).

Factors other than money keep minority Americans from seeing doctors. Both blacks (Hines, 1972) and Mexican Americans (Moustafa and Weiss, 1968; Madsen, 1973) tend to avoid contact with professional medicine to some degree. This is in part cultural, as these groups tend to rely on folk medicine or on the advice of friends and relatives. However, it is also partly caused by a lack of trust for professionals, a result in some cases of impersonal treatment in the past or of cultural imcompatibilities between minority poor patients and white upper-middle-class health professionals. These patterns are not universal among blacks and Chicanos and may be on the decline, but for those whose family and friends hold such attitudes, they can be a powerful factor keeping people away from the doctor (Cockerham, 1978, pp. 67–74). Resentment of and distrust toward the medical establishment also appear fairly widespread among Indian people (Allen and Tolliver, 1974). As we shall see in greater detail later in this chapter, part of the problem is a lack of black, Hispanic, and American Indian doctors. Medical underutilization is also partly the result of social class: A study of the poor in a New York state community revealed that fewer than one third regarded fainting spells, chest pain, chronic fatigue, shortness of breath, or persistent headaches to be symptoms requiring medical treatment (Koos, 1954, p. 32). To the poor, who generally do not enjoy good health to the same extent as the rest of the population, such conditions may be viewed as the normal state of affairs.

Availability of Health Care Personnel

Once minority group members do decide to seek medical assistance, they sometimes find that medical services are not readily available. Inner-city neighborhoods with large minority populations usually have relatively few practicing physicians. Nationally, metropolitan areas have about one doctor per 500 people. In the inner city ghettos, however, the picture is quite different. In the central district of Baltimore, there is only one doctor per 3,000 people and in one neighborhood with about 100,000 residents, the figure was one per 6,600 residents. In the South Bronx district of New York City, one of the nation's poorest areas, there was in 1968 only one doctor per 10,000 residents. Studies of Chicago and Los Angeles showed similar patterns of doctor shortages in low-income minority neighborhoods (Haynes and Garvey, 1969).

There are a number of reasons for this shortage. In a system where health care is based on ability to pay, a low-income ghetto is not an attractive place for a doctor to locate: They can earn more money in middle or upper-class (and often predominantly white) neighborhoods. In addition, health care personnel in large part locate according to the availability of health care facilities. The best-equipped hospitals tend to attract the most doctors and the best doctors, who prefer to locate where they can take advantage of the most up-to-date and elaborate technological innovations available. Such elaborate and well-equipped hospitals are rarely located in the ghetto or barrio. More basically, the hospital facilities available to the minority poor have recently *decreased* in many cities. In New York City, St. Louis, and other cities, public hospitals serving minority populations were closed during the 1970s as a result of the cities' fiscal problems.

Once established, the pattern of doctor shortages in minority neighborhoods tends to perpetuate itself. Frequently, physicians desire to locate their practice in proximity to other physicians, partly because of the convenience of referrals, but also because physicians, like other professionals, enjoy interaction with professional colleagues and will tend to avoid situations that deprive them of that opportunity.

Lack of Minority Physicians

There is another important reason for the lack of doctors in urban minority neighborhoods. Relative to the numbers of minority group members in the population, there are simply very few minority doctors. In the white population, for example, there is about one doctor per 750 population. There is, however, only one black physician per 3,500 black population (Hines, 1972). About 2 percent of all doctors are black, compared to the roughly 12 percent of the total population that is black (Sindler, 1978, p. 48). In 1970, 3.7 percent of doctors in the United States were Hispanic, a figure close to the proportion of the population that was Hispanic (U.S. Department of Health, Education, and Welfare, 1979). However, this figure is very misleading: Most of these doctors are not members of the two major disadvantaged Hispanic minority groups, Chicanos and Puerto Ricans. Some are immigrants who received their medical education in any of a variety of Spanish-speaking countries. A more enlightening source of information can be found in the more specific data available on medical school enrollments. During the 1968–1969 academic year—before the establishment of minority admission programs—only 0.2 percent of medical students were Chicano and fewer than 0.1 percent were Puerto Rican (U.S. Department of Health, Education, and Welfare, 1979, p. 12). These figures suggest a serious shortage of physicians among these groups, and even the corresponding figures of 1.6 percent and 0.5 percent for the 1976–1977 academic year indicate considerable underrepresentation, as these groups are presently estimated at 3.3 percent and 0.8 percent of the total U.S. population. The shortage of Chicano and Puerto Rican doctors can be seen in other ways. In California and Texas—the two states with the largest Chicano populations—11.9 percent and 16.4 percent respectively of the 1970 population was Hispanic, but only 5.1 percent and 10.3 percent of the doctors were Hispanic. In New York state, which has the bulk of the Puerto Rican population, 7.4 percent of the population but only 0.4 percent of the doctors were Hispanic in 1970 (U.S. Bureau of the Census, 1973a; U.S. Department of Health, Education and Welfare, 1979, p. 24).

Indian people are also seriously underrepresented in the medical profession. About 0.5 percent of the U.S. population is Indian; based on this figure we would expect about 1,400 Indian physicians nationally in 1970. The actual figure was 175 (U.S. Department of Health, Education, and Welfare, 1979, p. 10).

These figures indicate a serious need to increase the number of minority doctors. Such action would probably improve access to health care among black, Hispanic, and Native Americans, since minority physicians are more likely than others to locate in minority areas (though they, too, are subject to the same pressures that tend to keep physicians out of minority areas). Since anyone who wants to be a doctor must get into and through medical school, the participation of minority students in medical education today is a crucial determinant of the number of minority doctors in the future. This in turn has at least some bearing on access to health care among minority group members generally. Thus, decisions such as the *Bakke* case, which concerned minority admissions to medical school, may have important effects on future health of minority Americans. The crucial issue of who is admitted to medical schools, as well as the legal and social implications of the *Bakke* case, will be discussed in Chapter 13.

Thus far, we have explored a number of factors related to the ability of black, Hispanic, and Indian people in the United States to get needed health care. The cost of care, the availability of health care facilities and personnel in minority areas, the cultural incompatibility between middle-class medicine and some minorities, and the lack of minority physicians have all combined to create a situation in which minority group members do not, on the average, get health care to the extent that members of the dominant white group do. However, even when they do get health care, the kind of care they get is sometimes quite different from that which the white middle class is accustomed to. We shall explore these differences next.

Places and Types of Care:
Race and Class Differentials

Not everyone goes to the same kinds of places to get medical care, nor does everyone get care of comparable quality. Indeed, there are very important differences along the lines of social class both in where people go for care and in the kind of care that they get. Because minority Americans are so overrepresented among the lower-income groups, these differences also tend to occur largely along the lines of race and ethnicity.

Middle-class people are likely to have a private personal or family physician who is their regular source of medical assistance. This carries a number of advantages. First, the doctor's office maintains records containing a detailed medical history of the patients. This is helpful in diagnosis, as a new symptom may be related to a past problem and thus explained more readily than it would be if a medical history were not available. It is also helpful in treatment, since treatment for one condition can sometimes adversely affect another. The physician who has available a complete and detailed medical history is more likely to be aware of existing conditions that may be worsened by treatment for some new condition. Finally, the regular personal or family physician is more likely to get to know the patient as a person. Since we are becoming increasingly aware of the social, psychological and emotional aspects of illness, we know that such personal knowledge and concern can be of great importance in the treatment of illness.

The poor, however, receive their treatment not from private physicians but in other types of facilities: emergency rooms, hospital clinics, public hospitals, and sometimes so-called Medicaid mills. We shall explore the treatment of the poor under the Medicaid program in a following section; our focus here will be on the various hospital facilities in which the poor frequently receive medical treatment.

One problem common to emergency rooms and hospital clinics is that the patient tends not to see the same doctor on a regular basis and thus loses all the advantages of having a regular doctor discussed in the section above. Emergency rooms present particular problems. Since they are readily available and one does not have to "know" a doctor in order to go there, emergency rooms are becoming important sources of *primary care,* particularly among the poor (Gibson et. al., 1970; Satin, 1973; Satin and Duhl, 1972). (By primary care, we mean health care that is sought out by the patient as opposed to care that results from referral by physicians.) All in all, however, emergency rooms are far from ideal as a source of primary care. They tend to be concerned with relief of immediate symptoms and any seriously threatening conditions, rather than the exploration of underlying causes of the problem. Detailed medical histories are not taken, and use of lab tests to diagnose problems is usually minimal. In addition, emergency room physicians (often rotating interns or residents) usually have no medical history of the patient. Thus, emergency room care is often fragmented and commonly fails to get to the roots of the problem.

When their condition requires hospitalization, low-income patients frequently find themselves in public hospitals or Veterans Administration hospitals; middle-

A medical care facility in a minority neighborhood. Such facilities tend to be fewer in minority neighborhoods, and the type of care received there is often not the same as in the private facilities typically found in white middle-class neighborhoods. Marc Anderson.

class patients are usually hospitalized in private hospitals. As a general rule, private hospitals are better staffed and better equipped than the public hospitals, which must operate on very limited funds. Understaffing is a common problem in public hospitals, and limited money available for salaries may keep the best-qualified medical personnel away. In addition, public hospitals often lack the sophisticated, up-to-date diagnostic and treatment equipment found in many private hospitals. Even things regarded today as more or less essential are sometimes missing in public hospitals. In St. Louis, for example, City Hospital lacked air conditioning for years, despite that city's sweltering summers and despite the fact that extreme high temperatures can be seriously harmful to people in weakened physical condition. Only when a near-record heat wave struck the city in 1980, with day after day over 100 degrees (inside the hospital as well as out) was air conditioning finally installed on a temporary, emergency basis. Even then, it took a public outcry led by the local media to get the air conditioning installed.

Sometimes, when they are sick enough, low-income people are able to get admitted to university hospitals as ward patients. When this happens, the patients receive the most *technically* advanced treatment available. Even here, however, important differences exist between the way poor and nonpoor patients are treated. The nonpoor patient typically has a private or semiprivate room, and one physician is responsible for overseeing his or her care. Poor patients on the other hand, are

256

likely to be placed on a large ward shared with a number of other patients, and they are generally treated by interns and residents, sometimes on a rotating basis, rather than by a regular private physician. Again, their care is more likely to be impersonal and disjointed than that of the middle-class patient. Attitudes of medical personnel toward low-income patients are also less than ideal. Indeed, in the hierarchy of roles within the hospital, the role of patient is generally at the bottom of the ladder with respect to esteem, regardless of class (Reynolds and Rice, 1971). The position of the lower-status patient is even worse: Because of cultural differences between patient and practitioner, and because practitioners at the bottom of the hierarchy among physicians (interns and residents) are responsible for their treatment, low-income patients are often viewed as burdens and tend to remind interns and residents of their own low status within the medical hierarchy.

To summarize, the poor patient (and because of poverty, very often the black, Latino, or Indian patient) is generally hospitalized in a different kind of hospital, and within the hospital, in a different kind of setting. These differences frequently mean that the minority group patient receives lower-quality care, more fragmented care, or in some cases both. This, of course, happens once the patient reaches the stage of hospitalization. The lower-income patient, however often goes longer before reaching the hospital, which sometimes makes the treatment of conditions more difficult because they are allowed to become more advanced.

The Medicaid Program

In recent years an important source of health care for lower-income Americans has been the Medicaid program. This program, established by the federal government in 1965 along with the Medicare program for the elderly, provides federal funding (with required state matching funds) for medical treatment of the poor. At a minimum, the program must cover persons receiving welfare; in some states it is limited to such persons. Others may be included at the discretion of the states, subject to various limitations. The program is administered by the states, which of course means that there is considerable variation from state to state in the administration of the program. Basically, Medicaid is a program targeted at a small and very poor segment of the population. In 1976, only 5.8 percent of the population was covered by Medicaid; about twice that many Americans were poor by federal definition. Clearly, many poor people are not receiving the benefits of Medicaid. In addition, one must keep in mind that the federal definition of poverty is very conservative, and many people with very limited means are not included. Because Medicaid is so limited, it misses this near-poor population, many of whom cannot afford health insurance. Thus, Medicaid, as presently established, fails to cover millions of needy Americans. This failing can only be made even worse by cutbacks in the Medicaid program initiated by the Reagan administration.

As in other areas we have examined, minority Americans, because of their disproportionate poverty, are more reliant on Medicaid than white Americans. In 1976, 19.0 percent of minority Americans were covered by Medicaid, compared to only 3.8 percent of whites, who are much more likely than minorities to be covered by private insurance (U.S. Department of Health, Education and Welfare, 1978, p. 404). Still, this is below the roughly 30 percent of minorities who fall below the federal poverty level, indicating again that, among the minority poor, many are not covered by Medicaid. Even so, the Medicaid program clearly is the main source of payment for health care for a sizable number of minority Americans.

It should be said from the start that the Medicaid program has clearly improved access to health care among the very poor. Since the program began, poor people have seen doctors more often than before; indeed, they now see doctors more often than those just above the poverty level who do not qualify for Medicaid (Aday, 1976). Furthermore, such health indicators as life expectancy and, particularly, infant mortality in the United States have shown notable improvement in recent years. In 1979, for example, the infant mortality rate in the United States was 13.2 per 1,000 live births, compared to 16.1 in 1975, 20.0 in 1970, and 24.7 in 1965 (U.S. Department of Health, Education and Welfare, 1978, 1980). Among the black population, the infant mortality rate fell about 16 points between 1965 and 1976; among whites it fell only 8 points. (In spite of the greater improvement among blacks, the black infant mortality rate remains nearly twice as high as the white infant mortality rate.) There is no question that the improvement in public health generally, and minority public health in particular, results from a wide range of factors, only one of which is the Medicaid program. Furthermore, it is equally clear that major inequalities remain, as we have seen. There is little doubt, however, that the Medicaid program has resulted in *some* improvement in access to health care among poor and minority Americans, and it has probably led to some improvement in their health status. Having said this, it must also be said that the program is far from perfect, and that the care provided to the Medicaid patient is in many cases not as good as that provided to the middle-class patient. Let us examine some of the reasons for this.

To begin with, the Medicaid recipient must find a doctor willing to treat Medicaid patients. This is not always easy, since nearly half (45 percent, to be exact) of the nation's physicians do not accept Medicaid patients (Committee on the Budget, 1976, p. 125). Among those doctors who do accept Medicaid patients, some operate in "Medicaid mills," where large numbers of Medicaid patients are treated (or mistreated!) in assembly-line fashion. It is estimated that there are five hundred Medicaid mills in New York state alone, each billing the government, on the average, a whopping $500,000 per year for services to the poor (New York Times, February 15, 1977, p. 35). The emphasis in such Medicaid mills is to give as much treatment (sometimes, whether needed or not) as possible to as many people as possible in the shortest time possible. This can be highly profitable: Some physicians in the business have made *individual* collections in the hundreds of thousands of dollars in one year! It often means poor quality care for the patient, however. Among the more common problems are quick and superficial examinations, unnecessary lab tests and medical procedures, and "ping-ponging"—referring a patient with one problem to another doctor concerning another problem, whether the patient has the problem or not. All this is profitable for the doctors, who are paid once for each service they perform, but it is at best dehumanizing for the patient and, at worst, downright bad for the patient's health. Unnecessary operations and medical procedures are apparently fairly common in American medicine generally (Cockerham, 1978, pp. 140–141), but the problem is especially widespread among Medicaid patients. Not only does this waste public money; it threatens the lives and health of the Medicaid patients, since almost no medical procedure is entirely without risk. On the other hand, real problems may be missed because of the tendency of some Medicaid mills to run through as many patients as possible in a day. Thus, some Medicaid patients receive unneeded, costly, and potentially dangerous medical treatment; others fail to get treatment they really need. These problems result, in large part, because Medicaid retains the *fee-for-service* system that predominates in American medicine. By its nature, the fee-for-service system encourages doctors to perform as *many* services as possible in the shortest time. As third-party payments (by Medicare and private insurance companies as well as Medicaid) have become more common, the fee-for-service system has led to more abuses, and complaints about quick, impersonal treatment and unnecessary procedures have become more common.

Not all Medicaid patients are treated in Medicaid mills, but among those who are, the above-mentioned problems frequently stand in the way of high quality health care. In summary, we can say that the Medicaid program has made medical care available to millions of poor, largely minority Americans to whom it was not available in the past. The quality of that care, however, frequently does not match up to the quality of care enjoyed by middle-class Americans.

The American Health Care Institution: A Conclusion

Health care in America, as we have seen, is economically and racially stratified for two main reasons. First, poor people generally, and therefore a disproportionate number of black, Latino, and Native Americans, have a problem of *access* to medical care: They do not seek and/or cannot get care as readily as their white, middle-class counterparts. Second, when they do get care, it is often more fragmented, more rushed, and less holistic than the care received by the middle class. Thus, the American health care institution must be held at least partly responsible for the inferior health status of black, Hispanic, and Indian people in the United States as compared to the health status of white people.

It has been said that the American health care system (or nonsystem, as some call it) is designed to fit the needs of the physician more than those of the patient or the general public (see Stevens, 1971). This observation is strikingly similar to the more general position held by the conflict perspective: Social institutions tend to serve the interest of the dominant and powerful elite who control them. In the United States, physicians have wielded great political power through their national organization, the American Medical Association (AMA). This organization has vigorously resisted any governmental effort to regulate or control the fees that doctors charge for their services. Its considerable power can be seen in the fact that the United States stands nearly alone in the industrialized world in its having neither national health insurance nor socialized medicine. It has staunchly opposed such programs, fearing that even national health insurance would interfere with the setting of fees by doctors.

The more limited programs of Medicaid for the poor and Medicare for the elderly, of course, retain an essentially unregulated fee-for-service system, despite the fact that this system leads to unnecessary procedures, hasty treatment of patients, and other problems. Furthermore, largely as a result of the AMA's political influence, the quality of American health care is still based mainly on ability to pay. Only the poorest of the poor—under 6 percent of the population—are covered by Medicaid, and only the elderly are covered by Medicare. Furthermore, under Medicare, the patients must pay part of their own expenses.

For the great majority covered by neither Medicaid nor Medicare, health care remains based on ability to pay, either through private insurance or out of the pocket. This system has done an excellent job of preserving the fee-for-service system, and it has kept the typically high incomes of doctors rising well ahead of the pace of inflation. It has not, however, served the needs of the public as well, particularly those who are poor. It has led to a maldistribution of health care, with much of it in wealthy suburbs, little of it in the ghettoes and barrios, and little of it in rural areas. It has also led to class and racial *channeling* in health care, as the nonpoor receive care from private personal or family physicians while the poor (disproportionately minorities) receive frequently inferior care from emergency rooms, hospital clinics, Medicaid mills, and, when hospitalization is required, public hospitals. The effects of all this are worsened by a system of medical education that produces few minority doctors and that attracts future doctors mostly from the upper social strata.

All in all, there appears to be much truth in the observation that the American health care institution places the needs of the physician above the public, and the needs of the poor and minorities lowest of all. The limited reforms of Medicaid and Medicare, while helpful, have not been able to change that basic truth. It appears that to obtain racial and economic equality, the minimum necessary step would be the establishment of national health insurance, as Canada and so many other countries have done. To develop a truly efficient system, one that places the needs of the patient on a par with those of the doctor, basic structural reforms, such as elimination of the fee-for-service system, may be necessary.

SUMMARY AND CONCLUSION

In this chapter we began by examining competing theories on the causes of racial economic discrimination and on who benefits from such discrimination. Undoubtedly, the causes are complex, and the relative importance of various factors has changed with time. Although deliberate discrimination has decreased substantially since the end of World War II, economic racial inequality has persisted. Clearly, minorities are harmed by such inequality, and a plausible argument can be made, based on studies like those of Reich and Szymanski, that many whites are also harmed by it.

Recognizing that the causes of inequality have changed, we then turned to examining practices and patterns that have become institutionalized in modern society and that harm the economic positions of minority group members. Among such institutionalized patterns and practices are the use of inflated educational requirements in hiring, the movement of employment opportunities out of minority areas, and the pervasive pattern of discrimination in housing. The latter two, along with the system of raising revenue through local taxes, have helped to create a fiscal crisis in America's great cities, a crisis that has also been disproportionately harmful to the minority populations who are heavily concentrated in those cities. All of these processes have tended to preserve racial inequalities resulting from past discrimination. In the case of the large minority "underclass" described in the previous chapter, these processes have probably made matters worse. Finally, the problem of racial economic inequality is unlikely to be resolved until these institutionalized practices and patterns are altered. Eliminating deliberate discrimination, though necessary, does not appear to be enough: Further improvement in the status of minorities (and *any* real improvement in the status of the "underclass") will require more fundamental types of change.

Much the same is true of the health status of minority group members. Certainly not all of the health disadvantages of minorities can be attributed to the health care system. Nonetheless, it is clear that a health care system such as ours, based heavily on the ability to pay, cannot serve the disproportionately low-income minority population as well as it serves the higher-income white population. Thus, it appears that to eliminate racial and ethnic inequalities in access to quality health care, it will be necessary to make fundamental changes in the system of health care financing or, more basically, to eliminate substantial racial inequalities in income and wealth, or to do both. Thus, both the problem of economic racial inequality and the more immediate (but largely economic) problems of poorer health and higher mortality among the minority population would appear to require basic and far-reaching changes in our social institutions.

GLOSSARY

Blockbusting   A practice by realtors or real estate speculators that attempts to panic whites into selling their house at a low price because blacks are supposedly moving into the neighborhood. The speculator purchases the house, then sells it to a black family, often at an inflated price. This practice exploits both black and white homeowners and encourages racial segregation and rapid racial turnover in urban neighborhoods.

Fee-for-service system   A system of health care payment whereby a fee is collected by the physician for each service performed, such as an office visit, operation, or reading of an X-ray. Under such a system, the doctor is paid for each service in this manner regardless of whether the payment is made by the person receiving the treatment, a private insurance company, or a government program. This system may be contrasted with systems in which physicians receive fixed salaries, such as health maintenance organizations (HMOs) or systems of socialized medicine.

Index of dissimilarity   A measure of the amount of housing segregation between any two groups, such as blacks and whites. It indicates the percentage of either group that would have to move to attain complete integration (the same mix of the two groups in every block or neighborhood). It can range from 0 (fully integrated) to 100 (totally segregated). It is also sometimes called the *segregation index.*

Marxist theory of discrimination   A theory based on the ideas of Karl Marx claiming that discrimination hurts working-class whites as well as minority group members by creating racial divisions within the working class.

Medicaid Program   A federally funded program administered by the states which provide medical care to the poor. The program is for the most part limited to the poorest of the poor, covering only welfare recipients in many states, and covering some additional low-income population in other states.

Medicare Program   A social insurance program, funded under the Social Security System, which provides medical insurance for the elderly.

Split labor market   A situation where laborers are divided into two groups, one higher-paid (often a majority or dominant group) and one lower-paid (often composed of minority group members). The higher-paid group attempts to maintain an advantaged status by excluding the lower-paid group from certain kinds of employment.

Racial steering   A practice whereby realtors show white customers houses in all-white areas and show black customers houses in all-black or racially mixed areas.

The American Political and Legal System and Majority-Minority Relations

10

In this chapter we shall turn our attention to the American political and legal systems and examine their impact on majority-minority group relations in the United States. Although the chapter will focus on political and legal processes, it is important to recognize that these processes are closely intertwined with the economic processes described in the previous chapter.

To begin with, there is clearly some linkage between economic wealth and political power. Although the strength of this relationship is debated (see Mills, 1956; Reisman, 1953; Domhoff, 1967), clearly, those who are wealthy exercise considerably more power, both directly and indirectly, than those who are poor, and political power can enable a group to protect or advance its *economic* position. Thus, we see something of a vicious circle: If a group is generally poor, it will tend to have less than its share of political power, which will tend to further weaken its economic position, and so on.

Political processes are also linked to economic process through the unintended economic effects of decisions made in the political arena. Such effects may work either to the advantage or disadvantage of minority groups. This can be illustrated by two examples from twentieth-century American history. Under the Roosevelt administration, various laws were passed to protect the rights of workers to organize into labor unions and to prohibit employers from engaging in unfair labor practices. According to Wilson (1978) these laws tended to reduce job discrimination against blacks and other minorities, even though this was not their main purpose. It happened because strikebreaking was made more difficult (and subsequently happened less often), so that discrimination associated with the use of minority group members as strikebreakers decreased. In heavy industry particularly, a new environment developed in which white and minority workers cooperated in labor unions rather than struggling to undercut each other's position.

Government actions can also have a negative impact on economically disadvantaged minority groups. In the previous chapter, we discussed the impact of the current urban fiscal crisis on minority groups. A further analysis of the urban fiscal crisis reveals that it is in part a product of federal governmental policies that sometimes had unforeseen consequences. Tax deductions, loan guarantees, and subsidies provided housing assistance to millions of middle-class (and mostly white) Americans after World War II, and in large part made possible the flight of the

An urban freeway. More often than not, it is poor people and minorities that are displaced by the construction of such freeways, and they are rarely if ever paid the full cost of their forced move. Furthermore, such freeways have enabled the middle-class population to flee to the suburbs, leaving the central cities too fiscally poor to meet the needs of their growing low income and minority populations. Marc Anderson.

middle class to the suburbs, which depleted central cities of their tax base. The construction of urban expressways, financed mainly by the federal government under the interstate highway program, had similar effects, contributing to suburbanization of both residences and jobs (Long and Glick, 1976, p. 40; Kasarda, 1976, p. 119). Furthermore, the costs of the freeway system have been disproportionately borne by blacks and other minorities, whose central city neighborhoods have frequently been bulldozed for freeway construction (Downs, 1970). Thus, the economic welfare of minorities was influenced both directly and indirectly by government housing, taxation, and highway construction policies that outwardly had nothing to do with race relations.

It is clear, then, that decisions made in the political system can influence the position of racial and ethnic minorities in a wide range of areas, and can do so for better and for worse. In the following section, we shall examine ways in which political decisions and the American political system itself have affected the well-being of American minority groups.

GOVERNMENT IN AMERICA: AGENT OF THE WHITE OPPRESSOR OR PROTECTOR OF MINORITY RIGHTS?

Historical Patterns: Governmental Policies of Discrimination

Throughout American history, Afro-Americans, Chicanos, and Native Americans have been directly affected by policies and actions of federal, state, and local governments. As is described in some detail in Chapter 5, the U.S. Army, acting upon the orders of the federal government, played a critical and central role in the conquest and subordination of both the Indian people and the Mexican citizens who lived in what is now the Southwestern United States. Similarly, until the Civil War the federal government recognized the legality of black slavery in the southern states, and a number of U.S. Presidents themselves had slaves. For purposes of apportionment of Congress, the U.S. Constitution regarded each black slave as three-fifths of a person, one of many federal "compromise" decisions recognizing the legality and legitimacy of slavery in the southern states (Franklin, 1969, p. 142). Other such "compromises" provided for the return of runaway slaves to their owners, even when the runaways had established residence in states where slavery was illegal. Thus, it is no exaggeration to say that from the very beginning, the federal government played a central role in creating and maintaining racial and ethnic inequality in the United States. This was particularly true for the three colonized minority groups (see Chapter 6): blacks, Chicanos and American Indians.

In addition to the position of the federal government, state governments during the early history of the United States also took strong antiminority positions.

In the South all states had laws providing for black slavery. Furthermore, some had slave codes requiring freed slaves to leave the state and forbidding that slaves be taught to read or write and forbidding slaves from conducting any business with whites.

Lest there be any confusion, however, we should recognize that openly racist state and local legislation was not limited to the South and not limited to the pre-Civil War era. Pennsylvania, for example, denied the vote to blacks in 1838; Indiana did the same in 1851. In "liberal" New York, blacks were subjected to property ownership and length-of-residence voting requirements not required of whites (Franklin, 1969, p 220). Indeed, the predominant stance of state and local legislation concerning race and ethnic relations was supportive of discrimination until around World War II, and in some areas it remained that way for a good while after the war.

As noted in Chapter 6, the one brief period that was something of an exception to this general pattern was the period immediately after the Civil War known as Reconstruction. During this short period, laws pertaining to race relations were liberalized in both the North and the South, though liberalization in the latter came mainly from federal intervention. During this period, the Fourteenth Amendment (equal protection) and Fifteenth Amendment (no denial of vote due to race) to the U.S. Constitution and federal civil rights laws were passed. Numerous blacks were elected to southern state legislatures, and between 1870 and 1901, twenty blacks were elected to the U.S. House of Representatives and two to the U.S. Senate (Johnson, 1943; Franklin, 1969, pp. 317–321). However, this period did not last long. Beginning with a political deal struck between Democrats and Republicans in 1876 (McWilliams, 1951, p. 265; Simpson and Yinger, 1972, p. 389), the control of the South was returned to white supremacists. A very important step in the process was the *Plessy* v. *Ferguson* ruling of the Supreme Court in 1896 upholding the doctrine of "separate but equal" facilities. As a result, in many parts of the country public facilities quickly became separate but rarely, if ever, equal. In addition, the federal Civil Rights Act of 1875, mentioned above, had by now been declared unconstitutional, so that before the turn of the century, government had returned largely to the position of sometimes tolerating and other times requiring discrimination. Governmentally supported discrimination was most important in the first half of the twentieth century in the areas of voting rights, education, segregation of public facilities, housing, and immigration.

Voting Rights   Although the Fifteenth Amendment to the U.S. Constitution, enacted in 1870, prohibited denial of the right to vote on account of race, many of the states, particularly in the South, developed ingenious ways of getting around the amendment and keeping minority group members from voting. Probably the earliest was the "grandfather clause", which provided that people could vote only if they, their father, and/or their grandfather had been entitled to vote at some date prior to emancipation (Simpson and Yinger, 1972, pp. 369–390). These laws, passed by several southern states in the late 1890s, kept blacks from voting because they or their fathers or grandfathers had been slaves—and therefore ineligible to vote—on the date specified. These clauses had the effect of making previous condition of servitude (slavery) a condition of voting, which was forbidden by the Fifteenth Amendment, and in 1915 the Supreme Court declared them unconstitutional. In the meantime, however, they had been used to effectively eliminate black voting rights in a number of states for nearly twenty years.

Two other practices that were, for a time at least, accepted as constitutional, were the poll tax and the "white primary." Both practices became widespread in the South. In many southern states, the only real election during the first half of the twentieth century was the Democratic primary: These states were so heavily Democratic that whoever won the primary always won the general election. In Texas and several other states, voting in the Democratic primary was, with legislative permission, restricted to whites. This practice was based on a 1921 Supreme Court decision that primaries were not elections but rather party matters, and after two initial Texas laws were struck down, the Supreme Court approved in 1935 a decision by the Texas Democratic party convention to restrict the primary to whites, so long as the party, not the state, paid for it. In 1944 the Supreme Court reversed itself again and struck down all forms of the white primary, but by then the practice had been in effect in one or more southern states at virtually all times since 1923—a period of over twenty years.

Around the turn of the century, ten southern states instituted poll taxes designed to keep blacks, who were disproportionately poor, from voting by attaching an unaffordable cost to voting (Simpson and Yinger, 1972, p. 390). In Texas the poll tax—in effect for about sixty years—also kept Mexican-Americans from voting (Moore, 1976, p. 142), as well, of course, as numerous poor whites. This discriminatory practice remained in effect in five states until 1964, when it was finally outlawed by the Twenty-fourth Amendment to the U.S. Constitution.

In addition to these measures, an important way of limiting minority voting in southern states has been to give voting registrars considerable discretion in deciding who to accept and who not to accept for voter registration. Scruggs (1971, p. 85) argues that this was one of the most important ways in which blacks were kept from voting.

Probably the most widespread requirement limiting minority voting has been the literacy test. This requirement has existed in various forms in numerous states in the South, West, and Northeast. Among the states that have required voters to pass literacy tests are New York, California, and Massachusetts. Literacy tests have tended to reduce voting opportunities for black, Hispanic, and Indian Americans. All of these groups have suffered extensive educational discrimination, and consequently, a higher percentage of their adult populations are unable to pass the tests. The literacy tests in New York and in several southwestern states, because they have been exclusively in English, have had especially strong impacts respectively on Puerto Ricans (Simpson and Yinger, 1972, p. 413) and Chicanos (Moore, 1976, p. 142), though the New York test was revised to recognize Spanish in 1965. In many instances, too, literacy tests were applied unequally, with more stringent demands being made of minorities than of whites. (see Chief Justice Warren's opinion in *South Carolina* v. *Katzenbach*, 383 U.S. 301, 1966; quoted in Dorsen, 1969).

These practices were largely ended by the Voting Rights Act of 1965. Nonetheless, even during the late 1960s and 1970s, some states have engaged in practices that reduce minority voter participation. Reports by the U.S. Commission on Civil Rights (1968, 1975) indicate that in some southern states blacks have been kept from registering by limited hours for registration, harrassment by registrars, and more stringent identification requirements than were set for whites. Another common practice that has removed disproportionate numbers of minorities from the voting rolls is periodic purging of voters who do not vote. In Arizona, for example, this is done every two years (that is, every state/federal election), and this practice has had very disproportionate effects on Indian and Chicano voters (U.S. Civil Rights Commission, 1975, pp. 85−86).

It is clear from this review of the history of voting restrictions that numerous states have had policies governing voter registration that have made voting easier for whites than for minority group members. Especially but not only in the South, the intent of these policies has been partly or entirely to discriminate. During the past forty years, court rulings, the Twenty-fourth Amendment, and the 1965 Voting Rights Act have made discrimination in access to the ballot box considerably more difficult. Nonetheless, even in recent years the problem has not entirely disappeared, as the 1975 Civil Rights Commission report demonstrates.

Public Facilities   Throughout the South and in some border states, such public facilities as libraries, museums, parks, swimming pools, golf courses, and public transportation were strictly segregated through most of the first half of the twentieth century. Such segregation was required by both state law and local ordinances (Myrdal, 1944, Chapter 29). The length to which such rules of segregation sometimes went can be seen in examples presented by Woodward (1966, pp. 117−118). In 1932 Atlanta passed an ordinance forbidding amateur baseball clubs of different races to play within two blocks of one another. During the 1930s, Texas passed a law prohibiting ''Caucasians'' and ''Africans'' from boxing or wrestling together, and federal law law was used to hinder the circulation of films showing interracial boxing. In Oklahoma, state law even required segregated fishing and boating. In general segregation of public facilities was the law in the South and in some border areas until the 1950s.

State and local governments in the South were not always content with requiring segregation in publicly owned facilities. In many instances legislation was also passed requiring the operators of privately owned facilities and services open to the public to discriminate. An example of this can be seen in the laws of Florida, Tennessee, and a number of other states, which required segregation of passenger trains (Scruggs, 1971, p. 84).

As a general rule, governmentally mandated segregation of public facilities was much more widespread in the South and border states than it was in the North

(Mydral, 1944, Chapter 29). Nonetheless, the North was also highly segregated, and frequently the segregation existed with subtler forms of support and encouragement from state or local government. Although some northern states did have civil rights laws prior to the 1950s, others did not, and even where there were such laws, enforcement was frequently weak or nonexistent. Frequently, public facilities were de facto segregated by placing them in all-white or all-black areas rather than in borderline or racially mixed areas. In Chicago, police in some instances enforced segregation of city beaches even though there was no law or ordinance requiring such segregation (Drake and Cayton, 1945, p. 105). The absence of civil rights laws in some states made it perfectly legal for businesses to post signs such as "whites only," and many did (Myrdal, 1944, Chapter 29). Such practices sometimes also occurred without interference even in states that had civil rights laws. Especially in smaller northern cities, rigid patterns of discrimination frequently existed without governmental interference. Lynd and Lynd (1929) noted a pervasive pattern of racial segregation in Muncie, Indiana, including a policy of segregation at the local YMCA. In his autobiography, Malcolm X (Haley, 1964, p. 3) reports telling Michigan State University students about his experiences while growing up in East Lansing, the town where that university is located. "In those days," he told the students, "Negroes weren't allowed after dark in East Lansing proper."

The best overall description of the stance of state and local governments toward discrimination in public facilities in the first half of the twentieth century would be something like the following. In the South public facility segregation and discrimination was generally required by law. In the border states such discrimination was typically encouraged and often required. In the remainder of the country the position of state and local governments varied. In some states there was a formal prohibition of at least some types of discrimination, though enforcement was often weak. In many nonsouthern states, however, there was no law against discrimination in the private sector, and subtler forms of public-sector discrimination and segregation were frequently practiced, particularly at the local level and particularly in smaller communities. The federal government, with the exception of an occasional Supreme Court ruling, did little or nothing to stop such discrimination before about World War II, and in some ways tended to encourage it.

Housing   In numerous ways the actions of federal, state, and local government promoted discrimination in housing. Past actions of government are an important cause of the pervasive pattern of housing segregation that is found in the United States today. One of the most important things that governments did to promote housing segregation was to enforce restrictive housing covenants. As you will recall from Chapter 9, a restrictive covenant is a provision attached to a deed or sales contract in which the buyer must agree not to sell or rent to a member of a specified group, such as blacks, Chicanos, or Jews. To be enforceable, these restrictive covenants needed the backing of law. Until 1948 they got it: state courts, North and South, enforced these agreements by ordering a buyer of the "wrong" race or creed to give up the property (Simpson and Yinger, 1972, p. 437). Thus, state enforcement was the crucial link that made the restrictive covenant an effective force maintaining discrimination. At one time the practice of restrictive covenants was so widespread that it has been estimated that up to 80 percent of all vacant land in Chicago and Los Angeles was closed to blacks (Abrams, 1971, p. 218) . In 1944 eleven square miles of Chicago and five and a half square miles of St. Louis were covered by restrictive covenants against blacks (Vose, 1959). In 1948 the Supreme Court ruled that state courts could not enforce such covenants, but the covenants themselves did not entirely disappear until after the Civil Rights Act of 1968 banned housing discrimination.

Federal actions also contributed to housing segregation. The present-day pattern of predominantly minority cities and white suburbs is a legacy of the tax subsidies and the FHA and VA programs that made suburban housing available to the middle-class masses after World War II. Most of the benefits of these subsidy programs went to whites; comparable levels of aid were not available to lower-income residents, who were more likely to be minorities. Thus, a situation was created that enabled whites to buy new housing in the suburbs and restricted minorities for the most part to poorer-quality housing in the central cities. There is, furthermore, evidence that this did not all happen by chance. The official manuals governing Federal Housing Administration policy from 1935 to 1950 contained warnings against "The infiltration of inharmonious racial and national groups," "a lower class of inhabitants," "the presence of incompatible racial elements," and "a lower level of society" (Larsen and Nikkel, 1979, p. 235). In fact, FHA materials even included a model restrictive covenant, with the name of the unwanted group left blank to be filled in! (Larsen and Nikkel, 1979, p. 235). Thus, federal housing policy emerges as a major culprit in the problem of housing discrimination and segregation.

Local governments also promoted housing discrimination. With the silent acceptance of the federal government many local housing authorities used federal dollars to run segregated public housing developments. According to Franklin (1969, pp. 537, 610), this practice was widespread until around the time of World War II. It was the rule in all southern cities that had public housing and in some northern and border cities as well. As late as the 1950s formally segregated public housing developments remained in some parts of the country.

Another approach widely used against minorities at the local level is zoning. Zoning has been used primarily in two ways that tend to discriminate against minorities. One is the use of rezoning to block proposed housing developments that would house minority group members, attempt to create an interracial environment, or be built for low-income populations. The other way is through what is known as snob zoning, which uses devices such as minimum lot sizes and prohibition of certain types of housing to keep out "undesirables." Both practices have been widespread in American local communities, and to a considerable degree both remain a problem today.

Clearly, then, despite open housing legislation in the 1960s, federal, state, and local governments have been actively and heavily involved in housing discrimination over the years. Although many of the discriminatory practices have been curtailed, some, such as snob zoning, continue to play a significant role in housing segregation today. Thus, government at all levels bears a significant responsibility for the pervasive pattern of segregation and inequality in housing found in American urban areas today.

Education   Although education is discussed in detail in a later chapter, we shall briefly show that in education, as in other areas, the orientation of governmental policies—particularly at the state and local level—generally ranged from acceptance of discrimination to requiring discrimination in education up to the time of the 1954 Supreme Court ruling against segregated schools. In the South and border states, school segregation was generally required by law. No less than seventeen states and the District of Columbia at one time had laws requiring segregation of schools (Myrdal, 1944, p. 632). In addition, many local school boards implimented a policy of segregation even where it was not required by state law. State-mandated educational discrimination has been used not only against blacks but against other minorities as well. An 1860 California law, for example, excluded Chinese and Indians, as well as blacks, from that state's public schools. In 1906 the city of San Francisco took action to segregate the Chinese and Japanese in its school system, (Bahr et al., pp. 81, 85). In much of the Southwest, Chicanos were also segregated from Anglos in the school systems, (Moore, 1976, p. 81). In at least some instances, school boards in Texas responded to court orders to desegregate schools by mixing black and Chicano students, leaving white Anglo students in all-Anglo schools (Moore, 1976, p. 81).

Another area of discrimination in the past was the refusal to provide bilingual teachers who could communicate with Spanish-speaking students. At one time, for example, it was against the law in California for teachers to use Spanish in the state's public schools.

As we have seen in the preceding pages, throughout the first half of the twentieth century and in much of the earlier American history, there was a widespread pattern of discrimination involving, in various ways, the local, state, and federal levels of government. Although we have emphasized the areas of voting, use of public facilities, housing, and education; publicly supported or required discrimination has not been limited to these areas. In earlier chapters we discussed legal restrictions placed on the freedom of travel of reservation Indians, laws forbidding Chinese and Japanese to enter the United States at times when other immigrants were accepted, the use of American law to deprive Mexican-Americans of their land in the Southwest, and the blanket imprisonment of Japanese-Americans during World War II. A careful examination of American history can yield only one answer: Government at all levels in the United States has engaged in discrimination in thousands of ways and must bear a substantial piece of the responsibility for racial and ethnic inequality in America today.

Contemporary Patterns: Government and Majority-Minority Relations Today

As was described in Chapter 6, the position of governments in the United States shifted gradually to an antidiscrimination stance, beginning around the time of World War II. The major legislation, presidential decisions, and court rulings against racial and ethnic discrimination are summarized in Table 10.1.

It is clear that the formal position of the federal government today, as well as state and local governments is, on the whole, opposed to racial and ethnic discrimination. Nonetheless, a strong case can be made that, in subtler ways, government continues to operate against the interests of minority group members. As we have seen, government has in the past played a major role in creating and maintaining the racial and ethnic inequality that is so widespread in American society today. In spite of this fact, governments today are doing very little to undo the effects of the discrimination which they are largely responsible for creating. Analysis of a few areas of federal government action (or inaction) can clearly illustrate this point.

Table 10.1   Major Federal Actions Against Discrimination Since 1935.

Year	ACTION
1938	*Missouri ex. rel. Gaines* v. *Canada*, 305 U.S. 337. Supreme Court rules that University of Missouri must admit a black applicant to law school because the state provided no comparable law school open to blacks.
1941	President F.D. Roosevelt issues presidential order against discrimination in defense plants and governmental agencies.
1946	Two federal courts rule that segregation in interstate travel is illegal
1948	President H.S. Truman issues a presidential order to integrate the U.S. armed forces.
1948	*Shelley v. Kraemer*, 334 U.S.1. Supreme Court rules that racial restrictive covenants in housing are not legally enforceable.
1954	*Brown v. Board of Education*, 347 U.S. 483. Supreme Court ends "separate but equal" doctrine and rules that school segregation is illegal.
1957	President D.D. Eisenhower orders federal troops into Arkansas to enforce a court order to desegregate Little Rock schools.
1957	Civil Rights Act of 1957. Established and gave certain enforcement powers to a Civil Rights Division in the U.S. Department of Justice and provided penalties for failure to obey court orders in voting rights cases.
1960	Civil Rights Act of 1960. Strengthened voting rights enforcement provisions of 1957 Civil Rights Act.
1964	Civil Rights Act of 1964. Banned discrimination (including sex discrimination) in employment and union membership. Prohibited discrimination by privately owned businesses providing public accommodations, such as hotels, restaurants, and theaters. Strengthened enforcement provisions against discrimination in education.
1965	Voting Rights Act of 1965. Suspended use of literacy tests and permitted federal review of requirements attached to voting or registration. Authorized federal registration of voters where states discriminated.
1968	Civil Rights Act of 1968. Banned discrimination in the sale and rental of housing.

Government Spending   One way to assess the priorities of any government is to see where it spends its money. Examination of governmental expenditures in recent years will clearly show that, contrary to some popular opinion, programs to improve the status of minority Americans have not been given high priority. The recessions of 1974 and 1980 have reconfirmed the old adage that minority group members are the "last hired, first fired." During the 1970s, for example, the proportion of blacks unemployed has been two to two and a half times as high as for whites, with black unemployment soaring to around 15 percent during the recessions. In spite of this, programs to provide jobs, which represent only a tiny fraction of the federal budget, were cut during 1980 as a way of combating inflation, even though defense spending was *increased* at the same time. These trends, already under way during the Carter Administration, accelerated sharply after the Reagan Administration took over in 1981. Despite governmental claims to the contrary, the efforts to combat inflation have been undertaken largely at the expense of the poor. An examination of the federal budget in any recent year will reveal that the five largest anti-poverty programs (Aid to Families with Dependent Children, Food Stamps, Medicaid, Supplemental Security Income, and General Assistance) combined are a small piece of the federal budget, about 9 percent. By comparison, defense expenditures alone are about 26 percent. These figures are based on the FY 1981 budget; Executive Office of the President (1980). Further allocations away from these programs have been recommended by the Reagan Administration. This affects minorities far more than whites, since they are far more likely to be poor and to depend on such programs. Even these figures overestimate the share of governmental spending going to minorities, because the government also "spends" money by foregoing revenue through tax breaks of various forms. These tax subsidies go mainly to the wealthy, few of whom are minority group members (for more discussion of tax subsidies, see Larson and Nikkel, 1979, pp. 124–130.)

Of course, the tendency to cut job-producing programs during times of economic difficulty is doubly devastating, since (1) it is minorities who have the highest level of unemployment and (2) the cuts come precisely when jobs are most needed. Given the relatively low priority the problem has received, it is not surprising that black unemployment has consistently been twice, (or more) as high as white unemployment, or that the employment situation in the early 1980s in urban ghettoes is worse than it was during the last major round of urban violence in the late 1960s.

A related pattern of government spending that is harmful to minorities can be seen by examining some geographic patterns of federal spending. Such an examination shows that the large urban areas, where the bulk of the minority population lives, have gotten less than their share of federal dollars. New York City, for example, paid the federal government $3.2 billion more in taxes than it got back in expenditures *each year* from 1965 to 1967, many times the $1 billion deficit that brought the city to bankruptcy. At the same time, other parts of the country were getting back *more* than they paid in (Melman, 1976). Abrahamson (1980, p. 317) notes that federal aid to cities, where most black and Hispanic-Americans live, was much smaller relative to local taxes in 1965 than in either suburbs or rural areas. By

1976 the situation had shown little improvement in cities with large minority populations such as Atlanta, Cleveland, Newark, and St. Louis. Under the Carter administration there was some improvement, though the effects of chronic underfunding relative to suburbs and rural areas have driven many of these cities to the brink of bankruptcy. (In 1978 Cleveland became the first U.S. city since the great depression of the 1930s to default on a debt payment.) However, reductions in federal assistance to cities proposed by the Reagan administration threaten to make the problem worse than ever.

Welfare Reform   Another area where the federal govrnment has shown a lack of concern for minority needs in recent years is in its failure to reform the welfare system. As it operates now, the system tends to keep poor people dependent and unable to become self-supporting. It does so in part by failing to provide incentives to work: Recipients lose their welfare if they work, so they end up little better and sometimes worse off for working. It is also not unusual for recipients to be denied welfare if they seek higher education, even though such training may be exactly what they need to become independent. Finally, it is widely accepted that the welfare system tends to break up families by taking needed aid away from women because of the presence of an adult male in the household. Despite awareness of all these things, efforts at a thoroughgoing reform of the welfare system, including the payment of a minimum subsistence level of income, have repeatedly failed in Congress since the years of the Nixon administration.

Public Transportation and Health Care   Two other areas that the United States government has neglected are public transportation and health care. Among the industrialized nations of the world, the United States ranks near the bottom in these areas. The efficient subway systems of London, Paris, Stockholm, and Moscow present a striking contrast to the crowded freeways and the limited and financially insecure bus systems in cities such as Los Angeles, Detroit, and St. Louis. In the area of health care, one of the major supporters of national health insurance in the United States, Senator Edward Kennedy, is fond of pointing out that, aside from South Africa, the United States is the only industrialized nation in the world without some kind of national health care coverage. (The problems of minorities in the American health care system are discussed in detail in Chapter 9.) Governmental failure to provide public transportation and health care protection once again affects minority group members more than other Americans, because their disproportionate poverty leaves them less able than others to afford private transportation or health care. Statistics on auto ownership show that minority group members are less likely than whites to own automobiles (U.S. Bureau of the Census, 1972c, 1972d), and health coverage statistics show that they are also less likely to have health insurance (U.S. Department of Health, Education, and Welfare, 1978). In spite of all this, the Reagan Administration has proposed further cuts in funding for both public transportation and the Medicaid health care program, even though the U.S. financial commitment to both areas was already far below that of most other industrialized countries.

One may argue, of course, that the problems discussed here are economic rather than racial. In fact, W. Wilson (1978) has argued that class, rather than race, has become the main reason for black disadvantage in the 1970s. Indeed, governmental policies are, as we have noted, nondiscriminatory when taken at face value. This line of reasoning, however, ignores two important facts. First, the economically disadvantaged position of minorities is in large part the *result of past discriminatory actions by government*. As an illustration, imagine the government as the organizer of a twenty-mile foot race. The race is started with one of the runners required to wear a ten-pound weight on each foot. Halfway through the race, the organizer decides that this is not fair and decides to remove the weights. By now, however, the runner with the weights is exhausted and far behind, but the organizer says that he must nonetheless continue the race from his present position. Because the weights are gone, says the organizer, there is no more discrimination. In your judgment, has the organizer run a fair race? Does governmental inaction today, in the context of a history of nearly two hundred years of governmental discrimination against black, Indian, and Hispanic Americans make for a ''fair race'' in society?

A second problem is that inequality continues to exist in certain institutions under the control of and funded by the public sector in the United States. The two best examples of this are probably the legal system and the educational system. The relationship of the legal system to majority-minority relations will be discussed in the second half of this chapter, and education will be covered in Chapter 11. The points to be made here, however, are these: (1) Governments have for the most part been unwilling or unable to undo the effects of their past discrimination on American minority groups, and (2) discriminatory practices continue in the legal and educational institutions which are funded by and to a greater or lesser degree controlled by the public sector in the United States. Thus, despite the passage of numerous laws against discrimination since World War II, government continues to operate in ways that contribute to the maintenance of racial and ethnic inequality.

Foreign Policy   The foreign and military policies of the U.S. government have also tended to work against the interest of minority group members in certain ways. The Vietnam war, though it occurred during and after the period when the major civil rights laws were passed, is a case in point. First, the war shifted priorities away from the Johnson administration's antipoverty programs as more and more of the government's resources were turned to the war effort. Beyond this, however, minority group members fought and died in the war in numbers disproportionate to their share of the population. Among soldiers from the southwestern states, for example, over 20 percent of the casualties were Spanish-surnamed, though only about 15 percent of the area's population was Spanish-surnamed (Moore, 1976, pp. 55, 146; see also Guzman, n.d.). Black Americans also died in the Vietnam War disproportionately to their numbers in the population. Data gathered by the Harris Poll organization indicate that while blacks in the military were only slightly more likely than whites to go to Vietnam (55 percent versus 47 percent), they were overrepresented among the casualties: 12.6 percent of those killed were black, while only 9.3 percent of those in the armed services were blacks. The pollsters correctly point out that this was the result of class inequity much more than any deliberate racial discrimination. Nonetheless, the *result* was racial inequality (see Harris Poll, 1980).

Another example from the area of foreign policy is the government's policy toward racist regimes such as South Africa. Despite that country's open discrimination against blacks and other people of color, the U.S. government continues to permit American corporations to do millions of dollars in business with South Africa each year. This presents a stark contrast with our strict economic embargoes against other countries whose actions we disapprove, notably Cuba and, more recently, Iran.

Barriers to Greater Minority Political Power

Obviously, one reason that a group's interest may be ignored by government is that the group may have insufficient power to get the government to pay attention to it. Undoubtedly, minority groups have greater political power today than in the past, yet it is clear that their power is still quite limited. If we examine various sources of power, we can see some of the reasons why.

One way to gain power is through *influence:* gaining favor and popular support among groups other than one's own. When the issue was clear—that is, when the problem was defined as deliberate discrimination such as segregated lunch counters—minority group members had significant influence among the white population. During the 1950s and 1960s, white attitudes toward minorities and civil rights became significantly more favorable. (For greater detail, review Chapters 3 and 6.) However, as the issues became less clear cut and many whites began to believe that the problem had been solved (or at least the white part of the problem had been solved) by the civil rights laws of the 1960s, minority influence began to wane. Since the late 1960s various opinion polls have shown that whites no longer blame whites or our social institutions for racial problems and whites by and large do not favor any further major actions to solve the problem. Schuman (1975), for example, shows that whites feel that, at least in their own towns, blacks are primarily at fault for their own disadvantages. Of those responding, 54 percent felt that poorer jobs, education, and housing among blacks were mainly the fault of the blacks themselves. Only 19 percent said such disadvantages were mainly due to discrimination; another 19 percent blamed both discrimination and blacks themselves.

Research by Feagin (1972) shows similar results. Of eleven possible causes of poverty, a national sample of Americans ranked racial discrimination eighth. Low wages, poor schooling, lack of jobs, and exploitation by the rich ranked sixth, seventh, ninth, and tenth, respectively. Again, as in Schuman's research, the poor themselves were blamed for poverty. The top four causes of poverty according to those responding were lack of thrift and poor money management by the poor, lack of effort by the poor, lack of talent among the poor, and loose morals and drunkenness. The survey also showed that about 64 percent of the population favored a policy of guaranteed employment. But if such a policy required a tax increase to pay for it, only 35 percent would be willing to support it. Other proposals to combat racial inequality, such as preferential hiring and school busing, also met opposition from a sizable majority of whites, according to most surveys taken in the past decade. It is apparent that the majority of whites during the 1970s felt little or no personal need to try to solve racial problems, and there was little support among whites for new governmental initiatives in that area. Whether public concerns over such events as the bloody Miami riots and the shooting of civil rights leader Vernon Jordan in 1980 will lead to significant attitude changes among whites during the 1980s remains to be seen.

Voting and Political Participation

Another source of power is through voting strength. This is particularly true if a group votes as a bloc, as minority group members sometimes do. This can be seen in several recent presidential elections. In 1964, 97 percent of the black vote went to the Democratic candidate, Lyndon Johnson. In 1972, 87 percent went to Democrat George McGovern, even though he lost badly in the total vote. In 1976, 82 percent of blacks voted for Democrat Jimmy Carter. Indeed, the black vote can be credited for the victories of Democrats John Kennedy in 1960 and Jimmy Carter in 1976: in a number of big states, their margin of victory was far less than the number of votes they received from blacks. In spite of this, it is important not to overestimate the voting power of minorities. The combined racial/ethnic minority population in the United States is only 15 to 20 percent of the total population, less among the voting age population, and still less among those registered to vote. Thus, minorities only have enough votes to make a real difference when the election is very close, as was the case in both 1960 and 1976. In landslide elections of 1964 and 1972, however, the minority vote made no difference. We have already noted that 87 percent of the black vote was not enough to save George McGovern from one of the worst defeats ever (in an election where racial and economic inequality were made an issue by the losing candidate), and in 1964, Lyndon Johnson's win was so overwhelming that he would have still won easily without any minority votes. Much the same was true in 1980: the black and Hispanic vote went heavily for Democrat Jimmy Carter, but Republican Ronald Reagan's lead in the much larger white vote was so substantial that the election was not even close. Even in the relatively close election of 1968, an overwhelming black vote for Democrat Hubert Humphrey did not save him from losing to Richard Nixon. It is clear that any time the electorate divides racially (as it did to an unusual degree in 1972), minorities will come out on the losing side.

One factor that does help strengthen the voting power of minorities is that, even though they are a relatively small percentage of the total population, they are concentrated in certain geographic areas, and in such areas, they may be a majority or near-majority of the population. In such cities as Washington, Atlanta, Detroit, and Newark, the black electorate has become large enough to control or heavily influence the local political apparatus. These cities and others like them have elected black mayors in recent years, and black majorities are beginning to appear on such elected bodies as city councils and school boards. Similarly, Chicanos have been able to gain control of the political apparatus in some towns and counties in south Texas where they are the majority of the electorate (Moore, 1976, pp. 153–154). In New Mexico, where Chicanos are not only numerous but have long been politically involved (although in a very conventional style), numerous Spanish-surnamed officials have been elected over the years, even to such high offices as Governor and U. S. Senator.

Even where they are in the majority and have elected members of their group to public offices, the power of minority group members is limited. One of the most important limitations is that the areas of concentrated minority population are typically low-income areas, which places severe restrictions on their tax bases. Consequently, they are often unable to provide needed services without outside help, and such help, if it is available at all, frequently comes with strings attached. Detroit and East St. Louis, Illinois, are two prime examples of cities where minorities are in solid political control, but where the cities have been in a more or less constant position of fiscal inadequacy. In such situations a black mayor is ultimately confronted with the same choices as a white mayor in the same situation: Cut jobs and services to make the budget balance, accept outside aid with undesirable conditions attached to it, or both. Indeed, the white mayor of New York City, the black mayor of Detroit, and the Chicano mayor of a small south Texas town are all faced with the same kind of unpleasant situation, and it must be recognized that this situation places a serious limit on the extent of black or Chicano political power, even where blacks or Chicanos are in the majority and have elected members of their own group to public office.

All these factors combine to create a situation that leaves minorities seriously underrepresented in the political system, despite some improvement in recent years. The unwillingness of whites to support further major action to improve the position of minorities means, of course, that current officials have little or no incentive to pursue such policy. It also makes it very difficult for outspoken minority group members to be elected where the electorate is mostly white. Black mayors have been elected in predominantly white cities such as Los Angeles and Grand Rapids, Michigan, and Edward Brooke, a black, was elected to the U.S. Senate by a predominantly white electorate in Massachusetts. However, these officials have held quite moderate views on intergroup relations. More outspoken officials, such as Mayors Coleman Young of Detroit and Richard Hatcher of Gary, Indiana, would have a difficult time getting elected without the large black electorates that exist in their cities. In Detroit, for example, a large majority of the white vote has gone to white opponents of Coleman Young when his main opponent has been white (though the black vote went even more heavily for Mr. Young).

Mayor Coleman A. Young of Detroit accepts applause after being sworn in for a second four-year term in 1978. During the 1970s, increasing numbers of black and Hispanic Americans have been elected to public office. Most of these officials have been elected in areas where, like Detroit, the black or Hispanic population is a numerical majority. In some cases, their ability to bring about needed changes has been hampered by the fiscal poverty of the areas they govern. UPI.

In any case, an examination of the districts from which black officials have been elected will reveal that most have predominantly black constituencies. It is largely for this reason that, as noted in Chapter 8, fewer than 1 percent of all elected officials are black, even though around 12 percent of the U.S. population is black. The underrepresentation is especially severe at the state and federal levels, where most of the important and far-reaching decisions are made. Given current voting and belief patterns, it appears unlikely that our political system can soon produce any major change: Nearly all statewide offices, and all but a handful of congressional districts, have electorates where the majority of voters (usually a large majority) are white. In most cases these voters simply will not elect a minority group member who speaks out in favor of major policy changes to improve the status of minorities. Thus, with the exception of a relative handful of big-city mayors and congressional representatives from districts with large minority populations, such input is nearly absent from the political system.

In the search for alternatives to this pattern, one that comes to mind is suggested by the internal policies of the Democratic political party since 1972. In order to assure representation of women and minorities, the party has established guidelines concerning the percentage of convention delegates that should be female and that should be minority. This has led to a substantial increase in female and minority representation in the party's 1972 and 1976 presidential nominating conventions. Such an approach or something similar might be possible in the larger political system as well (for example, by requiring parties to use such percentage guidelines in their nominations of candidates for public office). However, based on white reactions to such proposals as busing and preferential hiring for minorities, there would undoubtedly be intense opposition to such a proposal. Indeed, there has been considerable criticism of the Democratic party guidelines by some within the party who regard them as unfair reverse discrimination, a barrier to the free election of delegates, or both.

To summarize briefly, it is clear that the American political system still leaves much to be desired in its treatment of racial and ethnic minorities. Although deliberate discrimination is for the most part illegal today, government is doing relatively little to undo the effects of past discrimination, much of which was required or encouraged by laws and policies established by governments at various levels. Undoubtedly, part of the reason for this is that, despite considerable improvement, minorities are still seriously underrepresented among our elected officials. Furthermore, there appears to be a definite limit to how much more it *can* improve, within the context of present white attitudes, the distribution of voting power, and the system by which we elect our representatives. Thus, we must conclude that a sizable degree of institutional discrimination (though probably mostly of the nonconscious type) remains in our political system. Despite the ban against open and deliberate discrimination, that system continues to operate in a way that permits, and in some ways encourages, the continuation of racial and ethnic inequalities it played a central role in creating.

THE AMERICAN LEGAL SYSTEM
AND MAJORITY-MINORITY RELATIONS

Closely related to and substantially influenced by the American system of government is the nation's legal system. In the remainder of this chapter we shall examine the present-day treatment of minority group members by the American legal system. We shall attempt to answer the question, to what degree does the legal system serve to protect the rights of minority group members, or on the other hand, to keep them in a disadvantaged position.

As we have already seen, a number of important decisions by the federal courts in recent decades have gone against the legality of deliberate discrimination and have thereby worked to protect the rights of minority group members. Of course, it is important to point out that in the past, many decisions of the courts went the other way. We have already discussed the impact of these major, precedent-setting cases. Our concern in the remainder of this chapter is different: Here we shall examine the day-to-day operations of our criminal justice and judicial systems to see how they influence the well-being of black, Hispanic, and Indian people on a day-to-day basis. We shall emphasize two areas. First, we shall examine our criminal justice system and the process by which it accuses, assesses guilt, and assigns punishment. Second, we shall examine the effectiveness of the police and courts in protecting minority group citizens against crime and illegal exploitation.

The Criminal Justice System and the Minority Accused

In any discussion of the detection and punishment of crime by the criminal justice system, it is important to stress that there are numerous steps in the process. At each of these steps, decisions must be made, and at any such step, there is the potential for either fair and equal treatment under the law or for unfair and discriminatory treatment, whether intentional or not. Among the major steps in the criminal justice process are the following:

1. Detection of crime
2. Decisions by police to arrest a suspect
3. Decision by police or prosecutor of whether to press charges in court, and if so, in what type of court
4. Setting and administration of bail for accused persons
5. Decision of judge, judicial panel, or jury of whether accused is guilty or innocent
6. Sentencing—that is, decision concerning nature and severity of penalty for crime

In the following pages, we shall examine the experiences of majority and minority group Americans at each of these stages in the criminal justice process.

Detection   It may well be that in present-day American society, the greatest potential for unequal justice arises from the fact that the criminal justice system detects the crimes committed by some kinds of people but fails to detect the crimes committed by others. A look at conventional sources of data on crime, such as the FBI's *Uniform Crime Reports,* will quickly confirm that the arrest and conviction rates of minority group members are far above those of whites. Other sources of data, such as criminal victimization surveys and self-report studies, seem to confirm that minority group members commit considerably more crime than do whites. However, all of these conventional sources of data on crime share one crucial problem: They focus only on certain kinds of crime. The major crimes included in the FBI crime index (frequently referred to as index crimes), for example, include homicide, rape, robbery, assault, larceny, burglary, and auto theft. All are in the so-called "street crime" category. They are disproportionately committed by persons of relatively low socioeconomic status, and they are crimes with known and clearly identifiable victims. However, there is good reason to believe that the importance of these and similar crimes may be overstated compared to other crimes that do not so often appear in the statistics. We are speaking here of white-collar and corporate crime, including tax fraud, bribery, embezzlement, violation of antitrust laws and laws on job safety, and the sale of products known to be unsafe or defective. The economic and human costs of such crime are enormous. Each year about 100,000 workers die as a result of health hazards encountered on the job, and many of the largest and most prominent corporations are involved (Quinney, 1979, p. 199). In recent years, there have been several highly publicized cases where automobiles with defects known to be dangerous were sold anyway, resulting in numerous deaths. If we examine the dollar costs of corporate and white-collar crime, we see that it, too, is staggering. In 1961, for example, it was shown that bid-rigging by companies producing electrical equipment had been bilking taxpayers at all levels of government out of an average of nearly $2 billion per year (Barlow, 1978, p. 247). Indeed the cost of white-collar and corporate crime is probably considerably greater than that of common "street crime." In 1967, for example, a presidential commission estimated that while such crimes as robbery and burglary resulted in an annual loss of around $600 million, the annual loss from fraud was about 1.4 billion and from unreported employee theft, close to 1.3 billion (President's Commission on Law Enforcement and the Administration of Justice, 1967). A more recent report (Chamber of Commerce, 1974) placed the annual cost of occupational crime at $40 billion, and this does not even include the cost of antitrust or health and safety violations!

Obviously, racial and ethnic minority group members are relatively uninvolved in crimes of this nature. As we saw in the previous chapter, they simply are not represented in the board rooms where the most costly crimes of this nature occur. To put it as clearly as possible, minority group members, because of their relatively low socioeconomic status, are more likely to commit "street crimes"; whites, with their higher socioeconomic status, are more likely to commit "white-collar" and corporate crimes. As we have seen, most conventional measures of crime focus on street crimes rather than white-collar crimes. As a result, most conventional measures of crime focus on the crimes more likely to be committed by minority group members, and deemphasize the crimes more likely to be committed by whites.

There are a number of reasons for this. Certainly, to a large degree the cause is to be found in the economic and political institutions in our society and the supporting ideology. As the dominant economic institution in our society, the corporation exercises tremendous political power (Domhoff, 1967), which gives it substantial influence over the criminal justice system, including the reporting of crime. The values and beliefs of our society are also heavily influenced by the dominant groups and institutions in our society, and this tends to direct the public's attention *toward* crimes committed by those from subordinate groups and *away from* crime in the dominant elements of our society (see Quinney, 1979, pp. 41–52; Barlow, 1978, pp. 258–261).

Beyond these considerations, the ease of *detection* plays an important role in differences in both public awareness of and punishment of white-collar and street crimes. When there is a murder, rape, robbery, burglary, or assault, there is usually little or no doubt that a crime has in fact taken place, and little or no question as to who has been the victim. This is usually not true of white-collar or corporate crime. Although we are all aware that we are continuously paying the cost of white collar and corporate crime, we usually do not know when and where we have been victimized. If, for example, the price of a product is inflated because of price-fixing conspiracies in violation of the antitrust laws, we are usually unaware of it. Illnesses arising from exposure to pollutants encountered in the workplace, or the release of dangerous substances into the environment, may not be identified as such. Even where employers are the victims of white-collar crime, it frequently goes undetected. A good example of this is theft by computer, an increasingly common crime that is very difficult to detect.

Perhaps because of this greater awareness of the occurrence of street crimes, it is probably true that people are generally more *afraid* of street crimes than they are of white collar and corporate crimes. In other words, people are more worried about the possibility of being robbed, shot, or raped than about the possibility of being exposed to dangerous chemicals, killed in an automobile that was known to be unsafe, or cheated by antitrust law violations. Not only are we more *aware* of being the victims of street crimes; such crimes also tend to be more sensational. Because of this greater public fear of street crime, law enforcement agencies are undoubtedly under more public pressure to control such crime. Nonetheless, this may be starting to change to some degree: incidents such as the Love Canal toxic waste disaster and the sale of autos with exploding gasoline tanks may be making the public more aware of the dangers they face from at least some types of corporate crime.

Difficulty of detection, combined with political, attitudinal, and ideological influences, has created a situation with important racial and ethnic implications. First, there is a greater public awareness of types of crimes committed disproportionately by minority group members than of crimes committed disproportionately by whites. Consequently, there is a tendency to label minority group members as criminally inclined, because there is greater *awareness* of the kinds of crime they are more likely to commit. Secondly, it is easier to detect and "solve" street crimes (disproportionately committed by minorities) than it is white collar and corporate crimes (disproportionately committed by whites). Thus, it is easier to get away with crime if you are a white corporate executive than it is if you are an unemployed black, Chicano, or Indian.

Even in those instances where they commit the same crime, whites, because of differences in social class, frequently have a better chance of getting away undetected than do minority group members. Let us consider the "crime" of smoking marijuana, an illegal activity widespread among all racial, ethnic, and social class groups in the United States (see National Commission on Marijuana and Drug Abuse, 1972; National Institute on Drug Abuse, 1976). Nonetheless, there is a tendency in some areas for blacks to be overly represented among marijuana arrestees. The National Commission on Marijuana and Drug Abuse (1972) found, in a study of six areas, that in five of them marijuana arrest rates were quite representative of the area's racial composition. In one area, however, the picture was drastically different. In the Chicago area (Cook County, Illinois), where 22 percent of the population was black in 1970, fully 53 percent of those arrested for marijuana violations from July to December 1970 were black. Nationwide, statistics on drug arrests do not provide a clear answer, but they do suggest the possibility that blacks are overrepresented among marijuana arrestees. Although they are about 12 percent of the population, blacks are about 20 percent of all drug law arrestees, and over 70 percent of such arrests are for marijuana (Federal Bureau of Investigation, 1979). It is known that blacks are overrepresented among both users and arrestees for certain drugs such as heroin. However, these are a small part of the total, suggesting a strong possibility of black overrepresentation among marijuana arrestees. Another example of this can be seen in arrests for drunkeness. J. Q. Wilson (1978) studied four cities and found that in three of the four, blacks were two to three times as likely as whites to be arrested for drunkeness, another "victimless crime" common among both the black and white populations. One possible reason was a tendency in many cities for police to view black drunks, but not white drunks, as "homeless" or derelict. (Wilson, 1978, p. 160).

There are a number of reasons why minorities are sometimes more likely to get arrested than whites, even for the same violations. Many concern the ease of detecting the violation. As we have already seen, white-collar crimes are usually harder to detect than street crimes. Even when they commit the same violation, however, the middle and upper classes (which are disproportionately made up of whites) often have an easier time committing it undetected. Let us consider further the example of marijuana use. As is true with all victimless crimes, people are arrested for marijuana violations when the police *observe* them using, carrying, growing, or delivering the drug. Because the nonpoor have greater access to private space than the poor, they are less likely to be observed by the police engaging in illegal behavior such as marijuana smoking. Put simply, nonpoor pot smokers are likely to do their smoking in the privacy of their homes; poor ones are more likely to smoke in streets or parks. They are more likely to be observed by the police and are therefore more likely to be arrested. This principle, of course, applies to many illegal activities besides marijuana smoking, and it is an important reason why the poor are arrested more often than the nonpoor, even for comparable activities. Although this effect is mainly one of social class, it has important racial and ethnic effects, since Indian, Hispanic, and black Americans are much more likely to be poor than whites. This can be illustrated by Green's (1970) study of arrest rates in Ypsilanti, Michigan. Blacks were significantly more likely than whites to be arrested, with most of the differences linked to social status, occupation, and migration to the area from the South.

Decision to Arrest   One of the most critical stages of the criminal justice process is the police officer's *decision* on whether to make an arrest when an illegal act is suspected. Unfortunately, this is also one of the most poorly understood stages of the process, since it is one of the most difficult to study. Clearly, the police can and do exercise considerable discretion in making such decisions. They cannot and do not arrest every person they suspect of committing an illegal act (see Goldstein, 1960; Kadish and Kadish, 1973; La Fave, 1965).

Apparently, *police expectations* concerning the behavior and motivations of suspects heavily influence their decision on whether or not to make an arrest. Such expectations are shaped by two major factors. First, there are *police beliefs* about the kinds of people who may commit crimes and about how citizens should behave toward the police. Social class, race and ethnicity, age, dress, and appearance influence such police judgments about citizens. Police will "find" and "solve" more crime among groups they are suspicious of, for example, at least partly because they investigate more closely the activities of people in these groups. Thus, if the police are generally suspicious of a particular racial or ethnic group, they will probably be more likely to investigate, stop, and/or arrest members of that group.

The second major factor influencing police expectations about citizens is the demeanor and behavior of the citizens themselves toward the police. In one study (Piliavin and Briar, 1964), police officers themselves reported that in juvenile cases, the demeanor of the suspect was the main factor determining how they handled the situation in 50 to 60 percent of their cases. Of course, citizen demeanor toward the police is shaped by citizen perceptions of the police: Citizens who do not trust the police will be more likely to behave in a negative manner toward them.

Unfortunately, racial, ethnic, and class factors can influence the ways in which both police and citizens perceive one another. Police, on the one hand, frequently have prejudiced or sterotypical attitudes and beliefs toward minority group members (Black and Reiss, 1967, pp. 132–139). However, one should not be too quick to place all the blame on the individual police officers. The structure of the situation in which they must operate probably tends to make them prejudiced: The crimes they can most readily detect and are *expected* to detect are mainly the street crimes, which are disproportionately committed by the poor and by members of racial and ethnic minority groups. This leads to a situation in which a "criminal stereotype" of certain class and ethnic groups easily develops. The situation is worsened, of course, by the fact that minority groups are substantially underrepresented on nearly all police forces in the United States, though in recent years court orders and increased minority voting power have begun to change that. Lundman's (1980, pp. 91, 101) data for Columbus, Ohio in 1975 are probably quite typical: The city's population was 19 percent black, but fewer than 4 percent of the city's police officers were black. A nationwide study showed that in 1975, 6.5 percent of all police officers in the United States were black, compared to between 11 and 12 percent of the population (National Institute of Law Enforcement and Criminal Justice, 1978, p. 13). Projections based on the rate of increase in minority representation on police forces indicate that by 1985, minorities will still be underrepresented on police forces (National Institute of Law Enforcement and Criminal Justice, 1978, p. 13). As a result, minority neighborhoods in many cities are patrolled largely by white police forces. Clearly, one effective way to combat police prejudice and stereotyping about minorities is to have more minority police.

Race and ethnicity also influence the ways in which minority group citizens view the police. A survey of thirteen large American cities in 1975, for example, showed that blacks had a considerably less positive attitude about police effectiveness than whites (Parisi et al., 1979). These data are presented in Table 10.2. The survey also indicated that blacks were substantially more likely than whites to express dissatisfaction concerning inadequate amount of patrol or investigations in their neighborhoods, promptness, courtesy and concern, and discrimination.

There are a number of reasons for these dissatisfactions. Minority members are well aware of the stereotyping and prejudice among police, and many have apparently experienced discourtesy or excessive use of force. There is a tendency, accordingly, for some minority group members to counterstereotype the police. This may lead to a mutual *self-fulfilling prophecy:* The white police officer and the black or Hispanic citizen, each expecting the worst of the other, speak or behave in some negative way toward each other. This "confirms" the other's beliefs, "proving" the correctness of the stereotype (Kuykendall, 1970). Given the mutual distrust, it is easy to see how encounters between white police and minority citizens can more easily escalate into confrontations leading to arrest than, for example, encounters between white police and white citizens (particularly white middle-class citizens).

There are other reasons for minority antipathy toward police. It is widely believed among minorities, with some basis in fact, that police do not adequately patrol their neighborhoods and that they take crime against blacks less seriously than crime against whites (Parisi et al., 1979, p. 301; Wilson, 1978, 157–165). Another factor creating hostility between police and minorities is the role of police as agents of control during minority protests. Regardless of the target of the protest, it is the police who must control it, and this frequently places them in an adversary position to groups such as minorities seeking change through social and political protest. Because of their central role of controlling protest, the police become protectors of the status quo (Quinney, 1979, pp. 265–269), as indeed does the entire criminal justice system (see Balbus, 1973). In addition, police frequently overreact or treat people of different groups differently in situations of social unrest. We have already

Table 10.2   Rating of Local Police by Race, 13 American Cities, 1975. Question: "Would you say, in general, that your local police are doing a good job, an average job, or a poor job?"

RACE	GOOD	AVERAGE	POOR	DON'T KNOW	NO ANSWER
White:	47	37	9	7	0
Black and other:	24	50	19	7	0

Source: Parisi et al., 1979, p. 301.

mentioned the tendency of police to arrest minorities but leave whites alone in the racial clashes of the teens and forties. In the riots of the 1960s, most of those killed died as a result of police action, frequently including indiscriminate firing into buildings. Conot's (1967) study of the 1964 Los Angeles riots, for example, showed that most of the people killed were black, were killed by police, and were unarmed. Such situations surely create considerable hostility toward police. Indeed, hostility has been observed not only among minorities but among most groups seeking social change. It was notable, for example, among many labor unionists in the 1930s and among student and antiwar protesters in the 1960s. Certainly, this type of structured conflict between police and those seeking social change is an important reason for mutually hostile attitudes between police and minority group members. These attitudes, along with others we have discussed, tend to create a situation in which minorities are more likely than others to be arrested because the mutually negative attitudes between many minority people and many police officers lead to negative interactions that in turn lead to arrest (see Bayley and Mendelsohn, 1968, pp. 162–166). So long as the police remain a force to be used to control movements for social change, so long as predominantly white police forces patrol predominantly

Police attempt to restore order as they are confronted by an angry crowd during Miami's 1980 riots. Regardless of the causes of such uprisings, it is the police who are called on to control them. This frequently places police and minorities in adversary roles, and can create a good deal of mutual hostility between police and minority citizens (UPI)

black and Hispanic neighborhoods, and so long as minority populations remain disproportionately impoverished (and therefore likely to commit the kinds of crimes in the kinds of places that police most easily observe), the problem of racial and ethnic inequity in arrest is unlikely to go away.

Bail   Another point in the criminal justice system where a potential for unequal treatment exists is the setting and administration of bail. The purpose of bail is to guarantee that an accused person who has been released from jail will show up for his or her trial. It is a sum of money held by the court to assure appearance for trial. Once the defendent appears, the money is returned; however, if he or she does not appear, the bail is forfeited and kept by the court. In some states, law permits private bail bondspeople to collect fees of 10 or 20 percent of the bail amount to post bail for the defendant. In others, the defendant may be permitted to put up 10 percent of the bail amount. Regardless of how it is handled in any given jurisdiction, many people feel that bail is inherently discriminatory along lines of social class: The wealthier the accused person is, the more likely he or she will be able to afford the bail. Studies have shown that, depending on the crime, the locality, and the amount of bail, the proportion of persons unable to afford bail can range from 25 percent to 90 percent of the suspects (Foote, 1958; Silverstein, 1966). Since black, Hispanic, and Indian people have lower incomes than whites, it is likely that members of these groups are overrepresented among those who cannot make bail.

Beyond the economic problem, there is apparently a good deal of more deliberate abuse of bail. As Barlow (1978, pp. 414–415) notes, numerous factors besides the likelihood that a defendent will fail to appear (the basic legal consideration) in fact influence the setting of bail. A study by the U.S. Commission on Civil Rights (1970, pp. 48–52) demonstrated the widespread use of bail in the Southwest as a way of discriminating against Mexican-Americans. Bail was sometimes used to harass people by keeping them in jail over the weekend: In one case, a group of Chicano students and a teacher were arrested on a Friday night, with bail set a $1200 each. On Monday, the bail was lowered to $500 and eventually changed again to permit release on personal recognizance (no bail required). Similar tactics were used in Texas against United Farm Workers union organizers. In many cases, the bail set was much greater than the maximum fine for the violations the organizers were accused of. The commission also received similar complaints from Colorado and New Mexico. The following passage from the Civil Rights Commission Report indicates that the violations sometimes went far beyond mere harassment:

> Mr. Trujillo [an investigator for the Alamosa, County, Colorado District Attorney's Office] disclosed another and more serious problem resembling involuntary servitude or peonage [both of which are forbidden by federal law under a penalty of fine up to $5000, up to 5 years imprisonment, or both]. He stated that during the harvest season local farmers would go to the jails in the towns of Center and Monte Vista, Colorado, on Monday mornings and inquire about the number of Mexican American laborers arrested over the weekend. The farmers would select the best

workers and pay their fines for them. Upon their release, the men would have to repay the farmer by working for him. According to Trujillo, in Monte Vista the men were told by the police magistrate that if they did not remain on the farm and work off the amount owed to the farmer, they would be returned to jail. In addition, he said, the police magistrate would sometimes give the farmer a "discount." If the fine was set at $40, he would only require the farmer to pay $25. The magistrate, however, would tell the worker that the fine paid by the farmer was $40 and that he owed the farmer $40 worth of work. According to Mr. Trujillo, once the worker was released from jail, he usually was at the mercy of the farmer and often was ill-treated while on the farm. The chief of police and a patrolman in Center, and the police magistrate in Monte Vista confirmed the fact that workers are bailed out of jail or have their fines paid by local farmers and are obligated to work off the ensuing debt.

Another study by the commission (U.S. Commission on Civil Rights, 1965) showed that bail was also used to harass black civil rights workers in the South during the 1960s. Discrimination in bail is not always so blatant, however. Frequently, such factors as property ownership, employment, and middle-class status come into play. Apparently factors of this nature were significant in Korphage's (1972) finding that in Seattle, whites were more likely than either blacks or Indians to be released on personal recognizance when charged with misdemeanors.

Both because it inherently discriminates on the basis of income and because of racial discrimination ranging from subtle to blatant, it seems fair to conclude that the system of bail and pretrial release has generally served the interests of the white accused better than it has served the interests of black, Chicano, and Indian people accused of illegal behavior.

Prosecution and Conviction   Another crucial decision in the criminal justice process that carries a great potential for discrimination is the decision on whether or not to prosecute or refer a case to the court system. Such decisions are influenced by the police, by district attorneys or prosecutors and, where applicable, by juvenile delinquency officials. At this stage of the criminal justice process, there seems to be significant discrimination in some places but little or none in others. Moore and Roesti (1980) found no effect of race on the frequency with which juvenile offenders in Peoria, Illinois, were referred to the court system, and Terry (1967) obtained similar findings with data from Racine, Wisconsin. On the other hand, Arnold (1971) found that in a medium-sized Southern city, black juvenile offenders were more likely to be referred to court than white juveniles, and that differences persisted despite controls for prior offense record and the seriousness of the offense of which the juvenile was accused. Thornberry (1973), using data from Philadelphia, obtained similar findings: Black juveniles were about twice as likely as white juveniles to be referred to probation by the police and were also more likely to be referred to the courts by probation. In a medium-sized northern city, Ferdinand and Luchterhand (1970) found that, among first-time juvenile offenders, blacks were more likely to be referred by police to the court system than were whites. This relationship held regardless of the crime and regardless of the offender's age and sex. These studies indicate that while racial inequality in prosecution is not a problem in *every* part of the country, it does exist in many areas, North and South, and therefore must continue to be regarded as a fairly widespread problem.

There is also evidence that racial inequality sometimes occurs in making judgments of guilt or innocence, particularly when such decisions are made by juries rather than by judges (Bahr et al., 1979, pp. 393–394). Underrepresentation of minorities on juries is a major reason behind the problem, and such un-derrepresentation is a major complaint of minority group members about the criminal justice system. All-white juries, the conviction of a prominent black educator, and the acquittal or nonfiling of charges in several cases of police violence against blacks were major precipitating issues in the 1980 Miami riots that took fifteen lives. Indeed, studies of jury composition indicate that minority groups are underrepresented in juries throughout the United States (Overby, 1972, pp. 268–270). In part, this underrepresentation occurs because nonmiddle-class people are generally underrepresented on juries, and minority group members are less likely than whites to enjoy middle-class status.

Sentencing Probably the most widely studied aspect of the criminal justice process, as far as majority-minority inequality is concerned, is sentencing. Do black, Hispanic, and Native Americans receive longer or more severe sentences than whites in comparable circumstances? In many parts of the country, they apparently do. The studies by Arnold (1971) and Thornberry (1973) discussed in the previous section also showed black-white inequality in sentencing of juvenile offenders. Thomson and Zingraff (1978) obtained similar findings in a study of North Carolina sentencing patterns for assault and armed robbery using data from 1969 and 1977. There was, incidentally, little difference between the two years. Hall and Simkus (1975), in a study of a western state, found that Indian people convicted of crimes tended to receive more severe sentences than did convicted whites. All of these studies showed that the sentencing of minorities was still disproportionately severe after controls for such factors as seriousness of the crime and past criminal record. There does, however, appear to be some variation in the severity of such discrimination. Hindelang's (1969) literature review suggests that the problem is more widespread in the South than in the North. As we shall see, however, the problem does exist in some parts of the North. Hagan (1974) reviewed seventeen studies published prior to that year (including some of the earlier ones cited above) and found that, while a number of them did indeed show racial effects on sentencing after control for other relevant factors, the effect in most cases was quite small. Some more recent studies, however, have revealed larger effects. A study by Grams and Rohde (1976) of sentencing patterns in Minneapolis is especially striking in this regard. This study found that, among 3,390 convicted felons between 1973 and 1975, blacks and Indians were twice as likely as whites to receive straight jail sentences as opposed to some form of reduced sentence. A study of a subsample of felons showed that this remained true after control for such factors as type of crime, criminal record, and even education and occupation. This study and others have identified the public defender system as a central source of such inequalities. This study, as well as one by Nagel (1969), indicates that minority group members are less likely to have their own private attorney than whites, relying instead on court-appointed attorneys from the public defender's office. Grams and Rohde found that Minneapolis blacks and Indians represented by public defenders were three times as likely to get jail sentences as were blacks and Indians represented by private attorneys. In a similar study in Detroit, the Saul R. Leven Memorial Foundation (1959) found that defendants with court-appointed attorneys were twice as likely as others to get prison sentences. Thus, we have identified one reason for more severe sentencing of minority group members: They are more likely to be represented by public defenders, and people represented by public defenders get more severe sentences than those represented by private attorneys. However, the Minneapolis study came up with an even more disturbing finding: *blacks and Indians represented by public defenders were four times as likely to get straight jail sentences as whites represented by public defenders.* Thus, not only were minorities at a disadvantage because of their greater likelihood of having public defenders and the lesser effectiveness of such attorneys, but also because minorities with public defenders apparently received less effective representation than did whites with public defenders.

Apparently, the race of the *victim,* as well as the race of the offender, has some effect on severity of sentence in parts of the country. One would hope that things have changed since the early 1960s, when a southern police officer told a writer, "In this town there are three classes of homocide. If a nigger kills a white man, that's murder. If a white man kills a nigger, that's justifiable homicide. If a nigger kills a nigger, that's one less nigger" (Banton, 1964, p. 173). Studies in Virginia and North Carolina (Garfinkel, 1949; Johnson, 1941) seem to confirm that many criminal justice officials took this view. About half of all blacks arrested for killing whites ended up convicted and sentenced to death or to life imprisonment. However, neither study found a single white arrested for killing a black who received such a sentence. Whites accused of killing blacks were usually acquitted; when they were not, they received relatively light sentences. The problem is not entirely one of the past, however. A recent study by Zimring et. al. (1976) of sentencing in Philadelphia showed that blacks who killed whites were twice as likely to receive life imprisonment or death sentences as were blacks who killed other blacks. Studies also indicate that for types of crime that are frequently interracial, such as larceny and armed robbery, there is greater racial inequality in sentencing than for typically same-race crimes such as assault (Nagel, 1969; Thomson and Zingraff, 1978).

A final source of inequality in sentencing is related to the difference in *types* of crime committed by majority and minority group members discussed earlier in this section. White collar crime, committed by the predominantly white middle and upper classes, is almost always prosecuted in *civil* court. Street crime, on the other hand, is usually prosecuted in *criminal* court. This is a very important difference, since only criminal court can put a person in prison and only criminal court can give a person a record that labels them for life as a criminal. This is one reason why people are almost never imprisoned for conspiracies in restraint of free trade, selling unsafe products, bribing foreign officials, or violating occupational safety laws, despite the enormous cost of these crimes in lives, dollars, and human suffering. The fact that these offenders are usually white, whereas street crime offenders are more often black, Hispanic, or Indian, is another source of racial inequality in the definition and punishment of crime.

In addition, the overload of the criminal court system, combined with society's needs for order, has created a situation where due process is much much more an ideal than a reality. If, for example, every defendent were to be tried by jury trial, the court system literally could not process half the number of cases it must handle. Thus (particularly where the defendent has limited resources to call upon), the system has come to be characterized by a *de facto* presumption of guilt rather than innocence: The defendant is subject to intense pressure to plead guilty (sometimes to a "reduced" charge), even from his or her own attorney (see Balbus, 1973, chapters 1 and 5). The criminal court system tries to retain legitimacy in the eye of the public by outward emphasis on "fair trial" and "due process," but in the large majority of cases it does not and cannot work that way, because if it did, either social control or the court system would break down: either the police would have to arrest far fewer people, or the courts would collapse from overload. Consequently, the court system avoids this dilemma by placing defendants under tremendous pressure to plead guilty. Since this is a characteristic of the criminal court system where street crimes are processed, and since it impinges especially on the defendant with few legal or economic resources, it is obvious that it works to the disadvantage of the minority and poor accused. (For further discussion of these issues and their application to the processing of minorities arrested in civil disturbances, see Balbus, 1973, especially chapters 1 and 5).

Conclusion As we have seen, there are varying amounts of racial and ethnic inequality present in every stage of the criminal justice process, from detection to sentencing. While the inequality may be small at any particular stage (in some places, anyway), the cumulative effect is substantial. "Equal justice" simply appears to be more equal for whites than it is for black, Hispanic, or Indian people in the United States. The effects of this can go far beyond the criminal justice system itself, because of the *labeling* process associated with a criminal record. The person with a criminal record frequently experiences rejection in the areas of employment, credit, and social opportunity: This, in turn, can lead the person back to crime, and soon he or she is caught in a vicious circle. Thus, it is no exaggeration to say that inequality in the criminal justice system is a significant force tending to keep minority groups in an inferior social and economic position.

Protecting Minority Rights

In the previous section, we have explored the treatment of majority and minority offenders (and accused offenders) in the criminal justice system. But what of the "average citizen," not accused of any crime but with certain fundamental rights as an American citizen that he or she relies on the police and legal system to protect? It is this concern to which we turn in the remainder of this chapter. Our emphasis will be on three areas: police protection, courteous and legal treatment of citizens by the police, and protection of citizen rights by the civil courts.

Police Protection   As we have seen, among the most common complaints against the police among Americans of color are that they fail to adequately patrol minority neighborhoods and they do not respond adequately to calls for assistance from minority citizens. J. Q. Wilson's (1978, pp. 158–166) study of police behavior indicates that this is indeed a problem in at least some cities. In Newburgh, New York, interviews with both black citizens and white police officers confirmed that officers were frequently slow or reluctant to intervene in response to complaints in the black community. This occurred partly because of police fears about intervening, and partly because the police believed that blacks preferred to solve their problems themselves (a perception that interviews with black citizens suggest is frequently incorrect). A study in Denver by Bayley and Mendelsohn (1968) showed that black and Chicano citizens were less likely than whites to be satisfied with what the police did for them when called for help. Specifically, 47 percent of the whites, 34 percent of the blacks, and 31 percent of the Chicanos were satisfied (Bayley and Mendelsohn, 1968, p. 117). It is difficult to assess to what degree these feelings reflect actual police behavior, because it is difficult without being an "insider" to observe just how police do respond to requests for assistance. However, from studies such as Wilson's and from observations like the one that follows, we do know that the problem is real. Grossman (1974) reports a case in which a police dispatcher decided not to send a car in response to a call for assistance in part *because a caller's voice sounded Indian, and that group was known for its disproportionate use of police resources.* Subsequently, an assault took place that might well have been preventable had police been sent. Although it is difficult to tell how widespread such incidents are, the widespread minority dissatisfaction with assistance received from police, as shown by the Denver study and the national survey cited earlier (Parisi et al., 1979) suggests that such inequalities may be fairly common.

In part because of inadequate police protection and in part because of the link between poverty and street crime, minority Americans are significantly more likely than white Americans to be the victims of crime. In 1976, minority group members were more than twice as likely as whites to be victims of rape, robbery, purse snatching, and pocket picking. They were also more likely to be victims of assault, burglary, and auto theft. (Parisi et al., 1979, pp. 378, 397).

Police Brutality   It is difficult to define exactly what is and what is not police brutality. Perhaps the most common definition is the use of force beyond what is necessary to make an arrest, subdue a violent suspect, or protect the police officer from injury. However, even this definition is imprecise, because in many instances there will be a wide range of disagreement on how much force is necessary. Beyond this, many argue that brutality is not always physical: such things as verbal abuse, racial epithets, and only listening to one side of the story are regarded by many people as a form of brutality (Bayley and Mendelsohn, 1968, pp. 122–125) and at the very least, as improper harassment of citizens. However defined, it is apparent that police brutality is a major issue among people of color throughout the United States. Indeed, untoward incidents between citizens and police have been the triggering incidents in many, if not most, outbreaks of racial violence in the sixties, seventies, and eighties (see, for example, U.S. National Advisory Commission on Civil Disorders, 1968). Complaints about police brutality are much more widespread among black, Hispanic, and Indian Americans than among white Americans (see Bayley and Mendelsohn, 1968, pp. 122–129; Parisi et al., 1979, p. 301). As is the case for arrest decisions, the structure of the situation surrounding minority–police encounters frequently contributes to an increased likelihood of violent police behavior in such situations. Such behavior on the part of police is especially likely when citizens challenge their authority or when the police hold citizens in low regard (Lundman, 1980, pp. 160–165).

As we have seen, the mutual feelings of mistrust and fear that frequently exist between police officers and minority citizens often create just such situations. In addition, there is a tendency for the incidence of police brutality to increase during periods of social unrest and political protest (Quinney, 1979, pp. 288–289). Since such protest has in recent years disproportionately involved minority group members, they have experienced more than their share of such police violence. In fact, a large proportion of the injuries and deaths during such disturbances are the result of police action, and such action is often far beyond that required by the situation.

Examination of the circumstances surrounding the deaths and injuries in two Los Angeles riots (Watts in 1964 and the Chicano Moratorium in 1970) confirms that police action was the main cause of death and injury, and that those killed or injured by police were frequently unarmed. In the Watts riot, indiscriminate police firing into buildings, at vehicles, and into crowded areas caused a large proportion of the 34 deaths in the riot (Conot, 1967, pp. 245–375). In the 1970 Chicano moratorium, a massive protest by Chicanos against the Vietnam War, there is also evidence of excessive use of force by the police. The event had been mostly peaceful until police swept the park where the demonstration was being held in response to some minor incidents away from or on the fringes of the crowd. Most of the people in the crowd were not even aware of any trouble until the police moved into the crowd. The three deaths resulting from the subsequent riot all resulted from the actions of police. One of those killed was a television reporter who had been critical of police action in previous incidents; he died when his head was pierced by a ten-inch tear gas projectile fired into the bar where he was sitting even though there had been no disturbance in the bar (Acuña, 1972, pp. 258–263).

While excessive use of force by the police is commonplace during civil disturbances, it is very important to keep in mind that disturbances are the exception rather than the rule, and that police brutality toward minority citizens is fairly widespread during times of tranquility as well. Reiss (1968) in a participant observation of police behavior in Chicago, Washington, and Boston, found that about 3 percent of alleged offenders in encounters with police suffered unnecessary violence at the hands of police. For a city of 500,000, this rate of violence would suggest 2,000 to 4,000 incidences of police brutality per year. Both black and white suspects were victimized by police—indeed, white suspects at a somewhat higher rate than black suspects. But since, as we have seen, the black citizen is more likely to become a suspect than the white citizen, it is probable that, overall, blacks are somewhat more likely to suffer police brutality than whites.

If we consider the extreme use of police force, it is clear that minorities are more often the victim of police violence than are whites. Of the more than 4,700 persons killed by the police during the period from 1952 to 1969, over 2,300, or 49 percent, were nonwhite (Kobler, 1975). If the threat of death or severe injury to the police or to a third party is regarded as the criterion of justifiability, it appears that about 40 percent of killings by police are unjustified, and another 20 percent are questionable.

Taken together, the various facts we have reviewed in this section suggest very strongly that minority group members, for a variety of reasons, experience more unnecessary violence at the hands of the police than do whites. It should be said again that individual police officers should not bear all the responsibility for this: The structure of the situations in which police officers come in contact with minority group members virtually guarantees that this will be the case, just as it guarantees that people of color will be *arrested* more frequently than whites. Until there is fundamental change in the ways wealth, income, and power are distributed between majority and minority groups, this is likely to continue.

Protection of Legal Rights in the Court System Ultimately, it is the judicial system that protects the rights of citizens in a democracy. If a citizen feels that his or her rights have been violated by another citizen or by an agent of the state, it is the court system that is called on to protect that citizen's rights. As we have seen, the laws of the United States today provide for equal rights regardless of race, creed, or color. As a practical matter, however, there is serious reason to question whether the judicial system actually operates that way. We have already seen considerable evidence of racial inequity in the courts in cases involving accused criminals. However, our concern in this section is not with accused criminals but rather with how the courts protect the legal rights of ordinary citizens who are accused of no crime.

An investigation of the civil court system by an individual who is himself a U.S. Court of Appeals justice suggests that there are serious inequities in the civil court system (Wright, 1969). Ordinarily, a citizen turns to the civil court system when there is a reason to believe that her or his rights have been violated by another citizen or by the government. These courts have the power to award payments for damages and to issue injunctions against actions that illegally deprive citizens of their rights.

Wright's investigation of the civil court system indicated that, in many ways, the courts have failed to protect the rights of poor Americans. One widespread problem is the failure of the courts to protect the minority poor from abuses by ghetto merchants. Wright describes one case in Washington involving the repossession of goods bought by an indigent mother of seven who was living on relief payments of $218 per month. In this case a merchant sought to repossess $1800 worth of goods bought over five years, most of which she had already paid for, because she failed to make her payments on a stereo she had subsequently purchased. This was based on a line of fine print on the sales contract that any unpaid balance on *any* item purchased from the store would be distributed among *all* items previously purchased. Although this arrangement allowed the taking without payment of items the woman had completely paid for, several lower courts upheld the contract and ordered the woman to return all the items. Only when the case reached the U.S. Court of Appeals did the court reverse and rule that only the stereo could be repossessed.

As disturbing as this case is, the woman was, for a number of reasons, more fortunate than a great many others in a similar position. Many poor people lack both the awareness of how the legal system operates and the money to hire a lawyer. To have any legal representation at all, they must be able to find a legal aid lawyer who is willing and able to represent them. Unlike the criminal courts, civil courts in most cases make no presumption of the right to a lawyer, so indigent plaintiffs must often go unrepresented. Appeals through several levels of the court system such as the one described above are extremely expensive and time consuming. Accordingly, very few poor people ever have the resources to go as far as this woman was able to.

Wright (1969) notes that this woman was "lucky" in another regard. In her case, the store itself was attempting to make the repossession. Had the contract been sold to a finance company, the woman might have had an even more difficult time in the courts. Under the doctrine of "holder in due course," a finance company can in most jurisdictions purchase installment payments free of any responsibility for fraudulent practices by the dealers (this, again, is a standard clause contained in the fine print of sales contracts). Thus, the interests of the finance company are protected, but those of the buyer are not. Unless the buyer can prove that the finance company *knew* the dealer was fraudulent (which is almost impossible to prove in most cases), he or she is out of luck, even if the dealer skips town.

Another widespread practice criticized by Wright and others is wage garnishment. Under this arrangement, it is possible under certain conditions in many states for a creditor to collect on past-due amounts by obtaining a court order to take up to one half of the person's wages. This typically requires a deficiency judgment, which in effect is a legal declaration that the creditor was not able to resell a repossessed property at a sufficiently high price to cover the amount due. Once a wage garnishment order has been issued, the debtor frequently loses his or her job. The employer may be embarassed by the garnishment orders or may simply consider the required procedure too much of a bother. Thus, a poor person who fails to make payment on a property may lose his or her job as well as the property—a condition that beyond doubt perpetuates poverty.

One innovation established in many areas as a way of better protecting the legal rights of the poor is the small claims court system. In these courts, a citizen can, without legal counsel, sue for amounts up to a few hundred dollars. The idea behind the establishment of small claims courts was to enable those too poor to hire lawyers to nonetheless receive legal protection when the amounts involved are not excessive. However, in practice, small claims courts have not generally worked that way: The great majority of those suing in small claims courts have been landlords and businesses. Frequently, those sued in the courts have been poor. Thus, the system has had the opposite effect from that intended: it has largely helped wealthier interests extract debts from the poor, without helping to protect the poor from abuses by landlords and businesses, as had been intended. The apparent reason for this is that the wealthy are more aware of and used to operating in the system. Some landlords and collection agencies use it on a routine basis. The poor, on the other hand, are largely unaware of their rights and do not know how to sue in small claims court. Even well-intended reforms can frequently backfire in a context of economic and racial inequality.

Our discussion of the court system has, thus far, focused mainly on economic rather than racial factors. However, since black, Hispanic, and Indian people are so much more likely than white people to fall in the lower income brackets, all of these class-related inequalities in the protection of legal rights create de facto racial and ethnic inequalities as well.

A final area in which the courts have in signficant ways failed minorities in America is in protecting them against abuses by the state. Of particular salience here is the issue of police abuse of minority citizens. The failure of the judicial system to punish acts of violence by police against citizens has been a major source of tension in the 1970s and early 1980s in Houston, Philadelphia, Los Angeles, and other cities. It was a major precipitating factor, as we have already noted, in the 1980 Miami riot. In Philadelphia, federal action against police violence failed in the courts in 1980. In Houston, there was a highly publicized case in which a Chicano man, Joe Campos Torres, was taken to a vacant area by police, beaten, and thrown or forced to jump into a swift-flowing stream, where he drowned. The verdict in the case was misdemeanor negligent homicide, and the sentence was one year in prison. Although the police involved were also convicted of felony violations of federal civil rights laws, the federal conviction added only one day to their sentence, although the law provided for a penality of up to life imprisonment (New York Times, 1979, 1980). Although a few such cases are highly publicized, they represent a much more widespread pattern. Kobler's (1975) study of 1,500 homocides by police officers found only three cases in which *any* criminal punishment resulted—this despite the fact that about 40 percent of the killings appeared unnecessary. Since about half those killed were nonwhite, this must be regarded as a failure of the courts to protect the rights of minorities. Conot's (1967, pp. 396–409) examination of the inquests into deaths resulting from the 1964 Watts riot found much the same, with virtually all cases involving killings of citizens by police or national guardsmen adjudicated justifiable, though again, many in all likelihood were not. Much the same can be said of lesser offenses by police against citizens: They are rarely tried, and convictions are even rarer.

SUMMARY AND CONCLUSION

We have seen that a good deal of institutionalized racial inequality persists in the political and legal systems. Open and deliberate discrimination in these institutions has been greatly reduced, if not totally eliminated. However, subtler and often unintentional forms of inequality remain, and these have had the effect of blocking most opportunities for blacks, Hispanic Americans, and Indian people to improve their standing in the political and legal systems. Thus, minorities remain greatly underrepresented on voter lists and juries, and among political officeholders, the legal profession, and police officers. They are overrepresented among those arrested, convicted, and imprisoned, and on the casualty lists of American wars. Most often, these things happen because of institutionalized policies and practices which, though they are not openly discriminatory, nonetheless have the effect of helping whites or holding down minorities.

As a result of this analysis we can offer some ideas about how to and how not to go about trying to solve the problem of political, legal, and judicial inequality between the races. Our analysis suggests that dealing with individual white prejudices, as suggested by the social-psychological perspective, or dealing with particular acts of discrimination, as suggested by the functionalist perspective, may have gone about as far as can be realistically expected: These beliefs, attitudes, and deliberate acts are a relatively small part of the problem as it exists *today*. It also seems futile, as the "culture of poverty" version of functionalist theory argues, to try to change minority group members to "fit the system" better: Much of their disadvantage results from their poverty, and many of their attitudes, such as distrust of the police and lack of faith in the judicial system, seem well-grounded in fact. This leaves one kind of solution: Change the ways the legal and political institutions work (e.g. by requiring proportional representation of races and classes on juries, to cite just one possibility), or, similarly, alter the economic system to eliminate the poverty that is a sizable part of the problem. It is further clear that neither any one "band-aid" change nor a small set of such changes in our institutions will suffice to solve the problem. Our examination of the legal system showed, for example, that no one stage in the process could be identified as the main cause of racial inequality in treatment of accused criminals. Rather, it was a number of sometimes small inequalities scattered throughout the process, combined with differences in treatment of the types of crimes committed by majority and minority group members, that *added up* to substantial racial differences in the punishment of crime. Thus, to eliminate the racial inequality in the punishment of crime, the entire process must undergo fundamental change, change that threatens dominant elements of the majority group. One example would be redirection of social control toward white-collar crime, changing the law and the judicial process to imprison white-collar and corporate criminals in the same way we imprison street criminals. According to Feagin and Feagin (1978), it is because of such threats to the advantaged that there has not been a concerted attack on the problem of institutionalized racism. Privileged whites, and the owners of wealth in particular, do not want to think of themselves as racists—thus the reduction in openly expressed prejudice and deliberate discrimination. Yet, the authors argue (p. 178), these dominant elements are unwilling to give up the advantages they enjoy as a result of discrimination, and this is in large part why institutionalized racism, even though largely unintentional, persists. Put differently, changing our institutions in such a way as to eliminate the processes that maintain racial inequality would harm the interests of the privileged, and for this reason, they use their considerable power to oppose such change. Given this persistence of institutional discrimination, it is unlikely that racial and ethnic equality in our political and legal processes will be attained until those processes and systems themselves undergo significant change.

Education and American Minority Groups

11

Continuing our examination of the roles of minority group members in American social institutions and the ways those institutions influence the status and welfare of minorities in American society, we will now focus on the educational system.

As was discussed in Chapters 6 and 9, a series of court cases and federal actions, highlighted by *Brown* v. *Board of Education* in 1954, placed the legal position of the government clearly against segregated education. For a variety of reasons, however, these actions did not put an end to institutional discrimination in the educational system. To begin with, there was strong resistance to school desegregation in parts of the South, and actual change was slow to come in many areas. Second, the legal rulings applied only to relatively open and deliberate policies of school segregation. In both the North and South, residential segregation and subtler forms of discrimination in the drawing of school district boundaries have kept public schools *de facto* segregated—that is, segregated in fact if not by law. Third and most important, there are a number of ways schools can discriminate without being segregated. The debate over segregation, while important, has often turned public attention away from the numerous practices institutionalized in the education system that may—often unintentionally—place minority students at a disadvantage. Also frequently ignored, but possibly very important, is the role of education in the larger social and economic structure in which it exists. In this chapter, we shall seek to understand these relatively subtle and complex issues in the education of minority groups in America as well as the more widely debated issue of school segregation (both deliberate and *de facto*).

A BRIEF HISTORY OF SCHOOL SEGREGATION SINCE 1954

As noted above, the Supreme Court's 1954 ruling requiring desegregation of public schools met widespread resistance in the South. Probably the most dramatic resistance came in 1957, when Arkansas Governor Orval Faubus threatened to use the state's National Guard to block court-ordered school desegregation in Little Rock. To enforce the law, President Eisenhower had to order U.S. Army paratroopers into the city and federalize the state's National Guard. In many other parts of the South, resistance took subtler forms. Legislation was passed in an attempt to avoid the jurisdiction of courts ordering desegregation; efforts were made to block the NAACP's desegregation drives (six states passed laws prohibiting the NAACP from providing legal aid); students were given "tuition grants" to attend segregated private schools; pupil assignment laws were written that provided access to desegregated schools only on request for reassignment, and compulsory attendance laws were repealed (Simpson and Yinger, 1972, pp. 549−552). Some districts went so far as to close their public schools entirely. Such resistance continued for years after the 1954 *Brown* decision. It was in 1963 that Alabama Governor George Wallace (later a presidential candidate) declared, "I say segregation now, segregation tomorrow, and segregation forever!" in his inaugural address.

Despite such resistance, legally segregated education did gradually disappear in the border states during the late 1950s and early 1960s, and in the deep South later. By the mid 1970s about two-thirds of the nation's school districts had taken some action to desegregate their schools (U.S. Commission on Civil Rights, 1976). Action against legally segregated schools, widespread as it was, turns out to have been somewhat limited in its actual effects on patterns of racial segregation in public schools. In 1974 about 40 percent of the nation's black students continued to attend schools that were more than 90 percent black. By comparison, about 65 percent of black students attended such schools in 1965. Segregation, furthermore, remains widespread despite support for the general concept of integrated schools. As we saw in Chapter 3, 84 percent of white Americans in 1972 agreed that white children and black children should attend the same schools. We are faced, then, with a perplexing question. If most school districts have tried to desegregate and if Americans overwhelmingly favor the principle of integrated education, why do nearly half the nation's black students attend what amount to segregated schools?

The problem is in large part what is commonly called *de facto* segregation. Unlike *de jure* segregation, which involves an official policy of segregated schools, *de facto* segregation results from subtler processes. One such process, sometimes called *gerrymandering,* involves drawing school attendance districts in such a manner that they are racially homogeneous. While such gerrymandering is illegal today if racial intent can be shown, present-day segregation in some cities is at least partly the result of past decisions about school attendance districts. (One example of this is Boston, where black students were at one time bused through a white neighborhood to attend a predominantly black school.)

Another major factor contributing to school segregation is housing segregation. Where housing is highly segregated, the system of neighborhood schools often amounts to a system of segregated schools. Although housing segregation is largely produced by private sector transactions (buying, selling, and renting of housing and the actions of the real estate industry), it is produced at least partly by exclusionary zoning and housing policies in some suburban communities. Thus, even school segregation produced entirely by housing segregation must be regarded as *partly* the result of public action.

Although deliberate operation of segregated schools is illegal everywhere and although segregated schools are found in all parts of the country, there are significant regional differences in the level of segregation in schools today. The most recent data available indicate that black-white school segregation is greatest in the Midwest and Northeast, lowest in the South, and at a middle level in the West (see Table 11.1).

Segregation is *lowest* in the South apparently because much of the segregation there was of the *de jure* type. As we shall see later, *de facto* segregation is not illegal in and of itself. Accordingly, the *de facto* segregation of the North has been less changed by the 1954 *Brown* decision and subsequent events than has the *de jure* segregation of the South.

Although other minority groups, despite past patterns of segregation, are not as segregated as blacks, it is significant to note that their regional variations are similar to those for blacks. American Indians are more segregated in the North Central states (the Midwest) than anywhere else, and Hispanic Americans are most segregated in the Northeast.

Segregation also appears to be greatest in cities. For both blacks and Hispanics, segregation levels are much higher in cities than in either suburban or rural school districts. It is important to note, however, that both groups are underrepresented in suburbs and rural areas, so that there may be relatively few minority students attending any schools in such areas. Furthermore, it must be kept in mind that all these statistics refer to segregation *within* school districts. Much of the segregation that exists today is *between* districts, such as exists when a city whose school population is 75 percent black borders on a suburban district that is 95 percent white.

To summarize, then, open and deliberate policies of segregation in schools have been illegal for over twenty-five years, yet actual segregation remains widespread. Today, segregation is actually greater in the North than in the South, and it is greatest in central cities. Furthermore, the mere fact that deliberate segregation is illegal does little to eliminate the kind of segregation that remains

Table 11.1 Average Segregation Indices* for School Segregation between Minorities and Whites in U.S. Public Schools, 1976 by Region.

				REGION			
				SOUTH			
GROUP	Northeast	North Central	Border	Southeast	West South Central	West	U.S. Total
Blacks	39	47	23	17	28	34	30
Hispanics	34	4	4	20	14	15	17
Asians	1	1	4	2	2	5	3
American Indians	1	28	0	22	2	8	11
All Minorities	34	37	21	16	20	18	24
Number of School Districts	539	784	108	882	737	566	3616

Source: U.S. Commission on Civil Rights, 1979, p. 20.
*Same index as used in Chapter 9 to measure housing segregation. Ranges from 0 (no segregation) to 100 (total segregation).

today. Only more drastic remedies, such as busing or redrawing of school districts to combine cities and suburbs, hold any real hope of further reducing segregation in our schools. We shall return later in the chapter to these issues, exploring in particular the degree to which desegregation, through busing or otherwise, may offer improved educational opportunities to minority students. In the meantime, we shall explore other aspects of our educational system that influence the educational opportunities of racial and ethnic minority groups in the United States.

THE ROLE OF EDUCATION: TWO VIEWS

Before we explore some relatively specific aspects of organization and practice within education, it is important to explore briefly the role of the educational system in the larger American society. Sociology offers two contrasting viewpoints about the role of education in American society; we shall briefly explore each of them in this section.

The traditional view of American education, linked closely to the order, or functionalist, perspective in sociology, is that education provides a source of social mobility in society. In other words, it offers to all the opportunity to move up in society, and how far one moves depends on his or her ability and motivation. The educational system also serves as an efficient way of allocating people to professions by providing them with the training they need. Thus, education provides employers with qualified workers, and it offers individuals the opportunity for mobility by rewarding them on the basis of what they know and what they can do (achieved characteristics) rather than on the basis of who they are or what their background is (ascribed characteristics). (For further discussion, see Davis and Moore, 1945; Parsons, 1959.)

A contrasting view that has gained increasing support among sociologists of education is that education does *not* operate in a way that offers much opportunity for upward mobility to the poor. Rather, education reflects and reinforces the social inequality in society. This viewpoint, more consistent with the ideas of the conflict perspective, challenges the popular view that "education is the answer." According to this view, education cannot be expected to bring about equality when the larger social and economic system is based on inequality. One strong proponent of this viewpoint is Christopher Jencks (Jencks et al., 1972). Jencks argues that if society wants to move in the direction of social equality, the way to do it is not to "educate" everyone, but rather to pursue changes in the economic system that would bring about equalization of income. Jencks should not be misunderstood, as he sometimes has been, as opposing quality education for all. Rather, the point he argues is that economic advantage is more important than mere access to education, and making everyone into a high-school or college graduate would not necessarily alter the basic forces that make for economic inequality in the United States.

Conflict theorists in the sociology of education argue that one reason education may not provide much opportunity for mobility is because the true function of the educational system is to *reinforce* and *preserve* the inequalities that exist in society. According to this view, education, as Marxist theory says is true of *all* institutions, exists to serve the interests of the dominant or advantaged elite who reap most of society's benefits. The true purpose of education, then, is not to provide social mobility, but rather to *channel* students into roles and statuses relatively similar to those of their parents. This serves two functions for the dominant group. First, it assures that they can pass along their advantages to their children. Second, it provides employers with "appropriately" socialized middle-class workers who will fit into their work organizations and not cause trouble.

There is some reason to believe that there is merit in this challenge to traditional views about education and social mobility. First, a wide range of studies do show that predominantly middle-class and predominantly working-class or poor schools tend to stress different kinds of values. Schools with students predominantly from the lower classes mainly stress conformity and obedience; middle-class schools also stress control over one's situation and the ability to work independently, though within a context of hierarchical supervision—values already largely present in the middle class (Friedenberg, 1965; Cohen and Lazerson, unpublished). Furthermore, the higher one goes in the education system (from grade school to high school to college to graduate school) (1) the higher the average family income of the students and (2) the closer the educational approach approximates the middle-class model (Binstock, 1970). Thus, the educational system nurtures and reinforces the "appropriate" values of the middle class, while it "cools out" the aspirations of working-class students and prepares them for lower-paying, manual jobs (Lauter and Howe, 1970.)

This function of education can also be illustrated by the behavior and preferences of those who do the hiring for the better jobs in society. A variety of studies suggest that the *affective* things that are learned in school (values and habits) are more linked to income and occupational status than is *cognitive* learning (the learning of skills and content). To begin with, a review by Gintis (1971) of a number of studies showed that while years of school were strongly related to a person's job status and income, measures of *what the person actually knew* added very little to the explanation. Clearly, employers preferred educated workers for high-status jobs for reasons *other than* cognitive knowledge. Gintis argues strongly that the studies suggest that what they are really looking for is middle-class values and work habits—exactly the kinds of things that the school system teaches. Also consistent with this observation is the fact that education pays off better for the white middle class than for minorities and the poor, and better for academic training (mostly middle class) than for vocational training (mostly working class) (Jencks et al., 1972; Super and Crites, 1962; Weiss, 1968; Harrison, 1972). Apparently, it is what is learned in the so-called *hidden curriculum* that employers are looking for in applicants for higher-status jobs: values and work habits that will "fit in," rather than any concrete factual knowledge.

Surveys of employers confirm that this is the case. Their preference for more educated applicants for higher-status jobs is in many cases not related to what such applicants *know* in areas related to the job. In most cases, this is taught on the job. Rather, more educated employees are preferred because of their values, beliefs, and work habits (Hamilton and Roesner, 1972). Employers believe that such employees will adapt and fit in better to the work environment. As Berg (1975, p. 308) puts it, employers believe that with increased education, "the worker's attitude is better, his trainability is greater, his capacity for adaptation is more developed." It does not really matter that such employees are not necessarily more productive than other employees (Berg, 1971, 1975); it is the belief of employers that "desirable" values and work habits are found among more educated employees that counts (Bowles and Gintis, 1976).

All this raises serious questions about the role of the educational system as a source of mobility in American society. Undoubtedly it does operate that way for some individuals, but these studies suggest there is strong reason to believe that the overall effect of the American educational system is to preserve inequalities rather than to reduce or eliminate them. Since economic inequality in the United States falls largely along racial and ethnic lines, education may well be acting in ways that preserve racial and ethnic inequality as well.

We have seen, then, that an increasing number of sociologists are arguing that the function of the school system is to *preserve* and *pass along* inequalities from generation to generation more than it is to break those inequalities down and to offer opportunities for mobility. They are able to present some significant data in support of this view, and the general relationship between such variables as race and class and the attainment of education (see Chapter 8) is also supportive of such a viewpoint. If this is true, however, then what specifically does the educational institution do to reinforce patterns of race and class inequality? Two major possibilities have been suggested by educational sociologists. First, more money is spent, and thus the quality of education is greater, in areas where the students are white and middle class than in areas where they are black, Hispanic, Indian, and/or poor. The second possibility is suggested by our discussion of the functions of the educational system. This viewpoint holds that there are important cultural and behavioral differences between many minority students and the people who teach them and prepare their educational materials. In the following sections, we shall explore both of these general issues in greater detail.

FUNDING OF SCHOOLS

There is evidence that schools where most of the students are black, Hispanic, or Indian are underfunded in comparison to schools where most of the students are white. This is partly inherent in the way in which schools are funded. As we saw in Chapter 9, schools get about half of their revenue from the local property tax, and most of the rest from state aid. Since the amount that can be raised through the property tax depends on the value of property that is present in the community, this tax tends to bring in more revenue in wealthier communities and less in poorer ones. State funds are often allocated according to matching formulas, which reward with state money those school districts that raise more money locally. This type of matching formula tends to reinforce the inequities that arise from unequal property tax bases. Thus, substantial disparities exist both within and between states in such measures as spending per pupil and number of teachers per thousand students (National Center for Education Statistics, 1980, Chapter 7). These inequities tend strongly to occur along the lines of income: Districts with higher incomes tend to spend more per pupil on education than do districts with lower incomes.

Because minorities have lower incomes on the average than whites, one effect of this would appear to be that *less* money is spent per student on the education of minorities than on the education of whites. And although further investigation shows that expenditures in central cities, where the bulk of the minority population lives, are actually slightly higher than in other areas (Brown et al., 1978), these figures are misleading for two reasons. First, *costs* tend to be higher in such areas, so the greater expenditure does not necessarily mean better education. Second, the support of education is a greater burden in such areas: Relative to the value of their property, central-city residents must pay significantly higher tax rates. The severity of the problem is well-demonstrated by cases of bankruptcy and consequent school closings in Chicago, Toledo, Cleveland, Boston, and other central cities: The limited property tax base and state aid simply cannot keep up with the soaring costs of urban education. The result: severe cutbacks and, in the most extreme cases, bankruptcy.

In some states, property tax *equalization* efforts have been made to try to eliminate some of the inequities arising from property taxation and state matching formulas. In about a half dozen states—notably California, Connecticut, Iowa, Maine, Oklahoma, Rhode Island, and Vermont—significant reductions in funding disparities were achieved between the 1969−70 and 1976−77 school years (National Center for Education Statistics, 1980, pp. 280, 292−293). However, in about the same number of states the situation became worse, and taking the nation as a whole, there was no improvement and possibly a slight worsening of educational funding disparities (Brown et al., 1978). The impact of such funding inequalities on minorities is illustrated by a study of educational funding in Texas (U.S. Commission on Civil Rights, 1972). In districts with 10 to 20 percent Chicano students, per pupil expenditure was $464; in districts with 80 percent or more Chicano students expenditure was only $296 per pupil.

In addition to inequities *between* school districts, inequities also exist *within* school districts. Put simply, school boards allocate more money for some schools than they do for others. One study in Detroit, for example, compared spending for teachers' pay in schools that were 90 percent or more black to those that were 10 percent or less black in 1970. The finding: $380 per pupil in the mostly black schools; $432 per pupil in the mostly white schools (Michelson, 1975).

Although there are significant deficiencies in the funding of minority education, it has become increasingly clear in recent years that spending more money on minority education would probably by itself do little to improve minority education, much less minority income. An important source of evidence on this topic is a massive survey of 570,000 students and 10,000 teachers and principals in over 4,000 schools in the United States. This study, which has come to be known as the Coleman Report (Coleman et al., 1966), was mandated by the 1964 Civil Rights Act to explore the quality of education being received by American minority students, and it revealed a number of startling findings. Among the most important was that traditional measures of educational quality—class size, educational level of teachers, facilities and programs available in the schools, and so on—explained relatively little of the variation in what students actually knew, as measured by tests of ability and achievement. Overall, these factors appear to explain about 5 percent of the variance—a bit more for "ability" measures, a bit less for the supposedly more schooling-related "achievement" measures. There was some racial difference, however: Such inputs explained from about 10 to 15 percent of the variance in achievement and ability for black students; they explained only about 2 to 6 percent of the variance for white students (Coleman et al., 1966, p. 294). In short, while school quality did make more difference in learning for blacks (and probably for other minorities as well) than for whites, it did not make a great deal of difference for anyone.

What *did* explain how much students learned? Coleman was able to identify two main factors. The first was a set of background factors, including urban/rural background, parents' education, family size and composition, facilities and educational resources available in the home, and parents' interests and desires concerning the child's education. These factors explained from 15 to 25 percent of the variance in student learning—more for whites than for blacks (Coleman, 1966, p. 300). The other important source of variation in student learning was the attitudes of the students themselves. Coleman measured three kinds of attitudes: interest in learning, self-concept, and belief that the individual can control his or her environment. Again, Coleman found a significant relationship: These individual attitudes explained 15 to 20 percent of the variation in learning for blacks, and 25 to 30 percent for whites. In the overall sample, these individual attitudes correlated more closely to student achievement scores than anything else Coleman measured (Coleman, 1966, pp. 319, 321). Although some differences were found for groups other than blacks or whites (see Table 11.2), Coleman's overall finding was quite clear: The background and attitudes of students were more strongly correlated to what they learned in school than was *anything* about the school that was measurable or that varied substantially from school to school.

The figures referred to above contain some overlap—that is, school characteristics, background factors, and student attitudes all tend to be associated with one another. Thus, it can be difficult to estimate just how much of the effect on student learning is coming from each variable. However, through a method known as stepwise regression, it is possible to add one variable at a time to the analysis and thus measure the *additional* effect of that factor after all others are taken into consideration. Using such methods Coleman was able to identify the effects of

Table 11.2   Race/Ethnic Variation in Achievement Explained by Adding:

GROUP	1 All School-to School Variation *Not Linked* to Background	2 School-to-School Variation *Linked* to Background	3 Individual Variation in Background	4 Individual Variation in Attitude	5 All Factors Combined
White	7.41%	2.08%	16.94%	13.38%	40.09%
Black	14.83	6.07	6.41	10.87	38.18
Puerto Rican	22.69	0.71	3.35	4.79	31.54
Indian	23.42	0.71	10.68	8.80	43.61
Chicano	17.75	2.32	6.02	8.24	34.33
Asian	2.20	0.13	19.66	10.05	32.04

Source: Coleman et al., 1966 p. 229, Tables 3.221.1 and 3.221.2.

various factors on twelfth grade verbal achievement, as shown in the following table.

These data reveal that all variation between schools *not* related to the background of students attending those schools accounted for only 2 percent of the variation in achievement for Asian students, 7 percent for white students, and 15 percent for black students. Variation linked to backgrounds and attitudes was much more important for these groups. Attitude and background together accounted for 33 percent of the variation in achievement for whites, 30 percent for Asians, and 23 percent for blacks. Thus for these groups, which account for over 90 percent of all U.S. students, attitude and background factors correlated a lot more closely with achievement than did differences between schools. Thus, the importance of schools seems to be less than many believed, though probably greater for blacks than for whites. The other groups are a bit different. For Chicanos and Indians, variations between schools seem about as important as differences in attitude and background in explaining student learning. Only for Puerto Ricans did differences in schools seem more important than individual differences. Even where school differences were important, however, differences in the attributes of the student bodies of those schools seemed to make more difference than did either teacher quality or school facilities (Coleman et al., 1966, p. 302).

CULTURAL AND BEHAVIORAL FACTORS IN THE EDUCATION OF MINORITIES

The Coleman Report shocked the American educational establishment. It suggested that more support of education for minorities might not, by itself, make much difference. Regardless of the "quality" of the schools, it seems that students with certain kinds of attitudes and background were learning in our educational system, and students with other kinds of attitudes and background were falling behind. Subsequent research by others (see Jencks et al., 1972; Bowles and Gintis, 1976) has confirmed that this is largely true. That is not to say that the level of support for education makes *no* difference. Coleman did find that school inputs made more difference for minorities than for whites, and more recent research by Summers and Wolfe (1977) confirms that school inputs make a difference, particularly for less advantaged students. Furthermore, Coleman's study could not assess the effects of temporary school closings due to bankruptcy such as those that have occurred in several cities with large minority populations since Coleman did his study. Finally, there is some evidence from preliminary reports of studies by Coleman and by Greeley in 1981 that suggest that, even controlling for a variety of student characteristics, students learn more in private schools than in public schools—another indication that schools make a difference. Greeley argues that this finding is especially true for minority students. Nonetheless, Coleman's basic points still remain valid: (1) There is a limit to the return that can be expected simply by upgrading the same basic educational system we now have, and (2) cultural, attitudinal, and behavioral factors probably play an important role in explaining racial inequalities in learning. Accordingly, we shall turn our attention now to an exploration of how such factors influence the education of minorities in America.

The finding that cultural and background factors are closely associated with learning in American schools can be interpreted in two quite different ways. One interpretation, aligned with the functionalist perspective, identifies the source of the problem in "dysfunctional" attitudes and beliefs among poor people and among racial and ethnic minorities. The other view, aligned with the conflict perspective, sees the source of the problem in the educational institution, arguing that it demands conformity to an arbitrary norm and punishes those who do not conform. (We have already seen some of this viewpoint in our discussion of education and social mobility). Of course, how one views this issue is probably partly a matter of which cultural group (middle-class educators or minority poor, for example) he or she identifies with. Nonetheless, there is some sociological evidence pertaining to the issue. In the following sections, we shall explore the evidence concerning the functionalist view that the problem is one of *cultural deprivation,* and the conflict theory view that the problem is *cultural bias*.

Cultural Deprivation?

Recall Coleman's finding that absence of facilities and educational materials in the home was associated with poorer performance in school. Specifically, Coleman found lower levels of achievement among children from homes that lacked such things as television, a telephone, a record player, an automobile, or a vacuum cleaner. He also found that the lack of reading materials such as books, magazines, daily newspapers, encyclopedias, and dictionaries was correlated with lower levels of learning. This (along with other data on family structure and parental interest and encouragement of children's education) suggested to Coleman that children from certain kinds of homes entered school at a disadvantage. Put simply, they were deprived of many of the learning opportunities that other children enjoyed; thus, they could not compete on an equal footing with other children who enjoyed these advantages. Their disadvantage was in many cases worsened by the lack of parental encouragement of education and finally by the attitudes of the children themselves. Underachieving children, Coleman found, tended to (1) have a poor self-image, (2) be relatively uninterested in school and (3) believe that they could not control their environment—that is, that success was a result of "good luck," not "hard work." Of these three, self-image and belief in control of environment had much stronger effects than interest in school, especially among black students; and for students from minority groups (and probably poor whites), the most important factor was belief in control over one's environment (Coleman et al., 1966, pp. 319–324).

To Coleman this strongly suggested that the lack of facilities and encouragement in the home, *combined with* the attitudes that minority students brought to school, placed those students at a very substantial disadvantage to whites. The solution: Change the attitudes of disadvantaged students so that they could develop a positive self-image and believe that they *can* control their environment. Coleman was able to present one additional piece of evidence that lends further support to his argument. In his own words, he found that "as the educational aspirations and backgrounds of *fellow students* increase, the achievement of minority group children increases" (Coleman et al., 1966, p. 302). In short, he found that, all else being equal, a minority student attending school with students from advantaged backgrounds who had positive attitudes did better than a comparable minority student attending school with students from disadvantaged backgrounds who had negative attitudes. The apparent reason: The positive attitudes and study habits of the other students "rubbed off" and the minority student developed more positive attitudes and study habits. Of equal significance, the evidence did *not* show any harmful effect on the more advantaged students of attending school with students of less positive attitude and background. In fact, the white and Asian students, who on the average did better than others in school, were not much influenced by the characteristics of their fellow students. The influence of fellow students was mainly on black, Chicano, Puerto Rican, and to a lesser degree, Indian students. A finding that was to have great political importance in later years, and that follows quite logically from what we have seen here, is that racially and socioeconomically integrated schools were associated with higher achievement among minority group children. The suggestion was clear: desegregation of schools might lead to improved learning among minority students as they took on the attitudes and study habits of their more advantaged white middle-class peers. As we shall soon see, the findings of the Coleman Report became an important part of the battle over school busing for racial integration that began in the late 1960s and has continued into the 1980s.

Essentially, Coleman's interpretation of his findings was consistent with the functionalist perspective. He focused on the idea that minority students (and lower-income students in general) come to school with attitudes and backgrounds that do not "fit in" to the school system. Coleman's findings, and those of other studies showing background strongly linked to school achievement, have led to two kinds of suggestions for action that are in keeping with a general functionalist, or order, perspective. One of them, a *conservative* approach, argues that, because of their background (or, according to the most extreme conservatives, their genetics), lower-income minority children are uneducable, and we ought to stop throwing away money trying to educate them. Among the proponents of such a viewpoint are Jensen (1969, 1975), Eysenck (1971), and Banfield (1968). As we shall see, however, the success of some efforts in the areas of school integration, community control, and emphasis on learning of the "basics" show that, done properly, economically disadvantaged students *can* be educated and can be educated well. The evidence does not indicate that such students are incapable of learning; rather, it shows that under the conditions in most of our schools, they *are not* learning. The other version of the general functionalist interpretation, a *liberal* approach, is to emphasize efforts aimed at helping minority students to fit in and develop the attitudes they need to get ahead in the school system. Such programs as Head Start have been designed to accomplish this, as has, in large part, the policy of school busing for the purpose of racial integration. The degree to which busing has been successful in improving the achievement of minority students will be explored in the final section of this chapter, which focuses on educational social policy. In the meantime we shall turn to another interpretation of Coleman's findings that clashes with both the conservative and liberal versions of the functionalist viewpoint.

Cultural Bias?

Conflict theorists, including a number of minority group spokespersons, argue that the "cultural deprivation" viewpoint reflects the biases of the white middle class, the group to which most social scientists belong. According to the conflict theorists, the problem is not to be found in the characteristics of the minority groups, but rather in the schools. The reason for low achievement among those with certain attitudes and backgrounds, according to this view, is that the schools demand certain values, attitudes, and habits and, in effect, punish those who do not conform. As we have seen, conflict theorists believe that schools operate this way for two reasons. First, it allows the dominant elements in society to pass their advantage along to their children. Second, it provides employers with a well-socialized work force that will "fit in" and not cause trouble (Bowles and Gintis, 1976). Thus, the schools serve the interests of the advantaged, in spite of the widespread ideology that they serve everyone's interest. Social scientists who hold this viewpoint say that it is not surprising that Coleman's study and others found that more of the same kind of education does not do too much for minority student achievement: The problem is not the amount or quality (as traditionally measured) of education; rather, it is the *kind* of educational system we have and the role that that system plays in the larger society.

If there is merit in this viewpoint, it should be possible to identify some specific ways in which the educational system penalizes minority students. In the following section, we shall examine the educational institution to see if we can identify practices or structures that do in fact work to hold down learning by minority students.

Biased or Limited Coverage of Minority Groups in School Materials

Both white and minority school children form important impressions about their own racial group and other racial groups based on what they are exposed to in educational settings. Until very recently, what most school children have been exposed to has been quite stereotypical and biased. Two distinct tendencies can be noted. One is simply to exclude minorities from materials discussing U.S. history, or from general educational materials, such as "Dick and Jane" grade-school readers. One study found that of forty-five social science textbooks, only eight even mentioned Spanish-speaking Americans. The largest Hispanic group, Chicanos, was mentioned in only two of the books (Kane, 1970). Research by Bowker (1972) indicates that Indian people are similarly neglected in history books and that the problem actually got worse between 1960 and 1972. A popular educational film narrated by comedian Bill Cosby titled "Black History: Lost, Stolen, or Strayed?" graphically illustrates the elimination of blacks from popular accounts of American history. One example he cites is the important role played by blacks in Teddy Roosevelt's widely glorified "charge up San Juan Hill." (An event that undoubtedly is viewed with less glory by Hispanic Americans than by Anglos!) Cosby points out that the black participants "didn't get lost on the way up the hill. They got lost in the history books."

The other major problem—which many view as more persistent than the one we have been discussing—is distorted or stereotypical presentations of Americans of color. Consider, for example, this list of adjectives used by schoolbooks to describe Indian people:

Fig. 11.1   Adjectives Used in Textbooks to Describe American Indians

degraded	ungrateful
filthy	dumb
barely human	incompetent
inferior	servile
stupid	unreliable
lecherous	vagrant
murderous	weak
selfish	unscrupulous
treacherous	on the lowest stage of man's development

Source: Bahr et al., 1979, pp. 237–238.

Chicanos have been similarly stereotyped. Kane's (1970) study showed, for example, that they were often portrayed as "wetbacks" crossing the border illegally, or as lawbreakers and bandits who are not wanted in this country. Another common stereotype is that of the migrant farmworker. Textbook portrayals of the Mexican-American in this light undoubtedly help to explain why this image persists, even though Chicanos are actually more urbanized than the U.S. population as a whole. Similar stereotyping occurs in the presentation of blacks in educational materials. Too often, black Americans have appeared in low-status roles in our children's textbooks, when they have appeared at all.

In the past ten to fifteen years, awareness of these problems has been increasing, and minority group members have begun to appear in school materials in greater numbers and in less stereotyped roles than in the past. Most major textbook publishers, for example, have added recommendations to their authors' guides concerning inclusion of minorities and women in textbooks (Britton and Lumpkin, 1977). However, there remains considerable room for improvement. One study of forty-nine major school textbook series from 1958 to 1976 showed that there was only a small increase in the number of minority characters (Britton and Lumpkin, 1977). Furthermore, the study showed that minority characters were depicted in a much more limited range of occupational roles than were white characters. Another problem was identified by McCutcheon et al. (1979)—a tendency to portray everyone, including minority characters, according to a white middle-class role model. Thus, skin color or names may be changed, but no real effort is made to display the great cultural diversity of the U.S. population.

The absence and/or distortion of minority groups in educational materials (coupled with similar omissions and distortions in the media) can have serious effects on both majority and minority group children. Among majority group children the consequence can be to create or reinforce prejudices and stereotypes concerning members of groups other than their own. Among minority group children the result can be serious damage to the children's self-image or to their beliefs concerning the racial or ethnic group to which they belong. The *symbolic interactionist* school of social psychology has shown that reality is *socially constructed*. In other words, we acquire our knowledge, beliefs, and self-images through *what we are told by others* (Cooley, 1964; Mead, 1967). For majority group children this means that their beliefs about minority groups are formed on the basis of what they hear and read at home, at school, and in the media. This is especially true when, as very frequently happens, the children grow up in segregated neighborhoods and attend segregated schools. (For further discussion of the role of social learning in the perpetuation of prejudice among majority group members, see Chapter 2.)

As we have suggested, the absence or distorted presentation of minorities in school materials can seriously harm the self-image of minority group children. Cooley's (1964) concept of *looking-glass self* is highly relevant here. According to this concept, we develop beliefs about ourselves based on the messages we get from others. If those messages are negative, the self-concept will tend to be negative. It is not surprising, then, that a sizable body of evidence shows that black children have in the past developed serious problems in the area of self-image. Among the most widely cited studies in this area are the doll studies by Clark and Clark (1958) and by Radke and Trager (1950). These studies showed that, when given a choice of otherwise identical black and white dolls, black school children (as well as white children) showed consistent preferences for the white doll. In the Clarks' study, for example, two-thirds of the black children chose the white doll as the one they wanted to play with, and 60 percent said it was the doll that had a nice color. On the other hand, when asked which doll "looks bad," 59 percent of the black children chose the black doll. The study also showed that the children were aware of racial differences: 94 percent made the correct choice when asked which doll "looks white," and 93 percent when asked which doll "looks colored." Significantly, however, fully one-third of those same black children picked the *white* doll when asked which doll "looks like you"—an apparent denial of their own racial identity.

Another approach that has been used to assess self-image is to have children draw pictures of themselves or tell stories about themselves (Porter, 1971). Such studies have shown that black (and often poor white) children express less positive themes in their stories and pictures and are more likely to draw small pictures or pictures with missing limbs or features. Such findings are not limited to blacks. Rosenthal (1974), using pictures of white and Indian children, found that the preference for white children was even stronger for Indians than it was with other groups such as blacks and Asians, and that unlike some other groups, the pattern did not decrease with age (Rosenthal's data, however, apply only to Chippewa Indians and may not be true for other groups). Doll studies with Chicano children have also found a fairly widespread preference for white dolls (Werner and Evans, 1968).

In spite of this widespread evidence that the self-images of minority children have in the past been seriously harmed, there is also rather impressive evidence that this pattern is changing. A more recent doll study (Katz and Zalk, 1974) found that the preference among black children for the white doll no longer existed. In addition, when Rosenberg and Simmons (1971) administered paper-and-pencil self-esteem scales to both black and white school children, they found that the black children had self-images at least as positive as those of the white students. Other studies by Zirkel (1971), Zirkel and Moses (1971) and Baughman (1971) suggest the same thing. Though the evidence is much more fuzzy and limited on Chicano and Indian children, such changes may quite possibly be occurring among them, too, since some studies show very little difference in self-esteem between them and white children (see Fuchs and Havighurst, 1972; Carter, 1968). It is undoubtedly true, however, that some of the conflicting findings for Chicano and Indian children result from the fact that different measures tend to produce different results. Nonetheless, there is little doubt that, at least for black children, self-esteem in recent years has been significantly higher than in the past.

Why has self-esteem among black children improved in recent years? Undoubtedly, one factor has been the more balanced presentation of minorities in educational materials and the media, even though there remains much room for improvement. Of possibly greater importance, however, is the emphasis on black pride and self-identity that has come with the Black Power movement since the 1960s. A major emphasis of that movement has been a rejection of the negative black image presented by whites and a corresponding emphasis of the notion that black people can and should define their own identities. Considering the findings of studies in recent years, it appears that these efforts have been quite successful. Since similar ideas concerning ethnic pride have become increasingly widespread among Hispanic and Indian Americans, it is quite possible that a similar trend toward a more positive self-image is under way among the children of these groups. Of course, none of these positive changes can undo the harm that has been done to minority children in the past, but they do suggest that at least in the area of minority children's self-esteem, things are getting better.

Teacher Expectations and Tracking

In recent years, there has been increasing awareness of possible effects of *teacher expectations* on student performance. It is now evident that a *self-fulfilling prophecy* frequently operates in the classroom: Teachers expect more of some students and less of others, their expectations affect the way they interact with the students, and as a result, the expectations come true. The most widely known study of this process was published by Rosenthal and Jacobson (1968) in a book titled *Pygmalion in the Classroom*. In this famous experiment, the researchers began by giving a test to children in a California elementary school. The teachers in the school were told that the test was a new instrument designed to identify "academic spurters"—children who would greatly improve their performance in the coming academic year. Actually, the test was an ordinary IQ test, and the 20 percent of the children who were identified as academic spurters, supposedly on the basis of the test, were in fact randomly selected. The teachers, of course, did not know this.

At the end of the year, the children were given another IQ test. The results in the first and second grades were striking: The children who teachers thought were "spurters" showed improvements in IQ of 10 to 15 points relative to the other children. Recall that these children were *in fact* no different from the other children: They had been randomly selected. The only difference was that their teachers thought they were going to do better. It should be noted, too, that the measure used, IQ, is one that is *supposed* to be relatively immune to such social influences.

The effects of teacher expectations appeared to occur mainly in the first and second grades. Older children seemed less susceptible to such effects. This may be because they were more intellectually developed and therefore less subject to such influences. Another possibility, however, is that by then, the children had established reputations with the teachers, and these reputations had more effect on teacher expectations than did the supposed test results.

Apparently, the process by which teacher expectations influence student learning is quite subtle. Teachers, for example, did *not* on the average spend more time with the students labeled as spurters. Apparently, the difference was more qualitative: Subtle messages given to students that they were or were not expected to do well. This view is supported by other studies. Brophy and Good (1970), for example, found that teachers directed more criticism toward those they believed were poorer students, and more praise and encouragement toward those they believed to be better students.

It should be pointed out that there have been methodological criticisms of the Rosenthal and Jacobson study (Thorndike, 1969) and that not all studies using similar methods have been able to replicate the findings (Boocock, 1978). Nonetheless, an impressive array of studies does suggest that teacher expectations do tend to influence student performance (see Beez, 1968; Nash, 1976, especially Chapter 3; Brophy and Good, 1974). One of the most interesting of these, conducted by Rist (1970) again reveals the sizable effects of labeling in early education. In the school observed by Rist, students were assigned to three tables according to their teacher's beliefs about their ability. These assignments were made during the first eight days of kindergarten, and for many children were inconsistent with reading-readiness scores. By second grade, not one of the children who remained in the class had moved to a higher group, and those in the low group had fallen far behind in reading and had become socially labeled as "the clowns."

In other words, the initial assignment of children to groups, made largely without regard to available ability measures, had a long-standing effect on student performance. In effect, the students assigned to the "low" table never really had a chance.

In itself, the fact that student performance is influenced by teacher expectations may seem irrelevant to the issue of majority-minority relations. However, there is a large and growing body of evidence that teachers do in fact form their expectations of students at least partially on the basis of race and class. In a study by Harvey and Slatin (1975), for example, teachers were given photographs of children and asked to evaulate their chances of success. The result: Teachers had substantially higher expectations of white children and of children whom they perceived to be from the middle or upper classes. Research by Leacock (1969) similarly indicated racial and class effects on teacher expectations, to the extent that teacher expectations of black students were actually negatively related to IQ. The study by Rist discussed in the previous paragraph also showed that the students were placed at the "low" or "high" tables in kindergarten largely on the basis of social class—in spite of the fact that in this case both the students and teachers were black.

To summarize, the studies that have been done to date indicate that (1) what teachers expect of students influences how much those students learn and the degree to which they progress in the school system and (2) such teacher expectations are

Teacher-student interactions have important effects on student learning. One example of this is the self-fulfilling prophecy; when teachers expect students to do well, they tend to actually do better. When teacher expectations are lower, student performance is not as good. Joe DiDio, NEA.

formed at least partly on the basis of race and class, though the extent to which this is true varies greatly from classroom to classroom (Hurn, 1978; Brophy and Good, 1974). Although we do not know the precise strength of either relationship, it does seem clear that teacher expectations are a significant source of racial and ethnic inequality in the American education system.

A closely related issue is tracking. Tracking is a practice whereby students believed to be similar in ability are grouped together in separate classes or groups. The idea behind tracking is to enable students to proceed at a pace consistent with their ability, preventing the better students from becoming bored and the poorer ones from being left behind. The tracking system has become widely used in American education (National Education Association, 1968). In recent years, however, tracking has come under attack as a practice that works to hold down the educational attainment of minority, poor, and working-class students. The argument is that tracking acts as a self-fulfilling prophecy, much as teacher expectations do. Minority and lower-status students are placed into less advanced tracks, on the basis of race and/or class, and this inhibits their later learning and academic advancement. Research on the topic generally supports this viewpoint. Although again it is not clear just how strong the effects are, there appears to be fairly wide agreement in the literature both that placement in tracks is influenced by race, Hispanic origin, and class (Alexander and Eckland, 1975; Alexander and McDill, 1976; Alexander et al., 1978; Boocock, 1978; Schafer et al. 1972; U.S. Commission on Civil Rights, 1974; Brischetto and Arciniega, 1973), and that once students have been placed in a low track, their future educational experience is largely determined: They stay in the same track and have a significantly reduced opportunity to enter higher education, regardless of their initial ability (Schafer et al., 1972; Esposito, 1973; McGinley and McGinley, 1970).

The processes behind these patterns are complex and not well understood. However, the following generalizations seem valid: First, whatever tracking decisions are made at the elementary school level (where there is less reliable information to base them on, since the earlier the decision is made, the less of an academic record is available) tend to directly and indirectly (through student attitude and self-concepts) get passed on to the high school level. If such decisions are biased, the biases also get passed on. Second, social class (which, of course, is correlated to race) tends to influence student attitudes, beliefs, behaviors, and educational plans. These, in turn, influence track placement (see Alexander et al., 1978). Third, the racial differences in track placement seem to result from two main factors: First, race is, as we have said, related to social class, and children whose parents have less income and less education tend to get placed in lower tracks. Second, minority children score lower on the tests used to place students in tracks, and this tends to place them in lower tracks (Alexander et al., 1978). The issue of test bias will be explored later in this chapter.

The effects of track placement on children's performance and educational plans have also been noted. Effects on actual learning are probably greatest in the lower grades, where teacher expectations exert their greatest influence. In high school, on the other hand, tracking seems mainly to affect the self-expectations and plans of students: Those placed in lower tracks generally lower their expectations and do not plan on (and therefore do not attend) college. Track placement, then, has effects on future educational attainment that hold true even when we compare students who are in different tracks but have similar ability and achievement levels (Hauser et al., 1976). Alexander et al. (1978, p. 60), for example, found that "enrollment in a college preparatory track increases by about 30 percent the probability that students will plan in their senior year to continue their education in comparison to equally able, motivated, and encouraged youth in nonacademic programs."

Taken as a whole, the literature raises serious questions about the usefulness of tracking. In addition to the factors we have noted, it must be stressed that the decision to place students in tracks is haphazard at best: Two recent studies of high school track placement found that ability, achievement, and background variables combined explained only 30 to 40 percent of the variation in track placement, leaving 60 to 70 percent unexplained (Alexander et al., 1978, p. 55; Hauser et al., 1976, p. 318). For a process that is supposed to be a rational decision based on student aptitude and performance, these figures are not impressive. Beyond this, however, we are, as we have seen, talking about a process that contains racial and class biases, and that arbitrarily influences the future educational attainments of students. Viewed from this perspective, the practice appears highly questionable.

Linguistic Differences

Another area of difficulty has arisen from linguistic differences between minority students and their teachers. This has in various ways been a problem for black students, who frequently speak various forms of the dialect commonly called "Black English," for Spanish-speaking students, and for Indian students, who may be penalized for speaking their native languages. The issue here is not whether students should be able to speak standard English—most educators, white and minority, would agree that not being able to speak standard English is a serious disadvantage in our present-day society, and that students should learn how to speak standard English if they do not know how. Rather, the issues concern negative and incorrect labels attached to minority children because they do not enter the school speaking standard English, and in some cases, the *failure* of the school system to teach minority group children standard English.

We shall begin our examination of this issue with an exploration of Black English. Traditionally, Black English has been regarded by many educators as an inadequate or poorly developed version of English, linguistically inferior to standard English. Deutsch (1963, p. 174), for example, wrote ". . . It appears that speech sequences seem to be temporally very limited and poorly structured syntactically. It is thus not surprising to find that a major focus of deficit in the children's language is syntactical organization and subject continuity." In recent years, however, sociolinguistic research on Black English has shown this viewpoint to be incorrect. In fact, Black English has standard rules (although there is some regional variation) concerning tenses, subjects and verbs, and so on. In the past, educators tended to see it as an inferior or incomplete language largely because their cultural and linguistic background did not give them the knowledge necessary to understand Black English. Put simply, Black English is *different from* standard English, but equally regular in its rules (Baratz and Baratz, 1970). One difference is in the use of tenses: Black English has a wider variety of tenses than does standard English (Fickett, 1975, 67−75; Seymour, 1972; Dillard, 1972, pp. 39−72). One example is the "habitual" tense, a pattern that exists in Black English but not in standard English. Apparently, this tense has its roots in West African languages. Silverstein and Krate (1975, pp. 146, 166) present two examples. In Black English, there is an important difference in meaning between "he workin" and "he be workin." "He workin" (the present tense) means he is working right now, whereas "he be workin" (the habitual tense) means he works regularly or habitually. Similarly, "she sick" means she is sick today but will probably be over it soon, whereas "she be sick" means she is seriously or chronically ill—the illness is likely to be of long duration.

Fickett (1975, p. 77) presents a similar example from research in a Buffalo high school. She found that nearly all the black students knew that "I been seen him" was longest ago, "I done seen him" more recent, and "I did see him" most recent. White students, on the other hand, either could not answer the question or guessed wrong. Interestingly, the black students were surprised that white students did not know the difference; some commented, "Those kids gotta be dumb." The findings of these and other studies, then, refute the traditional view that Black English is less developed or less capable of expressing concepts and ideas. The problem was that white educators did not understand Black English. (Some might say that these educators were "culturally deprived.")

Because of these misperceptions on the part of educators (including even some middle-class black ones who have adopted norms against Black English—see Gouldner and Strong, 1978), black children have frequently been, and sometimes still are, labeled as "slow" or stupid because of their use of Black English. This misperception is compounded in many cases by the fact that, in a white or middle-class environment where the norm is standard English, black youngsters feel inhibited and consequently become withdrawn, answering questions from the teacher slowly and as briefly as possible. On the other hand, when given a less formal environment, a speaker who communicates with them in their own language, and topics they find more familiar and interesting, the same students will become highly verbal and compete with one another for a chance to talk (Labov, 1972, pp. 60−62). Again, then, the teacher who uses only standard English in a formal classroom setting will probably label the students as slow or withdrawn, whereas the behavior that led to that label was in fact a product of the situation, not the characteristics of the student. The consequence of these processes is that black (and other) students who do not speak standard English will be incorrectly labeled as "slow learners," with all the implications that carries for their educational growth (recall the self-fulfilling prophecy effect discussed earlier in this chapter).

In addition to the labeling problem, many teachers apparently are not succeeding at teaching some of their black students standard English. This problem apparently is most serious for those black students who are toward the lower end of the socioeconomic scale. Middle-class black students, on the whole, become adept at using both Black English (''everyday talk'') and standard English (''school talk'') (Wood and Curry, 1969). In fact, some middle-class blacks are a good bit more familiar with standard English than with Black English, indicating that such linguistic variation is at least partly based on social class. Many blacks— particularly in the middle class—use Black English among their friends and family but standard English in formal or work situations and other white-dominated settings. Wood and Curry's study indicated that middle-class black high school students in Chicago were quite adept at this type of ''code-switching.'' Apparently, for many blacks who know standard English but prefer to speak Black English, the use of the dialect reflects an affirmation of black culture and a rejection of white cultural dominance (Taylor, 1978).

For black students from poor families, however, the picture is apparently different. It appears that many of these students *do* have trouble learning standard English. Wood and Curry (1969), for example, found that black students from poor

A group of high school students. White teachers often incorrectly label black students as withdrawn, noncommunicative, or unable to verbalize, based on their behavior in the white-dominated classroom. If such teachers could communicate with their students in a more comfortable, less threatening setting, they would see a very different pattern. Marc Anderson.

families in the high school they studied were *not* adept at code-switching: Even when asked to speak in "school talk," their responses more closely resembled Black English than standard English. One difference may be that the middle-class black child's parents speak both Black English and standard English; the poor child's parents speak only Black English. Some difference of this type has been noted in the literature (see Labov and Cohen, 1967). In any case, it appears that the schools are not too successful at teaching standard English to those black students who are not familiar with it. One apparent reason for this is that a great many of the teachers who are trying to teach standard English to speakers of Black English do not themselves know how to speak in Black English (Baratz and Baratz, 1970; Fickett, 1975, p. 94). If a teacher cannot communicate with a pupil in language that the pupil understands, it is difficult for that teacher to explain to the student a new form of language. The situation is somewhat analogous to that of a person who knows absolutely no English attempting to teach an English-speaking person to speak Spanish. Although the linguistic differences between standard and Black English are less extensive, the difficulties involved are much the same. Thus, both inappropriate labeling of some black students because of the dialect they speak and the failure of the schools to teach some black students standard English have become important barriers to the education of black students. Recently, the implications of this issue for equal educational opportunity have become an issue in the judicial system. A court ruling in 1979 required the Ann Arbor, Michigan, school system to take steps to meet the educational needs of students who spoke Black English, stating that the previous failure of the school system to deal with this issue threatened the educational opportunities of the city's black students.

Much of what has been said about the difficulties imposed by the educational system also holds true (in some cases, even more so) for Hispanic students. About half the Chicanos in the United States (and many other Hispanic-Americans, too) speak Spanish in their homes, though most also know English (Moore, 1976, pp. 121−122). Many schools, however, continue to forbid or strongly discourage *any* speaking of Spanish in school (Moore, 1976, p. 84). This practice was found by one study (U.S. Commission on Civil Rights, 1972, pp. 15−16) to be relatively rare in California, but quite widespread in Texas—a rather shocking finding, since the inability to use English is much more common among Chicano students in Texas than in California. A related problem is the tendency of some teachers to look down on students who speak Spanish, contributing to the widespread negative labeling of Latino students (Moore, 1976). This negative attitude in part reflects the development of dialogues that are neither distinctly English nor Spanish. Switching and mixing of the two languages is common among Hispanic Americans, as is the use of Spanish forms of English words (*pochismos*) such as *el troque* (the truck) or *la ganga* (the gang) (Moore, 1976, p. 124). This, too, has led to negative labeling on the part of English-speaking teachers, and sometimes also on the part of educated Mexican-Americans concerned with preserving standard Spanish. Nonetheless, this *caló* (mixed language) has come to be recognized by many in the Chicano movement as a symbol of a distinct Chicano culture that is neither totally Mexican nor totally American. In spite of this, it is clear that many Hispanic students have been held back by an educational system that labels them negatively because they speak Spanish or mixed Spanish-English dialects yet frequently fails to teach them standard English. As with black students, it appears that the nonlearning of standard English is most common among the lower classes.

Part of the problem is that some teachers attempting to teach Hispanic children to speak and write in English are not able to communicate with the children in Spanish. In the late 1970's this problem received increasing attention through the development of bilingual education programs. Such programs teach the children in both English and Spanish; teachers, of course, must be proficient in both languages. A related program is the teaching of English as a second language. These programs, and some bilingual education programs, are designed mainly to develop proficiency in English. Other bilingual programs are designed to develop proficiency in both English and Spanish (Irizarry, 1978, pp. 6–7), and some emphasize the value of maintaining Spanish language and culture.

During the 1970s, bilingual education programs gained support at both the federal and state level, and by the late 1970s, the federal government and twenty states had passed legislation providing support for bilingual education. In twelve states school districts are required to offer bilingual education programs if they have more than some minimum number of non-English-speaking students, though the number varies substantially from state to state (Irizarry, 1978, pp. 2, 15–16). Most states place no limits on the grades covered, but among the five southwestern states where most Chicanos live, all but California target the program to the lower grades, generally providing no support for programs beyond eighth grade.

Regulations issued during the Carter administration generally strengthened bilingual education and required that such programs be made available to more students. The early part of the Reagan administration, however, was marked by elimination of most of these regulations, in line with that administration's opposition to all types of federal regulation and its feeling that such programs are culturally divisive. If such decisions are left to local school officials, there is no guarantee that bilingual education will be offered, since the concept remains highly controversial. Thus, the continued availability of bilingual education to Spanish-speaking (and other non-English-speaking) students remains uncertain at the time of this writing.

It is too early to evaluate conclusively the overall success of bilingual education, but there is evidence that the approach can in some instances be successful both in improving student learning and in improving student retention (Flores, 1978). Nonetheless, some difficulties remain. First, not all students who need bilingual education are getting it, though the approach became much more widely used during the 1970's. Second, some school systems limit both the number of students in bilingual programs and the length of time students may remain in these programs. Third, it is crucial that teachers be proficient in the use of *both* English and Spanish. Some bilingual education programs have come under fire for having teachers not adequately proficient in English. A successful program must *both* foster an appreciation of Spanish language and culture *and* teach students to speak proficiently in English. Such a program is not always easy to design and implement. Some programs have also been criticized for contributing to the segregation of Hispanic children and for isolating Hispanic children from contact with the dominant culture (Thernstrom, 1980). Controversy also continues as to whether it is better to have intensive short-term programs to teach English or to integrate the students' native language into the broader curriculum. Thus, bilingual education offers an important step toward undoing some of the harm that has been done to Hispanic students because of their linguistic differences, but it still has a way to go in both coverage and effectiveness. As Flores (1978, p. 118) notes, bilingual education should be seen as "neither a passing fad nor a panacea."

Most of what has been said about language differences and the education of Hispanic-Americans is also largely true of the education of Indian people in America. Through much of our history Indian education emphasized the assimilation of Indian people into the dominant white culture. In practice, this has frequently meant placing Indian students in boarding schools, separating them from contact with their tribal culture, and allowing them exposure only to English in the schools. Such practices were common as recently as the 1940s and 1950s (Ogbu, 1978, p. 230).

Today, about two-thirds of all Native American students are in public schools, as opposed to BIA (Bureau of Indian Affairs) Indian Schools and other special schools (Bahr et al., 1979, p. 408). In response to the repeated failure of assimilationist educational programs in the past and to the increasing demands of Indian people for self-determination, Indian education has begun to change, and many schools attended by Indian students now have bilingual education programs. Nonetheless, there is a long way to go and Indian students in white-dominated schools frequently continue to be labeled as slow learners simply because of linguistic differences—just as many black and Latino students are.

Test Bias

One of the most controversial issues in the social sciences in recent years has centered around differences in ability and achievement test scores between whites and various minority groups in the United States. There is no question that, on the average, minority group members score lower than whites on standardized tests, though, of course, some individual members of *all* minority groups score far above the white average. Why are their average scores lower?

Some, most notably Arthur Jensen (1969, 1973), argue that the cause of this is genetic, but it is significant that those who hold this viewpoint have not been able to demonstrate any genetic factor associated with a racial difference in intelligence (Ogbu, 1978, p. 60). The large volume of research done on the topic indicates rather clearly that a more fruitful place to look for an explanation is in the tests themselves, the testing situation, and the wider environment. Among the important factors that are known to influence IQ test scores, for example, are the following:

Culture-specific content in the tests
The test situation, including race of the tester and how the test is presented
Teacher expectations
Health and nutritional factors
Perceived usefulness of doing well on the test

The differences that can be created by these factors appear to be more than enough to explain the average IQ score differences of about 10 to 15 points that have been noted between whites and various minority group members. Indeed, even identical twins (twins with the same genetic makeup) raised apart display IQ differences on this order. Let us explore the various factors influencing IQ test scores.

Culture-Specific Content Although IQ tests are designed to assess ability (what one is capable of learning, not what one already knows), ability cannot in fact be directly measured (Vernon, 1969). All that any test can measure directly is knowledge: Either one knows the "correct" answer or one does not. It is hoped that the knowledge measured by IQ tests is associated with ability, but the strength of this association has come increasingly under question. What IQ tests in fact seem to measure is the knowledge, habits, and modes of thinking (all *learned* characteristics) that are valued by the dominant cultural group in any society (Ogbu, 1978, pp. 30–37; Berger, 1978). In other words, IQ tests are designed to predict school achievement, and they do correlate fairly well with later school achievement. The reason, however, is that they measure the knowledge, habits, and modes of thinking needed to get ahead in that school system—the cultural attributes of the dominant group. This can be illustrated in several ways. Today, the great majority of Americans would not take seriously the notion that persons of Italian, Russian, or Polish heritage are inherently less intelligent than persons of British or German heritage—nor do test scores suggest this. However, in the early twentieth century, when these immigrant groups were new arrivals unfamiliar with American culture, they *did* score lower on the tests. Furthermore, much of the intellectual community of the time believed that these groups were genetically inferior—a view obviously disproven by today's test scores. One author argued, for example, that 83 percent of Jewish and 79 percent of Italian immigrants were "feebleminded" (Henry Goddard, cited in Kamin, 1974). Obviously, the reason for the low scores was cultural, not genetic.

Another example can be seen in the Goodenough Draw-A-Man IQ test. Although the test was designed to be culture-free, it—like all tests—has not turned out that way. In general, groups whose cultures stress art do well on this test. Southwestern Indians—who generally have highly developed arts—are generally shown by this test to be more "intelligent" than whites. The same Indians, however, tend to score lower than whites on verbal IQ tests, which are geared to the white culture. Thus, the differences in "intelligence" between whites and Indians as measured by these tests turn out to be cultural, not genetic (Ogbu, 1978, p. 218).

The cultural biases in intelligence tests, and their effects on blacks and other minority groups, are well illustrated by an example given by black psychiatrist Alvin Poussaint (1977). (See also Kagan, 1971, pp. 92–93.) On one IQ test, there was a question, "Your mother sends you to the store to get a loaf of bread. The store is closed. What should you do?" The "correct" answer to this question was go to the next closest store and get it there. Analysis of children's answers indicated that there were important group differences in response to this question. For one thing, rural children got it "wrong"—in their case, the next closest store might be ten miles away. Inner-city black children also got the question "wrong." They answered that they would go back home and ask what to do. Poussaint argues that for these children, this was the right answer: Interviews with the children indicated that some felt going to another store might be unsafe, because of dangers associated with gangs who controlled the "turf" around the next closest store. Thus, these children were penalized, even though they gave what, *for them*, was the most intelligent answer. Pouissant, Kagan, and others argue that questions with interviews about why the student answered the way he or she did would give a more reliable measure of IQ than straight test items. Many in the field of intelligence testing agree, and some of the better tests follow this model. However, the time and expense limitations of mass testing do not always permit such a careful approach. Consequently, cultural differences in familiarity with the content of "intelligence" tests remain an important cause of majority-minority differences on IQ test scores. *Within* any group, inherent differences undoubtedly account for part (not all) of the variation in IQ test scores. This does *not* follow when we are looking at differences *between groups* in average IQ test scores, however. As our examples have shown, group differences in familiarity with the culture-specific knowledge and modes of thinking measured by the test probably offer the best explanation of such group differences in scores.

Problems of this nature, of course, are not limited to formal test situations. Students to some degree are continuously evaluated in the classroom. Thus, whatever a student says or does (or fails to say or do) may lead to a positive or negative evaluation from the teacher. A group of sociologists known as *phenomenologists* have focused on problems of this nature arising in everyday classroom situations. According to this view, people tend to emphasize different aspects of a situation: Some people will perceive one aspect, others a different one. Since both aspects are there, neither perception is "wrong"; both are simply different ways of seeing or organizing the same material. Furthermore, such perceptions and ways of organizing things vary from one cultural grouping to another. A child from a minority or lower-income family may attend to what the teacher or test-designer regards as an irrelevant aspect of a question. The answer may be "right" in terms of the child's perception, but wrong in terms of what the teacher intended to emphasize. Consequently, the child is mistakenly marked wrong (Hurn, 1978, pp. 169–179; Mehan, 1974; MacKay, 1974; Keddie, 1971).

Test Situation   In addition to the content of the test itself, certain aspects of the test situation have also been shown to be in part responsible for the lower average scores of minority group members. Some studies have shown that the typical formality of the test situation tends to lower the scores of poor and/or minority group children. When the test is given in an informal, supportive setting or in the context of play, the IQ scores of such children rise significantly (Haggard, 1954; Palmer, 1970; Zigler et al., 1973; Golden and Birns, 1968), and racial and social class differences are reduced or eliminated. Even Jensen noted increases of 8 to 10 points in the IQ scores of low-income children as the result of play therapy. Apparently, the minority and poor children are less comfortable in a formal test situation and consequently benefit more from a less threatening situation.

It has also been shown that the race of the tester can affect the scores of minority children. Although the literature is not unanimous on this point, some evidence suggests that black students score higher on IQ tests when the person giving the test is black.

Another problem is that of linguistic differences, which can lead to testing bias as well as the types of general classroom bias we have already examined. Some Hispanic children, for example, have been labeled as having low intelligence because they were given intelligence tests in English rather than Spanish. Such imputation of low intelligence on the basis of linguistic differences is both inaccurate and harmful to the child.

Teacher Expectations   We have already discussed this topic at some length, but it is important to remind ourselves that Rosenthal and Jacobson's (1968) classic study used IQ test scores as the dependent variable and found 10- to 15-point IQ differences in the first and second grades as a result of differences in teacher expectations. Accordingly, it seems reasonable to expect that when IQ tests are given to students who have been in school a year or two (so that teachers have had some time to form and act on expectations), the results will be to some degree influenced by teacher expectations—which, as we have seen, are in turn related to the race and social class of children.

Nutritional Factors   Even primarily hereditary physical characteristics like height are significantly influenced by nutrition and other factors related to physical health. Thus, it hardly comes as a surprise that such factors can also influence IQ. Because minority groups are greatly overrepresented in the nation's impoverished population, they are more likely than others to suffer prenatal and childhood deficiencies in nutrition that can later inhibit their ability to do well on IQ and other tests.

Reduced Payoff for High Test Performance   A recent work by Ogbu (1978) has raised another interesting factor that may help to explain low scores by minorities on standardized achievement tests. His theory centers around the fact—seen in our discussion of the work of Bowles and Gintis (1976) on education and mobility—that there is less payoff for education among minorities than among whites. Put simply, educational success provides a greater return in the form of high-paying jobs for whites than it does for minorities. (There is some evidence that this is starting to change as a result of affirmative action programs, but any change has been very recent.) Ogbu argues that this affects the scores of minority students on all types of educational tests and tasks: "Doing well on these tests, like doing well on academic tasks generally, is not as rewarding for caste minorities as it is for the dominant group. Thus, caste minority children often do not take such tests seriously enough to try for the best scores they can get" (Ogbu, 1978, p. 37).

White Anglo parents, according to Ogbu (pp. 235–236) will teach their children to "persevere in school regardless of the boredom and unpleasantness involved *because they will be rewarded in the future with desirable social positions and jobs*" (emphasis Ogbu's). Minority children, on the other hand, will not be so encouraged by their parents, because the experiences of minority group parents "are different: education has not usually brought the same desirable social and occupational rewards." Ogbu (p. 37) notes that there is real evidence of such underachievement on tests: Observations by psychologists generally indicate that minority children "communicate" with their peers, solve problems, and use concepts in ways typical of children who have IQ's of a Binet type 10 to 15 points higher than theirs.

Testing Bias—Summary

To summarize briefly, we have seen that numerous factors unrelated to ability tend to cause minority children to receive lower than average scores on intelligence tests and other kinds of standardized tests. This is very harmful in two ways. First, it leads to incorrect labeling of minority children as "slow learners," which, as we have seen, hurts their ability to learn, their self-image, and their relationships with their peers. Second, it leads to their placement in "slow" tracks or ability groups, with all the harmful consequences that has for their future development.

In addition to the negative labeling and tracking of individual children, however, test bias has more general harmful implications for minority groups. First, it has tended to reinforce racist thinking about the intelligence of minority groups by creating the belief that it can be "scientifically proven" that some groups are genetically inferior to others. This is true in spite of the fact that there is absolutely no proof of genetic differences related to intelligence between races, and that the test score differences can be well-explained by the biases and situational factors we have discussed.[1] Unfortunately, the public is often not exposed to the scientific critiques of works such as Jensen's (and other more extreme materials such as those of Eysenck (1971), Herrnstein (1971), and William Shockley, (1971a, 1971b) which have appeared following the publication of Jensen's 1969 article.) Thus, claims based on tests purported to measure intelligence are often taken at face value by the public, even though there may be little basis in fact for such claims and/or widespread scientific criticism of them.

---

[1]In addition, critics of the hereditary explanation note that neither blacks nor whites in America are genetically "pure" because there has been considerable racial interbreeding, and that the IQ scores of blacks and other minorities vary across the same range as those of whites.

Another problem follows directly from Jensen's work. He argued that the supposed hereditary aspects of the racial IQ-score difference make any effort at compensatory education largely hopeless. While he is correct in pointing out that many compensatory education programs have not been successful, it is quite another thing to argue that *no* program to improve the educational opportunities of minorities can be successful. Nonetheless this is the argument that has been made to some degree by Jensen, and more explicitly by many others. An example of how the public can react to such materials occurred just five days after Jensen's article was publicized by the popular press. In Virginia, it was used in a federal court case by opponents of school desegregation to "prove" that black students could not be helped by such integration (Brazziel, 1969). Thus, a real danger in the use of biased tests is that they will reinforce public beliefs that some races are superior to others, and that efforts to improve minority education are doomed to failure.

Gradually, awareness of the inaccuracies and biases of IQ tests have increased among educators, and as a result, some school districts have stopped using them. Nonetheless, the testing industry is a multi-million dollar business, and IQ testing and ethnically biased testing are far from eliminated. It is perhaps time for an objective appraisal by more educators of what real benefits accrue from intelligence testing, and how these benefits, if any, compare to the very real harm to minority and low-income students from the biases that are unavoidable in such tests.

Lack of Minority Role Models

A final factor associated with the nature of the educational institution that is relevant to the education of minorities is the lack of minority group role models. Minorities continue to be underrepresented among teachers, though there has been some improvement, particularly for blacks. One study (U.S. Commission on Civil Rights, 1971) indicated that in the Southwest there was one Anglo teacher for every twenty Anglo students, but only one black teacher for every thirty-nine black students, and only one Chicano teacher for every one hundred twenty Chicano students. Furthermore, the higher the position in the educational system, the fewer the minorities. Thus, there are proportionately fewer minority principals and superintendents than minority teachers. Similarly, the percentage of minority teachers declines as one moves from elementary school to high school to college. Surely this gives an important message to both minority and majority group students about the roles to which they might aspire.

RACIAL BIAS IN THE EDUCATIONAL SYSTEM: AN EVALUATION

All of the evidence we have reviewed, when taken together, strongly suggests that the present educational system operates in certain ways that prevent minority students from achieving their full potential. This impression is supported by the findings of Coleman (1966) and numerous others that the minority-white gap in learning starts out relatively small but *increases* over the course of the educational process. As we have seen, a big piece of the problem is related to the fact that those who control our educational institution and a great many minority students are, quite simply, *culturally different* from one another. To some degree, the problems of bias in educational materials and presentation of minorities in history, linguistic differences, teacher expectations, tracking, and testing *all* arise from such cultural differences. Given this reality, it is not so surprising that research shows that merely spending more money, or increasing the "quality" of minority education, will not do much good. The problem, at least in part, is that schools demand and reward certain values, beliefs, and habits, and that they (often unconsciously and unintentionally) put down and hold back those who do not have those values.

This leaves us with two questions. First, are the demanded values, beliefs, and habits really necessary in society? Or do they merely serve the interests or fit the whims of some dominant group? Second, *if the values are necessary,* what is the most effective way to teach them to those who do not now have them.

The first question is at least partly a matter of values and preferences. Functionalists, who favor cultural homogeneity and consensus, would tend to answer yes—the values are necessary. They would argue that such middle-class values and beliefs as self-motivation, belief in control over one's environment, and deferral of gratification lead people to work harder, be more productive, and thus create a more efficient and productive society. Because they are likely to see minorities as lacking in values and beliefs needed in society, these theorists are most likely to take a "cultural deprivation" viewpoint. Conflict theorists, not surprisingly, see the problem quite differently. They argue (see Bowles and Gintis, 1976) that middle class values are stressed mainly because they serve the interests of the dominant, wealthy elite in society. Thus, the belief that we determine our own fate leads us to view wealth as deserved and earned, so that the right of the rich to their wealth and power is not questioned—while *in fact* wealth is mostly inherited, not earned. Similarly, the acceptance of hierarchy is encouraged because it helps to "keep people in their place," while creativity is stifled because it could give rise to "dangerous" ideas that might threaten the ascendency of the wealth owners. Thus, from the conflict perspective, education functions to enforce the status quo and to pass along inequality by demanding a set of values and beliefs that are held by the dominant elements in society and serve the interests of those groups. These values, beliefs, and habits may be "necessary" to preserve the position of the elite, but, from this viewpoint, they certainly are not functional for the society as a whole. Accordingly, these theorists are likely to define the problem as one of "cultural bias."

Even if there was agreement on the need in society for general acceptance of some values and beliefs (which, as we have just seen, there is not), there would still be disagreement about the best way to "teach" those values. As a general rule, the functionalist would opt for relatively minor changes in the educational system to give minorities and other disadvantaged students a greater opportunity to learn the "needed" values, habits, and beliefs. This might be done through more intensive student-teacher contact or through attempts (as suggested by Coleman) to give minority students greater contact with white middle-class students, in the hopes that they will adopt the values and habits of these more "advantaged" students. The conflict theorist, on the other hand, would argue that such "band-aid" approaches are doomed to failure. The reason minority students believe in "luck" rather than "hard work," for example, is that, *for them,* hard work has not in the past paid off. Similarly, it is hard to believe that one controls one's own fate when one in fact does not. According to the conflict theorist, attitudes and beliefs cannot and will not change until *experiences* change, and the efforts suggested by functionalists to teach people beliefs contrary to their own experiences are doomed to failure. Some conflict theorists, such as Bowles and Gintis (1976) and Jencks et al. (1972), and more recently, Ogbu (1978), argue that trying to solve such problems through education is futile: The roots of inequality are in the economic system, and only altering the pervasive reality of gross racial economic inequality can make a difference. Others, however, argue that changes in the power structure of the educational system could be useful, claiming that if minorities had greater control over their education, their experiences and, hence, their beliefs would be different.

Having seen in a general way how functionalist and conflict theorists would approach solving the problem of racial and ethnic inequality in education, we shall in the remainder of the chapter explore some more specific approaches that are being advocated as possible solutions to the problem.

RESOLVING PROBLEMS OF MAJORITY-MINORITY INEQUALITY IN EDUCATION: FUNCTIONALIST AND CONFLICT APPROACHES

Approaches Suggested by the Functionalist (Order) Perspective

Conservatism: "Benign Neglect"   As we have seen, the unequal test scores of majority and minority group children, and the failure of some programs to improve minority education, have led some to conclude that it is hopeless to try to improve the educational opportunities of minority students. Those who hold this view frequently make the mistake of assuming that the tests are true indicators of ability—an assumption that, as we have seen, is largely incorrect because of various forms of bias in the process and content of "ability" testing. A slightly different version of this view holds that the *culture* of blacks and other minorities is the cause of the problem. They adopt the "culture of poverty" or "cultural deficit" model, arguing—as do a wide range of functionalist theorists—that the values, beliefs, family structure, and so on of minority group members make it impossible for them to advance educationally, and that there is little that can or should be done to change that situation (see Banfield, 1968, 1974). This view is clearly racist in the sense that it (1) blames minorities for their disadvantage, when the true source of that disadvantage is a long and continuing history of discrimination and (2) regards as completely acceptable—perhaps even desirable—a continuing pattern of racial inequality in education and most other areas. Nonetheless, it would be a mistake to underestimate the popularity of this view: As we have seen before (see Feagin, 1972; Schuman, 1975), a great many Americans *do* believe that minorities are to blame for their own disadvantage. Furthermore, this view has been carried over into politics, as support for programs to combat racism declined during the 1970s. One example can be seen in a statement by Daniel Patrick Moynihan (the author of the "Moynihan Report" on the black family; see Chapter 4), in his role as an advisor to President Nixon, that the problems of the ghetto might best benefit from a period of "benign neglect." Translated, this and other similar statements by politicians during the past decade mean that minorities may as well get used to inequality, because little or nothing is going to be done about it.

Liberalism: Compensatory Education   While a great many social scientists do hold views consistent with the "culture of poverty" or "cultural deficit" theories, many of them do not favor neglecting the problem of racial inequality. Instead, they favor programs to bring about *cultural assimilation:* to teach to minority students the values and habits they need to get ahead in school and in life. This viewpoint is clearly aligned with the order perspective in that it does not question the need to maintain consensus on dominant (middle-class) values and beliefs. It is, however, more liberal than the "benign neglect" viewpoint because it seeks to bring about more equal educational outcomes rather than accepting racial and class inequality as a given. One approach arising from this liberal version of the order perspective is *compensatory education.* This approach consists of preschool programs for low-income and minority children and, in some cases, supplementary programs within the regular educational setting. The idea is to expose disadvantaged children to educational materials and to teach them skills, habits, and values related to education, compensating for what is believed to be missing in the home. The largest and best known example of compensatory education has been the Head Start preschool program.

Although Head Start and other compensatory education programs have been quite popular among educators, there is reason to question their effectiveness in achieving their primary goal—reducing racial and class inequalities in learning. That is not to say they have done no good. As Ogbu (1978) points out, they have tended to reduce fiscal inequalities between city and suburban school systems by channeling money into school systems with large numbers of minority and/or poor students. They have also provided services in related areas, such as health and psychological services, that many of these children had not previously gotten. However, it appears that Head Start and other compensatory education programs have in many cases led to only a small improvement in what minority group and/or low-income children actually learn. Apparently, what sometimes happens is that children who participate in Head Start and other programs do show substantial gains on ability and achievement measures as a result of participating in the program, but as a general rule, most of the benefit disappears by the second or third grade, so that compensatory education has little if any long-term effect on reducing racial and class inequalities in learning. (For a more thorough review of this literature, see Ogbu, 1978, pp. 84−100. Among the major studies supporting these conclusions are White, 1970; Little and Smith, 1971; Stanley, 1973.) It should be noted that compensatory education programs in some places have been successful (a notable example is Ypsilanti, Michigan, where long-term positive effects have been demonstrated in a recent study by Weber et al., 1978; see also Luzar, 1981), but that has not been universally true. In many places, compensatory education programs have done relatively little to reduce racial and class inequality in education.

Different explanations can be given for this. Proponents of compensatory education note that the approach is a new one, and that it takes some time to learn what works and what does not. They stress that some individual programs—generally the most intensive ones (small groups with close interaction, parental involvement, and advance planning)—have in fact been successful. They argue that this proves that the programs can work and certainly that the view of Jensen and others that many minority children cannot be educated is wrong.

On the other hand, there are those who argue that compensatory education has in many cases not worked very well because its basic assumption—cultural deprivation theory—is wrong. According to this view, compensatory education is basically "more of the same"; it places on students the same demands for conformity to white middle-class culture as does the regular educational system. Thus, it fails for many of the same reasons (Ogbu, 1978; Baratz and Baratz 1970; Bowles and Gintis, 1976). The experiences of minority and/or poor children are simply different from those of whites; they require adaptation through different kinds of values, habits, and beliefs, and attempting to "teach" people cultural characteristics that are contrary to their own experiences cannot be expected to work.

Liberalism: Desegregation through Busing   Another, quite different, approach to minority education is the effort to combat urban *de facto* school segregation through busing. Although some see busing as a radical proposal, a thorough analysis of the theory underlying busing shows that it basically arises from the functionalist perspective's ideas on cultural deprivation and the need for assimilation of minorities. Much of the theoretical argument behind busing can be traced to the Coleman Report (Coleman, 1966) discussed earlier in this chapter. Let us turn our attention for a moment to that report and identify the parts that led to the suggestion that busing may be the route to equal educational opportunity for minority school children. You will recall that the study found that the background characteristics of *fellow students* were an important factor influencing the learning of minority and low-income students. Specifically, the more "advantaged" the background of their fellow students, the better the minority students did. When their *fellow students* came from homes where the parents were more educated and able to provide more materials such as books, newspapers, and television, minority and low-income students did better. When their fellow students had the attitudes and beliefs associated with educational success, minority and low-income students also did better (Coleman, 1966, pp. 302–305). Coleman's data also showed that, apparently for this reason, minority students generally learned more in integrated schools than they did in segregated schools (pp. 307–312, 330–331). At the same time, Coleman's data indicated that the learning of white students was *not* harmed by attending integrated schools, and that the white students indeed generally appreciated the contact with students from groups other than their own. Coleman suggests that the reason that minority students do better when they attend school with white middle-class students is that minority students adopt the attitudes, beliefs, and study habits of their fellow students, and consequently do better. In short, assimilation of minorities into the school system is accomplished through their contact with their ''culturally more advantaged'' white middle-class classmates. Thus, Coleman's suggestion fits well within the functionalist perspective and its emphasis on cultural assimilation.

Coleman's finding that minority students do better in integrated schools—coupled with a theory to explain why they did better—was seen by many as convincing proof that equal educational opportunity could come about only through the creation of an integrated school system. You will recall that *de facto* segregation remained widespread in the United States at the time the Coleman Report was issued. In other words, schools remained largely segregated, even though deliberate policies of segregation were illegal. A large part of the reason for this was that schools are based on neighborhood attendance districts, and neighborhoods are, as we have seen, usually quite racially segregated. Therefore, the only way to bring about school desegregation in many urban areas was to bus minority children to schools in white neighborhoods and/or white children to schools in minority neighborhoods.

Because of its findings on integration and learning by minority students, the Coleman Report was frequently cited in court cases over school desegregation as ''proof'' that equal educational opportunity for minorities required that schools be integrated, by means of busing if necessary. Since the Coleman Report was published in 1966, busing for the purpose of school desegregation has been initiated, on varying scales, in many cities. In some, lawsuits by the NAACP or other groups favoring integrated schools have led to court rulings requiring busing. Frequently, such rulings have been based on findings that the segregation resulted at least partially from actions of school officials, not entirely because of housing patterns. In other places, busing programs have been initiated without court action, either at the initiative of the local school board or in response to pressures from groups favoring desegregation. Busing has become sufficiently widespread over a period of ten to fifteen years to make it possible to begin addressing the question of whether busing and other forms of school desegregation have worked to improve the educational opportunity of minorities in the ways the Coleman Report suggested they might.

The best answer appears to be a qualified yes. Desegregation has worked, but only to a limited degree and only under certain conditions. Numerous studies have been made of the educational effects of school desegregation; some have shown beneficial effects and others have not. To begin with, it must be stressed that it is one thing to show, as Coleman (1966) did, that minority students in integrated schools tend to do better than minority students in segregated schools. It is quite another thing, however, to say that taking a set of minority students out of segregated schools and putting them into integrated schools will cause their performance to improve. The latter is the question that is most relevant in evaluating the effects of busing and other desegregation programs. In studies relating to this question, it appears that the success of desegregation in improving the achievement of minority students depends on (1) how the desegregation is carried out, (2) the racial and political climate in which it occurs, and (3) social and demographic characteristics of the urban area in which it occurs.

David J. Armor (1972), using data from his study of a voluntary busing program in Boston and five other studies of northern desegregation, reported that desegregation had failed to improve the achievement of black students, failed to narrow the black-white achievement gap, and failed to improve the educational aspirations of black students. The one area of success was that black students attending desegregated schools were considerably more likely to go on to college, but Armour argues that this was tempered by high college dropout rates. A subsequent report by Pettigrew and his associates (1973) reviews seven studies that, according to the authors, do show gains in black achievement associated with desegregation through busing. In addition, these authors criticize Armor's study, noting that in several cities the black-white gap failed to narrow because the learning of whites also improved after busing. They also argue that the dropout rate of black college students who graduated from integrated schools is not high compared to that of college students in general. A review of about one hundred studies of desegregation (St. John, 1975) gives an impression similar to that gained from the Armor and Pettigrew articles taken together: Some studies indicate a gain in minority achievement, others do not. There is no evidence for any significant harm to the achievement of minority group children, nor is there evidence of harm to white children, except possibly when they are transferred to schools where the large majority of students are black. There is some evidence that educational and occupational aspirations of minority children decline slightly, but this has been shown to sometimes be correlated with *improved* achievement, notably in cases where aspirations had been unrealistically high. Overall, then, the effect of school desegregation on minority student learning appears to range from negligible to somewhat positive. It has generally not harmed the achievement of white students, but, where implemented, it has certainly not *eliminated* racial inequality in learning, either.

School desegregation was also intended to improve intergroup relations in the schools. Recall from Chapter 3 that intergroup contact, when it is equal-status, nonthreatening, noncompetitive, and ideally, interdependent, can improve intergroup relations. Recall also that when these conditions are not present, contact can make intergroup relations worse. A major purpose of school desegregation, besides bringing about more equal educational opportunity, has been to improve intergroup relations. Again, the evidence of its actual success seems mixed: Intergroup relations in some schools have improved; in others, they have gotten worse. In large part—as our discussion of Boston's desegregation efforts in Chapter 3 showed—desegregation's success or failure in improving intergroup relations depends largely on the presence of the conditions we have mentioned: equal-status contact, interdependency, and the absence of threat and excessive competition. Having made these general observations, let us now explore in more detail the kinds of factors associated with success or failure of desegregation and busing in the areas of both minority educational opportunity and intergroup relations.

Effects of How the Desegregation is Carried Out. A number of factors related to the design and execution of school desegregation programs seem related to the success of the desegregation. It seems that the younger the children involved, the more effective desegregation is in both improving minority student learning and in improving intergroup relations in the schools (see St. John, 1975; U.S. Senate Select Committee, 1972). Accordingly, school desegregation probably is most effective in elementary school, particularly in the lower grades and kindergarten. Apparently, by high school both study habits and intergroup prejudices have become sufficiently ingrained that desegregation makes little difference. Unfortunately, much of the desegregation that has occurred has been done in a way directly *opposite* to what these findings suggest: Many desegregation plans have involved high schools to a greater degree than the lower grades. The reason appears to be political: The busing of younger children, even though it appears to be more effective, is more controversial than the busing of older children.

Another aspect of the school desegregation process is emphasized by Pettigrew (1969a, 1969b). He draws a distinction between mere desegregation—simply altering the proportion of white and black students attending the schools—and true integration. In true integration, not only are students reassigned to different schools but real efforts are made to bring about closer and more friendly relations between the races. The issues involved in the distinction are numerous. In some desegregated schools, tracking and other practices have led to a good deal of segregation *within* supposedly desegregated schools. Even seating arrangements in the classroom can reflect the presence or absence of true integration. The nature of materials used in the classroom can also affect the success of school integration. It is important that the materials reflect the degree of cultural diversity present in the classroom, and it is equally important that teachers avoid the use of materials that may either intentionally or subtly downgrade a minority group. In some cases, the use of materials that teachers did not realize were degrading to minority groups has caused problems in newly desegregated classrooms. It is also important that teaching staffs as well as students be integrated, so that there are minority teachers and principals as well as students. In short, true integration is much more than transferring pupils to different schools to achieve racial balance. It requires

Minority teachers can serve as important role models for minority students, and can be helpful in breaking down stereotypes among majority group students. Joe DiDio, NEA.

extensive planning, preparation, effort, and in many cases, changes in established practices.

A third central factor, which was mentioned when we discussed school desegregation in Boston in Chapter 3, is that to improve the educational performance of minority students, *socioeconomic* desegregation as well as racial desegregation is needed. The original findings of the Coleman Report strongly supported this view: The habits and beliefs that related to academic achievement were associated with social class just as they were with race and ethnicity. Subsequent experience has supported this, as the case of South Boston illustrates: Transferring poor black and poor white students between two schools that have always been characterized by low levels of learning can be expected to do little or nothing to help the learning of either black or white students.

Racial and Political Climate of the Community: The Role of Leadership. It goes without saying that learning cannot occur in conditions of endless disruption. In a few communities, opposition to busing has been so sustained, violent, and disruptive that, for a period of time, it was very difficult for anyone to learn anything in the schools affected by the conflict. (It is important to point out however, that even in cities where there is much disruption and conflict, most of the trouble often centers around only a few schools. In Boston, for example, there was serious trouble in only four of eighty schools involved in desegregation.) In communities where busing has led to serious violence, such as Boston, Louisville, and, several years earlier, Pontiac, Michigan, the actions of the leadership in the community apparently played an important role in creating the trouble. A national survey of 532 school districts (U.S. Commission on Civil Rights, 1976, p. 175) showed, for example, that in the 411 districts that had no serious disruptions associated with desegregation, 65 percent of the districts had business leaders who were generally supportive or neutral toward segregation, and 67 percent had political leaders who were supportive or neutral. On the other hand, among the 95 districts that *did* have serious disruptions, only 27 percent had supportive or neutral business leaders, and only 30 percent had supportive or neutral political leaders. Boston, Louisville, and Pontiac were all to some degree marked by local leadership that emphasized its adamant opposition to busing rather than emphasizing the need to cooperate with the program (U.S. Commission on Civil Rights, 1976, pp. 179–183). In some communities the leadership, intentionally or not, has given people the misimpression that if only they "raise enough hell" the requirement of segregation will somehow go away. This apparently encouraged much more adamant opposition than would otherwise have developed. In cities where the local leadership has taken the view that, regardless of its popularity, busing is there to stay and that violent opposition to it would harm the school children and worsen the situation, even large-scale desegregation programs have been implemented without serious disruption; Detroit and Columbus, Ohio, are two examples. Apparently, the actions and statements of local leaders do make a difference. Communities where the political, business, labor, and religious leadership makes a vigorous effort to prepare the community for desegregation are less likely to experience difficulties.

    Social and Demographic Characteristics of the Community. Some of the opposition to busing centers around problems associated with a long bus ride, which can require children to leave home for school earlier and get back later than they otherwise would or which can cut into the school day by using some of the time for transportation. There are also worries about the increased risk of accidents and the increased use of energy. However, except in the largest cities, these problems do not in fact appear sizable. In twenty-nine districts studied by the U.S. Commission on Civil Rights (1976), for example, there was only a small average increase in the percentage of students bused. For minority students, the numbers bused increased from 47 percent to 56 percent; for white students, from 50 percent to 53 percent. Furthermore, the bus rides were typically quite short. Even in one of the larger cities, Minneapolis, the average bus ride after desegregation was less than 20 minutes—about the same as it was before desegregation.

    In a few very large cities with large minority populations, long and potentially disruptive bus rides are sometimes required. In the sprawling cities of Los Angeles and Detroit, for example, the length of the bus ride has become a major issue. In addition, there is another problem in some of these large districts that makes desegregation increasingly difficult: There are not enough white students to desegregate all the predominantly black schools. In general, the literature on school desegregation suggests that benefits of desegregation can be expected to be the greatest when the minority population is somewhere in the general range of 20 or 25 percent to 50 or 55 percent: enough to go beyond mere tokenism (Rist, 1978) but not so great as to represent a lack of true desegregation. In some large cities, however, the public school enrollment is 75 percent or more black—too high to meaningfully integrate a sizable proportion of the city's schools, unless schools from nearby suburban districts are also included in the desegregation plan. In Atlanta, for example, the 1978 school enrollment was 89 percent black. In Baltimore, it was 76 percent nonwhite (nearly all black), and in Chicago, 60 percent black and 15 percent Hispanic; only about 23 percent of Chicago's students were white Anglos. Other cities with school systems whose students are 60 percent or more black include Detroit (82 percent), Kansas City (64 percent), Philadelphia (62 percent), and St. Louis (72 percent) (U.S. Commission on Civil Rights, 1979). One solution that has been proposed to deal with this difficulty is busing between predominantly black central cities and nearby white suburbs. In the early 1970s, lower courts ordered such remedies in Detroit and Richmond, Virginia, but in 1975, the Supreme Court ruled that such *cross-district* busing was not required by law unless deliberate governmental action had been taken to create city-suburb segregation. Accordingly, it ordered that cross-district busing could not be ordered by the courts in these cases.

An issue closely related to this which has received considerable attention from social scientists is the question of "white flight": Does desegregation through busing cause a substantial loss of white students from big-city school systems, thus leaving them even more segregated than they were before the desegregation program was put into effect? The argument was first raised by Coleman (1975), who had by now reversed his position and come out against mandatory busing for desegregation. Coleman presented data which, he said, showed that busing caused so many white students to be taken out of the public schools—either through movement to the suburbs or enrollment in private schools—that the schools ended up even more segregated than when desegregation started. His study was incomplete, however, and critics such as Pettigrew and Green (1976) and Farley (1975) argued that methodological problems in the study prevented any such conclusion. It has been pointed out, furthermore, that white flight from public school systems has been going on anyway, with or without busing. Therefore, busing at most can account for only a part of the "white flight" problem.

Probably the most comprehensive study of the question to date is one by Armor (1978). This study indicates that, *in certain kinds of districts,* there has probably been significant white flight as a result of desegregation. This occurs in districts with large minority enrollments and closely accessible, predominantly white suburbs. Through comparisons with projected rates of white flight and with the experience of cities that did not desegregate, Armor argues that in some cities that desegregated, the number of white students who left the school system over a period of several years just before, during, and after busing began was up to twice as great as it would otherwise have been. Keep in mind that these findings apply to only certain kinds of cities. In cities that are not highly suburbanized, or in cities with 20 percent or fewer minority students, white flight does not appear to be significantly associated with desegregation. It is for this reason that the U.S. Commission on Civil Rights (1976) found that in most school districts, desegregation has not been associated with white flight. In fact, in smaller cities without large minority populations, desegregation has proceeded more smoothly on all counts. Studies by the U.S. Commission on Civil Rights (1976) indicate that it is cities like Berkeley, California; Colorado Springs, Colorado; Kalamazoo, Michigan; Newport News, Virginia; and Waterloo, Iowa, that have made the greatest progress toward desegregating their schools. Despite their diversity in some regards, all these cities have relatively small populations (75,000 to 175,000), and small-to-moderate minority school enrollments (16 percent to 37 percent). Even large cities with relatively small minority enrollments can have very successful desegregation: Minneapolis (population 424,000; minority enrollment, 21 percent) has been cited as a city where desegregation has been very successful (U.S. Commission on Civil Rights, 1976). All things considered, then, in most cities, desegregation (including busing) *if* properly implemented and supported by community leaders, will tend to go smoothly and carries the potential for moderate improvement in both intergroup relations and minority student achievement.

The problem of white flight—both that induced by desegregation and that which would have happened anyway—makes the desegregation of predominantly minority school systems in large suburbanized cities a more difficult case. Since a sizable proportion of the minority student population lives in such cities, they are of considerable importance, even though relatively few cities are involved. One solution that might work is cross-district desegregation between city and suburbs. Armor presents some evidence that this would reduce the problem of white flight, but downgrades it in favor of voluntary desegregation, where those who choose could be bused to schools with a racial composition different from their own. The problem with such voluntary desegregation, however, is that for the most part, it does not work: Not enough students participate to make any real difference in the racial distribution of students (Bahr et al., 1979, p. 418). The metropolitanwide approach has been adopted in only a few areas, most of which had one countywide school district. As we noted, the Supreme Court has ruled against any requirements for cross-district busing in most situations, and it is unlikely that such desegregation will come about either voluntarily or through state or federal legislation. The reason: It is not popular with the public. Although most Americans favor the general principle of integrated education, their attitudes change if busing is required to achieve it. In recent years polls have shown that between 65 percent and 85 percent of whites oppose busing, and there is sizable opposition among blacks, too: According to the polls, between a third and a half of blacks have also indicated opposition to busing. Accordingly, the hope for desegregating schools in large, heavily minority cities surrounded by suburbs is not great; indeed in some such areas segregation has actually increased in recent years.

The Effectiveness of Busing: An Overview. We have seen that, if properly implemented, school desegregation can bring moderate improvement in minority student achievement and in majority-minority relations in the schools. Such improvement, however, is not sufficient to eliminate the racial gap in learning. Furthermore, under present social and political conditions, desegregation is hard to accomplish in big cities with large minority populations and readily accessible suburbs. Only cross-district desegregation would work there, and it is unlikely in the present legal and political situation. Furthermore, even if it were done, it would involve longer bus rides than in the smaller cities (or large ones with small minority populations) where busing seems to work better. Given these limitations we must ask, are there other alternatives available for improving the education of minority school children?

Approaches Arising from the Conflict Perspective

Those who view the cultural deficiency approach as incorrect, as most conflict theorists do, argue that strategies such as compensatory education and school desegregation, while possibly desirable, cannot be expected to solve the problem of racial inequality in education. The problem is not in the minorities; it is in the schools that, in effect, arbitrarily demand that minority students change their values, beliefs, and habits to conform with those supported by the school system. This is unfair and unrealistic, the conflict theorists argue, because those habits, beliefs, and values are well suited to the social conditions of minority students. The solution, then, is not to change the minority student (which all the strategies we have examined thus far somehow aim to do) but rather to either (1) change the school or (2) change the *social conditions* that create the values of poor and minority students, values that functionalists hold to be harmful.

Community Control of Schools   One approach that aims to make such changes is the movement for *community control* of schools in minority neighborhoods. A major objective is to change the *power structure* of education to give minority parents control over decisions influencing their children's education. To a greater or lesser degree, community control is a reality in white communities, particularly ones that are small enough for individual parents to have some influence over what goes on in the schools. In minority communities, the picture is often different. For one thing, minorities are more likely to live in large cities, where the massive bureaucracy necessary to run a school system makes any kind of public input more difficult. Of equal or greater importance, school boards that govern minority schools often tend to be dominated by whites. An example is Boston, where, during desegregation, the Boston School Committee was all white, despite the large numbers of black and Hispanic students in the city's school system. Finally, all the cultural differences and conflicts between the schools and minority students suggest a need for greater minority group control over the school system, argue the proponents of community control.

In addition to enabling minority group parents to alter the educational system to better fit their needs, it is argued that community control gives minority students and parents a way of developing the sense of control over their environment which Coleman (1966) and others have shown to be so important for achievement (Fantini, 1969, Fantini et al., 1970, pp. 192–193).

What of the evidence? Do community-controlled schools work as they are supposed to? The actual evidence is quite limited, because true community-controlled schools in minority communities remain a rarity. Community control represents a real threat to the power structure of education, since it typically involves the right of the community to hire and fire teachers and to demand accountability in teaching. This represents a real threat to the school boards and to the professional organizations and unions of teachers and school administrators, and they usually mount vigorous opposition to community control. Experiments in community control have, however, been tried in New York and Washington, and a more limited approach, decentralization, has been implemented systemwide in New York City and Detroit. However, as we shall see, the latter cannot be equated with community control.

Limited evidence on the effects of community control from Washington's Adams-Morgan school experiment shows, for example, that vandalism and suspensions decreased, and that Adams-Morgan was one of only six schools in the city where reading scores improved during the 1967−68 school year (Fantini, 1969). Washington is something of an exception, however, as the teachers' union and school board supported the concept of community control in this experiment and in a subsequent one at Anacostia school (Fantini and Gittell, 1973).

Unfortunately, New York's experience may be more typical. There, too, an experiment with community-controlled education was tried out in the Ocean Hill−Brownsville district. In the early stages of the project, there were signs of success—lower vandalism, less absence of both students and teachers, and greater parental interest and involvement in the schools. However, this experiment ran into a buzz-saw of opposition from the educational establishment. The fierce opposition of the teachers' union, the United Federation of Teachers, led to a citywide teachers strike in 1968. The central school board, too, came into conflict with the local, community-controlled Ocean Hill board. Following the teacher strike, which lasted two and a half months and was marked by violent conflict between the striking teachers and the black community, the local board was stripped of much of its power. These events led to a lengthy boycott of schools in the Ocean Hill area by parents and students, at times joined by nonunion teachers. Violence became more widespread, and charges of white racism and anti-Semitism flew back and forth between the black community and the largely Jewish teachers' union. Much of the school year was lost, and any gains in student learning were wiped out, as subsequent research by Ravitch (1973) showed. (For a good general description of the Ocean Hill−Brownsville case, see Baldridge, 1976, pp. 480−484). The extent of opposition revealed by this case illustrates the difficulty of implementing a policy that makes fundamental changes in the power structure of education and probably explains why even experimentation with community control has been extremely limited.

As we indicated earlier, another, more moderate, approach, decentralization, has been implemented in two cities, New York and Detroit. Under this plan, authority for running the schools is divided between a central school board and regional boards—thirty in New York, eight in Detroit. In general, however, there is little or no evidence thus far that decentralization has made any real educational difference (Ornstein, 1978). A possible reason—decentralization is *not* the same as community control (Fantini and Gittell, 1973). The regional districts created by decentralization are still large—25,000 to 38,000 students per district in Detroit, for example (Glass and Sanders, 1978). Thus, the direct parental involvement at the school level that occurs with community control is not created. Furthermore, in both New York and Detroit, minority representation on school boards actually *decreased* when decentralization was implemented (Fantini and Gittell, 1973; Ornstein, 1978), though it has since risen. Today, blacks have the majority of positions on both regional and citywide boards in Detroit. The large-scale organization of even regional boards tends to make it easy for well-organized groups that are not necessarily representative of the community to gain influence. Ornstein argues that ideological militants have been overrepresented, but even groups not connected with the neighborhood community often gain influence—in New York, many of the regional board positions were filled by candidates supported either by the teachers' union or by Roman Catholic groups concerned with aid to parochial schools.

The idea of decentralization should not been seen as entirely useless, however. In Detroit, it has provided the stimulus for some new experiments with neighborhood community-controlled schools, initiated by some of the regional school boards (Glass and Sanders, 1978, pp. 107–114). In addition, as black parents have gained influence in recent years, they have shown increasing concern with the achievement scores of minority students (Glass and Sanders, 1978), though it is too early to assess the actual effect on achievement of this changed emphasis. Clearly, however, the schools' accountability for student achievement has emerged as a major issue in Detroit.

It should, of course, be noted that the community control movement has its critics. Some claim that it fosters segregation and inhibits contact between the races. Apparently, decentralization in Detroit did get some support from whites who saw it as a way of avoiding school desegregation (Ornstein, 1978). Others have argued that it represents a threat to academic freedom, especially when it leads to demands to take away teacher tenure or to control the materials used in the classroom. This could lead to narrowmindedness and parochialism in education that would heighten, rather than reduce, intergroup prejudices. Indeed, the banning of books dealing with a variety of sensitive issues in *white* school districts, which do typically have a greater deal of community control, suggests this is a potential problem. Although this does not negate the potential benefits of community control, it certainly points to the need for some safeguards.

Community control, then, like other approaches, emerges not as a panacea, but rather as an approach that, if properly implemented, offers some promise as a way of improving the achievement of minority school children. Even more than with other reforms, however, community control has been very slow to emerge because it involves basic changes in the school system's power structure.

Change the Larger System   Another idea increasingly stressed by conflict theorists is that, in a structure of gross *economic* inequality, education cannot by itself change patterns of racial inequality. Because this view has already been discussed earlier in this chapter, we shall examine it only briefly here. Fundamentally, it argues that in a system of economic inequality, the educational system, by demanding certain values, beliefs, and work habits, insures the passing along of inequality from generation to generation. The root of the inequality is found not in the educational system, but in the economic system. The educational system is merely one of many mechanisms by which the inequality is passed from generation to generation. If, of course, there is economic inequality along the lines of race, it is racial inequality that will be passed along. Furthermore, it is probably true that even without the cultural differences between schools and students from low-income families, the lower-income students would be at a disadvantage in the schools. Poverty itself is a great disadvantage that carries over into every aspect of one's life. Poverty often means malnutrition, more common illness, unhealthy housing, and inability to afford educational materials that others take for granted. It also means more stress, which in turn can lead to mental and physical disorders or to alcohol or drug abuse in the parents of poor children. Thus, *regardless* of one's cultural adaptation to poverty, poverty itself is likely to be a serious handicap to a child's educational opportunity. Thus, there are many who argue that no matter how necessary educational reform may be (and, as we have seen, it *is* highly necessary), educational reform alone (while desirable and necessary) cannot solve the problem because it is not the root cause of the problem: Only economic reform can offer a real solution, according to this viewpoint (Jencks et al., 1972; Bowles and Gintis, 1976; Ogbu, 1978. For a contrary view, see Edmonds, 1979, who argues there are numerous individual schools that *have* eliminated racial and economic inequalities in learning.)

A Final Note: Increasing the Rigor of Minority Group Education

One other approach must be noted which in the past few years has been suggested as a promising possibility for bringing about improved learning in minority students. As we shall see, the approach is not altogether clearly associated with either the functionalist or conflict approach. Like the conflict approach, it rests on the assumption that schools have failed minority students, but like the functionalist approach, it does not *necessarily* demand a substantial change in the organization or power structure of education. It does, however, require significant changes in the behavior of teachers and, ultimately, of minority students as well. This approach is based on the fact that, as we have seen, low teacher expectations lead to low student achievement. One reason for this is that when teachers have low expectations of students, they demand only a low quality of work. Thus, the solution is to (1) convince teachers that low-income and minority students *can* learn as well as anyone else and (2) get those teachers to demand such learning of their students. It is striking that essays advocating this approach have recently appeared in both the conflict theory-oriented periodical *Social Policy* (Edmonds, 1979) and in the functionalist *The Public Interest* (Coleman, 1981; Fuerst, 1981). The studies reported in these papers—along with others such as those of Weber (1971) and Brookover and Lezotte (1971)—strongly suggest that minority students do better when:

1. Teachers *believe* that the students are capable of success, and believe that their efforts can make a difference in what the students learn.
2. The class is a pleasant place, relatively quiet and orderly. The *most* effective teachers are those who can maintain reasonable order *without* spending a great deal of their time and effort on keeping order.
3. There is emphasis on the learning of basic reading and math skills, both in terms of how teachers spend their time and in terms of the level of performance that they require of their students.

A recent study by Feurst (1981) of all-black schools in Chicago showed that the schools where black students excelled (in some of these schools, average reading scores substantially exceeded the norms in white suburban schools) displayed the patterns described above. Although different schools used various innovations, all demanded quality performance—students could not be promoted without it—and all had teachers who believed that black students could learn as well as anyone else—a pattern which, as we have seen, is not typical of most urban schools. As one teacher said, "The belief that children can succeed is more than half of the battle." Unfortunately, these patterns, according to Fuerst, existed in only a minority of Chicago's all-black schools. About 20,000 of Chicago's black public school students are attending such schools, and another 10,000 are atttending racially integrated schools and are also doing well. Unfortunately, about 145,000 other black students are in less advantageous settings, benefitting neither from these educational reforms nor from integration (Fuerst, 1981, p. 91).

A final piece of evidence comes from very recent studies by Greeley (1981) and by Coleman et al. (1981). These studies, summarized by Coleman (1981) in his article in *The Public Interest*, indicate that (1) minority students of comparable socioeconomic status do better in private schools than in public schools and (2) in Catholic schools, particularly, there is much less inequality in achievement along the lines of race and social class than in public schools. The reasons, according to Coleman, are that such schools expect and demand higher levels of achievement, and that they maintain better order. Furthermore, public schools that have these characteristics are also marked by better student achievement. What all this suggests is that minority students *can* do as well as anyone in school, and that, where teachers *expect* and *demand* it, they very often will. According to Edmonds (1979), there are a variety of ways that such a situation can come about. It may be the result of an informed and dedicated teaching staff, or of a demanding principal. It may also be a result of parental pressure, so that it could be an outcome of an effective community control program.

To summarize, the approach of increasing the rigor of minority education, like community control and desegregation through busing, shows promise where it has been implemented. On the other hand, it is also true that, just as there are very few schools that are truly community controlled or truly integrated, there are—as

Fuerst's Chicago study shows—few schools that really expect and demand high performance of minority students. Thus, in spite of this promising new development, most of our schools are continuing to fail in their quest to eliminate racial inequality in education.

SUMMARY AND CONCLUSION

In this chapter we have seen evidence of educational inequality that has persisted despite the elimination of formal educational discrimination. We have also explored functionalist (cultural deprivation) and conflict (cultural bias) theories about the causes of educational inequality. We have seen a number of mechanisms by which schools subtly (and often unintentionally) discriminate against minority children, including culturally biased educational materials and tests, teacher expectation effects, and tracking. While compensatory education has had rather limited success, possibly because of overreliance on the cultural deprivation model, other strategies such as desegregation and community control show somewhat greater promise, if properly implemented. Nonetheless, their use has been limited due to powerful opposition, and in many of the big cities where much of the minority population lives, education has changed only incrementally. The failure to institute large-scale reforms in education, along with the similar failure to reform the economic system (see Chapter 9) means continuing educational inequality for black, Hispanic, and Indian Americans, despite the elimination of formal discrimination and official *de jure* segregation.

GLOSSARY

De facto segregation   School segregation which is the result *not* of an official policy of having separate schools for different racial groups, but of other processes which tend to create segregated schools, even without an official policy to have segregated schools. The most important cause of *de facto* segregation is housing segregation, which leads to a situation in which neighborhood school attendance districts tend to be, for example, all-white or all-black.

De jure segregation   School segregation which is the result of an official or deliberate policy of having separate schools for different racial groups.

Gerrymandering   The practice of drawing odd-shaped school attendance districts as a way of promoting racial or ethnic segregation in the schools.

Self-fulfilling prophecy   Any situation in which the expectation of some event or outcome contributes to the occurrence of that event or outcome. In education, for example, teachers frequently expect a lower quality of work from minority students than from white students. As a consequence, they treat minority students in different ways that tend to produce the expected outcome.

IV

VALUES, GOALS, AND ISSUES OF THE PRESENT AND FUTURE IN MAJORITY-MINORITY RELATIONS

Changing Values and Goals: Racial and Ethnic Group Movements and Attitudes from the 1960s to the 1980s

12

In Chapter 6 we saw how the response of minorities to intergroup inequality shifted from adaptation toward increasing protest after World War II. As the tide of protest by minorities rose, the patterns of inequality in the United States began to change. As the last several chapters have shown, the mechanisms of racial and ethnic inequality are quite different than they were before World War II. The mechanisms of inequality are much more subtle than in the past, but as these chapters have shown, racial and ethnic inequality continues to be a very serious problem in American society.

As the mechanisms of intergroup inequality in American society have changed, both the tactics and goals of minority group members have also changed. Indeed, the diversity of minority viewpoints has increased tremendously since the late 1960s. One example of this can be seen in the issue of school desegregation. In the era of *de jure* segregation in the 1950s, virtually all blacks in the United States favored integrated schools. Today, however, a significant number of blacks are skeptical about the benefits of integrated schools, and many more object to the methods that are sometimes proposed to bring about such integration. Thus, in the 1980s, blacks as well as whites are deeply divided over the issue of busing for the purpose of school desegregation.

The change in attitudes on school desegregation is just one of many possible examples. At least in part, it reflects a change in what some blacks consider to be an ideal or model pattern of race relations. In this chapter we shall turn our attention to such changes. We shall examine changes, and increasing diversity, in the goals and values of minority (and majority) group members concerning what constitutes a desirable pattern of intergroup relations. Specifically, we shall explore changing attitudes toward three ideal models, as well as the arguments for and against each. The three models are *assimilation, pluralism,* and *separatism.*

THREE IDEAL TYPE MODELS OF INTERGROUP RELATIONS

Model 1: Assimilation

The general concept of assimilation was first introduced in Chapter 4 and has been referred to a number of times since. In this section we shall discuss the concept in greater detail and delineate several distinct types of assimilation. By way of review, the general concept of assimilation refers to a situation in which (1) the dominant group accepts the minority group or groups (at least in some aspects of social life) and (2) the majority and minority groups become integrated into a common culture and social structure. In many cases, the common culture and social structure are for the most part those of the dominant or majority group, though it may incorporate some features of the minority group as well. In other cases, however, the minority group influence is quite substantial. Accordingly, the balance of dominant and minority group cultural influences varies considerably from society to society.

Sociologists distinguish between two major kinds of assimilation, *cultural* and *structural* (Gordon, 1964, pp. 70–71). Cultural assimilation, as the name suggests, occurs when two or more groups come to share a common culture. By this, we mean that they have common attitudes, values, and life styles. Frequently, they will also come to think of themselves more and more as one common group, and less as distinct racial and ethnic groups. When cultural assimilation occurs, the common culture that evolves is usually mainly that of the dominant group, though, as we have suggested, certain aspects of minority group culture are sometimes also adopted.

Structural assimilation occurs when two or more social groups come to share one common social structure. By this, we mean that they share common social institutions, organizations, and friendship networks. When structural assimilation is complete, the two or more groups will not only share common institutions, organizations, and so on, but will also hold relatively equal positions in those social structures. Partly for this reason, structural assimilation tends to be more difficult to achieve than cultural assimilation (Gordon, 1964, p. 77). A minority group may change its culture (attitudes, beliefs, life styles) to conform with the dominant society, but such conformity does not guarantee that the group will be accepted into equal status roles in the society, which remains in the control of the dominant group. Furthermore, both majority and minority group members may prefer to develop friendships within their own group, even when cultural differences are not great. For these reasons, structural assimilation tends to occur to a significantly lesser degree than cultural assimilation.

Perhaps the most difficult type of structural assimilation is what Gordon (1964; p. 71) calls *marital assimilation*. Marital assimilation occurs only when there is widespread intermarriage between two racial or ethnic groups. If marital assimilation occurs and persists for an extended period of time, the assimilation of the groups involved becomes complete, and they gradually lose any identity as separate groups—an outcome known as *amalgamation*.

Although there has been much resistance in the United States to true structural assimilation, American ideology has always strongly supported the idea of cultural assimilation. Until recently, there has been great emphasis on the idea of America as a "melting pot" where citizens cease to think of themselves as "German," "Irish," "Polish," "Italian," "African," or "Mexican," and regard themselves instead as "American." Assimilation is also highly valued by the functionalist perspective in sociology, because it helps to bring about the common values and shared identity that functionalists believe are necessary in any society.

Assimilation can indeed lead to a system of racial and ethnic equality. For this to happen, however, there must be relatively complete *structural* assimilation as well as the often more superficial cultural type of assimilation. As we have seen this does not often happen easily. In addition, assimilation is more likely to lead to intergroup equality if it involves a true blend of the cultures and institutions of both groups. Unfortunately, assimilation often means that the minority group for the most part adopts the culture and social structure of the dominant group, so that the process is unbalanced from the start. As we shall see in more detail later in the chapter, this has been largely true of assimilation in the United States, though in some other societies such as Mexico (see Chapter 7) the assimilation process has been much more balanced. For these reasons, the existence of cultural assimilation in a society does not at all guarantee that the society will have intergroup equality.

Model 2: Pluralism

A second model of intergroup relations is known as *pluralism* (Higham, 1974). In pluralism some aspects of culture and social structure are shared in common throughout society; other aspects remain distinct in each racial or ethnic group. Under pluralism, there is a common culture and set of institutions throughout society, but only up to a point. To a large degree, each ethnic group maintains a distinct subculture, a distinct set of social institutions such as churches, clubs, businesses, and media, and a distinct set of *primary group* relations such as friendship neworks and families. Thus, under pluralism there exists one society made up of a number of distinct parts. In contrast to the melting pot, the pluralist model is often compared to a *mosaic*: one unit made up of many distinct parts.

Just as was the case with assimilation, we can subdivide the concept of pluralism into *cultural pluralism* and *structural pluralism*. Cultural pluralism occurs when groups in society each retain certain sets of attitudes, beliefs, and life styles, while sharing others in common. Similarly, structural pluralism exists when groups retain some social structures and institutions of their own, but share others in common. An example of this can be seen where several groups all willingly give allegiance to one government, speak the same language, and share the same monetary system, but at the same time go to their own churches, have different patterns of occupations, and marry within their own group.

In the sense that it involves the sharing of some common cultural and social structural features throughout a society, the pluralist model is in part consistent with the functionalist perspective in sociology. In other respects, however, the pluralist model is more closely aligned with the conflict perspective. Specifically, it denies the need for complete consensus, suggesting instead that society can benefit from diversity and the opportunity for change that diversity can offer. Furthermore, the distinct cultures and distinct sets of institutions found in a pluralist society offer a power base for the various racial and ethnic groups in the society. In the view of conflict theorists, the various social groups in any society do not all share the same self-interests. By retaining its own culture and set of social institutions, each group potentially has a power base to protect its legitimate interests.

Like assimilation, a pluralist society can be a society of racial equality. This will tend to occur if the power position of the various groups is relatively similar, and if the institutions they control have relatively similar resources. If these conditions are *not* present, equality will not exist either, though some conflict theorists might well argue that the mere existence of distinct groups with distinct cultures and social institutions guarantees something of a power base, which makes social change more possible than it is when assimilation is complete.

Model 3: Separatism

A third model of intergroup relations, at the opposite end of the scale from assimilation, is racial or ethnic *separatism*. Under separatism, two or more racial or ethnic groups occupying an area each have their own cultures and their own separate sets of social institutions and primary group relationships. Little or nothing is shared in common between the groups. If there is contact between the groups, it is the type of contact that occurs between two distinct societies or independent nations.

In many instances, separatism could occur only with *population transfer*. The reason is that separatism is virtually impossible unless each group involved has a distinct geographic base—a territory of its own. Therefore, unless the population distribution in a society is such that each group lives in distinct areas, it will be necessary for many members of one or both groups to move in order to bring about separatism.

Like assimilation and pluralism, separatism may or may not act as a means of bringing about intergroup equality. If separatism is voluntary on the part of the minority group, as in secession, where the minority group withdraws from the dominant group's society, if the two groups are able to gain similar levels of power, and if the geographic areas to which the groups move have similar resources, separatism can potentially offer an opportunity for intergroup equality. If, however, these conditions are not present, separatism may not only fail to bring equality but may lead to even more inequality. This is particularly true when separatism is imposed on the minority group against its will. A contemporary example of this is South Africa's policy of resettlement of the black population to *bantustans*, or "independent" black states. This policy inhibits any real movement toward black—white equality because (1) the policy is being imposed on the black population by the dominant whites, (2) the areas assigned to the black population are small relative to the size of that population and are limited in resources, and (3) the *bantustans* are not allowed the power that would be associated with true independence. In effect, they exist at the pleasure of and subject to the restrictions of the white regime in South Africa.

In general, sociologists of the functionalist viewpoint tend to frown on separatism because of the divisions within society that separatist movements create. Some conflict theorists, however, see merit in separatism, taking the view that, if it is voluntary on the part of the minority group, separatism can free the subordinate group from the control of the dominant group and give it the independent power base that it needs.

Each of the three models we have outlined—assimilation, pluralism, and separatism—has its supporters among the American population, both majority and minority. In the following section we shall explore changing attitudes toward the three models among the American population and, in particular, some ways that the goals of minority groups and their social movements have changed as they relate to assimilation, pluralism, and separatism.

TRENDS IN ETHNIC AND RACIAL GROUP VALUES CONCERNING ASSIMILATION, PLURALISM, AND SEPARATISM

Assimilation and Anglo-Conformity

There is no doubt that the dominant norm in the United States through nearly all of our history has been cultural assimilation. The dominant cultural group in the United States has been the so-called WASPs: White Anglo-Saxon Protestants. Such has been the influence of this group on American culture that many social scientists describe the cultural pattern of the United States as *Anglo-conformity*: All other groups in America have been expected to adopt the language, culture, and social structure of the white northern Europeans (Gordon, 1964, p. 85). As Feagin (1978,

Chapter 3) illustrates in a thorough chapter on "English-Americans and the Anglo-Saxon Core Culture," the most influential group has been British Protestants. A somewhat altered British Protestant culture came to be accepted as the dominant "American culture," and all ethnic groups in America have been expected to conform to this culture and its attendant institutions. Thus, though we are a "nation of immigrants," English remains our only official language, and everyone has always been expected to learn it and speak it, regardless of what their native language is. Even the concept of bilingual education was pretty much unknown prior to the 1960s, and it remains controversial today.

Indeed, education has played a central role in the assimilation of a variety of immigrant groups into the so-called WASP culture. Not only was American education based largely on a British model and heavily under the control of elite English-Americans during its formative years, but it also placed intense pressure on children to conform to the dominant Anglo culture. In Feagin's (1978, p. 66) words, "whether the children were Irish, Jewish, or Italian did not seem to matter. Anglicization of the children was designed to ferret out the harmful non-Anglo-Saxon ways, to assimilate the children in terms of manners, work habits, and the Protestant Ethic."

It *is* true that we are a relatively diverse nation religiously. Although the majority of Americans are Protestant, millions are not. The largest single religious group (since Protestants are really made up of numerous distinct religious groups) in the United States is Roman Catholics, and about half of the world's Jewish population lives in the United States. Even among the Protestant majority, tremendous diversity exists. In spite of this apparent diversity, however, much is held in common among all major American religious groups. The so-called Protestant work ethic, originally associated with Calvinist Protestantism, became widely accepted by Americans of all faiths. Even the non-Protestant religions have to some degree changed, as Sklare (1955) notes in his studies of American Jewish worship ritual and religious school adaptations (see also Herberg, 1960). The replacement of Hebrew by English in Reform Jewish services and of Latin by English in the Catholic Mass are further examples of such changes.

Although we have seen that schools and other agents of socialization did place a great deal of pressure on immigrant groups to culturally assimilate, not all that much pressure was needed in many cases: Many immigrants very much *wanted* to give up their old ways and assimilate into the dominant Anglo-American culture. This tended to be especially true of the children of immigrants, who generally oriented themselves much more closely to the "American" ways of their peers and the school system than to the "Old World" culture of their parents (see Gordon, 1954, pp. 107–108). Undoubtedly, these tendencies toward cultural assimilation among immigrant groups were largely the result of the strong pressure to assimilate that existed in American society (Gordon, 1978, Chapter 7). Nonetheless, the view that cultural assimilation was *expected* of American immigrants received little serious challenge, and the overwhelming majority of the immigrants did culturally assimilate to a very substantial degree.

Although cultural assimilationist tendencies were strongest among immigrant minorities, such tendencies also existed to a very sizable degree among such colonized minorities as Afro- and Hispanic-Americans. Such a theme can be seen, for example, in the Negro self-help movement of Booker T. Washington around the turn of the century. Washington—one of the very few blacks to gain widespread credibility among whites during that era—argued that rather than challenging white society, blacks should demonstrate their value to society through improved education, hard work, and demonstrations of loyalty to American society (Hawkins, 1962). Washington hoped that, by emulating the values and work habits of middle-class white society, blacks could eventually gain some greater degree of acceptance. Of course, part of the reason for such an emphasis on assimilation and accommodation was that, in Washington's era, a more direct challenge to the white power structure would probably not have been tolerated.

Even in the 1950s and early 1960s, when the civil rights movement developed to full blossom, assimilationist tendencies remained evident. It is true that the civil rights movement sought to plead, pressure, or force whites into accepting social change that many of them did not want. It is also true that the tactics of civil disobedience and direct action were a challenge to the white power structure. Nonetheless, if we examine the *goals and objectives* of the early civil rights movement, it is clear that the movement in many ways sought assimilation. The major issues of this era centered largely around desegregation—the elimination of "whites only" schools, lunch counters, buses, railroad stations, and so on. In effect, the demand was for full participation by black Americans in all aspects of the white-controlled society. The goal was not, during this period, to build new or radically different social institutions; rather, it was for blacks to be able to participate in American social institutions on the same basis as whites.

Although their continuing loyalty to the Spanish language reflects a significant tendency toward cultural pluralism, Mexican-Americans have in many ways sought assimilation into American society as well. Alvarez (1973), for example, notes strong assimilationist tendencies in what he calls the "Mexican-American generation." These children of migrants from Mexico, born in the United States and coming of age during the 1950s and early 1960s, generally lived an urban life somewhat better than that of their parents. Consequently, most of them began to think of themselves as more American than Mexican and as moving toward full participation in American life. Unfortunately, the acceptance by Anglos that would have been necessary for such full Chicano participation in American life was still missing.

Probably the one major racial or ethnic group that presents a clear exception to the pattern of seeking assimilation is Native Americans. The United States government has, over the years, used about every technique imaginable to get Indian people to give up their Indian ways and seek assimilation into white culture and society. Among these have been attempts to set up Indian people as small farmers, to isolate their children from native culture in white-controlled boarding schools, and to get them to leave the reservation to take industrial jobs in urban areas. Native rituals and languages have in some cases been banned (for further discussion of U.S. policy toward Indian people, see Chapters 5 and 6). All these efforts, however, have been notably unsuccessful in getting Indian people to seek assimilation into white culture. In part, this is true because Indians have, until very recently, lived in predominantly rural and predominantly Indian social settings: Thus, they have been able to maintain much of their culture, even in the face of sometimes powerful attacks. Even today, when there has in the past two decades been rapid urbanization of the Native American population, Indian people continue to resist pressures for assimilation. Steele (1972, 1975) has demonstrated the strong resistance by many urban Indians to white social and cultural influences. Apparently, an important reason for this is the close contact with nearby Indian reservations that is maintained by many urban Indians. Thus, Native Americans probably represent the one major exception to the general pattern whereby nearly all racial and ethnic groups in America have sought assimilation into the dominant culture and society during at least a significant portion of their history in the United States.

Critique: Have Social Scientists Exaggerated the Degree of Assimilation in American Society?

As we shall soon see, Americans from a wide variety of racial and ethnic groups have begun to turn away from assimilation in the past fifteen years or so. However, some social scientists have questioned whether there was *ever* as much assimilation in America as was widely believed. Glazer and Moynihan (1970), for example, found in their study of the six major ethnic groups of New York City (blacks, Puerto Ricans, Jews, Italians, Irish, and "WASPs") that ethnic groups remained important throughout the twentieth century, developing and retaining "distinctive economic, political, and cultural patterns" (p. xxxiii). These patterns may not have been particularly similar to the culture of the "old country," but they were distinct in American society.

To this we must add Gordon's (1964, 1978) reminder that *structural* assimilation occurs much less easily than cultural assimilation. Thus, for example, family and other primary group relations continue to be influenced to a substantial degree by race and ethnicity. Interracial marriage remains rare, and majority group members continue to associate and form friendships mainly within the majority group, while minority group members similarly associate mainly with other minorities. While *interethnic* marriage is not uncommon, the image of one great melting pot does not fit very well here, either. A study of eighty years of marriage data in New Haven by Kennedy (1944, 1952) revealed that patterns of interethnic marriage were far from random. In fact, there seemed to be three distinct marriage pools: a Protestant one among British, Germans, and Scandinavians; a Catholic one among Irish, Italians, and Poles; and a Jewish one (see also Greeley, 1970).

Although this tendency toward marriage within religio-ethnic groupings has decreased somewhat over time, it has not disappeared. Major occupational distinctions also exist, as can be seen in the well-known specialization of many Irish-Americans in police work, manufacturing, and politics; of Greek-Americans in fishing and the restaurant business; of Jewish-Americans in small business; and of Chinese-Americans in services, restaurants, and specialty shops. Research by Greeley (1977; 1974, pp. 51–55) and by Cummings (1980) confirms that different ethnic groups have different occupational structures. Thus, we can see that indicators of structural assimilation such as occupation, marriage and friendship patterns, and religious affiliation do indeed reveal a lower level of assimilation than we would expect if we considered only cultural assimilation. Thus, the belief that assimilation has been pervasive throughout American history appears overstated, particularly if we are talking about structural assimilation.

In summary, we can say that cultural assimilation has been the norm in American society, and that it has been widespread but not complete. It has occurred to a significant degree among nearly all groups, generally more so among immigrant groups and less so among colonized ones. Structural assimilation, however, has occurred to a substantially lesser degree: More so among "old" immigrant groups (British, Scots, Germans, Scandinavians, Irish), less so among "new" immigrant groups (eastern and southern Europeans, Asian-Americans), and only to a very limited extent among minority groups (blacks, Hispanics, Native Americans) who, as we have seen, remain largely outside the institutional power structure of America.

Recent Trends Away from Cultural Assimilation

As we have seen, most racial and ethnic groups have sought cultural assimilation throughout most of American history. Even minority group social movements were substantially assimilationist in their goals until around the mid-1960s although, as always, there were some exceptions to the rule. Since that time, however, important changes have taken place. In the remainder of this chapter, we shall examine both what those changes have been and the major reasons for the changes.

The Black Power Movement Probably the earliest and most important indicator of a shift away from seeking assimilation was the Black Power movement, which began during the 1960s. Although the Black Power movement was never a cohesive, single, centrally organized movement with a totally agreed-upon set of goals, certain viewpoints and objectives were fairly well agreed-on by the various groups and individuals who identified with the general concept of Black Power. On the whole, there was deemphasis on black–white integration as a goal in itself. There was also something of a turn away from the old civil rights movement's objective of full participation by blacks in American social institutions. Rather than integration or participation, the major goals of the Black Power movement were (1) for blacks to have full control of their own lives rather than having their roles and statuses defined by whites, and (2) full social and economic equality between blacks and whites. There was increasing skepticism among blacks that these goals of self-determination and equality could be achieved through assimilation. More and more blacks began to believe that as long as society's institutions remained under the control of white people, black people could not realistically expect to gain equality through participation in or integration into those white-controlled institutions.

As a result of these changing perceptions, Black Power proponents developed objectives and priorities quite different from those of the earlier civil rights movement. A central objective was that blacks should have much greater (in some cases, total) control over institutions affecting black people. Examples of this are the community control movement in education and, in higher education, the widespread demand for Black Studies and Black Culture programs *under the control of blacks*. The Black Power movement also placed great emphasis on pride in the accomplishments and the culture of black people in America. This was seen as important because of the value of black culture and the risk that much that was positive could be lost if there were total assimilation of blacks into white culture. It was also seen as important in building a positive self-concept among black people. More and more black Americans began to say, "We will determine our own reality

One place where the trend toward cultural pluralism since the 1960s is evident is in dress. Observe the African influence on the styles of clothing worn by these women. Marc Anderson.

and our own concept of ourselves as a people, rather than having it defined for us by white people.''

All this added up to a distinctly more pluralist and less assimilationist set of goals than had existed in the past. There began to be a good deal of serious discussion about the idea of black people building their own institutions and organizations to serve their own interests. At the same time, the distinct features of black culture attracted considerable interest, and there was a great renewed interest in the African heritage of American blacks. At the same time, many blacks (and some nonblacks) began to regard integration and assimilation as ways by which whites sought to preserve cultural domination of blacks and other minorities. In effect, many black people came to believe that, by promoting assimilation, many white people were seeking to impose white culture on blacks as a precondition for social equality. This perception, not surprisingly, aroused considerable opposition to the concept of assimilation.

The turn away from assimilation as a goal occurred to a sufficient extent that not only pluralist, but also separatist, goals enjoyed a sizable surge of support. Although never supported by the majority of black people, separatist movements such as Elijah Muhammad's Nation of Islam (commonly known as the Black Muslims) enjoyed greatly increased support from the middle 1960s into the 1970s. It should be pointed out that separatism was not a new idea in the 1960s. Marcus Garvey's ''Back to Africa'' movement had gained considerable support during the 1920s, though not on the scale enjoyed by the Muslims in the late 1960s and 1970s. The Nation of Islam, under Elijah Muhammad's leadership, existed as early as the 1930s (Pinkney, 1976, p. 156). However, it was not until the 1960s that the movement began to enjoy widespread support among black people in the United States. By the 1970s the membership of the group had reached somewhere between 100,000 and 250,000 (the organization does not release membership statistics), but its influence is broader than its numbers suggest: by the middle 1970s, its weekly newspaper, *Muhammad Speaks,* had a circulation of 600,000, the largest of any black-owned newspaper in the United States (Pinkney, 1976, pp. 159–160).

Until very recently this group has been distinctly separatist in both its goals and practices. Membership until the late 1970s was limited to blacks, and Elijah Muhammad argued that whites constituted an evil and inferior race. Though these aspects of the movement have been modified in recent years since Muhammad's death, the emphasis continues to be on building separate, membership-controlled institutions rather than relying on those of the dominant society. Thus, the Nation of Islam operates its own school system and finances its operation through ownership of numerous business enterprises including supermarkets, restaurants, a publishing house, and as of 1972, over 20,000 acres of farmland in several states (Pinkney, 1976, p. 162). A major long-range objective of the Muslims has been to establish an independent, black-controlled region in the United States. Although this goal has never been close to being attained, the movement has been successful in amassing a good deal of wealth and property, the benefits of which have been shared among the membership. One estimate, by the *New York Times* (1973), is that the value of the organization's holdings in 1973 totalled about $70 million. (For further discussion of the Muslim movement, see Hall, 1978; Lincoln, 1973.)

Along with a shift away from assimilation as a goal among Afro-Americans, there were also important changes in the tactics used by the black movement. Although the civil rights movement of the 1950s and early 1960s frequently used civil disobedience as a tactic, it was in nearly all cases unalterably nonviolent. Dr. Martin Luther King, for example, carefully studied the philosophy and tactics of the great nonviolent leader of India's struggle for independence, Mahatma Gandhi. With the coming of the Black Power movement in the middle 1960s, however, some important changes in tactics occurred. Among younger black activists, particularly, there arose considerable dissatisfaction with the "turn the other cheek" philosophy. The Black Muslims, the Black Panthers, and many leading individuals in the movement began to argue that when whites use violence against blacks, black people should fight back. Muslim leader Malcolm X, for example, said, "We should be peaceful, law-abiding, but the time has come to fight back in self-defense whenever and wherever the black man is being unjustly and unlawfully attacked." This statement was frequently quoted by Black Panther leaders Huey Newton and Bobby Seale, who have explained that the black panther, chosen as the symbol of their movement, symbolized an animal that will not attack but will tenaciously defend itself (Hall, 1978, pp. 123, 124).

In spite of this philosophy, the white media have tended to exaggerate the violent tendencies of the Panthers, Muslims, and other groups associated with the Black Power movement. The view of these organizations was, as we have seen, not that black people should *initiate* violence, but that they should defend themselves by whatever means necessary once violently attacked. The number of violent incidents involving either the Muslims or the Panthers was in fact relatively small, nearly always involving shootouts or other confrontations between group members and police, with some doubt as to who initiated the violence. In some cases, there is good reason to believe that the police were the instigators, such as the incident in 1969 in which fifteen armed law officers raided the Black Panther office in Chicago, which resulted in the death of party leaders Fred Hampton and Mark Clark and the wounding of four others. Subsequent investigations of the incident indicate that, contrary to police reports of a shootout, it is likely that the Panthers were attacked while sleeping. Both the American Civil Liberties Union and a staff report of the National Commission on the Causes and Prevention of Violence concluded that police action against the Panthers was widespread, excessive, and frequently violated the group's rights (Pinkney, 1976, pp 109–110).

Urban Racial Violence   Most of the violence committed by blacks in the 1960s was not initiated by any organized group such as the Muslims or Panthers but rather took the form of spontaneous ghetto uprisings with little organization and no preplanning. That these uprisings were as widespread as they were between 1964 and 1968 certainly indicates a major change in black attitudes toward violence. Indeed, nearly every city with a sizable black population (except some in the South) experienced at least one disorder during this period, and many had several. As indicated in Chapter 6, the worst outbreaks were in Los Angeles in 1965 and Newark and Detroit in 1967. However, according to the U.S. National Advisory Commission on Civil Disorders (1968), during 1967 alone, 164 disorders took place in all parts of the country. The following year also brought widespread violence. About 125 cities experienced disorders after the assassination of Dr. Martin Luther King in April 1968, and outbreaks of violence continued intermittently throughout the summer and early fall of that year. After 1968 the level of violence subsided, and the 1970s were relatively quiet, with the exception of widespread outbreaks of looting and arson in New York City's minority neighborhoods during a citywide power blackout in 1977. A new upsurge of urban violence occurred in 1980, however. Widespread rioting in Miami's black neighborhoods led to seventeen deaths and widespread property damage, and several other cities—mostly in southern and border states—experienced lesser disorders.

The riots of the 1960s were different from earlier riots in the United States in several important ways. Most previous riots involved mass fighting between whites and blacks or other minorities. Nearly always, these earlier riots started when white mobs attacked minority group members. The main targets of the rioters were people, not property, as the mobs sought to beat and in some cases kill members of the opposite racial group. In the riots of the 1960s, however, the target of the rioters was mainly property, not people. The violence primarily took the forms of window-breaking, looting, and arson. Relatively few whites were involved, either as victims or participants. The instances of personal violence between blacks and whites that did occur took place mainly between white police and black rioters. Resentment against police by ghetto residents was a significant factor in the rioting of the 1960s, and a great many of the outbreaks began with incidents between police and black citizens (U.S. National Advisory Commission on Civil Disorders, 1968, Chapter 11). As indicated in Chapter 10, most of the deaths and injuries in the disturbances resulted from police action against citizens in the riot areas. Other than the confrontations with the police, personal violence between black and white citizens was rare during the urban violence of the 1960s (see Feagin and Hahn, 1973).

As the urban violence spread during the 1960s, many frightened white Americans came to hold several beliefs that were proven incorrect by subsequent research. One such belief was that the disturbances resulted from ''outside agitators'' or some kind of nationwide black conspiracy (Campbell and Schuman, 1968). Numerous studies of the riots, however, uncovered no evidence of such a conspiracy (Williams, 1975, p. 147). Nearly all the rioters arrested lived in the city where they were arrested (Fogelson, 1971). Most of the riots were spontaneous uprisings by an angry and disillusioned black population; organized efforts to cause trouble apparently played little or no role in the disturbances, despite widespread beliefs to the contrary by whites.

Another widely believed but incorrect explanation of the trouble is the so-called ''riff-raff theory.'' This view holds that most of the trouble was caused by a criminal element out to make trouble, and that racial grievances were merely an excuse used by this small minority of blacks to make trouble. This explanation, too, has been soundly disproved by research. It is undoubtedly true that lawless elements took advantage of the trouble for personal gain, but this was not the cause of the bulk of the trouble. A variety of studies suggest, instead, that rioting was a fairly generalized response among young urban blacks who had become deeply disillusioned with the slow pace of change in the status of black Americans. Research by Fogelson (1971) on a dozen cities experiencing serious disorders estimated that the proportion of blacks who participated actively in the disorders ranged from 2 percent to 35 percent, and averaged somewhere around 10 percent (see also Fogelson and Hill, 1968). Thus, a sizable minority of blacks participated in the disturbances. Furthermore, studies of participants indicated that those who participated in the violence were *not* more likely than other blacks of similar age to have criminal records (Fogelson, 1971, p. 42). Also contrary to popular belief, rioters in Northern cities were *not* more likely than other black residents to have moved there from the South (Fogelson, 1971, pp. 41–42); in fact, if anything, the rioters were *more* likely than others to be lifelong residents of the riot city. In Detroit and Newark, for example, the majority of the rioters were lifelong residents, whereas the majority of the nonrioters had been born elsewhere (U. S. National Advisory Commission on Civil Disorders, 1968, pp. 130, 174). It is also true that, rather than being concentrated among the poorest, most down-and-out blacks, participation in the disturbances occurred across the full range of income and occupational levels (Geschwender and Singer, 1968; Fogelson, 1971).

Attitude surveys of urban black Americans also indicate that the rioting had the support of far more than a tiny "riff-raff" element of the black population. Research by Campbell and Schuman (1968), for example, revealed that about a third of blacks believed that the riots helped the cause of black rights, whereas only a quarter felt that they hurt. Most of the rest either thought they both helped and hurt, or thought they made no difference. The majority of ghetto residents felt that the riots had a purpose (Feagin and Hahn, 1973, p. 271). Thus, the position of the black majority appears ambivalent: the majority did not "favor" riots but did see them as resulting mainly from discrimination and unemployment (Campbell and Schuman, 1968), as having a definite purpose, and as being of at least some potential benefit. A sizable minority of blacks—about one third in Los Angeles, for example—did "favor" the riots (Fogelson, 1971), and about 12 to 17 percent of blacks responding to surveys in 1968 regarded violence as "the best way for Negroes to gain their rights" (Feagin and Hahn, 1973, pp. 276–277; Campbell and Schuman, 1968). All this suggests rather clearly that rioting was not created by a criminal "riff-raff" and was not caused by militant activists. Rather, it was an outburst of protest against what was, to a great many blacks, an intolerable situation that had not been much changed by earlier, more moderate forms of protest.

It is now clear that there were some fairly major changes in the thinking of black Americans during the 1960s. Many blacks, both those actively involved in protest and those who were not, turned away from assimilation as a goal and toward a more pluralist model. For some, the turn was more radical; as we have seen, support for separatism increased substantially. The turn away from universal acceptance of nonviolence indicates a similar change in attitudes and behavior, though the violence done by blacks in the 1960s and since pales in comparison to the violence directed toward blacks by whites in earlier years. Although the level of protest abated somewhat during the 1970s, the attitude changes that took place during the 1960s continue to influence the thinking of Afro-Americans today. In particular, assimilation remains today much less widely supported than it was before the mid 1960s. The emphasis on preserving black culture and on building an independent base of black political and economic power has been a continuing feature of black thought through the 1970s into the 1980s. Nonetheless, it would be a mistake to overgeneralize about black attitudes. As we have seen, the black community has become more diverse with regard to education, occupation, and income. (See, for example, W. Wilson, 1978.) This, combined with important regional differences in the mechanisms underlying inequality (see, for example, Farley, 1981), has led to increasing diversity in black political thought. Thus, studies during the 1970s in Chicago (Surgeon et al., 1976), Detroit (Schuman and Hatchett, 1974; Farley et al., 1979) and New York City (Boyce and Gray, 1979) all support the notion of diversity in black thought, both within each area and between areas (blacks in New York and Chicago, for example, responded quite differently to the idea of affirmative action programs involving preferential treatment of minorities.)

The level of tension at any given time and place influences black racial attitudes. The Detroit studies, for example, showed a hardening of blacks' attitudes during the years after the Detroit riot, but a return, by 1976, to attitudes very similar to those before the riot. Although there is as yet little data available, there is some indication of a new increase in black militancy in the early 1980s, perhaps related to such events as the Miami riots of 1980, the shooting of Vernon Jordan in 1980, the murders of young blacks in Atlanta in 1980 and 1981, and the policies of the Reagan administration which involve both massive and disproportionate cutbacks in programs benefitting minorities (e.g., the CETA job program, Food Stamps, Medicaid) and a reduced commitment or even opposition to such policies as bilingual education, affirmative action, and even, perhaps, the federal protection of minority voting rights (which has come under attack recently by conservative Southern legislators). Trends of this type virtually force greater cohesion among blacks and other minorities, and regardless of one's views on assimilation or pluralism, many of the programs and policies have nearly unanimous minority group support because they relate to jobs, health, and even the right to vote.

To summarize, the rather widespread support for assimilation which was evident in the 1950s is unlikely to return: substantial long-term changes in minority group thinking appear to have resulted from the tumultuous events of the 1960s. The increasing diversity of the experiences of blacks during the 1960s and 1970s has also led to diversity in black racial attitudes. At the same time, however, the events of the early 1980s, some of which threaten even the limited black gains of the

1960s, seem to be creating a good deal of black cohesion and solidarity around certain important issues, and raise the possibility of a black social and political movement in the 1980s more cohesive and more unified than was the case during the 1970s.

The Reasons Behind the Changing Goals and Values of Black Americans
As we have noted, the 1960s in particular were a period of substantial change in black racial attitudes. A number of reasons can be identified for the shift away from seeking assimilation and other changes in the thinking of black people during the 1960s. Among those most commonly mentioned are the inconsistent behavior of whites, who did not always live up to what they preached; the violent response by the white power structure to civil rights protest in the South; a growing realization that civil rights laws were not bringing real racial equality; a rejection of the "culture of poverty" and "cultural deprivation" models that had become popular among the white social scientists; and the continuing influence of black nationalism in Africa. Let us examine each of these factors in greater depth.

To blacks, the behavior of whites by the 1960s did not seem to reveal any serious or consistent commitment to the kind of open opportunity that true integration of black people into American society would have required. While white supporters of civil rights were urging other white people to open up their schools and businesses to blacks and telling black people that assimilation was the answer, other whites were doing everything possible to prevent any meaningful participation by black people in American society. By the mid-1960s even the moderate policies of the federal government in support of civil rights (regarded as totally inadequate by most blacks) were under heavy attack from whites (Skolnick, 1969, p. 134). Furthermore, even whites who professed support for equal rights often did not live up to those ideals in their own behavior. An event that perhaps illustrates this as clearly as any was the failure of the Democratic National Convention in 1964 to seat the delegation of the Mississippi Freedom Democratic Party (Carmichael and Hamilton, 1967; Skolnick, 1970). This was an integrated delegation formed to challenge the all-white delegation of the regular party in Mississippi. In spite of the self-proclaimed position of the national Democratic party against racial discrimination, it seated the all-white delegation. The only so-called compromise was an offer—viewed by most blacks as a insult—to seat two members of the challenge delegation along with the segregated regular delegation. To many black people, actions spoke louder than words, and this was a clear message that even liberal whites could not be trusted to practice what they preached.

Closely related was the widespread violence by whites against civil rights workers in the South, and the inability or unwillingness of the federal government to do anything about it. As Skolnick (1969, p. 132) writes, "Freedom Riders were beaten by mobs in Montgomery; demonstrators were hosed, clubbed, and cattle-prodded in Birmingham and Selma. Throughout the South, civil rights workers, black and white, were victimized by local officials as well as by nightriders and angry crowds." In most cases, the federal government—notably the Justice

Department, whose duty it is to enforce federal law—did little about it. Eventually, blacks in the South and elsewhere got tired of turning the other cheek or relying on the protection of a government that was not willing to protect them.

By the mid-1960s, it also was becoming clear to many black Americans that the passage of civil rights laws was not, as they had hoped, bringing about racial equality. Black unemployment continued to be twice as high as white unemployment, and black family income far below white family income. In the North especially, schools and neighborhoods remained as segregated as ever. To the poor or unemployed northern urban black, the civil rights movement of the 1950s and early 1960s had made almost no difference. Indeed, this group had never been greatly involved in that movement, which was by and large composed of the black middle-class and sympathetic whites, also mostly middle-class. Like others, however, the poor urban blacks of the North had had their hopes raised by the promises to end discrimination and poverty that came with the civil rights movement and the Johnson administration's "War on Poverty." When these hopes proved to be false, this group was deeply disillusioned. It is accordingly not surprising that militant separatist organizations such as the Muslims gained most of their support from this segment of the black population. To the poor urban black, it did little good to integrate a lunch counter if you were unemployed and couldn't afford to buy a lunch. Leaders such as Malcolm X and groups such as the Muslims and the Black Panther Party weren't talking about integrated lunch counters; they were talking about economic survival and self-defense, and these themes had great appeal to the urban black trapped at the bottom.

Among black intellectuals, important changes in thinking were also taking place. It was during the early and middle 1960s that "culture of poverty" and "cultural deprivation" theories were gaining great popularity among white social scientists and intellectuals. What we have called the functionalist, or order, perspective was dominant in American social science at that time, and it seemed to offer a logical explanation of black disadvantage to the white social scientists of the era: Because of past discrimination, black Americans had never had the opportunity to develop the values, habits, and skills necessary to get ahead in American society. This seemed reasonable and not at all racist to most white social scientists, but black social scientists and intellectuals saw it differently. To them, it amounted to saying that blacks, because of their culture and attitudes, were at fault for their own disadvantages. (As we have seen, many avowedly racist whites did use the theories to make exactly that argument.) Furthermore, this explanation placed the burden for change on blacks: They had to change their ways before they could hope to enjoy the benefits of American society, even though the cause of their disadvantage, as admitted by white social scientists, was past discrimination *by whites*. This hardly seemed fair. Finally, all this seemed like a put-down of black culture precisely when blacks were proving their capabilities through the civil rights movement. Many blacks had a great need for pride in their race, and black accomplishments were becoming more visible than ever. (They had always been there but had been kept largely hidden by white society.) Nothing that seemed like an attack on the culture and accomplishments of blacks was going to be tolerated. By the middle 1960s assimilation to many educated blacks seemed to be a message from whites that said "do it our way or don't do it." This was no longer acceptable.

A final factor that led to increased emphasis on black self-help and Black Power was the continuing development of independent black nations in Africa (Skolnick, 1969, pp. 137−139). This development served as a model to blacks in the United States: Blacks could, through their own efforts, throw off the domination and influence of whites, run their own affairs, and build their own power base. More than ever before, black people in the United States began to see this as a viable model for attaining black liberation here.

Thus, we have seen that a number of events and influences came together in the 1960s to bring profound changes in the thinking of many Afro-Americans and in the direction of their social movements. The influence was not limited to Afro-Americans, however. These trends in the goals and values of the nation's largest minority group helped lead to some much wider changes in the pattern of racial and ethnic relations in the United States. The thinking of nearly every racial and ethnic group in America was influenced by the Black Power movement, and today the pluralist model, as opposed to assimilation, is much more widely accepted than it was fifteen or twenty years ago. These broader changes in race and ethnic relations in America will be explored in the remainder of this chapter.

Pluralism and Militancy among Chicanos and American Indians   During the 1960s, Mexican-Americans also turned away from assimilation as a goal and began to emphasize such concepts as self-defense and building an independent power base. *Chicanismo*—a stress on pride in Chicano culture and heritage and a struggle to combat forced assimilation—became a widespread ideology, particularly among younger Mexican-Americans. As we have seen in earlier chapters, there was an increased emphasis during this period on the preservation of the Spanish language and of unique Chicano dialects that mixed Spanish and English. One manifestation of this trend was the spreading demand for bilingual education. Many Chicanos have advocated bilingual education not only as a way of helping Chicano children to speak English, but also as a vehicle to ensure the preservation of the Spanish language among young Mexican-Americans.

Important changes also occurred during the 1960s in the tactics used in the Chicano movement. In the early 1960s Chicano polical involvement was marked by the *viva Kennedy* movement, which was basically an effort to get Chicanos involved in the traditional American political process, which they have always shunned to some degree. This effort is frequently credited with carrying the crucial state of Texas for the Kennedy-Johnson ticket in 1960 (Acuña, 1972, p. 223). In the mid 1960s Cesar Chavez's use of Gandhian nonviolence to unionize Mexican-American and Filipino farmworkers was probably the most widely known segment of the Chicano movement. Though a more direct challenge to the system than the earlier voter registration efforts, Chavez's movement retained a belief that Chicanos could be integrated into basic American institutions, in this case the labor movement.

Today, both voter registration and turnout efforts and Chavez's United Farm Workers Union remain important parts of Mexican-American political involvement. The UFW, for example, has succeeded in unionizing a sizable portion of California's agricultural labor force and has led to great improvement in wages and working conditions among Chicano farmworkers. Nonetheless, by the latter part of the 1960s, many Chicanos were starting to turn away from traditional electoral participation and Gandhian nonviolence. The year 1967 saw formation of the Brown Berets, a group stressing militant self-defense tactics similar to those of the Black Panthers. A number of militant Chicano student groups were also formed in that year and subsequent years (Moore, 1976, p. 151). The imagination of younger Chicanos was captured by the militant actions of Reis Tijerina in New Mexico (see Chapter 6). By the late 1960s many younger Chicanos in particular had given up on integration and sought to build an independent Chicano power base. Furthermore, at least a minority felt that violence or the threat of violence was the only way to get the Anglo power structure to take seriously the demands of Chicanos. Finally, the turn away from assimilationist tendencies can be seen in the formation of a Chicano

United Farm Workers Union president Cesar Chavez (left) prepares to address a rally in support of the union's lettuce boycott. Chavez has sought to improve the status of Chicano farmworkers through participation in the labor union movement and through efforts to establish a broad base of support in the American population for boycotts of producers who refuse to negotiate with their workers' union. This approach reflects a basic belief that with sufficient pressure, Chicanos can become integrated into basic American institutions. Paul E. Sequeira, Rapho/Photo Researchers, Inc.

political party—*La Raza Unida* Party. This party won control of the school board and city council in Crystal City, Texas, and other nearby communities in 1970 and captured about 6 percent of the vote for governor in Texas in 1972 (Moore, 1976, p. 153; Acuña, 1972, p. 236). The party was also on the ballot in Colorado in 1970.

Moore (1976, p. 49) cites several factors that contributed to these changes in attitudes. A very important factor was the development of the Black Power movement during this period. That movement provided a role model, and both illustrated that legal equality did not guarantee social equality and "legitimized an ideology that rejected assimilation and fixed the blame on the larger society" for racial inequality. In addition, it demonstrated that blacks could at least get attention and promises by rioting, which at the time was more than Chicanos were getting. In addition to the Black Power movement, the antiwar movement and the general atmosphere of protest and rebellion helped produce a situation conducive to a militant Chicano protest movement. The Chicano movement, however, was not merely a response to the Black Power movement or other social movements. It represented, as did the Black Power movement, a response to the failure of assimilation-seeking to bring about equality. In the case of Chicanos the frustrations may have even been greater than they had been with blacks. As with blacks, the promises of the Kennedy and Johnson administrations and the War on Poverty had led to raised expectations. However, Chicanos soon found out that the government bureaucrats for the most part thought of poverty and intergroup relations in terms of blacks and whites. Chicanos were almost entirely forgotten in the early stages of the War on Poverty, and this proved an important stimulus to the militant Chicano movement (Acuña, 1972, pp. 226–227).

Today, the level of protest has subsided, but the ideology of *Chicanismo* continues to have considerable influence among Mexican-Americans. Such programs as bilingual education have grown tremendously (although they are seriously threatened by policy changes initiated by the Reagan administration), and have widespread support in the Chicano community. In these and other ways, the changes in Chicano thought that occurred during the 1960s continue to have widespread influence in the 1980s.

Among American Indians, the picture is somewhat different. The difference is that Indian people never sought assimilation to even the degree that black or Mexican-Americans did—thus, a turn away from assimilation was not possible. However, important changes did occur among Indian people during the 1960s and early 1970s. The most important was the upsurge in protest, which had been rare among Native Americans until the late 1960s. By 1970 Indian people had become much more involved in protest, and much of it took on a very militant tone. (For a review of some of the major instances of Indian protest, see Chapter 6.) From the beginning, the protest was largely separatist in nature, as Indian people reasserted land claims and their historic status as independent nations. Thus, the thrust of Indian protest ever since the 1960s has been mainly the return of Indian land and the reassertion of treaty and fishing rights—*not* elimination of barriers to participation in American society. As with the other groups militant protest has had the greatest appeal among younger Indians. Throughout much of the 1970s, both legal means, such as lawsuits demanding the enforcement of old treaties, and illegal means, such as the various occupations of land and buildings discussed in Chapter 6, have been used. Although these actions have not resulted in the return of large land areas to Indian ownership, there have been some important successes. There have, for example, been some large cash settlements in lieu of land claims, and historic Indian fishing rights have been reestablished in a number of states, despite strong opposition from sport fishermen and state fish and game departments.

There is little doubt that the civil rights and Black Power movements played an important role in stimulating protest among American Indians (see Day, 1972). Nonetheless, the distinctive history of Indian people led to some significant differences. This historic resistance among Indians to forced assimilation probably helps to explain why, although protest was slower to come among Indian people than some other groups, it was more militant and separatist from the start once it did come.

The "Ethnic Revival" among White Americans   The trend toward emphasizing ethnic cultural distinctiveness was not limited to those groups that most clearly fit the definition of minority groups (blacks, Latinos, and Indians). White ethnic groups, as well, have placed a renewed emphasis on ethnicity since the late 1960s. Much has been written about the "ethnic revival" among various white ethnic groups. There is considerable debate as to the nature and extent of this ethnic revival, but it seems clear that something has been happening. Outwardly, at least, Americans from a wide variety of groups have placed a greater emphasis on ethnicity and ethnic culture. This can be seen in the proliferation of ethnic festivals, the celebration of ethnic holidays, and so on. There is much debate as to whether the change is superficial—relatively few (but some, nonetheless) have learned the language of their ethnic place of origin, for example. There is also debate as to whether the changes are really based on ethnicity or whether they are mainly a class phenomenon (Gans, 1974, pp. xi, xii). The ethnic revival has been most notable among Catholic, Jewish East European, and predominantly working-class groups, and among these groups it has often taken on political overtones. In two ways, these changes seem to have grown out of the Black Power movement. First, the Black Power movement served as a role model. It showed all other groups that racial or ethnic group consciousness was a way of getting the political system to listen to the collective concerns of a group. Second, many white ethnic groups perceived the gains being made by blacks as a threat: They believed that any gains made by blacks would come at their expense, not at the expense of the middle classes (Novak, 1971; Goering, 1971). There was some basis in reality for this perception: rarely were middle class suburban white children bused, and rarely were middle class neighborhoods blockbusted. Unfortunately, the anger of working class white ethnics was sometimes turned against blacks and the gains they made rather than against the larger power structure (see Ransford, 1972). Thus, it is ironic that a trend which is in part a product of the Black Power movement now threatens the position of blacks: the white ethnic working class, because of its greater numbers and economic and political resources, and because of its majority group membership, probably has the advantage in any struggle against blacks. (For further discussion of this problem, see Patterson, 1977.) Nonetheless, some observers such as Novak (1971) argue that the dominant thrust *is* against a power structure that has ignored the concerns of the working class white ethnics. Issues such as these suggest that the "ethnic revival" was at least partly a social class phenomenon, although ethnicity had at least symbolic importance.

Another school of thought suggests that the ethnic revival of the 1970s is not entirely an outgrowth of the Black Power movement, however. It may have been partly a result of the length of time that some ethnic groups have been in the United States. Hansen (1952, 1966) developed a theory that an ethnic revival typically occurs in the third generation. The second generation, according to Hansen's view, seeks to get rid of all trappings of the ethnic background of their parents and to become fully assimilated. The third generation, generally more socially and economically secure, seeks to rediscover its ethnic culture and heritage. Hansen based his theory partly on his observations of Swedish-Americans. Studies of other groups (see Sandberg, 1974; Abramson, 1975), however, call into question the universality of a third generation ethnic revival. Nonetheless, Greeley (1971) sees the ethnic revival of the 1970s largely as an affirmation of Hansen's third generation hypothesis. According to Greeley, the fact that many white ethnic groups had become more secure and affluent than they were in earlier years made it more possible for them to assert their ethnicity and inquire into their origins. (Concerning the increased affluence of white ethnic groups, see also Greeley, 1974.)

Although there is debate as to its degree (see, for example, Gans, 1974, 1979), there is little doubt that there has been a revived interest in ethnicity and group culture since the late 1960s. In greater or lesser ways, this is true for virtually every racial, ethnic, and cultural group in America. The blank in the statement, "I'm ——— and proud" could be filled in "black," "Chicano," "Indian," "Polish," "German," "Italian," "Greek," "Irish," or numerous other ways. It could even go beyond ethnic groups and say "female," "gay," or perhaps "disabled." The extent and meaning of the change may be debatable, but there can be little doubt that cultural pluralism has become very fashionable in the United States since the late 1960s.

SUMMARY AND CONCLUSIONS

In this chapter we have seen that cultural assimilation has been the dominant mode of adaptation for racial and ethnic minority groups in American society. The dominant group has always demanded it, and for the most part, minorities have gone along with it, though there have been notable cases of resistance. Nonetheless, assimilation has never been complete, particularly at the structural, as opposed to cultural, level. Indeed, substantial structural pluralism has been maintained, even when cultural assimilation has been quite general. Thus, the ideology of Anglo-conformity has probably led many to believe that America has been more of a melting pot than it in fact ever was. In addition, there has been a noticeable shift away from cultural assimilation toward cultural pluralism since the 1960s. An important stimulus to this shift was the Black Power movement, which was at least partly the result of the failure of assimilationist efforts to bring equality for black Americans.

We have also seen that assimilation occurs less readily for exploited minorities of the colonized type (Blauner, 1972) than for immigrant minorities. In the United States, this has meant that Afro-Americans, Mexican-Americans, and Native Americans have experienced less cultural and structural assimilation than have immigrant groups from Europe such as Irish, German, or Polish-Americans. This is true for a number of reasons. First and foremost, white Americans have strongly resisted the assimilation of the historically oppressed and colonized groups. (For further discussion of the effect of the history of colonization, see Chapter 6.) Second, the racial identifiability of these groups has made discrimination against them easier. As a general rule, racial minorities are assimilated less easily than ethnic ones, because their distinct appearance makes it easier to discriminate against them. Both these factors suggest that a big reason blacks, Chicanos, and Indians have never been fully integrated into American society is that whites in large part have not wanted or permitted these groups to participate as equals. A third reason for a lack of assimilation is that colonized groups are likely to perceive the dominant group as an oppressor and resist the dominant group's culture for that reason. That has been especially true of Indian people in the United States, and in recent decades has also been increasingly true of black and Hispanic Americans as well. As these groups have seen that group consciousness can build an important base for seeking political power, these pluralist tendencies have been reinforced.

There are other factors we have not mentioned in this chapter (but have discussed elsewhere; see Chapter 7) that influence the likelihood of assimilation versus pluralism. Cultural and structural assimilation are less likely, for example, where a minority group is relatively large than where it is very small. A large group is both more likely to be perceived as a threat (and thereby resisted by the dominant group) and more capable of reinforcing and preserving its own culture. In the long run, however, this factor is probably less important than others: Irish-Americans and German-Americans are both more numerous and more assimilated than the typical ethnic group in America.

A final factor influencing the likelihood of assimilation is nearness to one's homeland. Groups that live near or on their homeland generally are more able to maintain their group culture than groups who are very distant from their homeland. In the United States the two minorities living on or near their homeland are Chicanos and American Indians. It is striking that these are probably the two groups that have preserved their group cultures and institutions to the greatest degree in the United States.

America has been marked by substantial elements of both assimilation and pluralism. Separatist movements have occurred and exist today, but they have never had more than minority support. While cultural assimilation mixed with a sizable amount of structural pluralism has been the norm, there have been important variations both from time to time and from group to group. Today the balance seems to have swung toward pluralism, though there is debate as to how much. The consequences of this shift continue to be debated. Functionalist theorists see a serious threat to national unity in such trends and thus urge a move back toward assimilation and consensus (see A. Thernstrom, 1980). Conflict theorists, on the other hand, see a potential for a fairer power balance if pluralism can enhance the power base of minorities such as blacks, Chicanos, and Indians. They worry, however, that racial divisions could play off the white and minority working classes against one another, thus enhancing the power of the elite. In large part, however, the extent, longevity, and consequences of the recent trend toward pluralism remain to be seen. (For further discussion of assimilation and pluralism in the United States, see Abramson, 1980.)

In the next and final chapter, we shall further explore the arguments for and against assimilation, pluralism, and separatism, as well as several other current controversies concerning majority-minority relations in the United States.

GLOSSARY

Amalgamation   The loss of distinct identities of two or more racial or ethnic groups in a society through widespread intermarriage between the groups.

Cultural assimilation   A type of assimilation in which two or more groups gradually come to share a common culture, i.e. similar attitudes, values, language, beliefs, lifestyles, and rules about behavior. Frequently, the shared culture is much more similar to that of the majority group than it is to that of the minority group, though this is not *always* the case.

Cultural pluralism   A pattern in which different racial, ethnic, or other groups retain cultural features that are distinct in each group, but hold some others that are common to all groups in society.

Structural assimilation   A type of assimilation in which two or more groups gradually come to share a common social structure, i.e. they share common institutions, organizations, and friendship networks, and have relatively equal positions within these structures. If structural assimilation is complete, widespread intermarriage (marital assimilation) will also occur.

Separatism   The establishment of, or attempt to establish, entirely separate societies made up of distinct racial, ethnic, or other groups which formerly existed within one society. Examples would include efforts by some French-Canadians to divide Canada into two independent countries, one English and one French, and efforts by some Afro-Americans to establish separate black states in what is now the U.S. South.

Selected Issues in the Future of Majority-Minority Relations in the United States

13

Thus far in this book our focus has been on the past and on the present. We have examined the historical roots of racial and ethnic inequality in the United States and have seen how the mechanisms of inequality have changed over time. We have also examined patterns of majority-minority relations in present-day America and elsewhere and have explored in detail the relationship between a number of America's basic social institutions and American intergroup relations. In this final chapter we shall turn our attention to the future. As we have seen throughout this book racial inequality remains today a serious problem that can be found in almost every aspect of American society. As such, it raises numerous issues that will demand important decisions in our future. Most of these issues are with us today; all promise to foster debate and controversy for the foreseeable future. No chapter—indeed no book—could do justice to all the issues and controversies that have grown out of the various aspects of majority-minority relations. Thus, a chapter such as this must be selective. We have chosen to focus on five issues we feel are among the most important in coming years. These are the affirmative action controversy, the continuing debate on the desirability of different models for intergroup relations (assimilation, pluralism, separatism), the relative importance of race and class in American society, the extension of legal protection to minorities other than racial and ethnic ones, and the future immigration policy of the United States. Continuing the theme of the previous chapter, we shall turn first to the debate over assimilation, pluralism, and separatism.

ALTERNATIVE MODELS FOR INTERGROUP RELATIONS

As we saw in the previous chapter, one major debate in the area of majority-minority relations concerns the question, what is the ideal model or pattern of intergroup relations? To put it a little differently, what is the ultimate goal we are striving for when we try to bring about "better" race and ethnic relations? As we saw in the last chapter, three major models have been proposed: assimilation, pluralism, and separatism. Although we have seen that pluralism has become more popular and assimilation less popular in recent years, there continues to be much debate as to which model we ought to be striving toward. In this section, we shall briefly explore the arguments being made for and against each of these models.

Assimilation

The Case for Assimilation   In large part, the idea that cultural assimilation is desirable arises from the view that a society needs to share common values and beliefs, a common culture, to develop the sense of solidarity, unity, and cooperation that it needs to grow and prosper. This idea, as you probably recognize, is closely aligned with the functionalist, or order, perspective. The underlying premise is that a society with severe internal divisions along the lines of race, ethnicity, or religion cannot work well as a society. Too much energy goes into infighting, everyone places their own group ahead of the good of the larger society, and cooperation becomes impossible. A society where everybody is thinking in terms of their own little group and nobody thinks about the good of the whole society is in trouble, they argue, and in the view of functionalists, such an outcome is inevitable unless all major groups develop an identity with the society as a whole and move toward a common culture. The recent trend away from assimilation has been a matter of great concern to many functionalists, who argue that there are signs in the United States today of all the problems outlined above, for the simple reason that more and more Americans in recent years *have* been putting their own group needs ahead of the needs of the larger society. These sociologists believe that we are becoming a nation of special interest groups, with nobody much concerned about the good of the larger society. (For an example of this viewpoint, see Thernstrom, 1980.)

Another reason for advocating assimilation is a belief by some that it is the only realistic way to obtain racial and ethnic equality (see Patterson, 1977). This viewpoint holds that people's tendency toward ethnocentrism is so strong that, wherever racial and cultural differences exist, prejudice and discrimination will occur. This, of course, is especially true in settings where there has been a long history of discrimination. This view argues that these evils can be eradicated only by eliminating the cultural differences that are the basis for prejudice and discrimination. In its most extreme form, it holds that *amalgamation*—the elimination of distinct racial groups through repeated intermarriage and interbreeding—is the most effective long-term solution to the problem. The advocates of this viewpoint sometimes point to certain Latin American countries where long-term mixing of the white, black, and Indian populations has largely erased racial distinctions and prejudices of a racial nature (although cultural differences not totally linked to race remain significant). Others argue, in a more moderate vein, that the widespread acceptance of racial intermarriage (which remains relatively infrequent today in the United States) would be a crucial step toward the solution of racial problems in this country.

The Case against Assimilation   A common argument against assimilation is that it amounts to forced conformity. Some advocates of assimilation view it, ideally, as a process of culture sharing, with the majority group adopting some aspects of minority group culture and the minority adopting some aspects of the majority group culture. Thus, a new culture and social structure emerges which is neither that of the majority group nor that of the minority group or groups. Critics, however, argue that in reality, the process is seldom that balanced. As we saw in Chapter 12, the norm in the United States through most of its history has been Anglo conformity—a demand that all immigrant and minority groups conform to the expectations of the dominant WASP (white Anglo Saxon Protestant) group. Other groups have certainly had some influence, but the influence of this dominant group has been quite disproportionate.

A related criticism of assimilation is that it promotes cultural homogeneity rather than heterogenity. Some view the absence of heterogenity as a serious loss. First, it would involve a loss in freedom of choice: In a plural or heterogeneous society, a person has a wide range of values and life styles to choose from. To the degree that this heterogeneity is lost, freedom of choice is lost—there is no choice but to conform to the dominant values and life style. The critics also argue that heterogeneity is an important source of adaptation and innovation in society. If we all become the same, the diversity that produces new ideas may be lost, and society may stagnate.

Pluralism

The Case for Pluralism   Many of those who see in assimilation the dangers we have just discussed support cultural pluralism as the ideal model of intergroup relations. One reason is that they see a need in society for diversity or cultural heterogeneity, and pluralism facilitates this. In other words, a certain amount of diversity—as long as it does not create deep divisions—is good for society because it provides a basis for innovation and for adaptation to new situations. Of course, there are other bases of diversity besides racial or ethnic ones, as critics of this view would hasten to point out. Some critics such as Patterson (1977) have also argued that *group* diversity can lead to *individual* conformity, because of pressures to conform to group norms. While general societal benefits of diversity might be stressed by some functionalist sociologists, a conflict theorist would see a different advantage in pluralism. This advantage would be that racial or ethnic group awareness can form a power base through which an ethnic group can take action on behalf of its self-interest. Thus, if blacks, or Italian-Americans, or Jews, or whoever develop a group identity, it can become a source of social and political power. This may occur through the ballot box (observe how candidates must court the vote of various racial and ethnic groups), or it may occur through collective protest. Either way, an ethnic or racial group can potentially gain power if it can develop a common identity and take some kind of political action. For groups not well-represented in the traditional political process, the kind of group consciousness that leads to collective action and/or bloc voting may be the only real chance to gain political influence or power. Thus, by providing such a potential power base, cultural pluralism may be an important basis by which minority groups act on behalf of their self-interests. Furthermore, where a group has been subjected to widespread attacks on its culture, as have several minority groups in the United States, group identity can be an important source of self-esteem for group members.

A third argument in support of pluralism points out that it is desirable in and of itself to preserve the distinct cultures of various racial, ethnic, religious, and social groups. Such diversity provides a richness in society that would be absent if everyone were the same culturally. Furthermore, this view holds that it is nobody's business to tell a group that it must change its ways to conform to some dominant norm.

The Case against Pluralism   The major argument commonly made against pluralism is that it creates divisions in society. This can be harmful in several ways. To the functionalist, any significant division is potentially harmful, because it destroys the consensus and solidarity that society needs and inhibits cooperation. Furthermore, given the usual social tendency toward ethnocentrism, the existence of cultural differences makes prejudice and discrimination likely. While pluralism may sound like a good idea in the abstract, say the critics, it will not work in real life. As an example they point out that the emphasis in America in recent years on black culture, Italian culture, Jewish culture, and so on is dangerous because it emphasizes what is different about us (and therefore a potential basis for conflict and discrimination) rather than what is the same.

Some conflict theorists also see dangers in pluralism. For one thing, it is rarely true that different racial and cultural groups have equal power. Thus, if ethnic or racial groups are used as a way of gaining power, the groups with greater political and economic resources are favored. Along this line, Patterson (1977) argues that the Black Power movement, by making ethnic political movements acceptable again, has made it easier, for example, for the Irish of South Boston to organize an ethnically based movement to keep the Irish in control of their community, which translates to keeping blacks out of the neighborhood (on this point, see also Killian, 1981).

A related argument can be seen in Marxist theory, which argues that growing awareness of racial and ethnic differences leads people to ignore the divisions in society that are really important. Thus, a working class where people think of themselves above all as black or white, Anglo or Chicano, or perhaps (as in Northern Ireland) Catholic or Protestant, cannot act together on behalf of its interests as a class. Thus, the masses of blacks and whites (and so on) are *hurt* by ethnic awareness because it divides them and prevents them from acting on behalf of their larger common interests.

Racial/Ethnic Separatism

The Case for Separatism   Obviously, separation of the races is one mechanism by which a dominant group can maintain its advantages over a subordinate group—as the experience in the U.S. South during the Jim Crow era so clearly illustrates. For this reason, racial separation has often been advocated by racists as a way of maintaining dominant group advantage. In the present day, two examples of this would be the position of the Ku Klux Klan in the United States, and the system of *apartheid* in South Africa.

Other arguments made for separatism, however, do not arise from the desire of one group to dominate another. Historically, separatist movements have arisen among minority groups (especially those with a geographic base within the larger society) as a way of trying to escape the inequality they have experienced in their contacts with the dominant group. In this vein, black separatist movements in the United States were discussed in the previous chapter, and French separatism in Canada was discussed in Chapter 7. In cases such as these, the main argument for separatism is that it allows each group to control its own social institutions and to make its own political decisions, rather than having these things controlled by an outside group. In addition, it has been suggested by some as the only way of creating consensus out of a deeply divided society: create two separate societies, each with its own set of values and its own way of doing things. Thus, consensus and cooperation would be possible within each separate society, where they would not have been possible in the previous, larger society. The division of the Indian subcontinent into the separate and religio-ethnically distinct countries of India, Pakistan, and Bangladesh is sometimes cited as an example of this.

The Case against Separatism   Those opposed to separatism counter that in theory the concept may work, but in practice it usually does not. They cite in support of this view examples such as the violent history of Ireland, which was partitioned, in effect, into a Catholic section and a Protestant section, or the situation in the Middle East, which arose out of an attempt to create separate Jewish and Palestinian states after World War II. Where conflict is deep, the two sides will in many cases merely become warring countries after the separation occurs. Furthermore, if the separation is not complete (for example, the continued presence of many Catholics in the "Protestant" section of Ireland), internal conflict and violence are also likely. For this reason, separatism is nearly impossible to put into effect in any situation where the minority group and majority group do not have distinct and nearly exclusive geographic bases. Canada approximates this model to some extent (Quebec is 80 percent French speaking, and the rest of the country is almost totally English speaking), but the United States does not even come close.

Thus, despite the advocacy of separatism among some black and Indian Americans, the strategy would probably be virtually impossible to implement in the United States. In this country, the real choice is probably between pluralism and assimilation. The desirability of these two models will probably continue to be the subject of much debate in the United States. Where one stands will depend partly on one's values and partly on one's beliefs about how society operates.

AFFIRMATIVE ACTION

A second major controversy in intergroup relations is more political, more concrete, and much more frequently seen in the headlines. This debate concerns *affirmative action*. The concept of affirmative action dates to 1967, when the term was first used in an executive order by President Johnson concerning enforcement of antidiscrimination requirements for agencies and businesses under contract with the federal government (Seabury, 1977, p. 99). The order said "the contractor will not discriminate against any employee or applicant because of race, color, religion, sex or national origin. The contractor will take affirmative action to ensure that employees are treated during employment, without regard to their race, color, religion, sex or national origin." This meant, in effect, that contractors were supposed to make special efforts to ensure that they were not discriminating. In subsequent orders, the emphasis of affirmative action shifted toward the *result* of hiring practices and decisions. Specifically, a requirement was added for "goals and timetables to which the contractor's good faith efforts must be directed to correct the deficiencies and thus, to increase materially the utilization of minorities and women, at all levels and in all segments of his work force where deficiencies exist." Thus, the requirement was now added that contractors must not only avoid discrimination, but must also (1) make an active effort to increase the number of female and/or minority employees where they are underrepresented, and (2) develop a specific set of goals and timetables that would serve as targets and as a measure of a contractor's success in hiring more minorities and women.

These measures have been required of organizations doing business with the federal government (including most colleges and universities), and some businesses and unions have taken similar measures voluntarily. Similar affirmative action programs exist in some colleges and universities in the area of student admissions. They are most common in professional schools, such as law and medical schools, but exist in other areas as well. The objective of these affirmative action admissions programs is to increase the number of students from underrepresented groups such as blacks, Chicanos, Indians, and women.

Although affirmative action programs in both hiring and student admissions became quite widespread during the 1970s, they also became controversial. Opponents of the programs have argued that they amount to unfair discrimination against white males, while supporters say that they are necessary in order to undo the effects of past and present discrimination against minorities and women. In the next few pages we shall explore the arguments of both sides on this issue, which has been debated in recent years nearly everywhere in America, from the classroom to the newspapers to the union hall to the U.S. Supreme Court.

"Undoing Discrimination"

The fundamental argument for making special efforts to hire more minority workers or to admit more minority students—even to the point of a preference for the minority applicant—is that such a practice is the *only* way to undo the harmful effects of past and present discrimination. Past discrimination has, according to this view, left minorities in a disadvantaged position, so that race-blind admission or hiring is *not* really fair: Minority applicants, after generations of discrimination, simply do not have all the advantages that white male applicants have. Recall the analogy used in Chapter 10 concerning the two runners, one of whom had to start with weights tied to his feet. Removing the weights halfway through did not make a fair race: The runner was by then far behind. Removing the weight of discrimination today, but doing nothing else to make the competition fair, will *not,* in the eyes of affirmative action supporters, eliminate the disadvantages suffered by minority group members.

The effects of past discrimination are not the only reason the supporters of affirmative action give for having such a program. In Chapters 9, 10, and 11 we explored a number of ways in which modern American social institutions discriminate, often without even being aware of it. Unless and until such subtle mechanisms of discrimination are eliminated, "race-blind" (as well as "sex-blind") competition cannot really be fair: Minorities and women are held back by institutional discrimination in ways that whites and men are not. According to this view, the *only* way to get some semblance of racial or sexual equality *today* (until the effects of past and institutional discrimination can be eliminated) is to have some kind of racial or sexual preference in hiring and/or admissions. To fail to do this would be to keep minorities and women in a position where, through no fault of their own, they have less than their proportionate share of jobs, education, political representation, and so on.

In effect, the supporters of affirmative action argue that the only way to break through the continuous cycle of discrimination is to pay attention to the *result*. They often point out that this was done in the South where, for example, schools were given guidelines as to what percentage of black and white students constituted an integrated school. In general, supporters of affirmative action see it as a temporary tactic for offsetting the effects of past and institutional discrimination. They argue that once the cycle of inequality has been broken, and minorities and women enjoy the same educational and occupational advantages that white males do, the need for special consideration on the basis of race and sex will disappear.

"Reverse Discrimination"

As we stated, the concept of "affirmative action" is controversial. Many regard any preference for minority or female applicants as discrimination in reverse, just as unfair as is discrimination, for example, against blacks, Chicanos, or women (see Glazer, 1976). People with this viewpoint argue that preferential treatment for minorities is especially unfair when there is no evidence that the firm or school to which they are applying has deliberately discriminated in the past. They feel this practice forces many whites (or males) who are *not* guilty of discrimination to unfairly pay the price for past discrimination that they had nothing to do with. In short, it is seen as unfair to such people to be, through no fault of their own, passed over in favor of women and minorities who are no more qualified (and sometimes, it is charged, less qualified) than they are, at least by traditional measures of qualifications.

The question of qualifications has become a central issue in the debate over affirmative action. Those against affirmative action, in addition to the above arguments, say that affirmative action undermines the quality of work forces and student bodies by giving positions to persons other than the most qualified applicants. If one accepts the traditional measures of qualifications as reliable, it does appear that this happens sometimes. In many law schools and medical schools, for example, minority applicants have been accepted with admission test scores and/or undergraduate grade point averages (GPAs) significantly lower than those generally required of whites (see Sindler, 1978).

Another barrage of criticism has been directed at affirmative action on the grounds that it amounts to a quota system. This view holds that the goals and timetables used in affirmative action programs end up as quotas that must be filled regardless of the qualifications of the candidates. Thus, if a firm has a goal of hiring so as to have a 10 percent black workforce in three years, it will end up having to hire some minimum number of blacks regardless of their qualifications. Perceptions that this is a problem have been increased by incidences of employers telling white male applicants that they have been passed over in favor of less qualified women or minorities in order to meet affirmative action goals (see Nisbet, 1977). The use of quotas is of special concern to some ethnic groups: Jewish-Americans, for example, remember that many Jews were kept *out* of American colleges and professional schools by quotas that specified a maximum percentage of Jews. In part for this reason, many Jews and others see a dangerous precedent in what they view as a reintroduction of the use of quotas (see Raab, 1978).

"Considering the Net Outcome"

Supporters of affirmative action generally do not agree that a preference for women or minority applicants amounts to reverse discrimination, or that affirmative action programs have brought about widespread use of quotas. On the issue of quotas, they argue that goals and timetables have never been intended as rigid quotas but rather as a target and a standard against which the performance of government contractors can be measured. It is acknowledged, for example, that there are sometimes good reasons why a goal cannot be met: The key criterion is good faith effort and some indication of progress (Pottinger, 1972). Furthermore, it is argued that, unlike the quotas that limited the numbers of Jews in American universities in the 1950s and earlier, the purpose of affirmative action (whether it involves quotas or not) is to get people *into* employment or school, not to keep them out.

In this vein, supporters of affirmative action deny the claim that affirmative action is leading to the hiring or admission of less qualified applicants. They acknowledge that women and minorities hired or admitted under affirmative action programs may score lower on traditional criteria, but they deny that this indicates that they have lower potential as a student or employee. They cite two reasons. First, the minority applicant may score lower on these criteria because of disadvantages arising from past and institutional discrimination, not because of lesser ability. Society imposes handicaps on minorities that are not imposed on white males; thus, the criteria measure the effects of this discrimination better than they measure the applicant's true potential as an employee or student. Second, the tests and criteria used may themselves be biased (see the discussion of test bias in Chapter 11). For both these reasons, then, traditional criteria may underestimate the potential of the minority applicant. Indeed, with the best criteria available, it is possible to make only rough estimates of how good a student or employee an applicant will turn out to be. Law school admission criteria, for example, typically explain only about 25 percent of the variation in first-year academic performance of law students (Sindler, 1978, pp. 115−116). In short, the use of traditional admission criteria for minority applicants is considered unfair because it does not compensate for effects of discrimination (unintentional as well as intentional) that the applicant has previously experienced. People who support affirmative action believe that the *net effect of failing to consider race* in admissions and hiring decisions is to discriminate against minorities: Nothing is done to compensate for the effects of past discrimination and the subtle processes of institutional discrimination that have had the effect of placing the minority applicant at an unfair disadvantage. Under affirmative action the white applicant may suffer some disadvantage at the point of decision, but this is offset by disadvantages suffered by the minority applicant at earlier stages, such as primary and secondary education (see Chapter 11). Thus, according to this view, the only way to avoid net discrimination is through affirmative action.

A final and related issue raised by the supporters of affirmative action is the need for minority professionals. As we saw in Chapters 10 and 11, a serious shortage of minority doctors and lawyers is one important reason why minority Americans have less access to medical care and legal representation. Without affirmative action in law and medical school admissions programs, this condition would probably continue well into the future. A national study of law school admissions (Evans, 1977) showed, for example, that without affirmative action, not more than about 2 percent of all those admitted in 1976 would have been black, and only 0.75 percent would have been Chicano—compared to the actual figures of 5.3 percent black and 1.3 percent Chicano. Put differently, the number of minority students admitted would have been less than half what it was, had there not been affirmative action. This almost certainly would have a substantial impact on the supply of minority lawyers, especially when repeated year after year. The situation is much the same in medical schools; a brief submitted in the *Bakke* case (discussed later in this chapter) by the Association of American Medical Colleges (Waldman, 1977) indicted that without affirmative action programs, minority enrollment would have dropped from 8.2 percent to a "distressingly low" level of about 2 percent.

Practical Consequences of Affirmative Action: Empirical Evidence

Data on employment and income of recent minority and white college graduates is helpful in assessing the actual effects of affirmative action hiring programs in recent years. Such data suggest that among recent college graduates (and people who have recently finished postgraduate work), blacks are earning incomes quite similar to those of whites, but *not* greater overall than those of whites (Freeman, 1978; U.S. Bureau of the Census, 1979d). A more precise breakdown shows that among recent college graduates, black males have slightly lower incomes than white males; black females slightly higher incomes than white females; however, females of both races have far lower incomes than white males, even among recent college graduates (see Table 13.1). Thus, it would appear that, *among persons with at least four years of college,* affirmative action has moved things in the direction of equality, though white male college graduates twenty-five to thirty-four continue to have an average income more than $1,000 higher than that of *any* of the other groups. It is this group of minorities—the recent college graduates—who have benefited most from affirmative action, though even they have not reached equity with the white male. Among less educated minorities, affirmative action has had less benefit, though it has made some difference among building trades contractors with the government, public employees, and in some blue-collar manufacturing jobs. As Wilson (1978, pp. 99–121) has pointed out, it has had almost no effect on low-income, poorly educated, chronically unemployed minorities. Thus, affirmative action has helped to offset the effects of discrimination for relatively more advantaged minorities, but it has neither given these groups an income advantage over the dominant white male group nor made much difference at all for minorities in the impoverished underclass. Mainly for this reason, minority groups taken as a whole remain substantially disadvantaged in income, employment, and education compared to whites as a whole, in spite of affirmative action.

Table 13.1   Mean Income, 1977, Recent College Graduates,* by Race and Sex.

Mean Income in Dollars

AGE	WHITE MALES	WHITE FEMALES	BLACK MALES	BLACK FEMALES
25–29	$13,017	8,526	12,124	9,917
30–34	18,482	8,346	16,893	**
25–34	15,753	8,452	14,622	9,999

Mean Income as % of Majority Group Mean Income

	WHITE FEMALES	BLACK MALES	BLACK FEMALES	
AGE	% OF WM	% OF WM	% OF WM	% OF WF
25–29	65.1%	92.6	75.8	116.3
30–34	45.2	91.4	**	**
25–34	53.7	92.8	63.5	118.3

*All persons in age group with 4 or more years of college
**Too few in category for reliable estimate.
Source: U.S. Bureau of the Census, 1979d.

Legal Aspects of the Affirmative Action Controversy

Not surprisingly, an issue as controversial as affirmative action has been widely debated in the courts as well as in other places. Those who are against it have argued that it violates the Civil Rights Act of 1964 and the equal protection clause of the Constitution by discriminating against whites and/or males. Those who support it argue that affirmative action is not discrimination against anyone but rather an effort to *include* underrepresented groups, and thereby it is not illegal. In general, because of the equal protection clause and the civil rights laws, the courts view race as a "suspect category." In effect, this means that anyone who in any way uses race as a basis of consideration must demonstrate that some compelling interest is served by doing so, and that the purpose is not to discriminate against or exclude anybody on the basis of race. Since most affirmative action programs do in some way involve a consideration of race, an early court test of their legality was inevitable. By 1971, affirmative action was beginning to find its way into the courts. *Anderson* v. *S.F. Unified School District,* a challenge against an affirmative action program in the employment of San Francisco school administrators, reached the federal courts in 1971 (Dreyfuss and Lawrence, 1979, pp. 33–34). Shortly thereafter, *DeFunis* v. *Odegaard,* a challenge of a law school admissions program at the University of Washington, reached the Washington Supreme Court, where the program was declared constitutional. This ruling was appealed to the U.S. Supreme Court, but it avoided the issue, declaring the case moot because the plaintiff had been allowed to attend law school despite his rejection, pending a ruling by the courts. Not until the *Allan Bakke* v. *Regents of the University of California* case in 1978 did the U.S. Supreme Court rule on the constitutionality of affirmative action. This case pertained to admission of students; the Court ruled in the following year on a case of equal importance pertaining to affirmative action in employment, *Weber* v. *Kaiser Aluminum and Chemical Corporation.*

The *Bakke* case was brought by a medical school applicant, Allan Bakke, who was twice denied admission to the University of California at Davis Medical School. That school admitted one hundred applicants per year, eighty-four of them under a "regular" admission program and sixteen under a "special" admissions program for "economically and/or educationally disadvantaged persons" (Sindler, 1978, p. 52). Although whites were eligible for consideration under the special program, only minorities were actually admitted under the program in 1973 and 1974, the years Bakke applied. Bakke contended that this amounted to illegal discrimination; the university claimed that the program was legal because it was designed to promote the inclusion of underrepresented groups. By the time it reached the U.S. Supreme Court, the case had attracted tremendous attention: Fifty-seven *amici* (friend of the court) briefs were filed in the case, more than had been filed in the 1954 *Brown* case and possibly more than in any Supreme Court case in history (Sindler, 1978, p. 242). Over one hundred organizations either sponsored or supported an *amicus* brief—nearly three-fourths of these supported the university's position that its affirmative action program was legal. When the Court issued its ruling on July 28, 1978, it neither totally pleased nor totally dissatisfied either side. The ruling said, in effect, that the consideration of race in the admission of students was legal as long as it had a legitimate purpose, but that the use of quotas was not. It ruled the University of California–Davis Medical School's admissions program illegal because it amounted to a quota system, and it ordered that Bakke be admitted. As Supreme Court Justice Powell, who announced the decision, noted, the Court spoke "with a notable lack of unanimity." Six out of the nine justices wrote opinions in the case, and the outcome was in effect a four-one-four split. Four of the justices felt that *any* consideration of race in admissions was illegal, and another four felt that quotas were legal as long as their purpose was to remedy the effects of the past mistreatment of minority groups by society. The deciding vote was cast by Justice Powell, who held that quotas were an unacceptable form of discrimination, but that for the goal of having a diverse student body, universities could consider race as one of many factors. In effect, then, racial preferences in college and law school admissions were legal as long as they did not amount to quotas and as long as race was one of a number of factors considered. This decision, however, applied only to the admission of students to educational institutions, not to employment. The legality of affirmative action in private sector employment was the subject of the *Weber* case, decided by the Court the following year.

The *Weber* v. *Kaiser Aluminum and Chemical Corporation* case reached the Supreme Court after a series of appeals in a case brought by Brian Weber, a white employee of Kaiser Aluminum in Gramercy, Louisiana. Weber claimed that he had been the victim of racial discrimination resulting from an affirmative action plan which had been agreed upon by Kaiser Aluminum and its union, the United Steel Workers Union. The plan was designed to improve the representation of minorities in skilled labor positions. It provided that until the percentage of minority workers in skilled positions was roughly equal to the percentage of minorities in the local population, one minority person would be placed in a skilled position for each white placed in such a position (Dreyfuss and Lawrence, 1979, p. 251). In the plant where Weber worked, there was a great discrepancy: before the affirmative action plan, only 5 percent of Kaiser's skilled work force was black, whereas the local community was about 43 percent black. It was exactly this kind of discrepancy that the affirmative action plan was designed to alleviate. Under the plan, half of those hired or promoted to skilled positions were to be black, and Weber was turned down when he applied for a promotion, even though some of the blacks promoted had less seniority than Weber. He sued, and the lower courts ruled in his favor: Since there was no judgment or admission that the particular plant involved had deliberately discriminated against blacks, there was no legal reason for the plant to now favor blacks over whites. The company and union appealed, and the case eventually reached the U.S. Supreme Court. The Court announced its decision on June 28, 1979—exactly eleven months after it had decided the *Bakke* case. On a five to two vote (with two justices not participating), it overturned the lower court rulings and ruled that the affirmative action plan was legal. The ruling went on to say that, *as long as the purpose is to increase the representation of groups who have been held back by past societal discrimination,* consideration of race in hiring is legal, *even if it involves the use of a quota.* The reason that private employers may use quotas in their affirmative action programs, while the university could not do so in student admissions, is that private employers are not subject to constitutional restrictions that apply to public universities. The only laws applicable to employers are the civil rights laws; and these were designed to improve the position of minorities. Since the purpose of the affirmative action program is the same, the Court ruled that they are not forbidden by the civil rights laws (*New York Times,* 1979). The *Weber* case was generally regarded as a victory by civil rights organizations and other supporters of affirmative action because it was clearer and less ambivalent than the *Bakke* case, which drew a careful line between preferences and quotas.

If we can summarize the position of the law after *Bakke* and *Weber*, it would be something like this: Public universities, in affirmative action programs for student admissions, may employ a racial preference so long as race is one of a number of factors and the program does not amount to a quota system. Private employers may also use a racial preference in hiring and promotion as long as the goal is to reduce the effects of past societal discrimination. Among private employers, however, the preference *can* take the form of a quota. Thus, affirmative action programs involving a racial preference are legal in both cases, but there are fewer restrictions on private employers' hiring programs than on public university admissions programs. Although the present legal status of affirmative action has been greatly clarified by the *Bakke* and *Weber* cases, it must be kept in mind that further changes are possible. First, there is always the possibility that the picture may be changed by further court rulings. Second, there remains significant opposition to affirmative action: As we have seen, many whites view it as a reverse form of discrimination. Should such opposition intensify (as it could during a period of tightening job opportunities), there is always the possibility that it could lead to legislation changing the legal status of affirmative action. With the election of Ronald Reagan to the presidency in 1980, this possibility becomes greater since Reagan has expressed some opposition to affirmative action. As far as the courts are concerned, however, affirmative action programs can remain an important tool used by employers and universities to combat the effects of societal discrimination against blacks, Hispanics, Indians, and women.

IMMIGRATION POLICY

A third major subject of controversy in the area of majority-minority relations is the immigration policy of the United States. As we have seen, immigration policy has long been controversial in the United States and has at times been used in more or less openly racist ways. For about the first half of the twentieth century, Oriental Exclusion Acts kept people from China, Japan, and other parts of Asia from migrating to the United States. Quota systems were also used until the 1960s to keep down the number of southern and eastern Europeans entering the United States; these dated back to 1921. The discriminatory nature of this system can be seen in the fact that about 84 percent of the national quotas went to northern and western Europe (Great Britain and Germany alone accounted for about 60 percent), 14 percent to southern and eastern Europe, and 2 percent to the rest of the world (Thomlinson, 1976, p. 301). The reasons for these restrictions appear to have been twofold. First, there was resistance to the whole idea of immigration on the grounds that immigrants contribute to the unemployment problem, and that—because they are sometimes willing to work for lower salaries than Americans—they put Americans out of work and hold down their wages. Second, much of the opposition to immigration arises from plain and simple ethnocentrism. Some Americans simply do not want to admit people who are "different from us," even though they or their ancestors were once immigrants, too. Thus, it is hardly surprising that anti-immigration groups such as the Know-Nothing party and the Ku Klux Klan have been not only anti-immigration, but also anti-Jewish, anti-Catholic, and antiblack.

In 1965 legislation was passed that phased out the quota system over a three-year period. The annual limits on immigration were changed to 120,000 from the Western Hemisphere and 170,000 from the Eastern Hemisphere, with a maximum of 20,000 from any one country in the Eastern Hemisphere. This policy has obviously made immigration much more open to people from outside northern and western Europe than was previously the case. In 1978 the hemisphere distinction was dropped, and immigration was simply limited to 290,000 per year, with not more than 20,000 from any one country. Although the theoretical limit on immigration is 290,000 per year, the actual number of legal immigrants per year is larger because some immigrants are exempted from these limits. The parents, spouses, and unmarried children of U.S. citizens may enter the United States without numerical restrictions, and exceptions to the limits are also made for political refugees. Thus, legal immigration during the 1970s averaged close to 400,000 per year. During years with large influxes of refugees, such as the Cubans and Haitians in 1980, the total can rise significantly above that level.

In spite of the law, we know that actual immigration into the United States is well above the legal limits. Just how much above we do not know—estimates vary from a few hundred thousand up to a million or more per year. It seems likely that illegal immigration is at least in the same general range of numbers as legal immigration, and it may be twice as great as legal immigration. One large source of illegal immigration is the Mexican border, where both Mexicans and others can cross the border unmolested; it is simply too long and remote to patrol without a force of thousands. However, a recent study (Siegel et al., 1980) suggests that this may be a less important source of illegal immigrants than is widely believed, simply because a great many of the illegal immigrants from Mexico return to Mexico of their own will. In fact, many of them are seasonal. Another source of illegal immigrants is the arrival by air or sea of immigrants from a variety of places who either present forged documents or present valid documents but overstay their visa. The possible magnitude of this problem can be seen in one recent study (Vining, 1979) that estimates that in recent years, 500,000 to 700,000 more people have arrived by air in the U.S. each year than have departed—a figure that exceeds the total legal limit by 100,000 to 300,000 and does not consider border crossings by land or sea. The most authoritative estimates are that between 3 million and 6

Immigrants arriving on an Atlantic liner. Many Americans who favor a restrictive policy on immigration seem to forget that they too are the children of immmigrants. (Library of Congress)

million people—as much as 3 percent of the population—are living in the United States illegally. Some estimates place the figure as high as 10 million to 12 million, though many demographers regard these estimates as quite unsubstantiated. The fact is that, since illegal immigrants obviously want to avoid detection, there is no way to count them accurately. There is little doubt, however, that illegal immigration is substantial, both in absolute numbers and relative to legal immigration.

The reasons for this large-scale immigration are many, but the bottom line comes down to two main factors: First, the United States is a relatively wealthy and prosperous country, far more so than most of the countries of the Third World— Asia, Africa, and Latin America. For this reason, Third World countries have been the source of a large share of immigration to the United States in recent years, both legal and illegal. In 1976, for example, the top five countries in immigration were Mexico, the Philippines, Korea, Cuba, and India (Bouvier, 1977, p. 27). Very simply, a great many people have sought to move from these less wealthy countries to the United States (as well as to Canada and a number of countries in Western Europe). Second, the United States has been quite restrictive in terms of the number of immigrants that it admits. The average admission of 400,000 immigrants in the late 1960s and 1970s in the U.S. amounted to about 1.8 immigrants per 1000 population. During the same period, Canada admitted an average of about 170,000 immigrants annually (Beaujot, 1978, p. 19), or about 7.7 immigrants per 1000 population—about four times the U.S. rate. Even at this rate, Canada has had problems with illegal immigrants. Thus, it is not hard to see why the United States, with its much lower rate of admission in the face of similar pressures, has a large number of illegal immigrants.

The current situation, then, presents the United States with a choice of three general alternatives. One, obviously, would be to do nothing, which would probably mean a continued high level of illegal immigration, since the resources currently being devoted to enforcement cannot adequately enforce the law. A second alternative would be to reduce illegal immigration, most likely through stepped-up enforcement of the present laws. This would be very costly (if it could in fact be done), but some people believe that it would reduce the problem of unemployment by eliminating illegals as competitors for jobs. Recent events have directed attention toward a more serious problem that can occur when a very large number of immigrants rapidly enter an area, overwhelming the system's ability to absorb them. This is illustrated by the difficulty of finding jobs and housing for the thousands of Cuban and Haitian refugees who flooded the Miami area in 1980. Such cases are exceptional, however, and usually relatively short in duration.

A third alternative would be to raise the legal limits on immigration to a number more in line with the actual pressure for immigration. Those who favor this approach argue that the present laws are impossible to enforce, and that immigration brings important benefits to society. Immigrants fill jobs where trained workers are in short supply in this country, and new jobs are created by the buying power of immigrants. Studies suggest, for example, that economic growth is correlated with population growth, and that immigration is one way to maintain population growth in the face of the low U.S. birth rate. Finally, many believe that the cultural diversity brought by immigrants is an important source of adaptability and innovation in society.

Undoubtedly, a great many Americans would like to see immigration reduced to a level lower than the present level. Indeed, this tendency is seen in nearly every country in the world that admits substantial numbers of immigrants—a fact that, if nothing else, certainly illustrates the near-universality of ethnocentrism. Nonetheless, it is important to keep in mind that the United States is a nation composed almost entirely of immigrants, and that—aside from sudden floods of immigrants that overwhelm an area's ability to absorb them—those who are here gain from immigration a number of benefits that are sometimes forgotten amid the worry about increased competition for jobs and the fears about cultures different from our own. Thus, it may well be that the benefits of immigration outweigh the costs. Finally, many argue that it is hardly fair for a nation with the great wealth of the United States, and a nation that consumes such a large share of the world's wealth, to post a "Keep Out" sign at its boundaries, particularly when that nation itself is populated by immigrants and the sons and daughters of immigrants.

EXTENSION OF LEGAL PROTECTION TO MINORITIES OTHER THAN RACIAL AND ETHNIC ONES

Early in this book, we stated that the principles of majority-minority relations can be applied to social groups other than racial and ethnic ones. Women, the handicapped or disabled, and gay people (homosexuals) have been compared, in terms of their role in society, to racial minority groups such as blacks. Thus, a good part of what has been said in this book about racial and ethnic groups could also be applied to these groups, though there are, of course, differences. It is certainly true, however, that these groups have been the victims of discrimination in such areas as jobs and housing. Consequently, the drive for civil rights laws prohibiting discrimination against racial minorities has given rise to campaigns for similar legislation concerning the rights of such groups as women, the disabled, and gays. It is impossible here to do justice to all the arguments that have been put forth concerning why each of these groups should or should not receive the same legal and/or constitutional protections accorded to racial and religious minorities. To do this would require the writing of another book. Nonetheless, we shall highlight some of the major issues in the debate and summarize the current state of legislation and court rulings concerning these three nonracial minority groups.

Women's Rights

Undoubtedly, the most widespread of these controversies centers around the issue of legal protection of the rights of women. Although the actual debate usually centers on legislation such as the Equal Rights Amendment to the U.S. Constitution, it actually arises out of greatly differing views about the role of women in American society. One view sees women as very clearly a minority group in the sociological sense (females are actually a majority of the U.S. population)—a group that has been dominated by males, exploited through low wages in the labor market, and generally placed in a subordinate role. Those who hold this view—feminists and their supporters—point out that in the family, males have traditionally held most of the power, in large part because they have controlled the purse strings. The idea that a woman should "love, honor, *and obey*" her husband even became a common part of the marriage ritual. Outside the family, sexual inequality is evident: working women receive only about 60 percent of the income that working men receive. Furthermore, the power structure of the United States is almost totally male-dominated: In both the public and private sectors, nearly all the positions at the top, such as corporate officers and boards of directors and high elected offices, are held by males. One example can be seen in the U.S. Congress: In 1980 there were only 16 women out of 435 representatives in the House and 1 woman out of 100 senators. Sociologically speaking, it is very difficult to conceptualize women as anything other than a minority or subordinate group. U.S. history further supports this view; to give just one example, women have only had the right to vote for about sixty years out of our over two hundred-year history.

Yet, there are some who argue that women are not really an exploited minority. These people, who might be described as anti-feminist, generally see the status of women as special and protected, one that prevents women from having to do the dirty work: Women are protected and spared from dangerous occupations, heavy physical labor, and military combat duty. This more traditional view also sees feminism as a threat to family life, because the increased assertiveness of women can lead to husband-wife conflicts and in some cases to divorce or separation.

Feminists counter these arguments by noting that women have paid a very high price in dependency and low pay for whatever protection is associated with traditional sex roles. Furthermore, many argue that if a woman *wants* to do dangerous work, she should have the same right to do so as anyone else. They also ask what advantage lies in giving dangerous work exclusively to one sex. Finally, they are not greatly impressed by the arguments that feminism has harmed family life, noting that in a family where all the power is in the hands of the male, and the female is denied the same freedoms to learn and grow that the male enjoys, a healthy relationship cannot be said to exist.

Regardless where one stands in the debate, there is no question that feminism has enjoyed a tremendous surge of support in the United States since the 1960s. Indeed, public opinion polls show that a very substantial majority of Americans, both male and female, support the Equal Rights Amendment, strongly suggesting that most Americans do view women as a minority group that needs certain legal protections.

The growth of feminism from the 1960s to the 1980s must be classified as one of the great shifts of public opinion in American history. Like blacks and other racial minorities, women have more and more come to reject the traditional, largely subordinate, role that society placed them in. In this section, we shall briefly examine the circumstances surrounding the growth of feminism in the United States, then review the legal and political status of women's rights today.

There is no question that the black civil rights movement of the 1950s and 1960s was an important stimulus to the development of the women's movement in the United States. Although feminism was far from a new idea in the United States in the 1960s, the women's movement had lain more or less dormant since before World War II. By the middle to late 1960s, however, this was changing. Recall from Chapter 7 that in order for a social movement to form, several conditions must be present: Collective dissatisfaction, a communication network, a sense of efficacy, and leadership network. There is little doubt that the civil rights movement (along with the movement against the Vietnam War) added greatly to the presence of these conditions among American women. It is undoubtedly true that women during the 1950s felt some real dissatisfaction with their roles. With modern labor-saving devices they had time on their hands as never before but were still largely restricted from setting out on careers of their own. Nonetheless, by its stress on the concept of oppressed minorities, the civil rights movement probably heightened whatever dissatisfaction women were already feeling. More important, the civil rights and antiwar movements became vehicles by which women who were dissatisfied were able to come in contact with other women who felt similarly (Freeman, 1973). A series of state meetings on the status of women organized in 1963 had a similar effect. Once women of a similar mind had been placed in contact with each other, the basis for a large-scale social movement had been laid. The communication network among the dissatisfied group had been established, and a leadership group was being identified. Both of these grew largely out of the civil rights and antiwar movements. In addition, the successes of these movements provided a role model, showing women that social protest could be effective. Thus, all the elements required for a social movement were present, and all, at least to some degree, grew out of the civil rights and antiwar movements.

Today, the feminist movement has made important gains in providing the same legal protections to women as are provided to racial and religious minorities. Employment discrimination on the basis of sex has been forbidden by the 1964 Civil Rights Act, and several states have amendments or clauses in their constitutions banning discrimination on the basis of sex. Increasingly, the courts are viewing sex as a "suspect category," much the same as race, which means that a person's sex may be a factor in decisions about that person only if there is a legitimate and compelling interest in considering it. In spite of these victories, the effort to afford women the legal protections that exist for racial and religious minorities has not been fully successful. The Equal Rights Amendment, which states that "Equality of rights under the law shall not be denied or abridged by the United States or by any state on account of sex," remained three states short of ratification by the required thirty-eight states as of mid-1981. Thus, constitutional protection against sex discrimination by the state and federal governments has not yet been attained.

The Rights of the Disabled

Another group that has increasingly come to be viewed according to a minority group model is the disabled. Although there is disagreement on the precise number of disabled or handicapped people in the United States, a compilation of various surveys suggests that from 13 to 16 percent of the U.S. adult population is disabled (see Krute and Burdette, 1978; U.S. National Center for Health Statistics, 1979; Nagi, 1972; Farley, 1980). Increasingly, the disabled have come to believe that it is not mainly their physical disabilities that place them at a disadvantage, but society's *reaction* to their disability. Employers, for example, are often reluctant to

A school for disabled students in Washington, D.C. Many sociologists feel that the disabled fit the definition of "minority group" as well as do racial and ethnic minorities. (W.A. Graham/United Nations)

hire the disabled, even when their disability in no way impairs them from doing the job. Physically disabled people must also frequently deal with nondisabled people who expect them to be *mentally* disabled as well, and therefore talk down to them, talk about them in their presence, or assume that they cannot do things when they really can. Similarly, the nondisabled frequently view the disabled in a unidimensional manner—as *disabled* people rather than as whole people, so that the single characteristic of disability becomes foremost in their minds. Behaviors such as staring, uncomfortable silence, or endless questions about their disability continuously remind disabled people that they are "different" (Schuchardt, 1980). In effect, the stigma the rest of society places on disabled persons can often become a greater handicap than the disability itself. Even the physical disability is often more of a handicap than it need be because of actions of the larger society. It is not particularly difficult, for example, to design sidewalks and buildings so that most disabled persons can use them. Until recently, however, this was rarely done.

Because of various prejudices about disabled people and socially imposed handicaps such as hiring discrimination, many disabled people have come to view themselves as a minority group and to behave accordingly. They have held demonstrations in recent years and engaged in political lobbying similar to that done by racial and ethnic minorities and women. The threat of a lawsuit, for example, led to the captioning of part of the television braodcast of the 1980 Democratic National Convention for hearing-impaired viewers. Increasingly, legislation and labor-management contracts have forbidden discimination on the basis of disabilities not related to job performance. Such discrimination is forbidden, for example, in federal employment and among private employers under contract with the federal government (Bruck, 1978). The disabled have also come to be regarded as a protected group under affirmative action programs, and many employers have made special efforts to hire and upgrade the disabled.

Nonetheless, such efforts cannot entirely eliminate the prejudices and fears of the nondisabled toward the disabled, and a big piece of the disadvantage that disabled people suffer in some way arises from one-to-one interactions with individuals who have such prejudices. Only a greater awareness of the perspectives of disabled people can solve this problem. Even good intentions are not enough; well-meaning expressions of concern often come off as paternalizing and end up making the disabled person feel powerless or unaccepted (Gliedman, 1979). As long as such problems exist, disabled persons are likely to view themselves as a minority group and respond accordingly. For them, too, the black civil rights movement served as an important role model and provided some worthwhile lessons both about how society responds to groups who are "different" and how to deal with that response. (For further discussion of the problems of the disabled, see Bruck, 1978; Stubbins, 1977; Cohen, 1977.)

Gay Rights

Probably the newest and certainly the most controversial issue relating to legal protection of minorities concerns homosexuals, or gay people. It is extremely difficult to estimate the number of homosexuals in the U.S. population, for a number of reasons. First, the term is hard to define. If it is defined as those who have had homosexual experiences, at least a third of the American adult male population and 15 percent of the female population would probably qualify, based on Kinsey's (1948, 1953) data on sexual behavior. It is usually defined more narrowly than that, however, since most of these cases involve only a few encounters in otherwise heterosexual lives. Moreover, some individuals are bisexual—more or less equally homosexual and heterosexual. On top of all this, good data are hard to come by—sexual behavior is a highly private matter and the social sanctions for homosexuality, as we shall see, can be especially severe. Although a precise estimate is impossible, the various sources of data suggest that the most plausible estimate is probably in the range of 5 to 10 percent of the adult population (see APA Monitor, 1974), if we define homosexuality in terms of an exclusive or substantial sexual preference. Among males, the figure is probably somewhat higher; among females, somewhat lower.

Historically, in the United States and some other societies homosexuality has been viewed as a form of social deviance. Homosexuals have been seen not as a minority group but rather as a group of people who have chosen to engage in evil and socially unacceptable behavior. Accordingly, homosexuality was made illegal in every state in the U.S. and remains so in the majority of states, though several states have in recent years eliminated laws restricting sexual activity among consenting adults. The length to which repression of homosexuality can go is illustrated by German Nazism under Hitler: Along with the six million Jews who died in the gas chambers were an estimated 800,000 homosexuals or suspected homosexuals—a fact not often noted in present-day discussions of the Holocaust (Humm, 1980).

In spite of this, many societies in the past and in the world today had or have *no* rule against homosexuality. The ancient Greeks, for example (regarded today as an especially civilized society) placed a high value on homosexuality and in some ways institutionalized it (Licht, 1932). Although most Western, Christian-dominated societies frown on homosexuality, some European countries such as the Netherlands and Denmark have no law against it; in Holland, there has been no such law for over 160 years (Weinberg and Williams, 1974, Chapters 5−7). In the United States, however, the dominant view has been that homosexuals are a deviant group who represent a threat to society and must be kept under control (see Weinberg and Williams, 1974, pp. 19−21). As an example, a 1970 survey showed that 60 percent of American adults *opposed* the legalization of homosexual behavior between consenting adults.

In spite of these popular views a persuasive case can be made for viewing homosexuals as a minority group similar in some regards to a racial or cultural minority. First, the view that homosexuality is a freely chosen mode of behavior, for which an individual should be held responsible, is highly dubious. While there is no proof of a genetic factor in homosexuality (Rosenthal, 1970; Tourney et al., 1975) or, for that matter, heterosexuality, there is evidence that social learning, early experiences, and labeling processes (messages received from others) are related to homosexuality. Thus, one's sexual preference is largely beyond individual control, and even a homosexual who would prefer to be heterosexual is frequently unable to change his or her sexual orientation. For some, sexual preference is no more possible to change than their race or sex or a physical disability. From this perspective, then, homosexuals do fit the concept of a minority group.

Aside from this issue, however, a more fundamental one exists, that of personal freedom. Those who view homosexuals as an oppressed minority argue that laws against homosexual behavior and the existence of antigay discrimination in society would still be repressive and unfair, even if it could be shown that homosexuality was a freely chosen behavior. This view holds that no group has the right to impose its values and beliefs on another. Thus, just as feminists hold that nobody has the right to tell women what role they must fill in society, gay rights advocates hold that nobody has the right to tell others what their sexual preference must be. In other words, as long as the behavior is taking place between consenting adults, nobody is hurt by it and nobody should be punished for it.

Others see it differently. These opponents of gay rights see homosexuality as a threat to the family and as an indication of a moral decline in American society. This view holds, in addition, that a basic consensus about right and wrong is needed in society, and such a consensus is threatened by the legalization of "deviant" behavior. Thus, the supporters of this view believe that the legalization of homosexual behavior and legislation forbidding discrimination against gay people merely give legitimacy to homosexuality, contributing to its spread. An especially intense fear is that children will be seduced into a homosexual life style. This viewpoint has considerable popular support. The best-known gay rights opponent, singer Anita Bryant, was instrumental in the vote to repeal a gay-rights ordinance in Dade County (Miami), Florida, and played a leading role in similar votes in St. Paul, Minnesota, and several other cities.

Supporters of gay rights, and civil libertarians more generally, see a danger in the actions of the groups opposing gay rights. In large part these groups base their opposition to gay rights on religious beliefs and argue that the law must uphold the Judeo-Christian religious values of the United States. Civil libertarians see this view as a serious threat to the principle of separation of church and state, a principle established early in American law to prevent any religious group from imposing its views on all others. The dangers of linking religion with government are perhaps well illustrated by the Khomeini regime in Iran, which has made the strict rules of Shiite Islam the law of the land, imposing penalties up to and including execution for those who do not comply. Thus, it is argued that separation of church and state is a wise policy that is threatened by arguments like those of Anita Bryant, who has argued that the "Biblical" injunction against homosexual behavior ought to be incorporated into American law.

In addition, it is argued that it is not necessary to restrict behavior among consenting adults in order to protect others from harm. Regarding the fears about children and homosexuality, the supporters of gay rights point out that laws exist everywhere against the molestation or solicitation of children, whether by homosexuals or heterosexuals—and that most such cases involve heterosexuals.

Clearly, homosexuals are increasingly coming to view themselves as an oppressed minority group. Gay rights groups have sprung up throughout the country, actively opposing discrimination against homosexuals and urging that people be open about their gayness rather than hiding it. These groups have helped to make the public aware of widespread discrimination against homosexuals in areas such as housing and employment. While anti-gay groups remain influential, there is no doubt that awareness of discrimination against gay people has risen among heterosexuals. About forty cities, including Detroit, Minneapolis, San Francisco, and Seattle have passed local ordinances forbidding discrimination on the basis of sexual preference. Openly gay candidates have been elected to public office in several cities and states, in some cases from districts where the electorate was not predominantly gay. In areas with large concentrations of gay population, such as San Francisco, events such as Gay Pride Week have drawn the participation of local officials, much the same as ethnic festivals and parades do. Despite the scattered successes of groups opposing gay rights, a referendum that would have authorized the banning of gay people from public employment in certain jobs was soundly defeated by the California electorate in 1978. Still as of 1981, there is no state or national legislation, and no federal court rulings, that prevent discrimination against homosexuals. Except in the cities that forbid it by local ordinance or where labor-management contracts forbid it, such discrimination remains legal. Given this situation, it is likely that the debate over legal protection of the rights of homosexuals will continue well into the future.

THE RELATIVE IMPORTANCE OF RACE AND CLASS IN AMERICAN SOCIETY

The final controversy to which we now turn is an intellectual debate more than a policy debate, but it carries important implications for public policy as well. This debate concerns the relative importance of *racial discrimination* versus *social class* as causes of inequality in American society today.

The controversy began with the publication of William J. Wilson's (1978) *The Declining Significance of Race,* parts of which have been discussed at some length in other parts of this book. The controversial part of Wilson's book is his conclusion, suggested by the title, that disadvantages linked to social class (income, education, occupation) have become much more important than *racial* discrimination as a cause of black social disadvantage today. He bases this conclusion on the following major observations. First, there has been a substantial decline in deliberate employment discrimination in the United States since World War II. In other words, it has become much less common (as well as illegal) for employers to either refuse to hire someone because he or she is black, or to have a policy of paying blacks less for the same work. (This change, along with many of the reasons for it, including those suggested by Wilson, is discussed at greater length in Chapters 6 and 8 of this book.) Along with these changes have come an increase in enrollment and graduation of blacks in higher education, so that by the mid-1970s, according to Wilson, black enrollment rates in higher education were very close to white enrollment rates. As we saw in Chapter 8 and again in our discussion of affirmative action in this chapter, *recent black college graduates* are doing nearly as well as recent white graduates in terms of income and education, largely because previously closed opportunities have been opened by affirmative action. Thus, Wilson concludes that there is a growing black middle class, and that the younger members of this middle class are doing quite well economically, though he acknowledges that they experience considerable discrimination in the residential, social, and educational arenas.

Totally apart from this, according to Wilson, is the large and perhaps growing black underclass. This group, mostly falling below the poverty level and living in the inner cities, is beset with problems of unemployment and underemployment and is, as we have seen in previous chapters, probably becoming *worse off,* not better off, in the 1970s and 1980s. Wilson argues, however, that it is not *racial discrimination* but poverty itself that is this group's main problem. Thus, while blacks are overrepresented in the group due to past discrimination, it is not present day discrimination that is *keeping* them in their unfortunate position. Rather, it is changes in the economy that make this group in large part unemployable. (For a rather different analysis, which reaches a somewhat similar conclusion, see Wilhelm, 1980, esp. pp. 108–109.) This has happened because as manufacturing employment has declined, the availability of low-skill jobs has also decreased. Because of *past* discrimination, however, lower-class, inner-city blacks lack the skills needed for jobs that *are* growing, and have available fewer and fewer low-skill jobs for which they can compete. Thus, they experience high unemployment, often have to move from one short-term, dead-end job to another, and have little chance to escape this unfortunate situation. Thus, the problem is *not* the refusal of employers to hire such persons because they are black, but rather their lack, because of past discrimination, of any marketable skills. Thus class, not race, is the primary cause of black disadvantage *today*, according to Wilson. (For elaboration of these arguments beyond those made in his book, see Wilson, 1979, 1980.)

Wilson's book, as we have said, is highly controversial. One reason most certainly is that it is easily misinterpreted to suggest that America's racial problem is solved (Pettigrew, 1980). Certainly Wilson never intended such an interpretation, but some critics and some supporters of the book have given it that interpretation (Willie, 1979). As the critics emphatically point out, there is nothing approaching economic equality between the races in America (on this point, see the data presented in Chapter 8 of this text). A careful reading of Wilson, however, will clearly show that Wilson certainly never intended to claim there is racial equality, though his choice of titles for the book does encourage misinterpretation (Pettigrew, 1980; Payne, 1979, p. 138). As Willie (1979, p. 16) points out, such broad

The growing middle class among American minority groups has led some observers to argue that social class has become more important than race as a determinant of well-being in American society. David Hume Kennerly.

generalizations as "economic class is now a more important factor than race in determining job placement for blacks" (Wilson, 1978, p. 120) also encourage the interpretation (which many whites would like to make) that America's *racial* problem is largely solved and little more needs to be done. In the judgment of this author, a careful reading of Wilson's entire book would not support such an interpretation at all, but the title and some overly broad generalizations probably do.

The more empirical criticisms of Wilson's work, however, focus on somewhat different issues. Wilson does not disagree with his critics that blacks on the whole have lower incomes than whites,[1] or that serious and rapid action is needed on the problem of black poverty (see Wilson, 1979, p. 175). The real argument, as has already been suggested, is over the *reasons* for black poverty and over the degree to which middle-class blacks have really gained a socioeconomic status

[1]Though he does argue that treating blacks "as a whole" masks important socioeconomic differences within the black population.

400

comparable to middle-class whites. On the latter point, there is some evidence that while the income gap has narrowed for younger, highly educated blacks and whites, it has not necessarily disappeared. Willie (1979, pp. 53–54) reports that even black professional and managerial workers have incomes 20 percent below those of white workers in these areas, and cites data from a U.S. Civil Rights Commission study (1978) showing that *even after controls for age, education, and occupation,* both blacks and Chicanos typically received income substantially below that of white Anglos. A similar analysis by Reynolds Farley (1979) using 1978 data showed that black males, even if they would have had the typical social characteristics of white males, would still have received only 88 percent of the white male income. Females of both races were substantially lower. This suggests significant racial inequality *independent of* class inequality (as Wilson's critics claim), though, in partial support of Wilson, Farley's analysis does show a narrowing over time since 1960 in black/white inequality. Furthermore, Farley found that a black-white gap persisted after controls for other factors even in the most highly educated group, though, again, the gap did narrow. Thus, evidence is found in this study for a declining *but continuing* "significance of race."

Edwards (1979) and Marrett (1980) have pointed to another potential problem in Wilson's argument: Even though the black middle class *has* grown and narrowed the gap with the white middle class, the position of blacks and other minorities in the middle class is much less secure than that of the white middle class. Historically—as Wilson himself stresses—blacks and other minorities have tended to gain in good economic times, and to lose in bad economic times. Given the economic uncertainty of the 1980s, as well as an apparent conservative trend in the American populace, there is certainly a risk of minority losses. Wilson notes correctly that middle-class minorities did *not* lose ground in the recession of the mid 1970s, but over the longer term this may not continue to be the case if there is a long period of economic difficulty. Indeed, with shortages of even middle-class jobs, white opposition to affirmative action has grown, and the Reagan Administration has expressed considerable reluctance to press affirmative action goals. A retreat on affirmative action would beyond doubt limit black entry into the middle class, and even with affirmative action, the principle of the last hired being the first to be laid off in a time of economic crunch still holds true. Thus, in Detroit for example, when layoffs became necessary in the city's police force, seniority rules required that most of those laid off be black, because it was blacks who were most recently hired under the city's affirmative action program. Finally, Edwards (1979) correctly notes that black enrollment in a number of major universities has declined proportionate to that of whites in the latter half of the 1970s (perhaps because both black students and their white supporters stopped engaging in militant protests demanding high minority enrollment). Thus, it seems a fair criticism of Wilson's work to warn that, however much race may have declined in importance relative to class, there is a very real danger that it could increase in importance again, especially given the chronic economic difficulty the country has experienced in recent years and may well continue to experience.

Another point on which Wilson has received considerable criticism concerns the reasons for the disproportionate number of blacks in the impoverished underclass and the reasons that the people in this underclass cannot escape from that unfortunate status. It is Wilson's claim that the blacks are overrepresented in the underclass because of past discrimination, and that they are unable to escape the underclass (as is everyone else in the underclass) because of the lack of low-skill jobs in today's economy. Accordingly, Wilson argues that *present-day racial discrimination* is *not* very important as a cause of disadvantage among the black underclass. On this point, Wilson is vulnerable to considerable criticism. As we have seen in previous chapters, past racial discrimination and present-day class discrimination (including the institutionalized variety) *are,* as Wilson says, important reasons for continuing black (and other minority) overrepresentation in the impoverished underclass. However, Wilson is widely and correctly criticized for failing to note the importance of present-day *institutionalized racial discrimination* as a cause of the problem (Payne, 1979, pp. 134–137). Consider our own exploration of institutional discrimination in Chapters 9 to 11 of this book. There is no question that much of the discrimination discussed there does occur on the basis of social class, affecting minorities disproportionately because they are overrepresented among the poor. However, there is also a good deal of institutional discrimination specifically along the lines of *race*. In education, we have seen such problems as *de facto* school segregation, linguistic biases against minority students, low teacher expectations of minority students, distorted presentations of minorities in texts and materials, and racial inequities in tracking. Although there most certainly are strong class biases in the educational system (Bowles and Gintis, 1976), all of the inequities mentioned here are specifically *racial*. Since Wilson notes lack of quality education as playing a central role in the perpetuation of the minority underclass, it seems clear that institutionalized racial inequalities in education play an important role in the problem. The same is true in other areas. To cite one example, we can point to housing discrimination. Wilson himself (1980, p. 23) states that "the lack of opportunity for underclass blacks forces them to remain in economically depressed ghettoes. . .," which along with poor ghetto education, ". . . reinforce(s) their low labor market positions." Wilson is right about the effects of ghettoization on black employment when jobs have largely left the ghetto (see, for example, Farley, 1981). However, he is incorrect in that he ignores the crucial role of racial discrimination as a cause of ghettoization. As we saw in Chapter 10, economic differences between blacks and whites are less important than race as a cause of black-white housing segregation. The primary cause of such segregation is racial, not economic. Since such housing segregation restricts black opportunities in both employment and education, it is, as Wilson notes, an important cause of the problems of the minority underclass. However, Wilson fails to recognize the degree to which racial, as opposed to economic, factors produce that segregation. Thus, we see here, too, an example of the continuing significance of race.

These and other processes of institutional racial discrimination, then, *do* help explain why blacks and other minorities are so overrepresented in the impoverished underclass and why they have so much trouble escaping from that underclass. Further evidence of racial discrimination can be seen in the fact that the minority underclass is worse off than the white underclass. Thus, we find that, at the lowest levels of occupation and education, blacks and other minorities have *substantially lower incomes than whites* (Willie, 1979, pp. 62−63), though this gap, too, has narrowed somewhat over time (Farley, 1979). On the other hand, black Americans are more than three times as likely as whites to fall below the poverty level, and this pattern has *not* changed significantly in recent years.

Perhaps Payne (1979, p. 136) has hit upon the best description of the process causing racial inequality in recent years with his statement that "it is entirely possible that the processes sustaining differentials in racial privilege have become a good deal more fragmented than they once were." In other words, there are a wider variety of factors causing racial inequality than there once were. At one time, deliberate acts of racial discrimination were the main cause of racial inequality in America. Today, deliberate acts of discrimination are not the sole cause and perhaps not the primary cause of racial inequality. Today's inequality is a product of a combination of acts of discrimination, the effects of past discrimination, economic disadvantages *and* institutional discrimination. Thus, Wilson is right about the changes in the economy and the decline of open and deliberate discrimination, but he understates the continuing effect of institutional racial discrimination in perpetuating minority poverty. He is right, too, in pointing to increasing class differentiation within the minority population. However, he understates the degree to which the position of the minority group middle class is insecure and could deteriorate in the hard economic times that may be coming. Thus, Wilson's *The Declining Significance of Race* makes an important contribution to the understanding of majority-minority relations in America, but at the same time underestimates the continuing importance of racial types of discrimination as a factor influencing the status of black (and other minority group) Americans today. Thus, both class *and* race continue to be economically significant, perpetuating a situation where the overall position of minorities relative to whites is little if any better than in the past, despite increasing class differentiation within minority groups.

CONCLUSION

In this chapter, we have explored some of the issues in intergroup relations that face the United States today: affirmative action, assimilation versus pluralism, immigration policy, the rights of minority groups other than racial and ethnic ones, and the relative importance of racial discrimination and social class. These and a host of other issues relating to intergroup relations remain unresolved. The upsurge of racial violence in Miami and other cities, the increasing visibility of the Ku Klux Klan, Nazis, and other racist groups, and the mysterious killings of black people in Atlanta and Buffalo, all of which took place in the first year of the 1980s, serve to remind us that problems of intergroup relations remain deeply rooted in American society, and remain unsolved despite the deceptive calm of the middle and late 1970s. An intelligent and effective response to these problems will require both compassion and informed knowledge on the part of the American public. Neither by itself is sufficient. It is hoped that this book will help in some small way to make people more informed about intergroup relations. People must be aware of the historical patterns and subtle institutional processes that keep minority groups in an inferior position in present-day American society. Furthermore, they must be able to look at the problem from a perspective other than that of their own group. If this book has helped to accomplish these two things, its author will regard it as a worthwhile endeavor. While knowledge and understanding are necessary, however, they alone are not enough. Americans must be *motivated* to solve problems of intergroup relations; they must *care* about what happens to people in groups less fortunate than their own. No book can make that happen. Only the American public, including you, the reader, can do that.

GLOSSARY

Affirmative action   Any deliberate effort to increase minority representation, such as in a work force or student body. Affirmative action may be limited to more vigorous efforts to recruit minorities, or may be extended to preferences in hiring or student admissions for minority group members, sometimes including the use of specific goals and timetables for minority representation.

References

Abrahamson, Mark. 1980. *Urban Sociology*, second edition. Englewood Cliffs, N.J.: Prentice Hall.

Abrams, Charles. 1971. *Forbidden Neighbors*. Port Washington, N.Y.: Kennikat Press.

Abramson, Harold J. 1980. "Assimilation and Pluralism." Pp. 150–160 in Stephan Thernstrom, Ann Orlov, and Oscar Handlin (eds.), *The Harvard Encyclopedia of American Ethnic Groups*. Cambridge, Mass.: Harvard University.

Abramson, Harold J. 1975. "The Religio-Ethnic Factor and the American Experience: Another Look at the Three-Generation Hypothesis." *Ethnicity* 2: 163–177.

Abramson, Harold J. 1973. *Ethnic Diversity in Catholic America*. New York: John Wiley & Sons.

Acuña, Rodolfo. 1972. *Occupied America: The Chicano's Struggle Toward Liberation*. San Francisco: Canfield Press.

Adam, Heribert. 1971. *Modernizing Racial Domination*. Berkeley: University of California Press.

Aday, Lou Ann, 1976. "The Impact of Health Policy on Access to Medical Care." *Milbank Memorial Fund Quarterly* 54: 215–233.

Adorno, Theodor W., Else Frenkel-Brunswick, D. J. Levinson, and **R. N. Sanford.** 1950. *The Authoritarian Personality*. New York: Harper & Row, Pub.

Alexander, Karl L., Martha Cook, and **Edward L. McDill.** 1978. "Curriculum Tracking and Educational Stratification: Some Further Evidence." *American Sociological Review* 43: 47–66.

Alexander, Karl, and **Bruce K. Eckland.** 1975. "School Experience and Status Attainment.'' Pp. 171–210 in S. D. Dragastin and G. H. Elder (eds.), *Adolescence and the Life Cycle: Psychological Change and Social Context.* Washington: Hemisphere.

Alexander, Karl L., and **Edward L. McDill.** 1976. ''Selection and Allocation Within Schools: Some Causes and Consequences of Curriculum Placement.'' *American Sociological Review* 41: 963–980.

Allen, Michael A., and **Michelle Tolliver.** 1974. ''Medical Delivery System for Urban Indians: Consumer and Providers Perceptions.'' Paper presented to Southwest and Rocky Mountain Division of the American Association for the Advancement of Science, Laramie, Wyoming.

Allport, Gordon W. 1954. *The Nature of Prejudice.* New York: Addison-Wesley.

Alvarez, Rodolfo. 1973. ''The Psycho-Historical and Socioeconomic Development of the Chicano Community in the United States.'' *Social Science Quarterly* 53: 920–942. Reprinted in Norman R. Yetman and C. Hoy Steele (eds.), *Majority and Minority: The Dynamics of Racial and Ethnic Relations.* Boston: Allyn and Bacon, 1975.

APA Monitor. 1974. ''Homosexuality Dropped as Mental Disorder'' Vol. 5 (February).

Armor, David J. 1972. ''The Evidence on Busing.'' *The Public Interest* 28: 90–126.

Armor, David J., and **Donna Schwartzbach.** 1978. ''White Flight, Demographic Transition, and the Future of School Desegregation.'' *The Rand Paper Series* #P-5931. Presented to Annual Meeting of the American Sociological Association, San Francisco, California.

Arnold, William R. 1971. ''Race and Ethnicity Relative to Other Factors in Juvenile Court Dispositions.'' *American Journal of Sociology* 77: 211–227.

Arrow, Kenneth J. 1972. ''Models of Job Discrimination,'' in Anthony H. Paschal (ed.), *Economic Life.* Lexington, Mass.: D. C. Heath & Co.

Asch, Solomon E. 1956. ''Studies of Independence and Conformity: A Minority of One Against a Unanimous Majority.'' *Psychological Monographs* 70, No. 9 (whole No. 416).

Ashmore, Richard D. 1970. ''Prejudice: Causes and Cures.'' Pp. 244–339 in Barry E. Collins (ed.), *Social Psychology.* Reading, Mass.: Addison-Wesley.

Bahr, Howard M., Bruce A. Chadwick, and **Joseph H. Strauss.** 1979. *American Ethnicity.* Lexington, Mass.: D. C. Heath & Co.

Balbus, Isaac D. 1973. *The Dialectics of Legal Repression: Black Rebels Before the American Criminal Courts.* New York: Russell Sage Foundation.

Baldridge, J. Victor. 1976. *Sociology: A Critical Approach to Power, Conflict, and Change,* first edition. New York: John Wiley & Sons.

Bandura, Albert, and **Richard H. Walters.** 1963. *Social Learning and Personality Development.* New York: Holt, Rinehart and Winston.

Banfield, Edward C. 1974. *The Unheavenly City Revisited.* Boston: Little Brown.

Banfield, Edward C. 1968. *The Unheavenly City.* Boston: Little, Brown.

Banton, Michael. 1964. *The Policeman in the Community.* London: Tavistock.

Barabba, Vincent P. 1976. ''The National Setting: Regional Shifts, Metropolitan Decline, and Urban Decay.'' Pp. 39–76 in George Sternleib and James W. Hughes (eds.), *Post-Industrial America: Metropolitan Decline and Interregional Job Shifts.* New Brunswick, N.J.: Rutgers University Center for Urban Policy Research.

Baran, Paul A., and **Paul M. Sweezy.** 1966. *Monopoly Capital.* New York: Monthly Review Press.

Baratz, Steven S., and **Joan C. Baratz.** 1970. ''Early Childhood Intervention: The Social Science Base of Institutional Racism.'' *Harvard Educational Review* 40: 29–50.

Barber, James. 1967. *Rhodesia: The Road to Rebellion.* London: Oxford University Press.

Barlow, Hugh D. 1978. *Introduction to Criminology.* Boston: Little, Brown.

Barrera, Mario. 1979. *Race and Class in the Southwest: A Theory of Racial Inequality.* Notre Dame, Ind.: University of Notre Dame Press.

Barritt, Denis F., and **Charles F. Carter.** 1962. *The Northern Ireland Problem.* London: Oxford University Press.

Barth, Gunther. 1964. *Bitter Strength: A History of the Chinese in the United States, 1850–1870.* Cambridge, Mass.: Harvard University Press.

Bastide, Roger. 1965. "The Development of Race Relations in Brazil." Pp. 9–29 in Guy Hunter (ed.), *Industrialisation and Race Relations.* London: Oxford University Press.

Baughman, E. E. 1971. *Black Americans: A Psychological Analysis.* New York: Academic Press.

Bayley, David H., and **Harold Mendelsohn.** 1968. *Minorities and the Police: Confrontation in America.* New York: The Free Press.

Beaujot, Roderic P. 1978. "Canada's Population: Growth and Dualism," *Population Bulletin* 33 (2).

Beck, E. M. 1980. "Labor Unionism and Racial Income Inequality: A Time-series Analysis of the Post-World War II Period." *American Journal of Sociology* 85: 791–814.

Becker, Gary S. 1957. *The Economics Of Discrimination:* University of Chicago Press. (Revised edition published in 1971.)

Beez, W. V. 1968. "Influence of Biased Psychological Reports on Teacher Behavior and Pupil Performance." *Proceedings of the 76th Annual Convention of the American Psychological Association* 3: 605–606.

Bem, Daryl J. 1970. *Beliefs, Attitudes, and Human Affairs.* Belmont, Calif.: Brooks-Cole.

Berg, Ivar. 1975. "Rich Man's Qualifications for Poor Man's Jobs." Pp. 306–313 in Scott G. McNall (ed.), *The Sociological Perspective,* fourth edition. Boston: Little, Brown. (Reprinted from *Transaction* 6: 1969).

Berg, Ivar. 1971. *Education and Jobs: The Great Training Robbery.* Boston: Beacon Paperbacks.

Berger, Brigitte. 1978. "A New Interpretation of IQ Controversy." *The Public Interest* 50: 29–44.

Berry, Brewton, and **Henry L. Tischler.** 1978. *Racial and Ethnic Relations,* fourth edition. Boston: Houghton-Mifflin.

Biggar, Jeanne C. 1979. "The Sunning of America: Migration to the Sunbelt." *Population Bulletin* 34 (1).

Binstock, Jeanne. 1970. "Survival in the American College Industry." Unpublished Ph.D. Dissertation, Brandeis University.

Black, Donald J., and **Albert J. Reiss, Jr.** 1967. "Patterns of Behavior in Police and Citizen Transactions," in President's Commission on Law Enforcement and Administration of Justice, *Studies in Crime and Law Enforcement in Major Metropolitan Areas.* Washington, D.C.: U.S. Government Printing Office.

Blake, R., and **W. Dennis.** 1943. "The Development of Stereotypes Concerning the Negro." *Journal of Abnormal and Social Psychology* 38: 525–531.

Blassingame, John W. 1972. *The Slave Community: Plantation Life in the Antebellum South.* New York: Oxford University Press.

Blauner, Robert. 1972. *Racial Oppression in America.* New York: Harper & Row, Pub.

Bloch, Herman D. 1969. *The Circle of Discrimination: An Economic and Social Study of the Black Man in New York.* New York: New York University Press.

Blumenthal, David, and **James Fallows.** 1974. "Health: The Care We Want and Need." Pp. 162–168 in Dushkin Publishing Group (eds.), *Annual Editions: Readings in Sociology '74–'75.* Guilford, Conn.: Dushkin Publishing Group.

Blumer, Herbert. 1965. "Industrialisation and Race Relations." Pp. 220–553 in Guy Hunter (ed.), *Industrialisation and Race Relations: A Symposium.* London: Oxford University Press.

Bonacich, Edna. 1976. "Advanced Capitalism and Black/White Relations in the United

States: A Split Labor Market Interpretation.'' *American Sociological Review* 41: 34–51.

Bonacich, Edna. 1975. ''Abolition, the Extension of Slavery, and the Position of Free Blacks: A Study of Split Labor Markets in the United States, 1830–1863.'' *American Journal of Sociology* 81: 601–628.

Bonacich, Edna. 1972. ''A Theory of Ethnic Antagonism: The Split Labor Market.'' *American Sociological Review* 37: 547–559.

Boocock, Sarane Spence. 1978. ''The Social Organization of the Classroom.'' Pp. 1–28 in Ralph H. Turner, James Coleman, and Renee C. Fox (eds.), *Annual Review of Sociology—1978*. Palo Alto, Calif.: Annual Reviews.

Boskin, Joseph. 1969. *Urban Racial Violence in the Twentieth Century*. Beverly Hills, Calif.: Glencoe Press.

Boskin, Joseph. 1965. ''Race Relations in Seventeenth Century America: The Problem of the Origins of Negro Slavery.'' *Sociology and Social Research* 49: 446–455.

Bouvier, Leon F., with **Henry S. Shryock** and **Harry W. Henerson.** 1977. ''International Migration: Yesterday, Today, and Tomorrow.'' *Population Bulletin* 34(2).

Bowker, Lee H. 1972. ''Red and Black in Contemporary History Texts: A Content Analysis.'' Pp. 101–110 in Howard M. Bahr, Bruce A. Chadwick, and Robert C. Day (eds.), *Native Americans Today: Sociological Perspectives*. New York: Harper & Row, Pub.

Bowles, Samuel, and **Herbert Gintis.** 1976. *Schooling in Capitalist America*. New York: Basic Books.

Boyce, Louis Henri, III, and **Susan H. Gray.** 1979. ''Blacks, Whites, and Race Politics.'' *The Public Interest* 54: 61–75.

Brazziel, William F. 1969. ''A Letter from the South.'' *Harvard Educational Review* 39: 348–356.

Brischetto, Robert, and **Tomas Arciniega.** 1973. ''Examining the Examiner: A Look at Educators' Perspectives on the Chicano Student.'' In Rudolph O. de la Garza, Z. Anthony Kruzezewski, and Tomas A. Arciniega (eds.), *Chicanos and Native Americans: The Territorial Minorities*. Englewood Cliffs, N.J.: Prentice Hall.

Britton, Gwyneth E., and **Margaret C. Lumpkin.** 1977. ''For Sale: Subliminal Bias in Textbooks.'' *The Reading Teacher* 31: 40–45.

Brody, David. 1960. *Steelworkers in America: The Nonunion Era*. Cambridge, Mass.: Harvard University Press.

Brookover, Wilbur, and **L.W. Lezotte.** 1977. ''Changes in School Characteristics Coincident with Changes in Student Achievement.'' East Lansing, Mich.: College of Urban Develoment of Michigan State University and Michigan Department of Education.

Brophy, Jere, and **Thomas Good.** 1974. *Teacher-Student Relationships*. New York: Holt, Rinehart and Winston.

Brophy, J. E., and **Thomas Good.** 1970. ''Teacher's Communication of Differential Expectations for Children's Classroom Performance: Some Classroom Data.'' *Journal of Educational Psychology* 61: 365–374.

Brown, Lawrence L., Alan L. Ginsberg, J. Neil Killalea, and **Esther O. Tron.** 1978. ''School Finance Reform in the Seventies: Achievements and Failures.'' Pp. 57–110 in Esther O. Tron (ed.), *Selected Papers in School Finance*. Washington, D.C.: U.S. Department of Health, Education, and Welfare.

Brown, Roger, 1965. *Social Psychology*. New York: The Free Press.

Bruck, Lilly. 1978. *Access: The Guide to a Better Life For Disabled Americans*. New York: Random House.

Burgess, Jane K. 1970. ''The Single Parent Family: A Social and Sociological Problem.'' *The Family Coordinator* 19: 137–144.

Camarillo, Albert. 1979. *Chicanos in a Changing Society: From Mexican Pueblos to American Barrios in Santa Barbara and Southern California.* Cambridge, Mass.: Harvard University Press.

Campbell, Angus, and **Howard Schuman.** 1968. "Racial Attitudes in Fifteen American Cities." Pp. 1–67 in *Supplemental Studies for the National Advisory Commission on Civil Disorders.* Washington, D.C.: U.S. Government Printing Office.

Carmichael, Stokeley, and **Charles V. Hamilton.** 1967. *Black Power: The Politics of Liberation in America.* New York: Vintage Books.

Carter, Thomas P. 1968. "The Negative Self-Concept of Mexican-American Students." *School and Society* 95: 217–219.

Catton, William J., Jr. 1961. "The Functions and Disfunctions of Ethnocentrism: A Theory." *Social Problems* 8: 201–211.

Chamber of Commerce of the United States. 1974. *A Handbook on White Collar Crime.* Washington, D.C.: National District Attorney's Association.

Clark, Kenneth B., and **Mamie P. Clark.** 1958. "Racial Identification and Preference Among Negro Children." Pp. 602–611 in Eleanor Maccoby, Theodore M. Newcomb, and E. L. Hartley (eds.), *Readings in Social Psychology,* third edition. New York: Holt, Rinehart and Winston.

Cockerham, William C. 1978. *Medical Sociology.* Englewood Cliffs, N.J.: Prentice Hall.

Cohen, D., and **M. Lazerson.** "Education and the Industrial Order." Unpublished.

Cohen, Elizabeth G. 1972. "Interracial Interaction Disability." *Human Relations* 25: 9–24.

Cohen, Elizabeth G., Marlaine F. Lockheed, and **Mark R. Lohman.** 1976. "The Center for Interracial Cooperation: A Field Experiment." *Sociology of Education* 49: 47–58.

Cohen, Elizabeth G., and **S. S. Roper.** 1972. "Modification of Interracial Disability: An Application of Status Characteristic Theory." *American Sociological Review* 37: 643–657.

Cohen, Shirley. 1977. *Special People.* Englewood Cliffs, N.J.: Prentice Hall.

Cohn, T. S. 1953. "The Relation of the F-Scale to a Response to Answer Positively." *American Psychologist* 8: 335.

Coleman, James S. 1981. "Public Schools, Private Schools, and the Public Interest." *The Public Interest* 64: 19–30.

Coleman, James S. 1975. "Racial Segregation in the Schools: New Research with New Policy Implications." *Phi Delta Kappan* 57: 75–78.

Coleman, James S., Ernest Q. Campbell, Carol J. Hobson, James McPartland, Alexander Mood, Frederick D. Weinfield, and **Robert L. York.** 1966. *Equality of Educational Opportunity.* Washington, D.C.: U.S. Government Printing Office.

Coleman, James S., Thomas Hoffer, and **Sally Kilgore.** 1981. "Public Schools and Private Schools." Paper presented to conference on "The High School and Beyond," National Center for Education Statistics, Washington, D.C.

Collier, John. 1947. *The Indians of the Americas.* New York: W. W. Norton and Company.

Committee on the Budget, U.S. House of Representatives. 1976. *Working Papers on Major Budget and Program Issues in Selected Health Programs.* Washington, D.C.: U.S. Government Printing Office.

Conot, Robert. 1967. *Rivers of Blood, Years of Darkness.* New York: Bantam Books.

Cooley, Charles Horton. 1964. *Human Nature and the Social Order.* New York: Schocken. (First published in 1909).

Cooper, E., and **Marie Jahoda.** 1947. "The Evasion of Propaganda: How Prejudiced People Respond to Anti-Prejudiced Propaganda." *Journal of Psychology* 23: 15–25.

Cousins, Albert N., and **Hans Nagpaul.** 1979. *Urban Life: The Sociology of Cities and Urban Society.* New York: John Wiley & Sons.

Cox, Oliver Cromwell. 1948. *Caste, Class, and Race*. Garden City, N.Y.: Doubleday.

Cronbach, L. J. 1946. "Response Sets and Test Validity." *Educational and Psychological Measurement* 6: 475−494.

Crouthamel, James L. 1969. "The Springfield, Illinois Race Riot of 1908." Pp. 8−19 in Joseph Boskin, *Urban Racial Violence in the Twenthieth Century*. Beverly Hills, Calif.: Glencoe Press. Reprinted from *Journal of Negro History*. July, 1960: 164−175, 180−181.

Cummings, Scott. 1980. "White Ethnics, Racial Prejudice, and Labor Market Segmentation." *American Journal of Sociology* 85: 938−950.

Davis, David Brion. 1966. *The Problem of Slavery in Western Culture*. Ithaca, N.Y.: Cornell University Press.

Davis, Kingsley, and **Wilbert E. Moore.** 1945. "Some Principles of Stratification." *American Sociological Review* 10: 242−249.

Day, Robert C. 1972. "The Emergence of Activism as a Social Movement." Pp. 506−531 in Howard M. Bahr, Bruce A. Chadwick, and Robert C. Day (eds.), *Native Americans Today*. New York: Harper & Row, Pub.

Debo, Angie. 1970. *A History of the Indians in the United States*. Norman, Oklahoma: University of Oklahoma Press.

De Fleur, Melvin L., and **F. R. Westie.** 1958. "Verbal Attitudes and Overt Acts: An Experiment on the Salience of Attitudes." *American Sociological Review* 23: 667−673.

Degler, Carl N. 1959a. *Out of Our Past*. New York: Harper & Row, Pub.

Degler, Carl N. 1959b. "Slavery and the Genesis of American Race Prejudice." *Comparative Studies in Society and History* 2: 49−66.

Dent, Preston L. 1975. "The Curriculum as a Prejudice-Reduction Technique." *California Journal of Educational Research* 26: 167−177.

Des Moines Register. 1978. "Latinos Likely to Become Dominant Minority in U.S.," by Michael Kilian. Copyright 1977, *Chicago Tribune*. Sunday, January 1, 1978.

Deutsch, Martin. 1963. "The Disadvantaged Child and the Learning Process: Some Social and Developmental Considerations." In A. H. Passow (ed.), *Education in Depressed Areas*. New York: Teachers Press.

Deutsch, Morton, and **Mary Evans Collins.** 1951. *Interracial Housing: A Psychological Evaluation of a Social Experiment*. Minneapolis: University of Minnesota Press.

Dillard, J. L. 1972. *Black English*. New York: Random House.

Dobyns, Henry F. 1966. "Estimating Aboriginal American Population: An Appraisal of Techniques with a New Hemispheric Estimate." *Current Anthropology* 7: 395−416.

Dobzhansky, Theodosius. 1962. *Mankind Evolving*. New Haven, Conn.: Yale University Press.

Dodd, C. H., and **M. E. Sales.** 1970. *Israel and the Arab World*. London: Routledge and Kegan Paul.

Domhoff, G. William. 1967. *Who Rules America?* Englewood Cliffs, N.J.: Prentice Hall.

Dorsen, Norma. 1969. *Discrimination and Civil Rights*. Boston: Little, Brown.

Douglas-Home, Charles. 1968. *The Arabs and Israel*. London: The Bodley Head.

Dowdall, George W. 1974. "White Gains from Black Subordination in 1960 and 1970." *Social Problems* 22: 162−183.

Downs, Anthony. 1970. "Losses Imposed on Urban Households by Uncompensated Highway and Renewal Costs." Pp. 192−229 in Anthony Downs, *Urban Problems and Prospects*. Chicago: Markham Publishing Company.

Drake, St. Clair, and **Horace R. Cayton.** 1945. *Black Metropolis*. New York: Harcourt Brace Jovanovich.

Dreyfuss, Joel, and **Charles Lawrence III.** 1979. *The Bakke Case: The Politics of Inequality*. New York: Harcourt Brace Jovanovich.

Driver, Harold E. 1969. *Indians of North America,* second edition. Chicago: University of Chicago Press.

Durkheim, Emile. 1965. *The Elementary Forms of Religious Life*. Joseph Wald Swain (tr.). New York: The Free Press. (First published in French, 1912.)

Durkheim, Emile. 1964. *The Study of Society*. George Simpson (tr.), New York: The Free Press. (First published in French, 1893.)

Dushkin Publishing Group. 1977. *The Study of Society,* second edition. Gilford, Conn.: Dushkin Publishing Group.

Edmonds, Ronald. 1979. "Some Schools Work and More Can." *Social Policy* 9, 5 (March/April): 28−32.

Edwards, Harry. 1979. "Camouflaging the Color Line: A Critique." Pp. 98−103 in Charles Vert Willie (ed.), *Caste and Class Controversy*. Bayside, N.Y.: General Hall.

Egerton, John. 1970. "Black Executives in Big Business." *Race Relations Reporter* 1 (17): 5.

Ehrlich, Howard J. *The Social Psychology of Prejudice*. New York: Wiley Interscience. 1973.

Elkins, Stanley M. 1959. *Slavery: A Problem in American Institutional and Intellectual Life*. Chicago: University of Chicago Press.

Epp, Frank H. 1970. *Whose Land Is Palestine?* Grand Rapids: William B. Erdmans Publishing Company.

Esposito, D. 1973. "Homogeneous and Heterogeneous Ability Grouping: Principal Findings and Implications for Evaluating and Designing More Effective Educational Environments." *Review of Education Research* 43: 163−179.

Evans, Franklin R. 1977. "The Social Impact of *Bakke*." *Learning and the Law,* Spring.

Ewens, William L., and **Howard J. Ehrlich.** 1969. "Reference Other Support and Ethnic Attitudes as Predictors of Intergroup Behavior." Revised version of paper presented to the joint meetings of the Midwest Sociological Society and Ohio Valley Sociological Society, Indianapolis, Ind., May.

Eysenck, Hans J. 1971. *The IQ Argument*. New York: Library Press.

Fantini, Mario D. 1969. Participation, Decentralization, Community Control, and Quality Education." *The Record* 71: 93−107.

Fantini, Mario D., and **Marilyn Gittell.** 1973. *Decentralization: Achieving Reform*. New York: Praeger Publishers.

Fantini, Mario D., Marilyn Gittell, and **Richard Magat.** 1970. *Community Control and the Urban School*. New York: Praeger Publishers.

Farley, John E. 1981. "Black Male Unemployment in U.S. Metropolitan Areas: The Role of Black Central City Segregation and Job Decentralization." Paper presented to annual meetings of the Society for the Study of Social Problems, Toronto, Ontario.

Farley, John E. 1980. "Handicapped Persons in Madison County and Their Housing Needs." Report to Madison County, Illinois Community Development Department. Edwardsville, Ill.: Southern Illinois University at Edwardsville Center for Urban and Environmental Research and Services.

Farley, Reynolds. 1979. "Racial Progress in the Last Two Decades: What Can We Determine About Who Benefitted and Why?" Paper presented to the Annual Meeting of the American Sociological Association, Boston, Mass.

Farley, Reynolds. 1977. "Trends in Racial Inequalities: Have the Gains of the 1960's Disappeared in the 1970's?" *American Sociological Review* 42: 189−208.

Farley, Reynolds. 1975. "School Integration and White Flight." Unpublished paper, Population Studies Center. The University of Michigan.

Farley, Reynolds, Suzanne Bianchi, and **Diane Colasanto.** 1979. "Barriers to the Racial Integration of Neighborhoods: The Detroit Case."*The Annals of the American Academy of Political and Social Science* 441 (January): 97−113.

Farley, Reynolds, Shirley Hatchett, and **Howard Schuman.** 1979. "A Note on Changes in Black Racial Attitudes in Detroit: 1968−1976." *Social Indicators Research* 6: 439−443.

Farley, Reynolds, Howard Schuman, Suzanne Bianchi, Diane Colasanto, and **Shirley Hatchett.** 1978. "Chocolate City, Vanilla Suburbs: Will the Trend Toward Racially Separate Communities Continue?" *Social Science Research* 7: 319–344.

Feagin, Joe R. 1978. *Racial and Ethnic Relations.* Englewood Cliffs, N.J.: Prentice-Hall.

Feagin, Joe R. 1972. "Poverty: We Still Believe That God Helps Those Who Help Themselves." *Psychology Today,* November.

Feagin, Joe R., and **Clairece Booher Feagin.** 1978. *Discrimination American Style: Institutional Racism and Sexism.* Englewood Cliffs, N.J.: Prentice-Hall.

Feagin, Joe R., and **Harlan Hahn.** 1973. *Ghetto Riots: The Politics of Violence in American Cities.* New York: Macmillan.

Federal Bureau of Investigation. 1979. *Uniform Crime Reports, 1978.* Washington, D.C.: U.S. Government Printing Office.

Fendrich, J. M. 1967. "Perceived Reference Group Support: Racial Attitudes and Overt Behavior." *American Sociological Review* 32: 960–970.

Ferdinand, Theodore N., and **Elmer G. Luchterhand.** 1970. "Inner City Youth, the Police, the Juvenile Court, and Justice." *Social Problems* 17: 510–527.

Fernandes, Florestan. 1971. *The Negro in Brazilian Society.* New York: Atheneum.

Festinger, Leon. 1957. *A Theory of Cognitive Dissonance.* Stanford, Calif.: Stanford University Press.

Festinger, Leon, and **J. M. Carlsmith.** 1959. "Cognitive Consequences of Forced Compliance." *Journal of Abnormal and Social Psychology* 58: 203–210.

Ficket, Joan G. 1975. "'Merican: An Inner City Dialect—Aspects of Morphemics, Syntax, and Semology." *Studies in Linguistics—Occasional Papers* 13.

Fineberg, S. A. 1949. *Punishment Without Crime.* New York: Doubleday.

Firestine, Robert E. 1977. "Economic Growth and Inequality, Demographic Change, and the Public Sector Response." Pp. 191–210 in David C. Perry and Alfred J. Watkins (eds.), *The Rise of the Sunbelt Cities.* Volume 14, *Urban Affairs Annual Reviews.* Beverly Hills: Sage Publications.

Flores, Solomon Hernandez. 1978. *The Nature and Effects of Bilingual Education Programs for the Spanish-Speaking Child in the United States.* New York: Arno Press.

Flowerman, Samuel H. 1947. "Mass Propaganda in the War Against Bigotry." *Journal of Abnormal and Social Psychology* 42: 429–439.

Fogelson, Robert. 1971. *Violence as Protest: A Study of Riots and Ghettos.* New York: Doubleday.

Fogelson, Robert, and **R. B. Hill.** 1968. "Who Riots? A Study of Participation in the 1967 Riots." Pp. 217–248 in *Supplemental Studies for the National Advisory Commission on Civil Disorders.* Washington, D.C.: U.S. Government Printing Office.

Foote, Caleb. 1958. "A Study of the Administration of Bail in New York City." *University of Pennsylvania Law Review* 106.

Ford, W. Scott. 1973. "Interracial Public Housing in a Border City: Another Look at the Contact Hypothesis." *American Journal of Sociology* 78: 1426–1447.

Foster, William Z. 1920. *The Great Steel Strike and Its Lessons.* New York: Huebsch.

Franklin, John Hope. 1969. *From Slavery to Freedom: A History of Negro Americans,* third edition. New York: Vintage Books.

Frazier, E. Franklin. 1966. *The Negro Family in the United States* (revised edition). Chicago: The University of Chicago Press.

Freeman, Jo. 1973. "The Origins of the Women's Liberation Movement." *American Journal of Sociology* 78: 782–811.

Freeman, Richard. 1978. "Black Economic Progress Since 1964." *The Public Interest* 52: 52–68.

Freud, Sigmund. 1962. *Civilization and Its Discontents.* James Strachey (tr.). New York: Norton. (First published in German, 1930.)

Freyre, Gilberto. 1946. *The Masters and the Slaves: A Study in the Development of Brazilian Civilization.* New York: Knopf.

Friedenberg, E. Z. 1965. *Coming of Age in America.* New York: Random House.

Frisbie, W. Parker. 1977. "The Scale and Growth of World Urbanization." Pp. 44–58 in John Walton and Donald E. Carns (eds.), *Cities in Change: Studies on the Urban Condition.* Boston: Allyn and Bacon.

Fuchs, Estelle, and **Robert J. Havighurst.** 1972. *To Live on This Earth.* Garden City, N.Y.: Doubleday.

Fuerst, J. S. 1981. "Report Card: Chicago's All-Black Schools." *The Public Interest* 64: 79–91.

Gans, Herbert. 1979. "Symbolic Ethnicity: The Future of Ethnic Groups and Cultures in America." *Ethnic and Racial Studies* 2: 1–20.

Gans, Herbert. 1974. Foreword in Neil C. Sandberg, *Ethnic Identity and Assimilation: The Polish American Community.* New York: Praeger.

Gans, Herbert. 1973. *More Equality.* New York: Pantheon Books.

Gans, Herbert. 1971. "The Uses of Poverty: The Poor Pay All." *Social Policy,* July/August.

Gans, Herbert. 1967. "The Negro Family: Reflections on the Moynihan Report." Pp. 445–457 in Lee Rainwater and William L. Yancey (eds.) *The Moynihan Report and the Politics of Controversy.* Cambridge, Mass.: The M.I.T. Press.

Garbarino, Merwyn S. 1976. *American Indian Heritage.* Boston: Little, Brown.

Garfinkel, Harold. 1949. "Research Note on Inter- and Intra-Racial Homocides." *Social Forces* 27: 369–381.

Geschwender, James A. 1964. "Social Structure and the Negro Revolt." *Social Forces* 43: 248–256.

Geschwender, James A., and **B. D. Singer.** 1970. "Deprivation and the Detroit Riot." *Social Problems* 17: 457–463.

Gibson, Geoffrey, George Bugbee, and **Odin W. Anderson.** 1970. *Emergency Medical Services in the Chicago Area.* Chicago: University of Chicago, Center for Health Administration.

Gilbert, G. M. 1951. "Stereotype Persistence and Change Among College Students." *Journal of Abnormal and Social Psychology* (April): 245–254.

Gintis, Herbert. 1971. "Education, Technology, and Worker Productivity." *American Economic Review* 61 (American Economic Association Proceedings): 266–279.

Glass, Thomas E., and **William P. Sanders.** 1978. *Community Control in Education: A Study in Power Transition.* Midland, Mich.: Pendell Publishing Company.

Glazer, Nathan. 1976. *Affirmative Discrimination.* New York: Basic Books.

Glazer, Nathan. 1971. "Blacks and Ethnic Groups: The Difference, and the Political Difference It Makes." *Social Problems* 18: 444–461.

Glazer, Nathan, and **Daniel Patrick Moynihan.** 1970. *Beyond the Melting Pot.* Cambridge, Mass.: The M.I.T. Press.

Glenn, Norval. 1966. "White Gains From Negro Subordination." *Social Problems* 14: 159–178.

Glenn, Norval. 1963. "Occupational Benefits to Whites from the Subordination of Negroes." *American Sociological Review* 28: 443–448.

Gliedman, John. 1979. "The Wheelchair Rebellion." *Psychology Today,* August.

Gobineau, Arthur de. 1915. *The Inequality of Human Races.* Adrian Collins (tr.). New York: Putnam's. (First published in French, 1853–1855.)

Goering, John M. 1971. "The Emergence of Ethnic Interests: A Case of Serendipity." *Social Forces* 49: 379–384.

Golden, Mark, and **B. Birns.** 1968. "Social Class and Cognitive Development in Infancy." *Merrill-Palmer Quarterly* 14: 139–149.

Goldstein, Joseph. 1960. "Police Discretion Not to Invoke the Criminal Process: Low

Visibility Decisions in the Administration of Justice.'' *Yale Law Journal* 69 (March).

Gonzales, Nancie L. 1967. *The Spanish Americans of New Mexico: A Distinctive Heritage*. Advance Report 9. University of California, Los Angeles: Mexican-American Study Project.

Gordon, Milton M. 1978. *Human Nature, Class, and Ethnicity*. New York: Oxford University Press.

Gordon, Milton M. 1964. *Assimilation in American Life*. New York: Oxford University Press.

Goren, Arthur A. 1980. ''Jews.'' Pp. 571–598 in Stephan Thernstrom, Ann Orlov, and Oscar Handlin (eds.), *Harvard Encyclopedia of American Ethnic Groups*. Cambridge, Mass.: Harvard University Press.

Gossett, Thomas F. 1963. *Race: The History of an Idea in America*. Dallas: Southern Methodist University Press.

Gouldner, Helen, with **Mayr Symons Strong.** 1978. *Teachers' Pets, Troublemakers, Nobodies: Black Children in Elementary School*. Westport, Conn.: Greenwood Press.

Grams, Robert, and **Rachel Rohde.** 1976. Unpublished report to Judges Committee, Hennepin County, Minnesota District Court.

Grant, Madison. 1916. *The Passing of the Great Race or the Racial Basis of European History*. New York: Scribner's.

Grebler, Leo, Joan W. Moore, and **Ralph C. Guzman.** 1970. *The Mexican-American People*. New York: The Free Press.

Greeley, Andrew M. 1981. ''Minority Students in Catholic Secondary Schools.'' Paper presented to conference on ''The High School and Beyond,'' National Center for Educational Statistics, Washington, D.C.

Greeley, Andrew M. 1977. *The American Catholic: A Social Portrait*. New York: Basic Books.

Greeley, Andrew M. 1974. *Ethnicity in the United States: A Preliminary Reconnaissance*. New York: John Wiley & Sons.

Greeley, Andrew M. 1971. *Why Can't They Be Like Us?* New York: Dutton.

Greeley, Andrew M. 1970. ''Religious Intermarriage in a Denominational Society.'' *American Journal of Sociology* 75: 949–952.

Greeley, Andrew M., and **Paul B. Sheatsley.** 1971. ''Attitudes Toward Racial Integration.'' *Scientific American* 225, 6: 13–19.

Green, Edward. 1970. ''Race, Social Status, and Criminal Arrest.'' *American Sociological Review* 35: 476–490.

Greenberg, Michael R., and **Nicholas Valente.** 1976. ''Recent Economic Trends in the Major Northeastern Metropolises.'' Pp. 77–100 in George Sternlieb and James W. Hughes (eds.), *Post-Industrial America: Metropolitan Decline and Interregional Job Shift*. New Brunswick, N.J.: Rutgers University Center for Urban Policy Research.

Grimshaw, Allan D. 1959. ''Lawlessness and Violence in America and Their Special Manifestations of Changing Negro-White Relationships.'' *Journal of Negro History* 64: 52–72.

Grossman, Barry A. 1974. ''The Discretionary Enforcement of Law.'' In Sawyer F. Sylvester and Edward Sagarin (eds.), *Politics and Crime*. New York: Praeger.

Guest, Avery M., and **James A. Weed.** 1976. ''Ethnic Residential Segregation: Patterns of Change.'' *American Journal of Sociology* 81: 1088–1111.

Guzman, Ralph. ''Mexican American Casualties in Viet Nam.'' *La Raza* 1 (n.d.): 12.

Hagan, John. 1974. ''Extra-Legal Attributes and Criminal Sentencing: An Assessment of a Sociological Viewpoint.'' *Law and Society Review* 8: 357–383.

Haggard, Ernest A. 1954. ''Social Status and Intelligence.'' *Genetic Psychology Monographs* 49: 141–186.

Haimowitz, Morris L., and **Natalie R. Haimowitz.** 1950. ''Reducing Ethnic Hostility Through Psychotherapy.'' *Journal of Social Psychology* (May): 231–241.

Haley, Alex (ed.). 1964. *The Autobiography of Malcolm X.* New York: Grove Press.

Hall, Edwin L., and **Albert A. Simkus.** 1975. "Inequality in Types of Sentence Received by Native Americans and Whites." *Criminology* 13, 2: 199−222.

Hall, Raymond L. 1978. *Black Separatism in the United States.* Hanover, N.H.: The University Press of New England.

Hamilton, Charles V. 1978. "Blacks and Electoral Politics." *Social Policy* 9: 21−27.

Hamilton, Gloria, and **J. David Roesner.** 1972. "How Employers Screen Disadvantaged Workers." *Monthly Labor Review* (September).

Handin, Oscar, and **Mary F. Handin.** 1950. "Origins of the Southern Labor System." *William and Mary Quarterly* 7: 199−222.

Hannerz, Ulf. 1969. *Soulside.* New York: Columbia University Press.

Hansen, Marcus L. 1966. "The Third Generation." Pp. 255−272 in Oscar Handlin (ed.), *Children of the Uprooted.* New York: Harper & Row, Pub.

Hansen, Marcus L. 1952. "The Third Generation in America." *Commentary* 14: 492−500.

Harding, John, Harold Proshansky, Bernard Kutner, and **Isador Chein.** 1969. "Prejudice and Ethnic Relations." Pp. 1−77 in Gardner Lindzey and Elliott Aronson (eds.), *The Handbook of Social Psychology,* second edition, Volume 5. Reading, Mass.: Addison-Wesley.

Harris Poll. 1980. "Most Vietnam Veterans Glad They Served, Would Again, Poll Says." *St. Louis Globe Democrat,* July 2, 1980.

Harrison, Bennett. 1972. *Education, Training, and the Urban Ghetto.* Baltimore: Johns Hopkins University Press.

Hartley, E. M. 1946. *Problems in Prejudice.* New York: King's Crown Press.

Harvey, D. G., and **G. T. Slatin.** 1975. "The Relationship as Hypothesis." *Social Forces* 54: 140−159.

Hauser, Robert M., William H. Sewell, and **Duane F. Alwin.** 1976. "High School Effects on Achievement." Pp. 309−341 in William H. Sewell, Robert M. Hauser, and David L. Featherman (eds.), *Schooling and Achievement in American Society.* New York: Academic Press.

Hawkins, Hugh. 1962. *Booker T. Washington and His Critics: The Problem of Negro Leadership.* Boston: D. C. Heath & Co.

Haynes, M. Alfred, and **Michael R. Garvey.** 1969. "Physicians, Patients, and Hospitals in the Inner City." Pp. 117−124 in John C. Norman (ed.), *Medicine in the Ghetto.* New York: Appleton-Century-Crofts.

Heer, David H. 1980. "Intermarriage." Pp. 513−521 in Stephan Thernstrom, Ann Orlov, and Oscar Handlin (eds.), *The Harvard Encyclopedia of American Ethnic Groups.* Cambridge, Mass.: Harvard University Press.

Helms, L. Jay, Joseph P. Newhouse, and **Charles E. Phelps.** 1978. *Copayments and Demand For Medical Care: The California Medicaid Experience.* Santa Monica, Calif.: Rand Corporation (Report Number R-2167-HEW).

Herberg, Will. 1960. *Protestant-Catholic-Jew,* revised edition. Garden City, N.Y.: Doubleday Anchor Books.

Hermalin, Albert I., and **Reynolds Farley.** 1973. "The Potential for Residential Integration in Cities and Suburbs: Implications for the Busing Controversy." *American Sociological Review* 38: 595−610.

Hernstein, Richard J. 1971. "I.Q." *Atlantic Monthly* (September): 43−64.

Hershberg, Theodore, Hans Burstein, Eugene P. Ericksen., Stephanie Greenberg, and **William L. Yancey.** 1978. "A Tale of Three Cities: Blacks and Immigrants in Philadelphia: 1850−1880, 1930, and 1970." *Annals of the American Academy of Political and Social Science* 441 (January): 55−81.

Higham, John. 1974. "Integration Vs. Pluralism: Another American Dilemma." *Center Magazine* 7 (July−August): 67−73.

Hill, Robert. 1972. *The Strengths of Black Families.* New York: Emerson Hall.

Hindelang, Michael J. 1969. "Equality Under the Law." *Journal of Criminal Law, Criminology, and Police Science* 60: 306−313.

Hines, Ralph. 1972. "The Health Status of Black Americans: Changing Perspectives." Pp. 40−50 in E. Jaco (ed.), *Patients, Physicians, and Illness,* second edition. New York: Free Press.

Hitler, Adolf. 1940. *Mein Kampf.* New York: Reynmal and Hitchcock, 1940. (First published in German, 1925−1927).

Horton, John. 1966. "Order and Conflict Theories of Social Problems as Competing Ideologies." *American Journal of Sociology* 71: 701−713. Reprinted in Norman R. Yetman and C. Hoy Steele, *Majority and Minority,* second edition. Boston: Allyn and Bacon (1975).

Hovland, Carl I., Irving L. Janis, and **Harold H. Kelly.** 1953. *Communication and Persuasion.* New Haven: Yale University Press.

Humm, Andrew. 1980. "The Personal Politics of Lesbian and Gay Liberation." *Social Policy* 11 (2): 40−45.

Hunt, Chester, and **Lewis Walker.** 1974. *Ethnic Dynamics: Patterns of Intergroup Relations in Various Societies.* Homewood, Ill.: The Dorsey Press.

Hunter, Guy. 1965. *Industrialisation and Race Relations.* London: Oxford University Press.

Hurley, Roger. 1971. "The Health Crisis of the Poor." Pp. 83−112 in Hans Peter Dreitzel (ed.), *The Social Organization of Health.* New York: Macmillan.

Hurn, Christopher. 1978. *The Limits and Possibilities of Schooling: An Introduction to the Sociology of Education.* Boston: Allyn and Bacon.

Hutchinson, Peter M. 1974. "The Effects of Accessibility and Segregation on the Employment of the Urban Poor." Pp. 74−96 in George M. von Furstenberg, Bennett Harrison, and Ann R. Horowitz (eds.), *Patterns of Racial Discrimination, Vol. 1: Housing.* Lexington, Mass.: Lexington Books.

Hyman, Herbert H., and **Paul B. Sheatsley.** 1964. "Attitudes Toward Desegration." *Scientific American* 211: 2−9.

Ichihashi, Yamato. 1969. *Japanese in the United States.* New York: Arno Press and the New York Times. (First published by Stanford University Press, 1932.)

Illinois Capital Development Board. 1977. *The East St. Louis Area: An Overview of State Capital Projects and Policies.* Springfield, Ill.: Illinois Capital Development Board.

Irizarry, Ruddie A. 1978. *Bilingual Education: State and Federal Legislative Mandates.* Los Angeles: National Dissemination and Assessment Center, California State University.

Jahoda, N. M. "X-Ray of the Racist Mind." *UNESCO Courier* (October, 1960).

Jaquet, Constant H., Jr. (ed.). 1979. *Yearbook of American and Canadian Churches, 1979.* Nashville: Abington Press.

Jencks, Christopher, Marshall Smith, Henry Acland, Mary Jo Bane, David Cohen, Herbert Gintis, Barbara Heyns, and **Stephan Michelson.** 1972. *Inequality: A Reassessment of the Effect of Family and Schooling in America.* New York: Basic Books.

Jensen, Arthur. 1980. *Bias in Mental Testing.* New York: Free Press.

Jensen, Arthur. 1973. *Educability and Group Differences.* New York: Harper & Row, Pub.

Jensen, Arthur. 1969. "How Much Can We Boost IQ and Scholastic Achievement?" *Harvard Educational Review* 39: 1−123.

Johnson, Charles S. 1943. *Patterns of Negro Segregation.* New York: Harper & Row, Pub.

Johnson, Guy B. 1941. "The Negro and Crime." *The Annals of the American Academy of Political and Social Science* 217: 93−104.

Joint Center for Political Studies. 1977. *National Roster of Black Elected Officials,* Vol. 7. Washington, D.C.: Joint Center for Political Studies.

Jones, James M. 1972. *Prejudice and Racism.* Reading, Mass.: Addison-Wesley.

Jordan, Winthrop D. 1968. *White Over Black.* Chapel Hill: University of North Carolina Press.

Jordan, Winthrop D. 1962. "Modern Tensions and the Origins of American Slavery." *The Journal of Southern History* 18: 18−30.

Josephy, Alvin M., Jr. 1968. *The Indian Heritage of America.* New York: Alfred A. Knopf. (Bantam Edition, 1969).

Kadish, Mortimer R., and **Sanford H. Kadish.** 1973. *Discretion to Disobey.* Palo Alto: Stanford University Press.

Kagan, Jerome. 1971. "The Magical Aura of the IQ." *Saturday Review of Literature,* December 4: 92−93.

Kain, John F. 1968. "Housing Segregation, Negro Employment, and Metropolitan Decentralization." *Quarterly Journal of Economics,* May: 175−197.

Kamin, Leon J. 1974. *The Science and Politics of IQ.* New York: John Wiley & Sons.

Kane, Michael B. 1970. *Minorities in Textbooks: A Study of Their Treatment in Social Science Texts.* Chicago: Quadrangle.

Kantrowitz, Nathan. 1979. "Racial and Ethnic Residential Segregation in Boston 1930−1970." *Annals of the American Academy of Political and Social Science* 441 (January): 41−54.

Karlins, Marvin, Thomas Goffman, and **Gary Walters.** 1969. "On the Fading of Social Stereotypes: Studies in Three Generations of College Students." *Journal of Personality and Social Psychology* 13: 1−6.

Kasarda, John D. 1976. "The Changing Occupational Structure of the American Metropolis: Apropos the Urban Problem." Pp. 113−136 in Barry Schwartz (ed.), *The Changing Face of the Suburbs.* Chicago: The University of Chicago Press.

Katz, Donald, and **Kenneth Braly.** 1933. "Racial Stereotypes of One Hundred College Students." *Journal of Abnormal Psychology.* (October−December): 280−290.

Katz, Donald, I. Sarnoff, and **C. McClintock.** 1956. "Ego Defense and Attitude Change." *Human Relations* 9: 27−46.

Katz, Phyllis A., and **Sue R. Zalk.** 1974. "Doll Preferences: Index of Racial Attitudes?" *Journal of Educational Psychology* 66: 663−668.

Keddie, Nell. 1971. "Classroom Knowledge." Pp. 133−160 in M.F.D. Young (ed.), *Knowledge and Control.* London: Collier.

Kelman, H. C. 1958. "Compliance, Identification, and Internalization: Three Processes of Attitude Change." *Journal of Conflict Resolution* 2: 51−60.

Kendall, Patricia L., and **Katherine M. Wolf.** 1949. "The Analysis of Deviant Cases in Communication Research." In Paul F. Lazarsfeld and Frank N. Stanton (eds.), *Communications Research, 1948−1949.* New York: Harper & Row, Pub.

Kennedy, Ruby Jo Reeves. 1952. "Single or Triple Melting Pot? Intermarriage in New Haven, 1870−1950." *American Journal of Sociology* 58: 56−69.

Kennedy, Ruby Jo Reeves. 1944. "Single or Triple Melting Pot? Intermarriage Trends in New Haven, 1870−1940." *American Journal of Sociology* 49: 331−339.

Killian, Lewis M. 1975. *The Impossible Revolution, Phase 2: Black Power and the American Dream.* New York: Random House.

Killian, Lewis M. 1968. *The Impossible Revolution?* New York: Random House.

Kinloch, Graham C. 1979. *The Sociology of Minority Group Relations.* Englewood Cliffs, N.J.: Prentice Hall.

Kinloch, Graham C. 1974. *The Dynamics of Race Relations: A Sociological Analysis.* New York: McGraw Hill.

Kinsey, Alfred. 1953. *Sexual Behavior in the Human Female.* Philadelphia: W. B. Saunders.

Kinsey, Alfred. 1948. *Sexual Behavior in the Human Male.* Philadelphia: W. B. Saunders.

Kitagawa, Evelyn M. 1972. "Socioeconomic Differences in Mortality in the United States and Some Implications for Population Policy." Pp. 153–166 in Charles C. Westoff and Robert Parke, Jr. (eds.), *Demographic and Social Aspects of Population Growth,* Volume 1, Commission on Population Growth and the American Future. Washington, D.C.: U.S. Government Printing Office.

Kitagawa, Evelyn, and **Philip M. Hauser.** 1973. *Differential Mortality in the United States: A Study in Socioeconomic Epidemiology.* Cambridge, Mass.: Harvard University Press.

Kitano, Harry H. L. 1974. *Race Relations.* Englewood Cliffs, N.J.: Prentice Hall.

Kloss, Robert Marsh, Ron E. Roberts, and **Dean S. Dorn.** 1976. *Sociology With A Human Face.* St. Louis: C. V. Mosby Company.

Kobler, Arthur L. 1975. "Police Homocide in a Democracy." *Journal of Social Issues* 31: 163–184.

Kohlberg, Lawrence. 1969. "Stage and Sequence: The Cognitive-Developmental Approach to Socialization." Pp. 347–480 in David A. Goslin (ed.), *Handbook of Socialization Theory and Research.* Chicago: Rand McNally.

Koos, Earl. 1954. *The Health of Regionsville.* New York: Columbia University Press.

Korfhage, Darlene W. 1972. "Differential Treatment in the Municipal Court System." Unpublished masters thesis, Washington State University.

Kramer, Bernard M. 1949. "The Dimensions of Prejudice." *Journal of Psychology* (April): 389–451.

Kroeber, Alfred L. 1939. *Cultural and Natural Areas of Native North America.* University of California Publications in American Archeology and Ethnology 38.

Krute, Aaron, and **Mary Ellen Burdette.** 1978. "Disability Survey '72: Disabled and Non-Disabled Adults. Report 10-Chronic Disease, Injury, and Work Disability." Washington, D.C.: Social Security Administration. Publication Number (55A) 78-11700.

Kutner, B., C. Wilkins, and **P. R. Yarrow.** 1952. "Verbal Attitudes and Overt Behavior Involving Racial Prejudice." *Journal of Abnormal and Social Psychology* 47: 649–652.

Kuykendall, Jack L. 1970. "Police and Minority Groups: Toward a Theory of Negative Contact." *Police* 15: 47–56.

Labov, William. 1972. "Academic Ignorance and Black Intelligence." *Atlantic Monthly* (June): 59–67.

Labov, William, and **P. Cohen.** 1967. "Systematic Relations of Standard and Nonstandard Rules in the Grammars of Negro Speakers." *Project Literacy Reports,* No. 8. Ithaca, N.Y.: Cornell University.

La Fave, Wayne R. 1965. *Arrest: The Decision to Take a Suspect Into Custody.* Boston: Little, Brown.

Lampman, Robert. 1962. *The Share of Top Wealth Holders in National Wealth.* Princeton, N.J.: Princeton University Press.

Landis, Judson T. 1962. "A Comparison of Children from Divorced and Nondivorced Unhappy Marriages." *The Family Life Coordinator* 11: 61–65.

La Piere, R. T. 1934. "Attitudes Versus Actions." *Social Forces* 13: 230–237.

Larson, Calvin J., and **Stan R. Nikkel.** 1979. *Urban Problems: Perspectives on Corporations, Governments, and Cities.* Boston: Allyn and Bacon.

Lauter, Paul, and **Florence Howe.** 1970. *The Conspiracy of the Young.* New York: Crowell.

Leacock, E. B. 1969. *Teaching and Learning in City Schools.* New York: Basic Books.

Lebergott, Stanley. 1976. *The American Economy: Income, Wealth, and Want.* Princeton, N.J.: Princeton University Press.

Legum, Colin. 1975. "Color and Race in the South African Situation." Pp. 98–105 in Norman R. Yetman and C. Hoy Steele (eds.), *Majority and Minority: The Dynamics of Racial and Ethnic Relations.* Boston: Allyn and Bacon. Reprinted from *Daedalus* 96 (1967): 483–495.

Lessing, Elise E., and **Chester C. Clarke.** 1976. "An Attempt to Reduce Ethnic Prejudice and Assess Its Correlates in a Junior High School Sample." *Educational Research Quarterly* 1 (2): 3–16.

Lewin, Kurt. 1948. *Resolving Social Conflicts.* New York: Harper & Row, Pub.

Lewis, Oscar. 1965. *La Vida: A Puerto Rican Family in the Culture of Poverty.* New York: Random House.

Lewis, Oscar. 1959. *Five Families: Mexican Case Studies in the Culture of Poverty.* New York: Basic Books.

Licht, Hans. 1932. *Sexual Life in Ancient Greece.* London: Routledge.

Lieberson, Stanley. 1961. "A Societal Theory of Race Relations." *American Sociological Review* 26: 902–910.

Light, Donald Jr., and **Suzanne Keller.** 1979. *Sociology.* New York: Alfred A. Knopf.

Lincoln, C. Eric. 1973. *The Black Muslims in America,* revised edition. Boston: Beacon Press.

Lipset, Seymour Martin. 1959. "Democracy and Working Class Authoritarianism." *American Sociological Review* 24: 498–501.

Lipset, Seymour Martin, and **Earl Raab.** 1973. "An Appointment with Watergate." *Commentary,* September: 35–43.

Litcher, J. H., and **D. W. Johnson.** 1969. "Changes in Attitudes Toward Negroes of White Elementary School Students After Use of Multiethnic Readers." *Journal of Educational Psychology* 60: 148–152.

Little, Allan, and **George Smith.** 1971. *Strategies of Compensation: A Review of Educational Projects for the Disadvantaged in the United States.* Paris: Organization for Economic Cooperation and Development.

Litwack, Leon F. 1961. *North of Slavery: The Negro in the Free States, 1790–1860.* Chicago: University of Chicago Press.

Long, Larry H., and **Paul C. Glick.** 1976. "Family Patterns in Suburban Areas: Recent Trends." Pp. 39–68 in Barry Schwartz (ed.), *The Changing Face of the Suburbs.* Chicago: The University of Chicago Press.

Lundman, Richard J. 1980. *Police and Policing: An Introduction.* New York: Holt, Rinehart and Winston.

Lurie, Nancy Oestreich. 1975. "The American Indian: Historical Background." Pp. 169–183 in Norman R. Yetman and C. Hoy Steele, *Majority and Minority: The Dynamics of Race and Ethnic Relations.* Boston: Allyn and Bacon.

Lynd, Robert S., and **Helen Merrell Lynd.** 1929. *Middletown: A Study in Contemporary American Culture.* New York: Harcourt Brace Jovanovich, Inc.

Luzar, Irving. 1981. "Early Intervention is Effective." *Educational Leadership* 38: 303–305.

McCutcheon, Gail, Diane Kyle, and **Robert Skovira.** 1979. "Characters in Basal Readers: Does 'Equal' Now Mean 'Same'?" *The Reading Teacher* 32: 438–441.

McGinley, P., and **H. McGinley.** 1970. "Reading Groups as Psychological Groups." *Journal of Experimental Education* 39: 36–42.

McGuire, William J. 1968. "Personality and Susceptibility to Social Influence." Pp. 1130–1187 in Edgar F. Borgatta and William W. Lambert (eds.), *Handbook of Personality Theory and Research.* Chicago: Rand McNally.

Mackay, Robert. 1974. "Standardized Tests: Objective/Objectified Measures of Competence." In Aaron Cicourel (ed.), *Language Use and School Performance,* New York: Academic Press.

MacKinnon, William, and **Richard Centers.** 1956. "Authoritarianism and Urban Stratification." *American Journal of Sociology* 61: 610–620.

McWilliams, Carey. 1951. *Brothers Under the Skin,* revised edition. Boston: Little Brown.

McWilliams Carey. 1949. *North from Mexico.* Philadelphia: Lippincott Company.

Madsen, William. 1973. *The Mexican-Americans of South Texas,* second edition. New York: Holt, Rinehart and Winston.

Mandelbaum, D. G. 1952. *Soldier Groups and Negro Soldiers.* Berkeley: University of California Press.

Marrett, Cora Bagley. 1980. "The Precariousness of Social Class in Black America." *Contemporary Sociology* 9: 16–19.

Marshall, Ray. 1965. *The Negro and Organized Labor.* New York: John Wiley & Sons.

Marx, Karl. 1971. *A Contribution to the Critique of Political Economy.* Maurice Dobb (ed. and tr.). New York: International Publishers. (First published in 1859.)

Marx, Karl. 1967. *Capital, a Critique of Political Economy.* Three vols., Friedrich Engels (ed.), Samuel Moore and Edward Aveling (trs.). New York: International Publishers. (First published in German, 1867–1894.)

Marx, Karl. 1964. *Selected Works in Sociology and Social Philosophy.* Thomas B. Bottomore and Maximilien Rubel (eds. and trs.). New York: McGraw-Hill.

Mason, Philip. 1971. *Patterns of Dominance.* London: Oxford University Press.

Mason, Philip. 1960. *Year of Decision: Rhodesia and Nyasaland in 1960.* London: Oxford University Press.

Masters, Stanley H. 1975. *Black-White Income Differentials: Empirical Studies and Policy Implications.* New York: Academic Press.

Mead, George Herbert. 1967. *Mind, Self, and Society.* Chicago: University of Chicago Press. (First published in 1934.)

Mehan, Hugh. 1974. "Accomplishing Classroom Lesson." In Aaron Cicourel (ed.), *Language Use and School Performance.* New York: Academic Press.

Meier, August, and **Elliot Rudwick.** 1970a. *From Plantation to Ghetto: The Interpretative History of American Negroes,* revised edition. New York: Athenium Publishers.

Meier, August, and **Elliott Rudwick** (eds.). 1970b. *Black Protest in the Sixties.* Chicago: Quadrangle Books.

Meier, August, and **Elliott Rudwick.** 1969. "The Boycott Against Jim Crow Streetcars in the South." *Journal of American History* 55: 756–759.

Meier, Matt S., and **Felicano Rivera.** 1972. *The Chicanos: A History of Mexican Americans.* New York: Hill and Wang.

Melman, Seymour. 1976. "The Federal Ripoff of New York's Money." Pp. 181–188 in Roger E. Alcaly and David Mermelstein (eds.), *The Fiscal Crisis of American Cities.* New York: Vintage Books.

Merton, Robert K. 1949. *Social Theory and Social Structure.* New York: Free Press. (Reprint of "The Self-Fulfilling Prophecy," 1948. Antioch Review: Summer.)

Michelson, Stephan. 1972. "The Political Economy of School Finance," in Martin Carnoy (ed.,) *Schooling in Corporate Society.* New York: McKay.

Middleton, Russel. 1960. "Ethnic Prejudice and Susceptibility to Persuasion." *American Sociological Review* 25: 679–686.

Mills, C. Wright. 1956. *The Power Elite.* New York: Oxford University Press.

Mittnick, Leonard, and **Elliott McGinnies.** 1958. "Influencing Ethnocentrism in Small Discussion Groups Through a Film Communication." *Journal of Abnormal and Social Psychology* 56: 423–441.

Molotch, Harvey. 1972. *Managed Integration: Dilemmas of Doing Good in the City.* Berkeley: University of California Press.

Montagu, M. F. Ashley. 1964. *Man's Most Dangerous Myth: The Fallacy of Race,* fourth edition. Cleveland: The World Publishing Company.

Montagu, M. F. Ashley. 1963. *Race, Science and Humanity.* Princeton, N.J.: D. Van Nostrand.

Mooney, Joseph D. 1969. "Housing Segregation, Negro Unemployment, and Metropolitan Decentralization: An Alternative Perspective." *Quarterly Journal of Economics,* May: 299–311.

Moore, Joan W. 1970. "Colonialism: The Case of the Mexican Americans." *Social Problems* 17: 463–472.

Moore, Joan W., with **Harry Pachon.** 1976. *Mexican Americans.* Englewood Cliffs, N.J.: Prentice Hall.

Moore, L. Aubrey, and **Paul M. Roesti.** 1980. "Race and Two Juvenile Justice System Decision Points: The Filing of a Petition and Declaration of Wardship." Paper presented to annual meeting of the Midwest Sociological Society, Milwaukee, Wisconsin.

Moore, Robert. 1972. "Race Relations in the Six Counties: Colonialism, Industrialization, and Stratification in Ireland." *Race* 14. Reprinted in Norman R. Yetman, and C. Hoy Steele (eds.), *Majority and Minority: The Dynamics of Racial and Ethnic Relations.* Boston: Allyn and Bacon. 1975.

Moustafa, A. Taher, and **Gertrud Weiss.** 1968. *Health Status and Practices of Mexican Americans.* Advance Report II, Mexican-American Study Project. Los Angeles: University of California of Los Angeles.

Murguia, Edward. 1975. *Assimilation, Colonialism, and the Mexican American People.* Austin, Texas: The University of Texas at Austin.

Myrdal, Gunnar. 1944. *An American Dilemma: The Negro Problem and Modern Democracy.* New York: Harper & Row, Pub.

Nagel, Stewart. 1969. *The Legal Process from a Behavioral Perspective.* Homewood, Ill.: Dorsey Press.

Nagi, Saad Z. 1972. "Tabulations from the OSU Disability Survey-1972." Columbus, Ohio: Ohio State University.

Nash, Gary B. 1970. "Red, White, and Black: The Origins of Racism in Colonial America." Chapter 1 in Gary B. Nash and Richard Weiss, *The Great Fear: Race in the Mind of America.* New York: Holt, Rinehart and Winston.

Nash, Roy. 1976. *Teacher Expectations and Pupil Learning.* London: Routledge and Kegan Paul.

National Center for Health Statistics, 1976. *Health Characteristics of Minority Groups.* Washington, D.C.: U.S. Government Printing Office.

National Commission on Marihuana and Drug Abuse. 1972. *Marihuana: A Signal of Misunderstanding,* Appendix, Part 4. Technical Papers of the National Commission on Marihuana and Drug Abuse. Washington, D.C.: U.S. Government Printing Office.

National Education Association. 1968. *Ability Grouping.* Research Summary 1968–53. Washington, D.C.: National Education Association.

National Institute of Law Enforcement and Criminal Justice. 1978. *The National Manpower Survey of the Criminal Justice System. Volume Two: Law Enforcement.* Washington, D.C.: U.S. Government Printing Office.

National Institute on Drug Abuse. 1976. *Young Men and Drugs—A Nationwide Survey.* Research Monograph Series 5. Rockville, Md.: National Institute on Drug Abuse.

Neuhaus, Robert, and **Ruby Neuhaus.** 1974. *Family Crisis.* Columbus, Ohio: Merrill.

New York Times. 1980. "3 Ex-Houston Policemen Begin Terms for Civil Rights Violations." April 12, p. 30.

New York Times. 1979. "A Tale of Two Cities," by Tom Wicker. November 2, p. 31.

New York Times. 1979. June 29. Pp. 14, 11B, 12B.

New York Times. 1973. February, 1973, p. 5.

Nisbet, Lee. 1977. "Affirmative Action: A Liberal Program?" Pp. 50–53 in Barry R. Gross (ed.), *Reverse Discrimination*. Buffalo: Prometheus Books.

Noel, Donald L. 1972a. "Slavery and the Rise of Racism." Pp. 153–174 in Donald L. Noel (ed.), *The Origins of American Slavery and Racism*. Columbus, Ohio: Charles E. Merrill.

Noel, Donald L. (ed.). 1972b. *The Origins of American Slavery and Racism*. Columbus, Ohio: Charles E. Merrill.

Noel, Donald L. 1968. "A Theory of the Origin of Ethnic Stratification." *Social Problems* 16: 157–172.

Novak, Michael. 1971. *The Rise of The Unmeltable Ethnics*. New York: Macmillan.

Office of Special Concerns. Office of the Assistant Secretary, U.S. Department of Health, Education, and Welfare. 1974. *A Study of Selected Socio-Economic Characteristics of Ethnic Minorities Based on the 1970 Census. Volume II: Asian-Americans*. Washington, D.C.: U.S. Government Printing Office.

Ogbu, John U. 1978. *Minority Education and Caste: The American System in Cross Cultural Perspective*. New York: Academic Press.

Organization for Economic Cooperation and Development. 1977. *Public Expenditure on Health*. Paris: Organization for Economic Cooperation and Development.

Ornstein, Allan C. 1978. *Metropolitan Schools: Administrative Decentralization Vs. Community Control*. Metuchen, N.J.: The Scarecrow Press.

Ossenberg, Richard J. 1975. "Social Pluralism in Quebec: Continuity, Change, and Conflict." Pp. 112–125 in Norman R. Yetman, and C. Hoy Steele (eds.), *Majority and Minority: The Dynamics of Racial and Ethnic Relations*. Boston: Allyn and Bacon.

Ossenberg, Richard J. 1971. *Canadian Society: Pluralism, Change, and Conflict*. Toronto: Prentice Hall of Canada.

Overby, Andrew. 1972. "Discrimination in the Administration of Justice." Pp. 264–276 in Charles E. Reasons and Jack L. Kuykendall (eds.), *Race, Crime, and Justice*. Pacific Palisades, Calif.: Goodyear Publishing Company.

Palmer, Francis H. 1970. "Socioeconomic Status and Intellective Performance Among Negro Preschool Boys." *Developmental Psychology* 3: 1–9.

Parisi, Nicolette, Michael R. Gottfredson, Michael J. Hindelang, and **Timothy J. Flanigan (eds).** 1979. *Sourcebook of Criminal Justice Statistics-1978*. Washington, D.C.: U.S. Government Printing Office.

Parsons, Talcott. 1959. "The School Class as a Social System." *Harvard Educational Review* 29: 297–318.

Patterson, Orlando. 1977. *Ethnic Chauvinism: The Reactionary Impulse*. New York: Stein and Day.

Payne, Charles. 1979. "On the Declining—and Increasing—Significance of Race." Pp. 117–139 (Chapter 11) in Charles Vert Willie (ed.), *Caste and Class Controversy*. Bayside, New York: General Hall.

Pearce, Diana. 1976. "Black, White, and Many Shades of Gray: Real Estate Brokers and Their Racial Practices." Unpublished Ph.D. Dissertation, The University of Michigan, Ann Arbor.

Pearl, D. 1954. "Ethnocentrism and the Self-Concept." *Journal of Social Psychology* 40: 137–147.

Pettigrew, Thomas F. 1980. "The Changing—Not Declining—Significance of Race." *Contemporary Sociology* 9: 19–21.

Pettigrew, Thomas F. 1976. "Race and Intergroup Relations," Pp. 459–510 (Chapter 10) in Robert K. Merton and Robert Nisbet (eds.), *Contemporary Social Problems,* fourth edition. New York: Harcourt Brace Jovanovich, Inc.

Pettigrew, Thomas F. 1973. "Attitudes on Race and Housing: A Social-Psychological

View.'' Pp. 21–84 in Amos H. Hawley and V. P. Rock (eds.), *Segregation in Residential Areas.* Washington, D.C.: National Academy of Sciences.

Pettigrew, Thomas F. 1971. *Racially Separate or Together.* New York: McGraw-Hill.

Pettigrew, Thomas F. 1969a. ''The Negro and Education: Problems and Proposals.'' Pp. 49–112 in Irwin Katz and Patricia Gurin (eds.), *Race and the Social Sciences.* New York: Basic Books.

Pettigrew, Thomas F. 1969b. ''Race and Equal Educational Opportunity.'' Pp. 69–79 in Harvard Educational Review Editors (eds.), *Equality of Educational Opportunity.* Cambridge, Mass.: Harvard University Press.

Pettigrew, Thomas F., and **Robert L. Green.** 1976. ''School Desegregation in Large Cities: Critique of the Coleman 'White Flight' Thesis.'' *Harvard Educational Review* 46: 1–53.

Pettigrew, Thomas F., Elizabeth L. Useem, Clarence Normand, and **Marshall S. Smith.** 1973. ''Busing: A Review of the Evidence.'' *The Public Interest* 30: 88–118.

Piaget, Jean. 1965. *The Moral Judgement of the Child.* Marjorie Gabain (tr.). New York: Free Press. (First published in French, 1932.)

Pierson, Donald. 1942. *Negroes in Brazil.* Chicago: University of Chicago Press.

Piliavin, Irving, and **Scott Briar.** 1964. ''Police Encounters with Juveniles.'' *American Journal of Sociology* 70: 206–214.

Pinkney, Alphonso. 1976. *Red, Black, and Green: Black Nationalism in the United States.* New York: Cambridge University Press.

Pinkney, Alfonso. 1975. *Black Americans.* Englewood Cliffs, N.J.: Prentice Hall.

Pitt-Rivers, Julian. 197 . *After the Empire: Race and Society in Middle-America and the Andes.* London: Oxford University Press.

Piven, Frances Fox. 1977. ''The Urban Crisis: Who Got What and Why.'' Pp. 132–144 in Roger E. Alcaly and David Mermelstein (eds.), *The Fiscal Crisis of American Cities.* New York: Vintage Books.

Population Reference Bureau. 1980. ''1980 World Population Data Sheet.'' Washington, D.C.: Population Reference Bureau.

Porter, Judith D. R. 1971. *Black Child, White Child.* Cambridge, Mass.: Harvard University Press.

Pottinger, J. Stanley. 1972. ''The Drive Toward Equality.'' *Change* 4 (8): 24.

Poussaint, Alvin. 1977. Presentation to Intergroup Relations Week Program, Concordia College, Moorhead, Minnesota.

President's Commission on Law Enforcement and the Administration of Justice. 1967. *Task Force Report: Crime and Its Impact.* Washington, D.C.: U.S. Government Printing Office.

Prothro, E. T. 1952. ''Ethnocentrism and Anti-Negro Attitudes in the Deep South.'' *Journal of Abnormal and Social Psychology* 47: 105–108.

Quinney, Richard. 1979. *Criminology.* Boston: Little, Brown.

Raab, Earl R. 1978. ''Son of Coalition.'' Paper presented to the 28th Annual Meeting of the Society for the Study of Social Problems, San Francisco, California.

Raab, Earl, and **Seymour Martin Lipset.** 1959. *Prejudice and Society.* New York: Anti-Defamation League.

Radke, Marian J., and **Helen G. Trager.** 1950. ''Children's Perceptions of the Social Roles of Negroes and Whites.'' *Journal of Psychology* 29: 3–33.

Rainwater, Lee, and **William L. Yancey (eds.).** 1967. *The Moynihan Report and the Politics of Controversy.* Cambridge, Mass.: The M.I.T. Press.

Ransford, H. Edward. 1972. ''Blue-Collar Anger: Reactions to Student and Black Protest.'' *American Sociological Review* 37: 333–346.

Ravitch, Diane. 1973. ''Community Control Revisited.'' *Commentary,* February: 70–74.

Reich, Michael. 1972. "The Economics of Racism." Pp. 313–321 in Richard C. Edwards, Michael Reich, and Thomas E. Weiskopf (eds.), *The Capitalist System*. Englewood Cliffs, N.J.: Prentice Hall.

Reisman, David. 1953. *The Lonely Crowd*. New York: Doubleday.

Reiss, Albert J., Jr. 1968. "Police Brutality—Answers to Key Questions." *Transaction* 5: 10–19.

Reynolds, Robert E., and **Thomas W. Rice.** 1971. "Attitudes of Medical Interns Toward Patients and Health Professionals." *Journal of Health and Social Behavior* 12: 307–311.

Richert, Jean Pierre. 1974. "The Impact of Ethnicity on the Perception of Heroes and Historical Symbols." *Canadian Review of Sociology and Anthropology* 11, 2 (May): 156–163.

Riordan, Cornelius, and **Josephine Ruggiero.** 1980. "Producing Equal Status Interracial Interaction: A Replication." *Social Psychology Quarterly* 43: 131–136.

Rioux, Marcel, and **Yves Martin (eds.).** 1964. *French Canadian Society*. Toronto: McClelland and Stewart.

Rist, Ray C. 1978. *The Invisible Children: School Integration in American Society*. Cambridge, Mass.: Harvard University Press.

Rist, Ray C. 1970. "Student Social Class and Teacher Expectations: The Self-Fulfilling Prophecy in Ghetto Education." *Harvard Educational Review* 40: 411–451.

Robertson, Ian, and **Phillip Whitten.** *Race and Politics in South Africa*. Edison, N.J.: Transaction Books.

Robinson, Jerry W., and **James D. Preston.** 1976. "Equal-Status Contact and Modification of Racial Prejudice: A Reexamination of the Contact Hypothesis." *Social Forces* 54: 911–924.

Roncal, Joaquin. 1944. "The Negro Race in Mexico." *Hispanic American Historical Review* 24: 530–540.

Rose, R. 1971. *Governing Without Consensus*. London: Faber and Faber.

Rosenberg, Morris, and **Roberta G. Simmons.** 1971. *Black and White Self-Esteem: The Urban School Child*. Washington, D.C.: American Sociological Association.

Rosenthal, Bernard G. 1974. "Development of Self-Identification in Relation to Attitudes Toward the Self in the Chippewa Indians." *Genetic Psychology Monographs* 90: 43–141.

Rosenthal, D. 1970. *Genetic Theory and Abnormal Behavior*. New York: McGraw Hill.

Rosenthal, Robert, and **Lenore Jacobson.** 1968. *Pygmalion in the Classroom: Teacher Expectation and Pupils' Intellectual Development*. New York: Holt, Rinehart and Winston.

Rubin, I. M. 1967. "Increased Self-Acceptance: A Means of Reducing Prejudice." *Journal of Personality and Social Psychology* 5: 133–238.

Rudwick, Elliott M. 1964. *Race Riot at East St. Louis, July 2, 1917*. Carbondale, Ill.: Southern Illinois University Press.

Ryan, William. 1971. *Blaming the Victim*. New York: Vintage Books.

Ryan, William. 1967. "Savage Discovery: The Moynihan Report." Pp. 457–466 in Lee Rainwater and William L. Yancey (eds.), *The Moynihan Report and the Politics of Controversy*. Cambridge, Mass.: M.I.T. Press.

St. John, Nancy H. 1975. *School Desegregation: Outcomes for Children*. New York: John Wiley & Sons.

St. Louis Post Dispatch. 1978. "Social Progress Slow for Chicanos." by Pete Herrera, United Press International. Tuesday, October 31, 1978.

Sandberg, Neil C. 1974. *Ethnic Identity and Assimilation: The Polish-American Community*. New York: Praeger.

Satin, George D. 1973. "Help?: The Hospital Emergency Unit Patient and His Presenting Picture." *Medical Care* 11: 328–337.

Satin, George, and **Frederick J. Duhl.** 1972. "Help?: The Hospital Emergency Unit as Community Physician." *Medical Care* 10: 248–260.

Saul R. Leven Memorial Foundation. 1959. Unpublished Report of Study of Detroit Recorder's Court over 20-month Period, November 1, 1957 through June 30, 1959.

Scanzoni, John H. 1977. *The Black Family in Modern Society.* (Phoenix edition). Chicago: The University of Chicago Press.

Schafer, Walter E., Carol Olexa, and **Kenneth Polk.** 1972. "Programmed for Social Class: Tracking in High School." Pp. 34–54 in Kenneth Polk and Walter E. Schafer (eds.), *Schools and Delinquency.* Englewood Cliffs, N.J.: Prentice Hall.

Schermerhorn, Richard A. 1978. *Comparative Ethnic Relations: A Framework for Theory and Research.* (Phoenix edition). Chicago: The University of Chicago Press.

Schuchardt, Thomas. 1980. "A Study of the Disabled in the Role of Social Deviant." Unpublished masters thesis, Southern Illinois University, Edwardsville, Illinois.

Schuman, Howard. 1975. "Free Will and Determinism in Public Beliefs About Race." Pp. 375–380 in Norman R. Yetman and C. Hoy Steele (eds.), *Majority and Minority: The Dynamics of Racial and Ethnic Relations.* Boston: Allyn and Bacon. Earlier version appeared in *Transaction* 7 (2): 44–48, 1969.

Schuman, Howard, and **Shirley Hatchett.** 1974. *Black Racial Attitudes: Trends and Complexities.* Ann Arbor, Mich.: Institute for Social Research.

Scruggs, Otey M. 1971. "The Economic and Racial Components of Jim Crow." Pp. 70–87 in Nathan I. Huggins, Martin Kilson, and Daniel M. Fox (eds.), *Key Issues in the Afro-American Experience,* Volume II. New York: Harcourt Brace Jovanovich, Inc.

Seabury, Paul. 1977. "HEW and the Universities." Pp. 97–112 in Barry R. Gross (ed.), *Reverse Discrimination.* Buffalo: Prometheus Books. (Earlier version appeared in *Commentary*: February, 1972.)

Seymour, D. Z. 1972. "Black English." *Intellectual Digest* 2.

Shanahan, J. L. 1976. "Impaired Access of Black Inner-City Residents to the Decentralized Workplaces." *Journal of Economics and Business* 28 (2): 156–160.

Sheatsley, Paul B. 1966. "White Attitudes Toward the Negro." *Daedalus* 95: 217–238.

Sherif, Muzafer, O. J. Harvey, B. Jack White, William R. Hood, and **Carolyn W. Sherif.** 1961. *Intergroup Conflict and Cooperation: The Robbers Cave Experiment.* Norman, Okla.: University Book Exchange.

Shockley, William. 1971a. "Negro IQ Deficit: Failure of a 'Malicious Coincidence' Model Warrants New Research Proposals." *Review of Educational Research* 41: 227–28.

Shockley, William. 1971b. "Models, Mathematics, and the Moral Obligation to Diagnose the Origin of Negro IQ Deficits." *Review of Educational Research* 41: 369–377.

Siegel, Jacob S., Jeffrey S. Passel, and **J. Gregory Robinson.** 1980. *Working Paper on Illegal Immigration Prepared for the Select Commission on Immigration and Refugee Policy.*

Silverstein, Barry, and **Ronald Krate.** 1975. *Children of the Dark Ghetto—A Developmental Psychology.* New York: Praeger Publishers.

Silverstein, Lee. 1966. "Bail in the State Courts: A Field Study and Report." *Minnesota Law Review* 50.

Simpson, George Eaton, and **J. Milton Yinger.** 1972. *Racial and Cultural Minorities: An Analysis of Prejudice and Discrimination.* New York: Harper & Row, Pub.

Sindler, Allan P. 1978. *Bakke, DeFunis, and Minority Admissions: The Quest for Equal Opportunity.* New York: Longman.

Sklare, Marshall. 1955. *Conservative Judaism.* Glencoe, Ill.: The Free Press.

Skolnick, Jerome H. 1969. *The Politics of Protest.* New York: Simon and Schuster.

Smith, W. C. 1942. "Minority Groups in Hawaii." *The Annals of the American Academy of Political and Social Science* 223: 41.

Spear, Allan. 1971. "The Origins of the Urban Ghetto, 1870−1915." Pp. 153−166 in Nathan I. Huggins, Martin Kilson, and Daniel M. Fox (eds.), *Key Issues in the Afro-American Experience,* Volume II. New York: Harcourt Brace Jovanovich.

Spencer, Metta. 1979. *Foundations of Modern Sociology.* Englewood Cliffs, N.J.: Prentice-Hall.

Stampp, Kenneth M. 1956. *The Peculiar Institution: Slavery in the Ante-Bellum South.* New York: Vintage Books.

Stanley, Julian C. (ed.). 1973. *Compensatory Education for Children, Ages 2 to 8, Recent Studies of Environmental Intervention.* Baltimore: Johns Hopkins University Press.

Staples, Robert. 1973. *The Black Woman in America.* Chicago: Nelson-Hall.

Steele, C. Hoy. 1975. "The Acculturation/Assimilation Model in Urban Indian Studies: A Critique." Pp. 305−314 in Norman R. Yetman and C. Hoy Steele (eds.), *Majority and Minority: The Dynamics of Racial and Ethnic Relations.* Boston: Allyn and Bacon.

Steele, C. Hoy. 1972. "American Indians and Urban Life: A Community Study." Unpublished Ph. D. Dissertation, University of Kansas, Lawrence, Kansas.

Sternleib, George, and **James W. Hughes.** 1976. *Post-Industrial America: Metropolitan Decline and Inter-regional Job Shifts.* New Brunswick, N.J.: Rutgers University Center for Urban Policy Research.

Stevens, Rosemary. 1971. *American Medicine and The Public Interest.* New Haven: Yale University Press.

Stinnett, Nick, and **James Walters.** 1977. *Relationships in Marriage and Family.* New York: Macmillan.

Stoddard, Lothrop. 1920. *The Rising Tide of Color Against White World-Supremacy.* New York: Scribner's.

Stotland, E., Donald Katz, and **M. Patchen.** 1959. "The Reduction of Prejudice Through the Arousal of Self-Insight." *Journal of Personality* 27: 507−531.

Stouffer, Samuel A., E. A. Suchman, L. C. DeVinney, S. A. Star, and **R. N. Williams.** 1949. *The American Soldier, Volume 1. Adjustment During Army Life.* Princeton, N.J.: Princeton University Press.

Stubbins, Joseph (ed.). 1977. *Social and Psychological Aspects of Disability: A Handbook for Practitioners.* Baltimore: University Park Press.

Stuckert, Robert S. 1958. "The African Ancestry of the White American Population." *Ohio Journal of Science,* May: 155−160.

Summers, Anita, and **Barbara L. Wolfe.** 1977. "Do Schools Make a Difference?" *Sociological Inventory Sample Issue.* Washington, D.C.: American Sociological Association.

Sumner, William Graham. 1906. *Folkways.* Boston: Ginn and Company.

Super, Donald E., and **John O. Crites.** 1962. *Appraising Vocational Fitness.* New York: Harper & Row, Pub.

Surgeon, George, Judith Mayo, and **Donald J. Bogue.** 1978. *Race Relations in Chicago: Second Survey: 1975.* Chicago: University of Chicago Community and Family Study Center.

Szymanski, Albert. 1976. "Racial Discrimination and White Gain." *American Sociological Review* 41: 403−414.

Taeuber, Karl E., and **Alma F. Taeuber.** 1965. *Negroes in Cities.* Chicago: Aldine Publishing Company.

Taylor, D. Garth. 1979. "Housing, Neighborhoods, and Race Relations: Recent Survey Evidence." *Annals of the American Academy of Political and Social Science* 441 (January): 26−40.

Taylor, Karyn J. 1978. "A Black Perspective on the Melting Pot." *Social Policy* 8 (5): 31−37.

Terry, Robert M. 1967. "Discrimination in the Handling of Juvenile Offenders by Social Control Agencies." *Journal of Research in Crime and Delinquency* 4: 218−230.

Thernstrom, Abigail M. 1980. "E Pluribus Plura—Congress and Bilingual Education." *The Public Interest* 60 (Summer): 3−22.

Thernstrom, Stephan, Ann Orlov, and **Oscar Hanlin** (eds.). 1980. *The Harvard Encyclopedia of American Ethnic Groups.* Cambridge, Mass.: Harvard University Press.

Thomlinson, Ralph. 1976. *Population Dynamics: Causes and Consequences of World Demographic Change,* second edition. New York: Random House.

Thompson, Wilbur. 1976. "Economic Processes and Employment Problems in Declining Metropolitan Areas." Pp. 187−196 in George Sternlieb and James W. Hughes (eds.), *Post-Industrial America: Metropolitan Decline and Interregional Job Shifts.* New Brunswick, N.J.: Rutgers University Center for Urban Policy Research.

Thomson, Randall J., and **Matthew T. Zingraff.** 1978. "A Longitudinal Analysis of Crime Sentencing Patterns." Paper presented to Annual Meeting of Society for the Study of Social Problems, San Francisco, California.

Thornberry, Terence P. 1974. "Race, Socioeconomic Status, and Sentencing in the Juvenile Justice System." *Journal of Criminal Law and Criminology* 64: 90−98.

Thorndike, Robert C. 1969. "Review of Pygmalion in the Classroom." *Teachers College Record* 70: 805−807.

Tilly, Charles. 1974. "The Chaos of the Living City." Pp. 86−108 in Charles Tilly (ed.), *An Urban World.* Boston: Little, Brown.

Tourney, Garfield, Anthony Petrilli, and **Lon M. Hatfield.** 1975. "Hormonal Relationships in Homosexual Men." *American Journal of Psychiatry* 132: 288−290.

Triandis, Harry C. 1971. *Attitude and Attitude Change.* New York: John Wiley & Sons. Princeton, N.J.: Princeton University Press.

Tumin, Melvin M. 1953. "Some Principles of Stratification: A Critical Analysis." *American Sociological Review* 18: 387−393.

UNESCO. 1952. "Statement on the Nature of Race and Race Differences—by Physical Anthropologists and Geneticists." New York: UNESCO. Reprinted in Ashley Montagu, 1963, *Race, Science, and Humanity.* Princeton, N.J.: D. Van Nostrand. Pp. 178−183.

UNESCO. 1950. "The UNESCO Statement by Experts on Race Problems." New York: UNESCO. Reprinted in Ashley Montagu, 1963, *Race, Science, and Humanity.* Princeton, N.J.: D. Van Nostrand. Pp. 172−178.

U.S. Bureau of the Census. 1981. *1980 Census of Population.* Age, Sex, Race, and Spanish Origin of the Population by Regions, Divisions, and States: 1980. (Report Number PC80-51-1.) Washington, D.C.: U.S. Government Printing Office.

U.S. Bureau of the Census. 1980a. *Current Population Reports: Population Characteristics.* "Persons of Spanish Origin in the United States: March, 1979." Series P-20, Number 364, Washington, D.C.: U.S. Government Printing Office.

U.S. Bureau of the Census. 1980b. *Current Population Reports: Consumer Income.* "Money Income of Families and Persons in the United States: 1978." Series P-60, Number 123. Washington, D.C.: U.S. Government Printing Office.

U.S. Bureau of the Census. 1980c. *Current Population Reports: Population Characteristics.* "Educational Attainment in the United States: March, 1979 and 1978." Series P-20, Number 356. Washington, D.C.: U.S. Government Printing Office.

U.S. Bureau of the Census. 1980d. *Current Population Reports: Population Characteristics.* "Field of Study of College Students: October, 1978." Series P-20, Number 351. Washington, D.C.: U.S. Government Printing Office.

U.S. Bureau of the Census. 1980e. *Current Population Reports: Population Estimates and Projections.* "Estimates of the Population of the United States by Age, Sex, and Race: 1976 to 1978." Washington, D.C.: U.S. Government Printing Office.

U.S. Bureau of the Census. 1979a. *The Social and Economic Status of the Black Population in the United States: An Historical View, 1970−1978.* Current Population Reports, Special Studies, Series P-23, Number 80. Washington, D.C.: U.S. Government Printing Office.

U.S. Bureau of the Census. 1979b. *Current Population Reports: Population Characteristics.* "Population Profile of the United States: 1978." Series P-20, Number 336. Washington, D.C.: U.S. Government Printing Office.

U.S. Bureau of the Census. 1979c. *Current Population Reports: Population Characteristics.* "Persons of Spanish Origin in the United States: March, 1978." Series P-20, Number 339. Washington, D.C.: U.S. Government Printing Office.

U.S. Bureau of the Census. 1979d. *Current Population Reports: Consumer Income.* "Money Income in 1977 of Families and Persons in the United States." Series P-60, Number 118. Washington, D.C.: U.S. Government Printing Office.

U.S. Bureau of the Census. 1979e. *Current Population Reports: Consumer Income.* "Characteristics of the Population Below the Poverty Level: 1977." Series P-60, Number 119. Washington, D.C.: U.S. Government Printing Office.

U.S. Bureau of the Census. 1979f. *Current Population Reports: Population Characteristics.* "School Enrollment: Social and Economic Characteristics of Students: October, 1978." Series P-20, Number 346. Washington, D.C.: U.S. Government Printing Office.

U.S. Bureau of the Census. 1978a. *Current Population Reports: Population Characteristics.* "Household and Family Characteristics." Series P-20, No. 236. Washington, D.C.: U.S. Government Printing Office.

U.S. Bureau of the Census. 1978b. "Governmental Finances in 1976−77." Series GF77, Number 5. Washington, D.C.: U.S. Government Printing Office.

U.S. Bureau of the Census. 1977. *Current Population Reports: Population Characteristics.* "Educational Attainment in the United States: March, 1977 and 1976." Washington, D.C.: U.S. Government Printing Office.

U.S. Bureau of the Census. 1973a. *1970 Census of Population.* "Characteristics of the Population," Volume 1, United States Summary. Washington, D.C.: U.S. Government Printing Office.

U.S. Bureau of the Census. 1973b. *Current Population Reports: Population Characteristics.* "Characteristics of the Population by Ethnic Origin: March, 1972 and 1971." Series P-20, Number 249. Washington, D.C.: U.S. Government Printing Office.

U.S. Bureau of the Census. 1973c. *1970 Census of Population.* "Subject Reports: Persons with Work Disability: Final Report." PC(2)-6C. Washington, D.C.: U.S. Government Printing Office.

U.S. Bureau of the Census. 1972a. *1970 Census of Population.* "General Characteristics: United States Summary." PC(1)-B1. Washington, D.C.: U.S. Government Printing Office.

U.S. Bureau of the Census. 1972b. *1970 Census of Population.* "General Social and Economic Characteristics: United States Summary." PC(1)-C1. Washington, D.C.: U.S. Government Printing Office.

U.S. Bureau of the Census. 1972c. *1970 Census of Population and Housing.* "Census Tracts: Final Report." PHC(1)-58: Detroit, Michigan SMSA. Washington, D.C.: U.S. Government Printing Office.

U.S. Bureau of the Census. 1972d. *1970 Census of Population and Housing.* "Census Tracts: Final Report." PHC(1)-181: St. Louis, Missouri-Illinois SMSA. Washington, D.C.: U.S. Government Printing Office.

U.S. Bureau of the Census. 1971. *1970 Census of Population.* "Number of Inhabitants: United States Summary." PC(1)-A1. Washington, D.C.: U.S. Government Printing Office.

U.S. Bureau of Labor Statistics. 1979. Current Labor Statistics: Employment Data from the Household Survey. *Monthly Labor Review* 102 (12): 67−71.

U.S. Commission on Civil Rights. 1979. *Desegregation of the Nation's Public Schools: A Status Report.* Washington, D.C.: U.S. Government Printing Office.

U.S. Commission on Civil Rights. 1978. *Social Indicators of Equality for Minorities and Women.* Washington, D.C.: U.S. Government Printing Office.

U.S. Commission on Civil Rights. 1976. *Fulfilling the Letter and Spirit of the Law: Desegregation of the Nation's Schools.* Washington, D.C.: U.S. Government Printing Office.

U.S. Commission on Civil Rights. 1975. *The Voting Rights Act: Ten Years Later.* Washington, D.C.: U.S. Government Printing Office.

U.S. Commission on Civil Rights. 1974. *Toward Quality Education for Mexican Americans.* Mexican American Study Report Number 4. Washington, D.C.: U.S. Government Printing Office.

U.S. Commission on Civil Rights. 1972. *Mexican American Education in Texas: A Function of Wealth.* Mexican American Education Study. Report Number 4. Washington, D.C.: U.S. Government Printing Office.

U.S. Commission on Civil Rights. 1970. *Mexican Americans and the Administration of Justice in the Southwest.* Washington, D.C.: U.S. Government Printing Office.

U.S. Commission on Civil Rights. 1970. *Racism in America and How to Combat It.* Clearinghouse Publication, Urban Series No. 1. Washington, D.C.: U.S. Government Printing Office.

U.S. Commission on Civil Rights. 1968. *Political Participation.* Washington, D.C.: U.S. Government Printing Office.

U.S. Commission on Civil Rights. 1965. *Law Enforcement: A Report on Equal Protection in the South.* Washington, D.C.: U.S. Government Printing Office.

U.S. Department of Commerce. 1977. *Social Indicators 1976.* Washington, D.C.: U.S. Government Printing Office.

U.S. Department of Health, Education, and Welfare. 1980. *Monthly Vital Statistics Report.* Vol. 28, No. 12. "Births, Marriages, Divorces, and Deaths for 1979." Washington, D.C.: National Center for Health Statistics.

U.S. Department of Health, Education, and Welfare. 1979. *Minorities and Women in the Health Fields.* Publication number (HRA) 79-22. Washington, D.C.: U.S. Government Printing Office.

U.S. Department of Health, Education, and Welfare. 1978. *Health—United States 1978.* Washington, D.C.: U.S. Government Printing Office.

U.S. Department of Housing and Urban Development. 1979. *Measuring Racial Discrimination in American Housing Markets: The Housing Market Practices Survey.* Washington, D.C.: U.S. Government Printing Office.

U.S. Department of Labor. 1965. *The Negro Family: The Case for National Action* (The Moynihan Report). Washington, D.C.: U.S. Government Printing Office.

U.S. National Advisory Commission on Civil Disorders. 1968. *Report of the National Advisory Commission on Civil Disorders.* New York: The New York Times Company, Bantam Books.

U.S. National Center for Health Statistics. 1979. "Current Estimates from the Health Interview Survey: U.S., 1978." *Data from the National Health Survey.* Series 10, Number 130. Washington, D.C.: U.S. Government Printing Office.

U.S. Senate Select Committee. 1972. *Report: Toward Equal Educational Opportunity* Washington, D.C.: U.S. Government Printing Office.

Valentine, Charles A. 1968. *Culture and Poverty: Critique and Counter-Proposals.* Chicago: The University of Chicago Press.

Van den Berge, Pierre L. 1978. *Race and Racism: A Comparative Perspective,* second edition. New York: John Wiley & Sons.

Van den Berge, Pierre L. 1965. *South Africa: A Study in Conflict.* Middletown, Conn.: Wesleyan University Press.

Van den Berge, Pierre L. 1958. "The Dynamics of Racial Prejudice: An Ideal-Type Dichotomy." *Social Forces 37:* 138−141.

Van der Horst, Sheila T. 1967. "The Effects of Industrialisation on Race Relations in South Africa." Pp. 97−140 in Guy Hunter (ed.), *Industrialisation and Race Relations: A Symposium.* London: Oxford University Press.

Van Valey, Thomas L., Wade Clark Roof, and **Jerome E. Wilcox.** 1977. "Trends in Residential Segregation: 1960–1970." *American Journal of Sociology* 82: 826–844.

Vernon, P. E. 1969. *Intelligence and Cultural Environment.* London: Methuen.

Vining, Daniel R. 1979. "Net Migration by Air: A Lower-Bound on Total Net Migration into the United States."

Vose, Clement E. 1959. *Caucasians Only.* Berkeley: University of California Press.

Wade, Mason. 1968. *The French Canadians, 1760–1967.* Toronto: Macmillan of Canada.

Waldman, B. 1977. "Economic and Racial Disadvantage as Reflected in Traditional Medical School Selection Factors: A Study of 1976 Applicants to U.S. Medical Schools." Study reported in *Amicus* brief, U.S. Supreme Court, *Bakke,* Association of American Medical Colleges.

Warner, W. Lloyd, and **Leo Srole.** 1945. *The Social Systems of American Ethnic Groups.* New Haven: Yale University Press.

Weber, C. U., P. W. Foster, and **D. P. Weikart.** 1978. "An Economic Analysis of the Ypsilanti Perry Preschool Project." *Monographs of High/Scope Educational Research Foundation* 5.

Weber, G. 1971. *Inner City Children Can Be Taught to Read: Four Successful Schools.* Washington, D.C.: Center for Basic Education.

Weber, Max. 1968. *Economy and Society: An Outline of Interpretive Sociology.* Guenther Roth and Claus Wittich (eds.), Ephriam Fischoff et al. (trs.). New York: Bedminster Press. (First published in four volumes in German, 1922.)

Weinberg, Martin S., and **Colin J. Williams.** 1974. *Male Homosexuals: Their Problems and Adaptations.* New York: Oxford University Press.

Weiss, Randall. 1968. "The Effects of Scholastic Achievement on the Earnings of Blacks and Whites." Unpublished honors thesis, Harvard University.

Welch, Finis. 1967. "Labor Market Discrimination in the Rural South." *Journal of Political Economy* 75: 225–240.

Werner, Norma E., and **Idella M. Evans.** 1968. "Perceptions of Prejudice in Mexican-American Pre-School Children." *Perceptual and Motor Skills* 27: 1039–1046.

Wescott, Diane W., and **Robert W. Bednarzik.** 1981. "Employment and Unemployment: A Report on 1980." *Monthly Labor Review* 104 (2): 4–14.

Wesley, Charles H. 1927. *Negro Labor in the United States: 1850–1925.* New York: Vanguard.

White, Sheldon. 1970. "The National Impact of Head Start." *Disadvantaged Child* 3: 163–184.

Willhelm, Sidney M. 1980. "Can Marxism Explain America's Racism?" *Social Problems* 28: 98–112.

Williams, Robin. 1977. "Competing Models of Multiethnic and Multiracial Societies: An Appraisal of Possibilities and Performances." Paper presented to plenary session of the American Sociological Association, 72nd Annual Meeting, Chicago.

Williams, Robin. 1975. "Race and Ethnic Relations." Pp. 125–164, in Alex Inkeles, James Coleman, and Niel Smelser (eds.), *Annual Review of Sociology.* Palo Alto, Calif.: Annual Reviews, Inc.

Willie, Charles Vert. 1979. *The Caste and Class Controversy.* Bayside, New York: General Hall.

Wilner, Daniel M., Rosabelle P. Walkley, and **Stuart W. Cook.** 1955. *Human Relations in Interracial Housing.* Minneapolis: University of Minnesota Press.

Wilson, James Q. 1978. *Varieties of Police Behavior: The Management of Law and Order in Eight Communities.* Cambridge, Mass.: Harvard University Press.

Wilson, William J. 1980. "A Response to Marrett and Pettigrew." *Contemporary Sociology* 6: 21–24.

Wilson, **William J.** 1979. "The Declining Significance of Race: Revisited But Not Revised." Chapter 14 in Charles Vert Willie (ed.), *Caste and Class Controversy*. Bayside, New York: General Hall. (Reprinted from *Society*, July/August, 1978.)

Wilson, **William J.** 1978. *The Declining Significance of Race: Blacks and Changing American Institutions*. Chicago: The University of Chicago Press.

Wilson, **William J.** 1973. *Power, Racism and Privilege*. New York: The Free Press.

Wood, **Barbara Sudene**, and **Julia Curry.** 1969. "Everyday Talk and School Talk of the City Black Child." *Speech Teacher* 18: 282−296.

Woodward, **C. Van.** 1971. *American Counterpoint: Slavery and Racism in the North-South Dialogue*. Boston: Little, Brown.

Woodward, **C. Van.** 1966. *The Strange Career of Jim Crow*, second revised edition. New York: Oxford University Press.

Wright, **J. Skelly.** 1969. "The Courts Have Failed the Poor." *The New York Times Magazine*, March 9.

Yetman, **Norman R.**, and **C. Hoy Steele.** 1975. *Majority and Minority: The Dynamics of Racial and Ethnic Relations*, second edition. Boston: Allyn and Bacon.

Yinger, **J. Milton**, and **George Eaton Simpson.** 1974. "Techniques for Reducing Prejudice: Changing the Prejudiced Person." Pp. 96−144 in Peter Watson (ed.), *Psychology and Race*. Chicago: Aldine Publishing Company.

Zigler, **Edward, E. F. Abelson,** and **V. Seitz.** 1973. "Motivational Factors in the Performance of Economically Disadvantaged Children on the Peabody Picture Vocabulary Test." *Child Development* 44: 294−303.

Zimring, **Franklin E., Joel Eigen,** and **Shiela O'Malley.** 1976. "Punishing Homocide in Philadelphia: Perspectives on the Death Penalty." *University of Chicago Law Review* 43: 227−252.

Zirkel, **Perry A.** 1971. "Self-Concept and the 'Disadvantage' of Ethnic Group Membership and Mixture." *Review of Educational Research* 41: 211−225.

Zirkel, **Perry A.**, and **E. Gnanaraj Moses.** 1971. "Self-Concept and Ethnic Group Membership Among Public School Students." *American Educational Research Journal* 8: 253−265.

Glossary

Achieved status A position of status attained by something a person does or accomplishes rather than by birth. In class systems, social standing is determined largely by achieved statuses, though ascribed statuses also have a sizable influence.

Affirmative action Any delibrate effort to increase minority representation, such as in a workforce or student body. Affirmative action may be limited to more vigorous efforts to recruit minorities, or may be extended to preferences in hiring or student admissions for minority group members, sometimes including the use of specific goals and timetables for minority representation.

Amalgamation The combination of two racial or ethnic groups into one through marriage or other sexual contact between the groups. Gradually, the distinction between the two groups becomes blurred, and they come to be regarded as a single group.

Annexation An expansion of territory by one group to take control over territory formerly under control of another group. This may be through military conquest, in which the outcome is much the same as in colonization. It may also be voluntary, as when residents of an area ask to be annexed. Some cases, such as purchases, fall somewhere between.

Anti-Semitism   Prejudice and discrimination against Jewish people.

Ascribed status   Any characteristic or status determined by birth, such as race, sex, or who one's parents are. In caste systems, one's social standing is determined on the basis of ascribed statuses.

Assimilation   A process whereby a minority group is gradually integrated into the culture and social system of the dominant group. Although the dominant group may adapt itself to the minority or absorb certain cultural characteristics of the minority group, it is more often the minority group that must adapt to fit into the culture and social system of the majority. See also *cultural assimilation* and *structural assimilation*.

Attitudinal racism   Racial or ethnic prejudice. See *prejudice*.

Blockbusting   A practice by realtors or real estate speculators that attempts to panic whites into selling their homes at a low price because blacks are supposedly moving into the neighborhood. The speculator purchases the house, then sells it to a black family, often at an inflated price. This practice exploits both black and white homeowners and encourages racial segregation and rapid racial turnover in urban neighborhoods.

Caste system   A system of social inequality with two or more rigidly defined and unequal groups, membership in which is determined by birth and passed from generation to generation. There is ordinarily no opportunity for a person in one group to move to another group of higher status.

Class system   A system of loosely defined, unequal groups in which there is significant, but not unlimited opportunity to move to a higher or lower status.

Cognitive dissonance theory   A theory that says we strive to make our attitudes consistent with our behavior, frequently by developing attitudes to support or justify preexisting behavior. This theory suggests that nondiscriminatory behavior (e.g., to comply with the law) may lead to unprejudiced attitudes. Similarly, racist behavior (e.g., for personal gain) may lead to racist attitudes as a justifying mechanism.

Colonization   A form of intergroup contact that occurs when one group migrates into an area occupied by another group and subordinates that indigenous group.

Colonized minority   A minority group that initially became a part of the society it lives in through conquest or annexation. In addition to such forcible entry, colonized minorities are usually subjected to some form of unfree labor and to attacks on their culture and social institutions.

Conflict perspective   A sociological perspective that sees society as dominated by a powerful elite, which controls most of the wealth and power in the society, to the disadvantage of other, less powerful members of the society. Because of this inequality, society tends toward conflict and change, though the power and/or prestige of the dominant group may for a time lead to a consensus in society, or the appearance thereof. This consensus, however, is temporary: the long-term tendency is toward conflict and change.

Cross-cutting cleavages   The situation in which societal divisions such as race, language, religion, and class all cut along different lines; there are, for example, religious divisions with racial groups. Cross-cutting cleavages tend to hold down the amount of intergroup conflict, because people have divided loyalties.

Cultural assimilation   A type of assimilation in which two or more groups gradually come to share a common culture, i.e. similar attitudes, values, language, beliefs, lifestyles, and rules about behavior. Frequently, the shared culture is much more similar to that of the majority group than it is to that of the minority group, though this is not *always* the case.

Cultural pluralism   A pattern in which different racial, ethnic, or other groups retain cultural features that are distinct in each group, but hold some others that are common to all groups in society.

***De facto* segregation**   School segregation which is the result *not* of an official policy of having separate schools for different racial groups, but of other processes which tend to create segregated schools, even without an official policy to have segregated schools. The most important cause of *de facto* segregation is housing segregation, which leads to a situation in which neighborhood school attendance districts tend to be, for example, all-white or all-black.

***De jure* segregation**   School segregation which is the result of an official or deliberate policy of having separate schools for different racial groups.

Displacement, or Displaced aggression   Similar in meaning to scapegoating.

Dominant group   Similar in meaning to *majority group*.

Ethnic group   A group of people who are generally regarded by themselves or others as a distinct group, with such recognition based on social or cultural characteristics such as nationality, language, and religion. Ethnicity, like race, tends to be passed from generation to generation and is ordinarily not an affiliation that one can freely drop.

Ethnocentrism   A tendency to view one's own group as the norm or standard and to view out-groups as not just different but also strange and usually inferior. The ways of the in-group are viewed as the natural way or the only way of doing things and become a standard against which out-groups are judged.

False consciousness   The acceptance—usually by a subordinate group—of values, beliefs, or ideologies that do not serve the self-interest of that group. In Marxian analysis, false consciousness frequently occurs when subordinate groups accept ideologies promoted by the wealthy elite to serve the interests of the elite at the expense of the subordinate groups.

Fee-for-service system   A system of health care payment whereby a fee is collected by a physician for each service performed, such as an office visit, operation, or reading of an X-ray. Under such a system, the doctor is paid for each service in this manner regardless of whether the payment is made by the person receiving the treatment, a private insurance company, or a government program. This system may be contrasted with systems in which physicians receive fixed salaries, such as health maintenance organizations (HMOs) or systems of socialized medicine.

Fluid competitive race relations   A pattern of race relations best described as a class system with racial inequalities remaining from a past racial caste system. There is little official segregation but often much de facto segregation. Minority groups have middle classes but are disproportionately poor. Racial conflict is usually present but kept to a controlled level.

Functionalist perspective   A sociological perspective stressing the notions that society is made up of interrelated parts that contribute to the effectiveness of the society, and that society tends toward consensus, order, and stability. These tendencies are seen as necessary if society is to be effective and efficient. According to this perspective, the absence of these conditions can pose a serious threat to the quality of life in the society and even to the society's ability to continue to function.

Gerrymandering   The practice of drawing odd-shaped school attendance districts as a way of promoting racial or ethnic segregation in the schools.

Ideological racism, or racist ideology   The belief that one race is superior to another biologically, intellectually, culturally, temperamentally, or morally. Such ideologies usually exist in order to rationalize or justify domination of one race or ethnic group by another, and tend to become institutionalized, or widely accepted within a culture.

Immigrant minority   A minority group that voluntarily migrated into the country or society in which it lives. Ordinarily, these minorities are more readily assimilated into the dominant society than colonized minorities.

Immigration   Migration of one group into an area controlled by another group. The entering group becomes a part of the indigenous group's society. Immigration may be either voluntary or, as in the case of slave importation, involuntary. Bonded or indentured laborers and political refugees are cases that fall somewhere between voluntary and involuntary.

Index of dissimilarity   A measure of the amount of housing segregation between any two groups, such as blacks and whites. It indicates the percentage of either group that would have to move to attain complete integration (the same mix of the two groups in every block or neighborhood). It can range from 0 (fully integrated) to 100 (totally segregated). It is also sometimes called the *segregation index*.

Indigenous group   A racial or ethnic group that is well established in an area prior to the arrival of some new group. An indigenous group may be, but does not have to be, native to the area in which it is established.

Individual racial discrimination, or *individual behavioral racism*   Any behavior by individuals that leads to unequal treatment on the basis of race or ethnicity. A restaurant owner's refusal to serve Chinese-Americans would be an example.

In-group   A group of which a person is a member, or with which he or she identifies.

Institutional racism, or *institutional discrimination*   Any arrangement or practice within a social institution or its related organizations that tends to favor one race or ethnic group (usually the majority group) over another. Institutional racism may be conscious and deliberate, as in discriminatory voting laws, or subtle and perhaps unintended, as in industrial location decisions that favor suburban whites over inner-city blacks.

Intergroup education   Any effort, by whatever means, to bring about factual learning about intergroup relations. Education is not primarily intended to change attitudes or opinions, although this may be a common result and is sometimes a latent objective.

Majority group   Any social group that is dominant in a society; i.e. it enjoys more than a proportionate share of the wealth, power, and/or social status in that society. Although majority groups in this sense are frequently a numerical majority, this is not always the case.

Marxist theory of discrimination   A theory based on the ideas of Karl Marx claiming that discrimination hurts working-class whites as well as minority group members by creating racial divisions within the working class.

Medicaid program   A federally funded program administered by the states which provides medical care to the poor. The program is for the most part limited to the poorest of the poor, covering only welfare recipients in many states, and covering some additional low-income population in other states.

Medicare program   A social insurance program, funded under the Social Security System, which provides medical insurance for the elderly.

Minority group   Any group that is assigned to a subordinate role in society; i.e. it has less than its proportionate share of wealth, power, and/or social status. Minority groups are frequently, but not necessarily, a numerical minority in society. Blacks in South Africa would be an example of a minority group that is a numerical majority.

Order perspective   See *functionalist perspective*.

Out-group   A group to which one does not belong and with which one does not identify. Frequently, this group is culturally or racially different from and/or in competition with the in-group.

Overlapping cleavages   The situation in which societal divisions such as race, religion, class, and language all cut along the same lines. In this situation there tends to be a great deal of conflict because no matter what the issue, people are always on the same side.

Paternalistic race relations   A pattern of intergroup relations usually found in agricultural, preindustrial societies. It is a form of caste sysem characterized by clearly defined and well-understood racial roles and much contact between races, but also with much ritual or etiquette denoting inequality, paternalism, and little outward conflict.

Perspective   A general approach to or way of looking at an issue. A perspective consists of a set of questions to be asked about a topic, a theory or set of theories about realities concerning that topic, and a set of values concerning potentially controversial issues related to the topic.

Persuasive communication   Any communication-written, oral, audio-visual, or otherwise-that is specifically intended to influence attitudes, beliefs, or behavior.

Prejudice   A tendency to think in a particular way, usually negative, toward an entire group. Prejudice can be cognative (involving beliefs about a group), affective (involving dislike of a group), or conative (involving the desire to behave negatively toward a group).

Projection   A process whereby people minimize or deny characteristics they see as undesirable in themselves by exaggerating these same characteristics in others. Since such characteristics are often projected onto members of out-groups, projection appears to be a significant factor in the dynamics of prejudice.

Race   A grouping of people generally considered to be physically distinct in some way from others and regarded by themselves or others to be a distinct group.

Racial group   A group of people who develop a group identity and/or common culture based on race. The main difference between a racial group and a race is that one need not have a strong group identity or be part of a cultural group in order to be a member of a race.

Racial steering   A practice whereby realtors show white customers houses in all-white areas and show black customers houses in all-black or racially mixed areas.

Racism   Any attitude, belief, behavior, or institutional arrangement that tends to favor one racial or ethnic group (usually a majority group) over another (usually a minority group). See also the four types of racism: prejudice (attitudinal racism); ideological racism; individual discrimination (individual behavioral racism); and institutional racism.

Rigid competitive race relations   A pattern of race relations resembling an unstable caste system. Race largely but not totally defines roles and statuses; division of labor is more complex than in the paternalistic pattern, with majority and minority workers sometimes competing because they do similar work, though usually at different wages. Strict segregation usually accompanies this pattern, as a way the majority group protects its threatened social status. The potential for major conflict is nearly always present. This pattern is usually found in newly industrializing societies.

Scapegoating   A tendency to take out one's feelings of frustration and aggression against someone or something other than the true source of the feelings. Often, racial, ethnic, or religious minorities are made the scapegoat for feelings of anger and frustration that have built up for reasons unrelated to the minority groups.

Self-fulfilling prophecy   Any situation in which the expectation of some event or outcome contributes to the occurrence of that event or outcome. In education, for example, teachers frequently expect a lower quality of work from minority students than from white students. As a consequence, they treat minority students in different ways that tend to produce the expected outcome.

Separatism   The establishment of, or attempt to establish, entirely separate societies made up of distinct racial, ethnic, or other groups which formerly existed within one society. Examples would include efforts by some French-

Canadians to divide Canada into two independent countries, one English and one French, and efforts by some Afro-Americans to establish separate black states in what is now the U.S. South.

Social institution A well-established structure, or form or organization, with supporting norms and values, that performs a central function in society. Examples would include religion, the family, and the economic, political, legal educational, and health care systems.

Sociological, or social structural, approach An approach to the study of majority-minority relations that emphasizes the characteristics of collectivities of people (e.g., groups, societies) rather than the characteristics of individuals. Issues of interest concern how a group or society is organized, its base of economic productivity, its power structure, its social institutions, and its culture.

Split labor market A situation where laborers are divided into two groups, one higher-paid (often a majority or dominant group) and one lower-paid (often composed of minority group members). The higher-paid group attempts to maintain an advantaged status by excluding the lower-paid group from certain kinds of employment.

Stereotype An exaggerated belief associated with a category such as a group of people. It is a tendency to believe that anyone or almost anyone who belongs to a particular group will have a certain characteristic; e.g., "Jews are money-hungry."

Structural assimilation A type of assimilation in which two or more groups gradually come to share a common social structure, i.e. they share common institutions, organizations, and friendship networks, and have relatively equal positions within these structures. If structural assimilation is complete, widespread intermarriage (marital assimilation) will also occur.

Structural pluralism A situation in which two or more groups operate within a common social structure up to a point (e.g. a common government and economic system) but have some institutions, organizations, and patterns of interpersonal contact that are distinct and separate in each group.

Subordinate group Similar in meaning to *minority group*.

Theory A set of interrelated propositions about some topic or issue that are believed to be true. Ideally, a theory should be testable, i.e., possible to evaluate in terms of its accuracy in describing reality.

Value A personal preference or an opinion or moral belief concerning goodness or badness, right or wrong, etc. A value, being a matter of personal preference, cannot be tested, proven, or disproven.

INDEX